Beginning SQL Server 2005 Express Database Applications

with Visual Basic Express and Visual Web Developer Express From Novice to Professional

Rick Dobson

Apress®

**Beginning SQL Server 2005 Express Database Applications
with Visual Basic Express and Visual Web Developer Express From Novice to Professional**

Copyright © 2006 by Rick Dobson

ISBN (pbk): 1-59059-523-8

Printed and bound in the United States of America 9 8 7 6 5 4 3 2 1

Trademarked names may appear in this book. Rather than use a trademark symbol with every occurrence of a trademarked name, we use the names only in an editorial fashion and to the benefit of the trademark owner, with no intention of infringement of the trademark.

Lead Editors: Tony Davis and Matthew Moodie
Technical Reviewer: Cristian Lefter
Editorial Board: Steve Anglin, Dan Appleman, Ewan Buckingham, Gary Cornell, Tony Davis, Jason Gilmore, Jonathan Hassell, Chris Mills, Dominic Shakeshaft, Jim Sumser
Project Manager: Beth Christmas
Copy Edit Manager: Nicole LeClerc
Copy Editors: Damon Larson and Freelance Editorial Services
Assistant Production Director: Kari Brooks-Copony
Production Editor: Kelly Winquist
Compositors: Dina Quan and Diana Van Winkle, Van Winkle Design Group
Proofreader: April Eddy
Indexer: Valerie Perry
Cover Designer: Kurt Krames
Manufacturing Director: Tom Debolski

Distributed to the book trade worldwide by Springer-Verlag New York, Inc., 233 Spring Street, 6th Floor, New York, NY 10013. Phone 1-800-SPRINGER, fax 201-348-4505, e-mail orders-ny@springer-sbm.com, or visit http://www.springeronline.com.

For information on translations, please contact Apress directly at 2560 Ninth Street, Suite 219, Berkeley, CA 94710. Phone 510-549-5930, fax 510-549-5939, e-mail info@apress.com, or visit http://www.apress.com.

The information in this book is distributed on an "as is" basis, without warranty. Although every precaution has been taken in the preparation of this work, neither the author(s) nor Apress shall have any liability to any person or entity with respect to any loss or damage caused or alleged to be caused directly or indirectly by the information contained in this work.

The source code for this book is available to readers at http://www.apress.com in the Source Code section. You will need to answer questions pertaining to this book in order to successfully download the code.

Contents at a Glance

PART 1 ■■■ Working with SQL Server Express

PART 2 ■■■ Working with Visual Basic Express and Visual Web Developer Express

Contents

PART 1 ■■■ Working with SQL Server Express

PART 2 ■■■ Working with Visual Basic Express and Visual Web Developer Express

About the Author

RICK DOBSON has written six books on database development with Visual Basic .NET, SQL Server, and Microsoft Access. In the past few years, he authored three DVDs on Visual Basic .NET, ADO.NET, and T-SQL. In addition, Rick has written countless articles for computer periodicals, including *SQL Server Magazine, Visual Studio .NET Developer, Visual Basic Developer, SQL Server Professional, SQL Server Solutions, Inside Microsoft Visual Basic,* and *Smart Access.*

Rick is also the webmaster for several websites. His most popular site, `http://ProgrammingMSAccess.com`, focuses on the needs of VB .NET and SQL Server developers, as well as Access developers. This site gets over 1 million page views annually, and thousands of site visitors register to receive a newsletter summarizing new developments and opportunities on the site. The site also contains extra material related to the book, including extra examples. Rick also founded the Database Developers Group, an international association of Microsoft database developers.

About the Technical Reviewer

CRISTIAN LEFTER is a SQL Server MVP, a former developer, a database administrator, a trainer, and the CEO of MicroTraining, a consulting and training company. In his spare time, he is a tech reviewer, author, and leader for two user groups (ITBoard and Romanian SQL Server User Group).

Acknowledgments

I am very fortunate to have worked with a very talented team in the preparation of this book. It brings me great pleasure to acknowledge them because they have each contributed so spectacularly to the final draft of the book. As the sole author of the book, I take full responsibility for anything that you do not like about it.

As a reader, you are my most important partner. Your opinions matter the most to me. Therefore, I invite your thoughtful, constructive feedback so that I can make future editions of the book better for readers. Feel free to send your feedback about the book (praise reports are especially welcomed) to me at rickd@cabinc.net.

My wife, Virginia Dobson, is my partner in life and in business. I am honored that she donated her services to this book project. She is a tireless proofreader with advanced technical skills, and she has experience as a technical editor for well known computer industry authors. If you find any passages especially clear and helpful, it is highly likely that she had a lot to do with urging me to write plainly and in a warm, cordial style.

Beyond my wife, I was professionally assisted by Cristian Lefter and Matthew Moodie. As the technical editor, Cristian Lefter carefully scrutinized all the code samples and step-by-step instructions. On several occasions, he detected errors that we fixed for you, and in other cases he made suggestions that resulted in simpler or more powerful solutions. Matthew Moodie served as the lead editor. In this capacity, he modified every page of the book to make it more succinct and easier to read. Both Cristian and Matthew asked many probing questions to force clarifications of the content in the book. If you find a Tip, Note, or Caution that is especially responsive to your needs, chances are Cristian or Matthew prompted me to insert it. This book is my seventh book project as a sole author, and I never recalled being so blessed by two such talented editors.

Just as the content of the book was so impeccably handled by the book's editors, the business side of the book was equally well handled by two Apress team members. My acquisition editor was Tony Davis. He was all that an author can hope for in an acquisition editor. He contracted with me in an expeditious fashion for the book project. Beyond that, he made excellent editorial suggestions on the first several chapters, which I applied to the remaining book chapters. There is no doubt that the whole book is easier to read because of his excellent suggestions for the first couple of chapters. Beth Christmas served as the book's project manager. She regularly urged me to stay as close as possible to projected deadlines while always allowing me enough time to prepare the best content that I knew how to author. In addition, she regularly assisted me in all the ways that a project manager can to make things move expeditiously and gracefully.

It is my practice to include an acknowledgment of my Lord and Savior, Jesus Christ. He is the author and finisher of my faith much as I am the author of this book and ultimately responsible for its content. Jesus is my inspiration for working tirelessly to write the best book that I can for you. It is my prayer that He blesses you so that you derive the maximum value possible from this book.

Introduction

This book ~~especially targets~~ *is about* SQL Server Express (SSE), Visual Basic Express (VBE), and Visual Web Developer Express (VWDE), all of which offer traditional fans of Microsoft technology an inexpensive and easy route for adapting, learning, and growing professionally. As their names suggest, these products are all compact versions of the full-blown products, and as such are easily downloaded from the Microsoft website, allowing you to try them out without any major investment of time or money. This also makes it easy for you to get the latest versions as soon as they are available without having to rely on other sources.

In addition, using the Express suite components that form the focus of this book is a great way for new developers and database administrators (or those who are new to Microsoft software) to learn about the latest Microsoft technologies.

Beginning SQL Server 2005 Express Database Applications with Visual Basic Express and Visual Web Developer Express From Novice to Professional gives you a solid introduction to these new technologies. After finishing this book, you will have had exposure to database, Visual Basic, and web development techniques. This book is both

- An introduction to SSE, VBE, and VWDE

- A cookbook that is full of practical examples for developing database solutions

The code samples and sample solutions in this book show you how to perform tasks that you will need to do as you build solutions for yourself, your colleagues, and small to mid-sized organizations.

While this book systematically explores how to perform many new and traditional database development topics, it does not exhaustively cover every new feature. The presentation of SSE emphasizes how to use T-SQL, Microsoft's implementation of Structured Query Language (SQL). You'll learn how to use T-SQL to formulate query statements, design data manipulation statements, and perform selected database administration topics. The integration of the .NET Framework into SSE is mentioned in the book. However, it is my belief that those migrating to SSE from MSDE, Access, earlier versions of SQL Server, or competitive database packages, will initially benefit the most from learning how to perform tasks with T-SQL.

This book also covers how to create Windows applications and web applications with VBE and VWDE. Again, the coverage of these products is highly selective. The main purpose of covering each of these is to equip you to use them with SSE to create database solutions.

I have written a number of books and articles, many of which I support through my website, `http://ProgrammingMSAccess.com`. You will find many samples of my work there, including material that complements this book. This includes extra examples and information relevant to Part 2 of this book, "Working with Visual Basic Express and Visual Web Developer Express." Feel free to visit or get in touch with me at `rickd@cabinc.net`. In addition, I have provided an online chapter that looks at advanced VWDE topics. You can view this chapter at `www.apress.com/book/bookDisplay.html?bID=459`.

1 *catchy*
2 *omissions*

Who Is This Book For?

Beginning SQL Server 2005 Express Database Applications with Visual Basic Express and Visual Web Developer Express From Novice to Professional is for several communities of users. The book's overall goal is to get any user started with SSE, including those who are working with SSE on a stand-alone basis, as well as those who run SSE through either or both VBE and VWDE. Included in this general summary are the following types of audiences:

- Database administrators in small and mid-sized organizations that will use SSE as their primary database

- MSDE and Access database developers and users who want to move from legacy Microsoft database technology so that they can position themselves to take advantage of new features not available in their legacy software

- Classic Visual Basic database developers who want to try creating database solutions with SSE and VBE or VWDE

- Business, scientific, or technical professionals who are not IT persons, but who need to create database solutions for their personal consumption or use by their organizational unit

- Computer hobbyists and students who want to learn about T-SQL and Visual Basic programming for Microsoft's latest database engine technology

- Professional developers who want to embed SSE in commercial packages marketed by their firms

What Does the Book Cover?

The book has two parts. The first part, "Working with SQL Server Express," focuses on SSE. The programming language for this part of the book is T-SQL. The second part of the book, "Working with Visual Basic Express and Visual Web Developer Express," highlights the use of the Visual Basic 2005 language in VBE and VWDE. You also gain exposure to powerful graphical development techniques for creating database solutions.

Selected topics addressed in Part 1 include

- Installing and configuring SSE

- Graphical and command-line tools for building SQL Server solutions

- Database design techniques and procedures for backing up, restoring, and copying databases

- Table design techniques, including how to manage relationships between tables

- Query design techniques, for the needs of data analysts and advanced database developers

- Programming examples for encapsulating and using T-SQL code in views, user-defined functions, stored procedures, and triggers

- SSE security administration issues with a special focus on authentication and authorization, along with selected new security topics, such as schema creation and management

| Totally catchy!

Selected topics addressed in Part 2 include

- Techniques for creating Windows applications with VBE, with special attention on the integrated development environment (IDE) and Visual Basic 2005 language programming samples
- Techniques for creating web applications with VWDE that highlight websites managed by the built-in VWDE web server or the Microsoft Internet Information Services (IIS) web server
- Numerous ADO.NET 2.0 code samples for programming SSE from within VBE and VWDE
- Coverage of visual database tools and graphical techniques for adding data-bound controls to forms with VBE and VWDE

PART 1

■ ■ ■

Working with
SQL Server Express

CHAPTER 1

■ ■ ■

Getting Started with SQL Server Express

The overall goal of this chapter is to get you started with SQL Server Express (SSE) by answering two overall questions:

- What is SQL Server Express good for, and who should use it?
- How do you install, configure, and get started using SQL Server Express?

The first two main sections in this chapter directly address the first question. The description of SQL Server Express users conveys an appreciation of the wide range of audiences and applications that SQL Server Express can serve. The chapter's third and fourth main sections contrast SQL Server Express with alternative database servers to clarify further the special benefits that SQL Server Express brings to the use of databases in organizations. Although SQL Server Express is technically a server application, it can run on workstation computers. See the "Performing a System Check for SQL Server Express" section for more detail of SQL Server Express requirements.

The last three main sections address the second question, first, by showing you how to install a SQL Server Express instance. SQL Server Express is a server application, and you consequently need a client application to take advantage of it. Therefore, this chapter then shows you how to do the following:

- Use a query tool adapted for use with SQL Server Express from the other SQL Server 2005 editions. This new query tool helps you program SQL Server Express with Transact-SQL (T-SQL), the special SQL (Structured Query Language) variant for Microsoft SQL Server.
- Use SQL Server Express with down-level, or legacy, clients. These may be the client applications or similar applications that you are currently using with SQL Server 2000 or SQL Server 7. Part 2 of the book drills down on Visual Basic Express and Visual Web Developer Express and explains how to use these applications with SQL Server Express.

What Is SQL Server Express?

SQL Server Express is the database component for the 2005 Express suite components from Microsoft. Other components in the suite include

- Visual Basic Express
- Visual Web Developer Express
- Visual C# Express, Visual C++ Express, and Visual J# Express

SQL Server Express is based on SQL Server 2005 technology. It uses the same database engine but is limited to 1 CPU, 1GB of RAM, and a maximum database size of 4GB. Although SQL Server Express explicitly removes the workload governor associated with MSDE, SQL Server Express still explicitly targets nonenterprise solutions. It is available free of charge, and it is designed to efficiently support smaller-scale database applications, with a definite emphasis placed on ease of development and use.

Just as MSDE versions offered a subset of the functionality of SQL Server 7 and 2000, so SQL Server Express offers a significant subset of SQL Server 2005 database engine features. However, given that SQL Server 2005 represents a major upgrade from SQL Server 2000, SSE also represents a major upgrade from MSDE with, among other things, a significantly expanded security model, enhanced techniques for handling large objects in either string or binary format, a hosted .NET CLR in the server, and the availability of new XML data types with supporting data. However, SSE does lack many of the enterprise features of other SQL Server 2005 editions.

As mentioned, SSE also places a much larger emphasis on ease of use and security. The following GUI components are freely available for use with SQL Server Express:

- *SQL Server Express query tool*: The new query tool enables developers and other users to write and save queries in T-SQL.

- *SQL Server Configuration Manager*: Another new client application for starting, stopping, and configuring an SSE instance (see the "Configuring SQL Server Express for Network Access" section for more on this client application).

- *SQL Server 2005 Surface Area Configuration*: Another new client tool that overlaps somewhat with SQL Server Configuration Manager, but provides additional capabilities for managing the availability of SQL Server Express features.

XCopy deployment dramatically simplifies copying a database between folders on the same computer or different computers. With XCopy deployment, you can copy or move database files so long as a database is not being actively used by an SSE instance. Earlier versions of SQL Server and even other editions of SQL Server 2005 do not release their database files so long as a SQL Server instance is running without the invocation of a special instruction (namely, sp_detach_db). XCopy deployment in SSE eliminates the need to invoke the sp_detach_db system-stored procedure, as well as the need to subsequently reattach database files to a SQL Server instance so that users can work with the database again.

Three SQL Server Express features support XCopy deployment: the availability of an AttachDBFileName argument for the connection string, the lack of the requirement to specify a logical database name, and the auto-close feature.

- Use the AttachDBFileName argument to point a connection string at a database file by its path and file name on the local computer.

- SQL Server Express can automatically create a logical database name based on the AttachDBFileName argument. In contrast, MSDE (and other editions of SQL Server 2005 besides SSE) require the designation of an explicit logical name through the Initial Catalog or Database connection string argument.

- The auto-close feature releases the locks on database files after the application using a database file closes. Invoking the Close method for an open connection merely returns a connection to the server instance's connection pool. The connection can remain open at the server until the connection item in the pool times out. ADO.NET developers can invoke the ClearPool method of a SQL Connection instance to remove a connection from the connection pool after invoking the Close method.

Several restrictions apply to the use of XCopy deployment. For example, the XCopy deployment feature is only intended for cases in which a SQL Server Express instance exists on the destination computer. When you use the `AttachDBFileName` argument in a connection string, it must appear along with a Data Source parameter. The Data Source parameter specifies the SQL Server Express instance name, such as .\SQLEXPRESS for the SQLEXPRESS named instance on the local computer. The use of an Initial Catalog or Database argument in a connection string is optional. If you do use either argument with XCopy deployment, do not assign a value to the logical name argument, because XCopy deployment automatically assigns a logical database name based on the path and file name for a database file.

■Note You'll receive more coverage in the "SQL Server Express vs. MSDE" section. Chapter 3 drills down on issues related to XCopy deployment in more depth.

Numerous wizards are available for use with SSE. The query tools for SSE offer wizards for tasks such as creating a database, adding a table to a database, and designing queries. Chapter 2 demonstrates several graphical wizard tools from a query editor tool for SSE. Wizards perform a task without the need for T-SQL code, but you can typically modify the output from a wizard with T-SQL code. Additionally, wizards and builders in Visual Basic Express and Visual Web Developer Express dramatically simplify creating a new database and a new table within a database. However, SQL Server Express is not limited to serving other Express suite components.

For example, Visual Studio 2005 developers can create database solutions that take advantage of SQL Server Express. Visual Studio 2005 developers will be able to use SSE just as they do any other edition of SQL Server 2005. This capability is especially important for nonenterprise solutions that target individual workstations or small workgroups and for which other SQL Server 2005 editions are not cost effective.

SQL Server Express can also support down-level clients, such as those created with Visual Studio 2003 and even Access 2003/2002/2000. After configuring SQL Server Express for connection from remote clients and referencing an appropriate connection string in the client for SQL Server Express, down-level clients can display or even manipulate data in a SQL Server Express database.

SQL Server Express is also the 2005 upgrade for MSDE. Developers creating new applications that were candidates for MSDE should consider SQL Server Express to gain the significantly improved scalability and functionality of SQL Server Express.

Who Is SQL Server Express For?

Within a broad pool of potential application contexts, there are several key constituencies for SQL Server Express. Four significant groups of potential users include the following:

- Hobbyists and other nonprofessional developers

- Business analysts

- Database administrators and operations specialists

- Professional developers in need of a free, modern database

As you review how each of these constituencies can benefit from SQL Server Express, other important groups of potential users may come to your mind. You may not belong to any of the key constituencies listed above, but SQL Server Express may still be a great database server for your needs. The mass appeal of SQL Server Express makes it suitable for a multitude of potential audiences and their application requirements.

■**Note** This book primarily highlights core database development skills with SQL Server Express that interface well with both Visual Basic Express and Visual Web Developer Express. To focus on integrating these three Express suite components, the book drills down on selected features that materially help you build integrated solutions with one, two, or all three Express suite components. If you currently create database solutions with Visual Basic, ASP, or VBA and Access for SQL Server databases, this book will likely help you to discover new ways to perform familiar tasks. In addition, the book equips you for moving on to more advanced tasks if those needs arise. If you're starting out with database development, you'll learn fundamental database development techniques that lay a foundation for growing your skills as you require more advanced techniques, such as creating database objects with the hosted .NET CLR and XML data-processing techniques.

Hobbyists and Other Nonprofessional Developers

If music is food for the soul, creating computer solutions may be food for the mind. In any event, a lot of us enjoy creating computer solutions. Many professional developers derive personal satisfaction even as they earn an income from creating database solutions, but hobbyists receive all their compensation from the sheer pleasure of making a solution work or from the appreciation that their solution generates in others. Sometimes a hobbyist will be a high school student, but other times a retired executive who wants to stay mentally alert can join the ranks of computer hobbyists. Mostly, hobbyists create solutions for themselves, but they may generate solutions for others, such as friends, fellow club members, or the church to which they belong.

Nonprofessional developers build solutions for work environments more commonly than hobbyists, but nonprofessional developers share an important trait with hobbyists. Nonprofessional developers gain no or very little income directly from programming. A nonprofessional developer may start by creating a solution that helps with personal job performance. Later, this developer may share the application with others and then train others on how to use it or interpret its results. The projects addressed by nonprofessional developers are typically too small in scope to merit the attention of a professional developer, although the completed project may bring significant value to one or more individuals in an organization.

One way that a nonprofessional developer can continue to grow is by building more projects—some of which may be for other organizations besides the developer's own. I have earned all my income from creating computer solutions since 1991, but I started creating computer solutions for myself, then others in my department, and ultimately for other organizations besides my employer's. I ultimately resigned to pursue a computer consulting practice on a full-time basis.

The Express suite of components, including SQL Server Express, is ideal for hobbyists and nonprofessional developers. This is because there is no charge for SQL Server Express, and database applications are very fast and easy to create. In addition, SQL Server Express offers a rich subset of SQL Server 2005 capabilities. If you're just starting out with .NET, as either a hobbyist or nonprofessional developer, SQL Server Express drives down the complexity of creating your first solution and offers a rich set of features with which to create subsequent solutions.

Business Analysts

Databases are important to organizations for many reasons—and one of the most important reasons is that they can provide valuable input for making decisions. When decisions need to be supported by data analysis below the enterprise level, organizations may not be able to afford assigning an information technology professional to provide computer support. In these cases, business analysts within a department may generate some tabular reports, charts, or computer displays that help executives within a department or branch office make decisions.

Business analysts bring special value to creating results that help executives run a business smarter. The results can be as simple as a list of customers who ordered a certain product last year or who are located in a particular part of the country. Because of their close interaction with executives, business analysts can often create summary reports that highlight critical business issues for the executives. Summaries can aggregate values, such as the number of stores in an area or the sales per store for a particular product line. What business analysts lack in development skills, they can sometimes make up for in their understanding of data as well as how to present that data to support decisions by executives.

SQL Server Express, either by itself or with other Express suite components, is great for crafting department and branch office solutions, for several reasons:

- An organizational unit needs no direct financial outlay to acquire a database server.

- Business analysts can easily run reports for managers from the convenience of their own desktop or laptop computers. These reports can be the output from simple T-SQL scripts running in a query tool for T-SQL or summary reports appearing on forms in a Visual Basic Express or Visual Web Developer Express solution.

- The SQL Server Express XCopy deployment capability simplifies how a business analyst can share a decision-support solution with computers used by managers. By copying a database solution to a manager's computer, business analysts can grow their worth in an organization as they leverage database resources.

Database Administrators and Operations Specialists

Database administrators (DBAs) and operations specialists are information technology professionals responsible for maintaining databases in their organizations. DBAs specialize in administrating databases. Operations specialists focus on a subset of computer operations that may or may not include database administration. When operations specialists work on databases, they often support DBAs. DBAs maintain databases for a community of professional database developers and sometimes for end users, such as business analysts and nonprofessional developers. DBAs and operations specialists also occasionally perform light application development tasks. SQL Server Express offers an easy and free way for DBAs and operations specialists to gain experience with and evaluate SQL Server 2005 technology for their organizations.

In this sense, SQL Server Express serves the same kind of role for SQL Server 2005 that MSDE played for SQL Server 7 and SQL Server 2000. This simplified migration of MSDE solutions to more advanced SQL Server editions, and the same is true for SSE.

Gaining familiarity with SQL Server Express can serve DBAs and operations specialists in two other ways. First, it will equip these professionals to create new databases for clients or to assist clients maintain databases that already exist. Second, administrators and specialists who know SQL Server Express well will understand that SQL Server Express is merely another edition of SQL Server 2005. Learning SQL Server Express will prepare these professionals to use any of a variety of standard techniques for migrating and upgrading SQL Server Express solutions to more enterprise-scaled SQL Server 2005 editions when such a migration becomes appropriate.

DBAs and operations specialists should have a working familiarity with several aspects of the SQL Server Express administrative interfaces. SQL Server Express installs securely by default. For example, unless you make special command-line settings during installation, SQL Server Express requires configuration for access over a network as well as from clients, such as Visual Basic Express, Visual Web Developer Express, and query tools, including a special edition of SQL Server Management Studio for SQL Server Express. You can manually configure SQL Server Express by enabling network protocols, restarting (or initially starting) the SQL Server Express instance, and starting the

SQL Server Browser service. The new SQL Server Configuration Manager utility enables these manual tasks. The SQL Server Browser service is a new service that allows a named SQL Server Express instance to listen on a port. The SQL Server Browser service does not start by default, but you can launch it from the Services MMC (Microsoft Management Console) or via a command prompt.

■**Note** See the "Configuring SQL Server Express for Network Access" section for more details about the SQL Server Browser service, including what specifically to use it for and how to use it.

The new `sqlcmd` utility, which builds on the capabilities of `osql` from earlier SQL Server versions, is a programming API that targets IT professionals, such as DBAs and operations specialists. The `sqlcmd` utility runs T-SQL statements and script files from a command prompt. Therefore, `sqlcmd` permits data access, data manipulation, database definition, and server administration.

Professional Developers in Need of a Free, Modern Database

It is common to think of professional developers within organizations as building almost exclusively enterprise solutions. However, many professional developers create solutions for midsize organizations or even departments in large organizations. In fact, independent developers and small consultancies regularly create solutions for small businesses. A significant percentage of solutions created for smaller organizational units do not demand the same kind of enterprise resources provided by most other SQL Server 2005 editions. In fact, it is largely enterprise features in SQL Server 2005 that are excluded from SQL Server Express, as you will see in the next section. As a consequence, SQL Server Express is ideally suited for professional developers who are creating solutions at the nonenterprise level, such as for a department or a branch office, within an organization.

Professional developers can also use SQL Server Express to create a solution that requires an embedded, lightweight database that does not add to the cost of their solution. SQL Server Express represents an excellent choice for this scenario. These embedded solutions are typically for packaged applications, which may need a database. For example, a contact manager application may have a built-in database to help manage contacts. MSDE used to be the recommended SQL Server edition for these applications, but SQL Server Express is the new recommended database.

SQL Server Express is fast, lightweight, and relatively independent. These features make SQL Server Express ideal for department-level and branch office solutions, as well as packaged applications that require a database to perform some task, such as contact management. You can readily deploy solutions using SQL Server Express over the Internet because of its small size versus other SQL Server 2005 editions.

- SQL Server Express has a customized data access mode (SQL Native Client), which installs along with SQL Server Express and does not require a distinct MDAC (Microsoft Data Access) library version.

- The availability of a custom data access mode helps to make SQL Server Express less dependent on the operating system because the MDAC library traditionally ships with an operating system.

- SQL Server Express is smaller than most other editions of SQL Server 2005, so it distributes as part of an application package efficiently over the Internet. SQL Server Express installs with a default name, which simplifies sharing a single SQL Server Express instance with multiple applications.

SQL Server Express vs. SQL Server 2005

By now I hope you've got the idea that SQL Server Express represents a powerful new tool for creating database solutions and performing database analyses and can be considered a sort of cross between MSDE and SQL Server 2005. SQL Server Express is basically a slimmed-down version of SQL Server 2005 and an upgraded version of MSDE with some very important enhancements. This section provides a technical comparison of SSE with SQL Server 2005, and the next section contrasts SSE with MSDE.

Similarities

SQL Server 2005 represents a major upgrade from SQL Server 2000. SQL Server Express inherits many of the improvements introduced with the SQL Server 2005 family of editions. This section identifies selected improvements and core database engine capabilities that are available through SQL Server Express.

The main SQL Server 2005 capabilities excluded from SQL Server Express are the enterprise features. The core database engine features are all available with SSE and other SQL Server 2005 editions. In fact, the SQL Server Express feature set extends beyond the needs of many environments that are likely candidates for adopting it.

T-SQL is at the heart of the core features in SQL Server Express for traditional database development chores. SQL Server Express permits you to use T-SQL statements to build the same kinds of queries and data manipulation statements that you can with SQL Server 2005. In addition, you can create many kinds of database objects that let you reuse data and T-SQL code. Examples of the kinds of objects that you can create with T-SQL in SQL Server Express solutions include the following:

- Tables
- Constraints
- Keys
- Indexes
- Views
- User-defined functions
- Stored procedures
- Triggers
- Logins
- Users

Beyond these core database objects, SQL Server Express developers inherit a variety of benefits and features because SQL Server Express is a SQL Server 2005 edition. The hosted .NET CLR is one of the more radical innovations introduced with SQL Server 2005, including its SSE edition. With the hosted .NET CLR, you can create database objects with .NET code as opposed to T-SQL code; this new capability enables you to take advantage of the vast functionality implemented with the .NET code libraries in your SSE database applications. Another substantial innovation is the introduction of the XML data type. You can use the XML data type to store XML documents within a column of a database table. You can also check XML documents to make sure they are valid according to a schema.

Other features are remarkable but not as radical as the hosted .NET CLR or XML data type. One of these new features is multiple active result sets (MARS), which enables a single data connection to permit simultaneous access to multiple result sets. You also gain the T-SQL enhancements introduced with SQL Server 2005, such as varchar(max), nvarchar(max), and varbinary(max). These latter three new data types simplify working with data formerly held in text, ntext, and image columns. Another large group of enhanced features relates to various security topics, such as an encryption hierarchy for key management. The following list enumerates several significant new benefits database developers get, because SQL Server Express is a SQL Server 2005 edition.

- Hosted .NET CLR
- Tight integration with other Express suite components, such as Visual Basic Express and Visual Web Developer Express
- Tight integration with Visual Studio 2005
- MARS (multiple active result sets on a single database connection)
- XML data type for processing XML documents with the database engine
- Varchar(max), nvarchar(max), and varbinary(max) for easier processing of data longer than 8,000 bytes
- PIVOT operator for easier preparation of cross-tabs based on relational tables
- Improved ranking to return the row number or percentile associated with rows in a result set
- Encryption by synchronous and asynchronous keys
- Signing clear text data with certificates
- Mapping logins and database users to certificates and keys
- Encryption key management through an encryption hierarchy
- Schema rather than direct-user ownership of database objects

Differences

Relative to SQL Server 2005, a major defining characteristic of SQL Server Express is the lack of, or abridged, support for enterprise database support features. The absent or weak enterprise support features are not a significant limitation given the target scenarios for which SQL Server Express is intended, such as use by hobbyists or business analysts creating departmental solutions, or where a database is embedded in another solution. Some of the significant enterprise support features present in SQL Server 2005, but missing from SQL Server Express, include the following:

- Integration Services (formerly DTS)
- Analysis Services
- Notification Services
- Database snapshots
- Fail-over clustering
- SqlMail and SQLiMail
- Partitioned views
- Native HTTP SOAP access

Other selected SQL Server 2005 features that are significantly abridged in its SQL Server Express edition include the following:

- SQL Server Express cannot host a Reporting Services instance, but SQL Server Express users will be able to compose reports on any SQL Server 2005 instance that is hosting Reporting Services.

- With the Service Broker, two SQL Server instances can exchange information. Service Broker is a new SQL Server 2005 resource that supports peer-to-peer communication between SQL Server instances as well as interprocess communication between two processes on the same computer. SQL Server Express instances cannot share information between two computers unless the two SQL Server Express peers pass through another, more advanced SQL Server 2005 edition, but Service Broker will permit communication between multiple SQL Server Express instances on the same computer.

- SQL Server Express can participate in SQL Server 2005 replication on a subscriber basis only. In addition, SQL Server Express does not support refreshing a pulled subscriber copy with SQL Server Agent (as is the case with other SQL Server 2005 editions). However, you can synchronize pulled subscriber copies of a database on a schedule to SQL Server Express instance via the Windows Synchronization Manager or Replication Management Objects (RMO).

SQL Server Express vs. MSDE

SQL Server Express is the upgrade for MSDE. As any good upgrade should, SQL Server Express offers enhancements that are powerful incentives for upgrading. Perhaps the most important incentive is the removal of the governor in MSDE that starts to degrade performance after five concurrent database connections. With SQL Server Express, you can connect as many users as you wish with no impact on performance other than the normal one from the load of users. In addition, the maximum database size grew from 2GB with MSDE to 4GB with SQL Server Express. With a modern computer that has a fast processor, ample memory, and large storage, SQL Server Express should deliver much better scalability than MSDE.

The adoption of MSDE was thwarted by the lack of a simple interface for creating queries, reusing queries, and simplifying basic administrative tasks. In response to user requests for help with these kinds of activities, Microsoft will have a dedicated edition of SQL Server Management Studio for creating and editing SQL query statements for use with SQL Server Express. You can use the dedicated edition of SQL Server Management Studio for SQL Server Express to open previously saved queries for reuse as well as to build database objects, such as stored procedures, which facilitate the reuse of T-SQL code. The dedicated edition of SQL Server Management Studio for SQL Server Express also offers an Object Explorer for examining the databases attached to a server and the objects within a database. In addition, you'll be able to use wizards and builders for common administrative tasks, such as creating or altering a database.

■Note The dedicated edition of SQL Server Management Studio for SQL Server Express was not set for release when SQL Server Express initially was scheduled to become available in November 2005. As I write this book, the dedicated edition of SQL Server Management Studio for SQL Server Express is promised by Microsoft in the first half of 2006.

XCopy deployment is another SQL Server Express database feature that uniquely distinguishes SQL Server Express from MSDE (and even other SQL Server 2005 editions). With XCopy deployment, you can copy to another destination computer a database file (.mdf) when the database file is not actively open. On another computer, an application, such as one prepared with Visual Basic Express, can readily connect to its local copy of the database file by pointing at the database file with the `AttachDBFileName` connection string argument. See Chapter 12 for a demonstration of the syntax for the `AttachDBFileName` argument. You can also send a SQL Server Express database file and optionally an application file as mail attachments. The person receiving the e-mail can then copy the attachment(s) so that the database file is at the location specified by the `AttachDBFileName` argument in the connection string of an application file (.exe).

Installing SQL Server Express

SQL Server Express aims to be the easiest edition of SQL Server 2005, and its ease of use begins with the installation of the package. You can run the SQL Server Express Installation Wizard in either of two styles:

- *Basic style*: Does not present advanced configuration options and offers a minimum number of wizard screens with some screens partially or fully populated with recommended entries.

- *Advanced style*: Adds several more screens to the basic style of running the installation wizard. These screens offer selections that are prespecified with the basic style of installation.

This section briefly describes both basic and advanced screens in the order in which they normally appear.

■**Tip** In addition to installing SQL Server Express from its installation wizard, you can invoke the SQL Server Express setup.exe file from command-line prompts, which are the same as those for other SQL Server 2005 editions. By using command-line prompts, you can perform silent installs that are convenient for applications that need to embed a database server as well as remote installs, which allow a user on one computer to install SQL Server Express on a different computer. For the details on how to perform SQL Server Express installation from a command-line prompt, see the "Running Setup from the Command Prompt" in a SQL Server 2005 Books Online. Search the Microsoft Download Center (`http://www.microsoft.com/downloads/search.aspx?displaylang=en`) for instructions on how to download Books Online.

Performing a System Check for SQL Server Express

Launch the SQL Server Express Installation Wizard by running sqlexpr.exe, which is a self-extracting cabinet file. Cabinet files are compressed files used in Microsoft installation packages. No matter whether you select the basic or advanced installation process, you must have the 2.0 .NET Framework installed on your computer before invoking the installation wizard. You can run the 2.0 .NET Framework side by side with either the 1.0 or 1.1 versions of the .NET Framework, but delete any subsequent .NET Framework versions, such as 1.2.

In addition to the 2.0 .NET Framework, SQL Server Express has other hardware and software requirements. The installation computer must have Microsoft Internet Explorer 6.0 installed, but it doesn't have to be the default browser. Acceptable operating systems include Windows 2000 SP4, Windows XP SP2, and Windows 2003. Minimum hardware requirements specify a minimum Intel Pentium 3 or a compatible with no less than 256MB of memory.

After you start the SQL Server Express Installation Wizard and advance past the Welcome and License agreement screens, the wizard will perform a system check for the suitability of your computer's software and hardware to run SQL Server Express. At the end of the process, you see a screen like the one in Figure 1-1. This screen can warn you of situations that you may care to remedy or tell you of errors that need to be fixed. For example, if your computer has less than 512MB of memory, you will receive a warning. In fact, Figure 1-1 shows such a warning for Windows 2000 computers. Warnings do not necessarily need to be fixed prior to installation, but errors can cause an installation to abort. Of course, you can correct the error and relaunch the installation wizard.

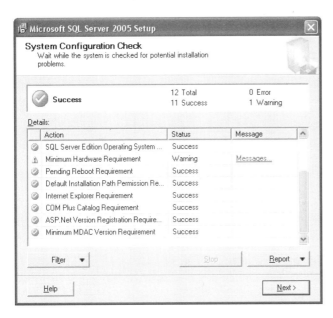

Figure 1-1. *The System Configuration Check screen helps you assess any remedial actions to take before completing the installation of SQL Server Express.*

Registration, Feature, and Instance Name Screens

The Registration Installation screen appears next. Unsurprisingly, you can designate user name and company. This screen includes a check box toward the bottom that allows you to suppress the display of subsequent screens showing advanced configuration options. The installation wizard automatically checks the box to hide the advanced configuration screens. You can clear the check box to view the default advanced configuration settings and optionally override them.

The Feature Selection screen appears next. You can use this screen to select any subset of SQL Server Express features that you care to install. No features or elements are initially selected for installation. You can save storage space by not installing the elements that you do not plan to use. A Feature description box on the screen offers a brief summary of the currently selected element as well as the amount of storage space for the element. Click the + to the left of the features to expand those features with one or more subelements below them. You can select the subelements individually. Figure 1-2 shows the Feature Selection screen with all SQL Server Express elements selected. I recommend that you select all elements (as Figure 1-2 shows) unless you have a compelling reason to do otherwise. The wizard will not let you proceed with an installation without making any selections from this screen.

The Instance Name screen can appear for either of two reasons. The installation wizard checks to see if an instance of SQL Server Express called SQLEXPRESS already exists on the computer. If not, then the wizard automatically assigns the name SQLEXPRESS to the instance it is installing. If a previously installed named instance has the name SQLEXPRESS, then the wizard shows the Instance Name screen so that you have the option to designate a new name for the new SQL Server Express instance that you are installing. Otherwise, the Instance Name screen does not show unless a user clears the Hide advanced configurations check box on the Registration Information screen.

Figure 1-2. *The Feature Selection screen lets you select which SQL Server Express elements you care to install.*

Service Account and Authentication Mode Screens

The Service Account screen appears next if you cleared the Hide advanced configurations check box on the Registration Information screen. The service account is the account under which the SQL Server Express service runs. Designating an appropriate service account is a delicate balance between granting sufficient permissions for "anything" that you want the SQL Server Express service to be able to do and not exposing the operating system of the computer on which SQL Server Express runs to hijacking. By default, the wizard designates a special account, such as the Network Service Account, that is a member of the local Windows Users group. If you are on a domain, you can select the Use a domain account radio button. Then, specify the user name, password, and domain name for the domain account. This screen also includes check boxes for starting the SQL Server Express and SQL Browser services automatically at the end of setup. You can change the default selection for either or both check boxes.

■**Tip** Microsoft recommends against using the Administrator account as a SQL Server Express service account. In any event, you may find it useful to have a domain account for a SQL Server Express instance with permissions to access data on another computer within a domain. Whenever you anticipate the need to join data from servers on two or more different computers, it is useful to have a service account that explicitly facilitates this objective. Finally, consider the security necessary for your operating environment and circumstances. If you have SQL Server Express running on a small network with no Internet access, and your business group has limited system resources to manage sophisticated security schemes, you may find the computer's Administrator account suitable for your needs. No matter which service account you use make sure it has a password that is not easy to hack. This caveat applies even more when your service account is the computer's Administrator account.

The Authentication Mode screen appears next. By default, the wizard selects Windows Authentication mode. This is the most secure authentication mode. It allows access to the SQL Server Express instance only via Windows operating system accounts. If a user does not have a systems account or SQL Server Express does not recognize a user's system account, then the user cannot connect to the SQL Server Express instance. Selecting the Mixed Mode radio button on the Authentication Mode screen enables connections to the SQL Server Express instance via both Windows operating system accounts and SQL Server Express administered logins. If your application environment doesn't allow you to control Windows accounts, or you haven't set up a user's Windows account as a valid SQL Server Express login, then mixed mode authentication may be an appropriate choice. If you anticipate a need for mixed mode authentication, you should make the choice here because there is no graphical user interface elsewhere for changing the authentication mode setting. You can programmatically alter authentication mode with SQL Management Objects (SMO). The Authentication Mode screen also requires you to set and confirm a password for the sa account in the SQL Server Express instance. Figure 1-3 shows the Authentication Mode with mixed mode authentication selection.

Figure 1-3. *The Authentication Mode screen enables you to specify an authentication mode and a password for the SQL Server sa login.*

Collation, Error Reporting, and Ready to Install Screens

The Collation Settings screen appears next if you are showing advanced configuration settings. Collation settings can impact the ability of two SQL Server instances to exchange information meaningfully. Collation settings control items, such as character set, sort order, and locale-specific settings. The wizard makes a default collation setting that matches the Windows Locale setting in your Windows operating system. If you need to exchange information with other SQL Server instances that have different collation settings, then you should make a collation setting that matches a target instance with which you seek to exchange information.

After the Collation Settings screen, you may notice the User Instances screen. This screen is optional. You can suppress its visibility by selecting the Hide Advanced Configuration check box. In addition, the visibility of this screen also depends on the selection of Database Services in the Features Selection screen, which nearly everyone installing SSE will select. A user instance is child instance of the SSE instance. The user instance runs under the credentials of the user.

The Error and Usage Report Settings screen permits you to control whether fatal errors send a report to Microsoft documenting the problem. You can also use this screen to send your installation selections to Microsoft. The usage reporting is anonymous, and it is meant to provide feedback on the features that SSE installations select. The error-reporting capability can be especially useful for a SQL Server Express instance dedicated to a critical business function in your organization because you ensure that Microsoft learns of problems causing your applications to fail. For casual use or prototype applications, the need to send reports to Microsoft may be less critical.

The final screen has the title Ready to Install. Click Finish and wait for the completion of the installation of the SQL Server Express instance. SQL Server Express can install "secure by default," so you actually have to start it before you can use it. In addition, because SQL Server is a server application, you need to run a client against it to verify that it is working properly.

Using SQL Server Express Query Tools

To use a SQL Server Express instance after you have installed it, you need to run applications, such as a query tool, suitable for using a SQL Server Express instance. However, before you can run client applications, you typically need to configure a SQL Server Express instance for use with client applications. This configuration process is crucial because SQL Server Express installs securely by default—not ready to use by default. Although you typically only need to configure SQL Server Express once, the configuration steps can be critical to your ability to run queries later.

This section begins by briefly reviewing a query tool that can serve as a client application for a SQL Server Express instance. This query tool is a dedicated SQL Server Management Studio version for SQL Server Express. Microsoft plans to release this tool in the first half of 2006, but a public beta version may be available before that date. Chapter 2 includes additional coverage and demonstrations on how the proposed query tool for SQL Server Express is likely to work. In the interim, SQL Server Express users can use SQL Server Management Studio from an evaluation or fully licensed copy licensed copy of SQL Server 2005 to perform queries.

Before you can run queries against a SQL Server Express instance, you nearly always need to configure the SQL Server Express instance and sometimes the Windows XP firewall. It is highly likely that you will not be able to connect to or run a query with a SQL Server Express instance unless you master the content in this section, which typically describes one of several approaches to configuring selected features of SQL Server Express. If your goal is to become an expert administrator for SQL Server Express, you can explore alternative configuration techniques that complement and extend the techniques described here. SQL Server Express Books Online is an excellent resource for starters.

■**Tip** Different versions and editions of SQL Server have a Books Online for documentation. SQL Server Express has its own version of Books Online with information specific to SQL Server Express. To find the most recent version of Books Online for SQL Server Express go to the Microsoft Download Center (`http://www.microsoft.com/downloads/`) and search for SQL Server Express Books Online.

I conclude this section by entering a simple query into SQL Server Management Studio, which serves as a surrogate for the future version of the SQL Server Express query tool. The discussion of this sample shows you one approach to connecting to a SQL Server Express instance. You also see the use of tabs as query tool elements for entering query statements and viewing results. Chapter 2 drills down on graphical techniques for running queries with SQL Server Express. The graphical tool covered in Chapter 2 is the one introduced in this section.

Query Tools for SQL Server Express

Part 1 of this book drills down on using T-SQL with SQL Server Express. To prepare you for subsequent chapters in Part 1, this section introduces the query tool mentioned previously for SQL Server Express. To provide SQL Server Express users with a query tool that is a subset of SQL Server 2005's tools, Microsoft plans to issue during the second half of 2006 a query tool based on a subset of features from the full version of SQL Server Management Studio. You can think of this query tool as SSMS for SQL Server Express. This query tool enables T-SQL queries. However, the SSMS version for SQL Server Express does not offer the enterprise features found in the full version of SSMS for other SQL Server 2005 editions. The lack of enterprise capabilities in the SQL Server Express version of SSMS is not generally a problem because SQL Server Express is not for enterprise solutions.

■**Note** The installation process for the SQL Server Express version of SSMS is likely to rely on an installation wizard. After running the wizard, you'll be able to start the SSMS-based application just like any other Windows program (from the Windows Start menu).

SSMS for SQL Server Express was developed so late in the SQL Server beta cycle that it was not available for hands-on testing in this book. In other words, not even a beta is available as I write this chapter. However, Microsoft assured me that users could get a hands-on feel for the second SQL Server Express query tool by using the full version of SSMS. Instead of focusing on the full range of features in the full SSMS version (or even the complete likely subset for SQL Server Express), this book focuses on how to

- Make connections to SQL Server Express
- Run queries against SQL Server databases

This chapter introduces SSMS after configuring SQL Server Express to work with it or another client application, such as Visual Basic Express or Visual Web Developer Express. Chapter 2 includes more extended coverage of the use of SSMS for SQL Server Express. The remaining chapters in Part 1 highlight the use of T-SQL to formulate query statements, maintain a database, and administer a SQL Server Express instance. Part 2 (Chapters 9 through 13) focuses on the use of Visual Basic Express and Visual Web Developer Express, including their use with SQL Server Express.

■**Note** Part 2 addresses connecting to SQL Server Express from Visual Basic Express or Visual Web Developer Express. I do not explicitly cover Visual Studio 2005 in this book because I do not assume that readers have a license for this more expensive application. However, Visual Studio 2005 will use the same connection strings that work for Visual Basic Express and Visual Web Developer Express.

Configuring SQL Server Express to Start Automatically

You can connect to a local SQL Server Express instance via the Shared Memory protocol, which the SQL Server Express installation process enables by default. After the installation of SQL Server Express, the instance does not necessarily start automatically, and the instance may not automatically start when you reboot your computer. This is part of what Microsoft means when it says that

SQL Server Express installs securely by default. You can configure a SQL Server Express instance (or the service for a SQL Server Express instance) to start automatically whenever the computer boots.

After you get SQL Server Express installed and running, you'll often want to set the local SQL Server Express instance so that it starts whenever the computer starts. You can accomplish this goal with a variety of tools. This section demonstrates the use of theSQL Server Configuration Manager. This tool is installed with any edition of SQL Server 2005, including SQL Server Express. To open the SQL Server Configuration Manager tool, choose Start ➤ All Programs ➤ Microsoft SQL Server 2005 ➤ Configuration Tools ➤ SQL Server Configuration Manager from the Windows XP Start button.

■**Note** Microsoft enabled the final version of the SQL Server Express Installation Wizard to configure SQL Server Express and SQL Server Browser so that they can start automatically whenever you reboot your computer. If SQL Server Configuration does not show these settings, you can use the instructions in this section to configure SQL Server Express and SQL Server Browser so that they do start automatically. In addition, you can adapt the instructions in this section to require the manual starting of SQL Server Express and SQL Server Browser.

After opening SQL Server Configuration Manager, you can assure that SQL Server Express starts automatically by performing two actions.

1. First, set the SQL Server Express service so that it starts automatically.

    a. Begin by selecting SQL Server 2005 Services in the left pane.

    b. Right-click anywhere on the SQLEXPRESS row in the right pane and choose Properties (see Figure 1-4).

    c. Next, select the Service tab for the SQLEXPRESS Properties dialog box.

    d. Then, as Figure 1-5 shows, open the Start Mode drop-down box and select Automatic.

    e. Click OK to commit your change and exit the dialog box.

2. While you have SQL Server 2005 Services in the left pane of the SQL Server Configuration Manager, set the SQL Server Browser to start automatically. The SQL Server Browser service facilitates the connection of remote computers to a SQL Server Express instance. The "Configuring SQL Server Express for Network Access" section later in this chapter describes the role of SQL Server Browser service. However, I describe how to turn it on automatically here because the process is so similar to automatically starting the SQLEXPRESS service.

    a. With SQL Server 2005 Services selected in the left pane, right-click anywhere in the SQL Server Browser service row within the right pane and choose Properties.

    b. Then, set the Start Mode attribute to Automatic on the Service tab of the Properties dialog box. The process for completing this task parallels the comparable function for the SQLEXPRESS service.

Figure 1-4. *Start to set the SQLEXPRESS named instance service so that it starts automatically by choosing its Properties in the SQL Server Configuration Manager.*

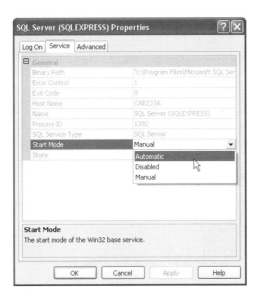

Figure 1-5. *Complete setting the SQLEXPRESS named instance service so that it starts automatically by opening the Service tab in the SQLEXPRESS Properties dialog box and selecting Automatic from the Start Mode drop-down box.*

Configuring SQL Server Express for Network Access

When connecting to a local instance of the SSMS-based query tool, you use a Shared Memory protocol. The Shared Memory protocol works locally on a computer and bypasses any network interfaces, which remote computers use to communicate with a SQL Server Express instance. The SQL Server Express installation process can disable network connectivity. This design helps to make a SQL Server Express instance secure by default immediately after installation. The feature also requires you to perform some additional steps if you require network access to a SQL Server Express instance.

The SQL query tool for SQL Server Express based on SSMS can connect to SQL Server Express from the same computer or another computer. In general, you can use SSMS to connect to SQL Server instances on multiple computers. To illustrate this design feature, the connection to SQL Server Express from the SSMS-based query tool in the next section is from a different computer than the one on which SQL Server Express runs.

■**Caution** You also require network access if you plan to communicate with a SQL Server Express instance from a down-level client even from a local computer. Down-level clients include any client application not based on the 2.0 .NET Framework or not using the new SQL Native Client. Examples of down-level clients include Visual Studio 2003, Visual Basic 6, and Access 2003.

There are two main steps to enabling network access to a SQL Server instance. The first step is to enable network protocols. With SQL Server Express, the network protocols are TCP/IP or Named Pipes. SQL Server Express does not support VIA protocols. You can enable the network protocols with the SQL Server Configuration Manager.

- Expand SQL Server 2005 Network Configuration in the left pane of SQL Server Configuration Manager.

- Then, select Protocols for the named instance that you are using, such as SQLEXPRESS.

- Next, enable the TCP/IP protocol. Figure 1-6 shows the right-click menu selection for enabling the TCP/IP protocol.

- Also, you can right-click the Named Pipes protocol and choose Enable. Named Pipes are a legacy protocol that you should not use unless necessary for older client applications or network settings.

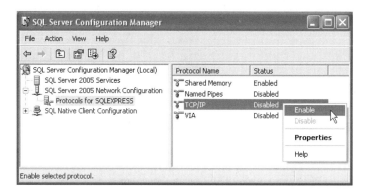

Figure 1-6. *Use SQL Server Configuration Manager to enable protocols.*

The second major step to enabling network access is to start the SQL Server Browser service (unless the installation wizard started SQL Server Browser automatically; Figure 1-4 illustrates how to determine the SQL Server Browser status). This service is new with SQL Server 2005. The service specifies on which port a SQL Server instance listens. The process for enabling the service parallels the process for enabling a SQL Server Express instance. Therefore, I described how to enable the SQL Server Browser service above in the "Configuring SQL Server Express to Start Automatically" section.

■**Caution** There is a potential conflict between the SQL Server Browser service and SQL Server 2000 instances, including those for MSDE without the SP3 update. The conflict results from both services (SQL Server Browser service and the SQL Server 2000 instance service) competing for port UDP 1434. One workaround for the problem is not to install SP3 for any SQL Server 2000 instances on a computer running a SQL Server Express instance.

After most major configuration steps, such as enabling the two network protocols and setting the SQL Server Browser service to start automatically, it is a good practice to restart the server instance to register your changes. You can begin to restart the service by right-clicking the SQL Server Express instance service in the right pane of SQL Server Configuration Manager with SQL Server 2005 Services selected in the left pane. Then, choose Restart from the context menu and wait for the service to stop and then start again. If the Restart command ends abnormally with an error, close Configuration Manager. Then, reopen Configuration Manager to confirm the status of SQL Server Express. If necessary, you can manually stop and then start SQL Server Express from Configuration Manager.

Configuring the Windows XP Firewall for SQL Server Express

If you are running SQL Server Express on a Windows XP computer, chances are you will need to configure the Windows XP firewall. A firewall blocks unexpected packets of information from getting behind the firewall and into the computer. If the firewall doesn't know about the information packet, then it doesn't get through. This can be pretty handy in blocking worms from getting into your SQL Server Express instance and causing failure, corruption, and other havoc. Unfortunately, firewalls can also block legitimate information if they are not properly configured.

■Note You do not necessarily have to configure the Windows XP firewall to enable SQL Server Express network connectivity. For example, if you install SQL Server Express on a Windows 2000 computer, then there is no Windows XP firewall to configure. Even on a Windows XP computer, you may disable the Windows XP firewall if you have another firewall that you prefer to use. In this case, you will have to configure the other firewall to permit network connectivity for SQL Server Express.

Developing a proper appreciation of firewalls is way beyond the scope of this book. However, you have to know a little bit about Windows XP firewall and how it interacts with SQL Server Express to be able to make network connections to a SQL Server Express instance running on a Windows XP computer. In this section I recommend one of several possible strategies for configuring the Windows XP firewall so that it expects input from the SQL Server Express and SQL Server Browser services. If a firewall knows about a source of legitimate input to a computer, it can let input from that source into the computer. Configuring the firewall so that it knows about your SQL Server Express and SQL Server Browser services permits you to pass login credentials to a SQL Server Express instance as well as T-SQL query statements from a remote computer.

The key to our approach to letting the Windows firewall work for SQL Server Express is to know the files and paths for the SQL Server Express and SQL Server Browser services.

- A SQL Server Express instance has a SQLservr.exe file that enables the service.
  - The path for this file is in one of the folders below \Program Files\Microsoft SQL Server\.
  - For example, if the SQLEXPRESS instance of SQL Server Express is the first named instance, then the rest of the path to its sqlservr.exe file is MSSQL.1\MSSQL\Binn\.
- The SQL Server Browser service is enabled by the sqlbrowser.exe file.
  - This file starts in the same root path (\Program Files\Microsoft SQL Server\) as the sqlservr.exe file.
  - The balance of the path to the file is 90\Shared\.

Now that you know the path and files to make exceptions for in the Windows firewall, you can launch the Windows XP Security Center from the Control Panel. The Security Center applet lets you manage the Windows XP firewall and other elements of Windows XP security.

1. In the initial page for the Security Center, click the Windows firewall link at the bottom of the page to open the Windows Firewall dialog box.
2. You can turn off the firewall from the General tab. This approach to managing access to a SQL Server Express instance is not recommended.
3. Select the Exceptions tab.
4. Click the Add Program button.

5. In the Add a Program dialog box, do the following:

    a. Use the Browse button to navigate to and select sqlservr.exe.

    b. Use the Browse button again to navigate to and select sqlbrowser.exe.

    c. Then, click OK to close the Add a Program dialog box.

6. Close the Security Center.

Connecting from the SSMS-Based Query Tool

After configuring SQL Server Express to start automatically and setting up network access, as well as optionally configuring the Windows XP firewall, you are ready to see how to connect to the SQLEXPRESS instance of SQL Server Express on one computer from another computer running SSMS. The preceding section on readying SQL Server Express for network access is especially critical because SSMS runs from another computer. SSMS serves as a surrogate for the SSMS-based query tool for SQL Server Express. Recall that a working version is not available, but the Express version of SSMS is similar to SSMS, except for enterprise features. The computer with an installed instance of SQL Server Express has the name CAB233A.

Launch the SSMS-based query tool from the Windows Start button, for example, by choosing Start ➤ All Programs ➤ Microsoft SQL Server 2005 ➤ SQL Server Management Studio. Selecting this menu item presents a Connect to Server dialog box over the SSMS IDE. SSMS automatically populates entries with the values from the last successful connection. If this is the first time you are opening SSMS, you may need to specify the entries on the Connect to Server dialog box.

SQL Server Express supports two types of authentication: Windows authentication and SQL Server authentication. With Windows authentication, SQL Server Express trusts the authentication of a user by Windows. With SQL Server authentication, SQL Server Express requests a user ID account and password instead of relying on a Windows security token associated with the user.

Figure 1-7 shows the Connect to Server dialog box for SSMS with a connection to the SQLEXPRESS instance on the CAB233A computer. Because the dialog box designates SQL Server Authentication, you can specify a user ID and password. During the installation steps in the "Installing SQL Server Express" section, saw the sa login, which is a SQL Server login. Enter the password that you specified for that login during setup. If you select Windows Authentication, then you can log in with your Windows account. In this case, the Login and Password dialog boxes are disabled. No matter which type of authentication you select, click Connect to launch an attempt to connect to the SQL Server Express instance specified in the Server name box.

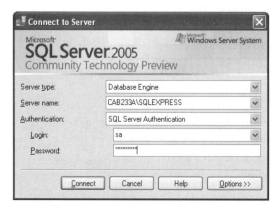

Figure 1-7. *The Connect to Server dialog box can connect to the SQLEXPRESS instance of SQL Server Express on the CAB233A with Windows Authentication.*

■**Note** The SSMS-based query tool will only support the Database Engine Server type in the Connect to Server dialog box. Other server types are reserved for other SQL Server 2005 editions that support enterprise features, such as Analysis Services and Reporting Services.

After SSMS makes a connection to SQLEXPRESS, you can click the New Query tool on the Standard toolbar to open an empty query window named SQLQuery1.sql. The Standard toolbar appears just below the menu in Figure 1-8. Immediately after installing and configuring SQL Server Express, you will only have the system databases on a server. Further, the master database, one of the system databases, is selected in the Available Databases drop-down control on the SQL Editor toolbar. The SQL Editor toolbar appears below the Standard toolbar in Figure 1-8.

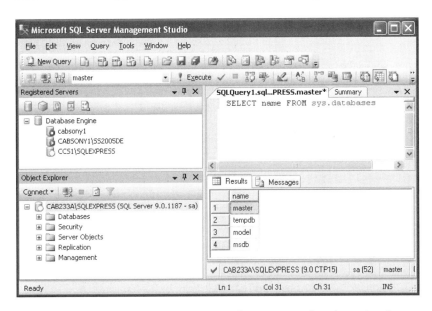

Figure 1-8. *By typing a T-SQL query statement into a query tab and running the statement, you can display the outcome from the query statement in the Results tab below the query tab.*

The selection of the master database in the Available Databases control means T-SQL statements run in the context of the master database. You can enter SELECT name FROM sys.databases in the SQLQuery1.sql window. This T-SQL statement selects name column values from the sys.databases system view, which contains a row for each database on the SQL Server Express instance. When executed against a newly installed SQL Server Express instance, this query returns the names for four built-in databases for a new instance. To run the query, press the F5 key or click Execute to see the results. Figure 1-8 shows the results from the SELECT statement in the Results tab below the SQLQuery1.sql tab. The Registered Servers and Object Explorer windows, which are discussed in Chapter 2, appear to the left of the SQLQuery1.sql and Results tabs.

Connecting from Remote Down-Level Clients

In this section I describe how to configure SQL Server Express for connection from remote, down-level (or legacy) clients, such as Visual Studio 2003 and Access 2003. Down-level (or legacy) clients that worked well with MSDE will not necessarily function in the same way with SQL Server Express. I restrict the focus to down-level clients in this section to give you a feel for how down-level clients work with SQL Server Express. To demonstrate how this works, this section starts with instructions for downloading several Microsoft sample databases. The AdventureWorks database is used in many chapters throughout the book.

There are really two sides to the issue of how to connect to SQL Server Express from remote clients. First, you have to configure SQL Server Express so that it is ready to receive connections from a remote client. You can perform this task with the techniques discussed in the "Using SQL Server Express Query Tools" section. Second, you have to create a connection in the client application that points at an appropriately configured SQL Server Express instance.

■**Caution** Even after you configure a SQL Server Express instance to interact with remote clients and you successfully connect with the SQL Server instance from a remote, down-level client, you may still not be able to view or edit data from a table directly because some down-level clients do not know how to process some schemas to which tables in SQL Server Express databases may belong. This is not an issue with down-level clients for tables or other objects that belong to a schema with a well-known name, such as dbo.

Installing Sample Databases

Part 1 includes a concentrated focus on T-SQL programming. One of the best ways to learn how to program any language is by studying code samples. Over time, three classic sample databases for SQL Server received substantial attention in SQL Server documentation (Books Online). The documentation is a good resource for T-SQL code samples. The sample database names are pubs, Northwind, and AdventureWorks. This section briefly describes how to obtain these sample databases for use with SQL Server Express.

Slightly updated versions of the classic pubs and Northwind database samples are available for download from the following URL: http://www.microsoft.com/downloads/details. aspx?FamilyId=06616212-0356-46A0-8DA2-EEBC53A68034&displaylang=en. You can download the SQL2000SampleDb.msi file from this URL. Running the .msi file that you download generates a folder that contains two T-SQL script files (.sql), which you can open and run individually from the SQL Server Express version of SSMS. When you run the scripts, you will create, populate, and attach the pubs and Northwind databases to the SQL Server Express instance to which you are connected. Both script files reside in the same folder, Microsoft SQL Server 2000 Sample Database Scripts, which is in the Program Files path. An HTML Readme file in the same folder with the script files describes the databases and gives more details on how to run the scripts.

Many of the code samples in the SQL Server 2005 documentation rely on the AdventureWorks database. It is therefore especially useful to become familiar with this database, which you can download from http://www.microsoft.com/downloads/details.aspx?FamilyID=2adbc1a8-ae5c-497d-b584-eab6719300cd&displaylang=en.

The AdventureWorksDb.msi file, in turn, generates support files for the AdventureWorks database. Running this .msi file generates two database files (AdventureWorks_Data.mdf and AdventureWorks_Log.ldf) in the Data folder of your SQL Server Express instance, which is often at C:\Program Files\Microsoft SQL Server\MSSQL.1\MSSQL\Data\. You can attach the database files as a database to your SQL Server instance by running the following script from a query tool:

```
USE master
GO

CREATE DATABASE AdventureWorks
ON PRIMARY (FILENAME = 'Data_folder_path\AdventureWorks_Data.MDF')
FOR ATTACH
GO
```

When it installs, its logical name is AdventureWorks. A detailed explanation of the operation of the FOR ATTACH clause of the CREATE DATABASE statement appears in Chapter 3.

Connecting to SQL Server Express from Visual Studio 2003

With Visual Studio 2003, you can connect with Server Explorer to a SQL Server Express database on a local or a remote computer. With this approach, you add a new data connection to Server Explorer for each SQL Server Express database that you want to reference from Visual Studio 2003. The process for connecting is the same whether you connect from a local or a remote computer. Once you have a valid data connection, you can use it in Visual Studio to examine databases and build database solutions.

Creating a Data Connection

Start to connect to a SQL Server Express instance by right-clicking Data Connections in Server Explorer and choosing Add Connection. This choice opens a Data Link Properties dialog box. So long as you have a SQL Server Express instance configured for remote connectivity, the instance will broadcast so that it appears in the server name drop-down box. For example, if a SQL Server Express instance named SQLEXPRESS resides on the CAB233A computer, then the drop-down box shows the server name as CAB233A\SQLEXPRESS. In some cases, a SQL Server instance may not be configured to broadcast its availability. If you can connect to such a server instance, then you can type the name into the server name box.

Next, you need to authenticate yourself to the SQL Server Express instance. If you are logged into Windows with an account to which the SQL Server Express instance grants access, you can choose Use Windows NT Integrated security. For example, you may have installed SQL Server Express after logging in as the Administrator of a computer. Then, you can choose Use Windows NT Integrated security, if you logged into Windows with the computer's Administrator account. If a SQL Server Express instance does not grant access to your Windows user account, then select the Use a specific user name and password radio button. Next, enter a valid SQL Server user ID and its password. You can use the sa user ID and its password in this case. Recall that the "Service Account and Authentication Mode Screens" section described how to permit the use of the sa account.

■**Note** To use a specific user name and password, your SQL Server Express instance needs to be configured for mixed authentication. See the "Service Account and Authentication Mode Screens" section in this chapter for instructions on how to permit mixed authentication during the installation of a SQL Server Express instance. You can also program SMO to permit mixed authentication after an instance is already installed.

If your Windows account is recognized by a SQL Server Express instance or you designated a valid SQL Server login and password, you can follow two steps to use the drop-down box below the Select the database on the server radio button. First, select the radio button. The drop-down box below the radio button shows the names of attached databases to the SQL Server Express instance designated in the server name drop-down box. Second, select the name of an attached database. After you click OK, Visual Studio 2003 sets up the connection in Server Explorer.

Using a Data Connection

One easy way to assess whether a data connection is working is to retrieve the values in a table. Figure 1-9 shows a data connection to the Northwind database on the CAB233A\SQLEXPRESS instance. The Tables collection for the instance is open. To the right of Server Explorer are the values from the Shippers table in the Northwind database. To generate an active display with the data from any table, you can right-click the table name in the Tables collection and choose Retrieve Data from Table. The display is active in the sense that you can modify table values from the display.

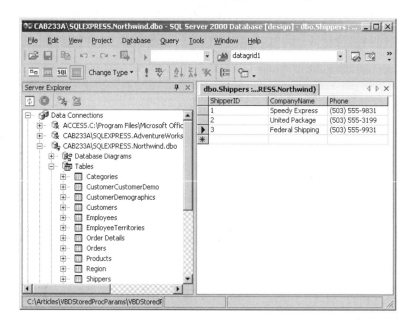

Figure 1-9. *Create a data connection to link Visual Studio 2003 to a SQL Server Express database.*

It is easy to work with a table in a SQL Server Express database in a Windows or Web form just like any table from earlier versions of SQL Server. Start by dragging a table name from Server Explorer to an empty form so Visual Studio 2003 creates SqlConnection and SqlDataAdapter objects. From the SqlDataAdapter object, you can generate a DataSet. Finally, you can assign the DataTable in the DataSet to the DataSource property of a DataGrid control and programmatically fill the DataSet when the form opens. By following these steps, the DataGrid will show the DataTable that the SqlDataAdapter fills when the form opens.

Disabling Network Access

Just as there are two main steps for enabling network access, there are two ways to disable network access to a SQL Server Express instance. You can stop the SQL Server Browser service to stop a SQL Server Express instance from broadcasting its availability. If you stop the SQL Server Browser service for a SQL Server Express instance, existing data connections in Visual Studio 2003 will still be able to function. However, you cannot create new data connections by selecting a SQL Server Express instance name from the drop-down box of server names in the Data Link Properties dialog box.

▩**Note** You can stop the SQL Server Browser service from SQL Server Configuration Manager. Select the SQL Server Browser service as if you are going to start it, but select Stop from the context menu instead of Start. See the "Configuring SQL Server Express to Start Automatically" section for instructions on opening the context menu for the SQL Server Browser service in SQL Server Configuration Manager.

The second way to disable network access actually disables the path to a SQL Server Express instance. This second route to managing network access disables from SQL Server Configuration Manager the server network protocols to a SQL Server Express instance. From the right-click menus for Named Pipes and TCP/IP items below the protocols for a server instance, choose Disable. Remember that you must restart the server instance to commit your changes. After making the changes, you totally secure a SQL Server Express instance from network access. In this case, previously existing data connections in the Server Explorer of a Visual Studio 2003 session will fail to operate.

Connecting to SQL Server Express from Access Projects

Access 2002 and 2003 share an identical COM-based technology—Access projects (.adp files)—for interfacing with SQL Server databases. Access 2000 has a very similar type of Access project for processing SQL Server databases. An Access project connects to a SQL Server instance through an OLE DB connection. You can use these projects to browse and edit table values as well as add new rows and delete existing rows. Access is popular as a report generator for SQL Server data. Business analysts frequently use Access to run ad hoc queries against a SQL Server database to support the information requirements of the decision makers in their organizational units. In addition, you can even create new objects, such as tables, stored procedures, and user-defined functions. As a consequence of the long history and power of Access projects for processing SQL Server instances, this section drills down on how to use Access projects with SQL Server Express databases.

Access 2002 and 2003 projects include a variety of visual designers that target the SQL Server 2000 database file format. As a consequence, these visual designers do not work with SQL Server 2005 editions, including SQL Server Express. Therefore, Access projects do not enjoy their full scope of functionality for SQL Server Express databases. However, the inability of the visual designers to run properly does not affect your ability to connect to SQL Server Express databases or your ability to browse, edit, update, and delete table values. In addition, you can run views and stored procedures, and you can even pass parameter values to stored procedures from pop-up boxes that automatically prompt for the parameter values that a stored procedure requires. Although the visual designers for creating new objects do not work, you can program new database objects with T-SQL from text-based templates in Access projects, such as the stored procedure template.

To create an Access project pointing at a SQL Server Express database, choose to create a new project with existing data. After you specify a name for your Access project file, Access presents a Data Link Properties dialog box. This dialog box works identically to the one for creating new data connections in Server Explorer within Visual Studio 2003, except that you establish a connection for the Access project instead of adding a new data connection to Server Explorer.

Figure 1-10 shows the Data Link Properties dialog box for the Access2SQLEXPRESS project, a sample Access project for this chapter. The dialog box in the figure points the project at the Northwind database attached to the CAB233A\SQLEXPRESS instance. The dialog box designates a SQL Server user ID (sa) and password. In production applications, you should avoid using the sa user. See Chapter 8 for a discussion of SQL Server security best practices as well as demonstrations of techniques for complying with those practices.

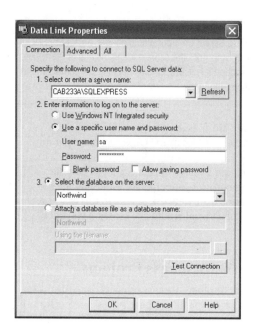

Figure 1-10. *Use a Data Link Properties dialog box to point an Access project at a SQL Server Express database.*

Figure 1-11 shows in its top pane a Datasheet view for the Shippers table in the Access2SQL-EXPRESS project. You can expose the view simply by double-clicking the Shippers table name in the Database window. Recall that the Access2SQLEXPRESS project points at the Northwind database on the CAB233A\SQLEXPRESS instance. A + sign precedes each row in the datasheet. Users can click the + before a set of column values for a row to show rows from the Orders table that point back to the shipper identified on the row with the +. This is all standard Access behavior that works automatically with an Access project pointed at a SQL Server Express database.

The bottom pane in Figure 1-11 presents a master detail (or main/sub) form generated with a single click to a toolbar control. As you can see from the pencil on the master form's record selector, a change to the current row is pending. Clicking the record selector commits the edited value to the SQL Server Express database.

Connecting to SQL Server Express from Access Linked Tables

ODBC linked tables are an even older Access-based technology than Access projects, suitable for showing SQL Server table values inside an Access application. Instead of relying on the newer .adp file type, linked tables work from traditional .mdb files. ODBC linked tables are an easy and popular technique for displaying table values from any ODBC-compliant data source, such as the AdventureWorks database on a SQL Server Express instance.

Although ODBC linked tables are not as flexible as Access projects in how they can interact with SQL Server data sources, ODBC linked tables are a very robust technology. For example, neither the Visual Studio 2003 technique demonstrated above nor the Access project approach can show values from tables in the AdventureWorks database on a SQL Server Express instance. However, this chapter's concluding demonstration reveals that ODBC linked tables within an Access .mdb file can display and join linked tables from a database with custom schema names, such as Sales, HumanResources, and Person.

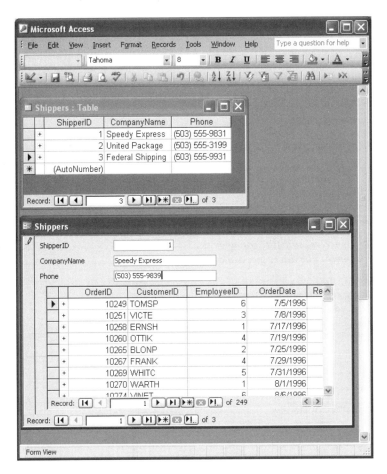

Figure 1-11. *Access projects make it easy to browse and edit table values in SQL Server Express databases.*

This ODBC linked table sample references the Sales.SalesPerson, HumanResources.Employee, and Person.Contact tables from the AdventureWorks database on the SQLEXPRESS named instance. To create the linked tables, you need a system DSN pointing at the AdventureWorks database on the SQLEXPRESS named instance. Then, reference the DSN from the Link dialog box in an Access database file (.mdb). Open the Link dialog box with the File ➤ Get External Data ➤ Link Tables command. Designate an ODBC Databases () file type. From the Machine Data Source tab of the Select Data Source dialog box, select the DSN for the AdventureWorks database and click OK. Then select the tables from the Link Tables dialog box and click OK. Figure 1-12 shows the three linked tables in the Database window of the AccessLinksSSE database file.

One significant advantage of linked tables is that Access developers can join them graphically to display combinations of column values from different tables. The top pane in Figure 1-13 shows the joining of the three linked tables from Figure 1-12. This query creates a telephone directory for sales persons in the AdventureWorks database. The bottom pane in Figure 1-13 shows an excerpt from the telephone directory returned by Query1. Access can use this query as a record source for an Access form or an Access report.

Figure 1-12. *ODBC linked tables in Access .mdb files can reference tables within custom schema names in the AdventureWorks database.*

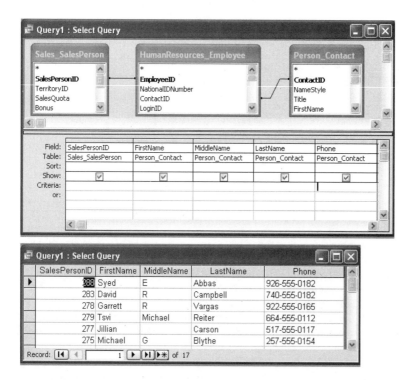

Figure 1-13. *Access developers can create custom views from ODBC linked tables from SQL Server Express databases.*

Summary

This chapter presented the background you need to get started with SQL Server Express. The chapter began by giving you a summary of what SQL Server Express is, and described four types of potential SQL Server Express users. Then it contrasted SQL Server Express with enterprise-scaled SQL Server 2005 editions and MSDE. Next, the chapter drilled down on how to install a SQL Server Express instance. The chapter concluded with two sections that demonstrated how to create client applications for SQL Server Express. One of these sections introduced the SSMS-based query tool for SQL Server Express, and the other section showed examples of down-level client applications interacting with SQL Server Express databases. In the process of preparing a SQL Server Express instance for connection from remote and down-level clients, you learned critical steps for configuring both a SQL Server Express instance and a Windows XP firewall.

CHAPTER 2

■ ■ ■

Graphical and Command-Line Query Tools

As with any modern general purpose database, administrators and developers can communicate with SQL Server Express via the SQL language. The variant of SQL optimized for Microsoft SQL Server is Transact-SQL (T-SQL). You can program T-SQL to return data, manipulate data, create tables for storing data, create other database objects with reusable T-SQL code, and administer a SQL Server instance (recall from Chapter 1 that SQL Server Express is just another edition of SQL Server 2005).

SQL Server Express users have two types of interfaces available to help program T-SQL. First, you can program T-SQL with a graphical query tool for SQL Server Express. Chapter 1 includes an introduction to a SQL Server Management Studio (SSMS)-based query tool. This chapter drills down on the SSMS-based query tool for SQL Server Express with tutorials covering how to

- Connect to SQL Server using Windows or SQL Server authentication.

- Explore SQL Server Express instances and their objects.

- Use built-in designers for creating databases, tables, and queries.

- Write, reuse, and automatically generate T-SQL code.

You can also invoke the `sqlcmd` utility to program T-SQL statements. The `sqlcmd` utility permits you to run T-SQL statements either typed into a command prompt window or from a script file containing T-SQL and `sqlcmd` instructions. Many database developers as well as beginning- to intermediate-level DBAs will prefer the SSMS-based graphical query tool, but advanced IT professionals and SQL Server power users who have to manage regularly recurring tasks, such as running a query for a weekly report or performing daily database updates, can often derive value from invoking command-line instructions with the `sqlcmd` utility. IT professionals and SQL Server power users can use `sqlcmd` statements in batch (.bat) files to group two or more `sqlcmd` statements, reduce the likelihood of typos on a command line, and automatically schedule the running of T-SQL statements.

Using the SSMS-Based Query Tool

As mentioned in the "Using SQL Server Express Query Tools" section of Chapter 1, Microsoft will make available for SQL Server Express a client application based on the SSMS tool found in other SQL Server 2005 editions. This SSMS-based query tool can help you write, debug, and run T-SQL statements in SQL Server Express instances. The SSMS-based query tool also provides an assortment of graphical features that help you to perform several essential tasks without even writing T-SQL code.

■**Note** To simplify referring to the SSMS-based query tool for SQL Server Express, in the remainder of this chapter, it is called Express SSMS.

Recall that Express SSMS is a subset of the full SSMS version found in other SQL Server 2005 editions. The primary change to SSMS for SQL Server Express is the removal of enterprise features, such as Analysis Services and Reporting Services; but selected convenience features, such as automatically scheduled tasks, are also omitted in the Express SSMS version. Despite these limitations, Express SSMS offers excellent functionality in a package that has a look and feel very similar to the full version of SSMS. Express SSMS is especially well suited for database development and administrative tasks implemented with T-SQL code or database objects that encapsulate T-SQL code.

Express SSMS occurred very late in the SQL Server Express beta period. During the early part of the SQL Server Express beta period, Microsoft offered a different query tool called Express Manager. Because of the incompatible feature set of Express Manager relative to SSMS, Microsoft decided to abandon Express Manager late in the SQL Server Express development cycle. Given that Express SSMS isn't available in even an alpha version at the time of writing, you'll see the use of a full SSMS version. However, the focus in this chapter is restricted to the features that Microsoft indicates are highly likely to be included in Express SSMS.

■**Note** It is almost certain that SQL Server Express may launch before Express SSMS is ready for final release. My recommendation is that early adopters of SQL Server Express use the SSMS in an evaluation copy of the SQL Server 2005 Developer Edition. Before the evaluation copy expires, these early adopters are likely to be able to download at least a beta copy of Express SSMS.

This section introduces Express SSMS by illustrating its use for a collection of common tasks.

1. Before you can do anything with a query tool, you have to connect to a database instance. Therefore, this section starts with several examples that illustrate how to achieve this essential step in two common ways.

2. After you connect to a SQL Server Express instance, you'll want to do something with it, such as create databases and tables as well as populate tables after you create them. You'll also learn how to create views that filter and manipulate the data in one or more tables. Express SSMS features enable these kinds of tasks without the need for T-SQL code.

3. The section concludes with additional examples that show how to write and reuse T-SQL statements. You'll even learn ways to automatically generate T-SQL code.

In the process of learning how to perform the common tasks just described, you will gain exposure to the Express SSMS user interface (UI). This UI is rich, and you can therefore use it in other ways beyond those demonstrated in this chapter. By learning the examples in this chapter, you'll acquire a background that enables you to adapt Express SSMS to perform other tasks that are important for your specific needs.

Connecting to SQL Server Instances

Express SSMS permits concurrent connections to multiple SQL Server instances. You can connect to SQL Server Express instances, other SQL Server 2005 instances, and SQL Server 2000 instances with Express SSMS. Express SSMS permits you to connect to server instances with either Windows or SQL Server authentication. Additionally, you can choose to connect to server instances running on the local computer or a remote computer.

You can choose to open multiple sessions to different server instances in the Object Explorer within Express SSMS. The Object Explorer caches (or saves) current connections within an Express SSMS session. As its name implies, you can use the Object Explorer to examine the databases and database objects within a server instance. The Object Explorer permits you to switch between multiple connections created within an Express SSMS session.

Connecting with SQL Server Authentication

Figure 1-7 in the "Connecting from the SSMS-Based Query Tool" section of Chapter 1 shows the Connect to Server dialog box settings for opening a new Express SSMS session to point at the SQLEXPRESS instance of SQL Server Express running on the CAB233A computer. Figure 2-1 shows Object Explorer to the left of the Document windows in SSMS immediately after the connection has been opened. The Summary tab's heading within the Document window reflects the name of the SQL Server Express instance and the computer on which it runs. The heading also includes the SQL Server version number as well as the user ID for the connection's login.

When a connection initially opens, you can view its top-level folders in Object Explorer. The Summary tab in the Document window shows the objects for the currently selected object in Object Explorer. When Express SSMS initially opens, Object Explorer and the Summary tab will show the same list of folders.

- The Express SSMS version will have at least the Databases and Security folders. SQL Server Express instances will, of course, have databases and logins. Databases populate the Databases folder, and logins are one of the types of items in the Security folder.

- The Server Objects folder is also likely to be in Express SSMS. This folder can contain backup devices, which are discussed in Chapter 3, and linked servers, which Chapter 5 demonstrates how to set up and use.

- The Express version of SSMS is not likely to have the Replication and Management folders because these folders pertain to enterprise features.

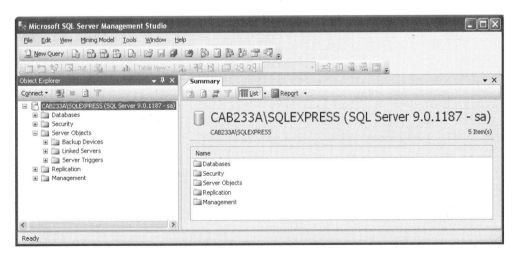

Figure 2-1. *Two important Express SSMS windows are Object Explorer (left) and the Document window (right).*

As mentioned, you can concurrently connect to multiple server instances within a single Express SSMS session. After an Express SSMS session is open, you can open the Connect to Server dialog box by clicking the Connect control on the toolbar within Object Explorer and selecting Database Engine from the drop-down list. Figure 2-2 shows the Connect to Server dialog box settings for connecting to a SQL Server Express instance on the CCS1 computer. Figure 2-3 displays another Connect to Server dialog box for connecting to the default SQL Server instance on the CCS1 computer, which is a SQL Server 2000 instance. Notice that you can use the same type of settings for connecting to SQL Server Express and SQL Server 2000 instances. You can also specify connections for other instances based on other SQL Server 2005 editions.

The Connect to Server dialog boxes in Figures 1-7, 2-2, and 2-3 all illustrate SQL Server authentication. Notice the selection in the Authentication drop-down box. When using SQL Server Authentication, you need to use a SQL Server login as opposed to a Windows login. For ease of use and simplicity (assuming you have very few logins set up on your server instances just now), the demonstration uses the sa login.

■**Tip** When building production systems, it is wise not to use the sa SQL Server login because it has the highest level of authority within a system. Production systems and the servers they run on become highly vulnerable if a hacker can attack an application and take over the sa account. However, the weakness of the sa account for production systems makes it attractive for demonstrations, such as those in Figures 1-7, 2-2, and 2-3. See Chapter 8 for detailed instructions on creating SQL Server Express security accounts that can eliminate the need for using the sa account.

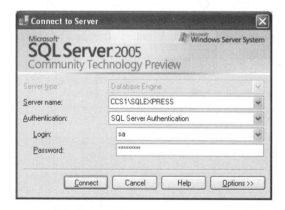

Figure 2-2. *This Connect to Server dialog box specifies a connection via SQL Server authentication to a named SQL Server Express instance on the CCS1 computer.*

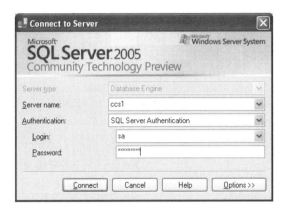

Figure 2-3. *This Connect to Server dialog box specifies a connection via SQL Server authentication to the default SQL Server instance on the CCS1 computer.*

Exploring the Objects in a Connection

Figure 2-4 shows Express SSMS after the three connections mentioned earlier are made from a single session. The connection information next to the CCS1 folder in Object Explorer refers to an 8.0 version of SQL Server, which designates a SQL Server 2000 instance. In contrast, the connection information for the CAB233A\SQLEXPRESS and CCS1\SQLEXPRESS folders refer to 9.0 versions of SQL Server, which designate two different preliminary versions of SQL Server Express.

▌**Note** As the development cycle for SQL Server Express and other SQL Server 2005 editions unfolded, there was a regular stream of new SQL Server Express versions that Microsoft called either beta or community technology preview versions. In the later stages of the SQL Server Express development cycle, the changes between versions were often minor and did not have a material impact on the typical range of features that most administrators and developers would use. This chapter uses the term *preliminary version* to refer to both beta and community technology preview versions.

The tree of objects within the CAB233A\SQLEXPRESS folder in Figure 2-4 is opened to allow the selection of the Tables folder within the Northwind database of the Databases collection on the CAB233A\SQLEXPRESS instance. You can open a folder by clicking the plus (+) next to it. You can collapse a folder by clicking the minus (–) next to it (see the Northwind and Databases folders). The Summary tab within the Document window in Figure 2-4 lists the names of all the tables within the Northwind database on the CAB233A\SQLEXPRESS instance. The Northwind database is one of the user-defined databases on the server instance. The Summary tab also shows a folder for the system tables on the server instance.

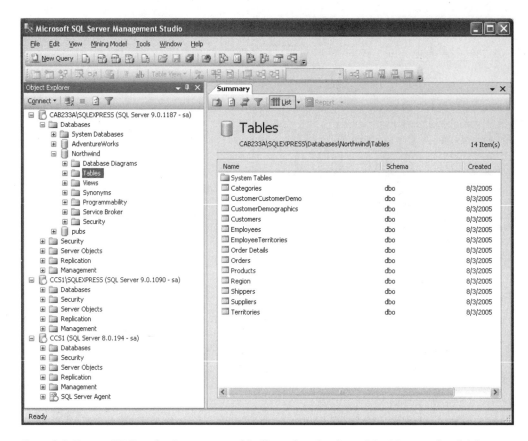

Figure 2-4. *Express SSMS makes it easy to graphically explore database objects in any of multiple concurrent connections pointed at different SQL Server instances.*

Connecting with Windows Authentication

When connecting to a server instance with Windows Authentication, the SQL Server Express instance trusts a Windows token that verifies the identity of a user. On the basis of Windows verification of a user, SQL Server Express authorizes a user to perform different tasks. The number of tasks that a user can perform depends on the permissions granted to the user's identity.

To help demonstrate Windows authentication, you can create two Windows accounts on a computer running a SQL Server Express instance. For example, I created two Windows accounts on the CAB233A computer named SSMSLogin and SSMSLoginLS. The SSMSLogin account belonged to the Windows Administrators group, which is granted a high level of permission within SQL Server Express. The SSMSLoginLS account belonged to the default Windows Users group. No special permissions are assigned to the members of the Windows Users group.

■Note SQL Server Express automatically recognizes Windows accounts belonging to either the Windows Users or Windows Administrators groups. Other SQL Server 2005 editions can recognize Windows accounts from both these groups, but the other editions do not automatically recognize members of the Windows Users group.

Figure 2-5 shows the Connect to Server dialog box for attempting to connect to the SQLEXPRESS instance on the CAB233A computer with the SSMSLogin Windows account. The dialog box has Windows Authentication selected in its drop-down Authentication box. As soon as you make this selection in the Authentication box, Express SSMS automatically disables the User name and Password boxes on the Connect to Server dialog box. In addition, the User name box shows the name of the current Windows account.

In order for CAB233A\SMSSLogin to appear in the User name box, you must log in to Windows with that account. The CAB233A refers to a Windows domain name. The SSMSLogin name is the domain account name. The dialog box could be from Express SSMS running on another computer that is not the Windows domain server.

■**Note** If you are not using a Windows domain server in your computer environment, you can simulate a comparable result to having an account on a Windows domain server by creating the same local Windows account name on a computer running SQL Server Express and another remote computer. Make sure the user account on the computer running SQL Server Express and the remote computer have the same name, group memberships, and individual permissions. The Connect to Server dialog box on the remote computer will display LocalComputerName\LocalWindowsAccountName in the User name box instead of DomainControllerName\DomainAccountName. However, the connection to the computer running SQL Server Express will run with the LocalWindowsAccountName, which is the same on the remote computer and the one running SQL Server Express.

Figure 2-5. *When you connect with Windows authentication, there is no need to specify a user name because SQL Server Express trusts the Windows verfication of a user.*

Recall that the SSMSLogin account belongs to the Windows Administrators group, whose members have a very wide scope of permissions on a SQL Server Express instance. Figure 2-6 shows an Express SSMS session for the SSMSLogin user. This user belongs to the Windows Administrators group, and the user therefore inherits a wide scope of permissions from its membership in the Windows Administrators group. The Express SSMS session shows the user navigating through the database objects in the AdventureWorks database and listing table names along with schema and date created.

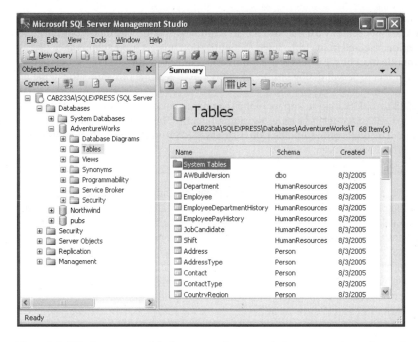

Figure 2-6. *Windows users with the appropriate permission can navigate through the database objects on a SQL Server Express instance.*

Figure 2-7 shows the Connect to Server dialog box for a user session of the SSMSLoginLS account. To log in with any Windows account, you must specify Windows Authentication. Express SSMS automatically detects the Windows security token validating a user and assigns the name of the Windows account to the User name box. Clicking Connect on the Connect to Server dialog box can successfully open an Express SSMS session to a SQL Server Express instance because SQL Server Express has a built-in login for members of the Windows Users group. All Windows accounts belong to this group (there's no way to have a Windows account without the account belonging to the Windows Users group).

Figure 2-7. *Any Windows account can connect to SQL Server Express with the same Connect to Server dialog box settings. All the user has to do is specify Windows Authentication.*

The Express SSMS session for the SSMSLoginLS account does not have any specific permissions to perform tasks on the SQLEXPRESS instance running on the CAB233A computer (other than to connect to the server instance). Therefore, the user cannot perform any tasks, such as run SELECT statements or navigate the database objects on a SQL Server Express instance. An attempt to expand the folder showing objects in the AdventureWorks database returns an error message saying that the AdventureWorks database is inaccessible (Figure 2-8). Recall that the same attempt succeeded for the SSMSLogin account that is a member of the Windows Administrators group.

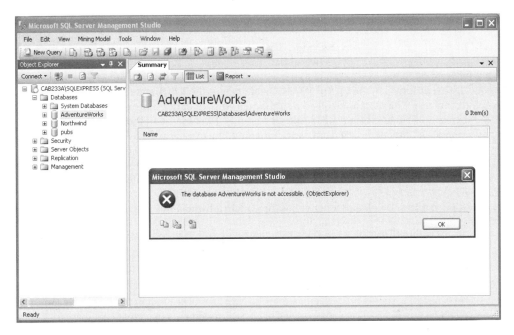

Figure 2-8. *Using a Windows account to connect to a SQL Server Express instance does not guarantee permission to perform even basic tasks, such as navigating through the objects within a database.*

Using Database, Table, and View Designers

Designers are graphical tools that help you perform several common tasks—perhaps by providing some default settings or otherwise constraining the full range of flexibility for performing a task with T-SQL statements. Designers are a great way to get started learning how some feature works. They are not the best tools for creating robust, powerful solutions that fully exploit SQL Server Express capabilities with T-SQL statements. In fact, designers typically insulate you from T-SQL code. With this background, I offer three guidelines about when to use (and not use) designers.

- Use designers to create solutions that do not need to be run often or that do not stress SQL Server Express in unusual ways, such as with a huge amount of data.

- Use designers to get a quick impression of how some SQL Server Express features work.

- Do not use designers when you need to create a custom solution with your own interface or that exploits options for performing a task not exposed by a designer.

In this section I demonstrate how three designers are used. All the designers are available through Express SSMS.

1. The first designer this section presents is used for creating databases. You'll learn how to open the Database Designer and how to run it. You'll also get exposure to a designer for dropping a database from a SQL Server Express instance.

2. Next, the section shows how to use a set of graphical tools for designing tables and populating them manually with data. The same tool available for initially populating a table with data is also available for editing the data in a table that already has data.

3. Finally, you'll see a popular type of graphical tool for creating views. The general design of this tool will be very familiar to anyone who has formulated queries graphically with earlier versions of SQL Server, Visual Basic/Visual Basic .NET, or Access.

Adding and Dropping a Database

As you'll learn in Chapter 3, the CREATE DATABASE statement is the T-SQL statement to invoke when creating a database. This statement offers a substantial amount of flexibility to enable you to create any kind of database that you may need. Some beginning developers and those migrating to SQL Server Express with other kinds of database or programming experience may find the New Database Designer an appealing shortcut to learning about creating databases. This designer offers a dialog box with multiple pages for graphically specifying the options for a new database. However, the designer will also assign default settings for all but one database attribute—the name of a database.

Learning the New Database Designer has three main advantages:

- The designer provides a very simple way to create a database. For those who prefer to avoid programming solutions, it is relevant to note that no T-SQL code is required.

- Learning how to invoke the New Database designer will familiarize you with a common way of invoking designers available within Express SSMS.

- You can readily view the T-SQL created by the New Database Designer and use that code as a starting point for creating your own custom T-SQL statements that create databases.

To invoke the New Database Designer, right-click the Databases folder for a SQL Server Express instance in Object Explorer to display the context menu shown in Figure 2-9. Then, select the New Database menu item. Right-clicking a folder in Object Explorer is a common way to find commands for manipulating the items in a folder, including how to create new items. Before progressing to the New Database Designer, you may want to note that Express SSMS offers additional designers to assist with other common database chores. For example, one of the most common requests at SQL Server newsgroups is how to attach database files to a server instance. Express SSMS offers a designer to help accomplish this task with SQL Server Express instances.

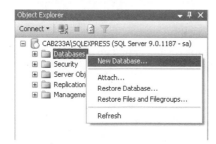

Figure 2-9. *Right-clicking a folder in Object Explorer will often expose a command for creating new items in the folder.*

After selecting the New Database item in the context menu for the Databases folder, Express SSMS opens the New Data Designer to its General page, which appears in Figure 2-10. All you need to do to create a database is assign a name for the new database in the Database name box and click OK. Figure 2-10 designates a name of ProSSEApps for a new database. The name that you assign to a database becomes its logical name, such as AdventureWorks, Northwind, or pubs for the names of Microsoft-supplied sample databases. If you click OK before assigning a database name, the New Database Designer automatically reminds you of the requirement to give the database a name before clicking OK.

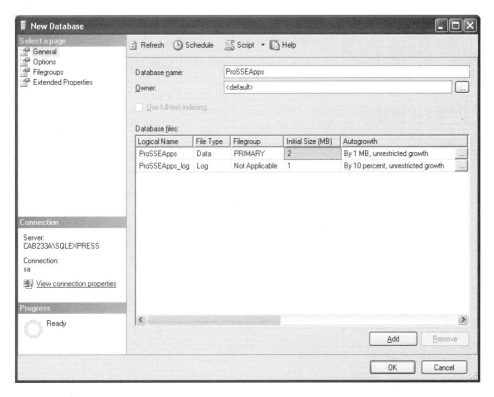

Figure 2-10. *The New Database Designer lets you create a new database as easily as assigning the database a name and clicking OK.*

A SQL Server Express database has a minimum of two files (in fact, just two files are common). The General window in the New Database Designer includes a grid with settings for each file. For example, the Database files grid shows the names of the Data and Log files as ProSSEApps and ProSSEApps_log. These names correspond to the entry in the Database name box at the top of the General page. Scrolling the grid to the right exposes additional database file attributes, such as their path. Ellipsis buttons let you specify nondefault paths for these files.

The icons along the top of the New Database Designer offer additional means of controlling the designer and the code created by it.

- The Refresh icon refreshes the data in the New Database Designer from the server instance.

- The Schedule icon will not be available in the Express version of SSMS. SQL Server Express users can resort to the Windows Scheduled Tasks applet to create schedules for the execution of program files, such as batch files (see the "Scheduling T-SQL Statements" section for instructions on how to do this).

- The Script icon lets you see the T-SQL code that your graphical selections make by opening a new query tab in the Document window of Express SSMS.

- The Help icon opens a Help window with instructions on how to complete the items on the current page in the designer. You can select pages other than the General page by clicking their name in the Select a page panel, which appears in the top-left corner of the New Database Designer.

Within the life cycle of a database, there can come a time to retire the database. Sometimes this happens early in a project when you are experimenting with different database designs, and you need to eliminate a database so that you can have a new one with the same name. Right-clicking a database name in Object Explorer and clicking the Delete menu item opens a Delete Object Designer. Removing a database can be as simple as clicking OK. In my use of the Delete Object Designer with databases, I have sometimes found it beneficial to clear the "Delete backup and restore history information for the databases" check box at the bottom of the designer. By default, the check box is selected, and you should use that option initially. If it fails, try clearing the check box.

■**Note** Both the "Adding New Tables and Populating Them with Data" and the "Viewing SQL Server Express Data" sections add database objects to the ProSSEApps database. See the "Attaching Databases with CREATE DATABASE" section in Chapter 3 for instructions on attaching the database files for the ProSSEApps database to the SQL Server Express instance that you are using.

Adding New Tables and Populating Them with Data

Building a new table for a database is one of the most critical database development activities that you can undertake. This activity can benefit from an in-depth knowledge of SQL Server Express data types as well as a grasp of normalization, primary keys, indexes, and foreign keys. An improperly designed table can lead to poor performance and even make it difficult to maintain valid data within a database.

The Table Designer in Express SSMS offers a shortcut to creating new tables and even modifying existing tables. This designer is similar to the designers in Visual Basic Express and Visual Web Developer Express for creating tables. Therefore, learning the Express SSMS Table Designer will help you with these other products.

The Express SSMS Table Designer permits you to create or modify a table without a working knowledge of the CREATE TABLE, DROP TABLE, and ALTER TABLE T-SQL statements. It simplifies making table settings by allowing you to create or edit a table's design through such actions as making selections from a drop-down box, entering values into a box, or making a menu item selection. The Table Designer is optimized for simplifying the settings for the individual columns within a table, but you can also use the designer to designate the primary key column(s) for a table as well as create foreign keys and column indexes.

■**Note** The Express SSMS Table Designer greatly simplifies the task of creating a table. However, the designer does not relieve you of the need for understanding best practices for table design as well as the implication of table-design decisions. One of the best ways to learn these critical topics is through a good understanding of T-SQL table-design techniques, starting with the CREATE TABLE statement. You will learn more about table-design issues in Chapter 4.

Just as you can create a new database by right-clicking the Databases folder for a server instance and choosing New Database, you can create a new table for a database by right-clicking the Tables folder within a database and choosing New Table. This menu selection adds a new tab to the Document window in Express SSMS. The tab contains two panes that let you specify successive columns in your new table.

- The top pane offers a grid for designating a column's name and data type as well as whether the column allows null values. Each new column in the table has its own row in the grid on the top pane. You can right-click a row for a column to refine your settings for that column, such as to designate a column as the primary key for a table.

- The bottom pane offers the same settings as the top pane along with a much wider selection of column properties. The settings showing in the bottom pane are for the currently selected table column in the top pane. In the bottom pane, you can control column properties such as the maximum number of characters that an nvarchar column value can contain, whether a column has an Identity property as well as the seed and increment values for the Identity property in a column, and the expression for a computed column.

Figure 2-11 shows the top pane for a new table in the ProSSEApps database created in the "Adding and Dropping a Database" section. The Table Designer was opened by selecting New Table from the Tables folder context menu of the ProSSEApps database in the Object Explorer. The figure shows a name (CustomerID), a data type (int), and the Allow Nulls check box cleared. The int data type is an integer data type that you can select with a drop-down box in the Data Type column. You can open a context menu for a column by right-clicking the column. The context menu for the CustomerID column has a Set Primary Key item available for selection to make CustomerID the table's primary key. After the selection, a key icon will show to the left of the CustomerID column.

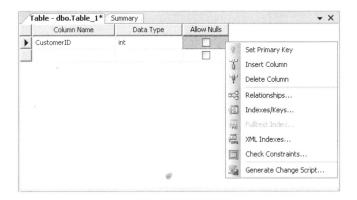

Figure 2-11. *The Express SSMS Table Designer lets you set the primary key for a table with a context menu selection.*

Figure 2-12 shows the top and bottom panes of the Table Designer with the `CustomerName` column selected in the top pane. The Table Designer uses a default data type for any column of `nvarchar` with a length of 10. This setting specifies a variable number of characters per column value with a maximum length of 10 characters. The bottom pane shows the `Length` property selected. The sample table will benefit from a larger upper limit, such as 40, for the maximum number of characters in a column value. By replacing the default `Length` property value of 10 with 40 in the bottom pane, you can set a new upper limit for the maximum number of values in a column.

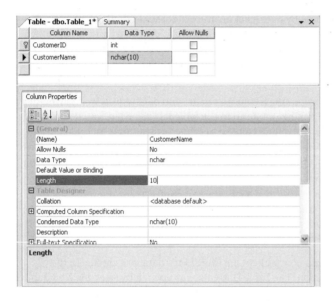

Figure 2-12. *The bottom pane in the Table Designer offers an extended set of properties relative to the top pane for specifying the columns in a table.*

The `Customer` table is to have an `Identity` property setting in this sample. An `Identity` property setting causes SQL Server Express to automatically assign values to a column starting from some seed value and growing by fixed increments for each successively inserted row.

1. To start making this property setting, select the `CustomerID` column in the top pane by clicking the area to the left of column name in the first row of the top pane.

    a. The row for the `CustomerID` column changes color to indicate that it is selected.

    b. In addition, the bottom pane settings pertain to the `CustomerID` column instead of the `CustomerName` column.

2. Expand the `Identity Specification` property for the column in the bottom pane by clicking the plus sign (+) next to the property.

3. Then change the nested (Is Identity) setting from No to Yes by altering the selection in the drop-down box.

4. After enabling the `Identity` property, Express SSMS automatically populates the nested `Identity Increment` and `Identity Seed` property values with one. You can override the default values, but leave them unchanged for the current demonstration. Express SSMS will then assign the seed to the first row inserted. When you add a new row, it will add the increment to the value in the preceding row and insert this new value into the new row. The process continues for each newly inserted row.

For this introduction to the Express SSMS Table Designer, the CustomerID and CustomerName columns are sufficient for the first of two tables in the ProSSEApps database. Notice from the tab name for the table in Figures 2-11 and 2-12 that the table's default name is dbo.Table_1. This table refers to the Table_1 table in the dbo schema. The asterisk after the table's name indicates the table design includes settings not committed to the database.

In general, you will not want to assign the default name (Table_1) to a table. In any event, the table is not committed to the database until you click the Save button on the Standard toolbar or choose File ➤ Save. When you issue a save command by either method, you can designate a name to replace the default name (or accept the default name) in the Choose Name dialog box. In this demonstration, the table in Figure 2-12 has the name Customer. Clicking OK commits the table to the database with the name in the dialog box. Clicking Cancel leaves the table open for further editing.

Figure 2-13 shows the design for a second table in the ProSSEApps database. The table is already saved with the name CustomerContact. The Customer and CustomerContact tables have a common column, CustomerID. Therefore, you can relate the two tables with this common column of values in both tables.

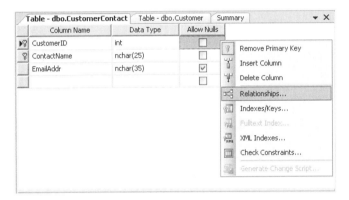

Figure 2-13. *Selecting the Relationships context menu item for one or more columns in a table opens the Foreign Key Relationships dialog box for linking the current table to another table.*

The selection of the Relationships menu item for the CustomerID column in Figure 2-13 opens the Foreign Key Relationships dialog box. You can use this box to link the CustomerContact table with the Customer table by their CustomerID column values.

1. Start to build the relationship by clicking the ellipsis button in the Tables and Columns Specification section of the dialog box. This action transfers control from the Foreign Key Relationships dialog box to the Tables and Columns dialog box.

2. Make selections like those in Figure 2-14 for the Tables and Columns dialog box so that

   a. Customer appears as the name of the Primary key table.

   b. CustomerContact appears as the name of the Foreign key table.

   c. CustomerID appears as the linking column for both tables.

3. Click OK to commit your specification.

4. Click Close to exit the Foreign Key Relationships dialog box.

5. Save the change to the CustomerContact table design.

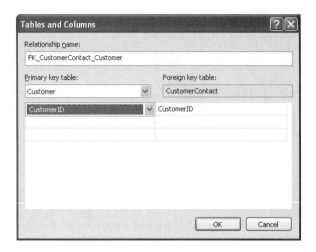

Figure 2-14. *Use the Tables and Columns dialog box to designate how two tables relate to one another through a foreign key constraint.*

The foreign key created by the preceding steps specifies that one row in the Customer table can have zero or more corresponding rows in the CustomerContact table. Rows correspond by their CustomerID column value. This foreign key constraint means that you must populate the Customer table with a row for a customer before you can add any rows for that customer to the CustomerContact table.

You can add data to the Customer table by right-clicking the table in Object Explorer and choosing Open Table. This opens a new tab (Table-dbo.Customer) with a form for entering new values and modifying existing values in the table. Because the CustomerID column has an Identity property setting, you merely designate a value for the CustomerName column and click the Pencil icon, which is to the left of the first column, to commit a row to the table. SQL Server Express automatically populates the CustomerID column value based on the Identity property settings. The Identity column value appears after the row commits to the table. You can optionally move to another row to commit the current row to the table.

Figure 2-15 shows the addition of a third row to the Customer table on the way to completion. The first two rows have CustomerID column values of 1 and 2. The Identity property setting will cause SQL Server Express to assign a value of 3 to the CustomerID column value in the third row. Clicking the Pencil icon to the left of the CustomerID column populates the row from SQL Server Express.

	CustomerID	CustomerName
	1	First Congregational Methodist Church
	2	Dee-Luxe Talent Agency
🖉	*NULL*	Database Developers Group|
＊	NULL	NULL

|◀ ◀ [3] of 3 ▶ ▶| ▶ (❉) Cell is Modified. 🖉

Figure 2-15. *By selecting the Open Table menu item for a table you can open a form like this one for adding new column values to a table.*

You can use the same process to add new rows of column values to the `CustomerContact` table. A similar process was used to add five new rows of data to that table. The View Designer in the next section will display these values.

Viewing SQL Server Express Data

The Express SSMS View Designer creates a view using a very popular type of visual designer tool. A view is a T-SQL `SELECT` statement that returns a result set of column values from a data source. The View Designer is important because it allows SQL Server Express users to create queries graphically. There are four panes within the View Designer. The names for these panes are, in order: Diagram, Criteria, SQL, and Results. This type of designer is very popular because it simplifies the design of queries. The following points summarize main considerations when designing a query with the View Designer:

1. First, you add one or more data sources, such as tables or other views, to a design surface (the Diagram pane).

2. Second, the View Designer will automatically join the data sources if it can detect a relationship between the sources, but you can also graphically join the data sources if there are relationships that the View Designer does not detect.

3. After you specify the data sources, you can designate a subset of the columns that you want to appear in the result set from the `SELECT` statement for your view. The selected columns appear in the Criteria pane. You can display a view's result set in the Results tab within the View Designer.

4. The View Designer creates a `SELECT` statement for you in the SQL pane. You specify the `SELECT` statement by

   a. Clicking check boxes to indicate which columns from the Diagram pane you want to appear in the Criteria pane.

   b. Specifying in the Criteria pane expressions to filter rows based on selected column values.

   c. Indicating in the Criteria pane which, if any, columns on which to sort rows.

   d. Specifying which sets of rows to group together when computing aggregate values, such as `COUNT` and `SUM`.

   e. Optionally specifying computed columns to assist with sorting, filtering, grouping, and aggregating rows.

As you build a `SELECT` statement graphically in the View Designer, you can optionally display the T-SQL for the `SELECT` statement in the SQL pane. Express SSMS does not offer a visual query designer for stored procedures, but you can use the View Designer to compose T-SQL query statements and then copy the SQL pane contents to a `CREATE PROCEDURE` statement.

You can open the View Designer by right-clicking the Views folder within a database in Object Explorer and clicking New View. In the Add Table dialog box that opens, you can designate data sources that you want in your view. Despite the dialog box's name, you are not restricted to tables as data sources for a view. You can use other sources, such as another view. For now, select the `CustomerContact` table in the `ProSSEApps` database. In the Diagram pane, select the (All Columns) check box.

Figure 2-16 shows the View Designer for a view that returns all columns for all rows from the `CustomerContact` table. Click the Execute SQL control (!) to populate the Results tab.

- The top pane is the Diagram pane with the `CustomerContact` table. The check box (All Columns) is selected.

- There are no filter criteria or sorting criteria in the second Criteria pane.

- The third pane, which is the SQL pane, shows the `SELECT` statement generated by selecting the (All Columns) check box for the `CustomerContact` table in the Diagram pane.

- The bottom pane is the Results tab. It shows the values entered for the `CustomerContact` table.

Figure 2-16. *The View Designer offers four panes to help you understand a view.*

After specifying a view, you can save it for future reference. Click the Save View control on the Standard toolbar, or select the Save View item from the File menu. In the Choose Name dialog box, you can override a default name, such as `view_1`, with a custom name, such as `vCustomerContact`. By saving the view in this way, you can refer to its underlying query statement instead of generating a new view with the same `SELECT` statement the next time you want that view of the data from the `CustomerContact` table.

Views are particularly powerful because of their ability to manipulate data from two or more data sources. The `vContactName` view in Figure 2-17 shows a view that both filters and sorts values from two different tables.

- The View Designer automatically determines a one-to-many relationship between the `Customer` and `CustomerContact` tables based on the foreign key in the `CustomerContact` table. The line connecting the two tables in the Diagram pane denotes a primary key on one end (the `Customer` table) and a foreign key on the other end (the `CustomerContact` table).

- The `ContactName` column has a descending sort order. The corresponding `ORDER BY` clause in the SQL pane causes Reverend Ron Walker to appear before Pastor Louis Coleman.

- `PATINDEX` in the fourth row of the Criteria pane is a T-SQL function that allows the filtering of rows from the full set of five rows for the underlying result set.

  - `PATINDEX` returns the starting character position of Church in the `CustomerName` column value or zero if Church does not exist in the `CustomerName` column value.

  - By filtering for values greater than zero on this criterion, the query returns only rows with Church in the `CustomerName` column value.

  - By default, rows in the Criteria pane appear in the result set for a view. Clearing the `Output` column for the `PATINDEX` function row in the Criteria pane allows the criterion to be a part of the query without generating any output in the result set.

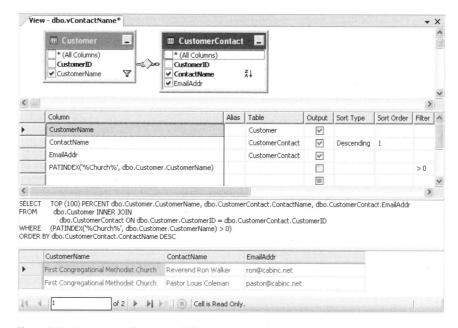

Figure 2-17. *You can easily sort and filter data with the View Designer.*

Designing, Running, Saving, and Rerunning SQL Scripts

As useful and powerful as the Express SSMS designers are, writing T-SQL queries for data access, data manipulation, and database and server administration can be even more powerful. However, writing queries in T-SQL can also be tricky. Therefore, it is especially useful to be able to save a query statement and open it later for use as-is or for editing before use.

In addition to writing your own T-SQL code, you should be aware that Express SSMS offers several tools for helping you to write T-SQL.

- With View Designer, you create a `SELECT` statement graphically. You can copy the contents of the SQL pane in View Designer to a query tab in the Express SSMS Document window.

- You can also right-click many objects in Object Explorer to uncover a Script menu item. You can often script an object in different ways. For example, you can script a table to create it, select data from it, or insert data into it. Choose the type of script that you want to open a query in a new tab within the Document window.

- Template Explorer offers a wide selection of T-SQL code samples that you can customize. Code samples are organized by topic, such as Database, Table, and Login. You can drag a predefined template from Template Explorer to an existing query tab, or you can open a new query tab expressly for a template.

Opening a Query Tab to Write a Query

You can open a tab for writing T-SQL in the Document window of Express SSMS by clicking New Query on the Standard toolbar. This may open a Connect to Server dialog box that lets you specify and open a connection to a SQL Server Express instance. The T-SQL in the query tab will connect to a SQL Server Express instance through the connection that you specify in the Connect to Server dialog box. The first query tab opened during an Express SSMS session will have SQLQuery1.sql. If you are not prompted with a Connect to Server dialog box, Express SSMS uses the currently active connection for the query tab.

A query tab can hold multiple T-SQL statements. You can run all statements within a query pane by pressing the F5 function key. If a pane contains multiple blocks of T-SQL statements that you want to run separately, you can select any block of contiguous T-SQL statements. Pressing F5 runs all selected T-SQL statements in the active query tab.

You can also populate separate query tabs with individual blocks or groups of T-SQL code. Click New Query to open a tab with the current connection for a new block of T-SQL code. A new tab appears with a tab title, such as SQLQuery2. If you have multiple connections to different server instances in Object Explorer, you can right-click an instance name in Object Explorer and choose New Query. This opens a new query tab in the Document window with a connection to that server.

T-SQL statements within a query tab operate within a connection context and a database context. You set the connection context when you open a query tab. You can set the database context with a USE statement that references a specific database. If you do not specify a database context, then T-SQL statements execute in the context of the default database, which is frequently the master database. Recall that the master database is one of the special system databases set up when you install SQL Server Express. Therefore, unless you explicitly want your statements to operate in the context of the master database, always specify a USE statement when running query statements in a query tab.

T-SQL statements that operate within an Express SSMS session can generate results in one of three formats.

- You can display the result set from a query statement in a grid within a Results tab that appears below the query tab. Ancillary information—such as the number of rows returned, warnings and error messages, and user-supplied messages returned by a T-SQL script—appears in a Messages tab. This style of output is the default output mode unless you change it.

- You can display the result set from a query statement in a text window within the Results tab. In this case, there is no Messages tab because all types of output appear in the text layout within the Results tab.

- You can send the output to a text file. This is a very basic way of generating a report. When the query runs with this setting, you are prompted with a dialog box for a file name in which to store the results.

Three controls on the SQL Editor toolbar allow you to select any of these output modes. You can also select the Options item from the Tools menu to set the default output mode for queries for the next time that you open an Express SSMS session.

Figure 2-18 shows the T-SQL statements for a query based on one SELECT statement with a result set (you can open the code in SQLQuery1_f0218.sql). The query returns the SalesPersonID, SalesYTD, and SalesLastYear column values for the top three rows ordered by SalesYTD from the Sales.SalesPerson table in the AdventureWorks database. The USE statement sets the database context to the AdventureWorks database for the SELECT statement. The USE and SELECT statements appear in the SQLQuery1 pane at the top of Query Editor. The Results tab below SQLQuery1 shows the result set in a grid layout format. Figure 2-18 displays the Messages tab, but not its content, which includes a statement about three rows being affected.

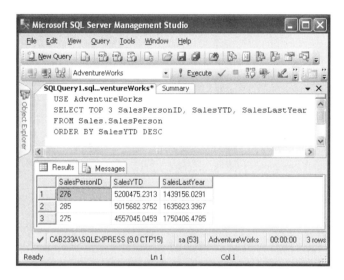

Figure 2-18. *A query tab has multiple areas (SQLQuery, Results, and Messages tabs) for displaying statements and results.*

Figure 2-19 shows a block of T-SQL code in the SQLQuery2 tab of the Document window of Express SSMS that creates two result sets each with just a single number that reports a count of rows. The first SELECT statement in the block of code returns the number of rows in the Sales.SalesPerson table, and the second SELECT statement returns the number of rows in the HumanResources.Employee table (you can open the code in SQLQuery2_f0219.sql). The Results to text control in the SQL Editor toolbar is selected so that output appears in a text layout. The Results tab presents the output from both SELECT statements in a text layout format. With a text layout format, notice that the number of rows affected appears in the Results tab as opposed to the Messages tab. In fact, if a syntax error exists in one or more statements, the statement's error message appears in the Results tab as opposed to the Messages tab when the result set has a text layout format.

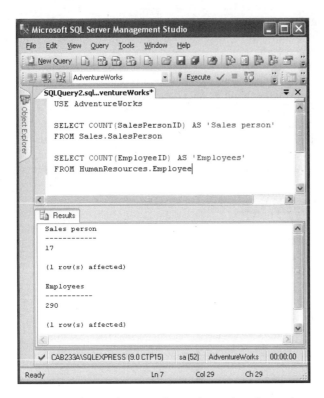

Figure 2-19. *The Results to text format intermixes the result set values with any messages about the number of rows affected or errors in the Results tab.*

Generating T-SQL Code Automatically

The preceding T-SQL statements are to illustrate the use of T-SQL in a query tab within Express SSMS. Practical applications of T-SQL often require considerably more complex T-SQL statements. Happily, there are at least three aids that Express SSMS offers to help you automatically generate T-SQL statements. As mentioned earlier, these techniques involve the use of the following:

- The SQL pane in the View Designer
- The Script context command for objects in Object Explorer
- The Template Explorer, a built-in library of T-SQL code samples

■**Note** You can also download a substantial code library for the chapters in this book. Chapters 3 through 8 focus on a wide range of T-SQL samples with numerous code samples.

Figure 2-17 displays View Designer joining two tables, filtering based on a computed column value, and sorting rows in descending order. Unless you regularly write T-SQL statements, constructing a T-SQL statement like this one might be tricky. T-SQL, like any other programming language, has syntax rules that can be easy to forget. On the other hand, the View Designer always remembers the rules, and it displays the code that you generate graphically in its SQL pane. After you complete the crafting of a statement with View Designer, you can just copy the T-SQL generated in View Designer's SQL pane to a query tab. If necessary, you can edit the T-SQL code generated by View Designer.

The query statement in the View Designer in Figure 2-17 returns the two contact persons for the customer with Church in the name. Let's say a need arose for contact persons from customers without Church in their names. One way to construct such a query is to copy the SQL pane code from the view represented by Figure 2-17 and edit the WHERE clause to return rows without Church in their CustomerName column value instead of those with Church in their CustomerName column value.

Figure 2-20 shows the original and edited versions of the T-SQL statement from the view along with the Results tab showing the outcome of the original and edited T-SQL statements. The .sql file with the query statements in the figure are in SQLQuery1_f0220.sql.

- A USE statement at the top of the query tab sets the database context to ProSSEApps.
  - The USE statement is not necessary within the view because you save the view in a database, and the view refers to that database by default.
  - When you copy the T-SQL statement from the view to an ordinary query, the USE statement, or some equivalent means, is necessary for setting the database context.
- The original T-SQL statement from the View Designer, which appears first, is cropped partially in order not to change the statement in any way even though it is unnecessarily wide. Enough of the statement shows to confirm it is merely the copied code from the SQL pane in Figure 2-17.
- The edited version of the T-SQL statement appears after the original version.
  - The edit is to change the WHERE clause criterion expression to replace > 0 with = 0.
  - By searching for rows with a PATINDEX('%Church%', dbo.Customer.CustomerName) value equal to zero, the query returns rows for customers that do not have Church in their name.
  - Some minor reformatting improves the readability of the T-SQL statement within the query tab.
- The Results tab shows the two contacts for the T-SQL original statement over three contacts for the modified T-SQL statement.

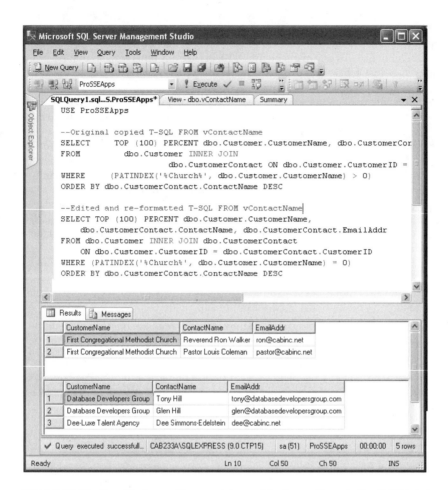

Figure 2-20. *The View Designer offers a quick, graphical way of generating T-SQL statements for use with stand-alone query statements.*

Most database objects in Object Explorer have a Script context menu item. This type of command generates a T-SQL script, which can have template parameters to help you customize it. Right-click an object in Object Explorer to expose its Script menu item. Figure 2-21 shows the Script command for the CustomerContact table in the ProSSEApps database. As with many Express SSMS menu commands, the Script menu command follows the command, Script, with the name of the type of object, Table, to which the command applies. The Script item itself has a menu for other items that, in turn, offer a menu of items.

- For example, the Script context command for the CustomerContact table offers menu items such as Create, Drop, Select, and Insert. The Insert menu item writes a script for adding a new row to the table.

- With the Insert item selected in Figure 2-21, you can see several options for where the script is to be written. Selecting the New Query Editor window item generates an Insert script in a new query tab within Express SSMS.

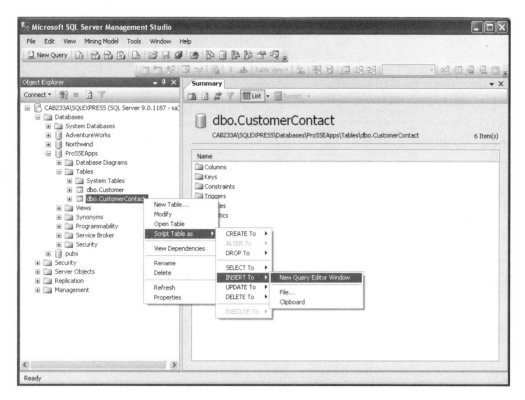

Figure 2-21. *The context Script menu command provides a range of commands for generating custom T-SQL code for an object.*

Figure 2-22 shows the Insert script for the CustomerContact table in a query tab. Following the VALUES keyword are three template parameters named ContactID, ContactName, and EmailAddr. Within the script, the parameters are enclosed within angle brackets (<>). You can designate values for the parameters by typing over them, or you can choose the Specify Values for Template Parameters item from the Query menu. Place column values in single quotes when inputting character values. The menu command opens a dialog box with a form for entering parameter values. After you complete entering the values and click OK, Express SSMS updates the statement in the query tab. You can then run the script to add a new row with the designated parameter values. The edited script is available as SQLQuery1_f0222.sql.

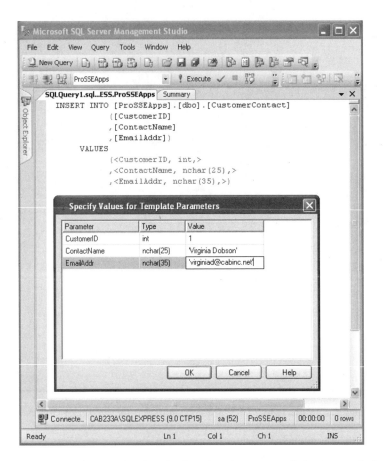

Figure 2-22. *The Specify Values for Template Parameters dialog box can help you to customize a T-SQL script generated with the Script context menu command.*

As mentioned previously, the Template Explorer is a library of T-SQL scripts. These scripts are not tied to any particular object, as are those that you generate with the Script context menu command. In addition, Template Explorer scripts typically address intermediate or high-level topics. The Template Explorer appears as a window on the right-hand side of Express SSMS. If the Template Explorer does not show, choose Template Explorer from the View menu. Template Explorer scripts exist as items within folders. Figure 2-23 shows the drop database script dragged from the Database folder to a query tab with a connection to a database. You can also add a template by right-clicking and choosing Open. This opens a Connect to Database Engine dialog box that lets you specify a server instance context in which the script will run. You can use the Specify Values for Template Parameters dialog box.

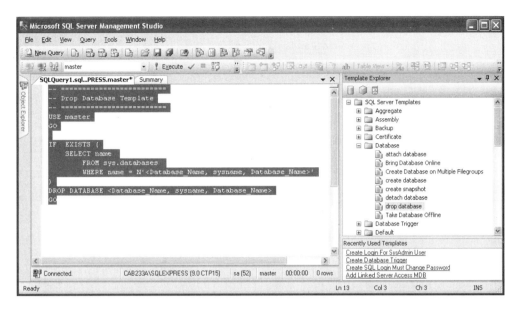

Figure 2-23. *Use the Template Explorer to add any of a large variety of T-SQL scripts to a query tab.*

Saving and Opening .sql Files

You can save the contents of a query tab in the Document window with any of the following:

- The Save icon on the Standard toolbar
- The "File ➤ Save query tab name As" command
- The "File ➤ Save query tab name" command

Before you initially save a query tab, you are always prompted with a File ➤ Save As dialog box. The dialog box suggests the default name, such as SQLQuery1.sql, but you can override the default name. If you do not append a .sql file extension to the file name, Express SSMS automatically assigns that extension.

After you initially save a query tab (or open a previously saved query tab), choosing an option to save a query tab automatically copies over a previously existing version of the .sql file for the query tab. However, you can explicitly choose a Save As command to save an existing or a modified query with a new name.

Note Unlike the full version of SSMS, Express SSMS does not allow you to work with query files as elements in a database project. When using Express SSMS, you can only work with query tabs as individual files.

There are three ways to open a previously saved query tab:

- Click the Open File icon on the Standard toolbar.
- Choose File ➤ Recent Files and then select the file from among the recently used files.
- Choose File ➤ Open ➤ File.

All the ways to open a .sql file create a new query tab for the file and prompt you to specify a connection for the new query tab. In this way, you can run an old query with a new and different database from the one last used with the query. After you open a previously saved query file, you can edit it to create a new query. Later, you can save the modified query with a new file name.

Using the sqlcmd Utility

The sqlcmd utility provides a command-line tool for running T-SQL statements. Although the rich ease-of-use features in Express SSMS makes it a desirable tool for a wide variety of users in different scenarios, the speed and convenience of a tool that operates from a command prompt has appeal as well. This section examines the sqlcmd utility. In this section, you'll discover how to connect to a SQL Server instance from the sqlcmd utility as well as how to run T-SQL statements. The section even shows how to make T-SQL statements dynamic at runtime to gain runtime flexibility in how T-SQL statements perform. The section concludes by demonstrating a workaround based on batch files for a sqlcmd utility weakness. Storing sqlcmd instructions in batch files significantly reduces the chance of creating a typo in a command line. Another very beneficial advantage of using batch files is that you can tap the Windows Scheduled Tasks applet to schedule the automatic execution of sqlcmd instructions at designated intervals.

Connecting to SQL Server Instances

Job one with any database application, such as Express SSMS or the sqlcmd utility, is connecting to a database server. When working with Microsoft SQL Server Express, this means logging into a SQL Server Express instance. The sqlcmd utility provides a couple of approaches to this critical task.

All sqlcmd approaches for connecting to a SQL Server instance, including a SQL Server Express instance, start by invoking the sqlcmd.exe program from a command prompt (>). You do this by opening a command prompt window and then typing sqlcmd at a command prompt. Follow sqlcmd with one or more switches. Each switch has a name, such as -S for server name or -o for output file. Many switches require an argument value, such as a server instance name for -S. You can specify connection as well as other argument values when you invoke sqlcmd.exe from a command prompt.

■Tip You can view all sqlcmd switches by typing sqlcmd -? at a command prompt. This sqlcmd statement generates a list of all the switches with a very brief summary of each switch. See Books Online for detailed documentation on sqlcmd switches and commands.

Connecting with Windows Authentication

The sqlcmd utility connects with Windows authentication by default. Therefore, you do not need to designate Windows authentication. However, you must specify a server name. Follow sqlcmd with the -S switch and the name of the server. If you wish, you can explicitly designate Windows authentication with the -E switch (this is strictly optional). Therefore, connecting to a SQL Server instance from the sqlcmd utility with Windows authentication requires syntax like the following:

```
C:\>sqlcmd –S SQLServerInstanceName –E
```

After the sqlcmd utility connects successfully, you see a prompt (1>) to enter your first sqlcmd or T-SQL statement in a batch of statements. If a statement does automatically execute, such as the sqlcmd :serverlist statement, then you do not need to type GO on a line by itself to invoke the statement. You can type GO on a line by itself following a batch of T-SQL and sqlcmd statements that do not automatically execute by themselves. The :serverlist sqlcmd keyword returns a list of locally configured SQL Server instances and SQL Server instances broadcasting over the network on which a client resides. You can terminate a sqlcmd session by typing EXIT on a line by itself.

Note The Dedicated Administrator Connection (DAC) is especially designed for use when a server instance is unresponsive to other connection types, such as Windows or SQL Server authentication. Although the DAC integrates tightly with the sqlcmd utility, which is available through SQL Server Express, the DAC feature does not operate with SQL Server Express instances.

Figure 2-24 shows a command prompt window with a sqlcmd session. The session starts by invoking the sqlcmd.exe with the -S switch. The instance name references the SQLEXPRESS instance on the local server. This statement attempts to connect via Windows authentication, which is the default authentication route for sqlcmd. After the login completes, the session continues by running a simple query. This task confirms that the connection is operational. Three additional sqlcmd statements on lines 1>, 2>, and 3> return a result set with the value of the number of sales-persons in the SalesPerson table within the Sales schema of the AdventureWorks database. The result set appears after the GO keyword, which launches the current batch of statements and readies sqlcmd for a new batch. The 1> prompt that appears after the result set shows sqlcmd is ready to start a new batch of statements. The EXIT keyword closes the sqlcmd session and returns control to the operating system command prompt window.

Figure 2-24. *You only need to specify the server instance name to connect from sqlcmd with Windows authentication.*

Connection via SQL Server Authentication

When using SQL Server authentication, you need to specify a login name and its password. Most database applications refer to a login name with userID or userid. Therefore, sqlcmd names its switch for the login name -U. There are several ways to specify the password for a login. For example, there is a -P switch for designating the password value when you invoke sqlcmd. However, sqlcmd shows your password in clear text so that anyone who can view your screen can learn your password. Another approach is to omit the -P switch when connecting with SQL Server authentication. In this scenario, sqlcmd prompts for the password after processing the sqlcmd statement but before granting access to a server instance. When you type your password into the prompt, no onscreen feedback appears. Thus, your password remains secure from those who can view your screen.

Figure 2-25 shows the syntax for a sqlcmd session using SQL Server authentication. The session uses the sa login. Notice that you still need to specify a server instance name with the -S switch. In addition, you need to designate a login name, which is sa, in the figure. The sqlcmd statement syntax without a -P switch causes the Password: prompt. A user must enter a valid password for the login specified with the -U switch before the sqlcmd utility permits access to the server. The display of the 1> prompt after the Password: prompt confirms the granting of server access. Although you must enter a valid password to get to the 1> prompt, no password shows on the screen.

Figure 2-25 demonstrates the use of the :serverlist keyword. Recall that this statement returns a list of visible SQL Server instances. If you are not sure of an instance name or you want to confirm that an instance is broadcasting its availability, this command is very convenient. The command executes automatically so there is no need for the GO keyword. The figure concludes with the EXIT keyword, which closes the sqlcmd session.

Figure 2-25. *By not using the -P switch with SQL Server authentication, you can secure your password from those who can view your screen.*

Running Statements from a File

The whole purpose for connecting to a SQL Server instance with sqlcmd is to perform database chores—namely, those that you can perform with T-SQL and sqlcmd statements. The sqlcmd utility is natively best for those chores that have short command statements and generate little or no output to the screen. An administrative statement, such as CREATE LOGIN, is ideal for the sqlcmd utility. Another example is any SELECT statement that generates an aggregate. The T-SQL statements in Figure 2-6 show how convenient it is to count the unique values in a column with the sqlcmd utility.

■**Note** The CREATE LOGIN statement adds a new login to a SQL Server Express instance. See Chapter 8 for extensive discussion and demonstrations on how to use this T-SQL statement.

You can work around the short input and output rule for the sqlcmd utility by using additional sqlcmd statement switches beyond those demonstrated already. When you need to run more than a couple of lines of statements, you can put the code into a file and then reference the file from a sqlcmd statement. There are two ways to accomplish this. First, you can use the -i command-line switch following sqlcmd. The argument for the -i switch is the path and file name containing the statements that you want to reference. There is no need to delimit the path and file with quotes (unless there are special characters, such as spaces, in a path name). Second, you can enter the :r sqlcmd keyword in response to a sqlcmd prompt, such as 1>. This keyword takes a string in double quotes to denote the path to a file.

With either the -i switch or the :r keyword, you can replace a set of statements with a single reference to a path and file. In fact, you can even debug the statements in Express SSMS and later run the statements in the file quickly and easily with the sqlcmd utility. The sqlcmd utility is ideally suited for rerunning a set of T-SQL statements whenever an IT professional or power user needs those statements run.

Using the –i Switch to Reference a File of Statements

The statements in a file that you reference with the -i switch can contain T-SQL statements, sqlcmd statements, or both types of statements. The three statements in Figure 2-5 start with the USE keyword to set the database context for two SELECT statements that follow it. The USE keyword is valid in both Express SSMS and the sqlcmd utility. The code portrayed in Figure 2-19 is saved as SQL-Query2_f0219.sql in the C:\ProSSEApps\Chapter02 path on my test computer.

The command prompt window in Figure 2-26 shows the syntax for the -i switch pointing at SQLQuery2_f0219.sql. Notice the statement's compact form. The statement has just two switches: one to denote a server instance name (-S) and another to denote a file with statements (-i). The argument for the -i switch points at Query2_f0205.sql in its path on the C drive of the local computer. The code in SQLQuery2_f0219.sql changes the database context to AdventureWorks and runs two SELECT statements.

The output, which appears below the sqlcmd statement, shows the outcome from each SELECT statement. When you use the -i switch with a sqlcmd statement, the sqlcmd utility never presents a prompt for interactive use. Instead, the statements within the file pointed at by the -i switch run, and control returns to another command prompt. You do not have to exit the sqlcmd utility to get to another command prompt.

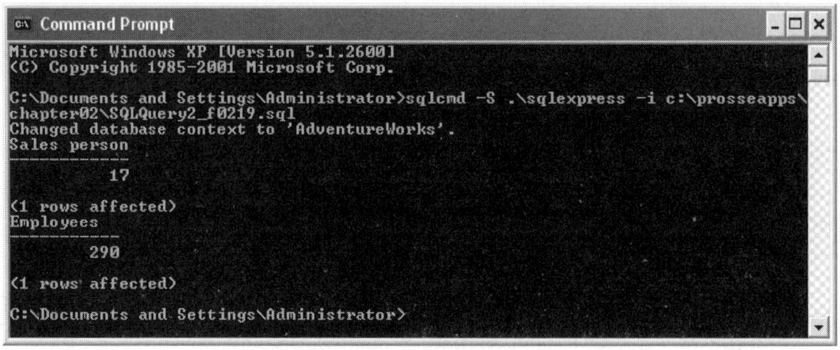

Figure 2-26. *Use the –i switch in a sqlcmd statement to refer to a file with statements to run.*

Using the :r keyword to Reference a File of Statements

The :r keyword operates from within the sqlcmd utility. When you run a statement with the keyword, control remains within the sqlcmd utility. Unlike statements with the :serverlist keyword, statements with the :r keyword do not automatically execute. You need to invoke the GO keyword to run a batch of statements that includes the :r keyword.

It takes a minimum of two statements to run a statement with the :r keyword. The first statement starts with the keyword followed by the path and file name containing the T-SQL or sqlcmd statements that you wish to run. The path and file name must appear in double quotes. The following sample uses a script saved from Express SSMS with a .sql file extension. However, you are not restricted to reading from .sql files. For example, you can specify a .txt file type instead of a .sql file type. The essential point is that the file referenced by the :r keyword must contain valid T-SQL and sqlcmd statements. Unless you add a second line with the GO keyword, the code in the file pointed at by the :r statement will not execute.

The following script excerpt shows necessary lines for running the code in SQLQuery2_f0219.sql. The statements generate output within the sqlcmd utility that looks like that within Figure 2-26.

```
1>:r "c:\prosseapps\chapter02\SQLQuery2_f0219.sql"
2>GO
```

Saving Output to a File

The statements that you run with either the –i switch or the :r keyword can generate richly structured data with multiple columns, each having many rows. You can also generate output with multiple result sets based on multiple SELECT statements. In fact, whether or not you use the –i switch or the :r keyword, you can produce richly structured data as output from a sqlcmd session. Your output's complexity is limited only by your ability to construct output with T-SQL statements. One way of handling relatively rich output is to save it to a file.

Saving your sqlcmd output to a file offers at least three benefits. First, you can edit and format the returned values with any application that can read a .txt file. Second, you can review the return values from the session without having to rerun the statements that create the output. Third, you can mail the output as an attachment to an e-mail message or even copy the output to the message body.

You can save the output from a sqlcmd session by adding the –o switch to the sqlcmd statement that launches a session. The argument value for the switch is the path and file name in which you want to store the output from a session. A very common file type for saving output is .rpt, but any file type will suffice. The file represents output with ANSI character codes by default. Therefore, you can read and even format the output with any other application that processes text files with ANSI character codes. If the file designated as an argument value for the –o switch does not exist, the sqlcmd utility automatically generates it.

■**Caution** If the target file already exists for a –o switch argument, the sqlcmd utility writes over any previous content in the file. The sqlcmd utility issues no warning before copying over prior values in a target file.

Figure 2-27 shows the syntax for sending the output from an :r statement to a file named saved_data.txt. The sample starts by adding the –o switch to a sqlcmd statement that connects to the SQLEXPRESS instance on the local server. The addition of the –o switch causes all output during the session, including error messages, to go to the file specified by the –o switch argument. The statements toward the top of Figure 2-27 show the syntax for running the Query2_f0205.sql file with the :r keyword. Notice that no output values appear within the session because of the –o switch in the sqlcmd statement. An EXIT statement terminates the sqlcmd session. A command prompt window type keyword displays the contents of the saved_data.txt file, which is an argument for the –o switch, after the close of the sqlcmd session.

Figure 2-27. *Use the –o switch in a sqlcmd statement to designate a file for saving the output from a sqlcmd session.*

Dynamically Running and Batching sqlcmd Statements

There are three more ways of running the sqlcmd utility that make it more dynamic and easier to use. You can make sqlcmd statements dynamic at runtime by using scripting variables. These variables let you create T-SQL scripts that include variable values for such items as database, table, and column names. Save your T-SQL scripts with the scripting variables as .sql files. At runtime, a sqlcmd statement can reference the T-SQL script and assign values to the variables in the script. This feature gives you the capability to reuse the same script with different variable values.

As useful as scripting variables are, they actually make using the sqlcmd utility more cumbersome in one way. This is because you have to assign scripting variable values in a sqlcmd statement. Some sqlcmd statements are already long when using more than one switch, and including variable assignments only makes the statements longer to type at a command prompt. Including one or more sqlcmd statements in a batch file enables you to edit your sqlcmd statements with the aid of your favorite text editor—for example, the Windows Notepad applet. Additionally, you can use the full range of command prompt window instructions and syntax conventions. For example, you can append the output from one sqlcmd statement to the output from a previously run sqlcmd statement with the >> operator so that you have a single output file for all the sqlcmd statements run from a batch file.

Another advantage of batching sqlcmd statements in .bat files is that you can schedule when .bat files run with the Windows Scheduled Tasks applet. The applet does not allow you to schedule sqlcmd statements outside of a .bat file. The capability to schedule sqlcmd statements is particularly important for SQL Server Express users because Express SSMS does not support scheduled tasks. The SSMS version for other SQL Server 2005 editions does support scheduled tasks, so there is no need to resort to an external resource for scheduling tasks, such as the Windows Scheduled Tasks applet.

Using Scripting Variables

Scripting variables enable you to invoke a dynamic T-SQL script from a sqlcmd statement. A T-SQL script can have one or more scripting variables. A sqlcmd statement can assign string values to the scripting variables that then replace the scripting variable in the T-SQL script when a sqlcmd statement invokes the script. Scripting variables are very flexible because they can designate any part of a T-SQL statement, including a database name, a table name, and a column name. It is the ability to replace a scripting variable with a value at runtime that makes the T-SQL dynamic.

The format for a scripting variable is: $(variablename). You can place one or more scripting variables anywhere in a T-SQL script to be run by a sqlcmd statement. When using sqlcmd scripting variables, you'll always have at least two elements. First, you need a script file with one or more T-SQL statements containing scripting variables. Second, you need a sqlcmd statement that assigns values to the scripting variables and references the file containing the T-SQL code with the scripting variables. It is typical to use a .sql file type to hold the T-SQL script. Express SSMS is not a particularly appropriate editor for T-SQL with scripting variables because its parser for T-SQL does not properly interpret sqlcmd scripting variables. An application such as Notepad makes an acceptable editor for scripting variables.

There are several rules and conventions that you should follow when assigning names to scripting variables.

- Scripting variable names are case sensitive.
- T-SQL variable names should not have the same form as scripting variable expressions, such as $(variablename).
- Variable names should be in quotation marks if they contain spaces.
- Quotation marks within a variable name need to be escaped (represent " as "").
- White space (e.g., nonprinting characters) should not be used in variable names.

The following T-SQL script is from ListColumnValues.sql. It contains a T-SQL script with three sqlcmd scripting variables. The variable names are DBName, CName, and TName. The USE statement sets a variable database context based on the value of DBName. The SELECT statement returns the values for the CName column from the TName table, view, or table-valued function.

```
USE $(DBName)
GO
SELECT $(CName) FROM $(TName)
GO
```

Figure 2-28 shows how to use the ListColumnValues.sql file in a sqlcmd statement that returns the company names for the shippers from the Northwind database. Notice the sqlcmd statement has three switches. The first switch (-S) designates a server. The second switch (-v) precedes a set of three assignment statements—one for each scripting variable. The assignments designate the CompanyName column in the Shippers table within the Northwind database. The third switch (-i) specifies the T-SQL script file with the scripting variables.

All three of these switches for a sqlcmd statement invoking a script file with scripting variables must be synchronized. For example, the variable assignments after the -v switch must be for scripting variables in the file specified by the argument for the -i switch. In addition, the script file must pertain to the server instance denoted by the server name following the -S switch.

The command prompt window in Figure 2-28 includes the output from the sqlcmd statement. By setting the database name to Northwind, the table name to Shippers, and the column name to CompanyName, the sqlcmd statement returns the company names of shippers from the Northwind database. You can generate other output by changing the assignment statements for the scripting variables.

Figure 2-28. *Scripting variables let you reuse T-SQL scripts from sqlcmd statements.*

Batching sqlcmd Statements

Typing one or more sqlcmd statements into a text file and saving the file with a .bat extension can simplify the use of sqlcmd statements. Windows operating systems (and MS DOS too) recognizes .bat files as batch files. A batch file can include one or more cmd.exe commands and other commands, such as sqlcmd statements, that you can execute from a command prompt. The contents of a batch file are plain text that you can enter and edit from Notepad or any text editor.

■**Note** cmd.exe is an outgrowth of command.com for MS DOS. cmd.exe ships with Windows NT, Windows 2000, Windows XP, and Windows 2003.

Figure 2-29 shows Notepad open with a file named ListColumnValues.bat. The sqlcmd statement in ListColumnValues.bat is the same one in Figure 2-10, with one minor enhancement. The enhancement sends the output to the ColumnValuesOut.rpt file instead of the command prompt window.

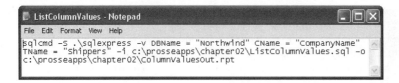

Figure 2-29. *You can easily edit sqlcmd statements in a batch file.*

When you need to rerun or edit a sqlcmd statement, having the statement in a batch file simplifies the task. For example, you can edit the batch file by opening it in Notepad, making your changes, and saving the file with your modifications. Using a sqlcmd statement when it is in a batch file is easier as well. To run the batch file, just type the path and file name for the batch file. You can optionally change the current directory with the CD command to the path containing the batch file. Because batch file names are typically much shorter than sqlcmd statements with multiple switches, this batching approach simplifies the use of sqlcmd statements.

Figure 2-30 shows a second batch file named ListColumnValues2.bat. This second batch file contains two sqlcmd statements. Both statements use the ListColumnValues.sql file with its scripting variables. The first sqlcmd statement is identical to the one in Figure 2-11, but the second sqlcmd statement changes the assignment statements for the scripting variables to return customer, instead of shipper, company names. In addition, the second sqlcmd statement uses the >> operator to append its output to the end of the previous output generated by the first sqlcmd statement in the batch file.

Figure 2-30. *Using a batch file, you can run multiple sqlcmd statements sequentially.*

The output file (ColumnValuesOut.rpt) for the two sqlcmd statements in the ListColumnValues2 batch file contains extended characters, such as an acute accent i (í) and an umlaut o (ö). The Notepad applet does not represent these extended characters properly when it opens ColumnValuesOut.rpt. However, you can copy directly from the cmd.exe window after invoking the type command for the output file.

Figure 2-31 shows an excerpt from the output generated with the type command. Figure 2-32 shows the same excerpt copied from the cmd.exe window to Excel. Notice in both figures that the extended characters appear correctly.

■**Note** The normal Ctrl+C shortcut does not work for copying content from a cmd.exe window. To copy text, first you highlight (or mark) the content that you want to copy. Choose the Edit ➤ Mark command and then highlight the area of the cmd.exe window that you want to copy. After marking the area, choose Edit ➤ Copy from the window's menu or press Enter (you can open the window's menu by clicking the icon in the window's top-left border area). You can paste content that you copy from a cmd.exe window into another application, such as Excel, in the same way that you do from any other application.

Figure 2-31. *You can view the output file from a sqlcmd statement with the type command in the cmd.exe window.*

Figure 2-32. *You can copy sqlcmd output from the cmd.exe window to Excel.*

Scheduling T-SQL Statements

A common requirement is to run some T-SQL statements on a regular basis automatically. For example, you may want the ColumnValuesOut.rpt file to refresh for the Northwind database daily, weekly, or monthly. You might even want a report file to update multiple times per day when working with website traffic data or any fast-changing data. Frequently updating this kind of task assures reasonably current data and relieves the load on a SQL Server Express instance (instead of multiple users repeatedly querying a server, they can read a file).

Another common use for scheduling tasks is to perform differential backups on a regular basis—say, once every few hours. Chapter 3 describes techniques for backing up and restoring SQL Server Express databases. By running backup .sql files from .bat files, you can schedule when backups are performed and build a history of backups.

You can get a feel for how to schedule repeated runs of a .bat file by scheduling the ListColumnValues.bat file. This .bat file invokes a sqlcmd statement that writes the current values of the Shippers table in the Northwind database to the ColumnValuesOut.rpt file. The "Batching sqlcmd Statements" section originally described ListColumnValues.bat. The Windows Scheduled Tasks applet lets you schedule this .bat file on any schedule according to your requirements. Follow these steps to schedule the running of ListColumnValues.bat:

1. Open the Scheduled Tasks applet from the Control Panel.

2. From the opening screen, double-click the Add Scheduled Task icon.

3. Click Next in the first Scheduled Task wizard screen.

4. On the next wizard screen, click Browse and navigate to ListColumnValues.bat.

5. Assign the task a name, such as ListColumnValues, and designate when the task should run, such as daily (even if you want the task to run more often than daily, select daily here); see Figure 2-33.

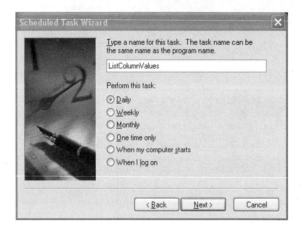

Figure 2-33. *After you pick a .bat file that implements your task, assign the task a name and designate when to run the task.*

6. On the next screen, refine your schedule by designating whether a program should run every day, on weekdays only, or every other day, and assigning a start time for the days the program should run. If you select weekly or monthly as the interval for rerunning a task, then you get refinement options appropriate for that interval.

7. Specify a Windows account name and password for running the task.

8. On the next, and potentially final, screen, you can click Finish and exit the wizard or open a task properties dialog box for refining your settings, such as specifying the interval between successive runs of a task per day.

   a. Select the only check box on the screen before clicking Finish to refine your timing specifications per day (or other aspects of your task settings).

   b. Then click the Schedule tab on the properties dialog box and click Advanced.

    c. Select the Repeat task check box on the Advanced Schedule Options screen, and designate a time interval between successive runs of a task—see Figure 2-34 for a setting that runs a task every 10 minutes.

    d. Clicking OK on the Advanced Schedule Options dialog box and the task properties dialog box commits the schedule for the task and exits the wizard.

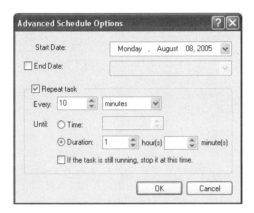

Figure 2-34. *Use the Advanced Schedule Options screen after completing the main wizard screens to specify the interval between successive runs of a task program more precisely than you can with the main wizard screens.*

Summary

This chapter drilled down on two tools for running T-SQL statements. Express SSMS is a rich graphical tool for running T-SQL statements. Express SSMS is especially designed for SQL Server Express, although you can use it to run T-SQL statements for other SQL Server 2005 editions and even other SQL Server versions, such as the MSDE version of SQL Server 2000. This chapter demonstrated many of the most important Express SSMS features, including how to

- Connect to different SQL Server Express instances
- Use three powerful designers for creating databases, tables, and views
- Write, save, and reuse T-SQL code

Chapters 3 through Chapter 8 examine in-depth T-SQL coding techniques that you can use from within Express SSMS (or any other query tool).

    The second tool covered in this chapter is the sqlcmd utility. This command-line application also runs T-SQL statements, but it offers no graphical user interface. The sqlcmd utility is especially designed for IT professionals and SQL Server power users. What the sqlcmd utility lacks in ease of use it compensates for by exposing an interface that makes it fast to invoke T-SQL statements without the overhead of a graphical user interface. In addition, the coverage of the sqlcmd utility included an example showing how to schedule the automatic running of sqlcmd tasks using the Windows Scheduled Tasks applet.

CHAPTER 3

■ ■ ■

Exploring, Creating, and Recovering Databases

Many database developers and business analysts have a way of taking databases for granted. These database users focus almost myopically on what's inside a database, such as its tables, stored procedures, and other database objects. However, before you can have a database application, someone, such as a DBA, lead developer, or power user, must create a database. The settings for a database at the time of its creation can significantly impact its suitability for different kinds of applications. These settings are often referred to as *database meta data*—namely, data about a database, as opposed to what's in a database. Even after a database is initially created, you can tweak database meta data to optimize the performance of a database or repurpose a database to meet new objectives.

This chapter presents the skills that you need to know to create and manage databases. You'll learn how to find the files that support a database and how to explore and manipulate database meta data. The content within this chapter trains you to create databases programmatically with T-SQL. You can run the T-SQL code from Express SSMS, which Chapter 2 introduced. This chapter also shows you how to attach database files copied from another computer.

In addition, you'll learn how to apply XCopy deployment and constraints that can inhibit this SQL Server Express (SSE) feature from being available. This chapter concludes by training you to protect your valuable database assets through coverage of backup and restore techniques. The discussion of backup and restore scripts at the end of this chapter presents easy-to-follow commentary describing which clauses and argument values to use for specific recovery scenarios.

Overview of Databases

Before you create and manage databases, it is very helpful to learn about important database features and the different kinds of databases. This section provides a quick introduction to these topics.

Databases are core objects inside of any SSE instance. In this section I briefly introduce databases, particularly as they pertain to SSE specifically and SQL Server 2005 generally. Another goal of this section is to highlight the interplay among XCopy deployment, the auto-close feature, and whether a database is attached to a database server. You'll also receive a quick overview of database types with a special focus on system databases. A basic understanding of these databases, particularly the master database, can help you avoid making disastrous mistakes or facilitate your recovery from what might otherwise be a fatal flaw.

Introducing Database Concepts

Databases are containers within an SSE instance. If you install SSE multiple times on the same computer, each installation creates a new SSE instance. It is common to refer to a specific server instance as a database server because a server instance serves, or makes available, the contents of a database. Just as you can install multiple instances of SSE on a single computer, a database server can contain multiple databases.

The relationship between SSE instances and a computer places limits on how you can organize databases on a computer. You can install up to 50 instances of SSE per computer. The maximum size of an SSE database is 4GB. The maximum number of databases per database server is 32,767. If you have a database that needs to grow beyond 4GB in size, you can reorganize the contents of a database so that it resides in two or more databases within one or more server instances. If you prefer not to segment a database that does (or will eventually) require more than 4GB of storage into multiple databases, you can migrate your solution to another edition of SQL Server 2005. Other commercial SQL Server 2005 editions can accommodate a single database that is over 1,000,000TB in size. SSE is clearly optimized for databases that will never grow beyond 4GB. Happily, many database applications fit comfortably within this size limit.

A database can contain typical database objects, such as tables, views, user-defined functions, and stored procedures. It is common to use a database as a container for multiple database objects relating to a common project. An accounting database, for example, can track customers, sales, accounts receivable, and accounts payable. You can use individual tables within the accounting database to track separate types of objects, such as customers in one table and sales in another table. You can use views to show subsets of a single table or joins of multiple tables, such as sales by customer in the current month. User-defined functions can perform computations, such as tax by jurisdiction. Stored procedures can perform various tasks, such as computing monthly or quarterly totals.

One especially distinguishing feature of SSE databases is the auto-close feature. Chapter 1 briefly introduced XCopy deployment as it surveyed important SSE features. Recall that prior SQL Server versions and other editions of SQL Server 2005 typically manage the files in a database whether or not a user is actively using the files. Because SQL Server used to manage files as long as a SQL Server instance was on, the file could not be copied or modified except through SQL Server. SQL Server Express typically manages databases so that the databases close when there are no active users of a database.

The auto-close feature, which enables XCopy deployment, radically simplifies the deployment of SSE databases. With XCopy deployment, you can copy the files for a database between SSE instances and computers as simply as copying database files from one computer to another, without any other special steps. If you turn off the auto-close feature, then you can copy the files for a database only after you first detach them from a database server. After making a copy of a database's files, you must reattach the original database files to the database server before you can use them. Later, you can attach the copied database files to a new server instance on the same or another computer.

■**Tip** See the "Attaching and Detaching Databases" section in this chapter for an overview of attaching and detaching databases as well as code samples that you can adapt for your specific requirements.

When working with SQL Server, you will typically have a database context. When you connect to an SSE instance, you must have a valid login account for the database server. Specify a database within a server that you want to use with the USE keyword in T-SQL. This database becomes the context for all subsequent T-SQL statements until you close your application or specify a new database context. Even with one database declared as your database context, you can still refer to data from other databases and even other servers. This allows you to perform analyses that draw on multiple databases spread across multiple server instances.

Types of Databases

There are two main types of relational databases in SSE. These are user databases and system databases. Individual database users with appropriate permissions can create user databases. Developers and database administrators can learn design guidelines from studying the objects in sample databases, and the standard SQL Server documentation (Books Online) references the sample databases. The "Installing Sample Databases" section in Chapter 1 describes the process for installing three Microsoft-supplied sample databases. If you did not previously install those databases, please do so now. The three sample databases are examples of user databases.

System databases can help you manage your user database as well as an overall server instance. There are five built-in system databases:

- The *master database* records all instance-level information for an SSE instance. This database tracks all logins to a SQL Server instance and all other databases in a server instance. You should always maintain a current copy of the master database.

- The *model database* is a system database that serves as a template for all new databases on an SSE instance. If you want a database object in all new databases, such as a table or a stored procedure, then you can update the model database with the database object that you want in all new databases.

- The *tempdb database* stores all temporary content during an SSE session. This database holds all temporary tables and temporary stored procedures along with other objects. When you close a SQL Server session, SQL Server drops the tempdb database. When you start a new SQL Server session, SQL Server creates a new tempdb database.

- The *msdb database* supports SQL Server Agent, which is not implemented with the SSE edition of SQL Server 2005.

- The *mssqlsystemresource database* is a new system database to help support fast upgrades. This database does not start up when a SQL Server instance begins to run, but its files reside in the default Data folder for an SSE instance.

■**Caution** If a server instance's master database gets corrupted or damaged and you do not have a current backup, you may be able to reattach your databases to the last available backup of the master database. If you do not have a backup of the master database, you may be able to attach your files for a database to a new SSE instance on the same or a different computer.

Getting Meta Data About Databases

Meta data describes the structure of a database server—such as an SSE instance—and its databases, as opposed to specific values from within a specific database. An enumeration of the database names on a database server is an example of meta data. A listing of the database names on a server provides feedback about the structure of a database server. A result set with the names of tables within a specific database is also an example of meta data. This example gives information about the structure of a specific database on a database server.

There are at least four ways to retrieve meta data from an SSE instance, each of which offers a special perspective or benefit:

- *Through the Express SSMS user interface—namely, Object Explorer*: Express SSMS's Object Explorer window displays selected meta data in a hierarchical tree format, such as the names of databases and the tables within those databases, for an SSE instance. See the "Exploring the Objects in a Connection" section in Chapter 2 for more detail on exploring meta data graphically with Express SSMS.

- *Using a system-stored procedure in T-SQL, such as* sp_helpdb: With this method, you can run system-stored procedures to gather preprogrammed information about database objects, such as the size of a database or when a database was created.

- *Referencing system catalog views, such as* sys.databases, *in T-SQL statements*: Because you can use system catalog views in the FROM clause of a SELECT statement, you can precisely designate a custom subset of meta data that you want to retrieve.

- *Using Windows Explorer to uncover the files for a database on a computer*: This approach is particularly convenient when you want to copy the files for a database between computers.

Using sp_helpdb for Database Help

A system-stored procedure named sp_helpdb can provide information about databases in either of two ways. First, you can run the system-stored procedure without naming a specific database to return summary meta data about all the databases on a database server. Second, you can designate a specific database name to return more detailed meta data about a particular database.

■**Tip** T-SQL supports a large variety of sp_help system-stored procedures for many different types of database objects. In fact, T-SQL even has an sp_help system-stored procedure that reports on all the objects in a database. It is worth searching for sp_help in the SQL Server 2005 Books Online when you seek information about database objects to see which variation of an sp_help system-stored procedure is best for your needs.

Getting Meta Data About All Databases

You can run the sp_helpdb system-stored procedure without naming a specific database. With this format, sp_helpdb returns a single result set. The result set contains seven columns of information for all the databases known to the SQL Server instance to which you are connected. Figure 3-1 shows Express SSMS with the syntax and a sample result set for invoking the sp_helpdb system-stored procedure without a database name (see SQLQuery1_f0301.sql for the listing). The Results tab in Query Editor shows the result set returned by the system-stored procedure. The USE statement merely designates a specific database context for the EXEC statements. The GO statement after the USE statement forces the USE statement to run before the sp_helpdb system-stored procedure executes. Because sp_helpdb extracts information from the sys.databases view in the master database, you can invoke the command with any legitimate database context for a server instance. Remember that the master database has a guest account that allows any user access to it.

■**Note** The EXECUTE statement, which is frequently abbreviated as EXEC, executes system-stored procedures, such as sp_helpdb. In general, you always need an EXEC (or EXECUTE) before a system-stored procedure, except when the system-stored procedure is the first one in a batch of T-SQL statements. You can also use EXEC to execute extended stored procedures, user-defined stored procedures, and scalar-valued user-defined stored procedures.

The result set in the Results tab of Figure 3-1 is from the `EXEC sp_helpdb` statement. The result set has eight rows—one for each of the three sample databases, a custom `ProSSEApps` database created in Chapter 2, and four system databases shown in Figure 3-1. The four system databases were all created during the SSE installation process by the sa user. The `Northwind`, `ProSSEApps`, and `pubs` databases were also created for the server with a connection for the sa user. The computer administrator (CAB233A\Administrator) ran the script to attach the `AdventureWorks` database files, and this account is therefore the owner of the `AdventureWorks` database. The output shows that the `AdventureWorks` database is the largest of the databases, with a size of slightly over 166MB. The status column values are truncated. This column includes a comma-delimited list of database options, such as whether a database is `ONLINE` or `OFFLINE`. An `OFFLINE` database cannot be modified. The default value for this database option is `ONLINE` sa user. The `dbid` column returns a numeric database ID that uniquely identifies a database on a database server—just as a database's name uniquely identifies a database. The `compatibility_level` column values designate which version of SQL Server to apply for selected behaviors.

Note The `sp_dbcmptlevel` system-stored procedure lets you specify a SQL Server version for invoking selected behaviors within a database, such as assigning a name to a database object. SQL Server 2005 editions, including SSE, recognize compatibility level settings, such as 70, 80, and 90. These level settings pertain, respectively, to SQL Server 7.0, SQL Server 2000, and SQL Server 2005. For example, when using a database with a compatibility level of 80, assigning the name `PIVOT` to a database object is legitimate. If you revise the compatibility level setting to 90 with `sp_dbcmptlevel`, then `PIVOT` is no longer a valid name because SQL Server 2005 introduces the `PIVOT` reserved word. Chapter 6 discusses how to use the `PIVOT` reserved word.

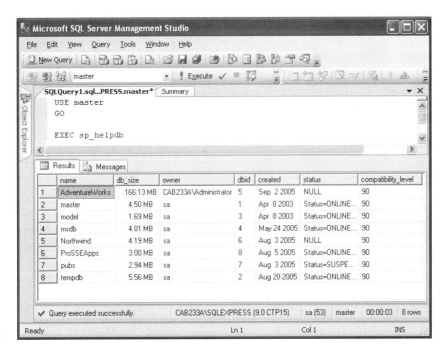

Figure 3-1. *Use the sp_helpdb system-stored procedure without naming a database to return meta data about all databases in an SSE instance.*

Getting Meta Data About a Particular Database

You can also invoke sp_helpdb and assign the name of a database to the @dbname parameter for the system-stored procedure. This format returns two result sets. The first result set has a single row with column names that match those for getting meta data for all the databases on a database server. The column values for the row correspond to the row from the result set for all databases with a name column value equal to the setting for @dbname. The second result set gives information about the database files for the database named by the @dbname parameter, such as the file names.

The first and second result sets in the Results tab of Figure 3-2 are from the EXEC sp_help @dbname statement (see SQLQuery1_f0302.sql for the listing). The @dbname value denotes the Northwind database. The first result set has a single row for the Northwind database. This row generally repeats the column values from the Northwind row in the result set showing in Figure 3-1. One obvious exception is the status column value. The result set for all databases shows a NULL value for this column for the Northwind database, but the first result set in Figure 3-2 displays comma-delimited values in its status column.

■**Caution** When converting a database, such as the Northwind database, from SQL Server 2000 to SQL Server 2005, you may discover some variance in meta data results returned by running sp_helpdb against the master database versus the actual converted database. In general, the sp_helpdb system-stored procedure with @dbname set to a database returns more timely and accurate meta data than sp_helpdb result set values derived from a master database.

The second result set includes information about the primary data file (.mdf) and the log file (.ldf). The filename column values are truncated in Figure 3-2. The filename column points at the C:\Program Files\Microsoft SQL Server\MSSQL.1\MSSQL\DATA\ path. The data file name is northwnd.mdf, and the log file name is northwnd.ldf. The second result set also denotes the current size of each file as well as how large and in what increments the file can grow automatically. The filegroup column refers to the topic of groups of database files, which does not apply to the overwhelming majority of the databases that you create and use with SSE instances.

■**Note** The primary data and log file are two of the three types of database files. The "Searching for and Copying Databases with Windows Explorer" and the "Using CREATE DATABASE" sections in this chapter drill down deeper into the topic of database files.

Using System Catalog Views

SQL Server System tables contain meta data for all of the objects in a server instance. However, you should not attempt to work with system tables directly because the structure of these tables can change, according to the needs of Microsoft, from one version to the next.

Instead, you can obtain this meta data from system catalog views. These are a richer set of views for obtaining information from SSE system tables than the older INFORMATION_SCHEMA view technology available in earlier SQL Server versions. Microsoft returns consistent result sets between versions for its system catalog and INFORMATION_SCHEMA views. One way of expressing the extra richness of system catalog views is to note that the count of system catalog views exceeds 250, whereas the number of INFORMATION_SCHEMA views is about 20. This section demonstrates the use of the sys.databases, sys.tables, and sys.columns system catalog views.

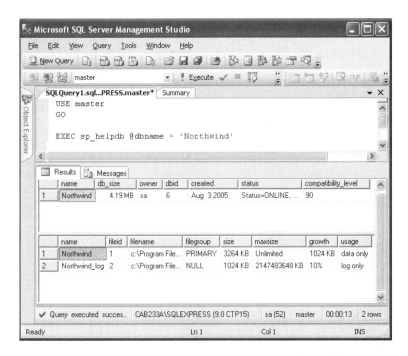

Figure 3-2. *Use the sp_helpdb system-stored procedure with its @dbname parameter to return meta data about a single database on an SSE instance.*

Using sys.databases

The sys.databases catalog view returns one row per database in a server instance with scores of columns of information on each database. This section demonstrates the use of the name and is_auto_close_on columns. The remaining columns cover just about every aspect of a database, such as the database's numeric ID (database_id), the security identifier of the database's owner (owner_sid), whether the database is read only (is_read_only), and the recovery model for a database (recovery_model and recovery_model_desc).

The name column value is the name of a database. The is_auto_close_on column value pertains to XCopy deployment. When the value is 1, you can merely copy the files to another directory or computer for their use elsewhere. When the is_auto_close_on column value is 0, you cannot copy the files for a database until you either detach the database or shut down the SSE instance containing the database.

■Note When is_auto_close_on equals 0, the database is attached to the database server. You must detach the database files from the server before you can copy them elsewhere. Then, you must reattach the database files if you want to use the database on the database server.

The following T-SQL script, which is available in SQLQuery2_f0303_f0304.sql, returns the name and is_auto_close_on column values from the server instance connection referenced in Figure 3-1. The USE statement designates the master database as the database context for the following SELECT statement. You can reference a system catalog view, such as sys.databases, from any database context on a server instance.

```
USE master
GO

SELECT name, is_auto_close_on
FROM sys.databases
```

Figure 3-3 shows the result set generated by the preceding SELECT statement. The three sample databases all have an is_auto_close_on value of 1. This makes them ready for XCopy deployment. However, all four system databases and the custom ProSSEApps database have is_auto_close_on values of 0. Therefore, the system databases and the ProSSEApps database are not available for XCopy deployment. However, you can readily make backup files for databases with an is_auto_close_on meta data column value of 0 through a BACKUP DATABASE statement even while a SQL Server instance is running. You can recover a backup for a system database with the RESTORE DATABASE statement.

■Tip The "Searching for and Copying Databases with Windows Explorer" section provides additional detail on how to perform XCopy deployment with Windows Explorer.

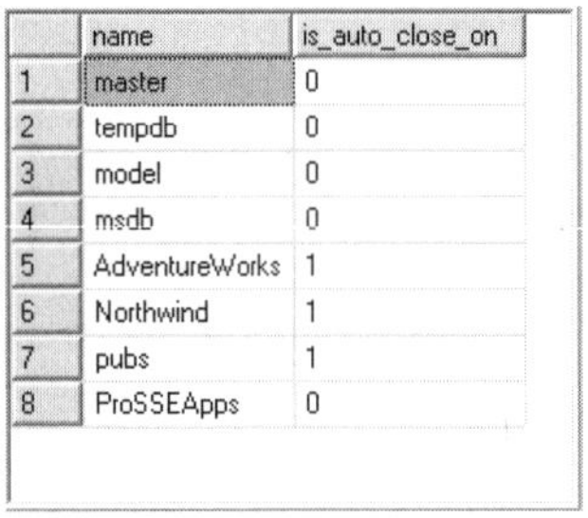

	name	is_auto_close_on
1	master	0
2	tempdb	0
3	model	0
4	msdb	0
5	AdventureWorks	1
6	Northwind	1
7	pubs	1
8	ProSSEApps	0

Figure 3-3. *The sys.databases catalog view can help you discover the names of databases on a server instance and determine whether the databases are ready for XCopy deployment.*

Modifying is_auto_close_on Column Values

You are not allowed to modify column values of system catalog views with direct UPDATE statements. However, the sp_dboption system-stored procedure allows you to change a variety of database-level options, including one named autoclose. You set values to the autoclose option with the sp_dboption system-stored procedure for a database by setting the option to TRUE or FALSE. You can return the autoclose setting for a database by running sp_dboption without specifying a value. In this case, the system-stored procedure returns a value of ON or OFF. An autoclose option value of TRUE or ON maps to an is_auto_close_on column value of 1, and an autoclose value of FALSE or OFF corresponds to a column value of 0.

The following T-SQL script queries the is_auto_close_on column value in sys.databases for the Northwind database row before and after changing the database's autoclose property to FALSE. See SQLQuery2_f0303_f0304.sql for the query file. After the option assignment via sp_dboption, the is_auto_close_on column value will be 0. The column value could be 1 before the invocation of sp_dboption (Figure 3-3 confirms that it is 1 for the Northwind database). Then, the script sets the is_auto_close_on column value to 1 by using sp_dboption to set the Northwind autoclose database option to TRUE. A final SELECT statement from sys.databases confirms the impact on the is_auto_close_on column value. The script generates three result sets—one for each SELECT statement from sys.databases.

```
USE master
GO
SELECT name, is_auto_close_on
FROM sys.databases
WHERE name = 'Northwind'
GO
sp_dboption 'Northwind', 'autoclose', 'FALSE'
GO
SELECT name, is_auto_close_on
FROM sys.databases
WHERE name = 'Northwind'
GO
sp_dboption 'Northwind', 'autoclose', 'TRUE'
GO
SELECT name, is_auto_close_on
FROM sys.databases
WHERE name = 'Northwind'
GO
```

Returning Hierarchical Meta Data

The following script draws on sys.tables and sys.columns as well as sys.databases to return the column names within a particular table of a database. Recall that sys.tables and sys.columns are two system catalog views. Although SELECT statements from sys.databases are independent of the database context, SELECT statements from either sys.tables or sys.columns are dependent on the database context. A USE statement before queries against either sys.tables or sys.columns causes the queries to return rows for tables and columns from the database specified in the USE statement. By default, a query from sys.columns returns meta data about columns from all user-defined tables in a database. However, you can code a join between sys.columns and sys.tables so that a query from sys.columns returns rows for columns from a designated table instead of rows for all columns from all tables in a database.

The next T-SQL code sample shows an approach to returning meta data about the columns within a particular table within a database. The script, which appears in the lower portion of SQL-Query2_f0303_f0304.sql, starts by declaring two local variables and assigning values to them. The @DBName local variable is for the database name, and the @TBLName local variable is for the table name. Both the database and table names are SQL Server identifiers.

```
USE master
GO

DECLARE @DBName nvarchar(128)
DECLARE @TBLName nvarchar(128)
SET @DBName = N'Northwind'
SET @TBLName = N'Shippers'
```

The first SELECT statement, which is from sys.databases with a master database context, returns the name of the @DBName database.

```
SELECT name
FROM sys.databases
WHERE name = @DBName
```

SQL SERVER IDENTIFIER RULES

Names for SQL Server objects, such as a database or a table, are commonly referred to as identifiers. SQL Server object names must conform to rules for identifiers. There are five rules for regular and delimited identifiers.

First, start with a Unicode character letter or an underscore (_), "at" sign (@), or number sign (#). Because identifier names beginning with @ and # can have special meanings, it is best to avoid starting identifiers with these characters unless you mean what the special character denotes. The @ is for local variables and parameters, and the # is for temporary objects.

Second, you can have up to 127 characters after the first character. These characters can consist of Unicode characters for letters and decimal numbers. In addition, you can also include @, dollar sign ($), and _.

Third, do not use SQL Server reserved keywords as identifiers. Search for the "Reserved Keywords" topic in SQL Server 2005 Books Online for an exhaustive list of all reserved keywords to avoid as identifiers.

Fourth, avoid the use of embedded spaces or other special characters beyond those mentioned in this list, such as _.

Fifth, identifiers that fail to comply with all four of the preceding rules must be delimited by either brackets ([ ]) or quotation marks (" "). Therefore, a table name of Order Details can appear in brackets ([Order Details]). Use quotation marks as delimiters for identifiers only when the quoted identifier database option is true. You can use the `sp_dboption` system-stored procedure or `SET QUOTED_IDENTIFIER ON` to make this setting.

A second USE statement references the Northwind database. For the results to make sense, the second USE statement must designate the same database to which the @DBName local variable points, which in this case is the Northwind database in the following script. You cannot use a local variable as an argument in a USE statement.

```
USE Northwind
SELECT name, object_id
FROM sys.tables
WHERE name = @TBLName
```

The object_id column in the result set from sys.tables denotes a table identification number. You can use the object_id column value from sys.tables to retrieve matching rows from sys.columns. The final SELECT statement demonstrates a subquery design with one SELECT statement nested in another, whereby the WHERE clause matches rows in the sys.columns view to a row in the sys.tables view.

```
SELECT name, column_id, object_id
FROM sys.columns
WHERE object_id IN
    (SELECT object_id
     FROM sys.tables
     WHERE name = @TBLName)
```

Figure 3-4 shows the three result sets from the preceding script in the Results tab of Express SSMS. The sequence of result sets correspond to the sequence of SELECT statements in the script. The first SELECT statement displays a database name. The second SELECT statement returns the name of a table from the database displayed in the first SELECT statement. The third SELECT statement generates a result set with the column names from the table name returned by the second SELECT statement.

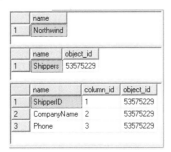

Figure 3-4. *You can report hierarchical relationships for a database's meta data by processing system catalog views.*

Searching for and Copying Databases with Windows Explorer

Windows Explorer lets you search for and copy SQL Server files for a database. Use the `sp_helpdb` system-stored procedure to gather information about the path and file names for the files in a database. Recall that you must designate a database name after `sp_helpdb` to obtain this information. If you follow recommended conventions, the files will have one of three extensions.

- *.mdf*: This extension is for the primary data file. This file is the logical start of a database. You can think of it as the startup file for opening a database. Although there can be other secondary files, it is not unusual for the primary data file to be the exclusive data file.

- *.ndf*: Microsoft recommends an .ndf extension for secondary files.

- *.ldf*: This is the recommended extension for log files. The log file holds log information necessary for the recovery of databases. SQL Server automatically creates a log file for a database if there isn't one already.

Database files will often, but not always, reside in the Data folder for a SQL Server instance within the Program Files directory. The .\sqlexpress instance used in this chapter is the first named instance of SQL Server on the test computer used to develop the examples for this book. Therefore, its files appear in the MSSQL.1 directory in the Program Files\Microsoft SQL Server path. Figure 3-5 shows the selection of the Data folder for the .\sqlexpress named instance in the left pane of Windows Explorer. In the right pane, you see files for databases, which consist of eight pairs. Each pair has one .mdf file and one .ldf file. When you copy a database, you should copy all the files for a database, including .mdf, .ldf, and .ndf files. Recall that files that are either open by a user or the system are not available for copying to another location. In addition, you cannot copy the files for a database to another location unless the `autoclose` database option is set to `TRUE`.

The auto-close feature of SSE makes it easy to store database files with other files for a project and to open your database files only when an application needs them. If an application does store its database files with other project files, you may therefore need to search other folders besides the Data folder for an SSE instance to discover all the database files on a computer. You can search for files with an .mdf extension because every database must have one file with this extension. Once you locate the path to a desired .mdf file, you can search for similarly named .ldf and .ndf files to locate all the files for a database.

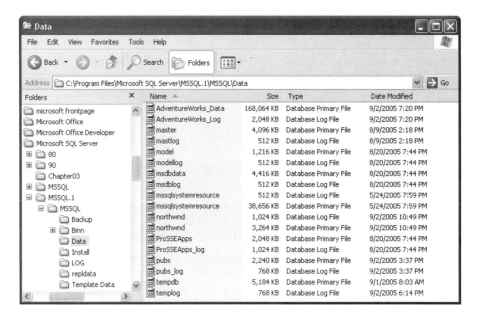

Figure 3-5. *You can navigate to the files for a database with Windows Explorer.*

Using CREATE DATABASE

T-SQL's CREATE DATABASE statement provides very rich capabilities for initializing a database in an SSE instance. This section introduces you to the CREATE DATABASE statement and core database design issues, as it demonstrates how to apply CREATE DATABASE with an emphasis on techniques that are typical for applications using SSE. This section also demonstrates the use of the DROP DATABASE statement. All the T-SQL scripts in this section are available from SQLQuery4_f0306_f0307_f0308.sql.

Just Naming the Database

The CREATE DATABASE statement performs three main tasks as it creates a new database:

- It copies the model database as a starting point for your new database.
- It makes customization changes based on argument values in its clauses.
- It initializes a database's data and log files by writing system data to the files and populating the rest of the files with empty pages.

The easiest way to use the CREATE DATABASE statement is to just name the database. All database names within a server instance must be unique. One advantage of just naming the database is that you do not have to specify any additional clauses. You can rely exclusively on the model database and take advantage of the CREATE DATABASE statement's native features to modify the model database as it creates your new database. The syntax for this style of using a CREATE DATABASE statement this way appears as follows:

```
CREATE DATABASE your_database_name
```

The following T-SQL script applies this syntax to create a new database named Database_2. Because this is the first invocation of a CREATE DATABASE statement, the script contrasts the new database with the model database. By contrasting the output from the `sp_helpdb` system-stored procedure with that for `Database_2`, you can see changes that the `CREATE DATABASE` statement makes to the model database design when creating a new database with no clauses.

In addition, the script concludes by dropping `Database_2` because there is no need to persist the new database. The `DROP DATABASE` statement removes whatever database you name as an argument when you invoke the statement. This statement operates similarly to the Delete command in Object Explorer for a database, except that it does not automatically refresh the Object Explorer listing of databases.

```
EXEC sp_helpdb model
CREATE DATABASE Database_2
EXEC sp_helpdb Database_2
DROP DATABASE Database_2
```

Figure 3-6 shows the four result sets that the preceding script generates. The first two result sets are for the model database, and the second two result sets are for `Database_2`. The `CREATE DATABASE` statement assigns the database name to the primary data file. The statement appends `_log` to the database name for the name of the log file.

Figure 3-6 shows `Database_2` settings nearly exactly match settings for the model database. The size of `Database_2` is nearly identical to that of the model database (the difference is just 8KB for the log file). The size of the data file in the primary file group is the same in both the model and `Database_2` databases. In addition, the growth column values are identical for the data and log files in both databases. The model database explicitly states an `UNLIMITED` maximum size for its data and log files. `Database_2` has essentially unlimited size for both its data and log files. For example, the maximum size of its log file exceeds the capacity of an SSE database (4GB).

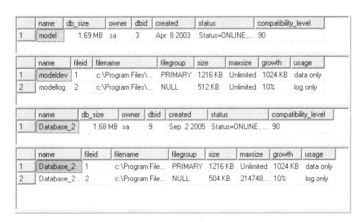

	name	db_size	owner	dbid	created	status	compatibility_level
1	model	1.69 MB	sa	3	Apr 8 2003	Status=ONLINE,...	90

	name	fileid	filename	filegroup	size	maxsize	growth	usage
1	modeldev	1	c:\Program Files\...	PRIMARY	1216 KB	Unlimited	1024 KB	data only
2	modellog	2	c:\Program Files\...	NULL	512 KB	Unlimited	10%	log only

	name	db_size	owner	dbid	created	status	compatibility_level
1	Database_2	1.68 MB	sa	9	Sep 2 2005	Status=ONLINE,...	90

	name	fileid	filename	filegroup	size	maxsize	growth	usage
1	Database_2	1	c:\Program File...	PRIMARY	1216 KB	Unlimited	1024 KB	data only
2	Database_2...	2	c:\Program File...	NULL	504 KB	214748...	10%	log only

Figure 3-6. *Using the CREATE DATABASE statement without clauses creates a near-replica of the model database.*

Designating Data Files in the ON Clause

The `ON` clause for the `CREATE DATABASE` statement lets you specify one or more data files for a database. These files hold the system and user data in a database. Recall that a database can have just one primary data (.mdf) file. The primary data file is the start of a database. Other data files (besides the primary data file) listed in the `ON` clause are secondary data (.ndf) files. A database can have only one primary data file, but it can have multiple secondary data files. These secondary files can hold data that does not fit in the primary data file or facilitate spreading the data for a database across multiple storage devices with each secondary data file being on a separate storage device.

Tip The vast majority of applications using SSE should have no need for secondary data files. This is because SSE especially targets smaller database applications in which all data can conveniently fit within the primary data file. In addition, SSE does not support the enterprise features normally associated with advanced hardware options, such as multiple storage devices, and secondary data files are optimized for use with multiple storage devices.

Data files have logical and operating system file names. In the ON clause, use the

- NAME keyword to designate a data file's logical name
- FILENAME keyword to denote the operating system file name, including its path

You can specify multiple files in the primary file group, and you can even specify multiple file groups in an ON clause. However, it is common for databases to have a single data file in a single file group. This sole data file serves as the primary data file in the primary file group. The database file specification design of a single data file in a single file group is likely to be particularly common on SSE instances.

You can optionally use the PRIMARY keyword in the ON clause to designate the primary file group. The primary file group consists of the primary data file and any secondary files that you include in the file group. If there is just one file group without any other file groups specified, the file group is, by default, the primary file group. Use the FILEGROUP keyword to designate other file groups besides the primary file group.

The following script demonstrates the syntax for specifying the primary data file in a CREATE DATABASE statement. As with the preceding CREATE DATABASE sample, this sample concludes by displaying sp_helpdb results for the newly created database. The last line in the following sample drops the database because the only purpose for the database is to show syntax rules.

The script's ON clause opens the specification for the primary file group, which has just one data file. A data file's location is not restricted to the Data folder for an SSE instance in the Program Files directory. Notice that the FILENAME argument points at the chapter03 folder within the prosseapps directory on the C: drive. The directory and folder names are for the main test computer used for the book. You can use any directory and folder names on your computer. Although a file's logical name and file specification point to the same file, the logical name and file name in the specification do not have to be the same. Notice the NAME argument has a suffix (_dat) appended to the end of the argument value for the FILENAME keyword.

In addition to specifying the names and locations of data files, you can also assign argument values to control the initial size of a file, the maximum size of a file, and how a file grows from its initial size to its maximum size.

- The SIZE keyword lets you specify the initial size. You can designate the argument value for this keyword as kilobyte (KB), megabyte (MB), gigabyte (GB), or terabyte (TB) units. Fractions are not recognized, but you can designate half a megabyte as 512KB.
- The MAXSIZE keyword specifies a file's maximum size. You can specify units as KB, MB, GB, and TB. In addition, you can use UNLIMITED to designate a file's maximum size. If you specify a number for either SIZE or MAXSIZE without designating a type of unit, the T-SQL interpreter assumes MB.
- The FILEGROWTH keyword designates how to grow a data file when a database requires more space. The FILEGROWTH argument value cannot exceed the MAXSIZE argument value. You can specify FILEGROWTH in KB, MB, or percentage units.

■**Caution** You can set the SIZE, MAXSIZE, or FILEGROWTH keywords only to values for data files on mapped drives (drive:\pathname\filename). These keywords are not available for assignment with data files mapped to a UNC path (\\computername\sharename\filename) in their FILENAME keyword.

```
CREATE DATABASE Database_2
ON
(NAME = Database_2_dat,
    FILENAME = 'c:\prosseapps\chapter03\database_2.mdf',
    SIZE = 2MB,
    MAXSIZE = 20,
    FILEGROWTH = 10%)
EXEC sp_helpdb Database_2
DROP DATABASE Database_2
```

Figure 3-7 displays the two results from the execution of the sp_helpdb system-stored procedure in the preceding script. Notice the _dat suffix in the data file name for the sole file in the primary file group. This is the logical name of the file specified as the argument for the NAME keyword. The filename column value for the file in the primary file group has the name database_2.mdf. You can widen the filename column to show the full path and file name for the primary data file. Notice the size and maxsize column values for the primary data file are 2MB and 20MB, respectively. The T-SQL inter-preter used the default unit type (MB) for the MAXSIZE argument because the script did not explicitly specify a type of unit.

You can compare the sp_helpdb output from Figure 3-7 with the comparable output in Figure 3-6 to gain additional insight about how the CREATE DATABASE statement works. Figure 3-7 has a growth column value of 10%, whereas Figure 3-6 shows a growth column value of 1,024KB for its primary data file. The FILEGROWTH setting in the immediately preceding script superseded the value inherited from the model database of 1,024KB. However, the column values for the log file in Figure 3-7 exactly match those for the log file in the model database (see the second sp_helpdb result in Figure 3-6). The maxi-mum size of 2,147,483,648KB is essentially unlimited. The corresponding specifications for the model and Database_2 databases in the preceding script are because the preceding script made no assign-ments for its log file.

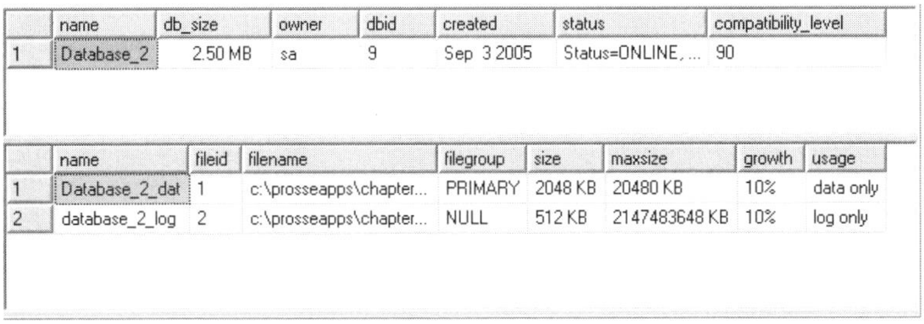

	name	db_size	owner	dbid	created	status	compatibility_level
1	Database_2	2.50 MB	sa	9	Sep 3 2005	Status=ONLINE, ...	90

	name	fileid	filename	filegroup	size	maxsize	growth	usage
1	Database_2_dat	1	c:\prosseapps\chapter...	PRIMARY	2048 KB	20480 KB	10%	data only
2	database_2_log	2	c:\prosseapps\chapter...	NULL	512 KB	2147483648 KB	10%	log only

Figure 3-7. *Using the CREATE DATABASE statement with an ON clause lets you designate data file specifications.*

Using the LOG ON Clause

The LOG ON clause for the CREATE DATABASE statement works for log files the way the ON clause func-tions for data files in a database. Log files can contain a history of all the changes to a database. Because of this feature, log files can facilitate recovery procedures to permit recovery to a point in time, or use other sophisticated recovery methods. You can specify one or more log files for a database in the LOG ON clause, but there is never more than one file group for the log files in a database.

You can assign values for SIZE, MAXSIZE, and FILEGROWTH keywords for log files just as you can for data files. The following script shows the syntax for assigning argument values to SIZE, MAXSIZE, and FILEGROWTH. The LOG ON clause permits the assignment of logical and physical, or operating system, file names. Use the NAME keyword for a logical name and the FILENAME keyword for a physical file name. After designating the logical and physical names, the code sets the log file size arguments. Notice the syntax for a log file is the same as for a data file. The specifications for a data file size appear in the ON clause, and the specifications for a log files are in the LOG ON clause.

```
CREATE DATABASE Database_2
ON PRIMARY
(NAME = Database_2_dat,
    FILENAME = 'c:\prosseapps\chapter03\database_2dat.mdf',
    SIZE = 2MB,
    MAXSIZE = 20,
    FILEGROWTH = 10%)
LOG ON
(NAME = Database_2_log,
    FILENAME = 'c:\prosseapps\chapter03\database_2log.ldf',
    SIZE = 4MB,
    MAXSIZE = 10MB,
    FILEGROWTH = 20%)
EXEC sp_helpdb Database_2
DROP DATABASE Database_2
```

Figure 3-8 shows the output from the preceding script, which adds functionality for constraining the log file. For example, the code sets a maximum of 10MB for the maximum file size. Figure 3-8 displays this upper limit, instead of UNLIMITED or a value that represents unlimited size. Although the default growth column value in the model database for a log file is 10%, the preceding script assigns a value of 20% to the FILEGROWTH keyword. The FILEGROWTH setting in the script overrides the model log file FILEGROWTH setting from which Database_2_log inherits.

	name	db_size	owner	dbid	created	status	compatibility_level
1	Database_2	6.00 MB	sa	9	Sep 3 2005	Status=ONLINE, ...	90

	name	fileid	filename	filegroup	size	maxsize	growth	usage
1	Database_2_dat	1	c:\prosseapps\ch...	PRIMARY	2048 KB	20480 KB	10%	data only
2	Database_2_log	2	c:\prosseapps\ch...	NULL	4096 KB	10240 KB	20%	log only

Figure 3-8. *Using the CREATE DATABASE statement with a LOG ON clause lets you designate log file specifications.*

Attaching and Detaching Databases

When you finish making a new database with the CREATE DATABASE statement, the SQL Server instance for your connection clearly knows about the database and log files for the database. However, there are at least two situations when database and log files can exist without a SQL Server instance having a corresponding database that refers to the files. First, if you copy the files for a database from one path to another on the same or a different computer, then no server instance has a database matching the copied database and log files. Second, if a master database becomes corrupt, you may be able to recover by replacing the corrupted master database with a backup copy of the master database or by installing a new server instance. With either approach to recovery, the most recent master database may not know about the database and log files for one or more databases.

Attaching a database is the process of informing a server instance of the availability of database and log files for a database. After attachment, users can reference the database on the server. Before attachment, the files for a database may exist, but users cannot connect to them through a server instance because the server instance does not know about the database and log files.

SQL Server Express normally manages user data and log files in a way that is different from other SQL Server 2005 editions as well as earlier SQL Server versions. The two points of divergence relate to whether the files are actively managed by a server instance and whether the files have restricted access. Earlier SQL Server versions and other SQL Server 2005 editions have an "always-on" connection for their database and log files. In addition, these other SQL Server versions and editions restrict access to the database and log files via the Windows operating system. In contrast, SSE normally does not connect to data and log files after an application closes its connection to the database, and the files are freely available to anyone with file access permission no matter what their permission is inside a SQL Server instance.

The auto-close feature lets an SSE instance release database and log files for a database when the server instance has no open connections to the database. During the time that SSE is not actively managing a database's data and log files, you can copy, move, or delete these files. Therefore, the auto-close feature brings some of the convenience of Access applications to SSE applications. However, releasing data and log files is not as secure as keeping them managed by a server instance at all times. Other SQL Server 2005 editions, as well as earlier versions of SQL Server, manage their data and log files as long as they are running.

Recall that you can turn off a database's auto-close feature so that SSE does not release a database's data and log files, except when a server instance closes. After you disable the auto-close feature, you may at some point in the future need to release the data and log files from a database without closing the server instance. The `sp_detach_db` system-stored procedure permits you to detach the data and log files for a database even when the auto-close feature is turned off.

■**Note** Just as T-SQL offers an `sp_attach_db` system-stored procedure, T-SQL also supports `sp_attach_db` and `sp_attach_single_file_db` statements. Microsoft recommends against using either of the attach system-stored procedure statements because they will be removed in the future. For this reason, this section highlights the `CREATE DATABASE` statement with the `FOR ATTACH` clause, which enables the same functionality as `sp_attach_db` and `sp_attach_single_file_db`.

The next section drills down on techniques for attaching and detaching data and log files to a server instance. The section contrasts two techniques for attaching data and log files. You'll also learn about a technique for detaching data and log files from an SSE instance.

Attaching Databases with CREATE DATABASE

Attaching data and log files with the `CREATE DATABASE` statement is the approach that Microsoft recommends for exposing data and log files as a database on a server instance. You have to make three settings when you attach data and log files with `CREATE DATABASE`.

- Assign a database name. Do this in the normal way right after CREATE DATABASE.

- Specify the path and file name for the primary data file. The CREATE DATABASE statement can derive the name and location of any other data and log files from systems information in the primary data file. If you just specify the primary data file, any other data and log files must reside in the same location that they occupied when the primary data file copy was initially created.

- Indicate that you are going to attach files with either the FOR ATTACH or FOR ATTACH_REBUILD_LOG clause.

  - The FOR ATTACH clause requires the availability of all previously existing log file(s).

  - The FOR ATTACH_REBUILD_LOG clause allows the building of log files if one or more original log files are missing.

The most elementary syntax for using the FOR ATTACH clause in a CREATE DATABASE statement appears next. The argument value for the FILENAME keyword specifies the path and file name for the primary data file. The statement uses the primary data file to derive the names and paths for a database's other data and log files. Therefore, your copied data and log files must have the same paths that they had on the initial server instance from which you copied the files. The inclusion of the PRIMARY keyword after ON is optional when designating the only data file for a database.

```
CREATE DATABASE your_database_name
ON PRIMARY (FILENAME = 'drive:\path\filename.mdf')
FOR ATTACH
```

Caution You can specify any location for the primary data file with the FILENAME keyword in a CREATE DATABASE statement with a FOR ATTACH clause. However, the statement automatically infers the names and locations of other data and log files from the primary data file. If the other files are not in locations that correspond to original file paths, you can generate an error or faulty operation of the database based on incorrect file references. You can circumvent this problem by explicitly designating all other files besides the primary data file. See the "Designating the Primary Data and Log Files" section in this chapter for an example of how to accomplish this task.

To illustrate the operation of the FOR ATTACH clause in a CREATE DATABASE statement, this section implements the statement with two syntax styles. First, it illustrates the syntax for using just the primary data file. Second, it shows how to reference both the primary data file and log file for a database.

Designating Just the Primary Data File

The scripts for this section and the next one use Database_1a, which is an arbitrary database. With appropriate updates to the sample code, you can replace Database_1a with ProSSEApps (originally created in Chapter 2), any of the sample databases, or a version of Database_2 from earlier in this chapter that you did not drop. For your easy reference, I list the very simple script for creating a database named Database_1a:

```
CREATE DATABASE Database_1a
```

All the sample code in this section is available from two batch files (copydb_1afiles.bat and recoverdb_1afiles.bat) and one T-SQL script (SQLQuery5_f0310_f0311.sql). Code segments from the script appear within the section to highlight various syntax and operational issues for using the FOR ATTACH clause in a CREATE DATABASE statement.

Database_1a does not have its autoclose option set to FALSE; the default autoclose option value for a database created with CREATE DATABASE in SSE is TRUE. Therefore, you can copy its data and log files when the database is not open. By using the xp_cmdshell extended stored procedure, you can programmatically copy, rename, and delete files with command-line instructions from within your T-SQL code. The sample demonstrating the FOR ATTACH clause starts by invoking xp_cmdshell to run a batch file. The batch file makes copies of the Database_1a data and log files for testing and recovery.

The xp_cmdshell system-stored procedure provides an extremely high level of flexibility within the operating system for the computer on which a database server runs. In the interest of security, Microsoft turns the feature off by default. This is part of what Microsoft means when it says SSE is secure by default. You can expose the capability to invoke xp_cmdshell with the help of the SQL Server Surface Area Configuration tool. You can use this tool to configure a local instance of SSE (or any other SQL Server 2005 edition).

1. Start the SQL Server Surface Area Configuration tool by choosing from the Windows Start button All Programs ➤ Microsoft SQL Server 2005 ➤ Configuration Tools ➤ SQL Server Surface Area Configuration.

2. From the tool's initial screen, click the Surface Area Configuration for Features link.

3. Expand the Database Engine in the list box to show the features available for configuration.

4. Select the xp_cmdshell feature.

5. Click the check box labeled Enable xp_cmdshell to select it (see Figure 3-9).

6. Click OK and close the SQL Server Surface Area Configuration tool.

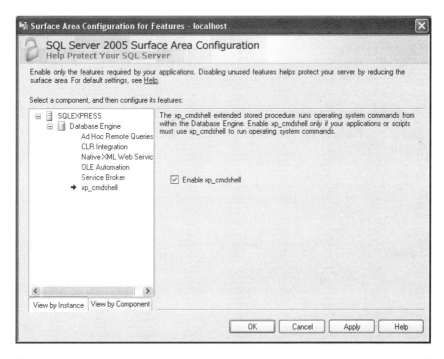

Figure 3-9. *The SQL Server Surface Area Configuration tool lets you enable the use of the xp_cmdshell extended system-stored procedure along with selected other SQL Server features.*

The data and log files for `Database_1a`, which are Database_1a.mdf and Database_1a_log.ldf, reside in the Data folder for the first named instance of SQL Server in the Program Files directory. The `FOR ATTACH` sample uses a copy of these files in the chapter03 folder of the c:\prosseapps directory. The following batch file (copydb_1afiles.bat) clears any prior data or log files for `Database_1a` from the chapter03 folder before making two sets of copies. First, the batch file makes a fresh set of copies in the chapter03 folder of the data and log files for `Database_1a`. Second, another set of backup copies of the data and log files (.bak) are created in the Data folder within the Program Files directory so that the sample can recover from an error that the demonstration purposely throws.

```
REM Erase old data and log files
cd c:\prosseapps\chapter03\
ERASE Database_1a*.*

REM Copy new data and log files to new folder
REM and to .bak files in the same folder
cd c:\program files\microsoft sql server\mssql.1\mssql\data\
copy Database_1a*.* c:\prosseapps\chapter03\
copy Database_1a.mdf Database_1a.bak
copy Database_1a_log.ldf Database_1a_log.bak
```

The following `xp_cmdshell` statement illustrates how to invoke the batch file from T-SQL.

```
xp_cmdshell 'c:\prosseapps\chapter03\copydb_1afiles'
```

The sample does one more step before using the `CREATE DATABASE` statement with the `FOR ATTACH` keyword. The step displays a summary of the databases on the server instance as well as returns values for the data and log files for `Database_1a` from `sp_helpdb`. The following short T-SQL script performs these tasks, and Figure 3-10 shows the three result sets—one from the `SELECT` statement and two from the `sp_helpdb` system-stored procedure. The top result set shows eight databases on the server instance, including `Database_1a` plus three Microsoft-supplied sample databases and four system databases. The two results provide information about `Database_1a`, including the path and file names for the data and log files.

```
SELECT name, database_id FROM sys.databases
EXEC sp_helpdb @dbname = N'Database_1a'
```

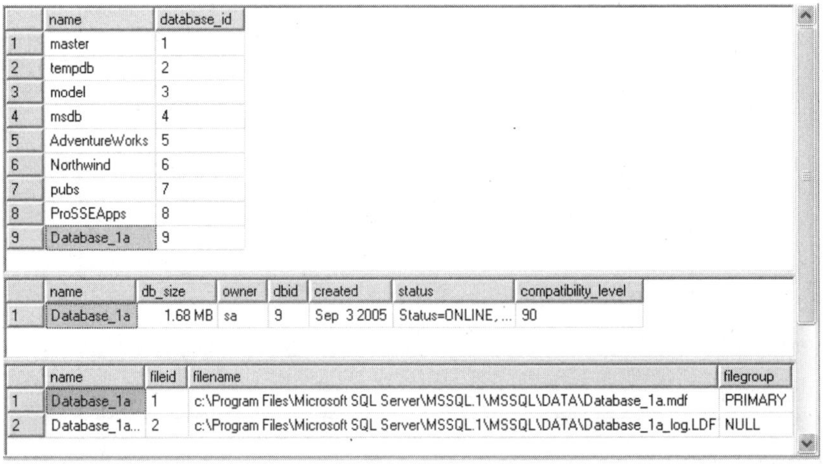

	name	database_id
1	master	1
2	tempdb	2
3	model	3
4	msdb	4
5	AdventureWorks	5
6	Northwind	6
7	pubs	7
8	ProSSEApps	8
9	Database_1a	9

	name	db_size	owner	dbid	created	status	compatibility_level
1	Database_1a	1.68 MB	sa	9	Sep 3 2005	Status=ONLINE, ...	90

	name	fileid	filename	filegroup
1	Database_1a	1	c:\Program Files\Microsoft SQL Server\MSSQL.1\MSSQL\DATA\Database_1a.mdf	PRIMARY
2	Database_1a...	2	c:\Program Files\Microsoft SQL Server\MSSQL.1\MSSQL\DATA\Database_1a_log.LDF	NULL

Figure 3-10. *Summary of the databases on an SSE instance and the data and log files for Database_1a*

The next script segment presents the most basic syntax for generating a database named Database_1b with the FOR ATTACH clause of a CREATE DATABASE statement. The script just references the primary data file (Database_1a.mdf). As a result, the code derives the log file path and file as the one showing in Figure 3-10 for Database_1a. Therefore, Database_1b and Database_1a share the same log file! This is not a good idea, and, in this case, it makes Database_1a unusable. The root problem is the failure to specify a separate log file name and path for Database_1b. Figure 3-11 confirms the addition of Database_1b (see the name column value matching database_id 10). In addition, Figure 3-11, as compared to Figure 3-10, shows that the log file name and path for Database_1b points directly at the log file for Database_1a.

```
CREATE DATABASE Database_1b
ON PRIMARY (FILENAME = 'c:\prosseapps\chapter03\Database_1a.mdf')
FOR ATTACH
GO
SELECT name, database_id FROM sys.databases
EXEC sp_helpdb @dbname = N'Database_1b'
GO
```

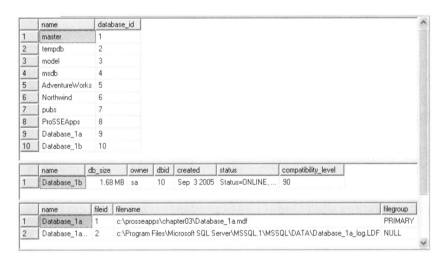

Figure 3-11. *When referencing a single file, Database_1b shares its log file with Database_1a.*

The failure to explicitly reference a log file name and path in the preceding CREATE DATABASE statement generates a need to remove Database_1b as well as Database_1a. The CopyDB_1aFiles.bat batch file initially created backup files (.bak) for the original data and log files for Database_1a. Therefore, the sample can start to restore the corrupted Database_1a by renaming the backup file extensions to .mdf and .ldf. Another xp_cmdshell extended system-stored procedure pointing at a second batch file (recoverdb_1afiles.bat) can rename the extensions for the backup files. The batch file appears next.

■**Tip** If bad things happen to your good database, a set of backup files for your database can prove to be a valuable resource. You can simply drop the database that has been corrupted or damaged, rename the backup files (if necessary), and then attach them with the name of the database that you dropped.

```
cd c:\program files\microsoft sql server\mssql.1\mssql\data\
rename Database_1a.bak Database_1a.mdf
rename Database_1a_log.bak Database_1a_log.ldf
```

The sample concludes by recovering with the following T-SQL script. The script begins by dropping the two databases as well as the unused log file (Database_1_log.ldf) copied to the chapter03 folder. The DROP DATABASE statement removes the data and log files for both databases. An xp_cmdshell statement erases the unused log file. After renaming the backup files by invoking the recoverdb_1afiles batch file, the code invokes CREATE DATABASE with a FOR ATTACH clause. The syntax is the same as the preceding one, but this time it works successfully because the data file points at the correct log file in the appropriate path. The script concludes with a SELECT statement to list the databases on the server instance along with sp_helpdb information on the newly recovered Database_1a. The output from these two statements is the same as that showing in Figure 3-10. This outcome confirms that these steps illustrate one approach to recovering a corrupted database.

```
DROP DATABASE Database_1b
GO
xp_cmdshell 'erase c:\prosseapps\chapter03\Database_1a_log.ldf'
GO
EXEC sp_helpdb @dbname = N'Database_1a'
DROP DATABASE Database_1a
GO
xp_cmdshell 'c:\prosseapps\chapter03\recoverdb_1afiles'
GO
CREATE DATABASE Database_1a
ON (FILENAME =
'C:\Program Files\Microsoft SQL Server\MSSQL.1\MSSQL\Data\Database_1a.mdf')
FOR ATTACH GO
SELECT name, database_id FROM sys.databases
EXEC sp_helpdb @dbname = N'Database_1a'
GO
```

Designating the Primary Data and Log Files

As the preceding section demonstrates, specifying a single database file—that is, the primary data file—for a CREATE DATABASE statement with a FOR ATTACH clause can sometimes be appropriate and other times lead to catastrophic failure. Designating just the primary data file is particularly appropriate when you can copy data and log files between computers so that they are in the same path on both computers. This situation may apply when you have a staging computer and a production computer. As the preceding sample illustrates, designating a single primary data file when basing a new database on copied files between paths on a single computer requires a different approach.

If you specify the data file(s) and the log file(s) separately, then you can successfully create a new database with the copied files. In addition, the new database will not disrupt the database from which files were copied. The syntax for designating both the primary data file and the log file in a CREATE DATABASE statement with a FOR ATTACH clause appears next.

```
CREATE DATABASE your_database_name
ON PRIMARY (FILENAME = 'drive:\path\filename.mdf')
LOG ON (FILENAME = 'drive:\path\filename.ldf')
FOR ATTACH
```

The following script excerpt is from SQLQuery6_f0312.sql. The excerpt starts by invoking an xp_cmdshell statement to copy files for Database_1a to the chapter03 folder in the c:\prosseapps directory. After the files become available in the folder, the code executes a CREATE DATABASE statement with references to the recently copied primary data file and log file in the chapter03 folder.

The excerpt concludes by listing the databases on the server instance and the displaying sp_helpdb result sets for the new database, Database_1b.

```
xp_cmdshell 'c:\prosseapps\chapter03\copydb_1afiles'
GO
CREATE DATABASE Database_1b
ON PRIMARY (FILENAME = 'c:\prosseapps\chapter03\Database_1a.mdf')
LOG ON (FILENAME = 'c:\prosseapps\chapter03\Database_1a_log.ldf')
FOR ATTACH
GO
SELECT name, database_id FROM sys.databases
EXEC sp_helpdb @dbname = N'Database_1b'
GO
```

Figure 3-12 shows the results from the SELECT and sp_helpdb statements in the preceding script excerpt. As you can see from the first result set, the script adds a new database named Database_1b. In addition, both the primary data file and the log file for the new database point to the copied files in the c:\prosseapps\chapter03 path. This result leaves the previously existing Database_1a unaffected by the addition of Database_1b.

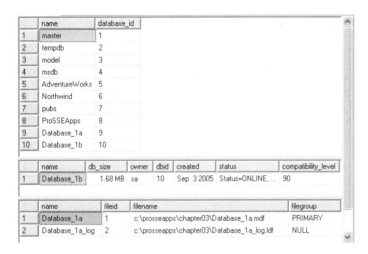

	name	database_id
1	master	1
2	tempdb	2
3	model	3
4	msdb	4
5	AdventureWorks	5
6	Northwind	6
7	pubs	7
8	ProSSEApps	8
9	Database_1a	9
10	Database_1b	10

	name	db_size	owner	dbid	created	status	compatibility_level
1	Database_1b	1.68 MB	sa	10	Sep 3 2005	Status=ONLINE, ...	90

	name	fileid	filename	filegroup
1	Database_1a	1	c:\prosseapps\chapter03\Database_1a.mdf	PRIMARY
2	Database_1a_log	2	c:\prosseapps\chapter03\Database_1a_log.ldf	NULL

Figure 3-12. *When referencing a data file and a log file, Database_1b is independent of Database_1a. The log file in Figure 3-11 is not independent of the log file for Database_1a (see Figure 3-10).*

Copying Files, the Auto-Close Feature, and sp_detach_db

All other editions of SQL Server 2005 besides SSE protect their data and log files in a couple of ways. First, regular SQL Server instances manage their database files whenever the server instances are running. Second, data and log files are protected with restricted access from the Windows operating system. SQL Server Express normally eliminates these two layers of file security when creating a new database in favor of ease of use by enabling its auto-close feature. However, you can disable the auto-close feature for added security if you decide that you prefer safety over ease of use. In addition, if you invoke the CREATE DATABASE statement with a FOR ATTACH clause, you cannot copy database file(s) because Windows secures the file for exclusive use with the SSE instance.

The process for disabling and then reenabling the auto-close feature can be symmetric in the sense that you can just toggle the auto-close feature. All you have to do to disable the auto-close feature is to set the autoclose database option to FALSE with the sp_dboption system-stored

procedure, and you can reenable the auto-close feature by setting the autoclose database option to
TRUE. However, this symmetric toggling of the feature does not independently expose the two layers
of protection mentioned in the preceding paragraph when the auto-close feature is disabled. In
practice, this means that you are not able to copy database files that are attached to a server
instance even if the autoclose database option is TRUE.

If you detach a database from its server, then the server no longer knows about the database.
For example, you will generate an error if you try to set a database context to a detached database.
You can detach the files for a database from its server by invoking the sp_detach_db system-stored
procedure. This system-stored procedure essentially removes a database from a server, but
sp_detach_db leaves the files for the database on the computer. The Windows operating system no
longer restricts access to database files for a database after you detach a database for its server. You
can ultimately manipulate the files by reattaching the files for the database. This step implicitly
reinitializes the autoclose database option to a setting of TRUE. However, recall that an attached file
is not accessible for XCopy deployment because Windows restricts access to the database files. The
file with code sample discussed in this section resides in SQLQuery7_f0313_f0314_f0315.sql.

The script in SQLQuery7f0313_f0314_f0315 begins by creating Database_2 with the same syntax
as in the "Using the LOG ON Clause," except that the concluding DROP DATABASE statement is omitted.
This leaves Database_2 available for use. The two database files are database_2dat.mdf and data-
base_2log.ldf. Both files reside in the c:\prosseapps\chapter03\ path. Because the script creates
Database_2 with a CREATE DATABASE statement that creates new database files, the autoclose database option is TRUE, and the files are available for manipulation through the file system. The
following excerpt from SQLQuery7_f0313_f0314_f0315.sql confirms these features. First, the
SELECT statement confirms the autoclose database option value is TRUE, which corresponds to an
is_auto_close_on value of 1. Next, two xp_cmdshell statements copy the .mdf file for the database to
a .bak file and then erase the .bak file. The main point of the sample is that if you create a database
in the normal way with a CREATE DATABASE statement, you can copy its database files. This capability
is necessary for XCopy deployment.

Note Notice the use of a string with the xp_cmdshell extended system-stored procedure. Using a string
that you can reassign makes your code more flexible, but it also requires a slightly more complex syntax. Either
approach is valid for designating an operating system command for the xp_cmdshell extended system-stored
procedure statement.

```
SELECT name, database_id, is_auto_close_on
FROM sys.databases WHERE name = 'Database_2'
DECLARE @str1 nvarchar(90)
SET @str1 = 'copy c:\prosseapps\chapter03\database_2dat.mdf ' +
    'c:\prosseapps\chapter03\database_2dat.bak'
EXEC master..xp_cmdshell @str1
SET @str1 = 'erase ' +
    'c:\prosseapps\chapter03\database_2dat.bak'
EXEC master..xp_cmdshell @str1
GO
```

Figure 3-13 shows the output from the preceding script. First, you see a result set for the SELECT
statement that confirms the autoclose database option is TRUE. The second result set confirms the
.mdf file for Database_2 copied to database_2dat.bak. The NULL by itself in the third result set confirms the erase of the .bak file succeeded.

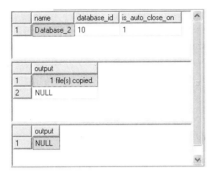

Figure 3-13. *You can copy a file created in the normal way with an autoclose database option value of 1.*

The next segment of the script shows the syntax for detaching the Database_2 database. This statement is not strictly necessary because the file is not attached in the first place. You only require sp_detach_db when a file is explicitly attached to a server, which is not normally the case for SSE databases. Detaching a database makes it unavailable to a server instance (almost as if you dropped the database). Unlike a DROP DATABASE statement, a sp_detach_db statement does not remove the files associated with a database. The following script excerpt confirms the existence of the database files for Database_2 with a dir command.

```
EXEC sp_detach_db @dbname = N'Database_2'
GO
SELECT name
FROM sys.databases WHERE name = 'Database_2'
DECLARE @str1 nvarchar(90)
SET @str1 = 'dir ' +
'c:\prosseapps\chapter03\database_2*.*'
EXEC master..xp_cmdshell @str1
GO
```

Figure 3-14 shows the result sets from running the segment. Notice the first result set is empty. This is because there is no database on the server instance named Database_2 after the execution of the sp_detach_db statement. You should also note the output from the dir command for the two database files.

	name

	output
1	Volume in drive C has no label.
2	Volume Serial Number is D83C-69C1
3	NULL
4	Directory of c:\prosseapps\chapter03
5	NULL
6	09/03/2005 07:30 PM 2,097,152 database_2dat.mdf
7	09/03/2005 07:30 PM 4,194,304 database_2log.ldf
8	2 File(s) 6,291,456 bytes
9	0 Dir(s) 3,933,962,240 bytes free
10	NULL

Figure 3-14. *Even after you detach a database, its files are still available for use.*

The final segment from SQLQuery7_f0313_f0314_f0315.sql attaches the files left after the execution of the sp_detach_db statement. By using a CREATE DATABASE statement with a FOR ATTACH clause, we can re-create a new version of the Database_2 database. The new version has an autoclose database option value of TRUE. However, you cannot copy its database files. The following script demonstrates these features. Contrast this performance with the initial version of Database_2, which did allow access to its files.

■**Note** If you need to copy files for an attached database, you can accomplish the task in three steps. First, detach the database. Second, copy its files. Third, reattach the database files to a server instance.

```
CREATE DATABASE Database_2
ON PRIMARY (FILENAME = 'c:\prosseapps\chapter03\Database_2dat.mdf')
LOG ON (FILENAME = 'c:\prosseapps\chapter03\Database_2log.ldf')
FOR ATTACH
GO
SELECT name, database_id, is_auto_close_on
FROM sys.databases WHERE name = 'Database_2'
GO
DECLARE @str1 nvarchar(90)
SET @str1 = 'copy c:\prosseapps\chapter03\database_2dat.mdf ' +
    'c:\prosseapps\chapter03\database_2dat.bak'
EXEC master..xp_cmdshell @str1
GO
```

Figure 3-15 shows the output from the preceding script excerpt. Two points are especially noteworthy. First, the autoclose database option is set to TRUE. This normally means the files for a database can be copied unless the file is open. Second, when you create a database by attaching database files to a server, the server, even an SSE instance, keeps the database files open all the time. As a result, the database files are in use all the time by the process for the database server, and the database files cannot be copied even when no user is actively using the database.

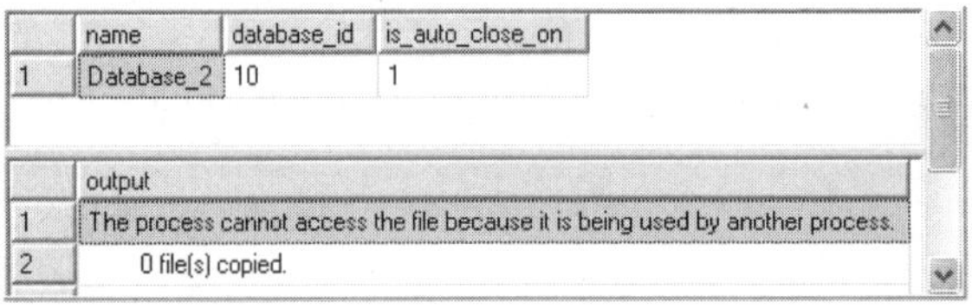

Figure 3-15. *You can't copy the database files for a database created with a FOR ATTACH clause.*

Backing Up and Restoring Databases

Although the CREATE DATABASE statement with a FOR ATTACH clause and the sp_detach_db system-stored procedure offer some support for backing up and restoring databases, these techniques are not optimized for backing up and restoring databases. When your primary objective is backing up and restoring your databases, consider using the BACKUP DATABASE and RESTORE DATABASE statements. There are a variety of related statements and concepts that can help you apply BACKUP DATABASE and RESTORE DATABASE statements so that they meet your specific objectives.

Recovering databases is an exceedingly rich SQL Server administration topic. This section aims to convey an overview of the topic and provide you with some practical samples that you can readily adapt for your own database backup and recovery solutions. The techniques demonstrated in this section will be sufficient for the database recovery needs of many database developers and small businesses served by an individual database developer. Those of you with advanced database recovery requirements can use this section as a foundation for moving on to more complex techniques, such as the bulk-logged recovery model and the full recovery models that permit the most flexible database restoration to a specific point in time.

Overview of Database Recovery Models

SQL Server 2005, including its SSE edition, provides three database recovery models. The techniques for each recovery model offer contrasting advantages and limitations. All SQL Server databases have a recovery model property. The setting for this property indicates the recovery techniques that apply to a database. You can modify a database's recovery model property with the `ALTER DATABASE` statement.

Three Recovery Models

The three recovery model names are simple, full, and bulk-logged.

- The *simple recovery model* is the easiest to use and understand.
- The *full recovery model* is the most robust and complicated approach to database recovery. This backup and restore approach can slow performance and be resource intensive.
- The *bulk-logged recovery model* can save storage space and speed performance even while it provides many (but not all) of the benefits available from the full recovery model.

Summary of the Full and Bulk-Logged Recovery Models

The full recovery model logs all transactions and retains them in the log file(s) for a database until after they are backed up. This model provides both recovery of a full database as well as recovery to any point in time. The latter feature is very convenient for backing out data when an application or user enters invalid data in a database. This model also captures bulk operation input, such as those from the `BULK INSERT` statement or the `bcp` utility, and new index values generated with a `CREATE INDEX` statement.

The bulk-logged recovery model is an adaptation of the full recovery model. Like the full recovery model, this approach captures all transactions to the log, except for selected minimally logged tasks. Examples of tasks that are minimally logged include `BULK INSERT`, `CREATE INDEX`, and the inputting of text and image column values. By minimally logging very large blocks of data, you can speed the operation of these tasks as you dramatically reduce the size of log files. The reduced-log-size file, in turn, simplifies database administration. With the bulk-logged recovery model, all data can be readily recovered, except for data that's minimally logged. However, you can fully recover your data by repeating the tasks that are minimally logged.

Types of Backups with the Full and Bulk-Logged Models

There are three main types of backups with a full or bulk-logged recovery model:

- *Data backup*: Generates an image of the data files for a database
- *Differential backup*: Contains only data that has changed since a preceding base backup, such as a full data backup
- *Log backup*: Contains only log records not backed up in a previous log backup

As you can see, backups normally build a natural sequence. The sequence consists of an initial data backup followed by one or more differential backups. However, it is possible to build a copy-only backup that is out of the bounds of the normal series of backups. This fourth type of backup can apply to data and log files. A copy-only backup is especially well suited for making a test version of a database on another computer.

Each of the four types of backups for the full and bulk-logged recovery models can implement different styles of backup. For example, a data backup can be for all the data (full data backup) or a subset of data files (partial data backup). Differential backups can also reference a subset of the data in a database. You will often have collections of one or more differential backups that refer to a base backup. The individual differential backups represent successive snapshots of database content relative to a base. Each successive differential backup is like a time-lapse image. A log backup can be for pure log data or log data plus data associated with bulk operations.

Note The advantages of the full recovery and bulk-logged recovery models are substantial, but so is the complexity of grasping the related conceptual details and administrative procedures. Organizations planning to use either of these recovery models should consider having a full-time database administrator as well as possibly migrating to an edition of SQL Server 2005 besides SSE.

The Simple Recovery Model and SQL Server Express

The simple recovery model retains log files for maintaining database consistency in the event of a crash and until the log file contents are used in a database backup. There are no log backups with a simple recovery model. This simplifies recovery planning and database administration because the size of log files is dramatically smaller.

With the simple recovery model, you can recover your data to the last backup but not to any arbitrary point in time. Data entered since the last backup is lost with this recovery model. You can mix full data and differential backups to minimize your potential for lost data. If your applications cannot tolerate any data loss and you must use SSE, consider backing up your input data sources outside of SSE to facilitate recovery of the most recent data beyond the last differential backup.

Database Recovery Model Settings

There are several techniques for checking which recovery model applies to a database. A newly created database inherits its recovery model property setting from the system model database. Therefore, by changing the recovery model for the model database, you can determine the recovery model for all new databases. Use the SET RECOVERY clause in an ALTER DATABASE statement to assign a recovery model. You can specify FULL, BULK_LOGGED, or SIMPLE as arguments in a SET RECOVERY clause. For example, use the following syntax to set the recovery model for a database to simple.

```
ALTER DATABASE database_name
SET RECOVERY SIMPLE
```

After the creation of a database, you can find its recovery model with either the sp_dboption system-stored procedure or sys.databases. When the trunc. log on chkpt. option is TRUE, the database has a simple recovery model. Otherwise, a database's recovery model is either full or bulk-logged. The syntax for returning the trunc. log on chkpt. option setting for a database is

```
EXEC sp_dboption 'database_name', 'trunc. log on chkpt.'
```

Two result set column values from sys.databases provide information about the recovery model for databases. Recovery_model column values are numbers from 1 through 3, with 1 indicating a full model; 2, a bulk-logged model; and 3, a simple model. The `recovery_model_desc` column values are text strings of `FULL`, `BULK_LOGGED`, or `SIMPLE`.

You can modify the recovery model for user databases with an `ALTER DATABASE` statement. Follow the same syntax as that for specifying the recovery model for the system model database (see the first paragraph in this section). By modifying the recovery model for an individual user database with the `ALTER DATABASE` statement, you can change the recovery model for just one existing database instead of all new databases as you do when you change the recovery property for the system model database.

Choosing and Modifying a Database's Recovery Model

All the recovery samples work with the `NWCopy` database. This database derives from `Northwind` data and log files copied to the chapter03 folder in the c:\prosseapps directory. The following excerpt from the SQLQuery8_f0316_f0317.sql script creates the database:

```
DECLARE @str1 nvarchar(128)
SET @str1 = 'copy "c:\Program Files\Microsoft SQL Server\' +
    'MSSQL.1\MSSQL\DATA\northwnd.mdf" ' +
    'c:\prosseapps\chapter03'
EXEC master..xp_cmdshell @str1
SET @str1 = 'copy "c:\Program Files\Microsoft SQL Server\' +
    'MSSQL.1\MSSQL\DATA\northwnd.ldf" ' +
    'c:\prosseapps\chapter03'
EXEC master..xp_cmdshell @str1
CREATE DATABASE NWCopy
ON PRIMARY (FILENAME = 'c:\prosseapps\chapter03\northwnd.mdf')
LOG ON (FILENAME = 'c:\prosseapps\chapter03\northwnd.ldf')
FOR ATTACH
GO
```

The recovery model property for a database is one of the most important elements of a database's design when you back up and restore a database. You can find the recovery model property with the `recovery_model` and `recovery_model_desc` columns from `sys.databases`. Recall also that a `SET RECOVERY` clause in an `ALTER DATABASE` statement lets you modify the recovery property for a database.

This next excerpt from SQLQuery8_f0316_f0317.sql lists the `recovery_model` and `recovery_model_desc` column values for all the databases on a server. The excerpt also demonstrates the syntax for changing the recovery model of a user database (`NWCopy`). First, the script sets the recovery model to full, but it concludes by assigning the database a simple recovery model. After each change, the script verifies its impact by displaying the `recovery_model` and `recovery_model_desc` column values from `sys.databases` for the `NWCopy` database.

```
SELECT name, recovery_model, recovery_model_desc
FROM sys.databases

ALTER DATABASE NWCopy
SET RECOVERY FULL
GO
SELECT name, recovery_model, recovery_model_desc
FROM sys.databases
WHERE name = 'NWCopy'
ALTER DATABASE NWCopy
SET RECOVERY SIMPLE
GO
```

```
SELECT name, recovery_model, recovery_model_desc
FROM sys.databases
WHERE name = 'NWCopy'
GO
```

Figure 3-16 presents the output from the preceding script. Notice that the Northwind sample database has a simple recovery model. Therefore, the NWCopy database, which derives its initial settings from the Northwind database, also has simple recovery. However, the script invokes the ALTER DATABASE statement to modify the NWCopy recovery model to full. Then, the script restores the initial setting of a simple recovery model to the NWCopy database.

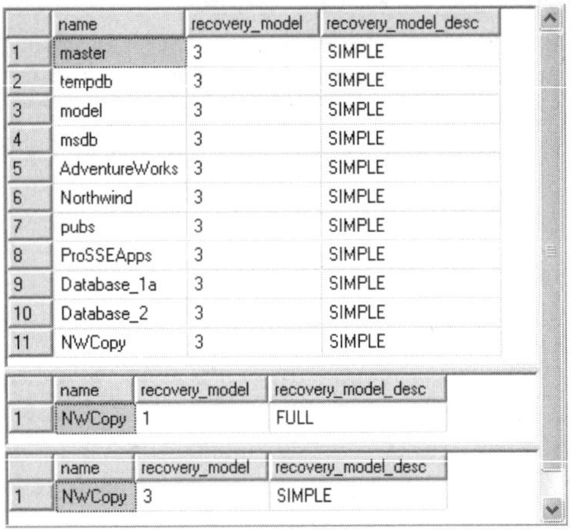

	name	recovery_model	recovery_model_desc
1	master	3	SIMPLE
2	tempdb	3	SIMPLE
3	model	3	SIMPLE
4	msdb	3	SIMPLE
5	AdventureWorks	3	SIMPLE
6	Northwind	3	SIMPLE
7	pubs	3	SIMPLE
8	ProSSEApps	3	SIMPLE
9	Database_1a	3	SIMPLE
10	Database_2	3	SIMPLE
11	NWCopy	3	SIMPLE

	name	recovery_model	recovery_model_desc
1	NWCopy	1	FULL

	name	recovery_model	recovery_model_desc
1	NWCopy	3	SIMPLE

Figure 3-16. *Use the recovery_model and recovery_model_desc columns from sys.databases to discover the recovery model for a database.*

Performing a Full Data Backup and Restore

A full data backup lets you recover from a disaster as of the last backup. The following script from SQLQuery8_f0316_f0317.sql simulates a disaster by erasing NWCopy's primary data file. Without a backup, a disaster like the one simulated in the following script can cause you to lose all the data and database objects in a database!

The script starts by showing the syntax for making a backup for NWCopy. This process begins by changing the database context to the master database. This is a good general practice when working with creating or restoring a database. The next statement executes the sp_addumpdevice system-stored procedure to create a backup device. A backup device points at storage for the backup file(s), which can be either on disk or tape. The backup device has both a logical name and a physical name. The logical name is NWCopyBK_1. The physical backup device name is c:\prosseapps\chapter03\NWCopyBK_1.bak. The BACKUP DATABASE statement names the NWCopy database and specifies the NWCopyBK_1 backup device.

After creating the backup, the script confirms the availability of the database by performing a SELECT statement against the Shippers table in NWCopy. Then, the script causes the server to pause a second before erasing the primary data file, which is northwnd.mdf in the c:\prosseapps\chapter03 path. Erasing a database's primary data file obviously makes the database unavailable. However, by invoking the RESTORE DATABASE statement, the script permits a SELECT statement against the Shippers table to succeed again. For a full data restore, all you have to do is specify the database name (NWCopy) and the logical backup device name (NWCopyBK_1) in the RESTORE DATABASE statement.

```
USE master
EXEC sp_addumpdevice 'disk', NWCopyBK_1,
    'c:\prosseapps\chapter03\NWCopyBK_1.bak'
BACKUP DATABASE NWCopy TO NWCopyBK_1
GO

SELECT * FROM NWCopy..Shippers
GO
WAITFOR DELAY '00:00:01'
GO
xp_cmdshell 'erase c:\prosseapps\chapter03\northwnd.mdf'
GO

RESTORE DATABASE NWCopy FROM NWCopyBK_1
GO
SELECT * FROM NWCopy..Shippers
GO
```

Performing Differential Backups and Restores

Differential backups and restores are more flexible than full data backups. As a result, the syntax and procedures for differential backups and restores is more complicated. The presentation for this topic starts with a demonstration of how to create two differential backups for NWCopy. Before creating the first backup, the sample inserts a new row in the Shippers table. Then, the sample inserts another row in the Shippers table before creating the second differential back. Three recovery operations follow. First, the sample shows how to recover the data in the first differential backup, which has four rows in the Shippers table. Next, you learn how to recover the data in the second differential backup, which has five rows in the Shippers table. Finally, a third recovery occurs after a disaster (again simulated by erasing the primary data file).

Creating the Differential Backups

The next excerpt from SQLQuery8_f0316_f0317.sql shows the syntax for creating an initial full data backup, which is followed by two differential backups. The first BACKUP DATABASE statement reuses the NWCopyBK_1 backup device from the preceding full data backup and recovery. Therefore, this sample does not require the invocation of sp_addumpdevice to create a new backup device. Notice the INIT keyword in the WITH clause for the first BACKUP DATABASE statement. This clause causes the first backup, which is a full data backup, to copy over any other content in the file. Without this clause, a BACKUP DATABASE statement appends its backup content to any existing content in a backup device.

The second and third BACKUP DATABASE statements are both differential backups, which share a common syntax with one another. It is their order in the script and their preceding INSERT INTO statements that makes the two differential backups distinct from one another. You can make a differential backup by inserting a WITH DIFFERENTIAL clause in the BACKUP DATABASE statement. Except for the WITH DIFFERENTIAL clause, the syntax for a differential backup is the same as for a full data backup.

The absence of the INIT keyword in either of the two differential BACKUP DATABASE statements concatenates their output to the end of any preceding backups in the NWCopyBK_1 backup device. As a consequence, the NWCopyBK_1 backup device contains three backups. It is common to refer to each backup as a file in a backup device. The full backup is the first backup file in the NWCopyBK_1 backup device. The first and second differential backups are the second and third backup files in the NWCopyBK_1 backup device.

```
BACKUP DATABASE NWCopy
TO NWCopyBK_1
WITH INIT
GO

INSERT INTO NWCopy..Shippers
    (CompanyName, Phone)
    VALUES ('CAB, Inc.', '(123) 456-7890')
GO

BACKUP DATABASE NWCopy
TO NWCopyBK_1
WITH DIFFERENTIAL
GO

INSERT INTO NWCopy..Shippers
    (CompanyName, Phone)
    VALUES ('CAB Does It', '(456) -789-0123')
GO

BACKUP DATABASE NWCopy
TO NWCopyBK_1
WITH DIFFERENTIAL
GO
```

Restoring the First Differential Backup

The following code excerpt from SQLQuery8_f0316_f0317.sql shows the syntax for recovering NWCopy as of the completion of the first differential backup. Notice that a collection of differential backups lets you restore a database to different points in time—that is, the times you created each differential backup.

You need two RESTORE DATABASE statements to restore a differential backup. The first RESTORE DATABASE statement specifies the base for the differential backup series, which is normally the first full data backup. Use the NORECOVERY keyword in a WITH clause to avoid closing the log file before the restoration completes. The second RESTORE DATABASE statement points at one of your differential backup files for the base backup. By using FILE = 2 in the following script, the code designates the second backup file in the NWCopyBK_1 backup device. Recall that the first differential backup generates the second backup file.

```
RESTORE DATABASE NWCopy
FROM NWCopyBK_1
WITH NORECOVERY
GO

RESTORE DATABASE NWCopy
FROM NWCopyBK_1
WITH FILE = 2, RECOVERY
GO

SELECT * FROM NWCopy..Shippers
GO
```

Figure 3-17 shows the output from the preceding script. The output is for a SELECT statement from the Shippers table. Because the differential backup contains an added row for the Shippers table relative to the initial three rows in the table, the output shows four rows. You can match the column values for the fourth row to the values in the first INSERT INTO statement in the differential backup script.

	ShipperID	CompanyName	Phone
1	1	Speedy Exprexx	(503) 555-9831
2	2	United Package	(503) 555-3199
3	3	Federal Shipping	(503) 555-9931
4	4	CAB, Inc.	(123) 456-7890

Figure 3-17. *You can recover a database's content to the values for any differential backup in a collection of differential backups.*

Restoring the Second Differential Backup

The script for restoring the second differential backup appears next. It is identical to the script for restoring the first differential backup, with one exception. The only difference is that the first argument for the WITH clause in the second RESTORE DATABASE statement is FILE = 3. Recall that the third backup file pointed at the output from the second differential backup. The SELECT statement at the end of the script returns five rows. The column values in the last row correspond to the values in the second INSERT INTO statement in the differential backup script.

```
RESTORE DATABASE NWCopy
FROM NWCopyBK_1
WITH NORECOVERY
GO

RESTORE DATABASE NWCopy
FROM NWCopyBK_1
WITH FILE = 3, RECOVERY
GO

SELECT * FROM NWCopy..Shippers
GO
```

Selecting a Differential Backup to Restore from a Disaster

The main purpose of most backups is to be able to recover from a disaster. Differential backups permit this in the same way that full data backups let you recover from major software or hardware failures. The following script simulates a disaster by erasing the primary data file for NWCopy. The final SELECT statement returns four rows because the second RESTORE DATABASE statement points at the first differential backup after the first full data backup. Modifying FILE = 2 to FILE = 3 in the second RESTORE DATABASE statement will cause the output to show five, instead of four, rows.

```
xp_cmdshell 'erase c:\prosseapps\chapter03\northwnd.mdf'
GO

RESTORE DATABASE NWCopy
FROM NWCopyBK_1
WITH NORECOVERY
GO

RESTORE DATABASE NWCopy
FROM NWCopyBK_1
WITH FILE = 2, RECOVERY
GO

SELECT * FROM NWCopy..Shippers
GO
```

Cleaning Up the Backup and Restore Scripts

You have already seen how to drop databases and delete files when you have finished using them. It is a good practice to drop databases and delete files for demonstration applications when you no longer need the files supporting the demonstration, because you are more likely to be able to rerun the same script later without any conflicts from an earlier use of the script. You should not, of course, drop operational databases and other important production files.

This sample introduces a backup device. Use the sp_dropdevice system-stored procedure to remove a backup device when you finish using it. The following closing excerpt from SQLQuery8_f0316_f0317.sql shows how to combine this technique with others already presented to clean up a script that backs up and restores databases.

```
DROP DATABASE NWCopy
GO
EXEC sp_dropdevice @logicalname = 'NWCopyBK_1'
GO
xp_cmdshell 'erase c:\prosseapps\chapter03\NWCopyBK_1.bak'
GO
```

Summary

This chapter focused heavily on how to explore, create, and recover databases. In the area of exploring databases, the chapter covered system catalog views and selected stored procedures. sys.databases was the main catalog view covered in the chapter, but sys.tables and sys.columns were also given some attention. The system-stored procedures for learning about and manipulating databases covered here included sp_helpdb and sp_dboption. The review of creating databases focused on programmatic approaches; see Chapter 2 for a demonstration of graphical techniques for creating databases. This chapter illustrated how to create and manipulate databases programmatically with Express SSMS. You were also able to take a close look at the CREATE DATABASE statement from multiple perspectives, including creating a database from scratch as well as attaching data and log files copied from databases that already exist. The chapter's final major section drilled down on backing up and restoring databases. You learned core concepts and saw specific examples that illustrated how to build backup and restore solutions with the BACKUP DATABASE and RESTORE DATABASE statements.

CHAPTER 4

■■■

Data Types, Tables, and Constraints

The main purpose of most relational database managers, such as SQL Server Express, is to store data in a way that can help to model organizations or systems. Relational databases store data in tables. The tables frequently represent entities that are being modeled, such as the students and classes at a college. By expressing relationships between distinct tables, you facilitate the retrieval and maintenance of information for the tables in a database.

This chapter drills down on data types and table design techniques. You need to learn about SQL Server Express (SSE) data types, because picking the wrong data types can waste storage space and cause your database solutions to run slowly. Picking the right data types can give you faster, easier, and more flexible options for retrieving data from your database. This chapter begins by acquainting you with the dozens of data types that SSE makes available so that you can make informed decisions about which data types to use.

The chapter covers data design techniques, introducing you to the basics of creating tables, including the use of data types in table definitions. You also learn how to specify constraints in table definitions that help to manage the integrity and usefulness of the data in a database. Different types of constraints are optimized to enhance data integrity and the accessibility of data within tables. Several especially important constraint types that you'll learn about in this chapter include the following:

- A PRIMARY KEY constraint designates one or more columns that are unique across all rows in a table. This type of constraint can avoid duplicate rows within a single table and help to define relationships between tables.

- A CHECK constraint lets you specify a Boolean expression that must be satisfied for a row to enter a table. For example, you can specify a CHECK constraint to avoid a situation where a student inadvertently enters her birth date for a year in the future.

- FOREIGN KEY constraints in coordination with either PRIMARY KEY or UNIQUE constraints facilitate managing data integrity and accessibility between pairs of tables. FOREIGN KEY constraints are optimized for designating one-to-many and many-to-many relationships between tables.

Learning About Data Types

SQL Server Express supports dozens of native data types. The data type that you use to store a column's values says a lot about the data in that column. Some data types are tailored for storing characters, whereas others are best for holding large numbers or small numbers. Picking the right data type for a column can often save storage space and generate performance improvements. This section organizes data types into groups, and subgroups in some cases, to help you understand which data types to use in a particular situation. The three main categories are

- Numbers and dates
- Character and binary byte streams
- Miscellaneous

■**Note** As mentioned in previous chapters, SSE is merely an edition of SQL Server 2005. It shares a common core database engine with commercial editions of SQL Server 2005. This commonality between SSE and other SQL Server 2005 editions is particularly evident for data types. The SSE data types are exactly the same as those in other editions of SQL Server 2005. For this reason, you can refer interchangeably to SQL Server data types and SSE data types.

Numbers and Dates

Data types for numbers have four common characteristics: precision, scale, length, and a range of legitimate values.

- *Precision* refers to how accurately a data type can represent a number value. You can think of a data type's precision as the maximum number of digits available to specify a value.
- *Scale* refers to the number of digits to the right of a decimal point.
- *Length* designates the number of bytes used to store a value.
- The *range of legitimate values* for a data type provides a very concrete way of appreciating the role of a data type.

The precision, scale, length, and range of legitimate values relate to one another. A data type's length in bytes sets an upper limit on the precision of values that a data type can represent. The more bytes a data type has, the more precise the values that it can represent. The scale for a data type can never be greater than the precision. That is, you cannot have more digits to the right of the decimal point than the total number of digits in a value. The precision, scale, and length set constraints on the range of values that a data type can store.

■**Tip** You should generally select a data type for a column that has the smallest possible length and a legitimate range of values for all the values that a column can hold.

Number data types can represent values either precisely or approximately. Several data types for storing numbers support the storage of integer quantities, such as 1, 2, or 100. Other values, such as 1 divided by 3, cannot be represented precisely. To accommodate values that cannot be represented precisely or whose length would be prohibitive to represent precisely, SQL Server offers approximate data types.

In many cases, data types for precise numbers represent integer values with a scale of zero (no digits to the right of the decimal point). Some data types for numbers represent values precisely even while they permit the inclusion of digits to the right of the decimal point. Three data types like this are money, smallmoney, and decimal (or numeric).

■**Note** The decimal and numeric data types are synonyms for each other.

SQL Server offers two data types for representing date and time values, datetime and smalldatetime. These data types store their values as numbers with digits to the left and right of a decimal point. Digits to the left of the decimal point represent whole days. Digits to the right of the decimal point denote fractions of a day. The datetime and smalldatetime data types have different lengths, which enable these two data types to represent a different range of date and time values to different levels of accuracy.

datetime and smalldatetime have characteristics that closely resemble the characteristics for numbers. For example, number data types and data types for dates and times have fixed lengths. In addition, both sets of data types have a legitimate range of values (from a minimum number or beginning date and time to a maximum number or ending date and time). The accuracy of date and time data types (1 minute for smalldatetime vs. 3.33 milliseconds for datetime) corresponds roughly to scale.

Bit Data Type

The bit data type is for values that can be either 0 or 1. This makes the bit data type particularly appropriate for representing column values that can be either true (1) or false (0). Another common use for the bit data type is to represent a check box on a questionnaire that can either be checked (1) or not checked (0).

bit values can be unknown (or null) besides 0 or 1. A null value represents information that is not known. For a table describing businesses, you can have a column indicating whether a business is incorporated in the state of Delaware. At the time that you enter a row for a business, the characteristic can be yes, no, or unknown (because you do not have information about the state of incorporation for a business). Unknown is different from either yes for incorporated within Delaware or no for not incorporated within Delaware.

■**Note** Null data values, usually represented by the NULL keyword, can apply to nearly all SQL Server data types. Whenever a column value is not known or missing, the column's value is null. A null value is different from zero or an empty string. Before the introduction of null values, developers used to represent missing values with some arbitrary value and did not need to follow any standard from one database to another. Using null values to represent missing data ensures your database follows widely used standards. Null values have distinctive features. For example, any value concatenated with a NULL returns another NULL. A null value does not equal (=) another null value.

A bit data type can correspond to a bit within a byte of computer storage. The SQL Server database engine automatically groups bit data values to fill the bits within a byte. If a table has between 1 and 8 bit values per table row, SQL Server stores the values in a byte. Similarly, from 9 to 16 bit values are stored within 2 bytes.

Integer Data Types

The four integer data types are tinyint, smallint, int, and bigint. The precision of these data types ranges from 3 through 19 digits. The scale for all integer data types is 0; no digits appear to the right of the decimal point. The integer data types have lengths of 1, 2, 4, and 8 bytes, respectively. The tinyint data type is distinct from the other three integer data types because it represents just positive values and zero, but the other three data types represent positive and negative values, including zero.

- tinyint
  - range of values: 0 through 255
  - precision: 3
  - scale: 0
  - length: 1
- smallint
  - range of values: $-32,768$ (-2^{15}) through $32,767$ ($2^{15} - 1$)
  - precision: 5
  - scale: 0
  - length: 2
- int
  - range of values: $-2,147,483,648$ (-2^{31}) through $2,147,483,647$ ($2^{31} - 1$)
  - precision: 10
  - scale: 0
  - length: 4
- bigint
  - range of values: $-9,223,372,036,854,775,808$ (-2^{63}) through $9,223,372,036,854,775,807$ ($2^{63} - 1$)
  - precision: 19
  - scale: 0
  - length: 8

Currency Data Types

The money and smallmoney data types explicitly target the representation of currency values. Both data types have four digits to the right of the decimal point, but all values are precisely represented. These four places allow for the precise representation of a ten-thousandth of a currency unit. Aside from the explicit targeting of currency applications, the smallmoney and money data types are very similar to the int and bigint data types. The specifications for the smallmoney and money data types are

- smallmoney
  - range of values: $-214,748.3648$ through $214,748.3647$
  - precision: 10
  - scale: 0
  - length: 4
- money
  - range of values: $-922,337,203,685,477.5808$ through $922,337,203,685,477.5807$
  - precision: 19
  - scale: 0
  - length: 8

Date and Time Data Types

The datetime and smalldatetime data types represent date and time values similarly to the way that money and smallmoney represent currency values. The similarity follows from the fact that the money data type represents a wider range of currency values than the smallmoney data type, and the datetime data type can denote a wider range of dates than the smalldatetime data type. In addition, the datetime and money data types are both 8 bytes long, whereas the smalldatetime and smallmoney data types are both 4 bytes long.

The two data types for date and time values diverge in one major way from the two data types for currency. This is because the smalldatetime data type does not have the same level of accuracy for time that the datetime data type does. Recall that both money and smallmoney represent currency values to four places after the decimal point. The smalldatetime data type distinguishes time to the level of 1-second increments, but the datetime data type can represent time to the level of 3.33-millisecond increments. For most business applications, the finer resolution of the datetime data type relative to the smalldatetime data type is not a driving factor for choosing the datetime data type in favor of the smalldatetime data type. Remember, you should always choose the smallest possible data type for a column in a table.

The specifications for the two date and time data types have a different format than other data types for representing number values. Although SQL Server does internally represent dates and times as number values with a precision and scale, it is not relevant to think about time units in the metrics of precision and scale. Instead, you should use the date range and the time resolution specifications in the following list:

- smalldatetime
    - date range: January 1, 1900, through June 6, 2079
    - time resolution: 1 minute
    - length: 4
- datetime
    - date range: January 1, 1753, through December 31, 9999
    - time resolution: 3.33 milliseconds
    - length: 8

Decimal and Numeric Data Types

The decimal data type and numeric data type both describe the same kind of data. A table designer can specify both the precision (p) and scale (s) of table columns with either a numeric or decimal data type at the time that they designate the column for the table. The value of p must be less than or equal to 38, and the value of s must be greater than or equal to 0, as well as less than or equal to p. Although decimal and numeric data type values permit digits to the right of the decimal, they precisely represent values. For this reason, you can use decimal and numeric data types for currency applications in addition to the money and smallmoney data types.

■**Note** As indicated previously, the numeric data type is a synonym for the decimal data type. The numeric data type, despite the *Random House Unabridged Dictionary* definition for the term *numeric*, does not mean "of or pertaining to numbers." The term *numeric* when used with respect to SQL Server data types has a much more limited meaning. For these reasons, you should be careful how you use the word *numeric* when describing numbers in SQL Server applications.

Unlike other data types for numbers, the specifications for the decimal and numeric data types can vary depending on the values that a table designer explicitly assigns to p and s.

- decimal or numeric
  - range of values: $-10^{38} + 1$ through $10^{38} - 1$
  - precision: minimum of 0 and maximum of 38
  - scale: minimum of 0 and maximum of 38
  - length: varies (for p of 1–9, the length is 5; for p of 10–19, the length is 9; for p of 20–28, the length is 13; for p of 29–38, the length is 17)

An example may help to clarify how to use of the decimal data type as it approaches its limiting upper value. The following script declares the @dec1 local variable as a decimal data type with a precision of 38 and a scale of 0. Next, a POWER function nested within a CAST function creates a value of 1,000,000,000 in @dec1. Then, a SELECT statement with a product as its list value returns a decimal value of 1 followed by 37 zeroes for a total of 38 digits. The second item in the SELECT list with the FLOOR and LOG10 functions actually computes the number of digits in the product.

```
SET NOCOUNT ON
DECLARE @dec1 decimal(38,0)
SET @dec1 = CAST(POWER(10,9) as decimal(38,0))
SELECT @dec1 * @dec1 * @dec1 * @dec1 * 10 AS 'Large Decimal value',
    FLOOR(LOG10(@dec1 * @dec1 * @dec1 * @dec1 * 10)
    + 1) AS 'Number of digits'
```

The following listing shows the result generated by the preceding script. Notice the large decimal value has 38 digits. Attempting to generate a decimal data type value with 39 digits (e.g., by replacing the 10 in the product with 100) will generate an arithmetic overflow error because the result of the product expression is too large to represent as a decimal data type. The script generating this listing is available as Ch04Decimal.sql.

```
Large Decimal value                       Number of digits
--------------------------------------    ----------------------
10000000000000000000000000000000000000    38
```

Approximate Data Types

real and float data types can represent values approximately instead of precisely, as with integer data types, such as int and bigint. real and float data types have a null scale setting because all values have a floating decimal point. The real and float data types follow an IEEE (Institute of Electrical and Electronic Engineers) specification for approximate data types. Because approximate values are subject to rounding error, they are not suitable for financial operations or other cases where precise results are required.

■**Tip** Approximate data types are best suited for scenarios when you are working with engineering or scientific data values. Avoid using real and float data types whenever you need precise results, such as in currency calculations.

There are three advantages for approximate data types relative to precise data types.

- Some number values without a precise representation, such as 1 divided by 3, can only be represented approximately (you can't represent them precisely).

- In exchange for not representing values precisely, approximate data types can represent a wider range of values than corresponding integer data types.

- Approximate data types save storage space, compared to precise data types, because they have a smaller length.

Here are the specifications for the real and float data types:

- real
  - range of values: –3.40E + 38 through 3.40E + 38
  - precision: from 1 to 7
  - scale: Null
  - length: 4
- float
  - range of values: –1.79E + 308 through 1.79E + 308
  - precision: from 1 to 15
  - scale: Null
  - length: 8

The following script helps to contrast the float data type from the decimal data type. Notice that the script follows the same general design as the preceding script for computing a large decimal value, but this script uses a float data type instead of a decimal data type. As a consequence, you can compute larger values, such as those with 39 digits. By computing with a multiple of 100 instead of a multiple of 10, the following script generates a value that is an order of magnitude larger than in the preceding sample for the decimal data type.

```
SET NOCOUNT ON
DECLARE @float1 float
SET @float1 = CAST(POWER(10,9) as float)
SELECT @float1 * @float1 * @float1 * @float1 * 100 AS 'Large Float value',
    FLOOR(LOG10(@float1 * @float1 * @float1 * @float1 * 100)
    + 1) AS 'Number of digits'
```

The following listing confirms the operation of the preceding script. The computed value (@float1 * @float1 * @float1 * @float1 * 100) is a number with 1 followed by 38 zeroes, for a total of 39 digits. The preceding script with the float script will return an error if you run it with a decimal data type instead of a float data type. The script generating the following listing is available as Ch04Float.sql.

```
Large Float value     Number of digits
--------------------- ----------------------
1E+38                 39
```

The float data type represents values precisely whenever its internal architecture can avoid representing a value approximately. For example, 7 divided by 10 with float values results in precisely .7. Similarly, the float data type can precisely represent .0001. However, the difference between 7 divided by 10 and .0001 is a number that a float data type can only approximately represent.

The following script contrasts `float` and `decimal` data types to indicate how a `decimal` data type can return a precise value for a computation for which a `float` data type returns an approximate value. Four local variables (@dec1–@dec4) are declared, with a `decimal` data type having four places to the right of the decimal and a total of 15 digits. This matches the number of digits for `float` data type accuracy. Four local variables (@float1–@float4) are also declared with a `float` data type. The script computes the difference between the quotient of 7 divided by 10 less .0001. The computation demonstrates the contrasting results from `float` and `decimal` data types. The script generating the following listing is available as Ch04FloatDecimal.sql.

```
SET NOCOUNT ON
DECLARE @float1 float, @float2 float, @float3 float, @float4 float
DECLARE @dec1 decimal(15,4), @dec2 decimal(15,4),
        @dec3 decimal(15,4), @dec4 decimal(15,4)
DECLARE @pointseven decimal(15,4)
SET @float1 = 7
SET @float2 = 10
SET @float3 = .0001
SET @float4 = @float1/@float2 - @float3
SET @dec1 = 7
SET @dec2 = 10
SET @dec3 = .0001
SET @dec4 = @dec1/@dec2 - @dec3
SET @pointseven = .7
SELECT @float4 '@float4', @float3 '@float3',
        @pointseven - @float4 'float diff'
SELECT @dec4 '@dec4', @dec3 '@dec3',
        @pointseven - @dec4 'dec diff'
```

The following listing shows the difference between the `float` and the `decimal` results. The preceding script compares each difference with a local variable named @pointseven that is equal to .7. This local variable has a `decimal` data type. The `decimal` difference is precisely .0001. The `float` difference is approximately .0001, that is, 9.9999999999989E–05.

@float4	@float3	float diff
0.6999	0.0001	9.9999999999989E-05

@dec4	@dec3	dec diff
0.6999	0.0001	0.0001

Character and Binary Byte Streams

A sequence of 1 or more bytes is a byte stream. SQL Server Express can decode a byte stream to characters, such as letters, numbers, and symbols, or it can just save and retrieve a byte stream without decoding the byte(s). Two common ways for decoding byte streams are with a character code set based on a code page or with a Unicode character set. Decoded byte streams from a database frequently contain names, such as student names or class titles. Binary byte strings are saved and retrieved as raw byte values. A client application, such as a graphics viewer, can decode a binary byte stream into an image.

■**Note** A code page is a mapping that translates byte values to characters. There are many code pages associated with different languages and locales. Just as a single code page maps byte values to characters for a single language and locale, a Unicode character set maps byte values to characters for all modern languages. There is more than one Unicode character set. SQL Server Express uses the UCS-2 Unicode standard.

Character codes typically match characters to single-byte representations. When a database application is meant for use with one language in a single locale, such as United States English, then a character code set is an especially useful way of translating bytes to characters. This recommendation uses a single code page that translates bytes to characters.

As the number of regional locales that an application has to serve grows beyond a few, it can become exceedingly difficult to find a single code page for translating byte streams properly across all locales. In these circumstances, switching to Unicode characters, which use 2 bytes per character, simplifies the process of translating byte streams to characters in a consistent way across locales. Recall that Unicode character sets are applicable to all modern languages used for business throughout the world. Unicode characters are also especially appropriate for selected Asian languages with more characters than a single byte can represent, such as Simplified Chinese, Traditional Chinese, Japanese, and Korean.

Each of the three types of byte stream types (character, Unicode character, and binary) has three corresponding data types. The first basic data type is for fixed-length values, such as Social Security numbers or credit card numbers. The second basic data type is for variable-length strings. This kind of data type is particularly appropriate for columns storing names, such as first name or last name, in which the values within a column can vary substantially in length across a table's rows. The third basic data type is for byte streams that exceed 8,000 bytes. The column values designated by these long strings are sometimes called large objects.

■**Note** It is common in database applications to use a character data type to represent an identification "number," such as a credit card number or a postal code.

Because large objects can slow the retrieval of data from a table, you may wish to isolate large objects in a separate table that points back to another table with nonlarge objects. This limits the impact of retrieving large objects to occasions when you explicitly need to access them. By storing large objects in a database, you can secure access to them via database security features. Another option is to store large objects as files and then include path and file names in your database. This practice relieves a database of storing and retrieving large objects. In this second scenario, you can manage access to paths containing files with large objects via Windows access control lists.

Character Data Types

The three character data types are `char`, `varchar`, and `text`. These data types correspond, respectively, to the fixed-length, variable-length, and large object data types. They use a single byte per character to represent non-Unicode characters. Byte values are decoded to characters with the default code page for an SSE instance, which is automatically set to a computer's Windows regional setting unless you override this setting during installation. You can designate a character constant value by including the value in single quotes—`'this is a character constant'`.

Use the char data type for table columns that hold values that are all of almost the same length. A syntax such as char(n) represents the maximum number of characters in a column with the char data type, where the n parameter can assume values of 1 through 8,000. The char data type is very efficient for processing character data because SSE can process a fixed number of characters per column value without the need to determine when each character string ends.

The varchar data type is appropriate for columns that will hold character strings that differ substantially across rows. Use a syntax of varchar(n) to denote a varchar data type, where the n parameter represents the maximum number of characters. As with the char data type, n can assume values from 1 through 8,000. The actual length in bytes of a varchar column value is n + 2. When the column values are nearly all of the same length, a char data type will process faster and require less storage space than a varchar data type.

■Note When you have a need for a varchar data type that can accommodate more than 8,000 characters, use max instead of n. The varchar(max) syntax is particularly appropriate in situations where you might consider the text data type.

As with the other character data types, the text data type stores non-Unicode data. The maximum number of characters in a text data type is 2GB. The varchar(max) specification represents large objects—just like the text data type. Microsoft will ultimately phase out the text data type in favor of varchar(max), as it also adds features for processing large objects that have similar syntax to character strings. For example, the UPDATE statement in SQL Server 2005, including the SSE edition, has been augmented to allow you to modify portions of column values declared with a varchar(max) data type.

Unicode Character Data Types

The fixed-length, variable-length, and large object data types for Unicode characters are nchar, nvarchar, and ntext. When you designate a Unicode character constant, specify a preceding N, such as N'a Unicode character constant'. Recall that Unicode characters require 2 bytes per character as opposed to 1 byte per character for non-Unicode characters. Because the maximum number of bytes for Unicode and non-Unicode strings is the same, Unicode character strings can hold only half as many characters as non-Unicode character strings.

Designate a fixed-length Unicode data type with a syntax of nchar(n). The value of n can range from 1 through 4,000. The upper limit of 4,000 is the maximum number of characters that you can hold in a fixed-length Unicode string. A 4,000-character fixed-length Unicode data type value and an 8,000-character fixed-length non-Unicode data type are both 8,000 bytes long.

Specify variable-length Unicode strings with the nvarchar(n) syntax. Again, n can range from 1 through 4,000. The nvarchar data type also takes a max argument to specify large objects.

■Note SQL Server Express uses the sysname data type to reference database object names. The sysname data type is a built-in user-defined data type based on nvarchar(128).

The ntext data type is for large objects with Unicode characters. As with the text data type, the ntext data type will eventually be dropped in favor of the nvarchar(max) data type for large objects. If you require a Unicode string of more than 4,000 characters, use an nvarchar(max) or ntext data type. As with the text data type, large objects made up of Unicode characters can have a maximum byte length of 2GB. However, because each Unicode character takes twice as many bytes as non-Unicode characters, you can hold up to 1GB characters in either an ntext or nvarchar(max) data type versus 2GB characters in either a text or varchar(max) data type.

Binary Strings

The fixed-length, variable-length, and large object binary string data types are binary, varbinary, and image.

- Use binary(n) to designate the fixed-length binary string data type for a column of binary strings. The n parameter can assume values from 1 through 8,000.

- Use varbinary(n) to specify a variable length binary string data type. Values for n can range from 1 through 8,000.

- Use image or varbinary(max) to specify a data type for a large object binary string with image or varbinary(max). Because of the future obsolescence of the image data type (along with the text and ntext data types), use varbinary(max) for all new database applications.

Miscellaneous

The remaining SQL Server data types serve a variety of specialized purposes. Unless your database application has special needs, you may find no use for these data types.

timestamp

The timestamp data type is a good example of the specialized nature of the remaining data types. You can use this data type for timestamping table rows for an insert or identifying the last update. Instead of assigning a datetime value to a row, the timestamp data type assigns a sequential binary(8) number that is unique throughout a database. rowversion is another name for the timestamp data type. Eventually, Microsoft will make the timestamp data type obsolete in favor of the rowversion data type name because rowversion is a more accurate reflection of the data type's role. In addition, the rowversion name is more consistent with industry standards for SQL data types. The "Assigning the Current User, Date, and Time" section demonstrates the use of the timestamp data type and discusses how to convert from a timestamp data type to a rowversion data type.

uniqueidentifier

The uniqueidentifier data type holds globally unique identifier (GUID) values, which have a 16-byte length. It is common to express uniqueidentifier values with a 32-character hexadecimal representation (xxxxxxxx-xxxx-xxxx-xxxx-xxxxxxxxxxxx); two hexadecimal characters represent 1 byte. GUID values are unique in space and time. As a result, uniqueidentifier values are sometimes used instead of the IDENTITY property for a column to denote the primary key for tables in a replicated database because the GUIDs will be unique across all replicated copies no matter how geographically dispersed the replicas are.

You can assign either the NEWID function or the NEWSEQUENTIAL function to the DEFAULT setting for a table column to automatically generate new uniqueidentifier values for successively inserted rows. See the "Managing Data Integrity with Basic Constraints and Column Properties" section for commentary on and samples using the DEFAULT setting for a table. The NEWID function generates uniqueidentifier values in a random order. The NEWSEQUENTIALID function generates uniqueidentifier values in a sequential order. You can perform equality and inequality comparisons between two different uniqueidentifier values.

■**Tip** You can assign the ROWGUIDCOL property to a column declaration with a uniqueidentifier data type to specify a column of uniqueidentifier values. By adding the ROWGUIDCOL property to a column declaration, you gain the ability to return uniqueidentifier values in a result set by including the ROWGUIDCOL keyword in the list for a SELECT statement.

The uniqueidentifier data type is an advanced data type that the typical reader of this book should not use. It is very resource intensive because of its length. The introduction of the NEWSEQUENTIALID function with SQL Server 2005 makes uniqueidentifiers more comparable than in previous SQL Server versions to IDENTITY values as primary keys and index values generally. Nevertheless, there is still a substantial performance penalty associated with uniqueidentifier values relative to data types used with an IDENTITY property. You also do not have the same richness of processing options available for a column with a ROWGUIDCOL property that you do for a column with an IDENTITY property.

cursor

The cursor data type represents a result set, such as one returned from a stored procedure, that you can scroll through. Set techniques that you implement with SELECT statements are generally a much more efficient way to recover values from a data source than for scrolling through result set rows with a cursor. My own preference is to reserve the use of cursors for Visual Basic 2005 code that manipulates the values in a result set derived with an SSE SELECT statement.

sql_variant

The sql_variant data type can store values declared with data types, except for text, ntext, image, timestamp, sql_variant, and the max data types for varchar, nvarchar, and varbinary. The sql_variant data type is similar to the variant type in Visual Basic. An application can use it to store values when you are not sure what types of values a user will need to enter. For example, a sales person may benefit from a column into which can be entered miscellaneous data, such as a client's birth date, a spouse's name, and the price paid for a product in the last order. The availability of the new xml data type removes the need for the sql_variant data type to serve this purpose while providing a widely adopted standard format for exchanging data. For this reason, you should consider using an xml data type whenever a sql_variant data type may be appropriate.

xml

The xml data type enables you to assign an XML document or XML fragment as a value for a column in a table's row, a variable, or a parameter. An XML document consists of a single root element with one or more nested other elements. An XML fragment consists of one or more elements without an outer root element. You can assign values to an XML document or XML fragment with element values and attribute values. SQL Server Express can implicitly convert a character constant to XML and assign the converted value to a column, variable, or parameter declared with an xml data type.

xml data type values can be either typed or untyped. A typed xml data type value has one or more schemas. An untyped xml data type value does not have a schema. SQL Server Express automatically checks xml values to make sure they are well formed. A well-formed document follows XML document syntax. If an xml value is typed, then SSE checks the value assignments and structure of a document to make sure that they are valid relative to the schemas for the XML document.

■**Note** As indicated next, XML can quickly become an advanced topic that has very little to do with traditional database development topics. The terms *schema, typed xml, well-formed*, and *valid* are special terms in the XML nomenclature. A well-formed XML document is one that follows all general XML syntax rules. A schema is an XML document that represents the structure of one or more other XML documents. A typed xml value is one that references a schema. A valid xml value is one that follows the rules of a specific schema.

XML can quickly become an advanced topic that requires knowledge of many topics that are tangential to database design and analysis, such as XML document syntax and XML schema design. To keep the book's focus on core database development topics, I do not deal with xml data types beyond this section.

The following script illustrates three attempts to define an xml data type value with a character constant. These examples demonstrate how you can assign ad hoc values to a variable with an xml data type.

- The first attempt, which succeeds, starts with a declaration for the @xdata local variable. Notice the variable has an xml data type. Then, the script assigns a character constant for an XML document to the local variable and displays the data. The character constant includes a root element and two firstname elements within the root.

- In the second attempt, the local variable is reused with a character constant representing an XML fragment. Notice there is no root tag, but there are two properly specified firstname elements.

- The third attempt does not succeed in assigning a character constant to a local variable declared with an xml data type. The problem is that the initial firstname element misses a closing tag.

```
DECLARE @xdata xml
SET @xdata = '<root><firstname>Rick</firstname>' +
    '<firstname>Virginia</firstname></root>'
SELECT @xdata AS 'xml data'

SET @xdata = '<firstname>Rick</firstname>' +
    '<firstname>Virginia</firstname>'
SELECT @xdata AS 'xml data'

SET @xdata = '<root><firstname>Rick' +
    '<firstname>Virginia</firstname></root>'
SELECT @xdata AS 'xml data'
```

The following listing shows the outcome of running the preceding script. You can see that the first two attempts succeed. The value of the xml data type varies depending on the syntax used in the character constant for the first two attempts. The SSE XML parser correctly detects a syntax error in the third assignment of a character constant to the local variable with an xml data type. The script generating this listing is available as Ch04Xml.sql.

```
xml data
-----------------------------------------------------------------------
<root><firstname>Rick</firstname><firstname>Virginia</firstname></root>

(1 row(s) affected)

xml data
-----------------------------------------------------------------------
```

```
<firstname>Rick</firstname><firstname>Virginia</firstname>

(1 row(s) affected)


Msg 9436, Level 16, State 1, Line 10
XML parsing: line 1, character 59, end tag does not match start tag
```

table

The table data type can represent a result set from a SELECT statement. You can return a table value from a table-valued, user-defined function. The returned table value can be referenced by the FROM clause of a SELECT statement in a script or a stored procedure. table values can be assigned to local variables. The table data type also offers an alternative to using temporary tables in stored procedures. Using table values in a stored procedure requires fewer stored procedure recompilations than when a stored procedure uses temporary tables. Most likely, the most common way you will use the table data type will be with user-defined functions that return a table. The "Creating and Using IF User-defined Functions" section in Chapter 7 includes samples illustrating the use of the table data type.

alias

The alias data type corresponds to what was called a user-defined type in earlier versions of SQL Server. However, the introduction of user-defined types based on classes for the embedded CLR in SSE caused the introduction of the alias term for referring to traditional user-defined data types. The alias data type is suitable for use in defining table columns as well as for variables and parameters. You can create an alias type based on any of the other built-in SQL Server data types and further constrain the alias type by specifying any characteristics of the base data type as well as the nullability of the new alias data type. Recall that the sysname data type is really an alias of nvarchar with a value of n equal to 128. The sysname data type does not permit null values.

■**Note** The new user-defined data type based on the embedded CLR is outside the scope of this book because of its advanced programming concepts and its indirect relevance to traditional database development topics.

You can create a new alias type with either the

- sp_addtype system-stored procedure
- CREATE TYPE statement introduced with SQL Server 2005

The CREATE TYPE statement facilitates the creation of alias data types as well as the new embedded CLR-based user-defined type. The sp_addtype will become obsolete in a future version of SQL Server. Therefore, use the CREATE TYPE whenever possible. alias data types apply to only the database in which you create them unless you add an alias data type to the model database. Then, the alias data type is available for all new databases created after the addition of the alias data type to the model database.

Creating Tables and Using Data Types

The review of data types indicates the role that data types can play in adding structure to a table. In a very real sense, specifying a data type for a table's column helps to define the table. A table column defined with a `tinyint` data type cannot hold any negative values nor any positive values greater than 255. Similarly, a table column defined with an `int` data type cannot store names based on the letters of the alphabet nor even numbers with digits after a decimal point.

Before you can add a column to a table, you must first create a table. You can add a new table to a database with the `CREATE TABLE` statement. Within the `CREATE TABLE` statement, there are many specifications that you can add, such as

- Data types associated with columns

- Column property assignments

- Constraints associated with individual columns

- Constraints associated with more than one column

- Constraints that tie one table to another

■**Note** SQL Server Express requires you to have permission to invoke a capability, such as run a `CREATE TABLE` statement, before you can invoke the capability. Anyone who can connect to an SSE instance as a sysadmin member, for example, a computer's administrator, can invoke the `CREATE TABLE` statement. In addition, this security feature (availability to sysadmin members) is true for nearly all other SSE capabilities. SQL Server Express also offers much more granular control over the permission to invoke its capabilities. Permissions are part of SSE security, which is the topic for Chapter 8.

This section briefly introduces the `CREATE TABLE` statement to demonstrate the role of a table as a container for columns with data types. As mentioned, data type specifications for columns add structure to a table. In addition, tables can constrain how data types work within a table. This section highlights the interplay between several data types when they are in a table.

Creating a Table with Columns

In its most basic form, the `CREATE TABLE` statement can act as a container for a set of column specifications delimited by commas. Follow the `CREATE TABLE` keywords with a name for the table. A table's name must be unique throughout a database. In addition, table names must follow the rules for SQL Server identifiers (see SQL Server Identifier Rules in Chapter 3). You can optionally qualify a table name with a database name for the database containing the table and a schema denoting ownership for the table. Chapter 8 covers schemas along with other SQL Server security topics.

Place the column specifications for a table inside parentheses after the table's name. At a minimum, each column must have a name and a data type (with the exception of timestamp columns, which don't have to have a name). As with table names, column names must follow the rules for SQL Server identifiers. SQL Server Express automatically assigns the name `timestamp` to a column with a `timestamp` data type, but you can override this default name with a custom one. This section presents a series of samples demonstrating how to use the `CREATE TABLE` statement to achieve different results.

Specifying Fixed-Width Data Types for Table Columns

You can essentially add an infinite number of tables to a database (the actual upper limit is 2GB). Within any table, you can designate up to 1KB columns. This number of columns is more than sufficient for the overwhelming majority of tables that you are likely to build. However, the maximum width for rows with exclusively fixed-width data types, such as tinyint, int, real, and char, is 8,060 bytes. Actually, because SSE reserves 7 bytes for overhead, the upper limit for data within a row is 8,053 bytes. This limit is based on the way SSE organizes data on storage devices; it ignores the upper limit on row width when a row contains one or more columns with a variable-length data type, such as varchar, text, or varchar(max).

■**Note** The width of a column with a char data type can change before you run a CREATE TABLE statement. Once you run a CREATE TABLE statement including a column with a char data type, all column values in any row of the table will have the same width specified in the CREATE TABLE statement.

The following script shows the syntax for creating a table named T. The table's name appears immediately after the CREATE TABLE keywords. The table has three columns named c1, c2, and c3. The data types for the columns are int for c1 and char for both c2 and c3. After the first and second column specifications, a comma delimits the column setting for the designation of a new column. A trailing comma is not necessary for the third column because there are no subsequent column specifications.

```
CREATE TABLE T (
    c1 int,
    c2 char(49),
    c3 char(8000)
)
```

The T table illustrates how easy it is to reach the upper limit for a row's width. The char data type consumes 1 byte per character. The column widths for c2 and c3 total to 8,049 bytes. An int data type has a width of 4 bytes, which when added to 8,049 equals the upper limit (8,053 plus 7 bytes for overhead) for the width of a row exclusively composed of fixed-width data types.

As with many data definition statements, it is good practice to make sure that the name for a new object is unique. If the name for a new object is not unique, its data definition statement, such as CREATE TABLE, will fail. When you are initially designing a table, it is often convenient to remove any previously existing table with the name of the new table. This is because you will probably be iteratively refining the table's design and you will probably have sample data that's relatively easy to insert into the table (or even no data). Another strategy is to rename the old table so that you can preserve, and later recover, its data.

The following sample code merely drops any existing table with the name of the new table. You need to run the code before the preceding CREATE TABLE statement. For the sake of clarity, the code listing tests for a table's existence before repeating the CREATE TABLE statement that implements the table's design. The EXISTS keyword takes a SELECT argument that searches for a table named T. If the table exists, the code invokes a DROP TABLE statement for the prior version of the table before creating a new table named T. The following script is available from Ch04IntChar.sql.

■**Note** The sample files from this point on in the chapter reference use, via a USE statement, the
ProSSEAppsCh04 database. You can create this database with a statement as simple as CREATE DATABASE
ProSSEAppsCh04. Alternatively, you can add and drop tables from any existing database that you prefer to use
instead of the ProSSEAppsCh04 database. Either choice will allow the code samples listed in the book to work as
described. However, if you want to run the downloaded code sample files, then you must create ProSSEAppsCh04
or modify the USE statement in the sample files so that they point at another database which you prefer to use
instead of ProSSEAppsCh04.

```
IF EXISTS(SELECT name FROM sys.tables
    WHERE name = 'T')
    DROP TABLE T

CREATE TABLE T (
    c1 int,
    c2 char(49),
    c3 char(8000)
)
```

What if your application requirements change, and you need another character in the c2 column without decreasing the width of the c3 column? Well, you could increase the number of characters for c2 from 49 to 50, but this would cause the CREATE TABLE statement to fail because the row size exceeds the maximum allowable width. By changing the data type for c1 from int to smallint, you can reduce the row size enough to accommodate the extra character for c2 plus one more character.

Specifying Variable-Width Data Types for Table Columns

As mentioned in the "Character Data Types" section, SSE processes char data type values faster than varchar data type values, but the varchar data type is more flexible. One area of flexibility pertains to maximum column widths. When a row contains at least one column with a variable-width data type, such as varchar, then SSE does not enforce the 8,060-byte limit. If you are working with tables that can have substantial variability in the number of characters across rows, the varchar data type is definitely preferable to the char data type in spite of the speed advantage for the char data type.

The following script, which is available as Ch04IntVarchar.sql, shows a CREATE TABLE statement with the same general design as the preceding one. Two key differences are the swapping of the varchar data type for the char data type for columns c2 and c3. In addition, the row width is 8,064 (8,000 + 60 + 4) plus 7 more bytes for overhead. Although this row width exceeds the 8,060-byte limit for rows with fixed-length data types, using varchar data types for c2 and c3 allows the row to exceed the limit without generating an error that blocks the creation of the table.

```
IF EXISTS(SELECT name FROM sys.tables
    WHERE name = 'T')
    DROP TABLE T

CREATE TABLE T (
    c1 int,
    c3 varchar(60),
    c2 varchar(8000)
)
```

Specifying Table Columns with Unicode Data Types

Data types specifying Unicode characters follow the same rules about row widths as single-byte characters. Of course, Unicode characters require two bytes of storage for each character. Therefore, you can hold just about half as many characters per row when you are using exclusively fixed-width data types. The next script in the Ch04IntNchar.sql file implements the initial design for table T with nchar instead of char data types for columns c2 and c3. Notice how the width for c3 is set to 4,000 characters. This number of Unicode characters requires 8,000 bytes of storage. This leaves just 53 bytes for the remaining two columns. The c2 column specification of nchar(24) consumes an additional 48 bytes of the remaining 53 bytes. This leaves 5 remaining bytes, which is more than sufficient for the int specification for c1.

```
IF EXISTS(SELECT name FROM sys.tables
    WHERE name = 'T')
    DROP TABLE T

CREATE TABLE T (
    c1 int,
    c2 nchar(24),
    c3 nchar(4000)
)
```

Adding Data to Tables

After you design a table, it is natural to want to add data to it. This section presents a couple of approaches for inserting rows into a table. The basics of data manipulation, including inserting rows, are too important to cover from just one perspective. Therefore, data manipulation is revisited in Chapters 5 and 6.

- A couple of row insertion samples in this section highlight the varchar data type, which is a popular one for storing character data.

- This section also demonstrates a basic technique for recovering the data from an old version of a table even as you redesign the actual structure of the table. This capability to recover data from an old table version is especially important if you have important data in the table that you cannot just drop from a database.

Inserting Very Wide Character Data into a Varchar Column

Both the char and varchar data types let you enter values into columns that are up to 8,000 characters in width. However, what happens if you need more than 8,000 characters in a single column? This requirement can exist for some comment fields in a database application as well as for storing messages or documents in a database. This section illustrates a basic technique for populating a column with a varchar data type. You also learn a solution based on the varchar data type that allows the insertion of more than 8,000 characters as a column value for a row in a table.

The following script, which is the top part of the listing in Ch04InsertToVarchar.sql, shows a new specification for the T table with just two columns, c1 and c2. The varchar setting for c2 designates a width of 8,000 characters. This is the maximum discrete number of characters that you can specify without referencing max. Recall that designating max as a width for a varchar data type allows up to 2GB of characters in a single column.

The sample script contains two GO statements—one after conditionally dropping T and another after creating T. The GO statement can force the execution of a batch of T-SQL statements. The use of a GO statement is especially useful when some downstream statements require the completed execution of some upstream statements.

> **Note** GO is not a T-SQL statement itself. Instead, GO is an instruction to a query tool, such as sqlcmd or the graphical query tool for SSE based on SQL Server Management Studio, which you use to submit T-SQL statements for processing by SSE.

```
IF EXISTS(SELECT name FROM sys.tables
    WHERE name = 'T')
    DROP TABLE T
GO

CREATE TABLE T (
    c1 int,
    c2 varchar(8000)
)
GO
```

The bottom portion of the script in Ch04InsertToVarchar.sql attempts to insert two rows into the table (see the following code). The code declares a local variable, @v1, with a varchar(max) specification to hold a value for insertion into the c2 column in T. The script uses the @v1 local variable to attempt the insertion of two rows into T. When using this format for an INSERT statement, the correct syntax is to list values for all the columns in a table, which is T in this case. You list the column values for a row after the VALUES keyword in the order that they appear in the CREATE TABLE statement.

- The first @v1 value consists of 7,999 instances of A, generated with the REPLICATE function followed by a single instance of B. A concatenation operator (+) appends B to the end of the 7,999 instances of A. The attempt to insert a row with the first value of @v1 succeeds.

- The second @v1 value consists of the prior @v1 instance value with another B concatenated to the end for a total of 8,001 characters. The attempt to insert a row with the second value of @v1 fails because the @v1 local variable is too wide to fit in the c2 column of table T.

```
DECLARE @v1 varchar(max)

SET @v1 = REPLICATE('A',7999) + 'B'
INSERT T VALUES (1, @v1)
SELECT RIGHT(c2,2) 'Right 2 of c2' FROM T

SET @v1 = @v1 + 'B'
INSERT T VALUES (2, @v1)
SELECT RIGHT(c2,2) 'Right 2 of c2' FROM T
```

The listing from the SELECT statements after the two attempted inserts appears next. Notice the right two characters of the first row in T are A followed by B. The error message for the second attempt to insert a row explains that a column value must be truncated to fit in the table. This is because a value with 8,001 characters, the second @v1 instance, does not fit into a column specified for a maximum of 8,000 characters. Therefore, the last SELECT statement in the preceding script invokes the RIGHT function for the last valid c2 column value.

```
(1 row(s) affected)

Right 2 of c2
-------------
AB
(1 row(s) affected)
```

```
Msg 8152, Level 16, State 10, Line 9
String or binary data would be truncated.
The statement has been terminated.
Right 2 of c2
-------------
AB

(1 row(s) affected)
```

To accommodate the second row of input, the c2 column in table T needs a new data type specification. In particular, change varchar(8000) to varchar(max). This simple redesign of the table permits its c2 column to accept up to 2GB of characters. The following script from the top portion of Ch04InsertToVarcharMax.sql shows a CREATE TABLE statement with the modification for c2.

```
IF EXISTS(SELECT name FROM sys.tables
    WHERE name = 'T')
    DROP TABLE T
GO

CREATE TABLE T (
    c1 int,
    c2 varchar(max)
)
GO
```

The bottom portion of Ch04InsertToVarcharMax.sql attempts the same two inserts described for the earlier version of table T. However, in this case, both inserts succeed. The following listing shows the results. Notice, in particular, the two row values returned by the second SELECT statement. The two rightmost characters are AB for the first row and BB for the second row. The outcome for the second row reflects the successive concatenation on two occasions of B to a string starting out with 7,999 instances of A.

```
(1 row(s) affected)

Right 2 of c2
---------------------
AB

(1 row(s) affected)


(1 row(s) affected)


Right 2 of c2
---------------------
AB
BB

(2 row(s) affected)
```

Recovering Values from an Old Table for a New Table

All the prior table-creation samples dropped a previously existing version of a table with the same name as the new one to be created. This step ensures that a CREATE TABLE statement will not fail because of a previously existing table with the same name. However, dropping the table throws the data away along with the old design. What if you want the old data in a newly designed table? The sample in this section illustrates one approach to saving and reusing the data from an old version of a table in a newly designed table.

This sample creates yet another version of table T. The sample assumes that the old version of table T has some data that you want to reuse even if you have to redesign the table. In this case, the specification for c1 changes so that its data type has to be revised from int to bigint. This kind of change is common as the number of rows in a table grows beyond an original expectation. The sample in this section runs immediately after the script in Ch04InsertToVarcharMax.sql, which populates table T with a known set of values.

The following script from the top of Ch04CreateRecover.sql starts by checking if a table named T exists already. If there is a prior version of the table, the procedure uses the sp_rename system-stored procedure to rename the prior version to T_old. The sp_rename system-stored procedure cannot rename an object to an object that already exists in the database. Therefore, the script attempts to drop the T_old table with a DROP TABLE statement before invoking sp_rename. If the T_old table is not already there, the DROP TABLE statement generates an error message, but the rest of the script runs successfully. The CREATE TABLE statement illustrates the syntax for assigning the bigint data type to the c1 column.

```
IF EXISTS(SELECT name FROM sys.tables
    WHERE name = 'T')
    BEGIN
        PRINT 'T already.'
        DROP TABLE T_old
        EXEC sp_rename 'T', 'T_old'
    END
ELSE PRINT 'No T already.'

CREATE TABLE T (
    c1 bigint,
    c2 nvarchar(max)
)
```

The most significant advantage of the preceding script is that it saves the data from the prior version of table T in a new version of the T_old table. After the preceding CREATE TABLE statement creates a new version of table T, the table has no data. An INSERT statement for table T that selects rows from the T_old table can populate the new version of the T table with the data from the prior version of the T table. The following script from Ch04CreateRecover.sql illustrates how simple the syntax can be to accomplish this task. The script also includes a SELECT statement to confirm the copying of the row values.

```
INSERT T
SELECT * FROM T_old

SELECT c1, RIGHT(C2,2) 'Right 2 of c2' FROM T
```

The following listing confirms the operation of the code from Ch04CreateRecover.sql. As you can see, the script detected a prior version of T, and the sp_rename system-stored procedure issued a precaution about the impact of changing an object name that may have other objects dependent on it. Because we are creating a replacement version of table T, and our modification is very minor, the precaution does not apply in this case. The listing ends by showing the two rightmost characters from the first and second rows of the data copied to the new version of table T.

```
T already.
Caution: Changing any part of an object name could break
scripts and stored procedures.

(2 row(s) affected)
```

```
c1                   Right 2 of c2
-------------------- --------------
1                    AB
2                    BB

(2 row(s) affected)
```

> ■**Note** Another approach to modifying a table is to invoke the ALTER TABLE statement. Although the ALTER
> TABLE statement does facilitate many table modifications, it is not as flexible as the CREATE TABLE statement.
> In addition, you will always need the CREATE TABLE statement whenever you need to make a new table from
> scratch. When you are just starting out with T-SQL, there are many statements as well as syntactical and semantic
> issues to learn. My recommendation is that beginners should master the essential, general-purpose statements,
> such as CREATE TABLE, before investing their time in more specialized statements, such as ALTER TABLE. How-
> ever, as your skills and experience grow, I strongly recommend that you experiment with the ALTER TABLE
> statement.

Managing Data Integrity with Basic Constraints and Column Properties

Just as you can manage the data in a table by setting the data type for a column within a CREATE TABLE statement, you can also set column properties and basic constraints that help you control the data entering a table. This section introduces you to a popular subset of the constraints and column properties that you can apply to individual columns to manage the integrity of the data in a table.

- You can add a constraint to a column that determines whether SSE will reject new rows with a missing value for the column (by default, SSE accepts rows with missing data for any column).
- You can use the DEFAULT column property to designate a value to enter when no input is specified for a column.
- Designating a table's primary key constrains a column to reject null values, and a primary key designates columns that uniquely identify the rows in a table.
- The IDENTITY property can interact with the PRIMARY KEY phrase to simplify the setting of primary key values.

Inserting Data for a Subset of Table Columns

When you enter a new row into a table, you may not always have values available for every column in the row. Columns in a new row with no values at input time typically have null values; this is another way of saying the values for those columns are unknown or missing. Null values behave differently than other column values. The sample code for this section illustrates how you can generate null values and demonstrates some special handling procedures for null column values.

The following excerpt from the Ch04InsertWithMissingValues.sql file creates a table with five columns. The first four columns specify in order int, bit, varchar, and dec data types. The last column is a computed column whose value depends on the sum of the first and second columns with int and bit data types.

```
CREATE TABLE T (
    int1 int,
    bit1 bit,
    varchar1 varchar(3),
    dec1 dec(5,2),
    cmp1 AS (int1 + bit1)
)
```

You can think of a computed column as a virtual column that is not physically a part of the table. Unless you explicitly persist a computed column (with the PERSISTED keyword), SSE stores just the expression for the computed column values and automatically computes values for the column whenever they are needed. However, a persisted computed column is stored as actual column values that are updated when any of the inputs to an expression are revised.

A computed column value will be null if one or more of its inputs are null. In addition, arithmetic overflows or underflows can generate null values for a computed column even when none of its inputs are null. An overflow is an outcome that is larger than the biggest number that a data type can represent. Similarly, an underflow is smaller, or more negative, than a data type can denote.

■**Tip** You can ensure that a computed column never results in a null value by using the ISNULL function, which returns a constant instead of a null value. The general syntax for such an expression is ISNULL(computedcolumnexpression, constant).

The following excerpt from Ch04InsertWithMissingValues.sql inserts four rows into the T table resulting from the immediately preceding CREATE TABLE statement. Although there are five columns in the table, each INSERT statement specifies values for just two columns. Furthermore, the designated columns change from row to row. By the way, you never insert values for a computed column, such as the cmp1 column in table T, because its value is computed from other values. Notice that the INSERT statement, when used with the following format, has column names in parentheses immediately after the INSERT keyword. Values in a second set of parentheses after the VALUES keyword designate values for the new row in the order of the column names in the first set of parentheses.

```
INSERT T (int1, bit1) VALUES (1, 0)
INSERT T (int1, varchar1) VALUES (2, 'abc')
INSERT T (int1, dec1) VALUES (3, 5.25)
INSERT T (bit1, dec1) VALUES (1, 9.75)
```

So, the first INSERT statement inserts 1 into int1 and 0 into bit1, because of the order of the column names in the first set of parentheses and the order of values in the second set of parentheses.

The next excerpt from Ch04InsertWithMissingValues.sql shows some ways of extracting and processing table values some of which may be null.

- The first SELECT statement merely lists all column values for each row in the table. This will clearly show which column values have known values versus null values.

- The next SELECT statement counts all the rows in the T table.

- The third SELECT statement invokes the COUNT function for the values in the int1 column. Because aggregate functions, such as COUNT, do not process null values, the count reflects just rows with known values.

- Although the third SELECT statement *implicitly* filters null values with the COUNT function, the fourth SELECT statement *explicitly* filters null values as it counts just the rows with known values for the bit1 column. The IS NOT NULL phrase in the WHERE clause references exclusively known values.

- The fifth SELECT statement counts just the rows with null values for the bit1 column. The IS NULL phrase in the WHERE clause designates just unknown or missing values.

- The last SELECT statement invokes the AVG function to compute the average of values in the dec1 column. Because AVG is an aggregate function, it automatically ignores null vales. However, the AVG function can cast its output with different precision and scale settings than its input. The list in the SELECT statement applies the CAST function to ensure a return value with the same precision and scale settings for the dec1 column.

```
--All columns for all rows
SELECT * FROM T
GO

--Count all rows
SELECT COUNT(*) 'Rows in T'
FROM T

--Count int1 values (implicitly non-null)
SELECT COUNT(int1) 'int1 values in T'
FROM T

--Count non-null bit1 values
SELECT COUNT(*) 'Count of non-null bit1'
FROM T
WHERE bit1 IS NOT NULL

--Count null bit1 values
SELECT COUNT(*) 'Count of null bit1'
FROM T
WHERE bit1 IS NULL

--Average of dec1 values
SELECT CAST(AVG(dec1) AS dec(5,2)) 'Avg of dec1'
FROM T
WHERE dec1 IS NOT NULL
```

Running Ch04InsertWithMissingValues.sql generates a result listing like the following one.

- The first result set clearly identifies the null column values with the NULL keyword for each row within the T table.

- The second result set returns the count of all the rows in T.

- The third result set shows how many of the rows in T have a non-null int1 value.

- The fourth and fifth result sets display, respectively, the number of non-null and null column values in the bit1 column of T.

- The sixth result set presents the average across the non-null values in the dec1 column.

int1	bit1	varchar1	dec1	cmp1
1	0	NULL	NULL	1
2	NULL	abc	NULL	NULL
3	NULL	NULL	5.25	NULL
NULL	1	NULL	9.75	NULL

```
Rows in T
-----------
```

```
4

int1 values in T
----------------
3
Warning: Null value is eliminated by an aggregate or other SET operation.

Count of non-null bit1
----------------------
2

Count of null bit1
------------------
2

Avg of dec1
-----------
7.50
```

Not Allowing Null Values in a Column

As the preceding sample demonstrates, null values are permitted by default for columns with int, bit, varchar, and dec data types. The same default behavior applies to most other data types that do not have special settings to force the population of a column value. The timestamp data type is one exception that requires no special settings to avoid the possibility of a null value.

Some database applications require a known value for a column. For example, you may require users to say whether they smoke or not on a questionnaire for health insurance. Failing to answer the question can make it impossible to compute a life insurance rate estimate. In this kind of situation, you need a way to constrain the values within a column so that null values are not permitted.

The NOT NULL phrase on the line declaring a column in a CREATE TABLE statement causes a column's default behavior with respect to null values to change. When a column declaration includes NOT NULL, SSE rejects attempts to insert rows that have unknown values for the column. Inserts succeed when they specify a known value in the legitimate range for a column's data type.

The following excerpt from the Ch04NoBit1Nulls.sql file shows the syntax for specifying the NOT NULL constraint for a column with a bit data type. The same syntax applies to other data types. If you look back at the preceding sample, you'll recognize the CREATE TABLE statement as the same, except for the NOT NULL phrase on the bit1 column specification. Because of the NOT NULL constraint in the bit1 column specification, only INSERT statements with a bit1 column value of 0 or 1 succeed.

```
CREATE TABLE T (
    int1 int,
    bit1 bit NOT NULL,
    varchar1 varchar(3),
    dec1 dec(5,2),
    cmp1 AS (int1 + bit1)
)
```

The T-SQL code in Ch04NoBit1Nulls.sql is nearly identical to the code in Ch04InsertWithMissingValues.sql from the preceding sample. For example, the INSERT statements are exactly the same in both files. The two differences are the inclusion of the NOT NULL constraint for the bit1 column and the exclusion of all SELECT statements except for the first one in the Ch04NoBit1Nulls.sql. The first SELECT statement lists the column values for all rows in the table.

The following excerpt from the listing for running the script inCh04NoBit1Nulls.sql shows the rows that succeeded in entering table T. Notice that there are just two rows, although there are four INSERT statements (see the INSERT statements from the preceding sample). Each row of output includes a known value (0 or 1) for a bit data type in the bit1 column. The two omitted rows correspond to INSERT statements that did not specify a value for the bit1 column. This result confirms the impact of the NOT NULL constraint for the bit1 column in the preceding CREATE TABLE listing.

```
int1        bit1  varchar1 dec1 cmp1
----------- ----- -------- ---- ----
1           0     NULL     NULL 1
NULL        1     NULL     9.75 NULL
```

Designating Default Column Values

You can use the DEFAULT keyword in a column declaration to designate a default value for the column. If an INSERT statement or an UPDATE statement fails to specify a value for the column, then SSE assigns the DEFAULT value, instead of a null value, to the column in a new row.

Using a DEFAULT column property assignment makes sense when a null value has no meaning for a column, such as a column to designate whether a contract is signed and available for review. You can represent this type of column with a bit data type that is either 0 for not signed or not available, but 1 for signed and available. A null value makes no sense for this type of column (unless you assume it is possible to not know if a contract is signed and available for review).

A DEFAULT constraint can specify

• A constant, such as a constant value equal to a number or a sequence of characters

• A function's return value, such as the GETDATE() function to return the current date and time

• A SQL-92 niladic function, which can supply either the current user's name or the current date and time

• NULL, which is not necessary because data column values are null by default

You specify a column's default value by following the DEFAULT keyword in the column's declaration with a constant, built-in function, a niladic function, or another keyword (NULL). The SQL-92 niladic CURRENT_TIMESTAMP function and the built-in GETDATE() function both return the current date and time. Four different SQL-92 niladic functions return the user account name for the current user: CURRENT_USER, SESSION_USER, SYSTEM_USER, and USER.

■**Note** You can also specify default values independently of column declarations and bind the default values to columns in one or more tables. This capability will be removed from future versions of SQL Server, including its SSE edition. Therefore, you should use the DEFAULT constraint whenever possible.

Assign Zeroes Instead of Null Values

The Ch04NullToZero.sql file illustrates how to define a default value for a bit column that represents missing values as zeroes rather than the default of null values. The CREATE TABLE statement from the file shows the syntax for the DEFAULT keyword. There is no need for any parentheses after the DEFAULT keyword to designate the constant value (0).

```
CREATE TABLE T (
    int1 int,
    bit1 bit NOT NULL DEFAULT 0,
    varchar1 varchar(3),
    dec1 dec(5,2),
    cmp1 AS (int1 + bit1)
)
```

The script in NullToZero.sql includes the same four INSERT statements and the first SELECT statement from Ch04InsertWithMissingValues.sql. When you run these statements after the preceding CREATE TABLE statement, the following listing appears. All four rows appear in the output from the SELECT statement. The DEFAULT 0 constraint for the bit1 column in the CREATE TABLE statement assigns a value of 0 to rows with a missing value—namely, the second and third rows. The NOT NULL constraint is not strictly necessary because the DEFAULT constraint overrides it, but the inclusion of the NOT NULL phrase does not cause a compilation error.

■**Note** If you have prior experience with earlier versions of SQL Server, you may be familiar with severity levels for errors. Error levels are reported after one or more batches of T-SQL statements run; the error level numbers tell you that something went wrong and how severe it is after the T-SQL code runs. The SSE query tool based on SQL Server Management Studio introduces the notion of a compilation error for T-SQL code. A compilation error is detected by the SSE query tool before batch statements run. The query tool marks lines with syntax or semantic errors. As noted, the NOT NULL and DEFAULT 0 column properties for constraining bit1 column values do not conflict with one another. However, replacing NOT NULL with NULL in the Ch04InsertWithMissingValues.sql file generates a compilation error because a column cannot have a default value of zero and allow null values. If you change NOT NULL to NULL, the SSE query tool marks the changed line.

```
int1        bit1  varchar1 dec1 cmp1
----------- ----- -------- ---- -----------
1           0     NULL     NULL 1
2           0     abc      NULL 2
3           0     NULL     5.25 3
NULL        1     NULL     9.75 NULL

Command(s) completed successfully.
```

Assigning the Current User, Date, and Time

It is often desirable to track the user, date, and time associated with changes to the rows in a database. The following demonstration from WhoWhenDefaults.sql tracks who made the last change to a row and when the user either inserted or modified the row. The DEFAULT property used along with the USER and CURRENT_TIMESTAMP SQL-92 niladic functions can help you store this kind of information in a table. The demonstration also contrasts the datetime return value from the CURRENT_TIMESTAMP function with a timestamp data type value. Recall that the timestamp data type adds a binary(8) number to a row rather than datetime data type.

The following excerpt from WhoWhenDefaults.sql creates a table with five columns.

- The first two columns have int and bit data types along with constraints, borrowed from the preceding sample, for the bit1 column.

- The declaration for the third column shows how to assign a name (rvr1) to a timestamp column. With the current declaration syntax, you can replace timestamp with rowversion. The designation of a name for a timestamp column is optional. If you do not explicitly specify a name, SSE uses the default name of timestamp for the column. Unlike the timestamp data type, the rowversion data type requires a column name in its declaration.

- The fourth column's declaration assigns the return value from the USER function to the usr1 column. The USER function returns the name of the current user, which is a user account. SQL Server Express represents user account names with a sysname data type that you can store in a column with an nvarchar(128) data type.

- The last column's declaration stores the date and time for a change in a datetime format. The CURRENT_TIMESTAMP function returns this value.

```
CREATE TABLE T (
    int1 int,
    bit1 bit NOT NULL DEFAULT 0,
    rvr1 timestamp,
    usr1 nvarchar(128) DEFAULT USER,
    createtime datetime DEFAULT CURRENT_TIMESTAMP
)
```

The following excerpt from WhoWhenDefaults.sql inserts three rows into the T table at 1-second intervals. The two WAITFOR statements generate 1-second delays between the INSERT statements. Without the delays, it is possible for SSE to insert more than one row within a single datetime instance. You will not normally program delays when inserting rows, but using them in this context helps to clarify the values returned by the CURRENT_TIMESTAMP function.

```
INSERT T (int1) VALUES (1)
WAITFOR DELAY '00:00:01'
INSERT T (int1, bit1) VALUES (2, 0)
WAITFOR DELAY '00:00:01'
INSERT T (int1, bit1) VALUES (3, 1)
```

The last code excerpt from WhoWhenDefaults.sql in the following code listing starts by listing the values in T generated by the preceding INSERT statements with a SELECT statement. The fourth item in the SELECT list uses a CONVERT function to represent the binary(8) value generated by the timestamp data type as an integer. Next, an UPDATE statement revises the bit1 column value to 1 for the row with an int1 column value of 2 (this is the second row). This bit1 column value is set to 0 by the preceding codeblock. The concluding SELECT statement lists the T values after the revision of the bit1 column value.

```
SELECT int1, bit1, usr1,
    CONVERT(int, rvr1) 'Timestamp as int',
    createtime
FROM T
GO

UPDATE T
set bit1 = 1
WHERE int1 = 2
GO
```

```
SELECT int1, bit1, usr1,
    CONVERT(int, rvr1) 'Timestamp as int',
    createtime
FROM T
GO
```

An excerpt from the result listing for running the script in WhoWhenDefaults.sql appears next.

- SQL Server Express generates the first result set from the first SELECT statement immediately after the INSERT statements.
  - Notice that the timestamp values increase by a single integer value from one row to the next. The actual values start at 3104 and end at 3106.
  - In contrast, the createtime column, which results from the CURRENT_TIMESTAMP function, increases by about 1 second for each successive row.
  - The usr1 column values reflect the return value from the USER function. I ran the script as the dbo user.
- SQL Server Express generates the second result set after invoking the UPDATE statement, which changes the bit1 column value for the row with an int1 value of 2.
  - Notice that this second result set has a new value for the timestamp column as well as the bit1 column in the second row. The new timestamp column value is 3107.
  - Also, notice that the createtime column value does not change. This distinction between the timestamp and createtime columns results from the fact that the CURRENT_TIMESTAMP function in the CREATE TABLE statement only operates when SQL Server Express inserts a new row in the table, but the timestamp column receives a new value whenever a row is initially inserted as well as for each subsequent row update.

```
int1  bit1  usr1  Timestamp as int createtime
----- ----- ----- ---------------- -----------------------
1     0     dbo   3104             2005-04-02 18:57:03.227
2     0     dbo   3105             2005-04-02 18:57:04.230
3     1     dbo   3106             2005-04-02 18:57:05.290
int1  bit1  usr1  Timestamp as int createtime
----- ----- ----- ---------------- -----------------------
1     0     dbo   3104             2005-04-02 18:57:03.227
2     1     dbo   3107             2005-04-02 18:57:04.230
3     1     dbo   3106             2005-04-02 18:57:05.290
```

Designating a Column as a Primary Key

Primary key values provide a basis for uniquely identifying each row within a table. Use the PRIMARY KEY phrase in a column declaration to designate the column as the primary key for a table. A table can have only one primary key, which can be based on a single column or a set of columns. The values in a primary key column must

- Be unique for each row in the table
- Not be null for any row in the table

The primary key depends on an index created by SSE. This index can be clustered or nonclustered. Clustered indexes process faster than nonclustered indexes in the same way that columns with indexes process faster that columns without indexes. SQL Server Express permits 250 indexes per table. Only one table index can be clustered—that is, have rows arranged in storage according to the order of the index values. You can use the CLUSTERED keyword in a column declaration to make the index for a column clustered. However, the PRIMARY KEY phrase makes the index for a primary key clustered by default unless

- There is already a clustered index for another column in the table.
- You include the NONCLUSTERED keyword in the primary key's column declaration.

Note The PRIMARY KEY phrase defines a constraint that restricts the values in the columns defining a primary key to conform to the rules of a primary key, which include uniquely defining a table's rows and not allowing null values. The UNIQUE constraint is another type of constraint that allows the specification of unique values across the rows of a table. UNIQUE constraint columns are independent of PRIMARY KEY constraint columns. In addition, a table can only have one PRIMARY KEY constraint, but it can have multiple UNIQUE constraints.

It is frequently recommended that you assign an integer data type to a primary key column. The smallest possible data type with enough distinct values for the rows in the table is the best choice for optimizing performance. Legitimate data types for a primary key column include tinyint, smallint, int, bigint, and dec(p, 0). When you use an integer data type for a primary key column, you can further reduce the possibility for erroneous data by designating an IDENTITY property for the primary key column.

On the one hand, IDENTITY values are a relatively easy way of generating a unique value for every row in a table; recall that IDENTITY values are automatically generated. On the other hand, IDENTITY values have no structural relation to the other column values. If the natural primary key for a table is defined by multiple columns, you may frequently improve performance by using an IDENTITY column as the primary key instead.

- Some developers prefer the performance and automatic generation benefits of IDENTITY values.
- Other developers prefer to use meaningful column values to define a primary key even if the use of multiple columns negatively impacts performance.
- For a relatively small table of several hundred to a few thousand rows, performance differences rarely have a significant performance impact. As the rows in a table grow, performance tuning becomes more critical.

Using the PRIMARY KEY Phrase

The following excerpt from the Ch04UsingPrimaryKey.sql file shows how simple it is to include a PRIMARY KEY phrase in a column declaration. No additional constraints apply to the int1 column, but SSE treats the column as if it had both NOT NULL and UNIQUE constraints. The bit1 column is the only other column in the table. This column has a NOT NULL and its DEFAULT property set.

```
CREATE TABLE T (
    int1 int PRIMARY KEY,
    bit1 bit NOT NULL DEFAULT 0
)
```

The next excerpt from Ch04UsingPrimaryKey.sql includes five INSERT statements for the table created with the preceding CREATE TABLE index.

- The first three INSERT statements are valid because they contain unique int1 column values.

- The fourth INSERT statement has a missing int1 column value. Because int1 serves as the primary key for the table, the missing value causes the rejection of the whole row.

- The fifth INSERT statement specifies an int1 column value of 3, but the third INSERT statement previously added a row to the table with this value. Therefore, SSE rejects the row for the fifth INSERT statement because it has a duplicate primary key value.

```
INSERT T (int1, bit1) VALUES (1, 1)
INSERT T (int1, bit1) VALUES (2, 0)
INSERT T (int1) VALUES (3)
INSERT T (bit1) VALUES (1)
INSERT T (int1, bit1) VALUES (3,1)
```

The following listing shows the result of running the script in Ch04UsingPrimaryKey.sql. A SELECT statement for all the column values in each row within the table created by the preceding CREATE TABLE statement generates the following output (SELECT * FROM T). The first three INSERT statements succeed. Before the result set for the SELECT statement, you can see error messages returned by SSE. These error messages explain why two of the INSERT statements did not succeed.

```
Msg 515, Level 16, State 2, Line 8
Cannot insert the value NULL into column 'int1', table
'ProSSEAPPSCh04.dbo.T'; column does not allow nulls.
INSERT fails.The statement has been terminated.
Msg 2627, Level 14, State 1, Line 9
Violation of PRIMARY KEY constraint 'PK__T__145C0A3F'.
Cannot insert duplicate key in object 'dbo.T'.
The statement has been terminated.
int1        bit1
----------- -----
1           1
2           0
3           0
```

Using the IDENTITY Column Property

It is common to specify an IDENTITY property for a column with an integer data type that serves as a primary key. The IDENTITY property causes SSE to assign sequential column values starting from a seed value in fixed increments. Although the default seed and increment values for the IDENTITY keyword are both 1, you can override either or both. To change the default seed and increment settings, merely specify IDENTITY(seedvalue, incrementvalue) instead of IDENTITY.

When a column has an IDENTITY property setting, users do not have to specify a value for a column during the insertion of a new row because SSE automatically assigns a column value. If you attempt to insert a column value for a column with an IDENTITY property setting, SQL Server rejects the row by default. When you include an IDENTITY property setting for a column serving as the primary key, you do not have to worry about duplicate values because SQL Server automatically specifies sequentially unique values.

■**Tip** The IDENTITY property applies only to columns that have an integer data type. You cannot use it with columns that have a char or varchar data type.

The following excerpt from Ch04UsingIDENTITY.sql demonstrates the syntax for specifying an IDENTITY property for the int1 column. By not explicitly designating seed or increment values, the statement accepts the default value of 1 for both. The int1 column also serves as the table's primary key, and it has an int data type. The bit1 column has a bit data type with a NOT NULL constraint and its DEFAULT property set to 0.

```
CREATE TABLE T (
    int1 int IDENTITY PRIMARY KEY,
    bit1 bit NOT NULL DEFAULT 0
)
```

The next excerpt from Ch04UsingIDENTITY.sql shows three valid INSERT statements for the table generated by the CREATE TABLE in the sample file and one invalid INSERT statement.

- The first two statements merely assign values to the bit1 column.

- The third statement shows the syntax for not specifying any column values. The DEFAULT VALUES phrase in the INSERT statement tells SSE to use the default value for bit1. This is legitimate in this case because

    - int1 has an IDENTITY property setting, which causes its column values to be assigned by SSE.

    - bit1 has its DEFAULT property set to 0, which does not conflict with the column's NOT NULL constraint.

- The fourth INSERT statement fails because it attempts to assign a value to int1, which has an IDENTITY property. SQL Server Express does not by default permit a client application to set a value for an IDENTITY column.

```
INSERT T (bit1) VALUES (1)
INSERT T (bit1) VALUES (0)
INSERT T DEFAULT VALUES
INSERT T (int1, bit1) VALUES (4,1)
```

The following listing shows the result of running the script in Ch04UsingIDENTITY.sql, which ends with SELECT * FROM T. Notice that the int1 column values start at one and increment by one for each valid row through three. An error message before the result set explains the problem with the fourth INSERT statement: that while it is technically possible to insert a value to a column with an IDENTITY property, IDENTITY_INSERT must be set to ON. By default, IDENTITY_INSERT is set to OFF.

Tip The syntax for turning IDENTITY_INSERT on is SET IDENTITY_INSERT databasename.schemaname. tablename ON. The syntax for restoring IDENTITY_INSERT's default status is SET IDENTITY_INSERT databasename.schemaname.tablename OFF. Specifying databasename and .schemaname qualifiers for the tablename argument is optional. While IDENTITY_INSERT is ON, you enable the insertion of values to the IDENTITY column for only one table in a database—namely, the tablename argument value.

```
Msg 544, Level 16, State 1, Line 9
Cannot insert explicit value for identity column in
table 'T' when IDENTITY_INSERT is set to OFF.
int1        bit1
----------- -----
1           1
2           0
3           0
```

Managing Data Integrity with Sophisticated Constraints

Constraining the values that can enter a table improves the ease of using a table by ensuring high-quality data in a table. For example, by not allowing nulls into some or all columns of a table, your queries for a table do not have to account for the existence of null values. In addition, a PRIMARY KEY constraint for a column guarantees that you cannot have duplicate values in that column of a table.

This section presents additional concepts and samples in three areas to help you manage the integrity of the data in your tables.

- First, you learn about CHECK constraints. This flexible type of constraint can set limits on what specific values and patterns for values are valid for a table.

- Second, this section presents the syntax and demonstrates solutions for creating constraints that are at the table level instead of being a part of the declaration for a single column. A table-level constraint allows you to manage your data across multiple columns within a table.

- The third and concluding topic for this section drills down on FOREIGN KEY constraints. Just as a primary key helps to manage data integrity for a single table, a foreign key facilitates the management of data integrity between a pair of tables.

Using CHECK Constraints

When you write a column CHECK constraint for a specific column, you can limit the range of values and pattern of values for that column. The logic behind a CHECK constraint within a column is very simple.

- A Boolean expression specifies a condition for the insertion of values in the column.

- If the condition evaluates to True, the new value is valid.

- If the condition evaluates to False, the new value is invalid.

Any table can have multiple CHECK constraints. When the values in a row are valid for all constraints, SSE inserts the row in a table. If one or more values within a row fail to pass a constraint, SSE issues an error message describing the problem for the first failed constraint. The error message helps to guide users to refine their input so that it is valid for resubmitting to the table. Additional resubmittals may uncover other constraints for which the data are not valid.

There are two syntax conventions for adding a CHECK constraint to a column declaration in a CREATE TABLE statement. The easiest way to add a CHECK constraint is to follow the CHECK keyword with a Boolean expression. Insert the keyword and expression in the column declaration for which you want to constrain values. With this approach, SSE assigns a default name for the constraint that appears in error messages.

A second approach to declaring a CHECK constraint within a column allows you to assign a custom name for a constraint that will appear in error messages. A custom name will define the purpose for a constraint more precisely than the default name that SSE assigns. Custom constraint names can make it easier for users to determine how to fix their input so that it is valid. You can assign a custom name by preceding the CHECK keyword with CONSTRAINT followed by the custom name for the constraint.

Blocking Empty and Missing Character Input

The Ch04CheckTooShort.sql file includes a script for verifying that varchar data type values do not contain an empty string (' '). The CREATE TABLE statement in the script demonstrates the two syntax conventions for declaring a CHECK constraint within a column. The following CREATE TABLE statement from the file declares three columns.

- The first column serves as the primary key for the table. This column has an int data type with an IDENTITY property and a PRIMARY KEY constraint.

- The second column (vch1) illustrates the approach to defining a CHECK constraint where SQL Server Express assigns a default name to the constraint. The Boolean expression following the CHECK keyword uses the LEN function to specify that the number of characters in the vch1 column must be greater than 0.

- The declaration for the third column (vch2) demonstrates the syntax for assigning a custom name to a constraint. The name for the CHECK constraint for the vch2 column is CK_LEN_TOO_SHORT.

```
CREATE TABLE T (
    int1 int IDENTITY PRIMARY KEY,
    vch1 varchar(5)
        CHECK (LEN(vch1) > 0),
    vch2 varchar(5)
        CONSTRAINT CK_LEN_TOO_SHORT
        CHECK (LEN(vch2) > 0)
)
```

The following four INSERT statements from Ch04CheckTooShort.sql test the CHECK constraints in the preceding CREATE TABLE statement.

- The first statement inputs a row with valid vch1 and vch2 column values.

- The second and third statements input rows with invalid values for the vch1 and vch2 columns, respectively.

- The last INSERT statement highlights an issue that the CHECK constraints are not optimized to address, that is, the entry of rows with null values for vch1 or vch2. If you want to block zero-length strings (' '), chances are you also want to block null values. However, the CHECK constraints for the vch1 and vch2 columns do not block the input of null values.

```
INSERT T (vch1, vch2) VALUES('a','b')
INSERT T (vch1, vch2) VALUES('','b')
INSERT T (vch1, vch2) VALUES('a','')
INSERT T DEFAULT VALUES
```

An excerpt from the listing for running the script in Ch04CheckTooShort.sql appears next. The listing results from running SELECT * FROM T at the end of the script. Notice that SSE automatically assigns the name CK_T_1B0907CE to the CHECK constraint for the vch1 column. This name by itself is not too informative. In contrast, the CHECK constraint in the vch2 column declaration assigns a name (CK_LEN_TOO_SHORT) that conveys the meaning of the constraint (the length of the input is too short). An informative constraint name can make detecting and fixing erroneous input easier and faster.

```
Msg 547, Level 16, State 0, Line 3
The INSERT statement conflicted with the CHECK constraint
"CK__T__vch1__1B0907CE". The conflict occurred in database
"ProSSEAPPSCh04", table "dbo.T", column 'vch1'.
The statement has been terminated.
Msg 547, Level 16, State 0, Line 4
The INSERT statement conflicted with the CHECK constraint
"CK_LEN_TOO_SHORT". The conflict occurred in database
"ProSSEAPPSCh04", table "dbo.T", column 'vch2'.
The statement has been terminated.
(1 row(s) affected)

int1        vch1  vch2
----------- ----- -----
1           a     b
4           NULL  NULL
```

Notice from the preceding output that a CHECK constraint for a string need not have an impact on the input of null values (the second row contains two null values). If you want to block null values as well as zero-length strings (' '), just insert the NOT NULL phrase in the declaration for a column. The following CREATE TABLE statement from Ch04CheckTooShortNotNull.sql illustrates the syntax for column declarations that block null values as well as zero-length strings (' ').

```
CREATE TABLE T (
    int1 int IDENTITY PRIMARY KEY,
    vch1 varchar(5)
        CHECK (LEN(vch1) > 0)
        NOT NULL,
    vch2 varchar(5)
        CONSTRAINT CK_LEN_TOO_SHORT
        CHECK (LEN(vch2) > 0)
        NOT NULL
)
```

When you attempt to run the preceding four INSERT statements for the version of table T in Ch04CheckTooShortNotNull.sql, the final result set contains just one row (the one with values of a and b for vch1 and vch2). This outcome indicates that the addition of the NOT NULL phrase to the vch1 and vch2 column declarations blocks the entry of null values. For the specific input designated by the fourth INSERT statement, the NOT NULL phrase in the vch1 column blocks the input from the last INSERT statement. The NOT NULL phrase in the vch2 column declaration does not become active because the constraint blocking nulls for the vch1 column takes effect first.

Specifying a Pattern for Character Input

One of the special advantages that CHECK constraints provide is the ability to limit the characters that can appear in a column as well as just the number of characters for a column. Using the LIKE operator with a pattern expression in a CHECK constraint provides a flexible means of validating character input for a column. Because numbers, such as five-digit U.S. zip codes and part "numbers," are often stored as characters, this approach can be very flexible.

You can designate patterns in the following ways:

- One character at a time in square brackets ([character])
- As starting (characters%) or ending (%characters) with one or more characters
- By denoting one or several individual wildcard characters (_) within a sequence of fixed or other wildcard characters (characters_characters)

Besides designating which characters should appear, you can even write pattern expressions to designate which characters should not appear by using a preceding caret symbol (^). You can also denote a range of values for a single character by an expression within square brackets ([beginningcharacter-endingcharacter]).

Here's a list that demonstrates some pattern expressions with selected values that match the expression from the CustomerID column in the Customers table of the Northwind database.

- LIKE 'A%': ALFKI, ANATR, ANTON, AROUT
- LIKE '[A-B][L-N]%': ALFKI, ANATR, ANTON, BLAUS, BLONP
- LIKE 'A%' OR LIKE '%A': ALFKI, ANATR, ANTON, AROUT, FAMIA, FISSA, HILAA, MAGAA, SAVEA, WOLZA
- LIKE '[A-D]___[E-R]': ALFKI, ANATR, ANTON, BLONP, BONAP, BOTTM, COMMI, CONSH, DUMON
- LIKE '[A-D]___[^E-R]': AROUT, BERGS, BLAUS, BOLID, BSFEV, CACTU, CENTC, CHOPS, DRACD

The following CREATE TABLE statement from the Ch04CheckZipPattern.sql file verifies five-digit zip codes with two constraints.

- First, a CHECK constraint verifies that
  - The length of each zip code column value (psc1) has a length of exactly five characters.
  - Each of the characters in a psc1 value is a number character from 0 through 9.
- Second, a NOT NULL phrase adds a second constraint to restrict the input of rows with a null psc1 value.

```
CREATE TABLE T (
    int1 int IDENTITY PRIMARY KEY,
    vch1 varchar(5)
        CHECK (LEN(vch1) > 0)
        NOT NULL,
    vch2 varchar(5)
        CONSTRAINT CK_LEN_TOO_SHORT
        CHECK (LEN(vch2) > 0)
        NOT NULL
)
```

The following set of four INSERT statements generates just one valid row for the table defined by the preceding CREATE TABLE:

- The first statement successfully adds a row to the table.
- The second statement fails the CHECK constraint because its length is four, instead of five, characters.
- The third statement fails because its first character (r) is not a numeric character from 0 through 9.
- The fourth statement fails because it attempts to insert a null value into the psc1 column; a null value is the default value for most columns that do not have a DEFAULT property set to another value.

```
INSERT T (psc1) VALUES('40222')
INSERT T (psc1) VALUES('4022')
INSERT T (psc1) VALUES('r0222')
INSERT T DEFAULT VALUES
```

Using Multicolumn Constraints

It is sometimes convenient to define constraints across more than one column.

- One obvious reason for a multicolumn constraint is when you need to specify a primary key based on two or more columns, instead of just a single column. You'll need a multicolumn primary key whenever it takes two or more columns to uniquely specify any particular table row.

- In addition, the CHECK constraints discussed in the "Specifying a Pattern for Character Input" section apply to just one column, but some database modeling efforts require constraints specified by two or more table columns. For example, your application may approve an order amount column value over a fixed limit only if another column indicates the name of an approving manager.

Multicolumn constraints are sometimes referred to as table constraints because they are not bound to a single column. In fact, the syntax for declaring a multicolumn constraint applies to the table level. As you have seen, the CREATE TABLE statement comma delimits the specification for each column. This syntax declares each column at the table level—not within another column of the table. After specifying all the columns for a table within a CREATE TABLE statement, you can use commas to delimit additional specifications for each constraint that you want to apply to an overall table instead of one specific column.

■**Note** Multicolumn primary keys can be clustered or nonclustered just like single-column primary keys. The ordering of rows on the storage device for clustered multicolumn keys applies to the primary key index—not to any one column defining the index. You can designate a clustered multicolumn primary key by specifying the termed CLUSTERED immediately after the PRIMARY KEY phrase. You can optionally replace the CLUSTERED keyword by the NONCLUSTERED keyword for a nonclustered primary key. The syntax for a clustered primary key index is: CONSTRAINT PK_Name PRIMARY KEY CLUSTERED (Col1_Name, Col2_Name).

Using a Multicolumn Primary Key

Multicolumn primary keys are common in tables that connect two other tables in a many-to-many relationship. A classic many-to-many relationship is the relationship of students and classes. Any one student can register for multiple classes. Most classes have multiple students. A table for storing student grades across multiple classes can have at least three columns. One column can identify the class, such as a ClassID number. A second column can identify individual students with another number, such as StudentID. A third column can store the grade for the student in the class.

The CH04PKStudentGrades.sql file shows the syntax for defining a multicolumn primary key in a table called ClassGrades. The CREATE TABLE for the table follows.

- The ClassID and StudentID columns each have an int data type.

- The GradeLetter column stores grades. This column has a varchar(2) type. The first character of the GradeLetter column denotes a letter for the grade, and the second column optionally records a + or – for grades such as A+ or A–.

- The name for the primary key constraint is PK_ClassGrades. The two columns defining the primary key are ClassID and StudentID. Notice the declaration for this constraint appears at the same level as the column declarations.

```
CREATE TABLE ClassGrades(
    ClassID int,
    StudentID int,
    GradeLetter varchar(2),
    Constraint PK_ClassGrades
        PRIMARY KEY(ClassID, StudentID)
)
```

The following three INSERT statements attempt to add three new rows to the ClassGrades table.

- The first statement adds a grade of A for the student with a StudentID of 1 in the class with a ClassID of 1.

- The second statement adds a grade of B– for another student with a StudentID of 2 in the same class as the first student.

- The third INSERT statement designates a grade of C– for a student in the class with a ClassID of 1. This statement does not specify a value for StudentID. Because StudentID is a part of the table's primary key, SSE automatically imposes a NOT NULL constraint for the column. As a result of the missing value for StudentID, the third INSERT statement fails and does not add a new row.

```
INSERT ClassGrades VALUES(1,1,'A')
INSERT ClassGrades VALUES(1,2,'B-')
INSERT ClassGrades (ClassID, GradeLetter)
VALUES(1,'C-')
```

An excerpt from the listing for running the script in CH04PKStudentGrades.sql describes the error message for the null value for StudentID in the third INSERT statement. Then, the listing enumerates the two rows added to the ClassGrades table. The statement generating the following output is SELECT * FROM ClassGrades.

```
Msg 515, Level 16, State 2, Line 4
Cannot insert the value NULL into column 'StudentID',
table 'ProSSEAPPSCh04.dbo.ClassGrades'; column does not
allow nulls. INSERT fails.
The statement has been terminated.
ClassID     StudentID    GradeLetter
----------- ------------ -----------
1           1            A
1           2            B-
```

Using a Multicolumn CHECK Constraint

A CHECK constraint can also have multiple columns. In the context of the ClassGrades table, you can specify a set of valid letter grades and a range of valid integer values to denote classes. Rows with GradeLetter values outside the letter range or ClassID values outside of scope of valid numbers for classes can be rejected by a CHECK constraint.

The following CREATE TABLE statement is from the Ch04CheckPKStudentGrades.sql file. The file's contents are exactly the same as for the CREATE TABLE statement in the preceding sample, except for one constraint.

- The new constraint is the CK_GradeLetter_ClassID CHECK constraint at the end of the statement. Notice the new constraint is comma delimited from the preceding PRIMARY KEY constraint.

- The CHECK constraint has two expressions for restricting the content in two columns.

  - The first expression designates the range of legitimate letters for grades in the GradeLetter column, namely, A–F.

  - The second expression indicates that the most positive ClassID value is less than 1,000, namely, 999.

  - An AND operator joins the two expressions so that the data for a new row must comply with both expressions to be valid data according to the CK_GradeLetter_ClassID CHECK constraint.

```
CREATE TABLE ClassGrades(
    ClassID int,
    StudentID int,
    GradeLetter varchar(2),
    Constraint PK_ClassGrades
        PRIMARY KEY(ClassID, StudentID),
    Constraint CK_GradeRange_ClassID
        CHECK (LEFT(UPPER(GradeLetter),1)
        LIKE '[A-F]' AND ClassID < 1000)
)
```

The following set of five INSERT statements attempt to add five new rows, but only three attempts succeed. The third and fourth INSERT statements fail.

- The third statement fails because its GradeLetter value (V–) has a letter outside of the bounds for legitimate letter grades (A–F).

- The fourth statement fails because its ClassID value (1001) is greater than the upper limit for ClassID values (999).

```
INSERT ClassGrades VALUES(1, 1, 'C+')
INSERT ClassGrades VALUES(1, 2, 'A+')
INSERT ClassGrades VALUES(1, 3, 'V-')
INSERT ClassGrades VALUES(1001, 1, 'A')
INSERT ClassGrades VALUES(999, 2, 'A')
```

Using Foreign Key Constraints

A foreign key constraint is one or more columns in a secondary table that points at corresponding columns in a primary table. For example, if Classes was a primary table, then a secondary table could be ClassGrades. The secondary table, ClassGrades, can use its ClassID column to point back at the ClassID column in the Classes table. Any secondary table can point at multiple primary tables, and therefore have multiple foreign keys. For example, the ClassGrades secondary table can also point at a Students primary table.

SQL Server Express enforces referential integrity by maintaining consistent values in the FOREIGN KEY columns of a secondary table and the PRIMARY KEY columns or the UNIQUE constraint columns of the primary table. Referential integrity rules restrict

- Column values in FOREIGN KEY columns to those that match values in the corresponding columns of the primary table
- The revision or deletion of column values in a primary table that will orphan rows in a secondary table

You can use a FOREIGN KEY constraint to designate a relationship between columns in a secondary table that points at columns that are a PRIMARY KEY or UNIQUE constraint in a primary table. SQL Server Express permits the declaration of FOREIGN KEY constraints at the column and table level. A table-level declaration of a FOREIGN KEY constraint is essential when a single foreign key extends across multiple columns. However, table-level declarations for single-column foreign keys can also improve the readability of the declarations for the associated columns.

Foreign keys optionally allow the specification of rules to define how foreign key columns in a secondary table will change when corresponding column values in the primary table are updated or deleted. To designate how the secondary table can change in response to updates and deletes in the primary table, you need to include the ON UPDATE or ON DELETE phrases in the FOREIGN KEY constraint declaration. Follow the ON UPDATE or ON DELETE keyword with a keyword to specify the action you wish to happen.

- The default rule prohibits changes to a primary table that require a corresponding change in a secondary table. In other words, the default rule allows "no action" to the primary table that requires a corresponding change to the secondary table. You can optionally specify the NO ACTION phrase to designate the default rule. In fact, ON UPDATE and ON DELETE are not necessary when the default action is acceptable.

- CASCADE extends the action for a row in the primary table to the corresponding rows in the secondary table.

  - CASCADE after ON DELETE causes the deletion of rows in a secondary table that correspond to a deleted row in a primary table.

  - CASCADE after ON UPDATE causes the revision of foreign key values after matching column values are updated in a primary table.

- SET NULL causes foreign key column values to be set to null values when updates or deletes occur to matching values in a primary table.

- SET DEFAULT causes foreign key column values to equal their DEFAULT property setting when updates or deletes occur to matching values in a primary table.

Supporting Basic Referential Integrity with Foreign Keys

Foreign keys tightly link and synchronize a pair of tables through referential integrity. Unless you enable an action through a FOREIGN KEY constraint on the secondary table, you may not be able to perform the action on the primary table. This section systematically explores the barriers to actions. It also demonstrates how you can enable actions on both primary and secondary tables tied together by referential integrity.

The Ch04FKClassesClassGrades.sql file contains a lengthy script that illustrates the operation of referential integrity. The script works with two tables—a primary table and a secondary table. The primary table, named Classes, holds data about classes, including ClassID and ClassTitle. The following excerpt from Ch04FKClassesClassGrades.sql shows the syntax for creating Classes. Notice especially the PRIMARY KEY constraint specified in the ClassID column declaration. Recall that a primary table must have either a PRIMARY KEY or UNIQUE constraint.

```
CREATE TABLE Classes(
    ClassID int PRIMARY KEY,
    ClassTitle varchar(50)
)
```

The secondary table, named ClassGrades created in Ch04FKClassesClassGrades.sql, contains data about student grades in classes, including ClassID, StudentID, and GradeLetter. The CREATE TABLE statement for ClassGrades appears in the following code listing.

- The secondary table contains a FOREIGN KEY constraint.

- The REFERENCES keyword in the ClassId column declares the FOREIGN KEY constraint within the column. The REFERENCES clause ties the ClassID column in the ClassGrades table to the ClassID column in the Classes table.

- The CASCADE keyword after the ON UPDATE phrase allows updates for ClassID values in the Classes table to propagate to corresponding rows in the ClassGrades table. In effect, changes to the primary table cascade to the secondary table.

- The ClassID column in ClassGrades also participates in a PRIMARY KEY constraint for the secondary table declared at the end of the CREATE TABLE statement.

```
CREATE TABLE ClassGrades(
    ClassID int REFERENCES Classes(ClassID)
        ON UPDATE CASCADE,
    StudentID int,
    GradeLetter varchar(2),
    Constraint PK_ClassGrades
        PRIMARY KEY(ClassID, StudentID)
)
```

■**Note** Referential integrity can have an impact on the order in which operations can be performed. Several examples in the book illustrate this point. Additional comments in the script within Ch04FKClassesClassGrades.sql have useful hints about the order in which operations can be performed. For example, after you bind a secondary table to a primary table with a FOREIGN KEY constraint, you cannot drop the primary table until you first drop the secondary table. If you plan on taking advantage of FOREIGN KEY constraints in your database development projects, I urge you to study the comments about the order of operations in the book and in the script to sharpen your understanding of referential integrity.

The next excerpt from Ch04FKClassesClassGrades.sql initially populates both the Classes and ClassGrades tables. Because of referential integrity, it is necessary to run the INSERT statements for the Classes table before the INSERT statements for the ClassGrades table. Running the INSERT statements in the reverse order would generate an error based on a violation of the FOREIGN KEY constraint. Recall that column values for PRIMARY KEY or UNIQUE constraints must exist in the primary table before you can reference them from the secondary table.

```
INSERT Classes VALUES(1,
    'Learning SQL Server Express')
INSERT Classes VALUES(999,
    'Biographies of Jesus Christ')
GO

INSERT ClassGrades VALUES(1, 1, 'C+')
```

```
INSERT ClassGrades VALUES(1, 2, 'A+')
INSERT ClassGrades VALUES(999, 2, 'A')
GO
```

The following excerpt from Ch04FKClassesClassGrades.sql attempts to insert a new row in the ClassGrades table that points at a class with a ClassID value of 998. The statement fails when it is run at this point. The reason for the failure is that the INSERT statement references a ClassID value in the secondary table that does not exist in the primary table. This action violates referential integrity.

```
INSERT ClassGrades VALUES(998, 1, 'B')
GO
```

The next excerpt from Ch04FKClassesClassGrades.sql illustrates a typical kind of change that you will make when working with a pair of tables. The script shows the result sets from a SELECT statement before and after an update to a ClassTitle column value in the Classes table for the row with a ClassID of 999. The SELECT statement joins columns from both the Classes and ClassGrades tables. C is an alias for Classes and CG is an alias for ClassGrades. These alias names are used as qualifiers for the column names in the SELECT statement. Referential integrity does not have an impact on the ability to make an update to a ClassTitle column value in the Classes table because referential integrity in this sample does not apply to the ClassTitle. Referential integrity applies to ClassID.

```
SELECT CG.StudentID, C.ClassTitle, CG.GradeLetter
FROM Classes C, ClassGrades CG
WHERE C.ClassID = CG.ClassID
GO

UPDATE Classes
SET ClassTitle = 'The Life of Jesus Christ'
WHERE ClassID = 999
GO

SELECT CG.StudentID, C.ClassTitle, CG.GradeLetter
FROM Classes C, ClassGrades CG
WHERE C.ClassID = CG.ClassID
GO
```

The listing from running the preceding excerpt follows.

- The three rows in the two result sets follow from the initial INSERT statements to populate the Classes and ClassGrades tables as well as from the UPDATE statement in the immediately preceding script.
  - The number of rows affected by the first SELECT statement is three.
  - The intervening UPDATE statement affects one row.
  - The second SELECT statement also affects three rows.
- Notice the ClassTitle column value switches from Biographies of Jesus Christ to The Life of Jesus Christ between the first and second result sets. This is a consequence of the UPDATE statement.

```
StudentID   ClassTitle                 GradeLetter
----------- -------------------------- -----------
1           Learning SQL Server Express C+
2           Learning SQL Server Express A+
2           Biographies of Jesus Christ A
```

```
(3 row(s) affected)


(1 row(s) affected)

StudentID   ClassTitle                 GradeLetter
----------- -------------------------- -----------
1           Learning SQL Server Express C+
2           Learning SQL Server Express A+
2           The Life of Jesus Christ    A

(3 row(s) affected)
```

The UPDATE statement in the next excerpt does depend on referential integrity and the CASCADE keyword following the ON UPDATE phrase in the CREATE TABLE statement for ClassGrades.

- This is because the UPDATE statement revises a ClassID column value in the Classes table, and the ClassID column is also referenced by the FOREIGN KEY constraint in the CREATE TABLE statement for ClassGrades.

- Without special settings, a FOREIGN KEY constraint blocks changes to ClassID in the primary table that affects rows in the secondary table.

- However, the ON UPDATE phrase followed by the CASCADE keyword in the REFERENCES clause for ClassID does the following:

  - Permits the update

  - Enables the changes in the Classes table to propagate to the ClassGrades table

```
SELECT * FROM Classes
GO

UPDATE Classes
SET ClassID = 998
WHERE ClassID = 999
GO

SELECT * FROM Classes
GO

SELECT CG.StudentID, C.ClassTitle, CG.GradeLetter
FROM Classes C, ClassGrades CG
WHERE C.ClassID = CG.ClassID
GO
```

The next listing shows the output from running the preceding script. This output assumes that you are running the inserts and updates sequentially as described in this section. The SELECT statements from the Classes table show the Classes table before and after the update to the ClassID column value for the row with an initial ClassID column value of 999. After the update, the ClassID column value switches successfully from 999 to 998. If this change did not propagate to the ClassGrades table, the concluding SELECT statement that joins the Classes and ClassGrades table would fail for one row in ClassGrades because ClassGrades would have a ClassID value of 999 that did not exist in Classes.

```
ClassID     ClassTitle
----------- --------------------------
1           Learning SQL Server Express
999         The Life of Jesus Christ

(2 row(s) affected)



(1 row(s) affected)

ClassID     ClassTitle
----------- --------------------------
1           Learning SQL Server Express
998         The Life of Jesus Christ

(2 row(s) affected)


StudentID   ClassTitle                   GradeLetter
----------- ---------------------------- -----------
1           Learning SQL Server Express C+
2           Learning SQL Server Express A+
2           The Life of Jesus Christ     A

(3 row(s) affected)
```

The final excerpt from Ch04FKClassesClassGrades.sql contrasts an update and a delete to the Classes table. As you have already seen, an update succeeds.

- This is because of the ON UPDATE phrase and the CASCADE keyword.

- A delete to Classes fails for a similar reason—that is, the absence of an ON DELETE phrase followed by CASCADE in the REFERENCES clause for ClassID within the CREATE TABLE statement for ClassGrades.

- The following script sandwiches a DELETE statement for the row in Classes with a ClassID value of 999 between two UPDATE statements.

  - The statement preceding the DELETE statement ensures that the row with a ClassID of 999 is in the table to delete.

  - The statement trailing the DELETE statement restores the ClassID value of 998.

```
UPDATE Classes
SET ClassID = 999
WHERE ClassID = 998
GO

DELETE
FROM Classes
WHERE ClassID = 999
GO

UPDATE Classes
SET ClassID = 998
WHERE ClassID = 999
GO
```

Implementing Many-to-Many Relationships with Foreign Keys

The concluding sample for this chapter demonstrates how to support a many-to-many relationship with foreign keys between two pairs of tables.

- The sample many-to-many relationship is between students and classes. Therefore, the demonstration application creates tables called Students and Classes. These two tables are primary tables.

- Many-to-many relationships require an intermediate table between the two main tables in the relationship. In our sample, the intermediate table will be ClassGrades.

- You can build the structure for the many-to-many relationship by using the intermediate table as a secondary table to each of the primary tables.

The following excerpt from Ch04FKMany-to-many.sql shows the CREATE TABLE statements for the two primary tables—namely, Students and Classes. The Students table has a StudentID column defined with an int data type that serves as the table's primary key. The Students table also has a computed column named FullName. This column is the concatenation of the FirstName and LastName column values with an intervening space. The Classes table in Ch04FKMany-to-many.sql has the same CREATE TABLE statement as in the preceding sample. The primary key for the Classes table is based on the ClassID column.

```
CREATE TABLE Students(
    StudentID int Primary Key,
    FirstName nvarchar(30),
    LastName nvarchar(50),
    FullName AS (FirstName + ' ' + LastName)
)
GO

CREATE TABLE Classes(
    ClassID int Primary Key,
    ClassTitle varchar(50)
)
GO
```

The intermediate table, ClassGrades, has three columns and three constraints. The three column names are ClassID, StudentID, and GradeLetter. The main purpose for the ClassGrades table is to store student grades in classes.

- The rows in the ClassGrades table are unique by the combination of ClassID and StudentID. Therefore, the PRIMARY KEY constraint for ClassGrades, PK_ClassGrades, relies on both its ClassID and StudentID column values.

- The FOREIGN KEY constraint that references the ClassID column values in the Classes table with the ClassID values in the ClassGrades table has the name FK_Classes_ClassID. This constraint enables cascading updates but no cascading deletes from the Classes table to the ClassGrades table.

- The FOREIGN KEY constraint that references the StudentID column values in the Students table with the StudentID values in the ClassGrades table has the name FK_Students_StudentID. This constraint also supports cascading updates, but it does not enable cascading deletes.

```
CREATE TABLE ClassGrades(
    ClassID int,
    StudentID int,
    GradeLetter varchar(2),
    Constraint PK_ClassGrades
        PRIMARY KEY(ClassID, StudentID),
    Constraint FK_Classes_ClassID
        FOREIGN KEY(ClassID)
        REFERENCES Classes(ClassID) ON UPDATE CASCADE,
    Constraint FK_Students_StudentID
        FOREIGN KEY(StudentID)
        REFERENCES Students(StudentID) ON UPDATE CASCADE
)
```

The next excerpt uses INSERT statements to populate the Classes, Students, and ClassGrades tables with an initial set of values. A concluding SELECT statement displays the values input with a result set that draws on all three tables. The SELECT statement's FROM clause defines aliases of C, CG, and S for the Classes, ClassGrades, and Students tables. The SELECT list starts with the reference to the FullName computed column from the Students tables. Other items in the SELECT list include ClassTitle from the Classes table and GradeLetter from the ClassGrades table.

```
--Insert classes rows
INSERT Classes VALUES(1,
    'Learning SQL Server Express')
INSERT Classes VALUES(999,
    'Biographies of Jesus Christ')
GO

--Insert Students rows
INSERT Students VALUES(1, 'Poor', 'DBA')
INSERT Students VALUES(2, 'Better', 'DBA')
GO

--Insert ClassGrades rows
INSERT ClassGrades VALUES(1, 1, 'C+')
INSERT ClassGrades VALUES(1, 2, 'A+')
INSERT ClassGrades VALUES(999, 2, 'A')
GO

--Show table values after initial population
SELECT S.FullName, C.ClassTitle, CG.GradeLetter
FROM Classes C, ClassGrades CG, Students S
WHERE C.ClassID = CG.ClassID AND
    S.StudentID = CG.StudentID
GO
```

The output from the preceding SELECT statement appears next. As you can see, there are just two students with names of Poor DBA and Better DBA. The student with a FullName of Poor DBA earned a C+ in the Learning SQL Server Express class. The other student, Better DBA, earned grades of A+ and A, respectively, in the Learning SQL Server Express and Biographies of Jesus Christ classes. These values follow from the INSERT statements preceding the SELECT statement.

```
FullName    ClassTitle                 GradeLetter
----------  -------------------------- -----------
Poor DBA    Learning SQL Server Express C+
Better DBA  Learning SQL Server Express A+
Better DBA  Biographies of Jesus Christ A
```

The next block of code, which is an excerpt from Ch04FKMany-to-many.sql, updates the column values for both ClassTitle and ClassID in the Classes table.

- The ClassID value changes to 998 for the row with a ClassID value of 999.

- The ClassTitle value for the row with an initial ClassID value of 999 updates to The Life of Jesus Christ.

You can designate changes for multiple columns within a single UPDATE statement by following a single SET clause with a separate comma-delimited assignment for each updated column value. The following code sample uses two assignment statements, one for ClassID and another for ClassTitle. The UPDATE statement occurs between two SELECT statements that show the ClassID and ClassTitle column values from the Classes tables.

```
SELECT * FROM Classes
GO

UPDATE Classes
SET ClassID = 998,
    ClassTitle = 'The Life of Jesus Christ'
WHERE ClassID = 999
GO

SELECT * FROM Classes
GO
```

The following listing shows the results from the preceding script as well as an additional SELECT statement that generates a result set showing FullName, ClassTitle, and GradeLetter column values for all combinations of student and class. The syntax for this additional SELECT statement is the same one that shows the initial values of the Students, Classes, and ClassGrades tables. The preceding UPDATE statement changed both the ClassTitle and the ClassID column values in the Classes table. However, a cascading update working through referential integrity revises the ClassID column value from the ClassGrades table to match the corresponding changed ClassID value from the Classes table.

```
ClassID     ClassTitle
----------- ---------------------------
1           Learning SQL Server Express
999         Biographies of Jesus Christ

(2 row(s) affected)



(1 row(s) affected)

ClassID     ClassTitle
----------- ---------------------------
1           Learning SQL Server Express
998         The Life of Jesus Christ

(2 row(s) affected)



FullName    ClassTitle                  GradeLetter
----------  --------------------------- -----------
Poor DBA    Learning SQL Server Express C+
```

```
Better DBA Learning SQL Server Express A+
Better DBA The Life of Jesus Christ     A
```

```
(3 row(s) affected)
```

The final portion of the script in Ch04FKMany-to-many.sql makes a change to the last name of the student named Better DBA. Although this change does not directly depend on referential integrity, it is typical of the kind of change that will be made in applications that implement referential integrity.

Let's assume Better DBA marries a preacher named Inspirational Minister. Because she has already attracted attention as an exceptional DBA, Better DBA does not want to totally give up her former last name. After her marriage, she changes her name to a hyphenated form (DBA-Minister). Then, she goes to the Office of the Registrar at her school and submits a request to change her last name. The following excerpt shows the code to implement the update and a new version of the result set to confirm the revision. The result set derives from the standard SELECT statement for this sample joining the Classes, Students, and ClassGrades tables.

```
UPDATE Students
SET LastName = 'DBA-Minister'
WHERE StudentID = 2
GO
```

```
FullName            ClassTitle                 GradeLetter
------------------- -------------------------- -----------
Poor DBA            Learning SQL Server Express C+
Better DBA-Minister Learning SQL Server Express A+
Better DBA-Minister The Life of Jesus Christ    A
```

Summary

This chapter showed you how to create tables for the solutions that you build with SSE. Tables are at the heart of every custom database solution. If you can't build your own tables, you are limited to selecting from tables created by other developers and administrators. Even in this case, knowing about the table design issues covered in this chapter can help you to design smarter SELECT statements and to debug your SELECT statements faster.

- Because data types are so fundamental to your ability to create tables, the chapter commenced with a review that summarized and contrasted the more than two dozen SSE data types.

- Next, the focus shifted to creating tables with columns based on SQL Server data types. You also learned how to populate tables with data as well as how to recover data from an old version of the table and restore the data to a new version of the table.

- The chapter closed with two lengthy sections that drilled down on data integrity. By building tables that take advantage of the many features that SSE offers for managing the quality of data that enters a database, you ensure that your database solutions are never characterized as garbage in, garbage out.

CHAPTER 5

■■■

Creating Queries from a Single Database Object

In the previous couple of chapters, you learned how to create databases and tables to store data. This chapter switches attention to retrieving data. The process of retrieving data is frequently called data access. There are two major aspects of data access covered in this chapter.

1. First, you'll learn about specifying SELECT statements for data access. This topic includes designating items for a SELECT statement to return as well as indicating where to retrieve data from. In the process, you also acquire a variety of tips and techniques for displaying and processing date and time values as well as computing calculated values for display.

2. Second, you'll receive training in filtering, grouping, and aggregating values from a data source. These actions can summarize values from a data source to make result sets have a greater impact. Among the specific topics addressed are how to filter character data and how to use special operators that can help you filter characters and numbers.

In addition to covering core data access topics, this chapter also includes content on innovations or advanced features that help you get the most from a SQL Server Express instance.

- This chapter drills down on the TOP keyword to demonstrate how to select fixed and variable subsets of rows from the beginning rows of a result set.

- You learn a couple of ways of performing queries for data sources on remote SQL Server instances, including SQL Server Express, other SQL Server 2005 editions, MSDE, SQL Server 2000, and SQL Server 7.

Specifying Items to Select from a Data Source

The SELECT statement is the core SQL tool for expressing queries. Because this statement is so fundamental to so many tasks that you can do with SQL Server Express, previous chapters demonstrated the use of the SELECT statement to show the impact of various SQL Server Express features. Starting with this section, this chapter systematically explores many popular techniques for using SELECT statements to generate query results from a single data source.

In this section, you will specifically learn tricks and techniques for

- Specifying and calculating the column values in a result set

- Extracting a fixed number or percent of rows from a full result set

- Formatting the display of date and time values in a result set

- Designating a data source based on a single database in the current database context or another database

- Returning result sets from a remote server using either ad hoc queries or linked servers

Specifying SELECT List Items

Every SELECT statement for retrieving data from a data source must have two parts: a SELECT list and a FROM clause. The list specifies the columns you wish to return in the result set generated by the SELECT statement. The FROM clause designates a data source that the SELECT statement searches to generate a result set. This section drills down on several important aspects of SELECT list design. The samples discussed in this section appear in the SpecifyingSELECTListItems.sql file.

The following SELECT statement illustrates a number of SELECT statement features.

- A SELECT statement for a query always operates in the context of a database setting. The USE statement in the following code snippet instructs the SELECT statement to look for the data source specified in the FROM clause in the AdventureWorks database.

- Items in a SELECT list normally refer to columns in one or more data source arguments in the FROM clause. The ProductCategoryID and Name columns in the result set derive from the ProductCategory table in the Production schema.

- By specifying column names, you can filter which columns from a data source appear in a result set. Using the * wildcard can return all columns to a result set. Unless you really need all the columns from a data source, it is preferable to name a subset of columns for a result set. Queries specifying a subset of columns can run faster by returning just the column values that you need. For tables containing columns with long character sequences within many rows, this performance effect can be noticeable.

- You can specify a column alias to assign an alternative name to the column's name in the underlying data source. The use of Category name in the SELECT list within single quotes illustrates a common way to designate a column alias.

Tip A schema separates containership from ownership. A schema can contain a set of database objects without directly implying ownership. Chapter 8 addresses this topic in the context of security.

```
USE AdventureWorks
GO

SELECT ProductCategoryID, Name 'Category name'
FROM Production.ProductCategory
```

The preceding script returns a result set with four rows of two columns. The actual values appear next. Notice the second column heading in the result set is Category name instead of Name, which is the column name from the underlying data source. One significant advantage of a column alias is to assign a name that improves the clarity of the output relative to the column name from an underlying data source. Since the next example will also reference a column named Name from a different data source, giving an alias to the column in this query helps to distinguish between the two query statements and their output.

```
ProductCategoryID Category name
----------------- -------------
4                 Accessories
1                 Bikes
3                 Clothing
2                 Components
```

The next SELECT statement demonstrates the same design principles as the preceding statement. This statement extracts three columns from the ProductSubcategory table in the Production schema of the AdventureWorks database. The ProductCategoryID column values for this sample repeat for different ProductSubcategoryID column values from the same category. This script, and most of the other samples in this chapter, references the AdventureWorks database. Future sample descriptions will mention database context only when another database is being referenced.

Notice that the name of the third column in the SELECT list for this sample is the same as the name of the second column in the preceding sample. Recall that the different aliases for the column called Name in both samples distinguish the code and the result set values between the first and second samples.

```
SELECT ProductSubcategoryID, ProductCategoryID,
    Name 'Subcategory name'
FROM Production.ProductSubcategory
```

The next set of lines shows an excerpt from the sample extracting column values from the ProductSubcategory table. The total result set contains 37 rows of output—one line for each unique ProductSubcategoryID value, which is the primary key for the query's data source. The listing excerpt that follows shows the first five rows. The first three of these are from the Bikes category, which, as we know from the previous result set listing, has a ProductCategoryID value of 1. The next two rows are from the Components category.

```
ProductSubcategoryID ProductCategoryID Subcategory name
-------------------- ----------------- ----------------
1                    1                 Mountain Bikes
2                    1                 Road Bikes
3                    1                 Touring Bikes
4                    2                 Handlebars
5                    2                 Bottom Brackets
```

While SELECT statements often derive all the list items from column names in a data source, it is possible to derive list items from other sources. For example, the following script declares a local variable (@intvar) and then assigns a value to the variable. Next, the script includes the local variable as a list item. The SELECT statement is the same as the first sample, except for the new third column. You can also assign a constant, such as the value 1, as a list item. A variable value or constant assigned this way will define a column in the result set and repeat its value for each row within that column.

```
DECLARE @intvar int
SET @intvar = 1
SELECT ProductCategoryID, Name 'Category name',
    @intvar 'Local variable'
FROM Production.ProductCategory
```

This listing for the preceding script shows the same value for the Local variable column in each row. Otherwise, this listing is identical to the one from the first sample.

ProductCategoryID	Category name	Local variable
4	Accessories	1
1	Bikes	1
3	Clothing	1
2	Components	1

List items can also include calculated column values as well as aggregated column values. When a SELECT list contains a single aggregate function, the result set consists of a single scalar value, instead of an array of rows. The following aggregate function returns the number of rows in the ProductSubcategory table (37). See the "Calculating Computed List Items" section in this chapter for details on using calculated items in a SELECT list.

```
SELECT Count(*)
FROM Production.ProductSubcategory
```

Each of the preceding samples implicitly accepts the default ALL keyword after SELECT. The ALL keyword shows all rows from a data source in its result set whether or not there are duplicate rows.

It is sometimes necessary to return a result set with just nonduplicate values in each row. If you do not have permission to access another data source with nonduplicated column values (such as, ProductCategory), you can still return unique values by explicitly specifying DISTINCT before the items in a SELECT statement that draws on another data source, such as ProductSubcategory. The DISTINCT keyword causes a SELECT statement to return only rows with unique values.

In the following sample, if it were not for the DISTINCT keyword, the result set would consist of a single column with 37 rows—one for each row in the ProductSubcategory table. Because there are only four unique ProductCategoryID values, many of the rows would have duplicate values. However, the DISTINCT keyword causes the return of a result set with just four rows—one for each unique ProductCategoryID value. You can generate the list yourself from the last sample in the SpecifyingSELECTListItems.sql file.

```
SELECT DISTINCT ProductCategoryID
FROM Production.ProductSubcategory
```

Returning Top Values

It is often easier to write queries that return more rows than you actually need to answer a question about the contents of a database. Sometimes you may actually want all the rows, but you only need to review the first few to verify that a query is performing properly. In these kinds of scenarios, adding the TOP keyword in a SELECT statement can return a subset of rows from the original result set, which is either a fixed number or a fixed percentage of rows from the top of the original set of rows. The samples for this section reside in ReturningTopValues.sql.

■**Note** One innovation for the TOP keyword introduced with SQL Server 2005 (including SQL Server Express) is the ability to dynamically set the number or percent of rows that the SELECT statement returns. The first sample demonstrating the TOP keyword forces the return of just five rows from the ProductSubcategory table. You may recall this sample as nearly the same as an earlier one describing how to specify a list of items for a SELECT statement. I showed only the first five rows of the results from that earlier sample for reasons of brevity, but the following sample explicitly specifies the return of just five rows.

```
SELECT TOP 5 ProductSubcategoryID, ProductCategoryID,
    Name 'Subcategory name'
FROM Production.ProductSubcategory
```

As mentioned, you can dynamically set the number of rows returned. The following code sample declares a local variable, @n, and then assigns a value of 6 to it. By enclosing the local variable's name in parentheses after the TOP keyword, you can have a SELECT statement return the number of rows assigned to the local variable's value. Changing the value of the local variable modifies the number of rows that return from the SELECT statement with the TOP keyword.

```
DECLARE @n int
SET @n = 6
SELECT TOP (@n) ProductSubcategoryID, ProductCategoryID,
    Name 'Subcategory name'
FROM Production.ProductSubcategory
```

By adding the PERCENT keyword after the fixed or variable value, you instruct SQL Server Express to return a percentage instead of an absolute number of rows. In other words, the PERCENT keyword causes TOP to interpret its argument as a percentage of rows. Therefore, SELECT TOP 10 PERCENT list FROM data source designates the return of the top 10% of rows from the data source.

■**Tip** By inserting TOP 100 PERCENT into a SELECT statement, you instruct SQL Server Express to return all the rows from the original SELECT statement that did not use the TOP keyword. The TOP 100 PERCENT phrase is especially convenient with views that require the TOP keyword in order to sort a result set with the ORDER BY clause. Chapter 7 presents details on how to define views.

The precise number of rows returned with the PERCENT keyword depends on both the value specified as an argument for the TOP keyword as well as the number of rows in the original result set without the PERCENT keyword. A percent of a fixed number of rows will often result in a fractional number of rows, such as 4.07 rows. SQL Server Express returns rows to the nearest whole number above the computed number of rows.

The following script shows the syntax for designating the return of a variable percent of rows. The assignment of 11 to @n specifies 11% of the rows. Without the TOP keyword, the SELECT statement returns 37 rows. 11% of 37 rows is 4.07 rows. Therefore, the statement returns 5 rows, which is the nearest whole number of rows above 4.07 rows. Assigning values of 10 and 9 to the @n local variable computes raw row values of 3.7 and 3.33. Because of rounding up to the nearest whole number, both values (10 and 9) for the TOP keyword return 4 rows. Assigning 8 to the @n local variable computes the return of 2.96 rows. Therefore, specifying the return of 8% leads to a result set with 3 rows.

```
DECLARE @n int
SET @n = 11
SELECT TOP (@n) PERCENT ProductSubcategoryID, ProductCategoryID,
    Name 'Subcategory name'
FROM Production.ProductSubcategory
```

Calculating Computed List Items

Just as you can have computed columns in the design of a table, you can have calculated items in the list for a SELECT statement. By including expressions in a SELECT list, you can specify calculated items. Calculated items in a SELECT list are particularly convenient for decision-support tasks, where you are not likely to know some, or even many, of the computed column values you are likely to need until after you start analyzing some data. Using calculated list items in a SELECT statement helps decision-support analysts to experiment with new ways of looking at data to provide powerful input for executive decisions. The samples for this section reside in CalculatingComputedListItems.sql.

When thinking of calculated values, it is natural to think of quantities and currency data types. The following SELECT statement includes a calculated item that multiplies an int value, OrderQty, by a money value, UnitPrice. Both columns are from the SalesOrderDetail table in the Sales schema. As it turns out, the AdventureWorks database designates the UnitPrice column values to four places after the decimal point—that is, 1/10,000th of a currency unit. The product of OrderQty times UnitPrice represents the total for a line item in an order before any discounts. The LineTotal column value is a computed column value that represents the total for a line item after discounts.

```
SELECT TOP 3 SalesOrderID, OrderQty, UnitPrice,
    (OrderQty*UnitPrice) 'Line total before discount',
    LineTotal
FROM Sales.SalesOrderDetail
```

The following listing shows the result set from the preceding SELECT statement. The TOP 3 phrase in the SELECT statement designates the return of the first three rows from the full result set that doesn't use the TOP 3 phrase. None of the returned rows have discounts. Therefore, the Line total before discount and the LineTotal columns are identical. The first and third rows in the result set have OrderQty column values of 1 so that the product of UnitPrice and OrderQty is the same as UnitPrice. The second row has an OrderQty column value of 3.

SalesOrderID	OrderQty	UnitPrice	Line total before discount	LineTotal
43659	1	2024.994	2024.994	2024.994000
43659	3	2024.994	6074.982	6074.982000
43659	1	2024.994	2024.994	2024.994000

The next pair of SELECT statements illustrates the syntax for recasting Line total before discount column values. Recasting in this context is the process of changing the data type of a column value from one type to another. In this case, the recasting transforms the Line total before discount column values from a money data type with four places to the right of the decimal point to a decimal data type with two places to the right of the decimal point. While this recasting introduces a slight rounding error, it is appropriate for most invoice statements because you can pay currency to the nearest 1/100th of a currency unit (a cent)—as opposed to the nearest 1/10,000th of a currency unit (1/100th of a cent).

- The first SELECT statement shows the syntax for using the CAST function to recast from a money data type to a dec(10,2) data type. This function takes two arguments—the first one is the expression value to recast and the second is the designation for the new data type. The AS keyword separates the two arguments.

- The second SELECT statement performs an identical transformation with the CONVERT function. For this type of recasting, the CONVERT function also takes two arguments. However, in this case, the data type designation precedes the expression, computing a result that requires a transformation. The two arguments are comma delimited. The CONVERT function, just like the CAST function, also transforms its expression argument to a dec(10,2) data type.

```
SELECT TOP 3 SalesOrderID, OrderQty, UnitPrice,
    CAST((OrderQty*UnitPrice) AS dec(10,2))
    'Line total before discount',
    LineTotal
FROM Sales.SalesOrderDetail

--Conversion with CONVERT function for computated value
--with numbers in list
SELECT TOP 3 SalesOrderID, OrderQty, UnitPrice,
```

```
    CONVERT(dec(10,2),OrderQty*UnitPrice)
    'Line total before discount',
    LineTotal
FROM Sales.SalesOrderDetail
```

While the preceding two SELECT statements use different functions for recasting the Line total before discount column values, both statements transform the column values to the same data type. Therefore, the output is identical for both statements. The following listing shows the output from the first SELECT statement. You can confirm the slight rounding by comparing the values in the third column of the following output with the third column values of the preceding result set listing.

```
SalesOrderID OrderQty UnitPrice Line total before discount LineTotal
------------ -------- --------- -------------------------- -----------
43659        1        2024.994  2024.99                    2024.994000
43659        3        2024.994  6074.98                    6074.982000
43659        1        2024.994  2024.99                    2024.994000
```

You can also calculate expressions for string values, such as concatenating two column values from a table into one calculated item for a SELECT list. This type of transformation is common when merging the parts of a person's name into a full name. The Contact table in the Persons schema of the AdventureWorks database has three columns named FirstName, MiddleName, and LastName. These columns represent name parts that you can concatenate with the concatenation operator (+). Because you do not normally have the end of one name part immediately start the next name part, you should insert a blank space (" ") between the FirstName and MiddleName column values as well as between the MiddleName and LastName column values.

The following SELECT statement illustrates an expression for concatenating the FirstName, MiddleName, and LastName column values into a list item with an alias of Full name. Since some rows from the Contact table have NULL values for MiddleName, the expression uses the ISNULL function to transform these NULL column values to an empty string. Failing to do so will cause a NULL value for the Full name list item for these rows (with NULL values for MiddleName).

```
SELECT TOP 3 FirstName, MiddleName, LastName,
    FirstName + ' ' + ISNULL(MiddleName, '')
    + ' ' + LastName 'Full name'
FROM Person.Contact
```

The following listing shows the result set from running the preceding SELECT statement. Notice the Full name item concatenates the parts. In addition, rows with a NULL value for their MiddleName column value do not propagate the NULL value to the calculated Full name item. However, there is one problem. Rows with a NULL value for their MiddleName column value have two, instead of one, blank space between their FirstName and LastName column values.

```
FirstName MiddleName LastName    Full name
--------- ---------- ----------- -----------------
Gustavo   NULL       Achong      Gustavo  Achong
Catherine R.         Abel        Catherine R. Abel
Kim       NULL       Abercrombie Kim  Abercrombie
```

Unless you are a professional developer with a vast library of previously developed solutions, it is not uncommon to develop expressions iteratively, such as the one for the Full name item. There are several approaches to removing the extra blank space between the FirstName and LastName column values in the calculated Full name list item. The next SELECT statement demonstrates the use of the REPLACE function.

The REPLACE function can replace one string, such as two blank spaces, with another, such as one blank space, in yet another string, such as the expression value for the Full name list item. The REPLACE function takes three arguments.

1. The first argument is the string constant or expression value to have a replacement made in it. In the context of this example, this argument is the expression for the Full name list item before the transformation.

2. The second argument designates the string value to be replaced, which is two blanks (" ") in this example.

3. The third argument is the string value that replaces any instances of the second argument in the first argument. It is a single blank space in this example.

The following string shows the application of the REPLACE function for replacing the two blank spaces with a single blank space in the Full name list item for rows with NULL MiddleName column values. The REPLACE function simply wraps the initial expression for the Full name list item. Notice that the third argument has one fewer space than the second argument.

```
SELECT TOP 3 FirstName, MiddleName, LastName,
    REPLACE(FirstName + ' ' + ISNULL(MiddleName, '')
    + ' ' + LastName, '  ', ' ') 'Full name'
FROM Person.Contact
```

Displaying datetime Values

SQL Server Express stores datetime and smalldatetime values as numbers (see the "Date and Time Data Types" section in Chapter 4), but it displays date and time values as strings. This is because the internal representation of a datetime (and a smalldatetime) value is a number with digits to the right and left of the decimal point. On the other hand, the number's value is meaningful to most of us only when you decode the number to common date and time units, such as days, months, years, hours, minutes, and seconds.

- Each integer value in a datetime or smalldatetime value represents one day.
- Values to the right of the decimal point denote fractions of a day or the time since 12 a.m. (midnight).

Although you can perform arithmetic with this basic understanding of datetime and smalldatetime values, it is preferable to use the SQL Server Express built-in functions for processing date and time values, as well as the CONVERT function for formatting date and time values. The samples for this section, which demonstrate these guidelines, reside in DisplayingDatetimeValues.sql.

The first datetime example that follows shows the basic format for representing a datetime value and illustrates the basics of performing arithmetic with datetime values. The SELECT statement extracts two columns from the first row in the SalesOrderHeader table in the Sales schema. The SalesOrderID column value uniquely identifies the row, and the OrderDate column value is the datetime value for the order denoted by the SalesOrderID column value.

The OrderDate column value is processed three different ways in the list for the SELECT statement.

1. First, it is reported as it is in the SalesOrderHeader table.

2. Second, the column value is displayed with a value of 9 added to it. This adds a value to the left of the decimal point. The alias for this list item is OrderDate + 9.

3. Third, the column value shows with a value of .5 added to it. This adds a fraction of an integer to the right of the decimal point. The alias for this list item is OrderDate + .5.

```
SELECT TOP 1 SalesOrderID,  OrderDate,
    OrderDate + 9 'OrderDate + 9',
    OrderDate + .5 'OrderDate + .5'
FROM Sales.SalesOrderHeader
```

The following listing shows the output from the preceding SELECT statement.

- The OrderDate column displays its value in the default style for a datetime value format for my SQL Server Express installation (if you installed SQL Server Express outside the United States you may have a different default style).

  - First, it shows the year as a four-digit integer (2001).

  - Next, the month appears as a two-digit integer (07).

  - The final date component is the day (01).

  - The remaining values represent the hours, minutes, seconds, and milliseconds for an OrderDate column value. The hours, minutes, and seconds are delimited from each other by colons. The milliseconds are delimited from the other time components by a decimal point and represented in three digits.

- The date and time below the OrderDate + 9 column heading show the outcome of adding 9 to the original OrderDate column value. Notice that the number of days advances by 9.

- The date and time below the OrderDate + .5 column heading indicate the effect of adding a fraction of an integer—that is, .5. In this case, the time advances by 12 hours, which is half of the 24 hours in a day.

```
SalesOrderID OrderDate              OrderDate + 9           OrderDate + .5
------------ ---------------------- ----------------------- ----------------------
43659        2001-07-01 00:00:00.000 2001-07-10 00:00:00.000 2001-07-01 12:00:00.000
```

It is typically much more useful to display date and time values in some format that is more meaningful for users than the SQL Server Express default datetime format. The CONVERT function offers a large variety of style format values for controlling the representation of date and time values in a result set. You can review documentation for the full set of style format values in the CAST and CONVERT (Transact-SQL) topic for Books Online.

■**Note** Books Online is the Microsoft documentation for SQL Server. There is a new version of Books Online for each version of SQL Server. While Books Online does not install with SQL Server Express, you can download Books Online from the Microsoft website. At the time that this book publishes, the URL for SQL Server 2005 Books online is http://www.microsoft.com/technet/prodtechnol/sql/2005/downloads/books.mspx.

When using the CONVERT function to format a datetime value, you will typically specify three arguments. The first is the output data type. Use a character format, such as varchar, to represent the date and time values as a string of characters. The second argument is an expression for the datetime value. This can be as simple as a column name, such as OrderDate from the SalesOrderHeader table. The third argument is the style format value. This argument is optional with a default value of 100.

The following SELECT statement and its output listing contrast the default format style for datetime values with two different CONVERT function styles. The style values are 100, 101, and 103.

The alias for each column showing a style value denotes the format for representing a `datetime` value.

- A style value of 100 represents the date starting with the three-letter abbreviation for the month, followed by day and year values, and then hour, minute, and day part (a.m. or p.m.) values. If you do not specify a style format value, the `CONVERT` function uses the format for a style value of 100.

- A style value of 101 displays just the date portion of a `datetime` value, with month number before day number before year number. This format for representing dates is common in the United States.

- A style value of 103 shows just the date portion of a `datetime` value, with day number before month number before year number. This format for representing dates is common in Great Britain and France.

```
SELECT TOP 1 SalesOrderID, OrderDate,
    CONVERT(varchar,OrderDate,100) 'Mmm dd yyyy hh:mmdp',
    CONVERT(varchar,OrderDate,101) 'mm/dd/yyyy',
    CONVERT(varchar,OrderDate,103) 'dd/mm/yyyy'
FROM Sales.SalesOrderHeader
```

```
SalesOrderID OrderDate               Mmm dd yyyy hh:mmdp mm/dd/yyyy dd/mm/yyyy
------------ ----------------------- ------------------- ---------- ----------
43659        2001-07-01 00:00:00.000 Jul  1 2001 12:00AM 07/01/2001 01/07/2001
```

The next `SELECT` statement and output listing compares three additional formats for displaying just the time from a `datetime` value with the default representation for `datetime` values. There is no `FROM` clause in this `SELECT` statement because the statement merely displays the current value of the SQL Server Express `GETDATE` function, but the format styles apply to any `datetime` column value from a table. The aliases denote the format style values for 108, 114, and 113. You can see from the column value for the `Default` column that the `datetime` value includes both a date and time, but only the time values appear in the three columns following the `Default` column.

```
SELECT TOP 1 GETDATE() 'Default',
    CONVERT(varchar,GETDATE(),108) 'hh:mm:ss',
    CONVERT(varchar,GETDATE(),114) 'hh:mm:ss:mmm',
    CONVERT(varchar,GETDATE(),113) 'dd Mmm yyyy hh:mm:ss:mmm'
```

```
Default                 hh:mm:ss hh:mm:ss:mmm dd Mmm yyyy hh:mm:ss:mmm
----------------------- -------- ------------ ------------------------
2005-04-17 20:52:49.377 20:52:49 20:52:49:377 17 Apr 2005 20:52:49:377
```

When working with `datetime` values, you will often want to process them. For example, you may want to roll a date forward one month or determine the number of days between two dates. SQL Server Express offers a variety of built-in functions to help you process `datetime` values. See the Date and Time Functions (Transact-SQL) topic in Books Online for links that let you drill down to learn more about these functions.

This next code and result set listings illustrate how to use the `DATEADD` and `DATEDIFF` functions—two of the most popular functions for processing `datetime` values. After assigning `GETDATE` to the `@thisdate` local variable, the code invokes `DATEADD`. Within the sample, this function rolls the current `datetime` value forward one month. The `SELECT` statement following the assignments for the `@thisdate` and `@nextmonth` local variables uses the `DATEDIFF` function as a list item to compute the number of days between `@thisdate` and `@nextmonth`.

The DATEADD function adds an interval to a base datetime value. This function applies to dates and times within datetime values. The interval can be one of 11 durations from a number of milliseconds to a number of years. Each interval type has one or two abbreviations for use with the DATEADD function, such as yyyy for year, m for month, and ms for millisecond. The DATEADD function takes three parameters.

1. The first parameter is most often an abbreviation for the type of interval. You can optionally use the full name for a part of a date, such as Month instead of m.

2. The second parameter is an integer value denoting the number of interval units to apply to the base datetime value to compute a new datetime value. You can use smalldatetime values as well as datetime values. A positive parameter value rolls time forward, and a negative parameter value rolls time backward. A noninteger value results in the fractional part of the value being discarded.

3. The third parameter is the base datetime value. You can specify the datetime value with either a datetime or smalldatetime data type.

The DATEDIFF function computes the difference between two datetime or smalldatetime values. You can request the computation of the difference in any of 10 different time intervals, such as year, day, or millisecond. This function can be particularly useful for documenting the performance differences for two or more different ways of performing the same task. The DATEDIFF function takes three parameters.

1. The initial parameter designates the date or time unit in which to compute a difference.

2. The second parameter is the starting date and time.

3. The third parameter is the ending date and time.

```
DECLARE @thisdate datetime, @nextmonth datetime
SET @thisdate = GETDATE()
SET @nextmonth = DATEADD(m, 1, GETDATE())
SELECT CONVERT(varchar, @thisdate, 101) 'Today',
    CONVERT(varchar, @nextmonth, 101) 'One month from today',
    DATEDIFF(d, @thisdate, @nextmonth) 'Days between'
```

```
Today                          One month from today Days between
------------------------------ -------------------- ------------
04/17/2005                     05/17/2005             30
```

Using the Current Database Context or a Different Database

When specifying a FROM clause for a single data source, SQL Server Express looks for the data source in the current database context, unless you explicitly indicate otherwise—by, for example, using a three-part name to designate a table in another database on the same server as the database context. You can use a four-part name to reference a table in another database on a different server from the one to which the database context refers. Data sources are typically either tables or views. This section highlights techniques for running queries from a single database either from the current database context or from another database on the same SQL Server instance. The samples for this section appear in CurrentDatabaseOrDifferentDatabase.sql.

> ■**Note** SQL Server Express always internally tracks data sources by a unique four-part name. Depending on database context for a query statement and the data source that you want a query statement to reference, you can often specify less than four name parts. The full name for a database object serving as a data source is `server_name.database_name.schema_name.object_name`. You can omit the `server_name` qualifier for an object when referencing it on the same server as the database context. Using name parts can be tricky in the abstract, but designating the appropriate name parts is straightforward in actual practice—just be sure to include enough name parts to uniquely identify an object. Therefore, this book refers to name parts as needed when dealing with contexts that highlight their roles.

Running Queries from the Current Database Context or a Different Database

The following script contrasts the syntax for referencing a data source from the current database context versus from another database. A USE statement sets the database context to AdventureWorks on the server for the connection to a SQL Server Express instance.

- The first SELECT statement looks for the SalesOrderHeader table in the Sales schema within the AdventureWorks database. The FROM clause uses a two-part name, for which the top part designates a schema in the current database context, and the nested second part references a table.

- On the other hand, the reference to the Northwind database uses a three-part name. The top part references the database name. Nested immediately below the database name is the schema name—dbo. The bottom part is the table name (Orders).

```
USE AdventureWorks
GO

SELECT TOP 5 SalesOrderID 'Order ID',
    CONVERT(varchar,OrderDate,101) 'Order date'
FROM Sales.SalesOrderHeader

SELECT TOP 5 OrderID 'Order ID',
    CONVERT(varchar,OrderDate,101) 'Order date'
FROM Northwind.dbo.Orders
```

The following listing shows the output from the preceding script. The top five rows are from the SalesOrderHeader table in the AdventureWorks database. The second five rows are from the Orders table in the Northwind database.

```
Order ID    Order date
----------- ----------
43659       07/01/2001
43660       07/01/2001
43661       07/01/2001
43662       07/01/2001
43663       07/01/2001

(5 row(s) affected)


Order ID    Order date
----------- ----------
10248       07/04/1996
10249       07/05/1996
```

```
10250     07/08/1996
10251     07/08/1996
10252     07/09/1996
```

```
(5 row(s) affected)
```

You can change the database context so that the `Northwind` database is the default database context, and you reference the `SalesOrderHeader` table in the `Sales` schema of the `AdventureWorks` database. In this scenario, you can use a two-part—or even a one-part—name to reference the `Orders` table in the `Northwind` database. However, you must use a three-part name to reference the `SalesOrderHeader` table. The following script shows the syntax for expressing these references in its two `FROM` clauses:

```
USE Northwind
GO

SELECT TOP 5 OrderID 'Order ID',
    CONVERT(varchar,OrderDate,101) 'Order date'
FROM Orders

SELECT TOP 5 SalesOrderID 'Order ID',
    CONVERT(varchar,OrderDate,101) 'Order date'
FROM AdventureWorks.Sales.SalesOrderHeader
```

Running Queries from a View

Another variation for using a single data source is to use a view instead of a table. This book drills down on views in Chapter 7, but views are also relevant to this section because they allow you to reference a single database object, namely a view, in a `FROM` clause. Views act like virtual tables in that you can reference their columns like a table, but views are based on a `SELECT` statement. What's most important about views for this section is that you can derive the columns for a view from more than one table.

Because of the rules of normalization, many individual tables within a database aren't likely to have all the columns for many queries that you'll want to run. One workaround for referencing a single database object in your `FROM` clause in this kind of situation is to use a view instead of a table. This is because a single view can reference multiple tables. Referencing a view in a `FROM` clause, in turn, simplifies your `SELECT` statements.

■**Note** Normalization is a fundamental database development issue that provides guidelines for the design of tables in a database. The basic advantages of normalization include helping to maintain data accuracy and simplify some query statements. There are numerous normalization rules that allow you to state that a database is normalized to a specified level (based on how many and which rules are followed). Because of its fundamental nature, as opposed to its relevance to SQL Server Express or even T-SQL, in-depth coverage of normalization is beyond the scope of this book. If you feel that you need additional coverage of this topic, there are many excellent resources spread across the Internet. Use your favorite search engine to seek URLs that give you enough exposure to normalization to make you feel that you understand it sufficiently for your requirements.

The `SalesPerson` table in the `Sales` schema of the `AdventureWorks` database includes data about year-to-date sales in its `SalesYTD` column for individual sales persons identified by `SalesPersonID`. Unfortunately, the `SalesPerson` table does not contain the names of sales persons, which are often more informative than an arbitrary numeric identifier, such as `SalesPersonID`. The reasons for using the vSalesPerson view, instead of the SalesPerson table, to display sales person names along with year-to-date sales are as follows:

- The names for sales persons, along with all other contact names in the AdventureWorks database, reside in the Contact table that belongs to the Person schema. That is, the SalesPerson table does not contain sales person names.

- There is no direct link between the SalesPerson and Contact tables. However, the SalesPerson table does link to the Employee table in the HumanResources schema, and the Employee table, in turn, links to the Contact table.

- While it is possible to build a custom SELECT statement that models the path from the SalesPerson table to the Contact table, you can simply reference the vSalesPerson view in the Sales schema, which includes the desired connections along with other connections.

You can reference the vSalesPerson view just like any table in a FROM clause. The view links to multiple tables, and it makes columns from these tables available. For example, because the vSalesPerson references both the SalesPerson and Contact tables, it can return data about sales person names along with year-to-date sales. The following SELECT statement shows how simple it can be to use a view to report data from tables that don't even link directly to one another. The view appears in the FROM clause with a two-part name that designates the schema before the database object's name. The following listing shows the SELECT item values from the three rows returned by the view:

```
SELECT TOP 3 SalesPersonID, FirstName, LastName,
       CAST(SalesYTD AS dec(12,2)) 'YTD Sales'
FROM Sales.vSalesPerson
```

```
SalesPersonID FirstName LastName YTD Sales
------------- --------- -------- ----------
268           Stephen   Jiang    677558.47
275           Michael   Blythe   4557045.05
276           Linda     Mitchell 5200475.23
```

Specifying Queries from Another Server Instance

Queries that reference another server instance besides the local one are often called distributed queries. There are two main types of distributed queries.

- Ad hoc queries are performed on a one-time basis (or a very small number of times). The OPENROWSET function is a popular technique for implementing this kind of query.

- Other distributed queries are performed often or at least at regular intervals, such as quarterly. Linked servers are a popular way of performing these types of queries.

Using the OPENROWSET function requires little or no administrative permissions. If you have permission to connect to and query a data source on another server instance, then you can apply the OPENROWSET function with about the same skill necessary to make a comparable query on a local SQL Server instance. The OPENROWSET function is suitable for power-level decision analysts who may have to connect to any of a variety of server instances at short notice. As long as the analysts can obtain permission, they can use a target database on a database server instance.

Using linked servers requires you to modify a server instance by adding and administering a linked server. You will typically need to know about or at least consider other people's logins when you create a linked server. On the other hand, the syntax for referencing a linked server is substantially easier than the syntax for referencing a data source on another server instance with the OPENROWSET function. Therefore, linked servers are more appropriate for database administrators who facilitate distributed queries for use by others, such as decision-support analysts.

Both the OPENROWSET function and linked queries have additional features besides implementing distributed queries between SQL Server instances. However, this section highlights how you specify and implement distributed queries with each method. In addition to samples illustrating how to code each approach for distributed queries, this section presents commentary about special implementation details associated with each approach. The samples from this section are in OPENROWSETAndLinkedServers.sql.

■**Note** Microsoft disabled the OPENROWSET function for SQL Server Express just before the final release. This feature worked successfully throughout the beta program. It is my hope that they will re-enable it with an update to the initially released version of SQL Server Express. Therefore, this book retains coverage of the OPENROWSET function so that you can easily take advantage of the feature if it is ultimately re-enabled.

Running Ad Hoc Queries on Another Server Instance

It is possible to specify distributed queries that run across server instances with a single FROM clause argument. Several strategies exist for implementing queries across servers, but their availability can depend on settings on both the server instance initiating the request and the server processing the request. For example, you may have to use the SQL Server Service Manager to turn on the Distributed Transaction Coordinator for the destination or remote SQL Server instance.

■**Note** Distributed queries across server instances are known to run slower than queries on a single server, and distributed queries across server instances are more complex to design and implement than queries on a single server. Therefore, you should always consider running queries to two separate servers from a single client and consolidating the results in a client application.

When you want to perform ad hoc queries, one of the most straightforward techniques for implementing queries across servers is to use the OPENROWSET function in the FROM clause of a SELECT statement. The OPENROWSET function can return a row set from another SQL Server instance running on the same or another computer. In order to run SELECT statements with the OPENROWSET function in their FROM clause, you'll need to first enable the capability.

One way to enable ad hoc queries via the OPENROWSET function is with the SQL Server 2005 Surface Area Configuration Tool that installs automatically with SQL Server Express. You can invoke this tool by choosing Start ➤ All Programs ➤ SQL Server 2005 ➤ Configuration Tools ➤ SQL Server Surface Area Configuration. Next, click the Surface Area Configuration for Features link at the bottom of the SQL Server 2005 Surface Area Configuration window (see Figure 5-1). Then, from the Surface Area Configuration for Features screen, select the Ad-hoc Remote Queries feature for the SQL Server 2005 instance you are using to expose a check box with a label that reads "Enable OPENROWSET and OPENDATASOURCE support." Select the check box so that it is checked (see Figure 5-2) before clicking OK and closing the SQL Server 2005 Surface Area Configuration window.

After enabling the ability to run an ad hoc query with the OPENROWSET function, you need to specify a SELECT statement with the function in the FROM clause. The OPENROWSET function is exceptionally rich, and it can work with many data providers, including heterogeneous ones, such as those for Access, Excel, or Oracle. Extensive documentation on all the OPENROWSET capabilities is available from the OPENROWSET (Transact-SQL) topic in Books Online.

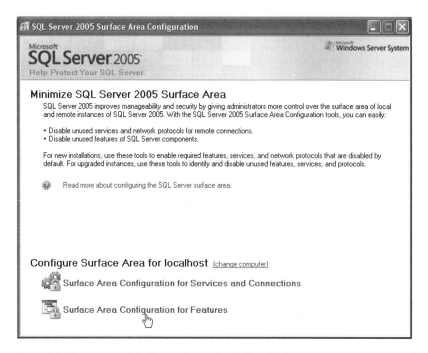

Figure 5-1. *You can graphically configure the ability of SQL Server Express to run ad hoc queries across server instances with the SQL Server 2005 Surface Area Configuration Tool.*

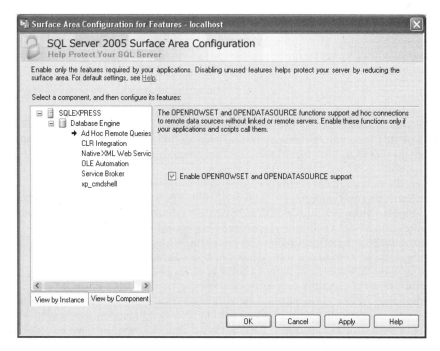

Figure 5-2. *From the Surface Area Configuration for Features screen, you can enable the running of ad hoc queries across server instances with the OPENROWSET function.*

The following SELECT statement specifies five arguments in the OPENROWSET function within the FROM clause. Each argument appears in single quotes (' '). The arguments are delimited by either a comma or a semicolon, depending on the argument type. The AS keyword in the FROM clause designates an alias named a for the result set returned by the query within the OPENROWSET function. This alias also appears as part of a SELECT list item. The a.* format for the list item uses the wildcard parameter to specify the return of all columns from the row set returned by the OPENROWSET function. The use of * in a SELECT list is valid with best practice guidelines because the OPENROWSET function's query statement denotes specific columns to return from the underlying data source on another server instance.

- The first argument (SQLNCLI) designates the SQL Native Client OLE DB Provider. You can use other provider names to connect in different ways and to other types of data sources, such as the OLE DB Provider for ODBC data sources or the OLE DB Provider for Jet.

- The second, third, and fourth arguments specify the server name, user ID on the remote server, and password for the user ID. You'll have to customize these for whatever server instance name and SQL Server login that you use in your computer environment. The instance name in this context will typically have a format like default_instance_name or computer_name\named_instance_name. If you use a different provider besides the SQL Native Client OLE DB Provider, then you're likely to need different argument settings.

- The fifth argument is a SELECT statement that references the Shippers table from the Northwind database for the database designated with the preceding four arguments.

■Tip The OPENROWSET function does not have a happy syntax. It can require a long list of parameters enclosed in quotes and separated by either commas or semicolons. My advice is to find a code sample that comes close to doing what you want done, and then tweak the parameters to complete your custom task. Use this base case OPENROWSET formulation to start developing your syntax for other applications.

```
SELECT a.*
FROM OPENROWSET('SQLNCLI','instance_name';'userid';'userid_password',
    'SELECT *
     FROM Northwind.dbo.Shippers') AS a;
```

The following output listing shows the result set returned by the preceding SELECT statement. Although this statement operates from a default database context of the AdventureWorks database on one computer, the statement still returns values from another database on a different server! While the syntax is a little arcane, I use this function regularly for ad hoc queries between server instances (and even other more exotic cases, such as between different types of data sources on different computers).

```
ShipperID    CompanyName       Phone
-----------  ----------------  --------------
1            Speedy Express    (503) 555-9831
2            United Package    (503) 555-3199
3            Federal Shipping  (503) 555-9931
```

Running Queries from a Linked Server

Linked servers offer another means of performing distributed queries and heterogeneous data access. Therefore, you can think of a linked server as representing any OLE DB data source. In addition, linked servers permit you to run stored procedures on another server instance. When you query a data source on a remote SQL Server Express instance, you can think of a linked server as one server instance that points at another server instance. Just as you could use a three-part name to point at another database on the same server, you can use the alias associated with a linked server in a four-part name to point at another server instance with an associated database name, schema name, and database object name. The alias represents all the connection and query parameter arguments in an OPENROWSET function with one name that identifies the linked server.

■**Note** A stored procedure is a collection of T-SQL statements saved on a server instance to be programmatically accessible. Chapter 7 drills down on stored procedures in greater depth.

The general syntax for using a linked server is

```
SELECT list FROM linked_server_name.database_name. schema_name.objectname
```

The linked_server_name part immediately after the FROM keyword is the alias for the linked server. Notice how simple the syntax is for using a linked server compared to the syntax of the OPENROWSET function.

Before you can apply the four-part name to reference a linked server, you must invoke the sp_addlinkedserver system-stored procedure to set up the alias for referencing a linked server. This system-stored procedure lets you associate the linked server name with connection information for a remote server and is exceptionally rich so as to accommodate the full feature set for linked servers. This section drills down on how to use a linked server to connect to another server instance on the same computer, as well as on another computer.

The sp_addlinkedserver syntax for these two objectives is essentially identical. In either case, SQL Server Express can map Windows accounts from the current server instance to a linked server instance. Because the Windows accounts are more likely to be different on two different computers, the default account mappings between the server instances is less likely to be valid when the linked server instance is on another computer. To set up a custom mapping of local server logins to remote server logins, use the sp_addlinkedsrvlogin system-stored procedure. In particular, the sp_addlinkedsrvlogin system-stored procedure permits three styles of mapping logins from a local server instance to a linked remote server instance.

- You can pass along account credentials for users on the local server instance to the remote server instance. This is also the default login mapping implemented by the sp_addlinkedserver system-stored procedure.

- You can designate a login on the remote server that all users on the local server can present when working with the linked server.

- You can specify individual remote logins for each individual local login that has access to a linked server.

Besides sp_addlinkedserver and sp_addlinkedsrvlogin, there are several other system-stored procedures that are worth getting to know when working with linked servers.

- The `sp_linkedservers` system-stored procedure returns a list of linked servers defined on the local server instance. This list will also include the local server instance—that is, the one from which you define the linked server. You are likely to find this system-stored procedure handy when you need to add and drop linked servers.

- The `sp_helplinkedsrvlogin` system-stored procedure lists the remote login mappings along with their properties. When you need to drop a login mapping, this command can be vital.

- The `sp_droplinkedsrvlogin` system-stored procedure removes a mapping between a local login and a remote login. You cannot drop a linked server until all the login mappings to the remote server are removed.

- The `sp_dropserver` system-stored procedure can drop a linked server alias on a local computer. This system-stored procedure is very convenient when you want to create a new linked server by the same name as an existing linked server because SQL Server Express allows only one name per linked server.

The following code sample shows the syntax for defining and using a linked server. The linked server is defined from a named instance of SQL Server Express to the default instance on the same computer with the default login mappings. There are two especially important elements in the listing that you can edit to make this code work in your computer environment.

- First, change all instances of the `MyLinkedServer` string in the code sample to whatever name you want to use for your linked server. Performing this step allows you to assign a meaningful name to your linked server, but the step is not strictly mandatory.

- Second, change the `default_instance_name` string to the name of your computer with a default instance of SQL Server already installed on it. Actually, you could just as easily apply this code to any named instance, such as one with a name in the following format: `default_instance_name\named_instance_name`. In any event, revising the `default_instance_name` string is mandatory for the code sample to work in your computing environment.

In the following listing, there are four batches of T-SQL with each one terminated by the `GO` keyword.

- The first batch sets up a default database context for the `AdventureWorks` database on the SQL Server Express instance for the current connection.

- Next, the `sp_droplinkedsrvlogin` syntax drops the default login mapping to the linked server named `MyLinkedServer`. The same batch also drops the `MyLinkedServer` linked server. It is important to drop the login mappings before attempting to drop a linked server.

- The third batch adds a new version of the `MyLinkedServer` linked server. Remember to change the setting for `@datasrc` so that it points at the name of a SQL Server instance on your computer.

- The final batch illustrates the proper syntax for a `SELECT` statement using the linked server. This statement runs on one server instance with a default database context for the `AdventureWorks` database. However, the statement pulls data from the `Shippers` table in the `Northwind` database on another server instance named `default_instance_name`. The result set generated by the `SELECT` statement is the same as the one illustrating the syntax for the use of the `OPENROWSET` function (see the "Running Ad Hoc Queries on Another Server Instance" section in this chapter).

```
USE master
GO

EXEC sp_droplinkedsrvlogin 'MyLinkedServer', NULL
EXEC sp_dropserver 'MyLinkedServer'
GO

EXEC sp_addlinkedserver
    @server='MyLinkedServer',
    @srvproduct= N'',
    @provider='SQLNCLI',
    @datasrc='default_instance_name'
GO

SELECT * FROM MyLinkedServer.Northwind.dbo.Shippers
GO
```

The next script illustrates the use of a linked server for connecting to a SQL Server instance on another computer. The script contains five T-SQL batches. In most cases the batches are identical to the preceding one for pointing a linked server to a SQL Server instance on the same computer. However, they are repeated in the following code for clarity. As with the preceding sample, you have the option of replacing all instances of the MyLinkedServer string to whatever name you want to use for your linked server.

There's a slight change in the third batch, which indicates an argument for the @datasrc parameter that points at the name of a SQL Server instance on another computer. Replace the @datasrc parameter with any appropriate name for your computing environment.

The new fourth batch illustrates the use of the sp_addlinkedsrvlogin system-stored procedure to enable all local user logins to connect to the linked server with remotelogin. The remotelogin login must exist on the server instance at which the linked server points.

The fifth batch in following script uses the same four-part naming convention of the preceding sample to reference the Shippers table in the Northwind database on the linked server. The output is identical as well.

```
USE AdventureWorks
GO

EXEC sp_droplinkedsrvlogin 'MyLinkedServer', NULL
EXEC sp_dropserver 'MyLinkedServer'
GO

EXEC sp_addlinkedserver
    @server='MyLinkedServer',
    @srvproduct= N'',
    @provider='SQLNCLI',
    @datasrc='instance_name_on_another_computer'
GO

EXEC sp_addlinkedsrvlogin 'MyLinkedServer', 'false',
    NULL, 'remotelogin', 'remotelogin_password'
GO

SELECT * FROM MyLinkedServer.Northwind.dbo.Shippers
GO
```

Filtering, Grouping, and Aggregating

Users very often need to see just a small excerpt of the rows in a data source. This capability of selecting a subset of rows based on column values is often called filtering. Another popular database application feature is the ability to summarize results by groups. This section highlights two `SELECT` statement clauses that let you implement these capabilities.

- The `WHERE` clause enables you to filter rows based on column values. This section demonstrates filtering rows based on columns with characters or numbers. You also learn about special operators that can help to specify criteria for filtering the rows that you seek.

- The `GROUP BY` clause helps you to group sets of rows in a data source. You'll often find use for this clause when you have aggregate functions, such as `COUNT` and `SUM`, in the list for a `SELECT` statement. This section also demonstrates how to format the output from a `SELECT` statement with a `GROUP BY` clause to exclude results for selected groups and to order how the group results appear in a result set.

■**Note** The `TOP` clause offers a limited capability for filtering when contrasted with the `WHERE` clause. When the features of the `TOP` keyword are sufficient for your needs, you should consider its use. See the "Returning Top Values" section earlier in this chapter for in-depth coverage of the `TOP` keyword.

Filtering for Exact and Approximate Character Matches

It is typical to perform searches for exact or approximate matches in a column of character values, such as columns with char or varchar data types. A simple equals comparison operator (=) enables exact character matches. The `LIKE` operator with wildcard characters is especially useful for expressing approximate matches.

If you are personally performing ad hoc searches, it is simple to directly code the comparison in the `WHERE` clause for a `SELECT` statement. When an ad hoc query escalates into one that is performed regularly, but with different search strings, then developing an expression for a `WHERE` clause can simplify the process for designating new search criteria. Local variables also add value when you are preparing a query statement for use by others who may not feel comfortable editing a clause in a `SELECT` statement.

All the samples in this section use the `Contact` table in the `Person` schema with searches on either the `LastName` or `Phone` column. The samples for this section are in ExactAndApproximate-CharacterMatches.sql.

A search for an exact match is convenient when you want to find one or a subset of rows in a data source that exactly match a criterion, such as everyone having the same last name. The following `SELECT` statement returns contact information, including e-mail address and phone number, for rows in the `Person` table with a `LastName` column value of `Blanco`. The use of the equals operator in a `WHERE` clause enables this kind of search.

```
SELECT FirstName, LastName, EmailAddress, Phone
FROM Person.Contact
WHERE LastName = 'Blanco'
```

Another common search is to find everyone whose last name begins with a particular letter. You can use the `LIKE` operator and a wildcard character to specify an expression for this kind of search. The following `SELECT` statement returns all rows from the `Contact` table whose `LastName` column value begins with b. The % wildcard character matches `LastName` column values with any number of characters after b. A couple of interesting variations of the criterion expression can search for all rows whose LastName column value ends with b (%b) or contains b (%b%). In addition, you are not restricted to using a single character (b)—you can also use any string of characters.

```
SELECT FirstName, LastName, EmailAddress, Phone
FROM Person.Contact
WHERE LastName LIKE 'b%'
```

Using a local variable with a wildcard character as an expression for a WHERE clause makes it easy to change a search criterion for a column of character values. When you specify such an expression for a WHERE clause, you need to use the concatenation operator (+) to merge the wildcard character with the local variable. The SELECT statement that follows illustrates how to use the concatenation operator following a local variable (@alpha) to merge the variable with a wildcard character. By declaring the local variable with an nchar(1) data type, you enable searches that begin with just one character. If you want to permit searches that begin with a variable number of characters, such as up to 10, you can declare the local variable with either nvarchar(10) or varchar(10).

```
DECLARE @alpha nchar(1)
SET @alpha = 'b'
SELECT FirstName, LastName, EmailAddress, Phone
FROM Person.Contact
WHERE LastName LIKE @alpha + '%'
```

The preceding sample is interesting because it suggests so many useful extensions. For example, instead of searching for LastName column values that begin with a character, you can switch the order of the wildcard character and the local variable in the WHERE clause of a SELECT statement to return rows that end with a character. In addition, you aren't restricted to using just one local variable.

The following SELECT statement includes a WHERE clause that searches for rows that start with one character and end with another. In this case, the beginning character is c and the ending character is o. The use of the % wildcard character is very powerful in this and other searches for a string of characters because % matches any number of characters. By modifying the SET statements assigning values to @alpha and @endalpha, you can search for LastName column values with different beginning and ending characters.

```
DECLARE @alpha nchar(1), @endalpha nchar(1)
SET @alpha = 'c'
SET @endalpha = 'o'
SELECT FirstName, LastName, EmailAddress, Phone
FROM Person.Contact
WHERE LastName LIKE @alpha + '%' + @endalpha
```

Aside from just searching for values that begin or end with one or more characters, you can also use the LIKE operator and the % wildcard character to represent the notion of "contained in." You can represent this notion by embedding a local variable between two wildcard characters. The WHERE clause in the following SELECT statement returns rows whose LastName column values contain bell either at the beginning, in the middle, or at the end of the string of characters within the column.

```
DECLARE @alpha nvarchar(10)
SET @alpha = 'bell'
SELECT FirstName, LastName, EmailAddress, Phone
FROM Person.Contact
WHERE LastName LIKE '%' + @alpha + '%'
```

To emphasize how flexible this kind of formulation is, an excerpt showing the first 10 rows from the result set returned by the preceding SELECT statement appears next. The first row shows bell beginning a LastName column value. The next three rows show bell at the end of their LastName column values. The fifth row has `bell` embedded with its name. The 10th row shows `bell` as the whole `LastName` column value. In this case, the beginning and ending wildcard characters represent a character string of zero length.

```
FirstName LastName EmailAddress                 Phone
--------- -------- ---------------------------- ------------
Shane     Belli    shane1@adventure-works.com   843-555-0175
Joan      Campbell joan0@adventure-works.com    700-555-0155
David     Campbell david14@adventure-works.com  756-555-0117
Frank     Campbell frank4@adventure-works.com   491-555-0132
Deanna    Sabella  deanna2@adventure-works.com  529-555-0100
David     Campbell david8@adventure-works.com   740-555-0182
John      Campbell john0@adventure-works.com    435-555-0113
John      Campbell john30@adventure-works.com   593-555-0100
Jean      Campbell jean7@adventure-works.com    827-555-0100
Alexandra Bell     alexandra7@adventure-works.com 987-555-0181
```

There are many ways in which you can combine exact and approximate matches for different column values. The following `SELECT` statement includes two expressions in its `WHERE` clause. The first expression specifies an exact search (`LastName` column value must equal `Blanco`), and the second expression designates an approximate search (`Phone` column value includes a country code of (`11`)). The `AND` operator between the two expressions additionally requires that rows in the result set must satisfy both expressions—instead of just either expression or even neither expression.

```
DECLARE @alpha1  nvarchar(30), @alpha2 nvarchar(10)
SET @alpha1 = 'Blanco'
SET @alpha2 = '%(11)%'
SELECT FirstName, LastName, EmailAddress, Phone
FROM Person.Contact
WHERE LastName = @alpha1 AND
    Phone LIKE @alpha2
```

Filtering for Values in a Range

Database applications often need to filter for rows based on whether column values are in a range or not. Three types of T-SQL operators in a `WHERE` clause help you to select a subset of rows with values for one of its columns in a range. By using subquery statements as arguments for these operators, you can add even more flexibility to your searches with these operators. We'll drill down on subqueries in Chapter 6.

- Comparison operations, such as >, >=, <, and <= are optimized for designating a range of values in a `WHERE` clause. For example, you can request all rows with a column value less than (<) a fixed value. By just replacing the < operator with a >= operator, you can return all rows that are equal to or more than the same fixed value. This kind of operator can accommodate more dynamic criteria, such as when you seek rows with one column value less than another column value.

- You can also use the `BETWEEN` operator to search for rows with column values from a lower bound to an upper bound.

- The `IN` operator lets you select a subset of rows with column values that match any of a discrete set of values.

You can find the samples for this section in FilteringforValuesInARange.sql.

Filtering Rows with <= and > Operators

The SalesPerson table in the Sales schema includes just 17 rows with several columns for tracking sales by SalesPersonID column values. The SalesQuota column has values with a money data type, and there are only three unique values across the 17 rows. You can think of each unique SalesQuota column value as denoting a range with just one entry in the range.

The following script includes a SELECT statement that uses the DISTINCT keyword to list each unique SalesQuota column value just once. It is often useful to run this type of query to determine the values that reside in a column before you decide to filter on the values. As you can see, the distinct SalesQuota column values include two quantitative values (250,000 and 300,000) and one null value.

```
SELECT DISTINCT SalesQuota
FROM Sales.SalesPerson
```

```
SalesQuota
---------------------
NULL
250000.00
300000.00
```

Three additional queries return rows matching each of the three SalesQuota column values. The next listing shows one query statement that returns all rows with a SalesQuota column value less than or equal to 250,000. The statement's WHERE clause includes a <= operator for comparing SalesQuota column values to a fixed value. When the criterion evaluates to True, a row's SalesQuota column value matches the criterion. A total of 11 rows with SalesQuota column values of 250,000 match this criterion. The result set listing below the query statement shows the SalesPersonID, SalesQuota, year-to-date sales (Sales this year), and last year's sales (Sales last year) for each of these rows:

```
SELECT SalesPersonID, SalesQuota,
    CAST(SalesYTD AS dec(12,2)) 'Sales this year' ,
    CAST(SalesLastYear AS dec(12,2)) 'Sales last year'
FROM Sales.SalesPerson
WHERE SalesQuota <=250000
```

SalesPersonID	SalesQuota	Sales this year	Sales last year
276	250000.00	5200475.23	1439156.03
277	250000.00	3857163.63	1997186.20
278	250000.00	1764938.99	1620276.90
280	250000.00	0.00	1927059.18
281	250000.00	3018725.49	2073506.00
282	250000.00	3189356.25	2038234.65
283	250000.00	3587378.43	1371635.32
285	250000.00	5015682.38	1635823.40
286	250000.00	3827950.24	2396539.76
289	250000.00	2241204.04	1307949.79
290	250000.00	1758385.93	2278548.98

You might think that just by swapping the <= operator for a > operator you can obtain any remaining rows with a different column value than 250,000. However, a null value cannot equal any non-null value. Therefore, checking for column values either above or below any fixed value will not return rows with a null value. The greater than operator (>) in the following query statement returns just the three rows with a SalesQuota column value of 300,000. The following listing shows the statement and its matching result set.

```
SELECT SalesPersonID, SalesQuota,
    CAST(SalesYTD AS dec(12,2)) 'Sales this year' ,
    CAST(SalesLastYear AS dec(12,2)) 'Sales last year'
FROM Sales.SalesPerson
WHERE SalesQuota >250000
```

```
SalesPersonID SalesQuota Sales this year Sales last year
------------- ---------- --------------- ---------------
275           300000.00  4557045.05      1750406.48
279           300000.00  2811012.72      1849640.94
287           300000.00  1931620.18      0.00
```

As you have seen, you cannot return rows with null values when you compare them to a fixed value with the <= or > operators. To select rows with null values in a column, use an IS NULL clause within a SELECT statement's WHERE clause. The following SELECT statement demonstrates the use of the IS NULL clause to return rows with null SalesQuota column values.

```
SELECT SalesPersonID, SalesQuota,
    CAST(SalesYTD AS dec(12,2)) 'Sales this year' ,
    CAST(SalesLastYear AS dec(12,2)) 'Sales last year'
FROM Sales.SalesPerson
WHERE SalesQuota IS NULL
```

```
SalesPersonID SalesQuota Sales this year Sales last year
------------- ---------- --------------- ---------------
268           NULL       677558.47       0.00
284           NULL       636440.25       0.00
288           NULL       219088.88       0.00
```

Filtering Rows with the BETWEEN Operator

The BETWEEN operator lets you select rows from a lower bound through to an upper bound.

- The BETWEEN operator specifies both ends of a range while the >, >=, <, and <= comparison operators explicitly specify just one end of a range.

- You can designate the lower and upper bounds for the BETWEEN operator with constants or expressions that are valid for comparison with a column's values (for example, you can compare an int value to a decimal value type, but you cannot compare an int value to a varchar value).

- Use the AND keyword to join the lower and upper bounds as arguments for a BETWEEN operator.

The following SELECT statement shows the syntax for using the BETWEEN operator to search for SalePerson rows with SaleYTD column values from 200,000 to 650,000. Notice that the AND keyword separates the lower and upper bounds for the range specified within the BETWEEN operator. The BETWEEN operator appears in the WHERE clause immediately after the name of the column to which it applies.

```
SELECT SalesPersonID, SalesQuota,
    CAST(SalesYTD AS dec(12,2)) 'Sales this year' ,
    CAST(SalesLastYear AS dec(12,2)) 'Sales last year'
FROM Sales.SalesPerson
WHERE SalesYTD BETWEEN 200000 AND 650000
```

The result set for the preceding SELECT statement returns two rows (see the following code block). Both of the Sales this year column values in the result set derive from the SaleYTD column in the SalesPerson table. As significantly, both Sales this year column values are in the range specified by the BETWEEN operator.

```
SalesPersonID SalesQuota Sales this year Sales last year
------------- ---------- --------------- ---------------
284           NULL       636440.25       0.00
288           NULL       219088.88       0.00
```

One interesting question is: are all the remaining SalesYTD column values non-null? There are several ways to answer this question. The following SELECT statement shows one way that relies on your knowing how many rows are in the SalesPerson table. The list for the SELECT statement develops a count of the rows meeting the criterion expression in the WHERE clause.

■**Tip** You can compute the number of rows in any data source with the following T-SQL statement:: SELECT COUNT(*) FROM data_source_name.

This next SELECT statement's WHERE clause expression is identical to the one in the preceding SELECT statement, with the addition of a NOT keyword before the BETWEEN operator. SQL Server Express considers NOT followed by BETWEEN to be an operator that designates the complement range of a BETWEEN operator with the same lower and upper bounds. In other words, the following SELECT statement counts the number of rows outside the range specified in the preceding SELECT statement.

```
SELECT Count(*) 'SalesYTD outside BETWEEN'
FROM Sales.SalesPerson
WHERE SalesYTD NOT BETWEEN 200000 AND 650000
```

The preceding SELECT statement returns a count of 15 rows. Since the SELECT statement without the NOT BETWEEN operator returned 2 rows, you know that all 17 rows have non-null SalesYTD column values. Any rows with null SalesYTD column values would fail to fall inside the ranges designated by the BETWEEN and NOT BETWEEN operators.

You can enrich your SELECT statements with BETWEEN criteria expressions by adding other criteria with comparison operators. The next SELECT statement uses the previous BETWEEN operator expressions to return two rows for sales persons with very low SaleYTD column values. However, the SELECT statement also complements the BETWEEN operator with a comparison operator that searches for sales persons with SalesYTD column values above 5,000,000. The WHERE clause combines the BETWEEN and > operator criteria with an OR operator that causes the SELECT statement to accept rows that meet either criterion.

```
SELECT SalesPersonID, SalesQuota,
    CAST(SalesYTD AS dec(12,2)) 'Sales this year' ,
    CAST(SalesLastYear AS dec(12,2)) 'Sales last year'
FROM Sales.vSalesPerson
WHERE SalesYTD BETWEEN 200000 AND 650000 OR
    SalesYTD > 5000000
```

The output listing for the preceding SELECT statement reflects the impact of both criteria expressions. The rows with SalesPersonID values of 284 and 288 meet the BETWEEN operator criterion. On the other hand, the rows with SalesPersonID values of 276 and 285 meet the criterion designated by the > operator.

SalesPersonID	SalesQuota	Sales this year	Sales last year
276	250000.00	5200475.23	1439156.03
284	NULL	636440.25	0.00
285	250000.00	5015682.38	1635823.40
288	NULL	219088.88	0.00

Filtering Rows with the IN operator

You can use the IN operator to determine if a column value matches an item value in a list. Therefore, this operator differs from the preceding two operators by dealing exclusively with discrete values—namely, those in the list. The list item values can be of any type that supports the equals (=) operator. In essence, you can think of criteria specified with an IN operator as equivalent to a series of equals comparison operators combined with OR operators. In other words

```
SELECT *
FROM table_name
WHERE column_name IN (list_item1, list_item2, list_item3)
```

is equivalent to

```
SELECT *
FROM table_name
WHERE column_name = list_item1 OR
    column_name = list_item2 OR
    column_name = list_item3)
```

As you can see, the SELECT statement with the IN operator is shorter and easier to read.

The following SELECT statement shows the syntax for the IN operator with a list of two numbers. These are the two unique, non-null SalesQuota column values in the SalesPerson table. The list item for the SELECT statement counts the number of rows meeting the criteria, which is 14 in this case. Using a NOT operator before IN will return a count of zero because the three remaining rows have null SalesQuota values.

```
SELECT COUNT(*)
FROM Sales.SalesPerson
WHERE SalesQuota IN(250000, 300000)
```

The next SELECT statement illustrates the use of the IN operator with a pair of character values (United States and Canada) in its list.

- This query is based on the vSalesPerson view, which draws on several tables, including SalesPerson and SalesTerritory in the Sales schema and CountryRegion in the Person schema.
  - The SalesPerson table has a SalesTerritoryID column value that maps to SalesTerritoryID in the SalesTerritory table.
  - In turn, the SalesTerritory table has a CountryRegionCode column that maps to the CountryRegionCode column in the CountryRegion table.

- The `CountryRegion` table provides the `CountryRegionName` column values in the list for the `SELECT` statement.

- The `SELECT` statement's `WHERE` clause specifies that the `CountryRegionName` list items compare with the items in the `IN` list.

```
SELECT SalesPersonID, CountryRegionName
FROM Sales.vSalesPerson
WHERE CountryRegionName IN ('United States', 'Canada')
```

The output listing that immediately follows shows the result set generated by the `SELECT` statement, with the `IN` operator having two character items in its list. Only rows from the `vSalesPerson` view with a `CountryRegionName` matching one of the two `IN` items appear in the result set. Notice also that there are 13 rows in the result set.

```
SalesPersonID CountryRegionName
------------- -----------------
278           Canada
281           United States
287           United States
275           United States
277           United States
282           Canada
280           United States
279           United States
276           United States
288           United States
268           United States
284           United States
283           United States
```

The series of relationships defining the `vSalesPerson` view and the actual values in the `SalesPerson` table enables a `SELECT` statement to obtain the `CountryRegionName` column values for all remaining rows.

- Although the `SalesPerson` table permits null values for its `SalesTerritoryID` column, all the rows in the `SalesPerson` table from the `AdventureWorks` sample database have non-null values for `SalesTerritoryID`, with matching values in the `SalesTerritory` table.

- Similarly, all the `SalesTerritoryID` values in the `SalesTerritory` table have matching `CountryRegionCode` values in the `CountryRegion` table.

- Therefore, all the `CountryRegionName` column values in the `vSalesPerson` view are non-null.

This series of relationships permits a slight modification to the preceding `SELECT` statement that returns the `CountryRegionName` value for all remaining rows in the `vSalesPerson` view. The modification is to insert the `NOT` keyword before the `IN` operator. The following listing shows both the modified code and its result set. Notice that none of the rows in the result set have a `CountryRegionName` column value equal to the United States or Canada. As you can see, the result set contains 4 rows, which when added to the 13 rows of the preceding `SELECT` statement, recovers rows for all 17 sales persons in the `AdventureWorks` database.

```
SELECT SalesPersonID, CountryRegionName
FROM Sales.vSalesPerson
WHERE CountryRegionName NOT IN ('United States', 'Canada')
```

```
SalesPersonID CountryRegionName
------------- -----------------
289           Germany
285           United Kingdom
286           France
290           Australia
```

Grouping and Aggregating

Grouping is another common database application requirement. The T-SQL GROUP BY clause for a SELECT statement is optimized for returning aggregates, such as counts and sums, by group. A common use for the GROUP BY clause is the computation of a query that returns values, such as sales by territory. The GROUP BY clause also facilitates calculating aggregate values for groups that nest within groups. If your organization defines regions in terms of sets of territories, then a GROUP BY clause can show to which region a territory and its sales total belongs. The samples for this section reside in GroupingAndAggregating.sql.

When you use a GROUP BY clause in a SELECT statement, you will sometimes be able to benefit from two other clauses.

- The HAVING clause performs filtering at the level of groups defined by a GROUP BY clause. This statement operates similarly to the WHERE clause. The WHERE clause filters individual rows in a data source before grouping, and the HAVING clause filters groups. You can filter with either or both WHERE and HAVING clauses.

- The GROUP BY clause organizes groups of rows, but it does not necessarily return values for groups in an order that is conducive to analysis or presentation. If you want to ensure a specific order for result set rows, you can use an ORDER BY clause.

The use of a GROUP BY clause in a SELECT statement places some restrictions on the entries in a SELECT list and other aspects of a SELECT statement. Regarding the list, you can only include

- Items that are also in the GROUP BY clause

- Expressions for computing aggregates, such as counts and sums

Legitimate data types for GROUP BY columns exclude text, ntext, and image types. The total number of columns that you can specify in a GROUP BY clause depends on the size of the GROUP BY columns, the aggregated column values, and the inputs to the aggregate values. The total length of all three sources can be no greater than 8,060 bytes.

A GROUP BY clause must appear after a WHERE clause if there is one in a SELECT statement. If your SELECT statement has a HAVING clause, the HAVING clause must appear after the GROUP BY clause. Finally, an ORDER BY clause must appear after all other clauses in a SELECT statement.

Grouping to Show Distinct Values

The core function of a GROUP BY clause is to show the distinct values across one or more columns of a data source. These distinct values are the groups by which you can report aggregate values with a GROUP BY clause. If you do not have column values that define the groups you want, then you can add calculated values to a SELECT list and use the values from the expression for the calculated values for grouping the rows from a data source.

The following code listing shows a pair of SELECT statements. The first statement uses the DISTINCT keyword to return unique TerritoryName column values from the vSalesPerson view in the Sales schema. This query statement generates a result set with a single column containing a separate row with the name of each unique value in the TerritoryName column from the view.

The second SELECT statement demonstrates a very simple use for the GROUP BY clause. The statement groups by TerritoryName value the rows returned by the vSalesPerson view. Despite the fact that this SELECT statement does not have a DISTINCT keyword and there are duplicate values in the TerritoryName column, all the column values in the result set are unique. These unique names serve as group names for the rows returned by the vSalesPerson view.

```
SELECT DISTINCT TerritoryName
FROM Sales.vSalesPerson

SELECT TerritoryName
FROM Sales.vSalesPerson
GROUP BY TerritoryName
```

Both of the preceding SELECT statements generate the same result set, which appears next. Including the null value, there are 11 distinct values in the TerritoryName column. Some of these values have multiple occurrences in the TerritoryName column, which means that more than one sales person serves the same area. The rows for three persons in the sales department are not assigned to a sales territory—that is, they have a null TerritoryName column value.

```
TerritoryName
---------------
NULL
Australia
Canada
Central
France
Germany
Northeast
Northwest
Southeast
Southwest
United Kingdom
```

Grouping and Nesting

The GROUP BY clause also allows you to nest groups within one another. Of course, to construct a result set having nested groups with a GROUP BY clause, the data source for the SELECT statement must itself have nested groups. In addition, columns representing groups that contain other groups must appear in the GROUP BY clause before the groups that they contain.

The vSalesPerson view has two geographically based column values that nest within one another. The TerritoryName column values nest within the TerritoryGroup column values. For example, the North America TerritoryGroup includes six TerritoryName values: Central, Northeast, Northwest, Southeast, Southwest, and Canada.

- The following SELECT statement shows how to define the nesting in a GROUP BY clause between the TerritoryGroup and TerritoryName column values. Notice TerritoryGroup, whose column values contain TerritoryName column values, occurs first.

- The SELECT statement counts the number of rows returned by the vSalesPerson view for each TerritoryName value. Using a SELECT list item of COUNT(*) returns the number of rows in each group. Aggregations, such as the counts in the following SELECT statement, always occur at the lowest nesting level.

```
SELECT TerritoryGroup, TerritoryName, COUNT(*) 'Sales persons'
FROM Sales.VSalesPerson
GROUP BY TerritoryGroup, TerritoryName
```

Probably the most common reason to use a GROUP BY clause is to perform some kind of aggregation. The following result set shows the number of sales persons in each TerritoryName group. You can also see to which TerritoryGroup a TerritoryName belongs.

```
TerritoryGroup TerritoryName  Sales persons
-------------- -------------- -------------
NULL           NULL            3
Pacific        Australia       1
North America  Canada          2
North America  Central         1
Europe         France          1
Europe         Germany         1
North America  Northeast       1
North America  Northwest       3
North America  Southeast       1
North America  Southwest       2
Europe         United Kingdom  1
```

There are a couple of deficiencies with the preceding result set listing.

- First, there really is no TerritoryName nor TerritoryGroup called Null. The Null keyword appears in the result to indicate that a sales person is not assigned to a TerritoryName.

- Second, the TerritoryName values are not ordered within the TerritoryGroup to which they belong. Notice the Canada and Central TerritoryName members of the North America TerritoryGroup are separated from the remaining four North America TerritoryGroup members by two members of the Europe TerritoryGroup.

The following SELECT statement addresses both of the deficiencies appearing in the preceding result set listing. The HAVING clause excludes from the result set any row with a null TerritoryGroup value. The ORDER BY clause groups the TerritoryName column values in ascending alphabetical order within TerritoryGroup column values, also sorted in ascending order.

```
SELECT TerritoryGroup, TerritoryName, COUNT(*) 'Sales persons'
FROM Sales.VSalesPerson
GROUP BY TerritoryGroup, TerritoryName
HAVING TerritoryGroup IS NOT NULL
ORDER BY TerritoryGroup, TerritoryName
```

■Note The ORDER BY clause receives in-depth coverage in Chapter 6.

The easiest way to appreciate the impact of the HAVING and ORDER BY clauses is to view the result set generated by the SELECT statement. The following listing shows that result set.

- First, notice that there are just 10 rows in this result set. This is because the HAVING clause includes IS NOT NULL, which eliminates the result set row with a null value for TerritoryGroup.

- Next, observe that TerritoryGroup column values appear in alphabetical order, and that TerritoryName column values appear in alphabetical order within a group. The ORDER BY clause specifies this outcome.

```
TerritoryGroup  TerritoryName   Sales persons
--------------  --------------  -------------
Europe          France          1
Europe          Germany         1
Europe          United Kingdom  1
North America   Canada          2
North America   Central         1
North America   Northeast       1
North America   Northwest       3
North America   Southeast       1
North America   Southwest       2
Pacific         Australia       1
```

It is often true that you can obtain the same results by using a HAVING clause after grouping as you would by using a WHERE clause before grouping. Unless one query statement runs substantially faster than another, which is not often the case, you can pick the statement syntax that appeals most to the query author. The following query statement is a reformulation of the preceding query statement, except that a WHERE clause replaces the HAVING clause. This statement, with the WHERE clause, generates identical results to the preceding statement.

```
SELECT TerritoryGroup, TerritoryName, COUNT(*) 'Sales persons'
FROM Sales.VSalesPerson
WHERE TerritoryGroup IS NOT NULL
GROUP BY TerritoryGroup, TerritoryName
ORDER BY TerritoryGroup, TerritoryName
```

Grouping for Aggregation

One of the most common uses of grouping is to show the results of aggregates by group and to filter the results based on the individual or aggregate values. This section presents a couple of samples to demonstrate techniques that you may find useful when using grouping to achieve these goals.

The first sample illustrates several different types of calculations and aggregations that you can perform to generate useful results with grouping. The following SELECT statement generates the number of employees and compensation by TerritoryID column value from the SalesPerson table in the Sales schema. The SELECT statement's WHERE clause excludes rows in the SalesPerson table that have no TerritoryID column value. The SELECT list includes five items.

1. The first item returns the TerritoryID. This item also appears in the GROUP BY clause.

2. The second item uses the COUNT aggregate function to return a count of the number of sales persons per territory.

3. The third item uses the SUM aggregate function to return the total by territory of a calculated item. The calculated item is the product of the CommissionPct and SalesYTD columns which returns commission compensation.

4. The fourth item is another aggregate, but this one is the sum of single column, Bonus.

5. The fifth item is the sum of commission compensation and bonus compensation. The item is built from the expressions for the individual items because T-SQL does not allow you to refer back directly within a SELECT list to the results calculated by expressions for other columns.

```
SELECT TerritoryID, COUNT(*) 'Persons/territory',
    CAST(SUM(SalesYTD*CommissionPct) AS dec(12,2)) 'Commissions',
    SUM(Bonus) 'Bonuses',
    CAST(SUM(SalesYTD*CommissionPct) +
        SUM(Bonus) AS dec(12,2)) 'Cs + Bs'
FROM Sales.SalesPerson
WHERE TerritoryID IS NOT NULL
GROUP BY TerritoryID
```

The following listing shows the result set prepared by the preceding SELECT statement. Because you're using the SalesPerson table instead of the vSalesPerson view, you only have TerritoryID values. The SalesPerson table does not have a column of TerritoryName values, and the vSalesPerson view does not include a CommissionPct column for the calculation of commission income. Notice that the fifth column in the result set is merely the sum of the third and fourth columns. This follows directly from the SELECT list items. In addition, there are just 10 rows in the result set because the WHERE clause in the SELECT statement excludes three rows in the SalesPerson table with null values for TerritoryID.

TerritoryID	Persons/territory	Commissions	Bonuses	Cs + Bs
1	3	79749.32	12400.00	92149.32
2	1	54684.54	4100.00	58784.54
3	1	57857.45	2500.00	60357.45
4	2	108194.38	5550.00	113744.38
5	1	28110.13	6700.00	34810.13
6	2	65489.73	5500.00	70989.73
7	1	61247.20	985.00	62232.20
8	1	40341.67	75.00	40416.67
9	1	31650.95	5650.00	37300.95
10	1	100313.65	5150.00	105463.65

The second sample highlighting aggregation techniques contrasts two approaches to aggregating column values from the SalesOrderDetail table in the Sales schema. The SalesOrderDetail table includes multiple rows per sales order. Each row for a sales order corresponds to a line item for that order. The results are for the first five sales orders that qualify for analysis. The SELECT list items returned by sales order are the number of different items ordered and the total price of the line items. The results are returned for the first five sales orders and the first five sales orders with a total price for the line items above the average price per order.

The technique for generating results for the first five sales orders depends on a single SELECT statement, which appears in the next code block. The SELECT statement includes a SELECT list with a FROM clause and GROUP BY clause. The TOP keyword and its argument specify a result set for just the first five rows.

- The FROM clause specifies that values come from the SalesOrderDetail table.

- The GROUP BY clause indicates that SELECT list items are to be grouped by SalesOrderID.

- The SELECT list specifies three columns.

  - The first column corresponds to the column named in the GROUP BY clause (SalesOrderID).

  - The second column counts the number of OrderQty column values to reflect the number of line items. You can count any column with non-null values to generate this result, or just use COUNT(*).

  - The third column sums the LineTotal column value, which reflects the price charged the customer for the line item represented by that row in the SalesOrderDetail table.

```
SELECT TOP 5 SalesOrderID, COUNT(OrderQty) 'Items ordered',
    CAST(SUM(LineTotal) AS dec(12,2)) 'Price of items ordered'
FROM Sales.SalesOrderDetail
GROUP BY SalesOrderID
```

The following script generates a filtered result set based on sales orders with an above average price, and uses some local variables to compute the overall average for sales orders. Then, the script uses the computed overall average price to return the first five orders that have above average prices.

Two SET statements compute and save the total sales across all orders and the total number of sales. The total number of sales is computed from the SalesOrderHeader table because this table contains just one row per sales order. Therefore, counting the number of rows in the SalesOrderHeader table returns the number of sales. The sum of the LineTotal column values from the SalesOrderDetail table reflects the overall revenue generated from sales. A SELECT list item expresses the formula for the average price as the total revenue divided by the number of sales orders.

```
DECLARE @totsales dec(12,2), @numofsales int
SET @totsales = (SELECT SUM(LineTotal) FROM Sales.SalesOrderDetail)
SET @numofsales = (SELECT COUNT(SalesOrderID) FROM Sales.SalesOrderHeader)
SELECT @totsales 'Total sales revenue',
    @numofsales 'Number of sales',
    @totsales/@numofsales 'Average revenue/sale'
```

After demonstrating the expression for representing the average price, a SELECT statement extracts the first five orders with summed LineTotal column values greater than the average price over all sales orders. This SELECT statement is almost the same as the first SELECT statement in the sample. The difference is the addition of a HAVING clause that filters for sales orders with summed LineTotal column values greater than the average price per sales order.

```
SELECT TOP 5 SalesOrderID, COUNT(OrderQty) 'Items ordered',
    SUM(LineTotal) 'Price of items ordered'
FROM Sales.SalesOrderDetail
GROUP BY SalesOrderID
HAVING SUM(LineTotal) > @totsales/@numofsales
```

The next result set listing shows the output from each of the preceding three code segments. There are three sets or rows in the result set—one corresponding to each code segment.

- The first code segment is the SELECT statement that gives the number of items ordered and the prices paid for those orders. There is no filtering for these orders. The SalesOrderID column values proceed sequentially in an uninterrupted path from 43659 to 43663.

- The second set of rows is just a single row. The third column in this row reflects the average revenue per order (4046.9467697441601) based on the total revenue across all orders (127337180.11) and the total number of orders (31465).

- The third result set includes five rows—just like the first result set. However, the price of items ordered for each order in the third result set is greater than the average revenue per order. Two sales orders (43660 and 43663) from the first result set with a price of items ordered below the average revenue are removed from the third result set and replaced by the next two other orders (43664 and 43665) with revenue greater than the average revenue for all orders.

```
SalesOrderID Items ordered Price of items ordered
------------ ------------- ----------------------
43659        12            20565.62
43660        2             1294.25
43661        15            32726.48
43662        22            28832.53
43663        1             419.46

(5 row(s) affected)


Total sales revenue Number of sales Average revenue/sale
------------------- --------------- --------------------
109846381.40        31465           3491.0656729699666

(1 row(s) affected)


SalesOrderID Items ordered Price of items ordered
------------ ------------- ----------------------
43659        12            20565.620600
43661        15            32726.478600
43662        22            28832.528900
43664        8             24432.608800
43665        10            14352.771300

(5 row(s) affected)
```

Summary

This chapter systematically reviewed the key SELECT statement clauses for implementing data access. These clauses include FROM, WHERE, GROUP BY, HAVING, and ORDER BY. You saw how to use these clauses together with SELECT list items to format the result sets generated by running SELECT statements. In the process of reviewing SELECT statement clauses, the chapter demonstrated numerous techniques, such as how to take advantage of traditional and innovative features for the TOP keyword, as well as how to format and process date and time values.

A central theme of this chapter was how to generate result sets from a single database object. That restriction still leaves substantial flexibility in the sources of data for a SELECT statement.

- If you need a column not provided by any single table, you may be able to specify calculated column values that meet your requirement.

- If that does not work, you may find the column you need in a view within the current database context that a USE keyword designates.

- If that does not work, you may be able to extract the values you seek from a database object in another database on the same server.

- Finally, you can resort to retrieving values from database objects on other database server instances connected via an OPENROWSET function or a linked server.

The next chapter will include coverage of techniques for concurrently retrieving data from multiple database objects, as well as other advanced data access techniques.

CHAPTER 6

■ ■ ■

Querying Multiple Database Objects and Manipulating Result Sets

The overall objective of this chapter is to present techniques to help you maximize the value of your organization's database investments. In the process, you learn ways of transforming data into information for decision making. The chapter covers two major areas:

- First, you learn how to build custom queries with techniques that enable you to reference your own ad hoc collections of database objects.

- Second, this chapter trains you to manipulate retrieved data in ways that highlight the most valuable content in one or more result sets.

As you discover the myriad ways for deriving information from data, you will be building solid relational data access skills. Examples of specific topics covered include

- Rich techniques for combining multiple data sources by merging and appending them to one another

- Techniques for integrating two or more query statements into a single one that can provide answers to complex questions

- Four new T-SQL functions for ranking and sorting data across all result set rows as well as within partitions of a result set

- New T-SQL techniques for reusing query statements and transforming data from a relational layout to a cross-tab format and back again

Joining Data Sources

You can join multiple data sources, such as tables or views, to enable simultaneous access to column values from the joined data sources. A result set from joined data sources merges the rows from the sources on one or more criteria. A *join* is a specialized kind of filtering that combines rows from different data sources when the rows comply with the join criteria.

A join is always between just two data sources. However, you can represent one data source in a join as the result set from joining another pair of data sources. In this way, you can join three data sources. SQL Server Express permits you to repeat this process to merge up to 256 data sources into a single SELECT statement.

There are several fundamental types of joins between data sources:

- An inner join, often simply called a join, merges rows from a pair of data sources when column values from both data sources match some criterion expression. Rows that do not comply with the criteria are excluded from the joined result set. Null values for any criteria column value cause a row to be excluded from the joined result set.

- An outer join merges rows from two data sources so that all rows from one data source enter into the result set. You can think of the first of a pair of data sources as a left data source, and the second data source as a right data source.

  - A left outer join combines all the rows from the first data source with rows that comply with the join criteria from the second data source.

  - A right outer join combines all rows from the second data source with rows that comply with the join criteria from the first data source.

  - A full outer join combines, without referencing criteria, all the rows from both data sources.

- A self-join merges the rows from a data source with a duplicate of itself. This kind of join is very convenient when two or more columns derive from a shared set of identification values, such as identification numbers for an employee and an employee's manager.

- A cross join individually merges all the rows from one data source with each of the rows in a second data source without regard to any join criteria. With even a modest number of rows in either or both data sources, a cross-joined result set can have an exceptionally large number of rows. For example, cross-joining two data sources with 10,000 rows each leads to a result set of 100,000,000 rows!

Joining can serve all kinds of data processing needs, such as

- Looking up column values in a table pointed at by a foreign key

- Ignoring rows that have no match in either data source

- Unconditionally merging all the rows from one data source with rows from another data source

- Filtering rows in one data source based on column values from another data source

- Grouping rows from one data source to aggregate column values from a matching second data source

Inner Joins

An inner join can merge rows from two data sources on one or more criteria values. There are two basic syntaxes for joining data sources in a SELECT statement:

- First, you can name the data sources in the FROM clause and specify the criteria for merging rows from two result sets in a WHERE (or even a HAVING) clause.

- Second, you can specify both the data sources and the criteria for matching rows in the FROM clause.

  - This second approach uses a keyword or phrase, such as JOIN or INNER JOIN, to specify which data sources to merge.

  - This approach uses an ON clause to designate the join criteria for the data sources.

When the same column name is in both data sources for a join, you must qualify references to the column name. You can qualify a column name with either the name for a data source, such as its schema and database object name, or an alias name. An alias name is like a nickname for a data source. You designate an alias name in the FROM clause of a SELECT statement.

The samples for this section appear in InnerJoins.sql. All the samples are for the ProductSubcategory table in the Production schema of the AdventureWorks database. Unless otherwise indicated, all samples throughout this chapter are for the AdventureWorks database.

A SELECT Statement That References a Foreign Key Value

One especially common use of an inner join is to look up a value in one table from another table. This is often convenient when a foreign key with a number data type points at a row in another table. Instead of showing the number value for the foreign key, you can show a name that designates a row at which the foreign key value points.

As an example in which a number is displayed instead of a name, the following SELECT statement includes three column names in its list. The ProductSubcategoryID column denotes the ProductSubcategory table's primary key, and the Name column value is the subcategory name from the ProductSubcategory table. The ProductCategoryID column value is a foreign key with an int data type that points at the ProductCategory table.

```
SELECT TOP 5 ProductSubcategoryID, ProductCategoryID,
    Name 'Subcategory name'
FROM Production.ProductSubcategory
ORDER BY ProductSubcategoryID
```

The TOP 5 phrase in the preceding SELECT statement shows just the first five rows from the underlying 37 rows in the ProductSubcategory table. These five rows appear in the following results. Notice that the middle column for ProductCategoryID shows a number value of either 1 or 2, which is not what you want.

ProductSubcategoryID	ProductCategoryID	Subcategory name
1	1	Mountain Bikes
2	1	Road Bikes
3	1	Touring Bikes
4	2	Handlebars
5	2	Bottom Brackets

Using FROM and WHERE Clauses

The consumers of a report such as the preceding one will often be more familiar with the name for a product category than its number. For this reason, you may wish to look up Name column values from the ProductCategory table and use them to replace the ProductCategoryID column values in the preceding report. An inner join can accomplish this task for you.

The next SELECT statement is a revision of the preceding one that joins the ProductCategory table to the ProductSubcategory table. The new SELECT statement uses the ProductCategoryID column value in the ProductSubcategory table to look up the corresponding Name column value from the ProductCategory table.

- The FROM clause references both tables with a comma delimiter between them.
- The WHERE clause specifies the join criteria for matching rows from the ProductCategory table with rows from the ProductSubcategory table.
- Because both joined tables have a Name column used in the SELECT statement, the SELECT list includes table name qualifiers to indicate which column values to use for the second and third columns in the result set.

```
SELECT TOP 5 ProductSubcategoryID,
    Production.ProductCategory.Name 'Category name',
    Production.ProductSubcategory.Name 'Subcategory name'
FROM Production.ProductCategory, Production.ProductSubcategory
WHERE Production.ProductCategory.ProductCategoryID =
    Production.ProductSubcategory.ProductCategoryID
ORDER BY Production.ProductSubcategory.ProductSubcategoryID
```

The following listing shows the outcome of the lookup. The first and third column values are identical to the previous listing. However, the second column of values shows category names instead of ProductCategoryID number values.

ProductSubcategoryID	Category name	Subcategory name
1	Bikes	Mountain Bikes
2	Bikes	Road Bikes
3	Bikes	Touring Bikes
4	Components	Handlebars
5	Components	Bottom Brackets

Although the output from the preceding SELECT statement is easier to interpret than the output from the statement it replaces, the revised statement is longer. This is mostly because of the use of table name qualifiers for column names. In the preceding example, SQL Server Express requires the designation of a schema name to qualify the table name.

One remedy for long table name qualifiers is to assign alias names to the tables. You can make your SELECT statements much more compact by replacing lengthy table names with shorter alias table names. These alias names do not require schema qualifiers. For example, the following SELECT statement replaces Production.ProductCategory with c and Production.ProductSubcategory with sc. You designate alias names, such as c and sc, in the FROM clause. After designating an alias, you must always use it in all other references that require a table name qualifier.

```
SELECT TOP 5 ProductSubcategoryID, c.Name 'Category name',
    sc.Name 'Subcategory name'
FROM Production.ProductCategory c, Production.ProductSubcategory sc
WHERE c.ProductCategoryID = sc.ProductCategoryID
ORDER BY sc.ProductSubcategoryID
```

Using a FROM Clause Only

The preceding two SELECT statements implement an inner join between the ProductCategory and ProductSubcategory tables by using both the FROM and WHERE clauses. However, you can place all the code for an inner join in the FROM clause of a SELECT statement. Placing all the syntax for a join in the FROM clause helps to isolate the filtering for a join from any other row filtering that you have in a WHERE clause. In addition, using JOIN or INNER JOIN along with ON in the FROM clause makes it easier to identify the elements of a join.

The following SELECT statement uses JOIN to delimit the ProductCategory and ProductSubcategory tables in the FROM clause. The argument within the ON clause specifies the criteria for merging rows. The SELECT list is the same whether you spread the join syntax across the FROM and WHERE clauses or place the syntax exclusively within the FROM clause.

Despite the absence of a WHERE clause and a redesigned FROM clause, the following SELECT statement generates an identical result set to each of the preceding two SELECT statements. This outcome confirms that you can express an inner join using the JOIN and ON keywords in the FROM clause interchangeably with denoting the data sources in the FROM clause and join criteria in the WHERE clause.

Using the WHERE clause is an older style of writing inner join queries, and the newer approach of including all the syntax for the inner join in the FROM clause is gaining in popularity. The SQL Server Express T-SQL compiler can optimize either syntax so you achieve equal performance with either way of expressing an inner join.

```
SELECT TOP 5 sc.ProductSubcategoryID, c.Name 'Category name',
    sc.Name 'Subcategory name'
FROM Production.ProductCategory c
    JOIN Production.ProductSubcategory sc
ON c.ProductCategoryID = sc.ProductCategoryID
ORDER BY sc.ProductSubcategoryID
```

Outer Joins

Outer joins include all the rows from the left, right, or both data sources for a join. This feature populates an outer join result set with rows whether or not those rows contain column values that comply with a join criterion. The introduction to the "Joining Data Sources" section explains how left, right, and full outer joins differ from each other conceptually.

There are two general reasons why a row from a data source can fail to comply with a join criterion:

- The column values for the join criterion expression can be present and not satisfy the condition represented by the expression.
- Column values for one or more join criteria can be null.

The samples for this section reside in OuterJoins.sql. As with selected other sections, you will find a few additional samples that illustrate topics that are related to this section but not explicitly discussed in the section.

Searching for Rows

Outer joins can help you search for null values that result from the joining of two data sources. The objective of this kind of search is to find the rows in one data source that are missing from a second data source. You can use outer joins to discover customers with no orders (maybe you should contact them about why they are not ordering) or customers without sales persons assigned to them (this could be why you have no orders from a customer).

The ProductSubcategory and Product tables in the Production schema of the AdventureWorks database contain many unmatched rows between them. In particular, 209 rows in the Product table include ProductSubcategoryID column values that are missing or null. Therefore, when you join these two tables with an outer join based on ProductSubcategoryID column values, you can include or exclude these rows with null values (depending on which way the outer join points) from the Product table that has missing or null values for ProductSubcategoryID.

The following pair of queries shows the number of rows with null and non-ProductSubcategoryID column values in the Product table. As you can see, there are 209 Product rows with null ProductSubcategoryID values. This is out of a total of 504 (209 + 295) rows in the Product table.

```
SELECT Count(*) 'Null SubcategoryID values in Product'
FROM Production.Product
WHERE ProductSubcategoryID IS NULL
```

```
Null SubcategoryID values in Product
------------------------------------
209
```

```
SELECT Count(*) 'Non-null SubcategoryID values in Product'
FROM Production.Product
WHERE ProductSubcategoryID IS NOT NULL
```

```
Non-null SubcategoryID values in Product
----------------------------------------
295
```

The next SELECT statement and result set shows the outcome of a right join between the ProductSubcategory and Product tables. The SELECT statement does a lookup of Name column values in the ProductSubcategory table based on ProductSubcategoryID column values in the Product table.

- The Product table is on the right so that all of its rows enter the result set whether or not they match rows in the ProductSubcategory table.

- All 209 rows with null ProductSubcategoryID column values in the Product table occur for rows with ProductID column values that are less than those for rows with non-null ProductSubcategoryID column values.

- Because the following SELECT statement contains an ORDER BY clause that sorts according to ascending ProductID values, rows with null values for the Name column of the ProductSubcategory table occur before rows with non-null Name column values.

The syntax for a right join is nearly identical to an inner join. In fact, the only difference is the keyword or phrase denoting the type of join. With a right join, you designate the type of join with either RIGHT JOIN or RIGHT OUTER JOIN. With an inner join, you specify the join with either JOIN or INNER JOIN.

```
SELECT TOP 5 ProductID, p.Name 'Product name', sc.Name 'Subcategory name'
FROM Production.ProductSubcategory sc RIGHT JOIN Production.Product p
ON sc.ProductSubcategoryID = p.ProductSubcategoryID
ORDER BY ProductID
```

```
ProductID   Product name            Subcategory name
----------- ----------------------- ----------------
1           Adjustable Race         NULL
2           Bearing Ball            NULL
3           BB Ball Bearing         NULL
4           Headset Ball Bearings   NULL
316         Blade                   NULL
```

If the direction of the join changes from a right join to a left join and all the other syntax remains the same, then only rows from the Product table with a match based on ProductSubcategoryID column values will enter the result set. As a consequence, all the Subcategory name column values in the result set will have non-null values. To redesign the SELECT statement for this outcome, all you need to do is change RIGHT JOIN to LEFT JOIN.

The following SELECT statement and result set show the syntax and outcome of a left join between the ProductSubcategory and Product tables based on ProductSubcategoryID column values. Notice all the Subcategory name column values in the result set are non-null. This is true for all Subcategory name values in the left join of the tables and not just the first five rows. The replacement of RIGHT JOIN with LEFT JOIN in the FROM clause within the SELECT statement only allows rows from the Product table with matching ProductSubcategoryID column values to enter the result set.

```
SELECT TOP 5 ProductID, p.Name 'Product name', sc.Name 'Subcategory name'
FROM Production.ProductSubcategory sc LEFT JOIN Production.Product p
ON sc.ProductSubcategoryID = p.ProductSubcategoryID
ORDER BY ProductID
```

```
ProductID    Product name                    Subcategory name
-----------  ------------------------------  ----------------
680          HL Road Frame - Black, 58       Road Frames
706          HL Road Frame - Red, 58         Road Frames
707          Sport-100 Helmet, Red           Helmets
708          Sport-100 Helmet, Black         Helmets
709          Mountain Bike Socks, M          Socks
```

Counting Rows

In addition to listing rows that match a join criterion, you'll often need to aggregate rows that meet a join criterion. For example, you may wonder if all the non-null ProductSubcategoryID column values in the Product table match at least one ProductSubcategoryID column value in the ProductSubcategory table. You can answer this question by counting the ProductID column values for a left join between the ProductSubcategory and Product tables as shown in the following SELECT statement. Recall that there are just 295 non-null ProductSubcategoryID column values in the Product table. Therefore, if the count of the ProductID column values equals 295 (as it does), then all the ProductSubcategoryID column values in the Product table match at least one ProductSubcategoryID column value from the ProductSubcategory table.

```
SELECT COUNT(p.ProductID) 'Product rows with non-null ProductSubcategoryID'
FROM Production.ProductSubcategory sc LEFT JOIN Production.Product p
ON sc.ProductSubcategoryID = p.ProductSubcategoryID
```

With many query designs, it is not uncommon to need some kind of aggregated summary. This kind of need regularly exists when working with outer joins. The following SELECT statement computes a count of the number of matching rows by ProductSubcategoryID value for a left join between the ProductSubcategory and Product tables. The query reveals the distribution of matching rows by ProductSubcategoryID value. This type of query task gives you a chance to combine a left join with a GROUP BY clause and an aggregate function—namely, COUNT. The left join automatically excludes all 209 rows from the Product table with null ProductSubcategoryID values. As a result, the sum across all 37 ProductSubcategoryID column values is 295. To conserve space, the listing from this query does not show, but you can easily generate the result set by running the last sample in OuterJoins.sql.

```
SELECT sc.ProductSubcategoryID, COUNT(p.ProductID) 'Count of products'
FROM Production.ProductSubcategory sc LEFT JOIN Production.Product p
ON sc.ProductSubcategoryID = p.ProductSubcategoryID
GROUP BY sc.ProductSubcategoryID
ORDER BY sc.ProductSubcategoryID
```

Cross Joins

A cross join merges each row in one data source with every row in a second data source. A cross join performs this merge unconditionally. In other words, there are no join criteria to specify. All you have to do is specify the name of the first data source, followed by the phrase CROSS JOIN, followed by the name of the second data source.

Despite the fact that a cross join is easy to specify, you are not likely to use it often. This is because even when you are using relatively modestly sized data sources as inputs, you can generate exceptionally large result sets. As noted in the introduction to the "Joining Data Sources" section, cross-joining two data sources with 10,000 rows each generates a result set of 100,000,000 rows.

Because of its ability to create such large result sets, it is important that at least one data source be exceptionally small—say one, two, or three rows. If one data source contains 10,000 rows and the second data source contains just 1 row, then the result set is still just 10,000 rows. When the second result grows to three rows, cross-joining it with another data source of 10,000 rows creates a result of just 30,000 rows. Therefore, cross joins are particularly appropriate when you want to add a short list of values or just one value.

To demonstrate a cross join, you can create a new table and add it to the AdventureWorks database. By using your own table you can control its properties and values precisely. In addition, you can drop the table from the database when the demonstration concludes so that the AdventureWorks database does not change permanently. The sample for creating the table, populating it with values, cross-joining it with the SalesPerson table, and dropping the special added table is in CrossJoins.sql.

The following excerpt from CrossJoins.sql shows the code for creating a table named CJTable. The table has a single column called myint and two rows with column values of two and four. The SET NOCOUNT statement suppresses the display of messages about how many rows are affected after each database operation, such as an INSERT statement or a SELECT statement.

```
USE AdventureWorks
GO

SET NOCOUNT ON

IF EXISTS(SELECT name FROM sys.tables WHERE name = 'CJTable')
    DROP TABLE CJTable
CREATE TABLE CJTable(
myint int
)

DECLARE @int1 int
SET @int1 = 2
INSERT CJTable VALUES(@int1)
SET @int1 = 4
INSERT CJTable VALUES(@int1)
```

The following code listing and result set demonstrate the syntax for implementing a cross join and show one use for the result set. The FROM clause shows the syntax for using CROSS JOIN. The cross join merges the rows of SalesPerson in the Sales schema with the CJTable table created by the dbo user. Because there are 17 rows in the SalesPerson table and two rows in the CJTable table, the result set for the cross join of the two data sources contains 34 rows. Each SalesPersonID column value appears twice in the result set because each row with a SalespersonID merges once with each row of the two rows in the CJTable table. The COUNT function for SalesPersonID therefore returns a value of 34 across the whole result set.

```
SELECT COUNT(SalesPersonID) 'Count of joined rows after adding 2 rows'
FROM Sales.SalesPerson CROSS JOIN dbo.CJTable
```

```
Count of joined rows after adding 2 rows
----------------------------------------
34
```

The next SELECT statement finds the maximum and minimum myint value from the first five rows sorted by SalesPersonID from the cross join result set. The SELECT list includes items for associated SalesPersonID and SalesQuota values for each row in the result set. The GROUP BY clause is critical in a couple of ways to the SELECT statement.

- First, it makes possible the use the MAX and MIN aggregate functions.

- Second, it enables these aggregate functions to process each distinct duo of SalesPersonID and SalesQuota column values. Each distinct duo of SalesPersonID and SalesQuota appears on two separate rows in the result set—once with a myint value of 2 and a second time with a myint value of 4.

The following SELECT statement and result set listing confirm the syntax for specifying a pair of aggregate values tied to a GROUP BY clause within a cross join. The TOP 5 phrase returns just the first five rows from the complete result set.

```
SELECT TOP 5 SalesPersonID, SalesQuota, MAX(myint) 'MAX(myint)',
    MIN(myint) 'MIN(myint)'
FROM Sales.SalesPerson CROSS JOIN dbo.CJTable
GROUP BY SalesPersonID, SalesQuota
ORDER BY SalesPersonID
```

SalesPersonID	SalesQuota	MAX(myint)	MIN(myint)
268	NULL	4	2
275	300000.00	4	2
276	250000.00	4	2
277	250000.00	4	2
278	250000.00	4	2

The next excerpt from CrossJoins.sql starts with the addition of a new row to the CJTable table. The myint column value for the new row is 8. Then, the script counts the rows in the cross join of SalesPerson and CJTable tables. The result set has 51 rows (17 rows from SalesPerson multiplied by 3 rows from CJTable). Next, the script excerpt lists the first 5 rows from a SELECT statement based on a cross join of the SalesPerson and CJTable tables. The output from the following script, which does not show, has the same layout as the preceding output, except that the MAX(myint) column values are all 8 instead of 4. This change is because the new third row for the CJTable table contains a myint value of 8.

```
SET @int1 = 8
INSERT CJTable VALUES(@int1)

SELECT COUNT(SalesPersonID) 'Count of joined rows after adding 3 rows'
FROM Sales.SalesPerson CROSS JOIN dbo.CJTable

SELECT TOP 5 SalesPersonID, SalesQuota, MAX(myint) 'MAX(myint)',
    MIN(myint) 'MIN(myint)'
FROM Sales.SalesPerson CROSS JOIN dbo.CJTable
GROUP BY SalesPersonID, SalesQuota
ORDER BY SalesPersonID
```

Self-Joins

A self-join is created when you join a data source, such as a table or a view, with itself. Essentially, the join works with two copies of the same data source—one on each side of the JOIN keyword. By assigning a different alias to each copy, you can refer to each copy separately. This kind of join is appropriate in at least two situations:

- The first scenario occurs when two columns in the same data source share common values, such as the EmployeeID and ManagerID columns in the custom vEmployeeDeptID view within the dbo schema of the AdventureWorks database. In this context, you can define a join criterion in terms of the two column values.

- The second scenario occurs when you can define a relationship between two or more different columns across both copies of a data source.

The samples in this section process a special view in the dbo schema of the AdventureWorks database. To create the view, log in as a dbo user, such as sa login or the computer administrator. Then, run the following script from the AdventureWorks database context with a query tool. The script creates the vEmployeeDeptID view in the dbo schema. The view has three columns, named EmployeeID, ManagerID, and DepartmentID. The WHERE clause in the SELECT statement only includes rows from the Employee table for employees who are still with the company (EndDate IS NULL). Chapter 7 examines the CREATE VIEW statement in much greater detail.

```
CREATE VIEW dbo.vEmployeeDeptID
AS
SELECT HumanResources.Employee.EmployeeID 'EmployeeID',
       HumanResources.Employee.ManagerID 'ManagerID',
       HumanResources.EmployeeDepartmentHistory.DepartmentID
FROM HumanResources.EmployeeDepartmentHistory INNER JOIN
       HumanResources.Employee
       ON HumanResources.EmployeeDepartmentHistory.EmployeeID =
       HumanResources.Employee.EmployeeID
WHERE HumanResources.EmployeeDepartmentHistory.EndDate IS NULL
```

The samples for this section reside in SelfJoins.sql.

Joining Rows When Values from Two Different Columns Match

The ManagerID and EmployeeID columns in the vEmployeeDeptID view make it possible to enumerate all employees who report to managers. Another way of saying this is to find all ManagerID column values that have at least one EmployeeID column value referencing them. The following SELECT statement shows one way to provide this enumeration with a self-join.

- The join criterion is satisfied when the EmployeeID column value from the e1 copy of the vEmployeeDeptID view equals the ManagerID column value from the e2 copy of the vEmployeeDeptID view. This expression finds all employees who report to a manager. Any employee who does not report to a manager, such as the top-level manager, is excluded by the criterion.

- The list items designate three columns (DepartmentID, ManagerID, EmployeeID) from the e2 alias.

- The ORDER BY clause orders the result set rows in ascending order by ManagerID within DepartmentID for the e2 alias.

```
SELECT e2.DepartmentID, e2.ManagerID, e2.EmployeeID
FROM dbo.vEmployeeDeptID e1 JOIN dbo.vEmployeeDeptID e2
ON e1.EmployeeID = e2.ManagerID
ORDER BY e2.DepartmentID, e2.ManagerID
```

The following excerpt from the result set listing for the preceding SELECT statement shows the first 10 rows. These rows enumerate all employees reporting to managers in departments with a DepartmentID value of 1 or 2. The full result set contains 289 rows, which is 1 less than the total of 290 employees. The excluded employee (EmployeeID 109) has a null value for ManagerID because he reports to no one else—this is the top-level manager. The following excerpt shows that the value of 109 does appear in the ManagerID column once because one employee from DepartmentID 1 reports to ManagerID 109.

Notice how ManagerID values sometimes repeat within a department. For example, there are four instances of 3 in the ManagerID column for DepartmentID 1. These duplicate values result from multiple employees reporting to the same manager within a department. You can start with these duplicate values to develop a list of nonduplicated managers for the employees within departments.

DepartmentID	ManagerID	EmployeeID
1	3	267
1	3	270
1	3	9
1	3	11
1	12	3
1	109	12
2	3	4
2	3	263
2	263	5
2	263	265

The following SELECT statement shows how to adapt the initial self-join to report just the nonduplicated managers within a department. The revised SELECT statement applies two design features to eliminate the repeated ManagerID values within a department.

- First, the new SELECT statement drops EmployeeID from its list. Without this step, rows with duplicate ManagerID values but different EmployeeID values within a department are distinct.

- Second, the addition of the DISTINCT keyword following SELECT eliminates the nondistinct rows in the result set.

```
SELECT DISTINCT e2.DepartmentID, e2.ManagerID
FROM dbo.vEmployeeDeptID e1 JOIN dbo.vEmployeeDeptID e2
ON e1.EmployeeID = e2.ManagerID
ORDER BY e2.DepartmentID, e2.ManagerID
```

An excerpt showing the first five rows from the result set for the preceding SELECT statement appears next. These rows show the ManagerID values for DepartmentID column values of 1 and 2. Notice particularly that the ManagerID column value of 3 appears just once for DepartmentID 1. Because employees from DepartmentID 1 and DepartmentID 2 report directly to the employee with an EmployeeID value of 3, the ManagerID value of 3 appears for both departments.

```
DepartmentID ManagerID
------------ -----------
1            3
1            12
1            109
2            3
2            263
```

Joining Rows Based on Two Criteria Expressions

The criteria expressions in the ON clause matching the JOIN keyword control which rows enter a result set. The preceding SELECT statement uses a single criterion expression. This expression, along with the DISTINCT keyword and the SELECT list, returned managers for the employees. Sorting by department showed the managers in a department.

The managers for employees within a department derived by the preceding SELECT statement can come from the same or a different department than the employees. For example, the preceding result set listing shows the employee with an EmployeeID value of 3 serving as a manager in two departments with DepartmentID values of 1 and 2. Because the vEmployeeDeptID view design allows a row to belong to just one department, the employee corresponding to EmployeeID 3 must manage a department to which she does not belong. Similarly, the employee corresponding to a ManagerID value of 109 manages employees in the department with a DepartmentID value of 1, but the manager actually works in a different department. Notice that 109 does not appear as an EmployeeID value for DepartmentID 1 within the result set before the last one.

Typically, higher-level managers reside in one department, but manage employees in one or more other departments. Therefore, you can find higher-level managers by searching for managers that manage employees from a different department than their own. You can find this elite group by specifying two join criteria expressions, as in the next SELECT statement.

- The first criterion expression is the same as the one in the preceding SELECT statement. It joins rows if they have other employees reporting to them.

- The second criterion expression identifies rows for which the manager's department in the e2 data source is not equal to (!=) an employee's department in the e1 data source.

By combining these two criteria expressions with an AND operator, the SELECT statement returns the intersection of employees who are managers and also have a different department from one or more direct reports.

■**Note** The != operator is equivalent to the <> operator.

```
SELECT DISTINCT e2.DepartmentID, e2.ManagerID
FROM dbo.vEmployeeDeptID e1 JOIN dbo.vEmployeeDeptID e2
ON e1.EmployeeID = e2.ManagerID AND e2.DepartmentID != e1.DepartmentID
ORDER BY e2.DepartmentID, e2.ManagerID
```

The result set for the preceding SELECT statement appears next. All of the ManagerID values in the listing are for departments other than the one they reside in. ManagerID value 109 appears as a manager for five DepartmentID column values, which is more than any other ManagerID value. Recall that the 109 ManagerID value points at the top-level manager.

DepartmentID	ManagerID
1	109
2	3
3	109
4	109
5	71
6	3
7	21
7	109
8	148
9	140
10	140
11	109
12	200
13	148
14	148
15	21

Depending on your requirements, it may be more valuable to obtain a list of ManagerID column values for employees who reside in the department that they supervise exclusively or with other managers. The following SELECT statement generates that list. The statement is identical to the preceding one except that the second criterion expression identifies managers with the same DepartmentID value as the employees that they supervise. The result set listing, which consists of 43 rows, does not appear to conserve space. However, you can generate the list for yourself by running the following SELECT statement, which resides in SelfJoins.sql.

```
SELECT DISTINCT e2.DepartmentID, e2.ManagerID
FROM dbo.vEmployeeDeptID e1 JOIN dbo.vEmployeeDeptID e2
ON e1.EmployeeID = e2.ManagerID AND e2.DepartmentID = e1.DepartmentID
ORDER BY e2.DepartmentID, e2.ManagerID
```

Joining Rows Based on Criteria Expressions in ON and WHERE Clauses

Until this point, the self-join samples illustrated techniques for retrieving the managers in each department. However, it is equally likely that you'll have to retrieve the employees in a department or the employees who report to a manager. You can segment employees in the same or a different department from their manager.

When analyzing the employees that report to a specific manager, you can perform two kinds of tasks:

- First, you need to develop a SELECT list that returns employees. The first self-join sample demonstrated how to do this.

- Second, you need to filter the rows returned by the SELECT statement so that they are all rows for a specific ManagerID value. You can place the filter in the ON clause for the JOIN keyword, or you can populate a WHERE clause with a filter selecting the rows that you seek.

The following SELECT statement returns employees reporting to the top-level manager where the employees come from a different department than the manager. This SELECT demonstrates a self-join in which a relationship is defined across two different columns in the same data source.

- The SELECT list retrieves EmployeeID column values and the ManagerID value for the manager to which the employees report.

- The FROM clause specifies two criteria expressions in its ON clause. These two expressions connected by an AND operator detect rows from the vEmployeeDeptID view where employees report to managers and the managers are from different departments than the employees.

- The WHERE clause filters for null ManagerID values. A null ManagerID value denotes a manager who does not report to another manager. There is only one employee with a null ManagerID column value. In the AdventureWorks database, this is the top-level employee with an EmployeeID value of 109.

```
SELECT DISTINCT e2.DepartmentID, e2.ManagerID, e2.EmployeeID
FROM dbo.vEmployeeDeptID e1 JOIN dbo.vEmployeeDeptID e2
ON e1.EmployeeID = e2.ManagerID AND e2.DepartmentID != e1.DepartmentID
WHERE e1.ManagerID IS NULL
ORDER BY e2.DepartmentID
```

The result set listing that appears next is for the preceding SELECT statement and denotes five employees. These are the people who report directly to the top-level manager and who come from different departments than the employee with an EmployeeID value of 109.

DepartmentID	ManagerID	EmployeeID
1	109	12
3	109	273
4	109	6
7	109	148
11	109	42

There is just one direct report that resides in the same department as the top-level manager. The following SELECT statement illustrates the syntax for retrieving the employee and the corresponding result set. The only change that you need to make to the SELECT statement is for the ON clause, in which you should replace the not equals operator (!=) with an equals operator (=).

```
SELECT e2.DepartmentID, e2.ManagerID, e2.EmployeeID
FROM dbo.vEmployeeDeptID e1 JOIN dbo.vEmployeeDeptID e2
ON e1.EmployeeID = e2.ManagerID AND e2.DepartmentID = e1.DepartmentID
WHERE e1.ManagerID IS NULL
ORDER BY e2.DepartmentID
```

DepartmentID	ManagerID	EmployeeID
16	109	140

Joins for More Than Two Data Sources

It is often useful to merge more than two data sources in a single SELECT statement. This is generally the case whenever the column values that you need for a result set reside in more than two tables. Highly normalized databases, such as the AdventureWorks database, increase the likelihood of needing to join more than two data sources. Even if you only need column values from just two tables, you will still need to join more than two tables if the columns you want to include in your result set are from tables in a many-to-many relationship. Many-to-many relationships between tables are described in the "Implementing Many-to-Many Relationships with Foreign Keys" section of Chapter 4. The samples for this section appear in MoreThanTwoJoins.sql.

Upgrading a Two-Table Join to a Three-Table Join

The first SELECT statement for this section shows a join between two tables that can benefit from the joining of a third table. The joined tables are the SalesPerson and Employee tables from the AdventureWorks database. The SELECT list includes SalesPersonID and SalesQuota from the SalesPerson table along with ContactID from the Employee table. However, the result set will not include any information about a sales person's name because column values for sales person names resided in neither SalesPerson nor Employee tables.

```
SELECT s.SalesPersonID, s.SalesQuota, e.ContactID
FROM Sales.SalesPerson s JOIN HumanResources.Employee e
ON s.SalesPersonID = e.EmployeeID
```

All the information for contact names of any type resides in the Contact table. The only way to link rows from the SalesPerson table to rows in the Contact table is through the Employee table. Both the Employee table and the Contact table contain a ContactID column. These two sets of column values let you join the Employee table to the Contact table based on ContactID column values. The preceding SELECT statement already shows you how to link rows from the SalesPerson table with rows from the Employee table.

The next SELECT statement indicates how to join the Contact table to the join of SalesPerson and Employee tables. You can add the Contact table by appending a new JOIN clause to the FROM clause in the preceding SELECT statement. The new JOIN clause references the Contact table in the Person schema. The ON clause for the new JOIN clause specifies the columns on which to merge rows. In this case, the ContactID column from the Employee table merges with the ContactID column from the Contact table.

```
SELECT s.SalesPersonID, s.SalesQuota, c.LastName
FROM Sales.SalesPerson s JOIN HumanResources.Employee e
ON s.SalesPersonID = e.EmployeeID
JOIN Person.Contact c ON e.ContactID = c.ContactID
```

By adding the Contact table to the join, you can replace in the SELECT list the ContactID column from the Employee table with the LastName column from the Contact table. Clients of database reports frequently prefer to view meaningful names, such as LastName column values, instead of cryptic code values, such as ContactID column values. The next result set listing is an excerpt of the first three rows generated by the preceding SELECT statement. It shows LastName column values next to the SalesQuota column values. The SalesQuota for the first row has a null value because the corresponding sales person is a manager.

```
SalesPersonID SalesQuota LastName
------------- ---------- --------
268           NULL       Jiang
275           300000.00  Blythe
276           250000.00  Mitchell
```

Specifying Four-Table Joins

In highly normalized databases, such as the AdventureWorks database, you will frequently have the opportunity to merge rows from four, or even more, tables when trying to compose a result set. Recall that when you merge rows from multiple tables, you need to consider how you are going to handle null values. Using a left join forces all rows from one table into the result set even if its rows have null values for merge columns. If you do not use a left or right join, then rows with null values may be excluded from a result set for a typical join between two data sources when merge column values equal each other. This section illustrates the syntax for both approaches.

The next SELECT statement shows a four-table join between the SalesPerson, Employee, Contact, and SalesTerritory tables. Adding the SalesTerritory table allows the use of Name column values from the SalesTerritory table instead of the more cryptic TerritoryID column values from the SalesPerson table. The fourth table, SalesTerritory, is appended to the end of the FROM clause from the preceding SELECT statement with a LEFT JOIN clause. The LEFT JOIN clause allows you to retain rows with null TerritoryID column values in the result set.

```
SELECT t.Name 'Territory name', s.SalesPersonID, s.SalesQuota, c.LastName
FROM Sales.SalesPerson s JOIN HumanResources.Employee e
ON s.SalesPersonID = e.EmployeeID
JOIN Person.Contact c ON e.ContactID = c.ContactID
LEFT JOIN Sales.SalesTerritory t ON s.TerritoryID = t.TerritoryID
ORDER BY s.TerritoryID
```

The next result set listing shows all 17 rows returned by the preceding SELECT statement. These rows correspond to the 17 rows in the SalesPerson table with added columns from the Contact and SalesTerritory tables.

- The Territory name column values in the result set are from SalesTerritory table.

- The LastName column values are from the Contact table.

The first three rows in the result set have null Territory name column values because these rows have null values for TerritoryID in the SalesPerson table. Without the use of a LEFT JOIN to add the TerritoryID column of values to the join of the SalesPerson, Employee, and Contact tables, the rows with null TerritoryID values would fail to be incorporated in the result set. The result set rows are ordered by TerritoryID values. Because TerritoryID column values map to territory names but don't reflect alphabetical order, the rows are grouped by Territory name but aren't in ascending alphabetical order.

```
Territory name  SalesPersonID  SalesQuota  LastName
--------------  -------------  ----------  -----------------
NULL            268            NULL        Jiang
NULL            284            NULL        Alberts
NULL            288            NULL        Abbas
Northwest       287            300000.00   Mensa-Annan
Northwest       280            250000.00   Ansman-Wolfe
Northwest       283            250000.00   Campbell
Northeast       275            300000.00   Blythe
Central         277            250000.00   Carson
Southwest       276            250000.00   Mitchell
Southwest       281            250000.00   Ito
Southeast       279            300000.00   Reiter
Canada          282            250000.00   Saraiva
Canada          278            250000.00   Vargas
France          286            250000.00   Varkey Chudukatil
```

```
Germany        289        250000.00  Valdez
Australia      290        250000.00  Tsoflias
United Kingdom 285        250000.00  Pak
```

Instead of just listing values, you will sometimes need to aggregate column values by group or even compute calculated columns for a result set. The next four-table join illustrates how to perform these tasks with a four-table join as a data source. The SELECT statement integrates design techniques from previous samples in this section.

- The SELECT list designates four columns:
  - The first column is the Name column from the SalesTerritory table.
  - The second and third columns are two aggregated columns that compute the sum of the SalesYTD and SalesLastYear column values from the underlying SalesPerson table.
  - The fourth column is a calculated column that uses the difference between the sum of SalesYTD and the sum of SalesLastYear column values to compute the percent change in sales between the two years.
- The FROM clause specifies the four tables that compose the data source. These input tables to the merged data source enable the computing of aggregates by territory name. An inner join merges the SalesTerritory table with the join for the preceding three tables. By using an inner join, rows with null TerritoryID column values from the SalesPerson table are dropped from the computation of aggregates. This is reasonable because you do not know to which territory you should assign the sales for the three sales persons without TerritoryID assignments.
- The GROUP BY clause groups rows in the data source with the same Name column value from the SalesTerritory table.
- The ORDER BY clause orders the result set rows in ascending alphabetical order.

```
SELECT t.Name 'Territory name',
    SUM(s.SalesYTD) 'YTD Sales',
    SUM(s.SalesLastYear) 'Sales last year',
    CAST(((SUM(s.SalesYTD) - SUM(s.SalesLastYear))/
    SUM(s.SalesLastYear))*100
    AS DEC(12,2)) 'Percent change'
FROM Sales.SalesPerson s JOIN HumanResources.Employee e
ON s.SalesPersonID = e.EmployeeID
JOIN Person.Contact c ON e.ContactID = c.ContactID
JOIN Sales.SalesTerritory t ON s.TerritoryID = t.TerritoryID
GROUP BY t.Name
ORDER BY t.Name
```

The result set listing for the preceding SELECT statement appears next. The listing contains just 10 rows—one for each of the sales territories. You may wish to revise the SELECT list so that YTD Sales and Sales last year columns appear with just two places after the decimal point. If you decided to make that adjustment, you should make a corresponding change in the calculated Percent change column. Otherwise, some consumers of the report may complain about the computational accuracy of your reports.

```
Territory name YTD Sales     Sales last year Percent change
-------------- ------------  --------------- --------------
Australia       1758385.926  2278548.9776    -22.82
Canada          4954295.2324 3658511.5515    35.41
```

```
Central         3857163.6332 1997186.2037    93.12
France          3827950.238  2396539.7601    59.72
Germany         2241204.0424 1307949.7917    71.35
Northeast       4557045.0459 1750406.4785   160.34
Northwest       5518998.6092 3298694.4938    67.30
Southeast       2811012.7151 1849640.9418    51.97
Southwest       8219200.7171 3512662.029    133.98
United Kingdom  5015682.3752 1635823.3967   206.61
```

Using Subqueries

A *subquery* is a SELECT statement that runs from within another SELECT statement. For this reason, a subquery is sometimes called an inner query, and the query in which it runs is called an outer query. You can use a subquery anywhere that you use an expression inside a SELECT statement.

You can think of subqueries as enabling you to ask two or more questions at once.

- The two questions can be independent or correlated.

- When the questions are independent, the inner query computes once no matter how many rows are in the outer query. SQL Server literature normally refers to these types of inner queries as subqueries or uncorrelated subqueries.

- When the two questions are correlated, the inner query computes for each row in the outer query. SQL Server literature frequently refers to these types of inner queries as correlated subqueries.

- Any one outer query can have more than one subquery within it. An outer query with two subqueries can have the subqueries reside in locations such as

  - A SELECT list

  - A SELECT list and a WHERE clause

  - A WHERE clause nested within another WHERE clause

- Multiple subqueries can nest within one another. SQL Server allows up to 32 levels of nesting, but it is possible to make queries too complex to compile before you reach this limit of 32 levels.

It is often possible to generate the output obtained from an outer query with an inner query as a join instead. The SQL Server Express T-SQL compiler attempts to optimize query statements no matter what syntax you use to express them. Although correlated subqueries can run more slowly than uncorrelated subqueries, correlated queries also provide more flexibility in the ways that you can query a database.

SQL Server Express is designed for relatively small databases used by relatively small numbers of people. For this class of application, the best way of expressing a query may be the way that is easiest for you to state. Therefore, learning how to use subqueries can increase the flexibility with which you can express queries with little or no performance penalty.

The samples for this section reside in Subqueries.sql.

Including a Subquery in a SELECT List

You can use a subquery in the SELECT list of an outer query like a customized function. For example, you can compute an average across all rows or a group of rows with the AVG function. However, the built-in AVG function does not allow you to select which rows count in the average. Using a SELECT statement as an expression in the SELECT list of an outer query allows you to use any subset of rows that a WHERE clause can specify. In this context, you should make the SELECT statement return a scalar value (i.e., a single value instead of a set, or column values within one or more rows).

The first subquery sample demonstrates the syntax for using a SELECT statement as an item in the list of an outer query. The outer SELECT list contains three types of items:

- Column names from the data source for the outer SELECT statement

- A subquery that returns a variation of the built-in AVG function

- A calculated item that derives from the difference between the subquery and one of the columns in the outer query

The data source for the outer query is an inner join of the Product and SalesOrderDetail tables. The join allows the result set to show product names (p.Name) from the Product table instead of ProductID column (sd1.ProductID) values from the SalesOrderDetail table. The SELECT list contains two subqueries:

- The first subquery returns the average LineTotal column value from the SalesOrderDetail table with OrderQty column values of more than 12. If you were just computing an average over all SalesOrderDetail rows, the subquery would add no value to the SELECT statement beyond what the built-in AVG could deliver.

- The computed item uses an inner query as a term in its expression. The design of the SELECT statement for the computed item is the same as the first subquery, except the second subquery does not use a data source alias name, such as sd2 in the first subquery.

■Note The use of an alias name for a data source in a subquery is optional. SQL Server Express attempts to resolve any column names for the data source inside the subquery. If a subquery's SELECT list specifies a column that is not in the subquery's data source, SQL Server Express attempts to find the column name in the outer query, unless you explicitly specify a qualifier for the column name.

```
SELECT TOP 10 sd1.SalesOrderID 'OrderID', p.Name, sd1.OrderQty,
    sd1.LineTotal,
    (SELECT AVG(sd2.Linetotal) FROM sales.SalesOrderDetail sd2
        WHERE sd2.OrderQty > 12) 'Avg. > 12',
    LineTotal - (SELECT AVG(Linetotal)
        FROM sales.SalesOrderDetail
        WHERE OrderQty > 12) 'Diff. from Avg.'
FROM Sales.SalesOrderDetail sd1
JOIN Production.Product p
ON sd1.ProductID = p.ProductID
WHERE OrderQty > 12
ORDER BY LineTotal DESC
```

The following result set listing shows the output from the preceding SELECT statement. The most important item to notice is that the values in the Avg. > 12 column are all the same. This indicates that the subquery defining this column is uncorrelated with the outer query. SQL Server Express computes the subquery's value for one row, and then uses the value for all other rows. The Diff. From Avg. column values are different from one row to the next, but this is because the LineTotal column values change from one row to the next.

OrderID	Name	OrderQty	LineTotal	Avg. > 12	Diff. from Avg.
55282	Touring-1000 Yellow, 46	26	27893.619000	1851.433973	26042.185027
43884	Mountain-100 Silver, 42	14	27055.760424	1851.433973	25204.326451
51131	Touring-1000 Blue, 60	21	26159.208075	1851.433973	24307.774102
43875	Mountain-100 Black, 38	13	24938.476108	1851.433973	23087.042135
57054	Touring-1000 Blue, 46	19	23667.854925	1851.433973	21816.420952
53460	Road-350-W Yellow, 48	30	22963.365000	1851.433973	21111.931027
51823	Touring-1000 Blue, 60	18	22422.178350	1851.433973	20570.744377
55282	Touring-1000 Blue, 46	18	22422.178350	1851.433973	20570.744377
55282	Touring-1000 Yellow, 60	17	21176.501775	1851.433973	19325.067802
63291	Mountain-200 Silver, 42	17	20607.311175	1851.433973	18755.877202

The next subquery sample illustrates how to have a subquery's value change depending on a value in the outer query. The outer query returns the first 29 rows from a query that returns the SalesOrderID, ProductID, and LineTotal column values from the SalesOrderDetail table. These column values are supplemented by a subquery that returns the SubTotal column value from the SalesOrderHeader table for the SalesOrderID column value in the current row of the outer query.

The WHERE clause in the subquery's SELECT statement links the inner query to the outer query by SalesOrderID column values. This makes the inner query a correlated subquery because the inner query's value can change depending on the value of the SalesOrderID column value for the outer query.

```
SELECT TOP 29 sd.SalesOrderID, sd. ProductID, sd.LineTotal,
    (SELECT sh.SubTotal FROM sales.SalesOrderHeader sh
        WHERE sh.SalesOrderID = sd.SalesOrderID) 'SubTotal'
FROM Sales.SalesOrderDetail sd
```

The following result set listing shows the first 15 rows of the output from the preceding SELECT statement. Notice that each of the three different values for the SubTotal column corresponds to a distinct SalesOrderID value.

SalesOrderID	ProductID	LineTotal	SubTotal
43659	776	2024.994000	24643.9362
43659	777	6074.982000	24643.9362
43659	778	2024.994000	24643.9362
43659	771	2039.994000	24643.9362
43659	772	2039.994000	24643.9362
43659	773	4079.988000	24643.9362
43659	774	2039.994000	24643.9362
43659	714	86.521200	24643.9362
43659	716	28.840400	24643.9362
43659	709	34.200000	24643.9362
43659	712	10.373000	24643.9362
43659	711	80.746000	24643.9362
43660	762	419.458900	1553.1035
43660	758	874.794000	1553.1035
43661	745	809.760000	39422.1198

Including a Subquery in a WHERE Clause

By placing a subquery in a WHERE clause, you can essentially write an expression that instructs the outer query which values to return. You can write your subquery to return either a single value or a collection of values depending on whether the outer query's WHERE clause takes a scalar value or an array of values.

- A subquery returning a scalar value in a WHERE clause argument is very flexible because the subquery will automatically revise whenever its underlying data source changes—which, in turn, can cause an alteration in the outer query's result set.

- A subquery is particularly advantageous as a WHERE clause argument when the array of values to check against is both numerous or subject to change. After you compose a valid SELECT statement for the subquery, the subquery will automatically return the correct list of values for a WHERE clause.

If your subquery returns a scalar value, you can use a comparison operator, such as >, to assess whether a column value from your outer query is greater than the value returned by your subquery. The following SELECT statement illustrates this use for a subquery. The outer query returns SalesPersonID, Salesperson name, and SalesYTD values. The subquery in the WHERE clause of the outer query returns the average value for SalesYTD from the SalesPerson table in the Sales schema. The > comparison operator along with the subquery in the WHERE clause selects just those rows from the SalesPerson table with a SalesYTD column value greater than the average for all the SalesYTD column values.

```
SELECT s.SalesPersonID,
    REPLACE(c.FirstName + ' ' + ISNULL(c.MiddleName, '') + ' '
        + c.LastName, ' ', ' ') 'Salesperson name',
    s.SalesYTD
FROM Sales.SalesPerson s
JOIN HumanResources.Employee e
ON s.SalesPersonID = e.EmployeeID
JOIN Person.Contact c
ON c.ContactID = e.ContactID
WHERE SalesYTD > (SELECT AVG(ss.SalesYTD) FROM Sales.SalesPerson ss)
ORDER BY s.SalesYTD DESC
```

The following result set listing contains the nine rows returned by the preceding SELECT statement. The subquery returns a value of 2,605,530.949 for the sample data that ships with the AdventureWorks database; this value does not appear in the listing. All the rows in the result set have SalesYTD column values above this average value. If you modify the SalesYTD values in the SalesPerson data by, for example, substantially increasing the SalesYTD column value for a sales person that is below the average, that person can be added to the result set, whereas another sales person may dynamically be dropped from the list. The subquery in the SELECT statement for the outer query makes this possible without any adjustment to the query statement.

```
SalesPersonID Salesperson name              SalesYTD
------------- ----------------------------- -----------
276           Linda C Mitchell              5200475.2313
285           Jae B Pak                     5015682.3752
275           Michael G Blythe              4557045.0459
277           Jillian Carson                3857163.6332
286           Ranjit R Varkey Chudukatil    3827950.238
283           David R Campbell              3587378.4257
```

282	José Edvaldo Saraiva	3189356.2465
281	Shu K Ito	3018725.4858
279	Tsvi Michael Reiter	2811012.7151

The next subquery sample demonstrates the use of a subquery that returns an array of values. This array of values serves as the argument for the IN operator in a WHERE clause. Recall from the "Filtering Rows with the IN Operator" section in Chapter 5 that a WHERE clause can select any row with a column value that matches one of an array of values. Therefore, by using a subquery that returns an array of values as the argument for an IN operator in a WHERE clause, you can dynamically designate the rows to enter a result set.

The following SELECT statement includes a subquery that returns the TerritoryID column values for the top three sales persons ordered by SalesYTD column values in the SalesPerson table within the Sales schema. The array of values returned by the subquery corresponds to the TerritoryID column values. For the sample data that ships with the AdventureWorks database, these TerritoryID values are 4, 1, and 10 in the order they are returned from the subquery. The IN operator in the WHERE clause for the outer query checks to confirm if the rows from its data source include a TerritoryID column value that matches the TerritoryID values for the top three sales persons.

The primary data source for the outer query in the following SELECT statement is the Customer table in the Sales schema. This table contains CustomerID and TerritoryID column values. A CustomerID column value corresponds to a store. The FROM clause for the outer query contains a series of joins that facilitate the return of store name along with contact information for persons at a store, including their name and phone number. The outer query returns this contact information only when the TerritoryID column value from the Customer table matches one of the three values returned by subquery.

```
SELECT cu.TerritoryID, cu.CustomerID, s.Name,
    REPLACE(co.FirstName + ' ' + ISNULL(co.MiddleName, '') + ' '
        + co.LastName, '  ', ' ') 'Store contact',
    co.Phone
FROM Sales.Customer cu
JOIN Sales.Store s
ON cu.CustomerID = s.CustomerID
JOIN Sales.StoreContact sc
ON sc.CustomerID = s.CustomerID
JOIN Person.Contact co
ON co.ContactID = sc.ContactID
WHERE cu.TerritoryID IN (SELECT TOP 3 TerritoryID
    FROM Sales.SalesPerson
    GROUP BY TerritoryID
    ORDER BY SUM(SalesYTD) DESC)
ORDER BY cu.TerritoryID, cu.CustomerID
```

The result set listing generated by the preceding SELECT statement contains hundreds of rows, but the following excerpt illustrates an important feature of the output. Notice particularly that the Progressive Sports store appears twice in the output. This is because there are two contacts for this customer. A store will repeat in multiple rows for as many distinct contacts as there are for a store.

TerritoryID	CustomerID	Name	Store contact	Phone
1	1	A Bike Store	Orlando N. Gee	245-555-0173
1	2	Progressive Sports	Geraldine T. Spicer	230-555-0100
1	2	Progressive Sports	Keith Harris	170-555-0127

The next subquery sample demonstrates how to use a subquery to search for character data with a wildcard argument. In addition, the subquery accepts user input via a local variable. The incorporation of a local variable makes the sample ready for adaptation with a stored procedure that accepts a parameter. The data source for the subquery is the CountryRegion table in the Person schema.

- The subquery's SELECT statement returns the Name column values from the CountryRegion table for rows that start with an nvarchar data type.

- The @alpha local variable accepts an assignment that specifies the beginning characters of a country name.

- For the AdventureWorks database, assigning the letter U to @alpha returns the names of countries and regions starting with the letter U, such as United States, United Kingdom, and U.S. Minor Outlying Islands.

The subquery's outer query in the following SELECT statement provides row counts for the Customer table in the Sales schema organized by Name column values from the CountryRegion table in the Person schema and the SalesTerritory table in the Person schema.

- A series of joins matches TerritoryID column values in the Customer table to corresponding Name values in the CountryRegion and SalesTerritory tables.

- The outer query's WHERE clause limits the Customer table rows that get counted to those with a country or region name matching one from the array of values returned by the subquery, which, in turn, depends on the value of @alpha.

- The GROUP BY clause in the outer query specifies the return of customer counts by the territory within a country or region.

- The concluding ORDER BY clause in the outer query orders by territory name within country or region name where both sets of names are sorted alphabetically.

```
DECLARE @alpha AS nvarchar(25)
SET @alpha = 'U'

SELECT cr.Name 'Country/Region', st.Name 'Territory',
    COUNT(*) 'Customer Count'
FROM Sales.Customer c
JOIN Sales.SalesTerritory st
ON c.TerritoryID = st.TerritoryID
JOIN Person.CountryRegion cr
ON st.CountryRegionCode = cr.CountryRegionCode
WHERE cr.Name IN (SELECT sq.Name
    FROM Person.CountryRegion sq
    WHERE sq.Name LIKE @alpha + '%')
GROUP BY cr.Name, st.Name
ORDER BY cr.Name, st.Name
```

The preceding listing assigns a value of U to @alpha. The following result set listing shows the outcome from this assignment. The United Kingdom and the United States are the only two country or region names beginning with U from the CountryRegion table that also match that TerritoryID column values in the Customer table. In addition, five distinct TerritoryID values exist within the Customer table. The following listing displays territory names nested within country names while presenting its counts for customers.

Country/Region	Territory	Customer Count
United Kingdom	United Kingdom	1953
United States	Central	71
United States	Northeast	64
United States	Northwest	3433
United States	Southeast	97
United States	Southwest	4581

Including a Correlated Subquery in a WHERE Clause

The first sample in the preceding section illustrated how to select just those rows with column values that exceed a value returned by a subquery. However, that sample code returned a constant value from the subquery for all rows in the outer query. It is sometimes necessary to make the value returned by a subquery depend on one or more column values in the outer query. Recall that this kind of query is often called a correlated subquery.

Using a correlated subquery requires the subquery to reference values from the outer query. When a subquery references a value from the outer query, the subquery can use the referenced value to modify its return values. The second sample in the "Including a Subquery in a SELECT List" section in this chapter demonstrated how to use a correlated subquery to specify a column for a result set. By contrasting the sample in this section with the earlier one, you can reinforce your understanding of correlated subqueries.

The outer query in the following SELECT statement returns three columns of values from the SalesOrderDetail table. However, the columns for a row are added to the result set only when the LineTotal column value exceeds the average LineTotal column value for all rows with the ProductID for the current row in the outer query. The inner query facilitates this objective by adjusting its output based on the ProductID value in the outer query. The WHERE clause in the inner query shows the syntax for varying the subquery's output based on the ProductID column value in the outer query (sd1.ProductID).

```
SELECT SalesOrderID, ProductID, LineTotal
FROM Sales.SalesOrderDetail sd1
WHERE sd1.LineTotal >
    (SELECT AVG (sd2.LineTotal)
     FROM Sales.SalesOrderDetail sd2
     WHERE sd2.ProductID = sd1.ProductID)
ORDER BY SalesOrderID, ProductID
```

An excerpt from the listing for the preceding SELECT statement appears next. The output shows the rows returned for SalesOrderID values 43659 through 43661. Although SalesOrderID 43660 has two rows associated with it, neither of these rows had LineTotal values that exceeded the average value for their ProductID. Although the outer query returned three rows for SalesOrderID 43659 and five rows for SalesOrderID 43661, the total number of line items for these SalesOrderID values is, respectively, 12 and 15.

SalesOrderID	ProductID	LineTotal
43659	709	34.200000
43659	711	80.746000
43659	777	6074.982000
43661	708	100.932500
43661	712	20.746000

```
43661       741        1637.400000
43661       775        6074.982000
43661       776        8099.976000
```

Explicitly Ordering and Ranking Rows

When a SELECT statement runs without any explicit instructions designating the order of rows, SSE does not ensure the result set rows will return in any particular order. With very few and very simple indexes for a data source, SELECT statements will often order rows by a table's primary key. However, several typical situations can cause exceptions to this outcome, including

- Indexes that overlap with each other in their outcome for the order of result set rows

- Indexes that have not been rebuilt since the addition of new rows

- Defragmentation of a hard drive

When your solution requires the rows of a result set in a specific order, you should use the ORDER BY clause of a SELECT statement or a related technique for precisely designating the order in which rows return.

- The ORDER BY clause has been available for many prior versions of SQL Server. You previously viewed its operation in the "Grouping and Aggregating" section of Chapter 5, and several samples up to this point in this chapter demonstrated the use of the ORDER BY clause. This section systematically explores how to use the ORDER BY clause in more depth, as well as outside of the context of grouping rows and aggregating column values.

- SQL Server Express, as part of SQL Server 2005, provides four new functions for ranking result set rows. The four new T-SQL function names are ROW_NUMBER, RANK, DENSE_RANK, and NTILE. When SQL Server Express ranks rows with one of these functions, it automatically orders the rows according to the rank values. This ordering can apply across all the rows of a result set or within subsets of rows (called partitions). To help you determine when and how to use these new features, this section shows the syntax and gives one or more demonstrations of each of these functions.

Controlling Row Order with the ORDER BY Clause

The ORDER BY clause lets you specify the order of rows in a result set according to the values in one or more columns. Delimit the column names by commas in an ORDER BY clause if you designate more than one column for sorting. You can add either ASC or DESC after each column name in an ORDER BY clause to designate the direction in which rows sort for a column's values.

- Using ASC causes the rows to sort in ascending order from the minimum column value to the maximum column value or from a to z for a column of character values. Because the default order for sorting is ascending, the use of ASC is optional.

- Using DESC causes column values to order themselves from the maximum value to the minimum value, or from z to a for columns with character values.

The ORDER BY clause also interacts in several ways with the TOP keyword in a SELECT statement. The TOP keyword does not apply to a result set to restrict the number of returned rows until after the ORDER BY clause operates (if a SELECT statement has an ORDER BY clause). In fact, including an ORDER BY clause in a SELECT statement with the TOP keyword is the only sure way to know the order in which the SELECT statement retrieves rows. By using DESC, you can cause the TOP clause to return the bottom rows from the original data source for a result set.

You can find the code samples for this section in OrderByClauseSamples.sql.

Tip Because rows returned by a SELECT statement without an ORDER BY clause are in an arbitrary order, a best practice guideline is to use an ORDER BY clause in SELECT statements that include a TOP clause. This practice ensures that you know how column values are ordered before a SELECT statement applies its TOP keyword.

Sorting Rows Based on a Single Column's Values

The following four SELECT statements highlight the impact of the ORDER BY clause with a single sort column.

- The first SELECT statement in the following listing is a repetition of Chapter 5's first SELECT statement. Although the ProductCategory table has ProductCategoryID as its primary key, the result set rows do not appear in the order of the primary key. Instead, the rows appear in a-to-z alphabetical order for Name column values.

- The second and third SELECT statements show how to ensure the rows appear in the order of the primary key for a primary key defined on a single column. These rules also apply to any column whether or not it is the primary key.

  - It is essential to include the primary key column name as the sole column after an ORDER BY clause.

  - By default, the rows will order in ascending order on the primary key column values. No keyword after a column name means that rows sort in ascending order.

  - To sort in descending order on primary key column values, use DESC after the column name.

- The fourth SELECT statement sorts rows in descending order based on Name column values.

```
SELECT ProductCategoryID, Name
FROM Production.ProductCategory

SELECT ProductCategoryID, Name
FROM Production.ProductCategory
ORDER BY ProductCategoryID

SELECT ProductCategoryID, Name
FROM Production.ProductCategory
ORDER BY ProductCategoryID DESC

SELECT ProductCategoryID, Name
FROM Production.ProductCategory
ORDER BY Name DESC
```

The output from the preceding SELECT statements appears next. The four result sets correspond to the SELECT statement listings.

- The first result set shows the order of the rows without any ORDER BY clause. Notice the rows do not appear in the order of the primary key column values. For example, the ProductCategoryID value for the first row is 4, and the column value for the last row is 2.

- The second result set shows the rows in the order of the primary key column values (ProductCategoryID). The ORDER BY followed by ProductCategoryID generates this result.

- The third result set lists the rows in the reverse order of the second result set. This reversed order is a consequence of the addition of DESC after the ProductCategoryID column name in the ORDER BY clause.

- The final result set shows the rows in descending alphabetical order by Name column values. This order follows from the specification of Name followed by DESC in the fourth SELECT statement.

```
ProductCategoryID Name
----------------- -----------
4                 Accessories
1                 Bikes
3                 Clothing
2                 Components
```

```
ProductCategoryID Name
----------------- -----------
1                 Bikes
2                 Components
3                 Clothing
4                 Accessories
```

```
ProductCategoryID Name
----------------- -----------
4                 Accessories
3                 Clothing
2                 Components
1                 Bikes
```

```
ProductCategoryID Name
----------------- -----------
2                 Components
3                 Clothing
1                 Bikes
4                 Accessories
```

Sorting Rows Based on More Than One Column's Values

Sorting on the values from more than one column is a very simple extension of sorting on the values from just one column. The simplest explanation of how to sort on more than one column is to add more column names to the ORDER BY clause, delimited by commas. In addition, if you want to sort in descending order on the values from a column, add DESC after the column name.

The next SELECT statement provides a telephone directory for the persons in the vSalesPerson view of the Sales schema. The ORDER BY clause sorts the SELECT statement's result set on two columns—TerritoryGroup and LastName. The first column name in the ORDER BY clause is the outer one in the sort order. This means that rows sort by LastName within TerritoryGroup.

```
SELECT TerritoryGroup, FirstName, LastName, Phone
FROM Sales.vSalesPerson
ORDER BY TerritoryGroup, LastName
```

The following output shows the telephone directory listing. Notice that rows are sorted by TerritoryGroup column values. Null values are sorted as the lowest values in a column, so they appear first in the implicit ascending order designated by the preceding SELECT statement. Within any type of TerritoryGroup value, including the absence of one denoted by NULL, rows appear in ascending order by LastName column value. Therefore, Abbas appears before Alberts, which appears before Jiang.

```
TerritoryGroup FirstName LastName          Phone
-------------- --------- ----------------- --------------------
NULL           Syed      Abbas             926-555-0182
NULL           Amy       Alberts           775-555-0164
NULL           Stephen   Jiang             238-555-0197
Europe         Jae       Pak               1 (11) 500 555-0145
Europe         Rachel    Valdez            1 (11) 500 555-0140
Europe         Ranjit    Varkey Chudukatil 1 (11) 500 555-0117
North America  Pamela    Ansman-Wolfe      340-555-0193
North America  Michael   Blythe            257-555-0154
North America  David     Campbell          740-555-0182
North America  Jillian   Carson            517-555-0117
North America  Shu       Ito               330-555-0120
North America  Tete      Mensa-Annan       615-555-0153
North America  Linda     Mitchell          883-555-0116
North America  Tsvi      Reiter            664-555-0112
North America  José      Saraiva           185-555-0169
North America  Garrett   Vargas            922-555-0165
Pacific        Lynn      Tsoflias          1 (11) 500 555-0190
```

Listing Top or Bottom Rows

You can fine-tune the operation of the TOP keyword by using it in a SELECT statement that includes an ORDER BY clause.

- By combining the TOP with an ORDER BY clause, you can control whether the rows selected by a SELECT statement with a TOP keyword are taken from the maximum values or minimum values for a sort order.

- In addition, by using the WITH TIES phrase with the TOP clause in a SELECT statement, you can control whether the statement returns all tied values for a rank or just a precise number of rows whether or not there are ties. The ORDER BY clause lets you uncover ties by allowing you to extract rows from both the top and bottom of a sort order.

This section presents samples that illustrate the use of the ORDER BY clause with the TOP keyword in these two contexts.

You can get the top two rows by using a TOP keyword and specifying the ORDER BY clause with a column name. Because the ORDER BY clause sorts in ascending order by default, you can get the lowest two values for a column whether you add ASC after the column name or not. The following code listing's result set output shows the top two rows from the SalesOrderHeader table for the SubTotal column values. By sorting in ascending order, the query returns the two lowest SubTotal values from the table.

```
SELECT TOP 2 SalesOrderID, SubTotal
FROM Sales.SalesOrderHeader
ORDER BY SubTotal ASC
```

```
SalesOrderID SubTotal
------------ --------
51782        1.374
51885        2.29
```

As it turns out, there are 138 other rows tied for second place with the second row in the preceding listing. Whenever it is useful to see all the ties for a rank, you can include a WITH TIES phrase in conjunction with the TOP keyword and its argument specifying how many rows or what percentage of rows to return. The following SELECT statement returns 140 rows of which 139 have a value of 2.29 for their SubTotal column value. These 139 column values tie for second place.

```
SELECT TOP 2 WITH TIES SalesOrderID, SubTotal
FROM Sales.SalesOrderHeader
ORDER BY SubTotal ASC
```

Very often when people refer to the top two rows, they mean the two rows with the highest column values as opposed to the lowest column values. Remember ascending order is the default order! By using DESC in an ORDER BY clause, you can force the rows with the highest column values to the top of a result set. If you also include a TOP keyword in your SELECT statement, you will choose the largest column values as opposed to the smallest ones.

The following code and result set listing reveal the syntax for returning the two rows with the largest SubTotal values from the SalesOrderHeader table. Just following the SELECT statement, you see the column values returned by the statement.

```
SELECT TOP 2 SalesOrderID, SubTotal
FROM Sales.SalesOrderHeader
ORDER BY SubTotal DESC
```

```
SalesOrderID SubTotal
------------ -----------
51131        224356.4831
55282        206097.4856
```

Ranking Result Set Rows

T-SQL has certain ranking functions for use inside the list of a SELECT statement. These ranking functions add a value to each row of a result set that indicates its rank in one way or another.

- The ROW_NUMBER function returns a number indicating the position of a row among all the rows of a result set or a partition of those rows, with one indicating the initial position in the sequence. When you designate a column to denote partitions, the sequential numbers restart at one for each new partition within the overall result set. You can think of a partition as similar to a group generated with a GROUP BY clause.

- The RANK function assigns a rank to each row. The rank increases for each distinct column value on which ranks are based, but more than one row can have the same rank if they have the same ranking column value. Whenever the column value changes, the rank for the new row is one plus the number of previously ranked rows.

- The DENSE_RANK function assigns a rank number that can be different from the one assigned by the RANK function if there are ties within the ranking column values. If the value of a ranking column for the current row is the same as the previous ranked row, then the rank of the current row is the same as the previous row. Whenever the ranking column value changes for a new row, the rank for the new row is one plus the value of the rank for the previous ranked row.

- The NTILE function creates n groups for all the rows in a result set or for each of the partitions within a result set once you have ordered the rows. The number of groups created by the function depends on the argument value that you pass to the NTILE function statement. Passing a value of 2 creates 2 groups, and passing a value of 10 creates 10 groups.

When you specify any ranking function for a SELECT list, you must also specify arguments for an OVER clause. This clause has one mandatory argument and one optional argument.

- You can specify one or more column names after the PARTITION keyword. The values for these columns define partitions within a result set. The PARTITION keyword and its column name arguments compose the optional argument for the OVER clause. If you use the optional argument, it must occur before the mandatory argument.

- The ORDER BY phrase takes one or more columns in the same way that a SELECT statement's ORDER BY clause does. The columns following the ORDER BY clause designate the order in which SQL Server Express applies the ranking function. The ORDER BY phrase and its associated column names compose the mandatory argument for the OVER clause.

You can find the code samples for this section in RankingRows.sql.

Assigning Row Number Values to Rows

A couple of code samples will demonstrate the syntax for the ROW_NUMBER function with and without the optional PARTITION keyword for its OVER clause. The first sample, which appears in the following code block, includes the ROW_NUMBER function as the last item in a SELECT list that draws its entries from the vSalesPerson view. The OVER clause for the ROW_NUMBER function designates the mandatory ORDER BY clause. This clause specifies that row numbers will be assigned according to SalesYTD column values in descending order.

```
SELECT FirstName + ' ' + LastName 'Name', SalesYTD, SalesQuota,
    TerritoryGroup,
    ROW_NUMBER() OVER(ORDER BY SalesYTD DESC) AS 'RowNumber'
FROM Sales.vSalesPerson
```

■**Caution** In the event of a tie between two or more underlying ORDER BY column values for the ROW_NUMBER function, the assignment of row number values to rows within the tie is indeterminate. If you need to avoid this indeterminacy, remove all ties by either adding more columns to the ORDER BY setting or changing the column for the ORDER BY setting.

The following output listing shows the result set generated by the preceding SELECT statement. Notice particularly the RowNumber column to the far right. The ROW_NUMBER function in the SELECT statement generates these values in the result set. The first row number corresponds to the largest SalesYTD column value. The DESC keyword following the SalesYTD column in the OVER clause specifies that rows should appear in descending order based on SalesYTD column values. Also, notice that the RowNumber column values start at 1 and extend through 17. This is because I haven't used a PARTITION setting, which would have caused the RowNumber column values to start over again for any subsets of rows within the result set.

Name	SalesYTD	SalesQuota	TerritoryGroup	RowNumber
Linda Mitchell	5200475.2313	250000.00	North America	1
Jae Pak	5015682.3752	250000.00	Europe	2
Michael Blythe	4557045.0459	300000.00	North America	3
Jillian Carson	3857163.6332	250000.00	North America	4
Ranjit Varkey Chudukatil	3827950.238	250000.00	Europe	5
David Campbell	3587378.4257	250000.00	North America	6
José Saraiva	3189356.2465	250000.00	North America	7
Shu Ito	3018725.4858	250000.00	North America	8
Tsvi Reiter	2811012.7151	300000.00	North America	9
Rachel Valdez	2241204.0424	250000.00	Europe	10
Tete Mensa-Annan	1931620.1835	300000.00	North America	11
Garrett Vargas	1764938.9859	250000.00	North America	12
Lynn Tsoflias	1758385.926	250000.00	Pacific	13
Stephen Jiang	677558.4653	NULL	NULL	14
Amy Alberts	636440.251	NULL	NULL	15
Syed Abbas	219088.8836	NULL	NULL	16
Pamela Ansman-Wolfe	0.00	250000.00	North America	17

The next SELECT statement adds a PARTITION setting to the OVER clause for the preceding SELECT statement. The column name following the PARTITION keyword designates partitions or rows within the result set based on TerritoryGroup column values. This leads to four subsets of rows—one for each of the TerritoryGroup column values plus one more subset for those rows with no TerritoryGroup column values.

```
SELECT FirstName + ' ' + LastName 'Name', SalesYTD, SalesQuota,
    TerritoryGroup,
    ROW_NUMBER() OVER(PARTITION BY TerritoryGroup
    ORDER BY SalesYTD DESC) AS 'RowNumber'
FROM Sales.vSalesPerson
```

The following output listing shows the result set generated by the second SELECT statement with a ROW_NUMBER function. Focus again on the RowNumber column. The values in this column no longer start at 1 and run through 17. Instead, the RowNumber column values increment by one based on the SalesYTD column values for each new row within a set of TerritoryGroup column values. At the first row for each new TerritoryGroup number value, the RowNumber column value resets to 1.

Name	SalesYTD	SalesQuota	TerritoryGroup	RowNumber
Stephen Jiang	677558.4653	NULL	NULL	1
Amy Alberts	636440.251	NULL	NULL	2
Syed Abbas	219088.8836	NULL	NULL	3
Jae Pak	5015682.3752	250000.00	Europe	1
Ranjit Varkey Chudukatil	3827950.238	250000.00	Europe	2
Rachel Valdez	2241204.0424	250000.00	Europe	3
Linda Mitchell	5200475.2313	250000.00	North America	1
Michael Blythe	4557045.0459	300000.00	North America	2
Jillian Carson	3857163.6332	250000.00	North America	3
David Campbell	3587378.4257	250000.00	North America	4
José Saraiva	3189356.2465	250000.00	North America	5
Shu Ito	3018725.4858	250000.00	North America	6
Tsvi Reiter	2811012.7151	300000.00	North America	7
Tete Mensa-Annan	1931620.1835	300000.00	North America	8
Garrett Vargas	1764938.9859	250000.00	North America	9
Pamela Ansman-Wolfe	0.00	250000.00	North America	10
Lynn Tsoflias	1758385.926	250000.00	Pacific	1

Assigning Ranks to Rows

Although ROW_NUMBER function values are equivalent to ranks when the sort order for all rows in a result set is distinct, the ROW_NUMBER function does not handle ties well from a ranking perspective. This is because the rank for two rows with the same column value should be the same, but the ROW_NUMBER function continues applying sequential numbers to rows whether or not there is a tie between two or more successive rows.

Like the ROW_NUMBER function, the RANK and DENSE_RANK functions assign incremental numbers to successive rows within a result set based on the ordering implied by one or more sets of column values. However, the RANK and DENSE_RANK functions both avoid the ROW_NUMBER function's deficiency in this respect. In the event of a tie between two or more successive rows, both the RANK and DENSE_RANK functions assign the same number to all rows with the same value. However, the number assigned will generally be different between the RANK and DENSE_RANK functions.

- The RANK function assigns a number to each successive row based on a new underlying non-tied value that is 1 plus the number of previously ranked rows. Therefore, if the first three rows are tied and the ranking column value for the fourth row is distinct, its RANK function value will be 4. The RANK function value for the first three rows is 1.

- The DENSE_RANK function assigns new ranks after a tie based on 1 plus the number of previously distinct ranks—not previously ranked rows. Therefore, if the first three ranking column row values are tied but the fourth row is unique, then the rank for the first three rows is 1, but the rank for the fourth row is 2.

Perhaps the best way to understand the differences between the RANK and DENSE_RANK functions is to compare them on ranking the same values. Let's use the same data source as for the preceding ROW_NUMBER function samples to help you grasp the distinctions between these three functions.

The following SELECT statement has both the RANK and DENSE_RANK functions in its list. The RANK and DENSE_RANK functions have identical syntax, except for the function name. Both functions order their ranks by SalesQuota column values from the vSalesPerson view, which has tied column values.

```
SELECT FirstName + ' ' + LastName 'Name', SalesYTD, SalesQuota,
    TerritoryGroup,
    RANK() OVER(ORDER BY SalesQuota DESC) AS 'Rank',
    Dense_RANK() OVER(ORDER BY SalesQuota DESC ) AS 'Dense Rank'
FROM Sales.vSalesPerson
```

The output listing appears next. For both functions, the rank values group by SalesQuota column values. There are two unique SalesQuota column values of 300,000 and 250,000 besides the null values for Amy Alberts, Stephen Jiang, and Syed Abbas. The null values rank lower than any actual assigned SalesQuota column values.

- The unique RANK function column values are 1, 4, and 15. The rank value is 1 for the first three rows with a SalesQuota column value of 300,000, and the rank value is 4 for the first row following the first three; 4 is also the rank for all other rows with a SalesQuota column value of 250,000. The rank for the last three rows with a NULL SalesQuota column value is 15.

- The unique DENSE_RANK function values are 1, 2, and 3. Notice that the DENSE_RANK function values increase based on the preceding unique rank values instead of the number of previously ranked rows. In addition, the DENSE_RANK function results in more intuitive values because it assigns a rank of 2, instead of 4, to all the rows that are tied for second place. The DENSE_RANK function applies the same type of meaningful value, 3, to those that tie for third place.

Name	SalesYTD	SalesQuota	TerritoryGroup	Rank	Dense Rank
Michael Blythe	4557045.0459	300000.00	North America	1	1
Tsvi Reiter	2811012.7151	300000.00	North America	1	1
Tete Mensa-Annan	1931620.1835	300000.00	North America	1	1
Jae Pak	5015682.3752	250000.00	Europe	4	2
Ranjit Varkey Chudukatil	3827950.238	250000.00	Europe	4	2
Rachel Valdez	2241204.0424	250000.00	Europe	4	2
Lynn Tsoflias	1758385.926	250000.00	Pacific	4	2
Pamela Ansman-Wolfe	0.00	250000.00	North America	4	2
Shu Ito	3018725.4858	250000.00	North America	4	2
José Saraiva	3189356.2465	250000.00	North America	4	2
David Campbell	3587378.4257	250000.00	North America	4	2
Linda Mitchell	5200475.2313	250000.00	North America	4	2
Jillian Carson	3857163.6332	250000.00	North America	4	2
Garrett Vargas	1764938.9859	250000.00	North America	4	2
Amy Alberts	636440.251	NULL	NULL	15	3
Stephen Jiang	677558.4653	NULL	NULL	15	3
Syed Abbas	219088.8836	NULL	NULL	15	3

There are several easy extensions of this sample that can generate different or supplemental ranking results. For example, you can add partitions so that the ranks occur within partitions of the result set instead of across the whole result set. You can also add another column name to the ORDER BY clause so that DENSE_RANK function values are unique for all rows. The RankingRows.sql file includes an example like this.

Assigning NTILE Numbers to Rows

Recall that the NTILE function divides a group of rows into a set number of groups. You specify the number of groups as an argument when you invoke the function. In the ORDER BY phrase of the OVER clause for the function, you can specify which column values to order rows with before dividing them into percentile groups. If the number of rows is not evenly divisible by the number of groups that you specify, then the NTILE function increases the size of each group by one until the group before the last group.

The following listing shows a SELECT statement that illustrates the syntax for invoking the NTILE function as well as a result set generated by the statement. Notice that the statement passes a value of 5 to the NTILE function, which tells it to generate 5 groups. When the SELECT statement runs, it sorts the rows by their SalesYTD column values and attempts to divide the rows evenly across the five groups.

The NTILE column values show the outcome of the attempt. Because there are 17 rows but 5 groups, the NTILE function can assign at least 5 rows to all 5 groups. However, this leaves two extra rows. Recall that the general rule is to assign one of the remainder rows to each of the groups up to the next to the last group. As a consequence, groups one and two each have four rows, and the other three groups have just three rows.

```
SELECT FirstName + ' ' + LastName 'Name', SalesYTD, SalesQuota,
    TerritoryGroup,
    NTILE(5) OVER(ORDER BY SalesYTD DESC) AS 'NTILE'
FROM Sales.vSalesPerson
```

Name	SalesYTD	SalesQuota	TerritoryGroup	NTILE
Linda Mitchell	5200475.2313	250000.00	North America	1
Jae Pak	5015682.3752	250000.00	Europe	1
Michael Blythe	4557045.0459	300000.00	North America	1
Jillian Carson	3857163.6332	250000.00	North America	1
Ranjit Varkey Chudukatil	3827950.238	250000.00	Europe	2
David Campbell	3587378.4257	250000.00	North America	2
José Saraiva	3189356.2465	250000.00	North America	2
Shu Ito	3018725.4858	250000.00	North America	2
Tsvi Reiter	2811012.7151	300000.00	North America	3
Rachel Valdez	2241204.0424	250000.00	Europe	3
Tete Mensa-Annan	1931620.1835	300000.00	North America	3
Garrett Vargas	1764938.9859	250000.00	North America	4
Lynn Tsoflias	1758385.926	250000.00	Pacific	4
Stephen Jiang	677558.4653	NULL	NULL	4
Amy Alberts	636440.251	NULL	NULL	5
Syed Abbas	219088.8836	NULL	NULL	5
Pamela Ansman-Wolfe	0.00	250000.00	North America	5

Manipulating Result Sets

After you initially compose a result set, you can reuse the result set to derive additional value for your applications. You can reuse a result set by manipulating it in any of a variety of ways. This section demonstrates four techniques for manipulating result sets to derive additional value from them (shown next).

- Save the result in a table for easy reference later. This technique lets you reuse the result set values without rerunning the query that generated the result set values.

- Append one result set to the end of another result set. This capability allows you to combine a subset of the columns from two or more different result sets.

- Temporarily keep one SELECT statement in scope and refer back to it from a second SELECT statement (or INSERT, UPDATE, DELETE statement as well). This technique can simplify query statements.

- With the PIVOT operator, designate column values to generate result sets with cross-tabulated values. This approach is useful for analyzing the values in a result set. With the UNPIVOT operator, you can restore the layout of relational data from cross-tabulated data.

Saving a Result Set with the INTO Clause

Using the INTO clause from within a SELECT statement makes it phenomenally easy to save a result set to storage. It takes a single argument, which is the name of a new table. The new table stores the result set generated by the list and clauses in a SELECT statement. You can position the INTO clause after the SELECT list and before the FROM clause. A SELECT statement with an INTO clause is commonly called a SELECT INTO statement. The following guidelines apply to the creation of a new table with a SELECT INTO statement:

- The new table resides in the current database context unless you explicitly specify otherwise with a three- or four-part name for the new table. Therefore, you can reference a data source within another database context using a three-part name in the FROM clause of a SELECT INTO statement to make a copy of the data source in the current database context.

- If the original data source or SELECT list has calculated column values, the SELECT INTO statement saves the values for the calculations—not the calculation expressions.

- If a table with the name for the new table already exists in the current database, then the SELECT INTO statement does not copy over the existing table.

The sample code for this section resides in SELECTINTOSamples.sql.

Making a Copy of a Table

The SELECT INTO statement that follows shows a very basic example that creates a copy of the ProductCategory table from the Production schema in the AdventureWorks database. The INTO clause designates MyCopy as the name of the new table to hold the copied values. Because a two-part name is used in the FROM clause, the statement assumes its database context is the AdventureWorks database. Use a three-part name to copy a table from another database or a four-part name to copy a table from another database on another server instance.

```
SELECT *
INTO MyCopy
FROM Production.ProductCategory
```

Immediately after running the preceding SELECT INTO statement, you have two tables, MyCopy and ProductCategory, with the values of ProductCategory. MyCopy is essentially a snapshot of ProductCategory at the time that you run the SELECT INTO statement. If you subsequently change values in ProductCategory, MyCopy still retains the original values (unless you explicitly revise MyCopy, too).

Although MyCopy contains the values in ProductCategory, it does not perfectly reflect the structure of the ProductCategory table. This is particularly so with respect to indexes. The following two SELECT statements echo the values from the two tables without any formatting. The result sets appear directly below the SELECT statements. The difference in the order of the rows between the ProductCategory and MyCopy tables indicates that the two tables are not identical although the tables contain the same values.

```
SELECT ProductCategoryID, Name
FROM Production.ProductCategory
```

```
ProductCategoryID Name
----------------- -----------
4                 Accessories
1                 Bikes
3                 Clothing
2                 Components
```

```
SELECT ProductCategoryID, Name
FROM MyCopy
```

```
ProductCategoryID Name
----------------- -----------
1                 Bikes
2                 Components
3                 Clothing
4                 Accessories
```

One area in which to look for differences between the two tables is the definition of their column values. The following pair of SELECT statements draws on the sys.columns and sys.types system views to characterize the columns in the MyCopy and ProductCategory tables. (Chapter 7 examines the topic of system views, such as sys.columns, in greater depth.)

In the current context, all you need to know is that you can obtain information about the columns and user-defined data types from the sys.columns and sys.types views. The OBJECT_ID function returns the database identification number of an object, which SQL Server Express uses to track database objects, such as tables.

The next pair of SELECT statements and their result sets show the column properties for the ProductCategory and MyCopy tables. Notice that the column names and the property values (the max_length column to the identity column) are identical in the two tables. However, the data type names are not identical. The ProductCategory table defines its Name column as a Name data type, which is a user-defined data type in the AdventureWorks database. The MyCopy table defines its Name column as an nvarchar data type with a maximum length of 100 bytes (or 50 characters because the column uses Unicode characters). In fact, the properties for the Name columns are the same in both tables although they have different type names.

```
SELECT c.name 'Column name', t.name 'Data type name',
    c.max_length, c.precision, c.scale,
    c.is_nullable 'nullable', c.is_identity 'identity'
FROM sys.columns c
JOIN sys.types t
ON c.user_type_id = t.user_type_id
WHERE object_id = OBJECT_ID('Production.ProductCategory')
```

Column name	Data type name	max_length	precision	scale	nullable	identity
ProductCategoryID	int	4	10	0	0	1
Name	Name	100	0	0	0	0
rowguid	uniqueidentifier	16	0	0	0	0
ModifiedDate	datetime	8	23	3	0	0

```
SELECT c.name 'Column name', t.name 'Data type name',
    c.max_length, c.precision, c.scale,
    c.is_nullable 'nullable', c.is_identity 'identity'
FROM sys.columns c
JOIN sys.types t
ON c.user_type_id = t.user_type_id
WHERE object_id = OBJECT_ID('MyCopy')
```

Column name	Data type name	max_length	precision	scale	nullable	identity
ProductCategoryID	int	4	10	0	0	1
Name	nvarchar	100	0	0	0	0
rowguid	uniqueidentifier	16	0	0	0	0
ModifiedDate	datetime	8	23	3	0	0

A much more significant difference between the two tables shows up when you compare the indexes for the two tables. You can use the sys.indexes system view to return information about the indexes and storage mechanism associated with a table. The following pair of SELECT statements illustrates the syntax for doing this:

- The first SELECT statement and its result set show that the ProductCategory table has three indexes. The PK_ProductCategory_ProductCategoryID index serves as the primary key, and it is clustered—meaning that rows are physically stored according to its values. Even in spite of these storage considerations, the rows do not automatically return in the order of the primary key column values.

- The second SELECT statement and its result set show that the MyCopy table has no indexes. The HEAP type description indicates this.

- This significant difference between the indexes for the two tables indicates that this is the source of the difference in row orders displayed previously.

■**Note** The difference in row orders and indexes for the ProductCategory and MyCopy tables is presented to reinforce the notion that you should always use an ORDER BY clause to ensure a specific order of rows in a result set. Of course, having an index for a column on which you plan to order rows can enhance the performance of your queries.

```
SELECT name 'Type name', type_desc 'Type description', is_primary_key
FROM sys.indexes
WHERE object_id = OBJECT_ID('Production.ProductCategory')
```

Type name	Type description	is_primary_key
PK_ProductCategory_ProductCategoryID	CLUSTERED	1
AK_ProductCategory_Name	NONCLUSTERED	0
AK_ProductCategory_rowguid	NONCLUSTERED	0

```
SELECT name 'Type name', type_desc 'Type description', is_primary_key
FROM sys.indexes
WHERE object_id = OBJECT_ID('MyCopy')
```

Type name	Type description	is_primary_key
NULL	HEAP	0

Copying Selected Rows from a Table

When working with a SELECT INTO statement, it is not necessary to copy all the rows of a table to another table. In fact, that's one of the advantages of the SELECT INTO statement, because you have access to the full array of SELECT statement clauses to formulate a result set that serves as the source for a new table. The following SELECT INTO statement selects the rows with a ProductCategoryID value greater than two for inclusion in the MyCopy table. The subsequent SELECT statement and its result set confirm the successful operation of the SELECT INTO statement.

■**Caution** You have to drop the MyCopy table for the code in this section to run as described. The sample code in SELECTINTOSamples.sql demonstrates how to accomplish this task.

```
SELECT *
INTO MyCopy
FROM Production.ProductCategory
WHERE ProductCategoryID > 2
GO

SELECT ProductCategoryID, Name
FROM MyCopy
GO
```

ProductCategoryID	Name
3	Clothing
4	Accessories

As mentioned, once you create a table with a SELECT INTO statement, you cannot copy over it.

- You can first drop the old version of a table with the DROP TABLE statement to save a new version with the same name.

- Alternatively, you can just copy the new version of the table with a different name.

If you run the following pair of batches, the initial SELECT INTO statement fails because it attempts to copy over a previously created table. The subsequent SELECT statement confirms that the values from the preceding SELECT INTO statement are still in the MyCopy table.

```
SELECT *
INTO MyCopy
FROM Production.ProductCategory
WHERE ProductCategoryID <= 2
GO

SELECT ProductCategoryID, Name
FROM MyCopy
GO
```

Appending Result Sets to One Another

The UNION operator in a SELECT statement allows you to combine the values from two data sources or two copies of the same data source. Although a join combines data values by matching rows from data sources on field values according a join criterion expression, the UNION operator appends the columns of a second data source behind those of a first data source. By default, if two data sources have rows with identical values, the UNION operator does not add the duplicate copy of a row to the combined result set. You can force the addition of duplicates by specifying the ALL keyword after UNION.

The syntax for the UNION operator is exceptionally simple: just place the UNION operator and a SELECT statement after an initial SELECT statement. The result sets from both SELECT statements must have the same number of columns. In addition, the columns in the two data sources must be compatible (e.g., you can't append an ntext column in the second SELECT statement to a bit column in the first SELECT statement).

```
SELECT statement1
UNION [ALL]
SELECT statement2
```

Several special rules apply to the use of UNION operators in SELECT statements.

- You can combine result sets from more than two SELECT statements by adding another UNION operator followed by another SELECT statement. In fact, you can add any number of SELECT statements by following the same process.

- By default, a UNION operator combines result sets in the order that they appear unless you override that order by enclosing two or more SELECT statements in parentheses.

- The use of an ORDER BY clause applies only to the last combined result set. An ORDER BY clause does not operate within a component SELECT statement that is in turn within a series of statements combined by UNION operators.

- GROUP BY and HAVING clauses apply only to individual SELECT statements combined by UNION operators and not the combined result set for the overall series of SELECT statements.

- You can save a result set for a combined series of SELECT statements by using a SELECT INTO statement for the initial SELECT statement in the series. Other SELECT statements connected by UNION operators append their result sets to the file initialized by the SELECT INTO statement.

The code samples for this section are in UsingUNIONOperators.sql.

Combining Result Sets with or without Duplicates

The first two UNION samples below demonstrate the operation of the UNION operator with and without its ALL keyword. Both of these UNION samples combine identical SELECT statements to show the contrast between the two forms of the operator. The first statement returns all rows from the ProductCatetory table with a Name column value beginning with C. The second statement returns all rows from the ProductCategory table with a Name column value beginning with CL.

In the ProductCategory table that ships with the AdventureWorks database, the first SELECT statement returns two rows, and the second one returns just one row. Furthermore, the single row returned by the second SELECT statement is a duplicate of one of the rows returned by the first statement.

- When the first UNION sample runs with its ALL keyword, all three rows are in the combined result set.

- When the second UNION sample runs without the ALL keyword, only two rows are in the result set because the duplicate in the second SELECT statement is rejected.

```
SELECT ProductCategoryID, Name
FROM Production.ProductCategory
WHERE Name LIKE 'C%'
UNION ALL
SELECT ProductCategoryID, Name
FROM Production.ProductCategory
WHERE Name LIKE 'Cl%'
```

```
ProductCategoryID Name
----------------- ----------
3                 Clothing
2                 Components
3                 Clothing
```

```
SELECT ProductCategoryID, Name
FROM Production.ProductCategory
WHERE Name LIKE 'C%'
UNION
SELECT ProductCategoryID, Name
FROM Production.ProductCategory
WHERE Name LIKE 'Cl%'
```

```
ProductCategoryID Name
----------------- ----------
2                 Components
3                 Clothing
```

Tracking Input Data Sources in a Combined Result Set

When working with data from multiple data sources, you may occasionally want to add an extra column that designates the data source. This technique is particularly appropriate for cases in which you are not working with such a highly normalized database as AdventureWorks. For example, the Northwind database has telephone and other contact data in multiple data sources, such as the Customers, Employees, Suppliers, and Shippers tables. This approach is not as elegant as the AdventureWorks design, which stores all kinds of contact data in the Contact table within the Person schema. If you are working with a database that is more like Northwind than AdventureWorks, you may find consolidating the contact telephone data with UNION operators provides you a virtual central repository for querying contact data even while you manage pools of contact data separately.

The following series of SELECT statements with UNION operators combines data from the Customers, Employees, and Shippers tables in the Northwind database. To make the combined result set compact, each SELECT statement includes TOP 3 to restrict its output to just three rows. The first three columns contain information related to contact name, phone, and fax. These column values are derived from the data sources, such as the Customers table. The last column denotes the data source that contains the contact information. The codes of Customer, Employee, and Shipper refer to the Customers, Employees, and Shippers tables in the Northwind database.

Notice the ORDER BY clause as the last clause in the series of SELECT statements. This clause applies to the overall combined result set. It does not just apply to the result set for the third SELECT statement. Using this kind of technique allows the grouping of rows from the same data source.

```
USE Northwind
GO

SELECT TOP 3 ContactName, Phone, ISNULL(Fax, '') 'Fax',
    'Customer' 'ContactType'
FROM Customers
UNION
SELECT TOP 3 FirstName + ' ' + LastName, HomePhone, '',
    'Employee' 'ContactType'
FROM Employees
UNION
SELECT TOP 3 CompanyName , Phone, '',
    'Shipper' 'ContactType'
FROM Shippers

ORDER BY ContactType
```

ContactName	Phone	Fax	ContactType
Ana Trujillo	(5) 555-4729	(5) 555-3745	Customer
Antonio Moreno	(5) 555-3932		Customer
Maria Anders	030-0074321	030-0076545	Customer
Andrew Fuller	(206) 555-9482		Employee
Janet Leverling	(206) 555-3412		Employee
Nancy Davolio	(206) 555-9857		Employee
Federal Shipping	(503) 555-9931		Shipper
Speedy Express	(503) 555-9831		Shipper
United Package	(503) 555-3199		Shipper

Reusing a Combined Result Set from a Table

When working with the UNION operators, you may sometimes generate some combined results that have many rows, though these combined result sets may take longer to generate than is suitable for your needs. If the information doesn't change very often, as is the case for quarterly or annual data, it may be helpful to copy the combined result set to a table and then reference the saved table. This will save your application the time of recreating the result set each time you need to query the combined data source.

The following pair of SELECT statements combined with a UNION operator generates two different result sets based on the ProductCategory table from the AdventureWorks database. The first SELECT statement adds two rows to the result set for Name column values that start with C. The second SELECT statement adds three rows to the result set—one from the row with a Name column value that begins with B and two more rows from product categories with Name column values beginning with C. Because you're using the ALL keyword, duplicate rows with Name column values beginning with C enter the combined result set.

The most significant feature of the code is not the SELECT statements that contribute to the combined result set, but rather the INTO clause in the first SELECT statement. This clause causes the combined result set for the following series of SELECT statements combined with one or more UNION operators to stream into the named data source. In this case, you copy the combined result set to the MyCopy table. The stand-alone SELECT statement at the end of the sample demonstrates the syntax for querying the newly created table. The sample result set after the sample code shows the values obtained with the SELECT statement.

■**Tip** Recall that a SELECT INTO will not copy into an existing table. Therefore, make sure that the MyCopy table does not exist before you run the sample to copy a combined result set into the table.

```
USE AdventureWorks
GO

SELECT ProductCategoryID, Name
INTO MyCopy
FROM Production.ProductCategory
WHERE Name LIKE 'C%'
UNION ALL
SELECT ProductCategoryID, Name
FROM Production.ProductCategory
WHERE Name LIKE 'C%' OR Name LIKE 'B%'

--Display table
SELECT ProductCategoryID, Name 'Name'
FROM MyCopy
```

```
ProductCategoryID Name
----------------- -----------
3                 Clothing
2                 Components
1                 Bikes
3                 Clothing
2                 Components
```

Reusing Queries with Common Table Expressions

A common table expression (CTE) is a new T-SQL tool introduced by SQL Server Express and the other SQL Server 2005 editions. With a CTE, you can specify one or more SELECT statements for reuse by another SELECT statement (or even an INSERT, UPDATE, or DELETE statement). You can also use a CTE within a CREATE VIEW statement. The use of a CTE in a CREATE VIEW statement is less critical than a SELECT statement because CREATE VIEW statements by definition store a SELECT statement for reuse.

- This tool helps divide a task into parts in which where one part builds on another. Just as a subquery inside an outer query enables more flexible query statements, so do CTEs. However, it is likely that many developers will find CTEs an easier way of expressing flexible query statements.

- CTEs also facilitate recursive tasks from within T-SQL. This feature is especially useful for processing hierarchical relationships, such as mapping relationships between managers and employees within an organization.

There can be as many as three parts to a CTE.

- You declare a CTE by using the WITH keyword to designate its name. This name is especially important because the name is the handle that another statement, such as a SELECT statement, uses to reference the CTE.

- You can optionally specify a list of column names that serve as handles for the column values returned by a CTE. Position the optional list of names after the CTE name and before the SELECT statements for the CTE. If you do not designate an optional list of column names, you can refer to a CTE's column values by the names that the CTE's SELECT statements assign to the columns.

- A CTE requires one or more SELECT statements to determine column values that it returns. You can specify a recursive CTE by designating a second SELECT statement that refers to a first SELECT statement from within the CTE. The multiple SELECT statements for a recursive CTE are linked by a UNION operator with the ALL keyword.

■**Caution** You must designate column names for the columns returned by a CTE. If you do not use an optional list of column names outside the one or more SELECT statements defining a CTE, then you must designate names for all columns from within the SELECT statements defining a CTE.

Several guidelines and restrictions apply to the design and use of SELECT statements in CTEs. Recursive CTEs have additional guidelines beyond those for nonrecursive CTEs.

A CTE must be followed by another statement, such as a SELECT statement, that refers to it. This is the only way to reuse the SELECT statements within a CTE. The CTE is not available for reuse beyond this single trailing statement.

- You cannot reference an ORDER BY clause in a SELECT statement for a CTE unless the statement also includes a TOP clause.

- You cannot designate an INTO clause for a SELECT statement within a CTE.

- When a CTE is part of a T-SQL batch, then the immediately preceding statement must terminate with a semicolon.

- SELECT statements within recursive CTEs cannot contain any of the following:
  - The DISTINCT keyword
  - The TOP keyword
  - GROUP BY or HAVING clauses
  - Outer joins (inner joins can be used)
  - Subqueries

- Guidelines applying exclusively to recursive CTEs include the following:
  - Within a view, CTEs can only be referred to by SELECT statements—not INSERT, UPDATE, or DELETE statements.
  - You should avoid infinite loops resulting from incorrectly designed CTE SELECT statements by using the MAXRECURSION hint or a column value to limit the number of iterations run.

The samples for this section are in UsingCTEs.sql.

Looking Up Values Based on CTE Column Values

The following code listing demonstrates basic design and guideline issues for using a CTE. The code illustrates two application steps that you must make whenever you are going to use a CTE. In addition, you'll look at an example of how not to use a CTE, to reinforce your understanding of one limitation associated with CTEs.

To start using a CTE, you use the WITH keyword followed by the CTE's name. You can optionally specify the columns returned by the CTE by adding a list of names in parentheses after the CTE's name. After the CTE and the optional column names, CTE syntax requires the AS keyword. This keyword precedes a set of parentheses that delimits one or more SELECT statements defining what values the CTE returns.

The SELECT statement inside the parentheses includes a SELECT list, a FROM clause, and a GROUP BY clause. The GROUP BY returns the average LineTotal column values grouped by ProductID column values. Recall that only nonrecursive CTEs, such as this one, are able to include GROUP BY clauses.

Immediately following the closing parentheses of the CTE is another SELECT statement that refers to the CTE.

- The reference from the SELECT statement to the CTE appears in the FROM clause. Notice that the first argument for the FROM clause is the CTE name. Therefore, the SELECT statement inside the CTE serves as one data source for the SELECT statement following the CTE.

- A JOIN clause merges the result set from the CTE with the Product table in the Production schema of the AdventureWorks database. This join allows the listing in the result set of Name column values from the Product table instead of ProductID column values from the CTE.

- A concluding ORDER BY clause sorts the result set rows by Name column values from the Product table.

Notice that there is a second SELECT statement after the CTE.

- This second SELECT statement fails to execute because the scope of the CTE extends only to the first statement following it.

- The statement immediately following a CTE can refer to the CTE more than once, but this is the only statement that can.

- If you need multiple references in different SELECT statements to a CTE, you can copy the CTE declaration and code once for each additional statement that needs to refer to the CTE. If you do copy a CTE declaration and its code in the same script, you can do one of two things:
  - Start a new batch with the CTE declaration as the first statement in the new batch.
  - Terminate the immediately preceding T-SQL statement in the same batch with a semicolon.

```
WITH ProductItemPrices AS
(
SELECT ProductID, AVG(LineTotal) 'AvgPrice'
FROM Sales.SalesOrderDetail
GROUP BY ProductID
)

SELECT p.Name, pp.AvgPrice
FROM ProductItemPrices pp
JOIN
Production.Product p
ON
```

```
pp.ProductID = p.ProductID
ORDER BY p.Name

SELECT * FROM ProductItemPrices
```

An excerpt from the result set is shown next, and confirms the operation of the CTE. The AvgPrice column name derives directly from a SELECT statement following the CTE. This SELECT list item, in turn, derives from the AvgPrice alias assigned to the return values from the AVG function within the SELECT statement inside the CTE.

```
Name                    AvgPrice
--------------------- ----------
All-Purpose Bike Stand 159.000000
AWC Logo Cap            15.147677
Bike Wash - Dissolver  13.871116
Cable Lock             62.462384
Chain                  37.510840
```

Using a CTE Instead of a Correlated Subquery

Aside from just passing along a value, such as a product identification number, to look up a product name, you can use CTEs to simplify more sophisticated tasks. The "Including a Correlated Subquery in a WHERE Clause" section earlier in this chapter describes a subquery application for listing rows from the SalesOrderDetail table with LineTotal column values that exceeded the average LineTotal values for rows with the same ProductID. The previous ProductItemPrices CTE generated a list with average LineTotal column values from the SalesOrderDetail table. Therefore, you can readily use it with a trailing SELECT statement to generate the same result set as the one provided by the correlated subquery sample. In essence

- The CTE serves as a correlated subquery.
- The CTE's trailing SELECT statement serves as an outer query.

A subquery in a WHERE clause is often a very compact way of expressing the relationship between inner and outer queries. However, specifying both queries can sometimes be tricky—especially when you are working with correlated subqueries. Using a CTE with a trailing statement to generate the same results can be simpler because it is often easier to specify the CTE SELECT statement and its trailing SELECT statement than a single SELECT statement with both inner and outer queries.

The following listing shows the code sample to list rows from the SalesOrderDetail table with LineTotal column values that exceed the average LineTotal column value for rows with the same ProductID. The list for the SELECT statement following the ProductItemPrices CTE includes three items from the SalesOrderDetail table (sd.SalesOrderID, sd.ProductID, and sd.LineTotal) along with one item from the CTE (pp.AvgPrice). The join merges the SalesOrderDetail table and the ProductItemPrices CTE based on matching ProductID column values. The WHERE clause restricts entry to the result set for the trailing SELECT statement to rows with an sd.LineTotal value greater than their pp.AvgPrice value.

```
WITH ProductItemPrices AS
(
SELECT ProductID, AVG(LineTotal) 'AvgPrice'
FROM Sales.SalesOrderDetail
GROUP BY ProductID
)
```

```
SELECT sd.SalesOrderID, sd.ProductID, sd.LineTotal, pp.AvgPrice
FROM Sales.SalesOrderDetail sd
JOIN
ProductItemPrices pp
ON pp.ProductID = sd.ProductID
WHERE sd.LineTotal > pp.AvgPrice
ORDER BY sd.SalesOrderID, sd.ProductID
```

An excerpt from the result set for the trailing SELECT statement appears next. The values in this listing match those from the earlier listing in the "Including a Correlated Subquery in a WHERE Clause" section. By including the AvgPrice column in this listing, you can also verify that the LineTotal column values for returned rows all exceed the average price for the ProductID of the current row.

```
SalesOrderID ProductID LineTotal   AvgPrice
------------ --------- ----------- -----------
43659        709       34.200000   32.236107
43659        711       80.746000   53.529649
43659        777       6074.982000 5644.018090
43661        708       100.932500  53.498343
43661        712       20.746000   15.147677
43661        741       1637.400000 1506.756382
43661        775       6074.982000 5726.483994
43661        776       8099.976000 5503.169878
```

In a production application of this sample, you might replace the ProductID column values with product names. This step was purposefully not taken to keep this sample as similar as possible to the previous correlated subquery sample. However, the preceding CTE sample demonstrates an approach to returning product names matching ProductID column values.

Mapping Hierarchical Relationships with a CTE

The next pair of samples demonstrates the use of recursive CTEs to map hierarchical relationships between employees and their managers. With a recursive CTE, you can track hierarchical relationships for employees down through all levels of an organization. The first sample starts with the top-level employee in the AdventureWorks database and shows who reports directly to that employee. Therefore, it tracks just the top two levels of employees with the database.

The sample begins by assigning a value of 109 to the @TopEmp local variable; this is the top-level employee in the company. The SET statement making an assignment ends with a semicolon because it precedes the WITH clause that designates Empcte as the CTE name. Notice that the Empcte CTE demonstrates the syntax for using an optional list of column names. The CTE's first SELECT statement generates the anchor row. This row contains EmployeeID, employee name, manager identification number, department name, and level (lvl) for the employee identification number specified in @TopEmp.

■**Note** The lvl column value returned by the CTE tracks iterations through the recursive loop and level for the employee within the organization. The recursive CTE assigns a value of 0 to the anchor row lvl value whether or not it is working with the top-level employee. This allows you to terminate the looping operation at a fixed number of iterations through the recursive CTE.

The anchor row is followed by a UNION operator and the ALL keyword. This operator and keyword in combination with a properly designed recursive SELECT statement allow the CTE to return the employees at each hierarchical reporting level in the organization starting right below the anchor employee.

- The last JOIN clause in the recursive SELECT statement selects all rows from the Employee table with a manager identification number (e.ManagerID) equal to the a.empid value, which is an employee identification number from the preceding level.

- The initial a.empid on the anchor row is 109 in this case. More generally, it is whatever value you assign to @TopEmp.

- All the rows selected by the recursive SELECT statement will have a lvl column value of 1 plus the lvl value for the anchor row or the lvl value for the preceding batch of rows selected—whichever is more recent.

- The iteration proceeds through all the employees at a level until it finds a level with employees who have no one reporting directly to them (or something external to the recursive CTE aborts further iterations).

```
DECLARE @TopEmp as int
SET @TopEmp = 109;

--Names and departments for direct reports to
--EmployeeID = @TopEmp; calculate employee name
WITH Empcte(empid, empname, mgrid, dName, lvl)
AS
(

  -- Anchor row
    SELECT e.EmployeeID,
    REPLACE(c.FirstName + ' ' + ISNULL(c.MiddleName, '') +
    ' ' + c.LastName, ' ', ' ') 'Employee name',
        e.ManagerID, dn.Name, 0
    FROM Person.Contact c
    JOIN HumanResources.Employee e
    ON e.ContactID = c.ContactID
    JOIN HumanResources.EmployeeDepartmentHistory d
    ON d.EmployeeID = e.EmployeeID
    JOIN HumanResources.Department dn
    ON dn.DepartmentID = d.DepartmentID
    WHERE e.EmployeeID = @TopEmp
    UNION ALL

  -- Recursive rows

    SELECT e.EmployeeID,
    REPLACE(c.FirstName + ' ' + ISNULL(c.MiddleName, '') +
        ' ' + c.LastName, ' ', ' ') 'Employee name',
        e.ManagerID, dn.Name, a.lvl+1
    FROM (Person.Contact c
    JOIN HumanResources.Employee e
    ON e.ContactID = c.ContactID
    JOIN HumanResources.EmployeeDepartmentHistory d
    ON d.EmployeeID = e.EmployeeID
```

```
JOIN HumanResources.Department dn
ON dn.DepartmentID = d.DepartmentID)
JOIN Empcte a
ON e.ManagerID = a.empid)
```

The SELECT statement for the preceding recursive CTE is shown next. This statement selects all column values from the CTE's result set for all lvl values less than or equal to 1. Because the lvl column value starts at 0, using a WHERE clause criterion expression of lvl <= 1 extracts the first two levels of employees at the company.

```
SELECT *
FROM Empcte
WHERE lvl <= 1
ORDER BY lvl, mgrid, empid
```

You can optionally use the MAXRECURSION hint to limit the number of levels reported. The following alternate version shows the syntax for using MAXRECURSION. The MAXRECURSION levels are zero-based, so a value of 1 designates the return of just the first two levels. The OPTION clause must come after all other clauses, but this position conflicts with the operation of the ORDER BY clause, which also should be the last clause in a SELECT statement. In any event, the OPTION clause argument with a MAXRECURSION hint and an ORDER BY clause does not return row values. Therefore, the ORDER BY clause is dropped. With this design feature, the following SELECT statement and the preceding one return the same rows.

```
SELECT *
FROM Empcte
OPTION (MAXRECURSION 1)
```

You can enhance your grasp of the syntax for using a recursive CTE by reviewing the result set from either SELECT statement. The following result set is from the SELECT statement with WHERE and ORDER BY clauses. Notice that the first anchor row has a lvl column value of 0. This row is for the top-level employee in the company (the row is also the result of the first iteration in the recursive CTE).

This manager has six other employees reporting directly to him. These employee rows in the result set all have lvl values of 1, which indicates they are one level down from the top-level employee of 109 (and are the result of the second iteration through the recursive CTE, where the anchor row SELECT statement counts as the first iteration). Because some of the direct reports to the top-level employee serve as a manager in more than one department, there are more than six rows in the result set with a lvl value of 1.

empid	empname	mgrid	dName	lvl
109	Ken J Sánchez	NULL	Executive	0
6	David M Bradley	109	Purchasing	1
6	David M Bradley	109	Marketing	1
12	Terri Lee Duffy	109	Engineering	1
42	Jean E Trenary	109	Information Services	1
140	Laura F Norman	109	Finance	1
140	Laura F Norman	109	Executive	1
148	James R Hamilton	109	Production	1
273	Brian S Welcker	109	Sales	1

You can use the Empcte CTE with different SELECT statements and assignment values other than 109 for @TopEmp. For example, you may be interested in mapping the employees reporting directly or indirectly to the employee with an employee identification number of 12. You can do this by assigning 12 to @TopEmp in the SET statement before the CTE.

You may also want to show the names of managers as well as their identification number. The following SELECT statement demonstrates the syntax for recovering the employee name corresponding to a manager's identification number. In addition, it sorts returned rows by lvl, mgrid, and empid column values, in that order.

```
SELECT empid, empname, mgrid,
    CAST(REPLACE(c.FirstName + ' ' + ISNULL(c.MiddleName, '') + ' '
    + c.LastName, '  ', ' ') AS nvarchar(18))
    'Manager''s name', dName, lvl
FROM Empcte ecte
JOIN HumanResources.Employee e
ON ecte.mgrid = e.EmployeeID
JOIN Person.Contact c
ON c.ContactID = e.ContactID
ORDER BY lvl, mgrid, empid
```

The result set for the preceding SELECT statement appears next. This result set includes three levels of employees reporting directly or indirectly to the employee with an identification number of 12; the employee's name is Terri Lee Duffy, who is the head of the Engineering department. Terri has people reporting directly and indirectly from the Engineering department as well as the Research and Development and Tool Design departments. The result set truncates the name of one department (Research and Development). Just one employee, Roberto Tamburello, reports directly to Terri. All the other employees in the result set report indirectly to Terri. Rob Walter appears twice as an employee because the EmployeeDepartmentHistory table in the HumanResources schema of the AdventureWorks database maps the EmployeeID for Rob Walter to two different departments (Engineering and Tool Design).

empid	empname	mgrid	Manager's name	dName	lvl
12	Terri Lee Duffy	109	Ken J Sánchez	Engineering	0
3	Roberto Tamburello	12	Terri Lee Duffy	Engineering	1
4	Rob Walters	3	Roberto Tamburello	Engineering	2
4	Rob Walters	3	Roberto Tamburello	Tool Design	2
9	Gail A Erickson	3	Roberto Tamburello	Engineering	2
11	Jossef H Goldberg	3	Roberto Tamburello	Engineering	2
158	Dylan A Miller	3	Roberto Tamburello	Research and Develop	2
263	Ovidiu V Cracium	3	Roberto Tamburello	Tool Design	2
267	Michael I Sullivan	3	Roberto Tamburello	Engineering	2
270	Sharon B Salavaria	3	Roberto Tamburello	Engineering	2
79	Diane L Margheim	158	Dylan A Miller	Research and Develop	3
114	Gigi N Matthew	158	Dylan A Miller	Research and Develop	3
217	Michael Raheem	158	Dylan A Miller	Research and Develop	3
5	Thierry B D'Hers	263	Ovidiu V Cracium	Tool Design	3
265	Janice M Galvin	263	Ovidiu V Cracium	Tool Design	3

Converting Between Relational and Cross-Tabulated Tables

You can think of a table in a relational database as representing classes, such as sales persons, employees, customers, sales orders, or products. Rows in a relational table denote class instances and columns denote their properties. This relational table format is convenient for storing, retrieving, and maintaining large amounts of data, but it is not the most common table format for analyzing data.

In contrast, cross-tabulation tables, or cross tabs, offer a popular format for analyzing data, but they are not a popular format for storing and retrieving data. A cross tab can aggregate one set of values based on two other sets of category values—one set each for the rows and columns of a cross tab. The row and column categories of a cross tab can be based on discrete values of two columns in a relational table. The values in a third column can provide items for aggregating within the body of a cross tab.

The PIVOT and UNPIVOT relational operators, which are introduced by the SQL Server 2005 family, allow you to translate between relational and cross-tab formats for data. The PIVOT operator allows you to transform data in a relational table to a cross tab, whereas the UNPIVOT operator allows you to convert data in a cross tab to a relational table. Earlier versions of SQL Server permitted you to specify a cross tab from a relational table based on a series of SELECT...CASE statements, although there was no operator for converting a cross tab to a relational table format.

Readers who are familiar with PivotTables from Excel or Access or who have extensive experience with cross-tab analysis may find the PIVOT and UNPIVOT operators have limited functionality. I like to think of these new operators as down payments on a more extended set of pivoting capabilities that Microsoft will build into future versions of T-SQL. In any event, SSE provides basic pivoting capabilities, and this section shows you how to tap those capabilities.

The code samples for this section are in UsingPIVOTUNPIVOT.sql.

Pivoting Relational Data to a Cross Tab

The best way to present the PIVOT operator may be to present a simple sample. The following code sample counts the number of employees by department in each of three shifts. Department names are row categories, ShiftID column values are column categories, and EmployeeID values are counted for the cells in the cross tab.

- The SELECT list for the outer query denotes the column name for the row category values (Name) followed by labels for three column category values ([1] AS 'Day', [2] AS 'Evening', [3] AS 'Night') in the cross tab. The row category values are Name column values from the Department table in the HumanResources schema. The column category values are ShiftID column values from the EmployeeDepartmentHistory table in the HumanResources schema. The labels cause the result set to use shift names instead of ShiftID values. If your application can use native column values, then you can use * as your sole SELECT list item.

- The FROM clause specifies a derived table with a SELECT statement that names three columns (EmployeeID, ShiftID, Name) for use in the cross tab. These columns are used explicitly and implicitly by the PIVOT operator to compose the cross tab. You must also assign a name to the derived table (st).

- The PIVOT operator specifically references two of three items in the derived table's SELECT list.

  - The COUNT function with the EmployeeID argument designates the values to show in the cross-tab cells. Any aggregate function for a list item from the derived table can populate cross-tab cell values.

  - The FOR keyword followed by a column name (ShiftID), an IN operator, and a list of specific ShiftID values denotes the column category values. The IN operator in this context can only take explicit values—not a subquery (boo!).

  - Values for the unreferenced list item (Name) from the SELECT statement for the derived table serve as row category values in the cross tab.

- The ORDER BY clause sorts the rows of the cross tab alphabetically by department name (Name).

> **Note** A derived table is a SELECT statement with an alias in the FROM clause of another SELECT statement. A derived table is similar to a subquery in that it allows you to compactly represent a data source with one SELECT statement that resides inside of an outer SELECT statement.

```
SELECT Name, [1] AS 'Day', [2] AS 'Evening',
    [3] AS 'Night'
FROM
(SELECT e.EmployeeID, edh.ShiftID, d.Name
FROM HumanResources.Employee e
JOIN HumanResources.EmployeeDepartmentHistory edh
ON e.EmployeeID = edh.EmployeeID
JOIN HumanResources.Department d
ON edh.DepartmentID = d.DepartmentID) st
PIVOT
(
COUNT (EmployeeID)
FOR ShiftID IN
( [1], [2], [3])
) AS spvt
ORDER BY Name
```

The result set listing from the preceding SELECT statement appears next. Notice that the column names for the result set correspond to the list items in the outer SELECT statement. The table appears as a cross tab with department names listed down the first column and shift names as column headings.

```
Name                        Day      Evening   Night
------------------------    -------- --------- ----------
Document Control            3        1         1
Engineering                 7        0         0
Executive                   2        0         0
Facilities and Maintenance  3        2         2
Finance                     11       0         0
Human Resources             6        0         0
Information Services        9        1         0
Marketing                   10       0         0
Production                  80       54        46
Production Control          4        1         1
Purchasing                  13       0         0
Quality Assurance           5        1         1
Research and Development    4        0         0
Sales                       18       0         0
Shipping and Receiving      3        2         1
Tool Design                 4        0         0
```

Saving a Cross-Tab Table

There are at least a couple of reasons for saving a cross tab created with the PIVOT operator.

- The saved copy makes it possible to recover values from the cross tab without having to rerun the underlying query. For large data sources that change infrequently, this can be a substantial benefit.

- If you want to use UNPIVOT to recover the exact relational table values that contributed to a cross tab, you need a saved version of the cross tab. When the original relational data have changed or are temporarily unavailable, this capability can be valuable—especially for verifying results.

You can use a SELECT INTO statement to generate a copy of a cross tab. The following example does so and saves the cross tab in the pvt table. Because the SELECT INTO statement does not copy over an existing table, the script starts by dropping the pvt table if it already exists.

Next, the SELECT INTO statement creates a cross tab that counts the number of purchase orders placed by four employees with vendors.

- The list items for the outer SELECT statement specify the following:

  - A column alias with row category values (VName). This alias points at the Name column in the Vendor table within the Purchasing schema.

  - Identification numbers and names of the four employees. The employee names, not the employee identification numbers, serve as column names in the saved cross tab.

- The INTO clause designates the table name (pvt) for the saved cross tab.

- The list items for the p-derived table designate three columns for use by the PIVOT operator in designating the cross-tab design. The data source for the columns is from the join of the PurchaseOrderHeader and Vendor tables in the Purchasing schema.

- The PIVOT operator explicitly designates the following:

  - The count of PurchaseOrderID column values for the cross-tab cells

  - Four employee identification numbers for four employees

- The PIVOT operator implicitly uses the VName column values from the p-derived table for row category values in the cross tab.

- The ORDER BY clause sorts the cross-tab rows in alphabetical order by VName values.

```
IF EXISTS(SELECT name FROM sys.tables WHERE name = 'pvt')
DROP TABLE pvt
GO

SELECT VName, [164] 'Mikael Q Sandberg', [198] 'Arvind B Rao',
    [223] 'Linda P Meisner', [231] 'Fukiko J Ogisu'
INTO pvt
FROM
(SELECT PurchaseOrderID, EmployeeID, v.Name as 'VName'
FROM Purchasing.PurchaseOrderHeader h
JOIN Purchasing.Vendor v
ON h.VendorID = v.VendorID) p
PIVOT
(
COUNT (PurchaseOrderID)
```

```
FOR EmployeeID IN
( [164], [198], [223], [231], [233] )
) pvt
ORDER BY VName
GO
```

The following SELECT statement and its result set show the first five rows for VName values beginning with the letter A. Mikael Q. Sandberg submitted four purchase orders for items from a vendor
named Advanced Bicycles. This means the PurchaseOrderHeader table contains four rows with both
the VendorID code for Advanced Bicycles and the EmployeeID value of 164, which is the value for
Mikael Q. Sandberg.

```
SELECT TOP 5 * FROM pvt
WHERE VName LIKE 'A%'
GO
```

VName	Mikael Q Sandberg	Arvind B Rao	Linda P Meisner	Fukiko J Ogisu
Advanced Bicycles	4	3	5	5
Allenson Cycles	5	3	5	5
American Bicycles and	5	1	5	5
American Bikes	6	2	5	5
Anderson's Custom Bike	4	2	6	4

Unpivoting a Cross Tab

Unpivoting a cross tab reconstructs a table in a relational format from a cross-tab data source. The
UNPIVOT operator is especially tailored for this exact task. To unpivot the pvt cross tab created in the
preceding section, you can run the following SELECT statement. The UNPIVOT operator comes after
the FROM clause of a SELECT statement that points at the pvt table.

- The SELECT statement for the outer SELECT keyword has a TOP 8 setting. This query statement
  returns the first two rows of four columns each from the cross tab in a relational table format.
  Because there are four columns per row in the cross-tab format, each cross-tab row transforms
  to four rows in a relational format. Therefore, the TOP 8 setting extracts the top eight rows from
  the relational format that correspond to the top two rows from the cross-tab format.

- The list item names in the outer SELECT statement are arbitrary. You can use any names that
  you wish for the first, second, and third columns of the result set.

- The list items for the derived table in the FROM clause of the outer SELECT statement must
  match the column names of the cross tab. These names appear in the preceding result set
  listing.

- The UNPIVOT operator explicitly references two sets of values and implicitly references a third
  set of values.

  - The designation of OrdCnt specifies a name to represent the cross-tab cell values in
    the result set. You can specify any name that you want, but the first argument for the
    UNPIVOT operator must match the third column name in the list for the outer SELECT
    statement.

- The second argument specifies a name called Employee after the FOR keyword, and then it uses an IN operator with a series of column names matching employees. The FOR keyword's argument must match the second list item in the outer SELECT statement. The IN operator arguments must reference the column names in the cross tab. You can print the cross tab to discover these names.

- The UNPIVOT operator does not reference a third set of values. The column with these values from the pvt table is VName, which is explicitly designated as the first list item in the SELECT statement for the derived table, p.

```
SELECT TOP 8 VName, Employee, OrdCnt
FROM
(SELECT VName, [Mikael Q Sandberg], [Arvind B Rao],
    [Linda P Meisner], [Fukiko J Ogisu]
FROM pvt) p
UNPIVOT
(OrdCnt FOR Employee IN ([Mikael Q Sandberg],
[Arvind B Rao], [Linda P Meisner], [Fukiko J Ogisu])
)AS unpvt
GO
```

The result set generated by the preceding SELECT statement appears next and is followed by a SELECT statement that extracts the first two rows from the cross tab in pvt. As you can see, unpivoting moves successive cross-tab cell values into a new third column. The first two columns become the corresponding row and column category values for the cell values in the third column. This outcome confirms the valid operation of the UNPIVOT operator as it successfully transforms a set of cross-tab values into a relational table format.

VName	Employee	OrdCnt
Advanced Bicycles	Mikael Q Sandberg	4
Advanced Bicycles	Arvind B Rao	3
Advanced Bicycles	Linda P Meisner	5
Advanced Bicycles	Fukiko J Ogisu	5
Allenson Cycles	Mikael Q Sandberg	5
Allenson Cycles	Arvind B Rao	3
Allenson Cycles	Linda P Meisner	5
Allenson Cycles	Fukiko J Ogisu	5

```
SELECT TOP 2 *
FROM pvt
ORDER BY VName ASC
GO
```

VName	Mikael Q Sandberg	Arvind B Rao	Linda P Meisner	Fukiko J Ogisu
Advanced Bicycles	4	3	5	5
Allenson Cycles	5	3	5	5

Summary

This chapter focused heavily on new and advanced data access topics for those creating solutions with SQL Server Express. The two main advanced topics include

- Implementing joins to build your own ad hoc collections of database objects for custom queries
- Using subqueries to create single SELECT statements that answer multiple and complex questions

The new topics include

- Four T-SQL functions for ranking and ordering data (ROW_NUMBER, RANK, DENSE_RANK, and NTILE)
- CTEs, which allow you to reuse query statements. They can drastically simplify the task of building complex queries and are especially well-suited for mapping hierarchical relationships
- Techniques for pivoting relational tables into cross tabs and reconstructing relational tables from data in a cross-tab format (PIVOT and UNPIVOT operators)

Between focusing on advanced and new topics, the chapter presented a variety of traditional database processing techniques that most database developers and administrators will find useful at one time or another. Some of these topics include

- Sorting your data multiple ways with the ORDER BY clause
- Appending result sets to facilitate asking queries across multiple data sources
- Saving result sets to new tables

CHAPTER 7
■■■

Leveraging Database Objects That Encapsulate T-SQL

Database objects that encapsulate T-SQL code make that code easier to reuse. This is an important technique because it lets you multiply the benefits of your investments in T-SQL code development. You will therefore find it more worthwhile to create solutions with T-SQL when you encapsulate your code in database objects.

SQL Server Express offers four database objects for packaging T-SQL code:

- Views
- User-defined functions
- Stored procedures
- Triggers

This chapter examines techniques for creating, managing, and referencing each of these four types of objects. You can leverage—that is, reuse—database objects by

1. Creating a database object with the code that you want to reuse
2. Referencing the database object in one or more other code blocks

Database object types distinguish themselves by the roles that they can play in a database solution. One goal of this chapter is to characterize the database objects in terms of the benefits that they bring to a solution. The skills that you gain in this chapter will motivate you to create and apply database objects in your custom database solutions.

Creating and Using Views

Views are virtual tables. That is, a view can represent a set of rows like a table. However, a view is not actually a table. Instead, a view is a SELECT statement that performs data access, such as many of the T-SQL code samples in Chapters 5 and 6.

The difference between a SELECT statement and a view is that a view encapsulates a SELECT statement as an object in a database. You can make a new view with a CREATE VIEW statement similarly to the way that you make a table with a CREATE TABLE statement. A CREATE VIEW statement contains a SELECT statement defining the rowset that a view represents, while a CREATE TABLE statement contains specifications for columns and constraints (see Chapter 4 for more detail on creating tables). You can drop and modify views with the DROP VIEW and ALTER VIEW statements.

A SELECT statement in a database object, such as a view, is more readily reusable than a SELECT statement in a .sql file.

- You can reference a view in the FROM clause of a SELECT statement because a view is a database object that acts like a virtual table. This capability to be referenced in a FROM clause dramatically enhances accessibility to the filtering, ordering, and aggregating features of a SELECT statement relative to a SELECT statement in a .sql file.

- You can also change a view's underlying data sources by referring to the view in the same way that you do a table in INSERT, UPDATE, and DELETE statements. If a view's concluding clause is WITH CHECK OPTION, you can force INSERT and UPDATE statements that reference the view to conform to criteria within a view's SELECT statement.

■**Tip** You can use constraints within a table's definition instead of the WITH CHECK OPTION in a view. If more than one view references the same table, using a constraint within a table's definition represents a more consistent technique for forcing inserts and updates to adhere to constraints.

A view does not accept arguments at runtime. Therefore, you cannot change the result set that gets returned from a view by changing the value of a parameter. Other database objects, such as user-defined functions and stored procedures, offer this capability.

There are three types of views, which are as follows:

- *Standard views* merely encapsulate a SELECT statement. You can place a complex SELECT statement in a view to make it easy to reuse. In addition to data access, standard views also support data modification.

- *Indexed views* work especially well when you want to aggregate many rows from multiple joined data sources. This type of view can deliver performance gains by creating a clustered index for the view. SELECT statements referencing data sources that change frequently because of new, deleted, or updated rows are not good candidates for indexed views.

- *Partitioned views* combine multiple tables via UNION operators from different storage devices on one computer or from different computers. This type of view can deliver performance benefits by scaling out across multiple servers or multiple storage devices on a single computer.

This section illustrates several typical ways of creating and using standard views. The other two view types are specialized extensions of standard views that you are not likely to need in the overwhelming majority of your SQL Server Express applications.

Performing Data Access with a View

There are two steps for using a view to facilitate data access.

1. Create the view with a CREATE VIEW statement.

2. Perform the data access task by referencing the view in the FROM clause of a SELECT statement.

When you create a view, you can create it in a custom schema for a database (such as the Sales schema in the AdventureWorks database), or as an object in a schema associated with a database user (such as the dbo user). The dbo user has a built-in schema with the same name as the user. A list of the built-in and custom schemas available for use in a database is available from the sys.schemas catalog view (SELECT * FROM sys.schemas) for a new database.

The assignment of a view to the schema for the dbo user can be implicit. If you do not explicitly designate a named view in a CREATE VIEW statement or the FROM clause of a SELECT statement as belonging to a specific schema, such as Sales, then SQL Server Express creates or searches for a view in the dbo schema. These naming conventions allow you to have multiple versions of a view with the same name in different schemas.

The samples for this section appear in ViewsForDataAccess.sql.

■ **Tip** The capability of having multiple view versions with the same name means that you should always designate a schema name for a view unless you explicitly mean to reference the default dbo schema.

Creating and Using a View in the dbo Schema

The following script shows the code for creating a view in the dbo schema. The IF statement uses the OBJECT_ID function to check if a view named vSalePersonNamePhoneEmail exists in the dbo schema. This function returns the identification number for an object in a database. If an object's identification number is NOT NULL, then the object exists. For this outcome (a non-null identification number), the code sample drops the view's current version. Without either dropping or archiving the current version, you would not be able to create a new version of vSalePersonNamePhoneEmail.

The CREATE VIEW statement in the code sample shows a basic syntax for creating a new view.

1. Specify the name of the new view after the CREATE VIEW phrase. The code sample explicitly designates the dbo schema name even though SQL Server Express will automatically assign a view to this schema if you do not explicitly designate another schema.

2. Follow the view's name with the AS keyword. This keyword serves as a transition from the view's declaration with CREATE VIEW to the SELECT statement specifying the rowset associated with the view. It is possible, but not necessary, to use additional clauses before the AS keyword to modify the way a view is saved or performs. For example, a WITH ENCRYPTION clause encrypts the text for the SELECT statement defining a view.

3. The SELECT statement in the script that follows joins three tables to provide contact data, such as name parts, phone, and email address, for sales persons in the AdventureWorks database.

```
IF OBJECT_ID('dbo.vSalePersonNamePhoneEmail', 'VIEW') IS NOT NULL
    DROP VIEW dbo.vSalePersonNamePhoneEmail
GO

CREATE VIEW dbo.vSalePersonNamePhoneEmail
AS
SELECT s.SalesPersonID, c.FirstName, c.MiddleName,
    c.LastName, c.Phone, c.EmailAddress
FROM Sales.SalesPerson S JOIN HumanResources.Employee e
ON s.SalesPersonID = e.EmployeeID
JOIN Person.Contact c
ON c.ContactID = e.ContactID
GO
```

Extracting data from a view is as simple as running a SELECT statement. The following SELECT statement returns all the columns, except for MiddleName, from the vSalePersonNamePhoneEmail view in the dbo schema. Notice that you do not need column prefixes to indicate the data source because all the columns derive from the vSalePersonNamePhoneEmail view. A filter restricts the return of rows to those whose LastName column value starts with A. You are not restricted to such simple SELECT statement designs. For example, you can perform grouping and ordering on result set rows.

■**Note** Recall the best practice guideline to include an ORDER BY clause whenever you require the rows in a precise order. This best practice applies especially to SELECT statements that reference one or more views in their FROM clause. A view can expose columns from multiple data sources that order rows by different criteria. In addition, you cannot include an ORDER BY clause in the SELECT statement defining a view unless the statement also includes the TOP keyword.

```
SELECT  SalesPersonID, FirstName, LastName,
    Phone, EmailAddress
FROM dbo.vSalePersonNamePhoneEmail
WHERE LastName LIKE 'A%'
```

The following output listing is the result set from the preceding SELECT statement. The rows appear sorted in alphabetical order by LastName column values—although SalesPersonID is the primary key for the SalesPerson table (one of the tables that serve as a data source to the vSalePersonNamePhoneEmail view). You can readily define other views that extract other subsets. If TerritoryID from the SalesPerson table were exposed through the view, you could filter by TerritoryID instead of the first letter in the LastName column value.

```
SalesPersonID FirstName  LastName        Phone         EmailAddress
------------- ---------  --------------- ------------- ----------------------------
288           Syed       Abbas           926-555-0182  syed0@adventure-works.com
284           Amy        Alberts         775-555-0164  amy0@adventure-works.com
280           Pamela     Ansman-Wolfe    340-555-0193  pamela0@adventure-works.com
```

Creating a View in a Named Schema

The preceding sample explicitly designated the dbo schema for the vSalePersonNamePhoneEmail view. As mentioned, there is no syntactical requirement to name the dbo schema when you want to create a view in it or use a view from it. However, you do need to designate a schema when you want to create or reference a view in a custom schema.

The following listing shows the code to create the vSalePersonNamePhoneEmail view in the HumanResources schema. Instead of using an OBJECT_ID function to specify a condition for an IF statement, an EXISTS operator tests for the existence of a prior instance of the vSalePersonNamePhoneEmail in the HumanResources schema (schema_id = 5) within sys.views. The two approaches are interchangeable for detecting a prior instance of a view. Instead of actually specifying the schema number (5), you can use the SCHEMA_ID function with the name of the schema. Therefore, you can replace a criterion expressed as schema_id = 5 with schema_id = SCHEMA_ID('HumanResources').

■**Caution** The OBJECT_ID function allows you to specify a view by its schema name and view name, such as schema.view. The sys.views catalog view has two distinct columns for view name and schema. In addition, the schema identification in sys.views is a schema identification number and not a schema name.

The CREATE VIEW statement in the following listing is identical to the one in the preceding code sample, except for the reference to the HumanResources schema. In this instance, both views return the same result set. In a `SELECT` statement referencing the `vSalePersonNamePhoneEmail` view in the `HumanResources` schema, you need to explicitly designate the schema name as a view qualifier in the `FROM` clause. This naming convention contrasts with a view associated with the `dbo` schema, which does not strictly require a schema name qualifier for it in the `FROM` clause.

```
IF EXISTS(SELECT *
    FROM sys.views
    WHERE name = 'vSalePersonNamePhoneEmail' AND schema_id =
            SCHEMA_ID('HumanResources'))
    DROP VIEW HumanResources.vSalePersonNamePhoneEmail
GO

CREATE VIEW HumanResources.vSalePersonNamePhoneEmail
AS
SELECT s.SalesPersonID, c.FirstName, c.MiddleName,
    c.LastName, c.Phone, c.EmailAddress
FROM Sales.SalesPerson S JOIN HumanResources.Employee e
ON s.SalesPersonID = e.EmployeeID
JOIN Person.Contact c
ON c.ContactID = e.ContactID
GO
```

Because you can have multiple views with the same names in different schemas, it is important to track views along with their schemas.

- The first `SELECT` statement that follows lists the `name` and `schema_id` column values from the `sys.views` system view, where the `name` column value equals `vSalePersonNamePhoneEmail`.

- The second `SELECT` statement that follows lists the `TABLE_NAME` and `TABLE_SCHEMA` from the `INFORMATION_SCHEMA.VIEWS` view, where `TABLE_NAME` equals `vSalePersonNamePhoneEmail`.

You can use either system view (`sys.views` or `INFORMATION_SCHEMA.VIEWS`) to track views in different schemas.

```
SELECT name, schema_id
FROM sys.views
WHERE name = 'vSalePersonNamePhoneEmail'

SELECT TABLE_NAME, TABLE_SCHEMA
FROM INFORMATION_SCHEMA.VIEWS
WHERE TABLE_NAME = 'vSalePersonNamePhoneEmail'
GO
```

The following result set listings are from the preceding two `SELECT` statements. The `sys.views` view returns a numeric index for the schema. (You can look up the schema name for the schema identification numbers in the `sys.schemas` view.) The `INFORMATION_SCHEMA.VIEWS` view refers to the view as a table—notice the first column's name in its result set is `TABLE_NAME`. Aside from these minor differences, both system views return the same information about the vSalePersonName➥ PhoneEmail views in the dbo and HumanResources schemas.

```
name                     schema_id
------------------------ -----------
vSalePersonNamePhoneEmail 1
vSalePersonNamePhoneEmail 5
```

TABLE_NAME	TABLE_SCHEMA
vSalePersonNamePhoneEmail	dbo
vSalePersonNamePhoneEmail	HumanResources

Performing Data Modification with a View

Performing data modification or data manipulation through a view is similar to performing data access.

1. First, you need to create a view.

2. Second, you need to run an INSERT, UPDATE, or DELETE statement that references the view.

Because views will often reference more than a single table and can present results that do not map to a column in a table, such as a computed value or an aggregate value, not all attempts to modify data sources through a view will succeed. Furthermore, even if some data modification does succeed, you may not be able to view the impact of the change. This can happen, for example, if a newly inserted row in one table does not have a matching column value in another table, and your view joins the two tables by the unmatched column value.

To help clarify the presentation of data modification via views, you can create a custom database with tables defined by a simple, easy-to-follow script. The portion of the script creating the ProSSEAppsCh07 database is minimal (see the following code block). With the master database set as the database context, the sample drops any previous version of ProSSEAppsCh07. The use of CREATE DATABASE merely assigns a name to the database. All the default database settings are accepted. See the "Using CREATE DATABASE" section in Chapter 3 for details about default database settings and additional coverage of how to invoke the CREATE DATABASE statement.

```
USE master
GO

--Create a database
IF EXISTS(SELECT name FROM sys.databases
    WHERE name = 'ProSSEAppsCh07')
    DROP DATABASE ProSSEAppsCh07
GO

CREATE DATABASE ProSSEAppsCh07
GO
```

The ProSSEAppsCh07 database has three tables related by foreign keys. Two of the tables, Classes and Students, are in a many-to-many relationship via the third table, ClassGrades. The script for creating and populating the table was initially presented and discussed in the "Implementing Many-to-Many Relationships with Foreign Keys" section of Chapter 4. The complete script for creating the ProSSEAppsCh07 database, populating it with tables, and populating the tables with initial values is in ViewsForDataModificationSampleDB.sql. The script with the sample code for demonstrating data modification through views is in ViewsForDataModification.sql.

Creating a View for the Classes, ClassGrades, and Students Tables

When you create a view, you should design it so that it serves its most popular applications well. Essential design considerations for a view include which underlying data sources to use as well as which columns to expose for those data sources. When working with views that you mean to use for data manipulation, it makes sense to limit or reduce design features that make data modification difficult or impossible. For example, don't compute aggregate values for views that you intend to use with data modification statements.

The following script drops a view called StudentGrades if one exists and replaces it with a new view. Notice that the WHERE clause for the SELECT statement subquery in the EXISTS operator contains criteria expressions for both name and schema_id. This enables you to check for the existence of the StudentGrades view in a schema with a schema_id of 1, which you will recall is the dbo schema identification number.

The following CREATE VIEW statement joins the Students and Classes tables through the ClassGrades table. Notice the view contains no aggregations. In addition, the view has no computed columns. This kind of view design maximizes the number of columns available for data modification through the view.

```
USE ProSSEAppsCh07
GO

IF EXISTS(SELECT *
    FROM sys.views
    WHERE name = 'StudentGrades' AND
    schema_id = SCHEMA_ID('dbo'))
    DROP VIEW dbo.StudentGrades
GO

CREATE VIEW dbo.StudentGrades
AS
SELECT s.StudentID, s.FirstName, s.LastName, s.Fullname,
    c.ClassID, c.ClassTitle, cg.Gradeletter
FROM Classes c JOIN ClassGrades cg
ON c.ClassID = cg.ClassID
JOIN Students S
ON s.StudentID = cg.StudentID
GO
```

Inserting a New Row

The first data-modification demonstration adds a new row to the Classes table through the StudentGrades view. The INSERT statement adds a new row for the Learning Visual Basic Express for DBAs class. The following four T-SQL statements and the result set listing from three of those statements show the syntax and outcome for inserting a new row through a view.

- The first SELECT statement on the dbo.StudentGrades view lists the distinct ClassID and ClassTitle column values. The DISTINCT keyword is necessary because ClassID and ClassTitle repeat in the dbo.StudentGrades view once for each student taking a class.

- The INSERT statement names the dbo.StudentGrades view as the target to receive the new row of ClassID and ClassTitle column values. The view, in turn, passes these values along to its underlying Classes table.

- The subsequent SELECT statement queries the dbo.StudentGrades view to show the new row. Although the insert of new column values through dbo.StudentGrades succeeded, the result set from the second SELECT statement against the view does not show the new class's identification number or title because there are no students enrolled in the new class.

- The final SELECT statement runs against the Classes table and confirms the insertion of the new row.

```
SELECT DISTINCT ClassID, ClassTitle
FROM dbo.StudentGrades
ORDER BY ClassID
GO

INSERT dbo.StudentGrades (ClassID, ClassTitle)
    VALUES (2, 'Learning Visual Basic Express for DBAs')
GO

SELECT DISTINCT ClassID, ClassTitle
FROM dbo.StudentGrades
ORDER BY ClassID
GO

SELECT ClassID, ClassTitle
FROM Classes
GO
```

```
ClassID      ClassTitle
-----------  ---------------------------
1            Learning SQL Server Express
999          Biographies of Jesus Christ
```

```
ClassID      ClassTitle
-----------  ---------------------------
1            Learning SQL Server Express
999          Biographies of Jesus Christ
```

```
ClassID      ClassTitle
-----------  --------------------------------------
1            Learning SQL Server Express
2            Learning Visual Basic Express for DBAs
999          Biographies of Jesus Christ
```

Inserting a Row for the Many-Side of a One-to-Many Relationship

When you are working with a view that connects two tables in a one-to-many relationship, you can generally insert new rows into the table on the one-side of the relationship through a view. The preceding example worked because the new row of class values was for the table on the one-side of the relationship. The next attempt to insert a row tries to add a new set of column values for a table on the many-side of a relationship, but fails. I'll then diagnose the problem and show you a remedial action.

■Tip When an attempt to insert a new row through a view fails, you can sometimes succeed by simplifying the process. If a view interprets your T-SQL statement as attempting to insert into two tables concurrently, rewrite the INSERT statement. For example, insert into just one table on the many-side of a relationship. Alternatively, write two separate INSERT statements that each add a row into a different table.

The following two pairs of INSERT statements show two different approaches to inserting a pair of class grades for the two students in the ProSSEAppsCh07 database.

- The statements that attempt to insert into the StudentGrades view both fail. This is because they are attempting to go through the view into the table on the many-side of a one-to-many relationship (one class can have grades for many students).

- SQL Server Express actually issues an error message about an attempt to insert into two tables. The ClassID and StudentID foreign key values in the INSERT statement, along with the one-to-many relationship in the StudentGrades view, cause this problem.

- The second pair of INSERT statements attempts to add two new rows directly into the ClassGrades table and succeeds. You can also insert the new rows into a view that points directly at the ClassGrades table instead of a view based on an inner join between the Students and Classes tables.

```
INSERT dbo.StudentGrades (ClassID, StudentID, Gradeletter)
    VALUES(2, 1, 'B')
INSERT dbo.StudentGrades (ClassID, StudentID, Gradeletter)
    VALUES(2, 2, 'A')
GO

INSERT ClassGrades (ClassID, StudentID, Gradeletter)
    VALUES(2, 1, 'B')
INSERT ClassGrades (ClassID, StudentID, Gradeletter)
    VALUES(2, 2, 'A')
GO
```

The following SELECT statement for the StudentGrades view is a repeat of the previous SELECT statement that listed just two classes after the Classes table was shown to have three rows.

- In this case, the SELECT statement for distinct ClassID and ClassTitle column values generates a result set with three, instead of two, classes.

- The previous invocation of this same SELECT statement returned just two rows.

- The difference is that this attempt follows the successful addition of rows to both sides of the one-to-many relationship for the Learning Visual Basic Express for DBAs class in Classes (one-side table) and ClassGrades (many-side table).

```
SELECT DISTINCT ClassID, ClassTitle
FROM dbo.StudentGrades
ORDER BY ClassID
GO
```

```
ClassID     ClassTitle
----------- -------------------------------------------------
1           Learning SQL Server Express
2           Learning Visual Basic Express for DBAs
999         Biographies of Jesus Christ
```

Updating a Row

Views also support the operation of other data manipulation statements, such as the UPDATE statement. The three statements that follow demonstrate the revision of a LastName column value in the

Students table with an UPDATE statement. The new LastName value of DBA-Minister replaces the former value of DBA for the student with a StudentID identification number of 2.

Before and after the UPDATE statement are SELECT statements. The result sets for these SELECT statements list class grades for all the students. The FullName column shows the name Better DBA for StudentID 2 in the result set for the first SELECT statement that runs before the UPDATE. FullName is a computed column value that concatenates FirstName and LastName with a space between them.

The second result set listing shows StudentID 2 with a FullName column value of Better DBA-Minister. This outcome confirms the success of the UPDATE statement on the LastName column value in the Students table through the StudentGrades view.

```
SELECT StudentID, FullName, ClassTitle, GradeLetter
FROM dbo.StudentGrades
ORDER BY StudentID, ClassID

UPDATE dbo.StudentGrades
SET LastName = 'DBA-Minister'
WHERE StudentID = 2
GO

SELECT  StudentID, FullName, ClassTitle, GradeLetter
FROM dbo.StudentGrades
ORDER BY StudentID, ClassID
```

StudentID	FullName	ClassTitle	GradeLetter
1	Poor DBA	Learning SQL Server Express	C+
1	Poor DBA	Learning Visual Basic Express for DBAs	B
2	Better DBA	Learning SQL Server Express	A+
2	Better DBA	Learning Visual Basic Express for DBAs	A
2	Better DBA	Biographies of Jesus Christ	A

StudentID	FullName	ClassTitle	GradeLetter
1	Poor DBA	Learning SQL Server Express	C+
1	Poor DBA	Learning Visual Basic Express for DBAs	B
2	Better DBA-Minister	Learning SQL Server Express	A+
2	Better DBA-Minister	Learning Visual Basic Express for DBAs	A
2	Better DBA-Minister	Biographies of Jesus Christ	A

Processing Meta Data with System Views

All SQL Server databases, including those for SQL Server Express, have a set of system views that provide meta data about the contents of a database. These are composed of both the older INFORMATION_SCHEMA views, such as INFORMATION_SCHEMA.VIEWS, and the newer system catalog views, such as sys.views. These two types of system views were used and discussed in the previous "Creating a View in a Named Schema" section, as well as in the "Using System Catalog Views" section of Chapter 3. The sample code for this section on meta data is in ViewsForMetaData.sql.

It is important to understand that these system views are data sources that you can use in SELECT statements as well as views and other database objects, such as stored procedures (discussed later in this chapter). All the tricks you learned about processing data sources in Chapters 5 and 6 apply to system views. This understanding empowers you to uncover and format a substantial amount of meta data about a database. For example, there are literally hundreds of system catalog views, and each of these views has multiple columns. In many cases, you can join system catalog views with the same techniques that you use for user-defined tables and views to reveal valuable meta data about a database.

Making sys.views Return INFORMATION_SCHEMA.VIEWS Columns

INFORMATION_SCHEMA.VIEWS and sys.views have different columns in their result sets, but you can join the sys.views view with another system catalog view and invoke a built-in function to return the same columns as the INFORMATION_SCHEMA.VIEWS views. The samples in this section work with a fresh copy of the vSalePersonNamePhoneEmail view in the dbo schema. The code at the top of ViewsForMetaData.sql removes the two prior versions of this view in different schemas and creates a new, single copy of the view in the dbo schema.

The next pair of SELECT statements and matching result sets reminds you of some of the differences between the sys.views and INFORMATION_SCHEMA.VIEWS system views. The sys.views view returns information about the schema that a view belongs to, such as a schema identification number. In addition, the sys.views view provides no information about the name of the database in which a view resides. On the other hand, the INFORMATION_SCHEMA.VIEWS view has separate columns in its result sets for a view's name, schema, and catalog (or database schema). The schema and catalog name appear as characters instead of as an identification number that requires a further lookup to derive a name.

```
SELECT name, schema_id
FROM sys.views
WHERE name = 'vSalePersonNamePhoneEmail'

SELECT TABLE_NAME, TABLE_SCHEMA, TABLE_Catalog
FROM INFORMATION_SCHEMA.VIEWS
WHERE TABLE_NAME = 'vSalePersonNamePhoneEmail'
GO
```

```
name                      schema_id
------------------------- -----------
vSalePersonNamePhoneEmail 1
```

```
TABLE_NAME                TABLE_SCHEMA TABLE_Catalog
------------------------- ------------ --------------
vSalePersonNamePhoneEmail dbo          AdventureWorks
```

By joining the sys.views view with the sys.schemas view and taking advantage of the DB_NAME function, you can return three columns from the sys.views view with the same information as the INFORMATION_SCHEMA.VIEWS result set. The following SELECT statement shows the syntax for achieving this outcome, and the result set listing confirms the operation of the SELECT statement.

It is not uncommon when working with system catalog views to benefit from joining two or more views to form a useful result set. In this case, you can retrieve the name of the schema in which a view resides by looking up the name column value from sys.schemas for the schema_id column value from sys.views. The DB_NAME built-in function returns the name of the current database context. Using this function in a SELECT statement allows you to return the name of the current database as part of the result set from the SELECT statement.

```
SELECT v.name 'View name',
    s.name 'Schema name',
    DB_NAME() 'Database name'
FROM sys.views v JOIN sys.schemas s
ON v.schema_id = s.schema_id
WHERE v.name = 'vSalePersonNamePhoneEmail'
GO
```

```
View name                    Schema name  Database name
--------------------------   -----------  --------------
vSalePersonNamePhoneEmail dbo              AdventureWorks
```

Reporting Column Meta Data for a View

When you are joining one or more columns of a view or entering data through a view, it can be useful to know the names, data types, and related kinds of information about the columns in a view. The following SELECT statement joins the sys.columns and sys.types views to report the data type for the columns in a view.

- The sys.columns view contains information about the columns in all objects within a database. Each row in the sys.columns view contains meta data about a column. The object_id column in sys.columns denotes the parent data source, such as a table or a view, for the column.

- The SELECT statement's WHERE clause includes a subquery that looks up the object identification number for the vSalePersonNamePhoneEmail view. By matching the return value from the subquery with the object_id column in the sys.columns view, the SELECT statement extracts rows from sys.columns that are for columns in the vSalePersonNamePhoneEmail view.

- The FROM clause performs a join between the sys.columns and sys.types views. The sys.types view contains information about user-defined types and system types in a database. The join has two criteria expressions combined with an AND operator.

  - The first expression evaluates equality between the system_type_id column values in sys.columns and sys.types.

  - The second expression evaluates equality between the system_type_id and user_type_id column values in sys.types. This second expression excludes any rows from sys.types for user-defined types that extend a system type. Without this second expression, the result set can include multiple types for each column in the vSalePersonNamePhoneEmail view.

- The SELECT list includes one item that references the name column from sys.types. This item looks up the data type name for the system_type_id value in the sys.columns view.

  ```
  SELECT c.name, t.name 'data type', c.max_length, c.is_identity
  FROM sys.columns c JOIN sys.types t
  ON t.system_type_id = c.system_type_id AND
      t.system_type_id = t.user_type_id
  WHERE object_id =
      (SELECT OBJECT_ID('dbo.vSalePersonNamePhoneEmail', 'VIEW'))
  ```

The result set for the preceding SELECT statement appears next. Notice the data type column shows the name of the data type for the columns in the vSalePersonNamePhoneEmail view. max_length defines the maximum width of a column in bytes. The is_identity column returns a

0 or 1 to show whether a column has an `IDENTITY` property setting (a value of 1 indicates a column with an `IDENTITY` property setting). Other meta data that could be added to the result set include such items as precision and scale of numbers in a column and whether the column is nullable or computed.

```
Column          data type max_length is_identity
------------    --------- ---------- -----------
SalesPersonID   int       4          0
FirstName       nvarchar  100        0
MiddleName      nvarchar  100        0
LastName        nvarchar  100        0
Phone           nvarchar  50         0
EmailAddress    nvarchar  100        0
```

Creating and Using User-Defined Functions

User-defined functions allow you to return the outcome of a scalar value—such as the result of numerical or string calculation—or a result set. User-defined functions can be programmed with T-SQL code, and they are database objects. Therefore, you can create, drop, and alter them. Unlike a view, a user-defined function can accept one or more input parameters, which enables users to change the output from a user-defined function at runtime.

There are three types of user-defined functions. These types depend in part on what a user-defined function can return. As mentioned, a user-defined function can return the output of a computation as a scalar value or it can return a result set as a table data type.

- A scalar user-defined function (FN) returns a single value, such as an `int` value or an `nvarchar` value. You can use an `FN` user-defined function to process numbers or characters, such as converting a temperature from centigrade to Fahrenheit or combining the parts of a name into a full name.

- Two types of user-defined functions return a table value. A table value can contain one or more rows of column values.

  - An inline user-defined function (IF) returns the output from a single `SELECT` statement. The structure of the returned table value automatically conforms to the structure of the columns in the result set. You cannot edit the values of a `SELECT` statement's result set from within an `IF` user-defined function.

  - A multi-statement table-valued user-defined function (TF) also returns a table value. However, a `TF` user-defined function requires you to declare the column values within the function, generate values for the table, and insert values in the returned table. This type of function provides more granular control over the contents of a returned table value than an `IF` user-defined function, at the expense of a more complex function.

You can use an `IF` user-defined function in the same way as a view, but an `IF` user-defined function provides one additional important advantage not available with a view. Both a view and an `IF` user-defined function can

- Represent a result set

- Allow you to modify the underlying data source behind a result set

However, an `IF` user-defined function accepts parameters so that you can modify its result set at runtime. This makes it possible to reuse the code in an `IF` user-defined function in substantially more situations than the code inside a view. The number of situations in which you can reuse an IF user-defined function is the number of legitimate, distinct values of the parameters for the IF user-defined function.

This section introduces you to programming techniques for user-defined functions by presenting samples of FN and IF user-defined functions with and without parameters. You'll learn how to create and drop these database objects. In addition, you'll learn how to invoke them after you create them. This section does not cover TF user-defined functions because they are substantially more complicated than the other types, and many of their special capabilities can readily be accomplished by standard T-SQL programming outside of a user-defined function or with other database objects.

Creating and Using FN User-Defined Functions

You can use a CREATE FUNCTION statement to create any of the three types of user-defined functions. After you create a new FN user-defined function, you can use it in the same way as a built-in function. One distinction between FN user-defined functions and built-in functions is that you must specify the schema for the FN user-defined function when you invoke it. For example, use dbo.FNFunctionName() instead of BuiltinFunctionName(). The samples in this section reside in FNUserDefinedFunctions.sql.

Working with an FN User-Defined Function Without Parameters

As with CREATE statements for other SQL Server objects, you cannot create a new instance of an FN user-defined function with the name of an existing FN user-defined function. Therefore, you need to insure that the name for your new user-defined function does not already exist. The following code excerpt establishes the AdventureWorks database as the database context and then searches for a previous instance of an FN user-defined function in the sys.objects view.

- The code sample designates the type of object by specifying FN for the type column value in the WHERE clause.

- Next, the code designates a search of the dbo schema by setting schema_id equal to 1 in the WHERE clause.

- Finally, the sample designates the name of the FN user-defined function through the name column value for the view.

If the FN user-defined function exists, the code simply drops the previous version. You can write code to archive prior versions if you prefer. The sp_rename system-stored procedure can assist with this task, but you may need to perform some object management if you want to maintain more than just a single backup version of a database object.

```
USE AdventureWorks
GO

IF EXISTS(
    SELECT * FROM sys.objects
    WHERE type = 'FN' AND schema_id = SCHEMA_ID('dbo')
    AND name = 'ufnCntCustomers')
    DROP FUNCTION dbo.ufnCntCustomers
GO
```

The next code excerpt demonstrates the syntax for an FN user-defined function that returns an aggregate value. The aggregate value is the count of the rows in the Customer table of the Sales schema. The designation of the owner (dbo) after CREATE FUNCTION as a name qualifier is optional,

but it is good programming practice because it explicitly reminds you of the schema for your new FN
user-defined function.

Every CREATE FUNCTION statement for an FN function must have a RETURNS clause, an AS keyword, and one or more lines of code within a BEGIN...END block. At least one statement within the
BEGIN...END block should be a RETURN statement because this statement specifies a return value from
the function.

- The RETURNS clause denotes the type of scalar value that a function returns. You can return
  any scalar data type from an FN user-defined function, except for text, ntext, image, or
  timestamp.

- The AS keyword marks a transition from the header area to the body area. The header area
  includes the CREATE FUNCTION phrase as well as the RETURNS clause. The body of the FN user-
  defined function is the code within the BEGIN...END block.

- You can have multiple lines of code within a BEGIN...END block, but even if your FN user-
  defined function has just a single line of code, it still requires a BEGIN...END block.

```
CREATE FUNCTION dbo.ufnCntCustomers()
RETURNS int
AS
BEGIN
    RETURN (SELECT COUNT(*) FROM Sales.Customer)
END
GO
```

After you create an FN user-defined function, the next step is to use it. The following listing
illustrates some code for invoking the ufnCntCustomers user-defined function in the dbo schema. In
particular, notice the specification of a schema name qualifier before the function name. Also, you
must add parentheses after the function—even if the function has no parameters. The listing also
shows how to drop the FN user-defined function with the DROP FUNCTION statement. In the current
database context, this step restores the AdventureWorks database to its initial state. The total count
of customers in the AdventureWorks database is 19,185.

```
SELECT dbo.ufnCntCustomers() '# of Customers'
GO

DROP FUNCTION ufnCntCustomers
GO
```

```
# of Customers
--------------
19185
```

Working with an FN User-Defined Function That Has a Parameter

One particularly powerful feature of user-defined functions is their ability to take one or more input
parameters. This capability enables a user to modify the output from a user-defined function at
runtime. You can use a function as all or part of the definition of a computed column value in a
SELECT statement, a CREATE VIEW statement, or a CREATE TABLE statement. One user-defined function can even call another. All this is possible and made more powerful because user-defined
functions can accept input parameters.

The next CREATE FUNCTION statement illustrates how simple it is to specify an input parameter
for a user-defined function. The following FN user-defined function uses the modulo operator (%) to

determine the remainder for dividing a number by 2. The number (@n) is an input parameter. Specifying an int keyword after the parameter assigns an int data type to the @n parameter. Unless the value of @n is null, the function returns a value of either 0 or 1.

- A return value of 1 indicates @n equals an odd number.

- A return value of 0 indicates @n is an even number.

- When ufnIsOdd returns a null value, the value of @n is not specified—that is, null.

```
CREATE FUNCTION dbo.ufnIsOdd (@n int)
RETURNS bit
AS
BEGIN
    RETURN (@n % 2)
END
GO
```

The following script and output listing show the syntax and results of invoking the ufnIsOdd user-defined function with an even number and an odd number as an input parameter. The code excerpt makes an assignment of a value to a local variable (@numb) before passing the local variable's value to ufnIsOdd. The output from the SELECT statements shows the local variable's value and the output of the ufnIsOdd user-defined function. If a user fails to designate a value for the @n parameter (by, for example, not assigning a value to the @numb local variable), the ufnIsOdd user-defined function returns a null value.

```
DECLARE @numb int
SET @numb = 6
SELECT @numb 'Number', dbo.ufnIsOdd (@numb) 'Is_odd = 1'
SET @numb = 7
SELECT @numb 'Number', dbo.ufnIsOdd (@numb) 'Is_odd = 1'
```

```
Number      Is_odd = 1
----------- ----------
6           0
```

```
Number      Is_odd = 1
----------- ----------
7           1
```

The next script and output listing show a SELECT statement with a computed column. The SELECT statement invokes the ufnIsOdd user-defined function to compute the fourth column of its result set. In this case, the ufnIsOdd user-defined function derives its input parameter value from the first column (SalesPersonID) in the result set.

```
SELECT TOP 5 SalesPersonID, FirstName, LastName,
    dbo.ufnIsOdd(SalesPersonID) 'ID_odd = 1'
FROM Sales.vSalesPerson
```

```
SalesPersonID FirstName LastName ID_odd = 1
------------- --------- -------- ----------
288           Syed      Abbas    0
283           David     Campbell 1
```

```
278        Garrett  Vargas   0
279        Tsvi     Reiter   1
277        Jillian  Carson   1
```

Creating and Using IF User-Defined Functions

An IF user-defined function is very similar to a view. Each type of database object is based on a single SELECT statement. Both a view and an IF user-defined function can return a set of rows with each row having multiple column values. In addition, you can update the underlying data sources for each database object type through the database object.

■Tip In spite of the fact that a view and an IF user-defined function can both return a result set, there is one especially important distinction—users can modify the result returned by an IF user-defined function that accepts one or more parameters.

IF user-defined functions also have important similarities and differences to FN user-defined functions. Among the similarities are the following two points:

- You create and drop each type of user-defined function with the CREATE FUNCTION and DROP FUNCTION statements.
- Both functions accept parameters with the same syntax.

Some of the important differences between FN and IF user-defined functions are as follows:

- The syntax for IF and FN user-defined functions is not the same in the body of the CREATE FUNCTION statement.
- The syntax for invoking IF and FN functions need not be the same.
- An FN function can output only a scalar value while an IF function can return a set of rows each with one or more column values.

The samples in this section reside in IFUserDefinedFunctions.sql.

Working with an IF User-Defined Function Without Parameters

If you want to return a result set for a specific data source with a SELECT that has no parameters, then a view is the typical way to return the result set. However, an IF user-defined function can perform the task as well. The syntax is slightly more tedious for this very basic task when you use an IF user-defined function. However, returning the result set with an IF user-defined function allows you to add parameters later if you subsequently need a more dynamic result set that is dependent on parameters.

The following excerpt from IFUserDefinedFunctions.sql shows the code for dropping a previously existing version of the uifListAllSalesPersons user-defined function before creating a new version of the user-defined function. The syntax for conditionally dropping an IF user-defined function is very similar to that for an FN user-defined function. In both cases, you can query the sys.objects view for an existing version of the function. However, if you want to limit the search by database object type for precision, then you should set the type column value criterion to IF for an inline user-defined function instead of FN for a scalar-valued user-defined function.

The RETURNS clause of the CREATE FUNCTION statement for an IF user-defined function should always have table as an argument. The only reason for using an IF user-defined function is to return a result set. After the AS keyword, you can specify the SELECT statement for the result set as an argument within the RETURN statement. You should also note that an IF user-defined function can have only one SELECT statement.

The SELECT statement in the following user-defined function draws on the SalesPerson, Employee, Contact, and SalesTerritory tables. All the joins are inner joins, except for the one merging the SalesTerritory table to the other three tables. Using a LEFT JOIN specification allows the result set to include those rows from the SalesPerson table that have a null TerritoryID column value. The whole reason for including the SalesTerritory table is to enable the lookup of territory names corresponding to TerritoryID column values. Notice the column alias of TerritoryName for st.Name—namely, the Name column in the SalesTerritory table.

```
IF EXISTS(
    SELECT * FROM sys.objects
    WHERE type = 'IF' AND schema_id = SCHEMA_ID('dbo')
    AND name = 'uifListAllSalesPersons')
    DROP FUNCTION dbo.uifListAllSalesPersons
GO

CREATE FUNCTION dbo.uifListAllSalesPersons()
RETURNS table
AS
RETURN (
    SELECT s.SalesPersonID, c.FirstName, c.LastName,
        st.Name 'TerritoryName', c.Phone
    FROM Sales.SalesPerson s
        JOIN HumanResources.Employee e
        ON s.SalesPersonID = e.EmployeeID
        JOIN Person.Contact c
        ON e.ContactID = c.ContactID
        LEFT JOIN Sales.SalesTerritory st
        ON s.TerritoryID = st.TerritoryID)
GO
```

Once you create an IF user-defined function, you can use it nearly like a view. The only extra requirement is that you include a pair of parentheses after the function's name. There is no need for a user qualifier as there is with FN user-defined functions. The following SELECT statement requests the first three rows from the result set returned by the uifListAllSalesPersons user-defined function. The result set that follows the SELECT statement shows the outcome. The NULL value for TerritoryName in the first row confirms the impact of the LEFT JOIN phrase within the uifListAllSalesPersons user-defined function.

```
SELECT TOP 3 * FROM uifListAllSalesPersons()
GO
```

SalesPersonID	FirstName	LastName	TerritoryName	Phone
268	Stephen	Jiang	NULL	238-555-0197
275	Michael	Blythe	Northeast	257-555-0154
276	Linda	Mitchell	Southwest	883-555-0116

Selecting from an IF User-Defined Function with a Parameter

When you specify a parameter for an IF user-defined function, the SELECT statement in the function will often use the parameter in the WHERE clause. The following CREATE FUNCTION statement for the uifListSalesPersonsInTerritory IF user-defined function demonstrates the syntax for this approach. The IF user-defined function's SELECT statement draws on the vSalesPerson view that comes with the AdventureWorks database.

- The parameter name (@t) initially appears in parentheses after the function name following CREATE FUNCTION. The parameter has an nvarchar data type.

- The IF user-defined function uses the parameter to specify the name for a territory. For this reason, the parameter name appears in the WHERE clause of the SELECT statement for the user-defined function. In this way, the user-defined function can vary its result set at runtime.

```
CREATE FUNCTION
    dbo.uifListSalesPersonsInTerritory(@t AS nvarchar(50))
RETURNS table
AS
RETURN (
    SELECT SalesPersonID, FirstName, LastName,
        TerritoryName, Phone
    FROM Sales.vSalesPerson
        WHERE TerritoryName = @t)
GO
```

You can pass a parameter to an IF user-defined function in a way that parallels passing a parameter to an FN user-defined function. However, you have more flexibility in how you invoke IF user-defined functions. With an IF user-defined function, the use of a user qualifier for the user-defined function name is optional.

The following script illustrates two different styles for invoking an IF user-defined function. The script starts by declaring a local variable (@t).

- The first example specifies a schema qualifier (dbo) for uifListSalesPersonsInTerritory, while the second example does not designate a qualifier for the IF user-defined function.

- Before you invoke uifListSalesPersonsInTerritory for the first time, you assign the value Canada to @t. This local variable appears as a parameter of the IF user-defined function, which, in turn, is the argument for the FROM clause of a SELECT statement. This first invocation returns data about sales persons in the Canadian sales territory.

- You assign the value Northwest to @t before the second invocation of uifListSalesPersonsInTerritory. The second SELECT statement returns sales persons serving the Northwest territory.

```
DECLARE @t as nvarchar(50)

SET @t = 'Canada'
SELECT * FROM dbo.uifListSalesPersonsInTerritory(@t)

SET @t = 'Northwest'
SELECT * FROM uifListSalesPersonsInTerritory(@t)
GO
```

The listing for the next two result sets shows the output from the first and second invocations of uifListSalesPersonsInTerritory. The first result set shows the sales persons assigned to the Canadian sales territory. The second result returns the name and phone numbers for the three sales persons handling customers in the Northwest sales territory.

The important point to take away from this output is that the same user-defined functions generated both result sets. To generate these two different result sets with views, you would need two different views—one for the Canadian sales territory and the other for the Northwest sales territory. A single IF user-defined function that takes a parameter can generate both result sets.

```
SalesPersonID FirstName LastName     TerritoryName Phone
------------- --------- ----------- ------------- -----------
278           Garrett   Vargas      Canada        922-555-0165
282           José      Saraiva     Canada        185-555-0169
```

```
SalesPersonID FirstName LastName     TerritoryName Phone
------------- --------- ----------- ------------- -----------
280           Pamela    Ansman-Wolfe Northwest     340-555-0193
283           David     Campbell    Northwest     740-555-0182
287           Tete      Mensa-Annan Northwest     615-555-0153
```

Updating from an IF User-Defined Function with a Parameter

In addition to just selecting rows with an IF user-defined function, you can also perform standard data manipulation statements, such as INSERT, UPDATE, and DELETE. This section demonstrates the operation of an UPDATE statement with the uifListSalesPersonsInTerritory function. The preceding section highlighted that this function takes a parameter. Therefore, you can apply an UPDATE statement to a subset of a full set of rows from a data source through an IF user-defined function that takes one or more parameters.

The following script tracks the status of two sales persons serving the Canadian sales territory. The first SELECT statement shows the rows before an update to the LastName column value. Next, the script uses an UPDATE statement to modify the LastName column value for the row with a SalesPersonID column value of 278. Another SELECT statement shows the updated value by displaying the rows for the sales persons serving Canada. A second UPDATE statement restores the LastName column value to Vargas, which is the original value for the column. A closing SELECT statement shows the restored column value for the sales person with a SalesPersonID of 278 as part of the two sales persons serving Canada.

```
DECLARE @t as nvarchar(50)
SET @t = 'Canada'
SELECT * FROM dbo.uifListSalesPersonsInTerritory(@t)

UPDATE dbo.uifListSalesPersonsInTerritory(@t)
SET LastName = 'Vargax'
WHERE SalesPersonID = 278

SELECT * FROM dbo.uifListSalesPersonsInTerritory(@t)

UPDATE dbo.uifListSalesPersonsInTerritory(@t)
SET LastName = 'Vargas'
WHERE SalesPersonID = 278

SELECT * FROM dbo.uifListSalesPersonsInTerritory(@t)
```

The output from the preceding three SELECT statements appears next. The middle result set shows the LastName column value for the sales person with a SalesPersonID value of 278 as Vargax. The third result set shows the LastName column value for SalesPersonID restored to Vargas, which matches the LastName column value before an update (see the first result set).

The most powerful aspect of the demonstration for this section is that it confirms that you can modify the underlying data source for an IF user-defined function through the function. The same rules that apply to data modification through a view also apply to data modification through an IF user-defined function. For example, you cannot modify a computed column value. If you need to change the value of a computed column, modify the inputs to the computed column so that they generate the result you seek for the column.

```
SalesPersonID  FirstName  LastName      TerritoryName  Phone
-------------  ---------  ------------  -------------  ------------
278            Garrett    Vargas        Canada         922-555-0165
282            José       Saraiva       Canada         185-555-0169
```

```
SalesPersonID  FirstName  LastName      TerritoryName  Phone
-------------  ---------  ------------  -------------  ------------
278            Garrett    Vargax        Canada         922-555-0165
282            José       Saraiva       Canada         185-555-0169
```

```
SalesPersonID  FirstName  LastName      TerritoryName  Phone
-------------  ---------  ------------  -------------  ------------
278            Garrett    Vargas        Canada         922-555-0165
282            José       Saraiva       Canada         185-555-0169
```

Creating and Using Stored Procedures

Stored procedures store and facilitate the reuse of T-SQL code. You can use a stored procedure for data access, data manipulation, or database administration. This section highlights the use of stored procedures for data access, and it also gives demonstrations of the advantages that stored procedures bring to data modification tasks.

While this section will not drill down on the use of stored procedures for server administration, several prior chapters (mainly Chapters 3 and 5) included coverage of system-stored procedures, which focus on server administration. All system-stored procedure names start with sp_. Selected system-stored procedures previously reviewed illustrate the kinds of tasks system-stored procedures do well.

- sp_helpdb returns information about a specified database, such as its owner, size, and files underlying it.

- sp_dboption lets you view and change database settings (or options), including such features as a database's auto-close setting, which facilitate the deployment of SQL Server Express databases.

- sp_attach_db and sp_detach_db facilitate attaching and detaching databases from a server instance.

- sp_rename enables you to rename user-created database objects.

- sp_addlinkedserver, sp_linkedsrvlogin, and sp_linkedservers help you to create and administer linked servers.

System-stored procedures are preprogrammed to perform a specific task. With a user-defined stored procedure, you can write custom T-SQL code and package it as an object to perform a task of your own choosing. Stored procedures in T-SQL are like procedures in other modern programming languages. You can pass them parameters to determine what they do, and they can return parameters as well as return status values that reflect what they did. A stored procedure can also return a result set.

Because a stored procedure is a database object, it is natural to compare it to other database objects that store T-SQL code, including views and user-defined functions.

- T-SQL offers several statements for managing stored procedures that are analogous to those that you can use to manage other database objects.

    - You create a new stored procedure with a CREATE PROCEDURE or CREATE PROC statement. You can drop a stored procedure or modify one with DROP PROCEDURE or ALTER PROCEDURE statements.

    - The most common way to invoke a stored procedure is with an EXECUTE or EXEC statement.

- A stored procedure can return one or more result sets. Views and table-valued user-defined functions also return result sets.

    - A view or a table-valued user-defined function can return only one result set, but a stored procedure can return multiple result sets.

    - On the other hand, the result set from a view and a table-valued user-defined function can serve as the argument for the FROM clause of a SELECT statement. A stored procedure cannot serve as the argument (or part of the argument) for a FROM clause in a SELECT statement.

- A stored procedure can accept input parameters—similar to user-defined functions.

    - Views do not accept parameters at all.

    - It is easier to tap the default value for a stored procedure parameter than for a user-defined function parameter.

- Both stored procedures and user-defined functions can return output parameters.

    - A stored procedure can return multiple output parameters while a user-defined function can return only a single parameter, which is represented by the function's value in the calling code.

    - A user-defined function's value can be used in another expression, but a stored procedure does not directly enable its returned parameters for this purpose.

- A stored procedure can pass back a return status value to code that calls it; the return status value is an integer value that can reflect how a stored procedure closes. Neither views nor user-defined functions pass back return status values.

Returning Result Sets Without Parameters

This initial section on developing solutions with stored procedures demonstrates the basics of creating and invoking a stored procedure that returns one or more result sets. Specifying a result set for a stored procedure is easy: just include a separate SELECT statement for each result set that you want your stored procedure to return. As with views and user-defined functions, you can add new stored procedures to a named schema or the default dbo schema. You can have multiple stored procedures with the same names in different schemas within a database. The samples in this section reside in StoredProcResultSets.sql.

Returning a Single Result Set

As when creating other database objects, you must make sure that an object with the same name as your new stored procedure object does not already exist. You can use the sys.objects catalog view to scan for existing objects with the same name as the new stored procedure you want to create.

The following excerpt from StoredProcResultSets.sql starts by designating the AdventureWorks database as the database context, which is the case with many of the examples in this section. Sections whose samples process another database will clearly show that they use a different database.

The following excerpt from StoredProcResultSets.sql searches the sys.objects catalog view for rows with a type equal to P. These are rows that represent stored procedure database objects.

- By scanning for a row with a specific name column value, such as usp_SalePersonNamePhone➡Email, you can determine if any existing stored procedure in the database has the name that you want to assign to your new stored procedure.

- The code sample that follows merely drops a previously existing version of the stored procedure in the default schema for a user. If you are a dbo user and your database does not use named schemas, this syntax is sufficient. If your database has multiple versions of the stored procedure in different schemas, then you should search for the stored procedure in a particular schema and use a schema qualifier for the stored procedure name in the DROP PROCEDURE statement. A subsequent sample for returning multiple result sets demonstrates this schema-sensitive approach.

- Instead of dropping an existing stored procedure version, you can create a backup copy of it with the help of the sp_rename system-stored procedure. See the "Recovering Values from an Old Table for a New Table" section in Chapter 4 for a code sample demonstrating the use of sp_rename.

```
USE AdventureWorks
GO

IF EXISTS(SELECT * FROM sys.objects
    WHERE type = 'P' AND
    name = 'usp_SalePersonNamePhoneEmail')
    DROP PROCEDURE usp_SalePersonNamePhoneEmail
GO
```

The following script shows how simple it can be to create a stored procedure. First, you add the name for your new stored procedure after the CREATE PROCEDURE phrase. If your stored procedure does not use parameters, then follow the stored procedure name with a space as a delimiter and then the AS keyword, which serves as a transition between the header and the body of the stored procedure. The sample that follows has just one SELECT statement, which joins the SalesPerson, Employee, and Contact tables to make available TerritoryID and contact information, such as last name, phone, and email address, in a result set.

The concluding GO keyword invokes the CREATE PROCEDURE statement. Failing to place a GO keyword at the end of a CREATE PROCEDURE statement may cause other statements after the CREATE PROCEDURE statement to become a part of the stored procedure. This, in turn, may cause unintended behavior from the stored procedure.

```
CREATE PROCEDURE usp_SalePersonNamePhoneEmail
AS
SELECT s.TerritoryID, c.LastName, c.Phone, c.EmailAddress
FROM Sales.SalesPerson S JOIN HumanResources.Employee e
ON s.SalesPersonID = e.EmployeeID
JOIN Person.Contact c
ON c.ContactID = e.ContactID
GO
```

To run a very simple stored procedure, you need only to provide the name of the stored procedure after EXEC. Notice you do not use a SELECT statement to extract the result from a stored procedure, which eliminates your ability to format a result set with the tools of a SELECT statement. If you require formatting, include it in your SELECT statement within the stored procedure.

The following listing illustrates the syntax for invoking the stored procedure created by the preceding CREATE PROCEDURE statement. After the EXEC statement, you see the result set returned by the stored procedure.

```
EXEC usp_SalePersonNamePhoneEmail
```

TerritoryID	LastName	Phone	EmailAddress
NULL	Jiang	238-555-0197	stephen0@adventure-works.com
2	Blythe	257-555-0154	michael9@adventure-works.com
4	Mitchell	883-555-0116	linda3@adventure-works.com
3	Carson	517-555-0117	jillian0@adventure-works.com
6	Vargas	922-555-0165	garrett1@adventure-works.com
5	Reiter	664-555-0112	tsvi0@adventure-works.com
1	Ansman-Wolfe	340-555-0193	pamela0@adventure-works.com
4	Ito	330-555-0120	shu0@adventure-works.com
6	Saraiva	185-555-0169	josé1@adventure-works.com
1	Campbell	740-555-0182	david8@adventure-works.com
NULL	Alberts	775-555-0164	amy0@adventure-works.com
10	Pak	1 (11) 500 555-0145	jae0@adventure-works.com
7	Varkey Chudukatil	1 (11) 500 555-0117	ranjit0@adventure-works.com
1	Mensa-Annan	615-555-0153	tete0@adventure-works.com
NULL	Abbas	926-555-0182	syed0@adventure-works.com
8	Valdez	1 (11) 500 555-0140	rachel0@adventure-works.com
9	Tsoflias	1 (11) 500 555-0190	lynn0@adventure-works.com

Returning Two Result Sets from a Single Stored Procedure

The next stored procedure shows how to return two result sets from a single stored procedure. If client applications need multiple result sets, you can sometimes conserve connection resources on a SQL Server Express instance by returning multiple result sets with a single stored procedure. The syntax for achieving this is very straightforward.

The sample stored procedure that will return two result sets is called usp_ProductCategory➡ CountSubcategory. The demonstration stores the stored procedure in the Production schema of the AdventureWorks database. The following script searches for this particular version of the stored procedure and drops the stored procedure if it exists already. To facilitate a search by schema name instead of schema_id number, the SELECT clause for the EXISTS operator joins the sys.objects view with the sys.schemas view. The SELECT statement references name column values from both views (s.name and o.name). The DROP PROCEDURE statement uses a schema name qualifier to identify the particular version of the stored procedure to remove from the database.

```
IF EXISTS(SELECT * FROM sys.objects o JOIN sys.schemas s
    ON o.schema_id = s.schema_id
    WHERE o.type = 'P' AND
    s.name = 'Production' AND
    o.name = 'usp_ProductCategoryCountSubcategory')
    DROP PROCEDURE
        Production.usp_ProductCategoryCountSubcategory
GO
```

The usp_ProductCategoryCountSubcategory stored procedure returns two result sets. The first result set lists the ProductCategoryID and Name column values from the ProductCategory table in the Production schema. The second result set contains a count of the number of rows in the ProductSubcategory table matching each ProductCategoryID value. The CREATE PROCEDURE statement shows the SELECT statements specifying each result set.

```
CREATE PROCEDURE
    Production.usp_ProductCategoryCountSubcategory
AS

SELECT ProductCategoryID, Name
FROM Production.ProductCategory
ORDER BY ProductCategoryID

SELECT ProductCategoryID, COUNT(*) 'No. Subcategories'
FROM Production.ProductSubcategory
GROUP BY ProductCategoryID
ORDER BY ProductCategoryID
GO
```

The EXEC statement and result sets for the usp_ProductCategoryCountSubcategory stored procedure appear next. Notice that the EXEC statement for this stored procedure, which returns two result sets, has the same syntax as one that returns a single result set. The number of result sets returned from a stored procedure depends exclusively on the number of SELECT statements in the CREATE PROCEDURE statement for the stored procedure in question. Furthermore, there isn't anything special that you need to do to retrieve more than one result set from a stored procedure that contains more than one SELECT statement.

```
EXEC Production.usp_ProductCategoryCountSubcategory
GO
```

```
ProductCategoryID Name
----------------- -----------
1                 Bikes
2                 Components
3                 Clothing
4                 Accessories
```

```
ProductCategoryID No. Subcategories
----------------- -----------------
1                 3
2                 14
3                 8
4                 12
```

Returning Result Sets and Input Parameters

You have just seen one of the special features of stored procedures—namely, the ability of stored procedures to return multiple result sets. Neither views nor table-valued user-defined functions support this feature. The ability to return a result set based on a parameter value is another special feature of stored procedures. Views do not offer this capability at all. User-defined functions can accept input parameters, but stored procedures are able to deal with default parameter values in a more elegant way than user-defined functions. The samples in this section reside in StoredProcInputParameters.sql.

Using a Parameter in a WHERE Clause

One obvious place to use an input parameter is in the WHERE clause for a SELECT statement that defines a result set for a stored procedure. The following stored procedure, named usp_SalesPersonInATerritory, illustrates how to declare a parameter for a stored procedure and how to use it. The stored procedure returns a result set with one row for each sales person in a sales territory designated when the stored procedure is invoked.

- You declare the parameter after specifying the name for the stored procedure. Like local variable names, parameter names start with @. Follow the parameter name with its data type. The following sample declares the @TID parameter with an int data type.

- If your stored procedure has multiple parameters, which is not the case in the sample that follows, you can delimit them with commas. For readability purposes, many stored procedure authors use commas and a new line to mark the start of each new parameter declaration.

- After you declare a parameter, you need to use it somewhere within the stored procedure. You can use a parameter anywhere in a SELECT statement where you can use a local variable (see Chapter 5 for examples of the use of local variables in SELECT statements). The following sample uses the @TID parameter in the WHERE clause for a SELECT statement.

```
CREATE PROCEDURE usp_SalesPersonInATerritory
@TID int
AS
SELECT s.TerritoryID, c.LastName, c.Phone
FROM Sales.SalesPerson S JOIN HumanResources.Employee e
ON s.SalesPersonID = e.EmployeeID
JOIN Person.Contact c
ON c.ContactID = e.ContactID
WHERE s.TerritoryID = @TID
GO
```

The following pair of EXEC statements invokes the usp_SalesPersonInATerritory stored procedure twice: once with a value of 1, followed by a second time with a value of 2. The result set for each invocation of the stored procedure follows the EXEC statements. A value of 1 for @TID returns three rows, and a value of 2 returns a single row.

```
EXEC usp_SalesPersonInATerritory 1
GO
EXEC usp_SalesPersonInATerritory 2
GO
```

```
TerritoryID LastName           Phone
----------- ----------------   ------------------
1           Ansman-Wolfe       340-555-0193
1           Campbell           740-555-0182
1           Mensa-Annan        615-555-0153
```

```
TerritoryID LastName          Phone
----------- ----------------- -------------------
2           Blythe            257-555-0154
```

The preceding sample code is very basic in several ways. First, the sample designates just one parameter. Second, it does not designate the name of the parameter when it assigns a value. For example, you could specify a value for a single parameter like this:

```
EXEC usp1 @param1 = value
```

If you had two parameters, you could designate them like this:

```
EXEC usp1 value1, value2
```

Or like this:

```
EXEC usp1 @param1 = value1, @param2 = value2
```

If a user fails to specify a parameter value for the preceding instance of the usp_SalesPerson➥ InATerritory stored procedure, an error will result. Sometimes you as the author may forget about a parameter declaration for a stored procedure, or another user may not even know of the need for a parameter. Either of these scenarios can generate an error. The following EXEC statement shows an attempt to invoke usp_SalesPersonInATerritory without a parameter. Instead of generating a result set, SQL Server Express returns an error message indicating the stored procedure expects a parameter for @TID.

```
EXEC usp_SalesPersonInATerritory
GO
```

Specifying a Default Parameter Value

If you specify a default value for a stored procedure's parameter, the stored procedure will succeed even if a user fails to specify a value for the parameter. The following script shows a variation of the preceding usp_SalesPersonInATerritory stored procedure. This instance of the stored procedure assigns a default value of 3 to the @TID parameter. With this assignment, if a user fails to specify a value for the @TID when invoking the stored procedure, the stored procedure will use the value of 3. If the user specifies another value, the user-specified value overrides the default setting.

```
CREATE PROCEDURE usp_SalesPersonInATerritory
@TID int = 3
AS
SELECT s.TerritoryID, c.LastName, c.Phone
FROM Sales.SalesPerson S JOIN HumanResources.Employee e
ON s.SalesPersonID = e.EmployeeID
JOIN Person.Contact c
ON c.ContactID = e.ContactID
WHERE s.TerritoryID = @TID
GO
```

Both of the following EXEC statements call the preceding instance of usp_SalesPersonInA➥ Territory. The first EXEC statement designates a value of 1 for @TID. The second EXEC statement does not set a value for @TID. Therefore, SQL Server Express uses the default value of 3. The result sets from the two EXEC statements appear after the pair of EXEC statements. Notice the second result set has a TerritoryID column value of 3, which corresponds to the default setting for @TID.

```
EXEC usp_SalesPersonInATerritory 1
GO
EXEC usp_SalesPersonInATerritory
GO
```

TerritoryID	LastName	Phone
1	Ansman-Wolfe	340-555-0193
1	Campbell	740-555-0182
1	Mensa-Annan	615-555-0153

TerritoryID	LastName	Phone
3	Carson	517-555-0117

Filtering for Null Values with a Stored Procedure

You can attempt to return rows from the SalesPerson table with unspecified TerritoryID column values from the preceding stored procedure, but the attempt will fail. The failure derives from the design of the WHERE clause. Consider the following EXEC statement, which submits a value of NULL for the @TID parameter. The SalesPerson table has three rows with null values for TerritoryID, but the result set generated by the following EXEC statement has no rows.

```
EXEC usp_SalesPersonInATerritory NULL
```

The reason there are no rows in the result set is because the WHERE clause does not have the proper syntax to filter null values. The WHERE clause in the preceding instance of the usp_SalesPersonInATerritory stored procedure is

```
WHERE s.TerritoryID = @TID
```

However, the appropriate syntax to filter for null values is

```
WHERE s.TerritoryID IS NULL
```

If you want to filter for values that can be non-null or null, then your stored procedure can have two separate SELECT statements. An IF statement can direct the flow of a stored procedure to one SELECT statement or the other based on the value of the @TID parameter. This kind of flexibility is one of the reasons that stored procedures are such popular tools with database developers.

The following CREATE PROCEDURE statement illustrates the appropriate syntax for a stored procedure that handles null parameter values. The name of the stored procedure is usp_SalesPersonInATerritoryOrNot. The CREATE PROCEDURE statement assigns a default value of NULL to its @TID parameter.

- If a user invokes the stored procedure with a non-null @TID value, the IF statement directs the control flow to the first SELECT statement. This is the same SELECT statement found in both of the two preceding two versions of the usp_SalesPersonInATerritory stored procedure.

- If a user invokes the stored procedure with a null @TID value, the IF statement directs the control flow to the second SELECT statement. This SELECT statement uses the correct syntax for filtering for null TerritoryID column values.

- If a user invokes the stored procedure without designating a value for @TID, the IF statement uses the default value for @TID and directs the control flow to the second SELECT statement.

```
CREATE PROCEDURE usp_SalesPersonInATerritoryOrNot
@TID int = NULL
AS
IF @TID IS NOT NULL
    SELECT s.TerritoryID, c.LastName, c.Phone
    FROM Sales.SalesPerson S JOIN HumanResources.Employee e
    ON s.SalesPersonID = e.EmployeeID
    JOIN Person.Contact c
    ON c.ContactID = e.ContactID
    WHERE s.TerritoryID = @TID
ELSE
    SELECT s.TerritoryID, c.LastName, c.Phone
    FROM Sales.SalesPerson S JOIN HumanResources.Employee e
    ON s.SalesPersonID = e.EmployeeID
    JOIN Person.Contact c
    ON c.ContactID = e.ContactID
    WHERE s.TerritoryID IS NULL
GO
```

The following listing shows three EXEC statements for the preceding stored procedure with corresponding result sets in the same order. If the user specifies a value for @TID, then the stored procedure returns information about sales persons serving that territory. On the other hand, if a user explicitly designates a null value for @TID or fails to specify a value for @TID, the stored procedure returns rows for sales persons that have null TerritoryID column values.

```
EXEC usp_SalesPersonInATerritoryOrNot 1
GO
EXEC usp_SalesPersonInATerritoryOrNot NULL
GO
EXEC usp_SalesPersonInATerritoryOrNot
GO
```

TerritoryID	LastName	Phone
1	Ansman-Wolfe	340-555-0193
1	Campbell	740-555-0182
1	Mensa-Annan	615-555-0153

TerritoryID	LastName	Phone
NULL	Jiang	238-555-0197
NULL	Alberts	775-555-0164
NULL	Abbas	926-555-0182

TerritoryID	LastName	Phone
NULL	Jiang	238-555-0197
NULL	Alberts	775-555-0164
NULL	Abbas	926-555-0182

Contrasting Input Parameters for User-Defined Functions and Stored Procedures

As noted, both user-defined functions and stored procedures can handle input parameters. In spite of this similarity, there are important differences. Perhaps the most notable difference is with respect to the default values.

- As you have seen, you can assign the default value to a stored procedure parameter just by omitting the parameter from the EXEC statement for the stored procedure.

- To assign the default value for a user-defined function parameter, you must explicitly reference the parameter with the DEFAULT keyword.

- Omitting a parameter value for a user-defined function generates an error even when the parameter has a default value.

The following CREATE FUNCTION and CREATE PROCEDURE statements compute whether a number is odd or even.

- The CREATE FUNCTION statement was initially described in the "Creating and Using FN User-Defined Functions" section within this chapter.

  - The scalar function returns a value of 1 for an odd input parameter and 0 for even input parameter.

  - The input parameter has a default value of 5; this feature was missing from the scalar function in the "Creating and Using FN User-Defined Functions" section.

- The usp_NumberIsOdd stored procedure uses the same modulo function (%) the user-defined function does to compute whether a number is odd or even.

  - The stored procedure generates a result set of two numbers—one for the input parameter and the other to indicate whether the input parameter is odd or even.

  - Like the user-defined function, the stored procedure assigns a default value of 5 to its input parameter.

```
CREATE FUNCTION dbo.ufnIsOdd (@n int = 5)
RETURNS bit
AS
BEGIN
    RETURN (@n % 2)
END
GO

CREATE PROCEDURE usp_NumberIsOdd
@n int = 5
AS
SELECT @n 'Number', @n % 2 'Is_odd = 1'
GO
```

The following listing shows three different invocations of the dbo.ufnIsOdd user-defined function.

- The first invocation passes a null value as an input parameter to the user-defined function. Notice that @numb is declared, but it is not assigned a value prior to its use in the first invocation. The output shows NULL for the input parameter value and whether the input parameter is odd (the remainder of dividing a null value by 2 is a null value).

- The second use of the dbo.ufnIsOdd user-defined function uses the default value for the function's input parameter. Notice the use of the DEFAULT keyword as a function argument. Since the default value is 5, the function indicates it is odd. However, the default input parameter value is not available to the code that calls the user-defined function because the sole return value from the function is the value indicating whether the function is odd or even.

- The dfo.ufnIsOdd function's third use occurs after @numb is set to 6. The function indicates this input parameter is even.

```
DECLARE @numb int

SELECT @numb 'Number', dbo.ufnIsOdd (@numb) 'Is_odd = 1'
SELECT @numb 'Number', dbo.ufnIsOdd (DEFAULT) 'Is_odd = 1'
SET @numb = 6
SELECT @numb 'Number', dbo.ufnIsOdd (@numb) 'Is_odd = 1'
```

```
Number      Is_odd = 1
----------- ----------
NULL        NULL
```

```
Number      Is_odd = 1
----------- ----------
NULL        1
```

```
Number      Is_odd = 1
----------- ----------
6           0
```

The next listing shows the code for calling the usp_NumberIsOdd stored procedure with the same three inputs you used for the dfo.ufnIsOdd user-defined function.

- Each call to the stored procedure invokes an EXEC statement.

  - The EXEC statements return a result set with the value of both the input parameter and the indicator of whether the input parameter is odd or even.

  - The second EXEC statement omits a parameter value. Recall that the second use of the user-defined function referenced the DEFAULT keyword to request the use of the input parameter's default value.

- The output from the first and third runs of the user-defined function and stored procedure is identical. However, the output for the second runs is different.

  - In particular, the stored procedure output shows the correct value for the default value. This is because the stored procedure passes back a result set with two values from the stored procedure—one value is for the input parameter and the other is for the indicator of whether the input parameter is odd or even.

  - The user-defined function output does not show the correct value for the default value because the default value is assigned within the user-defined function, but the function can return just one scalar value (the indicator for whether the input parameter is odd or even).

```
DECLARE @numb int

EXEC usp_NumberIsOdd @numb
EXEC usp_NumberIsOdd
SET @numb = 6
EXEC usp_NumberIsOdd @numb
```

```
Number      Is_odd = 1
----------- -----------
NULL        NULL
```

```
Number      Is_odd = 1
----------- -----------
5           1
```

```
Number      Is_odd = 1
----------- -----------
6           0
```

Returning Scalar Values with Output Parameters

As you have seen from the preceding sample, you can return scalar values from a stored procedure in a result set. However, it is more common to use output parameters when you have just a few scalar values to return from a stored procedure. Using an output parameter makes the output parameter values readily available for further manipulation in the code calling the stored procedure. You can concurrently use both output and input parameters in a single stored procedure.

The use of output parameters has design implications for both the CREATE PROCEDURE statement that makes a stored procedure and the EXEC statement that invokes a stored procedure.

- You declare output parameters similarly to the way that you declare input parameters. One important distinction between input and output parameters is that you must identify each output parameter with the OUTPUT keyword. If you don't do this, the parameter is an input parameter. You can optionally use the INPUT keyword to explicitly designate a stored procedure parameter as an input parameter.

- You must follow the stored procedure name in the EXEC statement with an assignment statement for each output parameter. The assignment statement designates a local variable to accept the output parameter's value. Mark the end of the assignment statement with the OUTPUT keyword.

■**Caution** The assignment statement for copying a stored procedure's output parameter value to a local variable has its two terms in the opposite order of typical assignment expressions. Specifically, the parameter name must appear on the left of the equals (=) sign. The local variable must appear on the right of the equals sign.

The samples in this section reside in StoredProcOutputParameters.sql.

Returning Values from a View as Stored Procedure Output Parameters

The first sample demonstrating the use of output parameters looks up some values in a view. This view, vSTRow_Numbers, serves as a data source in the subsequent sample as well.

- The CREATE VIEW statement for vSTRow_Numbers makes a view with two columns: one column contains the SubTotal column values from the SalesOrderHeader table in the Sales schema, and the second column (rn) contains values returned by the built-in Row_Number function. The "Assigning Row_Number Values to Rows" section in Chapter 6 reviews the syntax and operation for this function.

- For your purposes here, all you really need to know is that the Row_Number function sorts the view's rows by SubTotal value in ascending order. The first rn column value is 1, and the last column value equals the total number of rows returned by the view. This number will vary depending on the rows in the view's underlying source.

```
CREATE VIEW dbo.vSTRow_Numbers
AS
SELECT SubTotal, Row_Number() OVER (ORDER BY SubTotal) rn
FROM Sales.SalesOrderHeader
GO
```

The usp_MinMaxSubTotal stored procedure looks up the SubTotal values in the first row and the last row of the view. These values are returned as output parameters to the code calling the usp_MinMaxSubTotal stored procedure.

- The stored procedure's header section declares two output parameters named @minSubTotal and @maxSubTotal.

- The first SELECT statement in the stored procedure's body assigns the first SubTotal column value from the vSTRow_Numbers view to the @minSubTotal parameter.

- The second SELECT statement in the stored procedure's body assigns the last SubTotal column value from the vSTRow_Numbers view to the @maxSubTotal parameter.

```
CREATE PROCEDURE usp_MinMaxSubTotal
@minSubTotal money OUTPUT,
@maxSubTotal money OUTPUT
AS
SET @minSubTotal =
    (SELECT TOP 1 SubTotal
        FROM dbo.vSTRow_Numbers ORDER BY rn)
SET @maxSubTotal =
    (SELECT TOP 1 SubTotal
        FROM dbo.vSTRow_Numbers ORDER BY rn DESC)
GO
```

The following listing includes the EXEC statement invoking the usp_MinMaxSubTotal stored procedure and the output generated by running the stored procedure.

- Whenever you run a stored procedure with output parameters, it is imperative to have local variables to store the output parameter values locally. Therefore, the following script starts with a DECLARE statement for the @lclmin and @lclmax local variables.

- The EXEC statement shows the syntax for storing the two output parameter values locally.

- A SELECT statement formats the two local variables with the output parameter values for display, and the output shows the minimum and maximum SubTotal column values from the vSTRow_Numbers view.

```
DECLARE @lclmin money, @lclmax money
EXEC usp_MinMaxSubTotal @minSubTotal = @lclmin OUTPUT,
    @maxSubTotal = @lclmax OUTPUT
SELECT @lclmin 'Min. SubTotal', @lclmax 'Max. SubTotal'
```

```
Min. SubTotal         Max. SubTotal
--------------------  --------------------
1.374                 224356.4831
```

Returning a Computed Value as a Stored Procedure Output Parameter

The next sample reuses the vSTRow_Numbers view to compute its median SubTotal value. If the count of numbers over which you are computing a median is odd, then the median is the middle number from a sorted series of values. If you are computing the median for a series of sorted numbers with an even count, then there is no number that is exactly at the middle. However, you can compute the median as the average of the two numbers in the middle of the sorted series, such as SubTotal column values in the vSTRow_Numbers view.

The sample for this section uses the ufnIsOdd user-defined function. Recall that this sample was initially presented and discussed in the "Creating and Using FN User-Defined Functions" section of this chapter. The function takes an input parameter and returns a value indicating whether the input parameter value is odd (1) or even (0). The output from this function serves as the condition argument for an IF statement that allows the stored procedure to branch to one of two code blocks depending on whether the count of the number of SubTotal column values is odd or even.

The usp_MedianSubTotal stored procedure computes the median value of the SubTotal column value series.

- After local variable declarations, the stored procedure divides the number of rows in the vSTRow_Numbers view by two and stores the result in @rnval.

- Next, an IF…ELSE statement branches to one of two code blocks.

  - If the count of rows in the vSTRow_Numbers view is odd, the value of the @rnval local variable is one less than the row number of the middle value.

  - If the count of rows in the vSTRow_Numbers view is even, the value of the @rnval local variable points at the top row of the two middle rows needed for computing the median. After retrieving both of these values in a BEGIN…END block, the stored procedure computes the median as their average value.

- The stored procedure's @MedianVal output parameter returns the median value to the next line after the statement that invokes the usp_MedianSubTotal stored procedure.

■**Note** You could improve the design marginally by assigning the value of COUNT(*) to a variable and then reusing the variable. To simplify the presentation of the procedure's computing logic, I did not take advantage of this opportunity. However, it is a best practice in production solutions to compute function values just once and then reuse the computed value.

```
CREATE PROCEDURE usp_MedianSubTotal
@MedianVal money OUTPUT
AS

DECLARE @rnval int
DECLARE @midup money, @middown money

--Compute near middle row
SET @rnval = ((SELECT COUNT(*) FROM dbo.vSTRow_Numbers)/2)

IF dbo.ufnIsOdd
    ((SELECT COUNT(*)
        FROM dbo.vSTRow_Numbers)) = 1
    --get mediam for odd count
    SET @MedianVal = (SELECT SubTotal
    FROM dbo.vSTRow_Numbers
    WHERE rn = @rnval + 1)
ELSE
BEGIN
    --compute mediam for even count
    SET @midup =
        (SELECT SubTotal
            FROM dbo.vSTRow_Numbers
            WHERE rn = @rnval)
    SET @middown =
        (SELECT SubTotal
            FROM dbo.vSTRow_Numbers
            WHERE rn = (SELECT @rnval + 1))
    SET @MedianVal =
        (SELECT (@midup + @middown)/2)
END
GO
```

An EXEC statement can recover the output parameter that contains the median value from the usp_MedianSubTotal stored procedure. A subsequent SELECT statement displays the median value. The following listing shows the EXEC statement and the SELECT statement along with a DECLARE statement for the local variable (@MedValue) that holds the median value returned as an output parameter. The listing concludes by displaying the median value (782.99) for the SubTotal column value series.

```
DECLARE @MedValue money

EXEC usp_MedianSubTotal @MedianVal = @MedValue OUTPUT

SELECT @MedValue 'Median value'
GO
```

```
Median value
--------------------
782.99
```

Processing Return Status Values

Return status values serve as a kind of specialized output parameter. A stored procedure assigns a value to its return status just before exiting with a RETURN statement. Remember that a RETURN statement signals an end to the stored procedure and return of control to the line after the statement that invoked the stored procedure. A stored procedure can have multiple RETURN statements, a property that allows you to signal an exit from a stored procedure at different places. By adding an int value after the RETURN keyword, you can pass an integer back to the statement following the line that called the stored procedure. This is the return status value. The sample code for this section is in StoredProcReturnStatusValues.sql.

■Tip If you do not assign a return status value with a RETURN statement within a stored procedure, the default return status value is 0.

You recover a return status value in an EXEC statement for a stored procedure differently than an output parameter. To do so, you assign the stored procedure to a local variable within the EXEC statement. This local variable makes the return status value from the stored procedure available for subsequent use within the code block calling the stored procedure.

The following CREATE PROCEDURE statement illustrates the design of a stored procedure named usp_SalesPersonReport that returns a result set, an output parameter, and a return status value.

- The output parameter is called @BestSalesPerson. This output parameter holds the full name of the sales person with the highest year-to-date sales.

- The SET statement appearing immediately after the AS keyword assigns a value to the output parameter based on a SELECT statement with a subquery that finds the sales person with the highest SalesYTD column value.

- Next, a SELECT statement designs a result set for the usp_SalesPersonReport stored procedure to return to its calling code block.

- Finally, an IF statement specifies a return status value of 1 or 0.

  - The return status value is 1 if the SalesYTD column value is greater than the SalesLastYear column value for the best sales person.

  - Otherwise, the return status value is 0.

```
CREATE PROC usp_SalesPersonReport
@BestSalesPerson nvarchar(150) OUTPUT
AS

SET @BestSalesPerson = (SELECT REPLACE(FirstName + ' ' +
    ISNULL(MiddleName, '') + ' ' + LastName, '  ', ' ')
    FROM Sales.VSalesPerson
    WHERE SalesYTD =
    (SELECT MAX(SalesYTD) FROM Sales.VSalesPerson))

SELECT SalesPersonID, FirstName, MiddleName,
    LastName, SalesYTD
FROM Sales.VSalesPerson

IF (SELECT SalesYTD
    FROM Sales.VSalesPerson
    WHERE SalesYTD = (SELECT MAX(SalesYTD)
```

```
        FROM Sales.VSalesPerson)) >
        (SELECT SalesLastYear
        FROM Sales.VSalesPerson
        WHERE SalesYTD =
        (SELECT MAX(SalesYTD)
        FROM Sales.VSalesPerson))
        RETURN 1
    ELSE
        RETURN 0
    GO
```

The next listing shows the code for extracting the result set, output parameter, and return status value from the usp_SalesPersonReport stored procedure.

- The DECLARE statement makes instances of two local variables: @BestName for the stored procedure's output parameter, and @rsval for the return status value.

- The EXEC statement shows the syntax for assigning the return status value from the stored procedure to the @rsval local variable.

- An IF...ELSE statement after the EXEC statement for the stored procedure branches to one of two SELECT statements depending on the value in @rsval. This SELECT statement specifies the name of the best sales person and whether that sales person exceeds last year's sales this year.

- The output after the code shows the result set for all sales persons and the output from the SELECT statement branched to by the IF statement. Because any result set from a stored procedure always returns before output parameters and return status values, the result with the SalesYTD column values for all sales persons appears before the output for the best sales person, including their name and whether their sales this year exceeded their sales last year.

```
DECLARE @BestName nvarchar(150), @rsval int

EXEC @rsval = usp_SalesPersonReport
    @BestSalesPerson = @BestName OUTPUT

IF @rsval = 1
    SELECT @BestName  'Best sales person is:',
        'Yes' 'Exceeded last year:'
ELSE
    SELECT @BestName  'Best sales person is:',
        'No' 'Exceeded last year:'
```

SalesPersonID	FirstName	MiddleName	LastName	SalesYTD
268	Stephen	Y	Jiang	677558.4653
275	Michael	G	Blythe	4557045.0459
276	Linda	C	Mitchell	5200475.2313
277	Jillian	NULL	Carson	3857163.6332
278	Garrett	R	Vargas	1764938.9859
279	Tsvi	Michael	Reiter	2811012.7151
280	Pamela	O	Ansman-Wolfe	0.00
281	Shu	K	Ito	3018725.4858
282	José	Edvaldo	Saraiva	3189356.2465
283	David	R	Campbell	3587378.4257
284	Amy	E	Alberts	636440.251
285	Jae	B	Pak	5015682.3752

```
286       Ranjit   R      Varkey Chudukatil 3827950.238
287       Tete     A      Mensa-Annan       1931620.1835
288       Syed     E      Abbas             219088.8836
289       Rachel   B      Valdez            2241204.0424
290       Lynn     N      Tsoflias          1758385.926


Best sales person is: Exceeded last year:
--------------------- -------------------
Linda C Mitchell      Yes
```

Performing Data Manipulation

Data manipulation—sometimes called data modification—can be implemented via Data Manipulation Language (DML). Data manipulation lets you add to, change, and delete the values in a database. This section drills down on how to perform data manipulation via stored procedures—and especially with input parameters. For example, you can insert multiple rows into a table by rerunning a stored procedure with an INSERT statement. During each invocation of the stored procedure, you can submit different input parameters for the column values of a new row. This section also introduces you to bulk insert techniques that offer advanced features for transferring large quantities of data into SQL Server Express.

■Tip Use stored procedures with parameters to dramatically simplify data manipulation tasks.

To build on what you already know and still give you some feel for the complexity that you can encounter in your own data manipulation tasks, this section draws on the ProSSEAppsCh07 database. Recall from the "Performing Data Modification with a View" section in this chapter that this database contains three tables. Two of the tables, Students and Classes, are in a many-to-many relationship. A third table, ClassGrades, unites the other two tables. You can create this database and populate its tables with some initial values by running the script in ViewsForDataModification-SampleDB.sql.

■Note Even if you built the ProSSEAppsCh07 database earlier in this chapter, you should create a fresh copy of the database for this section. Run the script in ViewsForDataModificationSampleDB.sql to reinitialize the ProSSEAppsCh07 database.

Recall that the section in which you modified data through views used the StudentGrades view to change data in the ProSSEAppsCh07 database. This section also uses the StudentGrades view for some samples to help you appreciate the advantages of using input parameters for stored procedures over using T-SQL's native INSERT, UPDATE, and DELETE statements without input parameters. You can learn more about the StudentGrades view in the "Creating a View for the Classes, Class-Grades, and Students Tables" section. For your convenience, the file with the samples for this section, StoredProcsForDataModification.sql, starts by recreating the StudentGrades view in the ProSSEAppsCh07 database.

Adding a New Row

You can use the StudentGrades view to add new rows to some of its underlying tables. Whenever a change affects just one underlying table, such as the Classes table for the StudentGrades view, an attempt to change the table through the view will succeed. The main advantage of using a stored procedure to add a new row to an underlying table for a view is that all a user needs to do is specify the column values for the new row. There is no need to designate the data source or properly specify the INSERT statement syntax.

The following script shows a stored procedure named usp_AddClass that can add a row to the Classes table for a new class. The stored procedure requires two input parameters—one for each of the columns in the Classes table. The body of the stored procedure contains an INSERT statement that adds a row to the Classes table through the StudentGrades view. The VALUES clause of the INSERT statement uses the two input parameters as arguments. Therefore, users can specify the ClassID and ClassTitle column values for a new row in the Classes table by specifying these values as input parameters for the usp_AddClass stored procedure.

```
CREATE PROC usp_AddClass
@ClassIDval int,
@ClassTitleval varchar(50)
AS
INSERT dbo.StudentGrades (ClassID, ClassTitle)
    VALUES (@ClassIDval, @ClassTitleval)
GO
```

One obvious way to test this stored procedure is to perform a SELECT statement for the column values in the Classes table before and after adding a new row to the Classes table through the stored procedure. The following listing shows the syntax for this test along with the resulting output.

- The initial SELECT statement returns the original classes in the Classes table.

- The EXEC statement shows the syntax for adding a new row to the Classes table through the usp_AddClass stored procedure. The two input parameter values are for the ClassID and the ClassTitle column values.

- The ending SELECT statement shows the column values in the Classes table after the stored procedure has inserted a new row. The output from this SELECT statement confirms the operation of the usp_AddClass stored procedure.

```
SELECT ClassID, ClassTitle
FROM Classes
GO

EXEC usp_AddClass 2, 'Learning Visual Basic Express for DBAs'
GO

SELECT ClassID, ClassTitle
FROM Classes
GO
```

```
ClassID     ClassTitle
-----------  -------------------------------------
1           Learning SQL Server Express
999         Biographies of Jesus Christ
```

```
ClassID      ClassTitle
-----------  ---------------------------------------
1            Learning SQL Server Express
2            Learning Visual Basic Express for DBAs
999          Biographies of Jesus Christ
```

You may have noticed that the stored procedure adds a new row to the Classes table through the StudentGrades view, but the preceding demonstration did not look for the new row in the StudentGrades view. The reason for this is that the view will not show the new row in the Classes table until the ClassGrades table has at least one row for the newly added class. The inner join between Classes and ClassGrades enforces the requirement. The following SELECT statement and its output confirm that the new class added to the Classes table does not appear in the StudentGrades view.

```
SELECT DISTINCT ClassID, ClassTitle
FROM dbo.StudentGrades
ORDER BY ClassID
GO
```

```
ClassID      ClassTitle
-----------  ---------------------------------------
1            Learning SQL Server Express
999          Biographies of Jesus Christ
```

By adding rows to the ClassGrades table for the Learning Visual Basic Express for DBAs class, a SELECT statement for ClassID and ClassTitle column values in the StudentGrades view will show the new class. The ClassGrades table has three columns: ClassID, StudentID, and GradeLetter. Therefore, by inserting new values for these columns through the ClassGrades table, a stored procedure can indirectly add new rows to the StudentGrades view. The following CREATE PROC statement specifies the usp_AddClassGrades stored procedure for this exact task.

- The stored procedure has three input parameters—one parameter for each column value in the ClassGrades table.

- The body of the CREATE PROC statement includes the INSERT statement.

- Like the CREATE PROC statement for usp_AddClass, the usp_AddClassGrades stored procedure is designed for simple reuse. Just invoke the stored procedure with a new set of column values to add a new row.

```
CREATE PROC usp_AddClassGrades
@ClassIDval int,
@StudentIDval int,
@Gradeletterval varchar(2)
AS
INSERT ClassGrades (ClassID, StudentID, Gradeletter)
    VALUES(@ClassIDval, @StudentIDval, @Gradeletterval)
GO
```

The next listing demonstrates the syntax for adding two new rows to the ClassGrades table through the usp_AddClassGrades stored procedure.

- The first parameter designates the ClassID. The ClassID column value for the Learning Visual Basic Express for DBAs class is 2.

- The second parameter is for the StudentID. The two students in the Students table have StudentID values of 1 for Poor DBA and 2 for Better DBA.

- The third parameter is GradeLetter. The student with a StudentID of 1 earns a B, and the student with a StudentID of 2 receives an A.

```
EXEC usp_AddClassGrades 2, 1, 'B'
EXEC usp_AddClassGrades 2, 2, 'A'
GO
```

The next SELECT statement and its result set confirm the success of the attempt to insert two new rows into the ClassGrades table and the associated StudentGrades view. You can see the two grades earned by students in the class with a ClassID of 2. By the way, this is the same class (the one with a ClassID of 2) that did not appear in the StudentGrades view before the addition of grades to the ClassGrades table.

```
SELECT FirstName, LastName, ClassID, Gradeletter
FROM dbo.StudentGrades
ORDER BY ClassID
GO
```

FirstName	LastName	ClassID	Gradeletter
Poor	DBA	1	C+
Better	DBA	1	A+
Poor	DBA	2	B
Better	DBA	2	A
Better	DBA	999	A

Updating a Column Value

Updating a column through a stored procedure delivers the same kind of benefits that inserting a new row does. Namely, you simplify the task through code that is easier to reuse. A common task when working with tables holding personal names is changing the last name of a person, such as for a student in the Students table of the ProSSEAppsCh07 database. This can happen when a student marries and changes their last name.

When you want to modify a column value, such as LastName, for a particular person, it is best to use a unique identifier, such as a primary key, to designate the row corresponding to a person. If you have a primary key based on a numeric value and you want to change the last name of a person, you'll need two input parameter values—one parameter to identify the row for the person and a second parameter for the new LastName column value. The CREATE PROC statement for the usp_UpdateLastName stored procedure illustrates this design.

- The @StudentIDval parameter points at the StudentID column in the Students table. This input parameter designates a specific table row by specifying a column value for the table's primary key (StudentID).

- The @NewLastNameval parameter specifies a new value for the LastName column in the row pointed at by the @StudentIDval parameter.

- The UPDATE statement applies the parameters to update a single column value in the Students table through the StudentGrades view. Recall that the Students table is one of the underlying tables for the StudentGrades view.

```
CREATE PROC usp_UpdateLastName
@StudentIDval int,
@NewLastNameval nvarchar(50)
AS
UPDATE dbo.StudentGrades
SET LastName = @NewLastNameval
WHERE StudentID = @StudentIDval
GO
```

The next listing includes three components that show how to use the usp_UpdateLastName stored procedure, and confirms its operation.

- The first component is the EXEC statement for the stored procedure. It specifies that the LastName column value for the student with a StudentID value of 2 should change to DBA-Minister.

- The second component is a SELECT statement that returns data from selected StudentGrades columns, including LastName.

- The last component is the result set from the SELECT statement. It confirms the operation of the usp_UpdateLastName stored procedure. Notice that the name for Better DBA changed to Better DBA-Minister.

```
EXEC usp_UpdateLastName 2,'DBA-Minister'
GO

SELECT FirstName, LastName, ClassID, Gradeletter
FROM dbo.StudentGrades
ORDER BY ClassID
GO
```

FirstName	LastName	ClassID	Gradeletter
Poor	DBA	1	C+
Better	DBA-Minister	1	A+
Poor	DBA	2	B
Better	DBA-Minister	2	A
Better	DBA-Minister	999	A

Deleting a Row in One Table with Related Rows in Another Table

Deleting a row can be more complicated than it may initially appear. This is especially true when there are foreign key constraints between tables. For example, you frequently cannot delete a row from one table if it orphans rows in another table.

In the case of the ProSSEAppsCh07 database, you cannot remove a row from the Classes table that has matching rows in the ClassGrades table. The relationship between the Classes and ClassGrades tables requires you to remove matching rows from ClassGrades before removing a row from Classes, which may frustrate an inexperienced user trying to remove a row from Classes that still has matching rows in ClassGrades. However, to help in this kind of situation you can write a stored procedure to automatically delete rows from the matching rows in ClassGrades before attempting to remove a row from Classes. If you also add an archiving capability to your stored procedure, you can recover from situations in which rows are inappropriately deleted from one or more tables.

Note See the "Archiving Changes to a Table with Triggers" section later in this chapter for an example of how to create an archiving capability into your applications.

Because the DELETE statement is so basic, it is very straightforward to build solutions that cascade from one table to another. Even while you may prefer to block cascading deletes generally, you may need to enable this feature for a selected user. By granting EXECUTE permission for a stored procedure to just one or some users, you can restrict access to deleting rows in the Classes table and any related tables, such as the ClassGrades table.

The following CREATE PROC statement creates a new stored procedure named usp_DeleteGradesClasses that deletes matching rows in ClassGrades before attempting to delete a row in the Classes table. The stored procedure requires a single input parameter, @ClassIDval, which identifies the row to delete from the Classes table along with any related rows from the ClassGrades table. The stored procedure has two DELETE statements within it.

- The first DELETE statement removes matching rows from the ClassGrades table for the row that you want to delete from the Classes table.

- The second DELETE statement removes the target row from the Classes table.

- The order of the DELETE statements is critical for operating within the foreign key constraints between the ClassGrades and Classes tables.

```
CREATE PROC usp_DeleteGradesClasses
@ClassIDval int
AS
DELETE FROM ClassGrades
    WHERE ClassID = @ClassIDval
DELETE FROM Classes
    WHERE ClassID = @ClassIDval
GO
```

The following listing shows the syntax for invoking usp_DeleteGradesClasses to remove the class with a ClassID column value of 2. As you can see, the syntax is very straightforward—just follow the stored procedure name with the ClassID column value for the class that you want to remove. This simple action removes a row from the Classes table after first deleting matching rows from the ClassGrades table.

A subsequent SELECT statement and its result set confirm the operation of the usp_DeleteGradesClasses stored procedure. Notice that the StudentGrades view returns just three rows, instead of the five rows that were previously returned by the view. The missing two rows both have a ClassID value of 2.

```
EXEC usp_DeleteGradesClasses 2
GO

SELECT FirstName, LastName, ClassID, Gradeletter
FROM dbo.StudentGrades
ORDER BY ClassID
GO
```

```
FirstName LastName      ClassID     Gradeletter
--------- ------------  ----------  -----------
Poor      DBA           1           C+
Better    DBA-Minister  1           A+
Better    DBA-Minister  999         A
```

Performing Bulk Inserts

It is sometimes necessary to copy large quantities of data from an external file into a SQL Server Express table or view. The T-SQL BULK INSERT statement is optimized for this precise task. However, the BULK INSERT statement has a higher level of security and more exacting requirements surrounding its use than an INSERT statement.

The BULK INSERT statement offers a couple of key advantages over traditional data manipulation statements.

- First, it can bypass the insertion of data in a database's log file, which can increase performance. As the number of rows to insert grows, this performance enhancement becomes more significant.

- Second, you can accept data into a SQL Server table or view from a text file. There is no need for a live connection to another database on a different server. It is frequently relatively easy to export data from data storage systems in text format. Therefore, being able to import from a text file provides the capability to receive data from a very wide range of data storage systems.

The advantages of the BULK INSERT statement are partially offset by restrictions and rules associated with its use.

- Limited permission is available to run the BULK INSERT statement. You have to be a member of the sysadmin or bulkadmin fixed server role to invoke the statement.

- The user of the BULK INSERT statement must have read access to the source text file. This may involve copying a text file from its original source, though an ideal situation is one in which the source text file is on the same computer as the server, because this optimizes performance.

- It can be tedious to properly format the arguments for a BULK INSERT statement. If you have a repetitive requirement for importing many rows, the effort to perfect the argument list for the statement will be worth it. The sample in this section uses tab-delimited data, but you can adapt the BULK INSERT statement for use with files containing data in CSV and fixed-width formats.

A related option is to use the bcp command-line utility, which can both import and export large quantities of data. As its name implies, the BULK INSERT statement only imports data.

By default, the BULK INSERT statement will import data with tabs delimiting column values and linefeeds delimiting rows. Formatting your input data file in this fashion allows you to take advantage of default argument values for the BULK INSERT statement that simplify its use. The NewClasses.txt sample file has the default format. Figure 7-1 illustrates the look of this format inside the Notepad utility. As you can see, there are two new rows for the Classes table, with ClassID column values of 2 and 3.

Figure 7-1. *The default sample format used by the BULK INSERT sample for inserting two new rows into the Classes table*

If you create your input file for the BULK INSERT statement in the default format, you can specify as few as two arguments for the statement.

- The BULK INSERT statement's first argument is the name of the target table or view to which data will be copied.
- Next, specify the FROM keyword, and then the path and file name for the text file that contains the data that you want to import.

The following CREATE PROC statement for the usp_BULKINSERT stored procedure shows the syntax for a BULK INSERT statement that will insert data from the NewClasses.txt file into the Classes table within the ProSSEAppsCh07 database.

```
CREATE PROC usp_BULKINSERT
AS
BULK INSERT Classes FROM "c:\NewClasses.txt"
GO
```

After you have the stored procedure created, you can invoke it with an EXEC statement. In this very basic example, there is no need for any arguments.

```
EXEC usp_BULKINSERT
GO
```

As basic as this demonstration is, the usual process is to perfect the BULK INSERT statement and then wrap it in a stored procedure to simplify its use. Some usual steps to perfect a BULK INSERT can include the following:

- Getting the data file in the right format, such as the default BULK INSERT format
- Making sure that the user of the stored procedure with the BULK INSERT statement has permission to invoke the statement
- Making sure the user has read access to the input data file
- Developing BULK INSERT arguments that conform to a data file's format if it's not convenient to use the default BULK INSERT format

The following SELECT statement and result set show the outcome of running the usp_BULKINSERT stored procedure. The procedure adds two new rows to the Classes table. This very simple example confirms the kind of value you can derive from learning more about the BULK INSERT statement or even the bcp utility.

```
SELECT * FROM Classes
GO
```

ClassID	ClassTitle
1	Learning SQL Server Express
2	Learning Visual Basic Express for DBAs
3	Learning Visual Web Developer Express for DBAs
999	Biographies of Jesus Christ

Creating and Using Triggers

A trigger is like an event procedure. Depending on its type, a trigger can fire just before or just after an event, such as the insertion of a new row into a table. SQL Server Express enables DML and DDL (Data Definition Language) triggers.

- DML triggers fire in response to INSERT, UPDATE, and DELETE statements. You can use DML triggers to monitor changes to a database and enforce business rules dictating what kinds of changes are permissible on the values in a database.

- DDL triggers operate in response to DDL statements that begin with CREATE, DROP, and ALTER, such as CREATE PROCEDURE. DDL triggers permit an application to track operations that affect the database objects, as opposed to the data values, in a database.

Most SQL Server Express instances will have an individual administrator who controls the rules for creating, modifying, and dropping database objects, as well as when to deviate from those rules. Other SQL Server 2005 editions are much more likely to serve teams of users with multiple members having database creation capabilities. As a result, DDL triggers are best suited for other SQL Server 2005 editions.

On the other hand, SQL Server Express database applications are much more likely to require the capabilities of DML triggers because the need to add, modify, and delete data is much more common than the need to add, modify, and drop database objects. Therefore, this section devotes no further attention to DDL triggers. Instead, the remaining focus is on DML triggers.

There are two types of DML triggers.

- AFTER triggers fire after an operation, such as when an INSERT, UPDATE, or DELETE statement operates. The data manipulation event occurs within a transaction that you can roll back from within an AFTER trigger.

    - An AFTER trigger applies exclusively to table database objects.

    - You can have multiple triggers for the same type of event associated with an individual table.

- INSTEAD OF triggers fire instead of an INSERT, UPDATE, or DELETE statement. This type of trigger fires before—instead of after—a data manipulation statement. There is no need to roll back a change with an INSTEAD OF trigger. You can just omit making the change specified by the statement that fired the trigger.

    - INSTEAD OF triggers can apply to views as well as tables.

    - You can have only one INSTEAD OF trigger for a type of event with a database object.

A trigger is a database object that contains T-SQL code in a way similar to a stored procedure. Therefore, you can manage the life cycle of triggers with CREATE TRIGGER and DROP TRIGGER statements. You can also modify triggers with ALTER TRIGGER statements. Triggers can act as gateways to tables and views and enforce business rules for data that enters a database through those objects. If you need to temporarily suspend the operation of business rules enforced by a trigger, you can invoke a DISABLE TRIGGER statement. Later, you can restore the business rules with an ENABLE TRIGGER statement.

Two temporary tables are associated with each of the two types of DML triggers. These two tables have the names inserted and deleted.

- INSERT statements populate the inserted table.
- DELETE statements populate the deleted table.
- UPDATE statements populate both the inserted and deleted tables. New column values are in the inserted table, and old column values are in the deleted table.

You can use the inserted and deleted tables inside triggers for the following:

- Assessing whether business rules are followed
- Completing and refining actions associated with a DML statement
- Building custom archiving solutions for changes to a table or view

Learning to Reference Inserted and Deleted Tables

Understanding how to use the inserted and deleted tables is critical for the effective use of triggers. Therefore, the coverage of triggers commences with a demonstration that shows how to populate these tables with values and how to recover values from the tables. You populate the inserted and deleted tables with values by invoking DML statements that generate values for the tables. You can read values from the inserted and deleted tables with a SELECT statement inside a trigger.

The samples in this section and the next two sections reside in Triggers.sql. The samples for the fourth section on triggers reside in TriggerForView.sql. If you are going to run any of the sample code for triggers, you should first refresh the ProSSEAppsCh07 database by running the script in ViewForDataModificationSampleDB.sql.

Before you can use a trigger you must create one. As with any database object, it is always wise to check for the existence of a previous object of the same type with the name of the new object that you want to create. The following T-SQL statement uses sys.objects and sys.schemas to check for an existing instance of a trigger named trStudentsEcho in the dbo schema. If the trigger exists, a DROP TRIGGER statement removes it.

```
IF EXISTS(SELECT *
    FROM sys.objects o JOIN sys.schemas s
    ON o.schema_id = s.schema_id
    WHERE type = 'TR' AND
    s.name = 'dbo' AND
    o.name = 'trStudentsEcho')
    DROP TRIGGER trStudentsEcho
GO
```

The following CREATE TRIGGER statement for the trStudentsEcho trigger demonstrates some basic syntax for specifying an AFTER trigger. The specification of a trigger in the header section of a CREATE TRIGGER statement tells you a lot about what it does.

- The ON clause designates the object to which a trigger applies. In the following example, the trigger applies to the Students table in the current database context. A prior USE statement set this context to the ProSSEAppsCh07 database.
- The FOR clause designates the type of trigger (FOR indicates this is an AFTER trigger) as well as the types of events to which the trigger applies. The following code sample applies to UPDATE, INSERT, and DELETE statements that reference the Students table. You can designate a trigger for any combination of one, two, or three of these statements.

The body of the trigger starts immediately after the AS keyword. The body of a trigger can often be complex—though, in general, it will be as complex as necessary for the business rules and other tasks that it implements. This initial trigger sample merely displays the contents of the inserted and deleted tables. The contents of these tables will be displayed whenever an INSERT, UPDATE, or DELETE statement operates on the Students table in the ProSSEAppsCh07 database.

```
CREATE TRIGGER trStudentsEcho
ON Students
FOR UPDATE, INSERT, DELETE
AS
SELECT * FROM inserted
SELECT * FROM deleted
GO
```

The trStudentsEcho trigger fires in response to DML statements for the Students table. After each type of statement, you can see the contents of the inserted table followed by the contents of the deleted table. The following T-SQL statements display a heading (with Before INSERT) before invoking the INSERT statement to add a new student named Rick Dobson with a StudentID of 3 to the Students table.

- After the INSERT statement completes, the trStudentsEcho trigger fires and displays the contents of the inserted table followed by the contents of the deleted table.

- The first row of output shows the data added to the inserted table by the INSERT statement.

- The last row displays the data in the deleted table. This row is empty because an INSERT statement does not populate the deleted table.

```
SELECT 'Before INSERT'
INSERT Students (StudentID, FirstName, LastName)
    VALUES (3, 'Rick', 'Dobson')
```

```
-------------
Before INSERT

StudentID    FirstName LastName  FullName
-----------  --------- --------- -------------------
3            Rick      Dobson    Rick Dobson

StudentID    FirstName LastName  FullName
-----------  --------- --------- -------------------
```

The next two T-SQL statements illustrate the impact of an UPDATE statement on the inserted and deleted tables. In this case, the heading for the output is Before UPDATE. An UPDATE statement populates both the inserted and deleted tables. The new column values are in the inserted table. Notice that Rickie is the FirstName column value in the output for the inserted table. The old column values (the ones being updated) are in the deleted table. The FirstName column value being replaced (Rick) is in the deleted table.

```
SELECT 'Before UPDATE'
UPDATE Students
SET FirstName = 'Rickie'
WHERE StudentID = 3
```

```
-------------
Before UPDATE

StudentID   FirstName LastName  FullName
----------- --------- --------- -------------------
3           Rickie    Dobson    Rickie Dobson

StudentID   FirstName LastName  FullName
----------- --------- --------- -------------------
3           Rick      Dobson    Rick Dobson
```

The last two T-SQL statements for this demonstration show the impact of the DELETE statement on the inserted and deleted tables. Because the DELETE statement only adds content to the deleted table, the inserted table is empty. The deleted table contains the column values for the student with a StudentID column value of 3.

```
SELECT 'Before DELETE'
DELETE FROM Students WHERE StudentID = 3
```

```
-------------
Before DELETE

StudentID   FirstName LastName  FullName
----------- --------- --------- -------------------

StudentID   FirstName LastName  FullName
----------- --------- --------- -------------------
3           Rickie    Dobson    Rickie Dobson
```

Rolling Back in an AFTER Trigger

Just because you invoke a DML statement and an AFTER trigger fires, it doesn't mean that a change has to be committed to a table. For example, you can implement a ROLLBACK statement inside the trigger. Whenever you create a trigger for a statement, any change associated with the statement occurs within a transaction. The transaction commits when the trigger closes normally without any special events. One special event is the execution of a ROLLBACK statement within a trigger. Special events are normally highly customized for an application's context. For example, you might forbid updates of a column value unless a user belongs to a special role that gives them permission to change a column value, such as allowing a manager to change a register value, but not allowing a clerk to change the same value.

The ability to roll back a transaction is not new to T-SQL. While you could do this in earlier versions of SQL Server, there is a change to how you roll back a DML statement and continue the normal operation of a database application that may be confusing to those who are familiar with the feature from earlier SQL Server versions. The good news is that if you are learning how to roll back a DML statement for the first time, you have nothing to unlearn.

The CREATE TRIGGER statement for the trStudents_Insert_Rollback trigger illustrates the syntax for specifying the rollback of a DML statement. This trigger is for an INSERT statement on the Students table, but the same syntax applies to UPDATE and DELETE statements as well. The use of the TRAN keyword, which is an abbreviation for TRANSACTION, is optional. The PRINT statement provides feedback from the trigger. If control passes to the PRINT statement, then you know that the ROLLBACK statement did not cause the trigger to cease operating.

Note It is possible for the use of triggers to become substantially more complex if you nest triggers within one another. Many explanations of triggers, including the coverage in Books Online for SQL Server 2005, focus heavily on nested triggers. However, it is not necessary to use nested triggers to roll back DML statements. Therefore, this presentation does not focus on nested triggers.

```
CREATE TRIGGER trStudents_Insert_Rollback
ON Students
FOR INSERT
AS
ROLLBACK TRAN
PRINT 'INSERT statement rolled back.'
GO
```

If you have a trigger with a ROLLBACK statement within it, you are likely to want to bypass the trigger at least some of the time, such as for a certain user or users with special permission to modify the table. Instead of dropping and recreating the trigger, you can temporarily disable a trigger. You can then enable the trigger to enforce the no-changes rule after your special-handling scenario is over.

The following DISABLE TRIGGER statement shows how to temporarily disable a trigger. The capability to disable a trigger outside of an ALTER TABLE statement is a new capability introduced for all SQL Server 2005 editions, including SQL Server Express. The DISABLE TRIGGER statement takes the name of the trigger and the name of the table as arguments. The name of the table appears in an ON clause within the DISABLE TRIGGER statement.

The T-SQL batch starting with DISABLE TRIGGER includes four additional statements. The output from the statements appears following the GO keyword that executes the batch. The point of showing the output is to demonstrate that the INSERT statement works by adding a row to the Students table.

```
DISABLE TRIGGER trStudents_Insert_Rollback ON Students
SELECT * FROM Students
INSERT Students (StudentID, FirstName, LastName)
    VALUES (3, 'Rick', 'Dobson')
SELECT * FROM Students
DELETE FROM Students WHERE StudentID = 3
GO
```

StudentID	FirstName	LastName	FullName
1	Poor	DBA	Poor DBA
2	Better	DBA	Better DBA

StudentID	FirstName	LastName	FullName
1	Poor	DBA	Poor DBA
2	Better	DBA	Better DBA
3	Rick	Dobson	Rick Dobson

The next script sample starts with an ENABLE TRIGGER statement. This statement reimposes the operation of the trStudents_Insert_Rollback trigger with its ROLLBACK statement. When the INSERT statement in the following script passes control to the trigger, the trigger rolls back the transaction and aborts the batch—that is, the trigger concludes normally, but the batch invoking the trigger via an INSERT statement aborts abnormally. This is why the following code segment includes two GO keywords. The second GO keyword restarts the code after the trigger containing the ROLLBACK statement aborts the batch. The second SELECT statement confirms that no new row was added to the Students table.

■**Note** The syntax for the ROLLBACK statement is the same as in preceding versions of SQL Server—however, prior versions of SQL Server did not abort a batch after a ROLLBACK statement.

```
ENABLE TRIGGER trStudents_Insert_Rollback ON Students
SELECT * FROM Students
INSERT Students (StudentID, FirstName, LastName)
    VALUES (3, 'Rick', 'Dobson')
GO
SELECT * FROM Students
GO
```

```
StudentID   FirstName LastName  FullName
----------- --------- --------- ------------------
1           Poor      DBA       Poor DBA
2           Better    DBA       Better DBA
```

```
INSERT statement rolled back.
Msg 3609, Level 16, State 1, Line 7
The transaction ended in the trigger. The batch has been aborted.
```

```
StudentID   FirstName LastName  FullName
----------- --------- --------- ------------------
1           Poor      DBA       Poor DBA
2           Better    DBA       Better DBA
```

Archiving Changes to a Table with Triggers

One common application requirement is to monitor the changes to one or more tables in a database. Triggers offer a convenient vehicle for constructing this kind of solution. In the following example, you'll use two tables and three triggers.

- The first table is the Students table in the ProSSEAppsCh07 database. This is a resource table that gets monitored. You can replace the Students table in the sample application with any target resource table that your needs dictate.

- The second table is an archive table. The sample solution stores the changes to the Students table in the archive table. By reviewing the contents of the archive table, you can tell what changes were made in which order to the Students table (or any other resource table that you are monitoring with a variation of this sample). The archive table must have a pair of columns for each column in the original resource table that you are monitoring.

- One column in each pair is for the new column value in the resource table.

- The other column in each pair is for the original or deleted column value in the resource table.

- You may want several additional columns in the archive table to capture other items of interest, such as when a change occurred, what type of change was made, or which user made the change.

- You also need three triggers—one each for the INSERT, UPDATE, and DELETE statements that operate on the resource table. The main purpose of these triggers is updating the archive table with values from the inserted and deleted tables. You can also use the triggers to enforce business rules.

  - The INSERT trigger fires after the insertion of a new row. It transfers values from the inserted table to the archive table.

  - The DELETE trigger fires after the deletion of a row. It also copies values to the archive table, but its source table is the deleted table.

  - The UPDATE trigger is an INSTEAD OF trigger that copies values from the inserted and deleted tables to the archive table. In this example solution, this trigger allows changes to the FirstName and LastName column values, but it blocks changes to StudentID column values.

Setting up the Archive Solution

As mentioned previously, this sample application uses the Students table from the ProSSEAppsCh07 database as the resource table. The sample relies heavily on triggers, but it assumes that only the three triggers that follow are in the database. If you have worked on any prior samples that use the ProSSEAppsCh07 database, your current copy may have other triggers. Therefore, your first step should be to run the script in the ViewForDataModificationSampleDB.sql file. This will create a fresh copy of the ProSSEAppsCh07 database with no triggers for the Students table.

The following CREATE TABLE statement defines the columns of the archive table, which has the name StudentsArchive in the sample application.

- The AID column serves as the table's primary key. This column has an IDENTITY property setting.

- The type column is an nvarchar variable with up to six characters. The values for this column are INSERT, UPDATE, or DELETE.

- The whenchanged column has a default value that assigns the current date and time as a smalldatetime value.

- The table has one column, named StudentID, for recording StudentID column values. Only one column is required for StudentID column values because a business rule prevents users from changing this column in the original resource table.

- The FirstName and LastName column values each have two corresponding columns in the archive table.

  - Column names starting with the letter n are for values from the inserted table.

  - Column names starting with the letter o are for values from the deleted table.

```
CREATE TABLE StudentsArchive (
AID int IDENTITY(1,1) PRIMARY KEY CLUSTERED,
type nvarchar(6) NOT NULL,
whenchanged smalldatetime NOT NULL DEFAULT Getdate(),
```

```
    StudentID int,
    nFirstName nvarchar(30),
    nLastName nvarchar(50),
    oFirstName nvarchar(30),
    oLastName nvarchar(50)
    )
    GO
```

The INSERT trigger, which is an AFTER trigger, is called trStudents_INSERT. After the addition of a new row to the Students table, this trigger pumps values to the StudentsArchive table from the inserted table. The trigger uses three local variables, @StudentID, @FirstName, and @LastName, to store values from the inserted table and represent those values for insertion into the StudentsArchive table. The INSERT statement for the StudentsArchive table specifies a constant nvarchar value of INSERT for the type column.

```
CREATE TRIGGER trStudents_INSERT
ON Students
FOR INSERT
AS
DECLARE @StudentID int, @FirstName nvarchar(30),
    @LasName nvarchar(50)

SET @StudentID = (SELECT StudentID FROM inserted)
SET @FirstName = (SELECT FirstName FROM inserted)
SET @LasName = (SELECT LastName FROM inserted)
INSERT StudentsArchive (type, StudentID, nFirstName,
    nLastName)
    VALUES('INSERT', @StudentID, @FirstName, @LasName)
GO
```

The DELETE trigger is called trStudents_DELETE. This trigger is also an AFTER trigger and has a parallel design to trStudents_INSERT. The trStudents_DELETE trigger uses three local variables with the same names as in the trStudents_INSERT trigger to copy values to the StudentsArchive table. Instead of copying the @FirstName and @LastName local variables to the nFirstName and nLastName column values in the StudentsArchive table, this trigger copies its local variable values for FirstName and LastName column values to the oFirstName and oLastName column values in the StudentsArchive table. In addition, the nvarchar constant value for type is DELETE instead of INSERT.

```
CREATE TRIGGER trStudents_DELETE
ON Students
FOR DELETE
AS
DECLARE @StudentID int, @FirstName nvarchar(30),
    @LasName nvarchar(50)

SET @StudentID = (SELECT StudentID FROM deleted)
SET @FirstName = (SELECT FirstName FROM deleted)
SET @LasName = (SELECT LastName FROM deleted)
INSERT StudentsArchive (type, StudentID, oFirstName,
    oLastName)
    VALUES('DELETE', @StudentID, @FirstName, @LasName)
GO
```

The UPDATE trigger is radically different than both the INSERT and DELETE triggers. The UPDATE trigger, whose name is trStudents_UPDATE, is an INSTEAD OF trigger, rather than an AFTER trigger. This UPDATE trigger performs archiving and enforces a business rule blocking changes to StudentID column values. The use of an INSTEAD OF trigger makes it relatively easy to prevent a change in the Students table when a user attempts to make a change to a StudentID column value.

- This trigger uses five local variables to track StudentID column values and FirstName and LastName column values before and after a change.

- After declaring its local variables, the trigger checks to see if the StudentID value after the update from the inserted table is different from the StudentID value before the update. If the two StudentID values are different, the application returns an information message with a RAISERROR function. By including the RAISERROR function in the IF clause of an IF…ELSE statement, the trigger either returns the message, or, if the old and new StudentID values are the same, processes the update.

- The ELSE clause of the IF…ELSE statement has more than one statement, so it contains them in a BEGIN…END block. Three things happen within the BEGIN…END block.

  - First, the code populates the trigger's local variables from inserted and deleted column values.

  - Second, an UPDATE statement revises the FirstName and LastName column values for the StudentID row in the Students table with the local variables from the inserted table. Recall that an INSTEAD OF trigger happens instead of the change that fires the trigger. Therefore, if you want the change to take place, you have to program it. This disadvantage is offset by eliminating the need to roll back changes, as is sometimes necessary for AFTER triggers.

  - Third, an INSERT statement populates the StudentsArchive table with the local variable values. It also populates the type column with an nvarchar constant with a value of 'UPDATE'.

```
CREATE TRIGGER trStudents_UPDATE
ON Students
INSTEAD OF UPDATE
AS

DECLARE @StudentID int, @nFirstName nvarchar(30),
    @nLastName nvarchar(50), @oFirstName nvarchar(30),
    @oldLasName nvarchar(50)

IF (SELECT StudentID FROM inserted) <>
    (SELECT StudentID FROM deleted)
    RAISERROR ('You are not allowed to change StudentID.',
    10,1)
ELSE
BEGIN

--set local variables
    SET @StudentID = (SELECT StudentID FROM inserted)
    SET @nFirstName = (SELECT FirstName FROM inserted)
    SET @nLastName = (SELECT LastName FROM inserted)
    SET @oFirstName = (SELECT FirstName FROM deleted)
    SET @oldLasName = (SELECT LastName FROM deleted)

--write to table
    UPDATE Students
    SET FirstName = @nFirstName, LastName = @nLastName
    WHERE StudentID = @StudentID
```

```
-- write to archive
   INSERT StudentsArchive (type, StudentID, nFirstName,
       nLastName, oFirstName, oLastName)
       VALUES('UPDATE', @StudentID, @nFirstName, @nLastName,
       @oFirstName, @oldLasName)
END
GO
```

Demonstrating the Archive Solution

The main objective of the archive solution is to copy values from the inserted and deleted tables to the StudentsArchive table for changes in the Students table. This process creates an auditing trail for changes to a table. A secondary objective for the sample application is to enforce a business rule to disallow changes to StudentID column values in the Students table. Since the sample solution rejects an attempt to modify a StudentID column value, the StudentsArchive table should not update after such an attempt. After all, no change was made to the Students table.

■**Tip** In these times of heightened awareness of the need for accurate corporate reports, archiving changes to critical data sources is a valuable technique for assuring the validity of corporate reports.

The following script and result set show two T-SQL statements and an associated result set. The first statement inserts a new row into the Students table. As a result, the trStudents_INSERT trigger fires. This trigger adds a new row to the StudentsArchive table. The SELECT statement following the INSERT statement shows the new row in the StudentsArchive table. Notice the StudentID, nFirstName, and nLastName column values from the StudentsArchive table match arguments in the VALUES clause of the INSERT statement.

```
INSERT Students VALUES (3, 'Rickie', 'Hobson')
SELECT * FROM StudentsArchive
```

AID	type	whenchanged	StudentID	nFirstName	nLastName	oFirstName	oLastName
1	INSERT	May 28 2005 10:09PM	3	Rickie	Hobson	NULL	NULL

The next pair of T-SQL statements includes an UPDATE statement for the Students table followed by another SELECT statement for the StudentsArchive table. The second row in the StudentsArchive table reflects the changes made by the UPDATE statement. All columns in the row have non-null values. The new values specified for the FirstName and LastName column values in the UPDATE statement appear in the nFirstName and nLastName columns of the second row in the StudentsArchive table.

```
UPDATE Students
SET FirstName = 'Rick', LastName = 'Dobson'
WHERE StudentID = 3
SELECT * FROM StudentsArchive
```

AID	type	whenchanged	StudentID	nFirstName	nLastName	oFirstName	oLastName
1	INSERT	May 28 2005 10:09PM	3	Rickie	Hobson	NULL	NULL
2	UPDATE	May 28 2005 10:11PM	3	Rick	Dobson	Rickie	Hobson

The third pair of T-SQL statements highlights the operation of the business rule disallowing changes to StudentID column values. Notice the UPDATE statement attempts to modify the StudentID value of 3 to 999. However, the business rule in the trStudents_UPDATE trigger fails to implement the change. Since this trigger is an INSTEAD OF trigger, the trigger has to actually program the change for it to take effect. In addition to not carrying out the change, the trigger displays a brief message reminding the user that changes to StudentID column values are not allowed (this message is not shown in the following code). In addition to not modifying the Students table, the trigger does not change the StudentsArchive table. Therefore, the output from the SELECT statement matches the output from the preceding SELECT statement.

```
UPDATE Students
SET StudentID = 999
WHERE StudentID = 3
SELECT * FROM StudentsArchive
```

The final pair of T-SQL statements and the corresponding output from the SELECT statement illustrate the impact on the StudentsArchive table of a DELETE statement for the Students table. The following DELETE statement adds a third row to the StudentsArchive table through the trStudents_DELETE trigger. The nFirstName and nLastName columns have null values in the third row because a DELETE statement adds no new column values to a table. Although this is the fourth statement to attempt to change the Students table, the StudentsArchive table has just three rows because the third attempt failed by trying to modify a StudentID column value.

```
DELETE FROM Students WHERE StudentID = 3
SELECT * FROM StudentsArchive
```

AID	type	whenchanged	StudentID	nFirstName	nLastName	oFirstName	oLastName
1	INSERT	May 28 2005 10:09PM	3	Rickie	Hobson	NULL	NULL
2	UPDATE	May 28 2005 10:11PM	3	Rick	Dobson	Rickie	Hobson
3	DELETE	May 28 2005 10:13PM	3	NULL	NULL	Rick	Dobson

Using an INSTEAD OF Trigger with a View

The AFTER trigger type is appropriate for many scenarios. This type of trigger is especially convenient because you do not have to program changes if they are already valid (recall that the trigger does not fire until after the change is already made). However, AFTER triggers have their limitations. One significant limitation is that AFTER triggers apply only to tables. If your application needs to update a data source through a view, an INSTEAD OF trigger is your only option. This section demonstrates how to program an INSTEAD OF trigger that permits changes to two of the tables underlying a view.

Designing a Trigger That Performs Data Manipulation Through a View

The demonstration for this sample again works with the ProSSEAppsCh07 database. You should make a fresh copy of the database with the script in the ViewForDataModificationSampleDB.sql file if you want to run the sample code in this section. The sample also uses the familiar StudentGrades view. The code to create this view along with all other code from this section resides in the TriggerForView.sql file.

Although the StudentGrades view has been used in several previous sections, the code is shown here because it is so critical to the sample. As you can see, the view performs inner joins for the

Students, ClassGrades, and Classes tables in the ProSSEAppsCh07 database. Users can make changes to the Students and Classes tables through the view. However, users must still input valid entries when attempting to make a change to these tables. For example, users cannot input a new row to the Students table with a StudentID column value that already exists because this would generate a duplicate primary key value. For the same reason, users also cannot input a new row to the Classes table with a ClassID that already exists.

```
CREATE VIEW dbo.StudentGrades
AS
SELECT s.StudentID, s.FirstName, s.LastName, s.Fullname,
    c.ClassID, c.ClassTitle, cg.Gradeletter
FROM Classes c JOIN ClassGrades cg
ON c.ClassID = cg.ClassID
JOIN Students S
ON s.StudentID = cg.StudentID
GO
```

The trInsertClassStudentGrades trigger is an INSTEAD OF trigger for INSERT statements that reference the StudentGrades view. The trigger performs three main tasks.

- First, it checks INSERT statement data to make sure it is valid.

- Next, the trigger determines whether to implement an INSERT statement for the Students or Classes table through the StudentGrades view.

- Third, the trigger displays an informative message when the ClassID column value or the StudentID column value for a new row already exists in one of the underlying tables for the StudentGrades view.

Because the code in the trInsertClassStudentGrades trigger is longer than appropriate for a single listing, the trigger's presentation occurs through a series of code excerpts. The complete listing is in the TriggerForView.sql file.

After declaring a collection of local variables for use in the sample, the trigger's code assigns the ClassID and StudentID column values from the inserted table to the @ClassID and @StudentID local variables. If the inserted column value for ClassID is null because the user is attempting to enter a row in the Students table, the code assigns a null value to @ClassID. The code acts similarly for a StudentID column value in the inserted table and the @StudentID local variable.

```
SET @ClassID = (SELECT ClassID FROM inserted)
SET @StudentID = (SELECT StudentID FROM inserted)
```

Next, the code checks to see if the @ClassID local variable value already exists in the ClassID column of the Classes table or the @StudentID local variable value already exists in the StudentID column of the Students table. The value of the @ClassIDIn local variable is set to 1 if there is a match, or 0 otherwise. Again, the @StudentIDIn local variable follows a parallel pattern of being 1 if there is a match between the @StudentID local variable and a StudentID column value in the Students table, or 0 otherwise.

```
IF EXISTS(SELECT * FROM Classes WHERE ClassID = @ClassID)
    SET @ClassIDIn = 1
ELSE
    SET @ClassIDIn = 0

IF EXISTS(SELECT * FROM Students WHERE StudentID = @StudentID)
    SET @StudentIDIn = 1
ELSE
    SET @StudentIDIn = 0
```

Next, the trigger decides whether and how to handle an attempt to add a new row to the Classes table through the StudentGrades view.

- In order for an INSERT statement to add a row to the Classes table, there needs to be a non-null ClassID column value. In addition, if the attempt to add a new row is to succeed, the @ClassIDIn local variable should equal 0—that is, the ClassID for the new row should not already exist in the ClassID column of the Classes table. If both of these conditions are met, the trigger runs an INSERT statement against the StudentGrades view that will add a new row to the Classes table. Before running the INSERT statement, the trigger retrieves the ClassTitle column value from the inserted table.

- When the @ClassID local variable already exists in the ClassID column of the Classes table, the ELSE clause of the following excerpt displays an informative message about the nature of the problem.

```
IF @ClassIDIn = 0 and @ClassID IS NOT NULL
BEGIN
    SET @ClassTitle = (SELECT ClassTitle FROM inserted)
    INSERT dbo.StudentGrades (ClassID, ClassTitle)
        VALUES (@ClassID, @ClassTitle)
END
ELSE
    IF @ClassIDIn = 1
        RAISERROR ('ClassID already assigned.',10,1)
```

Corresponding, parallel code exists for the Students table in the trInsertClassStudentGrades trigger.

Demonstrating a Trigger That Performs Data Manipulation Through a View

The following code and output listing demonstrates an attempt to add a new row to the Students table through the StudentGrades view. SELECT statements before and after an INSERT statement monitor how the INSERT statement operates. As you can see, the new row is added to the Students table.

```
SELECT * FROM Students

INSERT dbo.StudentGrades (StudentID, FirstName, LastName)
    VALUES (3,'Virginia', 'Dobson')

SELECT * FROM Students
```

```
StudentID   FirstName LastName  FullName
----------- --------- --------- -------------------
1           Poor      DBA       Poor DBA
2           Better    DBA       Better DBA


StudentID   FirstName LastName  FullName
----------- --------- --------- -------------------
1           Poor      DBA       Poor DBA
2           Better    DBA       Better DBA
3           Virginia  Dobson    Virginia Dobson
```

The next sample attempts to add another new row to the Students table with the same StudentID as the preceding sample. Because this insertion attempt would generate a duplicate primary key value, the trigger does not try an INSERT statement. Instead, the trigger issues a warning message. The user can fix the problem by, for example, using a new StudentID column value, such as 4 rather than 3.

```
INSERT dbo.StudentGrades (StudentID, FirstName, LastName)
    VALUES (3,'Mary', 'Dobson')
```

The final code and output listing shows an attempt to add a new row to the Classes table through the StudentGrades view. The attempt succeeds because there is not an existing row in the Classes table with a ClassID column value of 2. The code within the trInsertClassStudentGrades trigger determines this and automatically runs the INSERT statement for the Classes table instead of the Students table.

```
SELECT * FROM Classes

INSERT dbo.StudentGrades (ClassID, ClassTitle)
    VALUES (2, 'Learning Visual Basic Express for DBAs')
GO

SELECT * FROM Classes
```

```
ClassID    ClassTitle
---------- --------------------------------------
1          Learning SQL Server Express
999        Biographies of Jesus Christ
```

```
ClassID    ClassTitle
---------- --------------------------------------
1          Learning SQL Server Express
2          Learning Visual Basic Express for DBAs
999        Biographies of Jesus Christ
```

Summary

This chapter provided coverage of database objects that encapsulate T-SQL code. In particular, you learned about four database objects: views, user-defined functions, stored procedures, and triggers. Selected applications for these database objects covered in this chapter included the following:

- Making available filtered, aggregated, and ordered virtual tables with views
- Returning meta data about database objects with views
- Performing data manipulation via views
- Providing custom, reusable expressions with user-defined functions
- Enabling "parametric views" through user-defined functions with input parameters
- Returning multiple result sets from a single database object with a stored procedure
- Making a stored procedure dynamic with input parameters

- Returning scalar values from stored procedures with output parameters and return status values
- Simplifying data manipulation with stored procedures
- Archiving changes to a table with triggers
- Enforcing business rules with triggers
- Managing data manipulation through a view via INSTEAD OF triggers

CHAPTER 8

■■■

Managing SQL Server Express Security

Security has always been a critical database application developer issue, but the growing activity of hackers and the extreme sensitivity of data in some databases escalates the importance of security as never before. SQL Server Express (SSE) extends traditional SQL Server security features and introduces new security technologies to secure your data in ways never before possible. Whether you manage departmental solutions or your data are available for access via an Internet connection, the content in this chapter is absolutely vital.

Overview of Security Concepts

The following are among the traditional security features available with SSE:

- SQL Server and Windows logins. The logins enable users to authenticate themselves (make a claim about who they are) to an SSE instance.
- SQL Server user accounts tied to logins grant database access.
- Fixed server roles and fixed database roles with preassigned permissions. These fixed roles allow you to simplify security management by simply assigning logins and users to fixed roles.
- The ability to grant, deny, and revoke permissions to users. GRANT, DENY, and REVOKE statements allow you to assign specific permissions to individual logins, users, and custom roles.
- The ability to assign permissions to users and custom roles has not changed, but the number of permissions has increased dramatically to make it more feasible to assign the minimum set of permissions.
- The ability to create custom roles with special sets of permissions; custom roles can simplify the management of permissions by setting up clusters of permissions to which you can add and drop users.

Selected new security features introduced with SSE include

- A reorganization of security elements into the following:
  - Principals: Entities that can perform actions on other things, such as create a database on a server or create a table on a database
  - Securables: Entities that are available for use by principals, such as tables, columns, and triggers
  - Permission: Actions that principals can perform on securables, such as create or drop a table from a database

- Execution contexts let one user write code that impersonates another user so that a third user with very limited permissions can still perform essential tasks; this new impersonation feature for custom code makes it more feasible than with prior SQL Server versions to assign very limited permissions to typical database users.

- Schemas serve as containers for other objects within a database. Unlike earlier SQL Server versions, user accounts do not own database objects. Instead, user accounts own schemas that contain database objects, such as tables, views, and stored procedures.

- The ability to create certificates, asymmetric keys, and symmetric keys facilitates encrypting and signing data. Even if hackers gain access to your SSE instance and falsely represent themselves as individuals authorized to view secure data, they still will not be able to view encrypted data.

Exploring and Creating Principals

A principal is an individual, group, role, or process that can make requests to SSE. A database solution can use a principal to request data from a data source or instruct a database object to perform a task, such as insert a row in a table. Data sources and database objects that can perform tasks are examples of securables; permissions enable principals to use securables.

Different types of principals can have different scopes, three of which are

- Windows-level principals, such a Windows local login, Windows domain login, or Windows group

- SQL Server–level principals, such as a SQL Server login or fixed server role

- Database-level principals, such as a database user or fixed database role

A principal can refer to an individual user or some entity associated with a group of users. Before an individual can access a database on a server instance, the individual must first gain access to the server instance. A login is a type of principal that can gain an individual access to a database server; before an individual can gain access to a server instance, the server instance must verify that the individual maps to a login. There are two ways to verify the authenticity of an individual with a login.

- A login can be based on a Windows user or group account. In this scenario, SSE accepts the authentication of the individual by Windows but maps the user to a login on the SQL Server instance.

- With a SQL Server login, SQL Server both authenticates an individual and maps the individual to a login.

A login can perform administrative tasks on a server based on permissions to perform individual tasks or through membership of fixed server roles, which provide permissions for clusters of server-based tasks.

After an individual user gains access to a server instance through a login, the individual will often need access to a database on a server. A login must map to a database user, often just called a user, to gain access to a database. A user is a second type of principal that represents an individual inside a database, and a login can map to multiple users—one user per database.

- Some logins, such as the login for the Windows administrator or the SQL Server sa login, map automatically to the dbo user. The dbo user has unlimited permissions within a database.

- You can map a login to a database user with the CREATE USER statement. Users can receive permissions, such as a SELECT permission for a table, to perform tasks within a database.

- If a login does not map to any user, it may still connect to a database and perform functions if the database has a guest user. A guest user enables logins that do not map to individual users to access and perform functions based on the permissions assigned to the guest user.

Yet another type of principal is a role, such as a fixed server role or a fixed database role. Fixed roles represent preconfigured sets of permissions to which you can add logins and users. In addition to the fixed roles, you can also create custom database roles to which you can assign any set of permissions that your database solution requires. By assigning logins and users to roles, the logins and users inherit the permissions for the roles to which they belong, which means that a role is a way for a group of individuals to share a set of permissions. One individual can belong to multiple roles.

■**Note** An application role is a special kind of role. It is a principal that associates an application name and password with a set of data. Individuals who log in with the proper name and password gain access to the data associated with the role. An application role suspends other types of SSE security.

Exploring Principals

There are two main system catalog views that you can use to explore principals (sys.server_principals and sys.database_principals). The code for this section resides in ExploringPrincipalsInModules.sql. Other system catalog views and system-stored procedures let you examine subsets of principals. For example, sys.syslogins and sys.sysusers are especially useful for verifying the existence of two types of principals—namely, logins and users. The next section ("Creating Principals") illustrates this use for the following two system catalog views.

- The sys.server_principals view provides information about server-level principals, such as logins and fixed server roles.

- The sys.database_principals view makes available information about database-level principals, such as users, fixed database roles, and custom database roles.

A system catalog view can provide meta data based on the principal that invokes it. The broader the permissions associated with a principal, the more information they return. This section uses the login for the Windows administrator. The "Assigning Permissions to Principals" section later in this chapter invokes system catalog views with other principals to highlight how the views' performance reflects the principal invoking them.

The sys.server_principals view provides information identifying server-based principals. Two key items of information include

- The name of the principal, which has a sysname data type (nvarchar(128))

- A principal identifier with an int data type

Another especially useful sys.server_principals column is type_desc. This column has a cryptic description that summarizes the type of each principal, such as

- SQL_LOGIN for SQL Server login

- WINDOWS_LOGIN for a login mapped to a Windows login

- WINDOWS_GROUP for a login mapped to a Windows group

- CERTIFICATE_MAPPED_LOGIN for a login mapped to a certificate (for internal system use only; not meant for typical developer use)

- SERVER_ROLE for a fixed server role

The following code shows the syntax for listing the noninternal server-based principals (internal principals are meant for the exclusive use of SQL Server). The name for internal server-based principals begins with ##MS.

You can see that the name and type_desc columns characterize principals, but the principal_id column values uniquely identify the principal type.

- There are eight fixed server roles that convey built-in special clusters of permissions. The fixed server role names start at sysadmin and run through bulkadmin.

- There are four logins, but others may appear depending on your settings.

    - The sa is a SQL Server login. This is a system administrator that is created when you enable SQL Server logins.

    - BUILTIN\Administrators is the Windows Administrators group on the local computer.

    - BUILTIN\Users is the Windows Users group on the local computer; availability of this login is optional.

    - NT AUTHORITY\SYSTEM is a special-purpose login not meant for use by typical SSE database developers.

- By assigning a login to a fixed server role, you cause the login to inherit the permissions associated with that fixed server role.

- All logins belong to the public server role whether or not they belong to one or more of the eight fixed server roles.

```
SELECT name, principal_id, type_desc
FROM sys.server_principals
WHERE LEFT(name, 4) <> '##MS'
```

name	principal_id	type_desc
sa	1	SQL_LOGIN
public	2	SERVER_ROLE
sysadmin	3	SERVER_ROLE
securityadmin	4	SERVER_ROLE
serveradmin	5	SERVER_ROLE
setupadmin	6	SERVER_ROLE
processadmin	7	SERVER_ROLE
diskadmin	8	SERVER_ROLE
dbcreator	9	SERVER_ROLE
bulkadmin	10	SERVER_ROLE
BUILTIN\Administrators	257	WINDOWS_GROUP
NT AUTHORITY\SYSTEM	258	WINDOWS_LOGIN
BUILTIN\Users	260	WINDOWS_GROUP

Three system-stored procedures help you to explore fixed server roles.

- sp_helpsrvrole returns the eight fixed server role names along with another column providing a brief description of each role. The syntax for this system-stored procedure is EXEC sp_helpsrvrole.

- `sp_helpsrvrolemember` returns a list of the logins that belong to a fixed server role. So, for example, running `EXEC sp_helpsrvrolemember 'sysadmin'` lists the principals that are members of the sysadmin fixed server role. By default, these principals are sa, BUILTIN\Administrators, and NT AUTHORITY\SYSTEM. You can add other logins to the sysadmin fixed server role, a process that is described in the "Assigning Permissions via the Fixed Server Roles" section in this chapter.

- A third system-stored procedure, `sp_srvrolepermission`, can list the specific permissions associated with a fixed server role. Invoking `EXEC sp_srvrolepermission 'bulkadmin'` lists the two permissions in the bulkadmin fixed server role. In contrast, the sysadmin role has well over 100 permissions associated with it.

The `sys.database_principals` view provides information about the principals in the current database context. By changing the database context, you can generate different results from this view (for the newly selected database context). If you run a `SELECT` statement for `sys.database_principals` with a newly created database as the database context, then you will return information about the default user accounts in a new database as well as the fixed database roles. As you add new users and custom roles and drop existing users and custom roles, the `sys.database_principals` views will reflect the changes that you make to the principals in a database over time. As the name of the category implies, you cannot make changes to or drop fixed database roles.

The following script shows the syntax for a `SELECT` statement that extracts a subset of columns from the `sys.database_principals` view for a new database named NewDB. The script starts by creating the database. Then it runs a `SELECT` statement for the view after changing the database context to NewDB.

```
USE master
GO

IF EXISTS(SELECT name FROM sys.databases
    WHERE name = N'NewDB')
    DROP DATABASE NewDB
GO

CREATE DATABASE NewDB
GO

USE NewDB
GO

SELECT name, principal_id, type_desc,
    default_schema_name, is_fixed_role
FROM sys.database_principals
```

The result set from the preceding `SELECT` statement is shown next. There are four default users in the new database: dbo, guest, INFORMATION_SCHEMA, and sys.

- The dbo user is a database owner user. Multiple logins can map to this account, such as the sa login and the login for the Windows Administrator. Also, any member of the sysadmin server role maps to the dbo user.

- The INFORMATION_SCHEMA and sys users are specialized principals meant exclusively for use with views that match their name.

- Logins that do not map to any other database user map to the guest user. If the guest account has no permissions in a database, then logins mapping to the account can connect to the database, but the logins have no permissions in the database. Alternatively, you can assign some minimum set of permissions to the guest user so that logins mapping to the user can perform one or more basic actions in a database, such as run a SELECT statement for one data source.

Note The guest user operates slightly differently in SSE and other SQL Server 2005 editions than in earlier versions of SQL Server. In particular, the guest user is always present in a database, and it is enabled by default. You can disable it with the sp_dropuser system-stored procedure and re-enable it with the sp_adduser system-stored procedure.

In addition to the listing of database principals for a new database, the result set includes database roles as well as users.

- There are two categories of database roles: fixed and nonfixed.

  - Fixed database roles have a prespecified set of permissions that you cannot change. By adding users to a role, the users gain those permissions.

  - Nonfixed roles can be either custom roles that you create or the default public role to which all users belong whether or not they belong to any other fixed or custom roles.

- The type_desc column indicates that 10 rows are for database roles.

  - Nine of those rows are fixed database roles. These rows start with the row for the db_owner role and end with the row for the db_denydatawriter role.

  - The public role is not a fixed role. This means that you can set custom permissions for it, but this is not a recommended practice.

- The following result set includes no principals for custom roles because the listing is for a new database. As you add custom roles, you will gain additional rows in the result set from sys.database_principals that reflect these roles.

name	principal_id	type_desc	default_schema_name	is_fixed_role
public	0	DATABASE_ROLE	NULL	0
dbo	1	WINDOWS_USER	dbo	0
guest	2	SQL_USER	guest	0
INFORMATION_SCHEMA	3	SQL_USER	NULL	0
sys	4	SQL_USER	NULL	0
db_owner	16384	DATABASE_ROLE	NULL	1
db_accessadmin	16385	DATABASE_ROLE	NULL	1
db_securityadmin	16386	DATABASE_ROLE	NULL	1
db_ddladmin	16387	DATABASE_ROLE	NULL	1
db_backupoperator	16389	DATABASE_ROLE	NULL	1
db_datareader	16390	DATABASE_ROLE	NULL	1
db_datawriter	16391	DATABASE_ROLE	NULL	1
db_denydatareader	16392	DATABASE_ROLE	NULL	1
db_denydatawriter	16393	DATABASE_ROLE	NULL	1

There are system-stored procedures to help you explore fixed database roles just as there are system-stored procedures for fixed server roles.

- Invoke the sp_helpdbfixedrole to list the names of the fixed database roles with a brief description of each role.

- The sp_helprolemember system-stored procedure returns a list of the users added to a role. For a new database, running EXEC sp_helprolemember 'db_owner' returns the dbo user for the database.

- Running EXEC sp_dbfixedrolepermission 'db_datawriter' returns a result set that shows INSERT, UPDATE, and DELETE permissions for any object in a database. These permissions are available to all members of the db_datawriter role.

Creating Principals

Two principals that database administrators and developers regularly need to create are logins and users. This section highlights techniques for creating both of these principals. In addition, you'll learn to verify the operation and explore the logins and users that you create. The samples for this section reside in CreatingPrincipals.sql.

Recall that there are two types of logins: SQL Server logins and Windows logins. As described in the introduction to the "Exploring and Creating Principals" section, these two login types follow different conventions for authenticating SSE users. In addition, the login types have different naming conventions within T-SQL. The authentication and naming convention distinctions have an impact on how you create the two different types of logins. The naming convention differences follow.

- SQL Server logins have one-part names, such as sa (a built-in name) or sqllogin1 (a custom name).

- Windows logins have two-part names; the parts are delimited by a backslash (\).

  - The first part is the name of the Windows computer or server.

  - The second part is the name of the Windows user or group within the computer.

  - The two parts together appear as computername\Windowsuserorgroup.

■**Tip** If you are working on a Windows domain instead of a workgroup, you can replace the computer or server name with the domain name when assigning a name to a SQL Server login.

Creating SQL Server Logins

When you create a SQL Server login, you can specify its name and a password, which is a very common way to create a SQL Server login. I describe this type of login next. Another, newer way to create a SQL Server login is by specifying a security element, such as a certificate or asymmetric key, instead of a password. The "Encrypting Data" section introduces you to the syntax for creating a certificate or an asymmetric key.

■**Note** Those running SSE on Windows Server 2003 and who are enforcing the `NetValidatePasswordPolicy()` API can require the use of complex passwords. Using complex passwords makes your databases and servers more resistant to invasion by hackers (and harder for typical legitimate users who must remember complex, meaningless character strings as passwords). The limited availability of built-in Windows support for complex passwords makes it unlikely that it will be an issue in most SSE instances.

A login is a database object in the same sense that a table or a view is an object. Therefore, you can create, modify, and drop it with `CREATE LOGIN`, `ALTER LOGIN`, and `DROP LOGIN` statements. Although you can track existing logins in `sys.server_principals`, it is more practical to use a system catalog view that especially focuses on logins when looking to see if the `name` for a new login already exists.

■**Note** You can still use the `sp_addlogin` and `sp_droplogin` system-stored procedures from earlier versions of SQL Server to add and drop logins. However, Microsoft has deprecated these system-stored procedures in favor of the newer `CREATE LOGIN` and `DROP LOGIN` statements, which are new in SQL Server 2005 editions, including SSE.

When you are creating a SQL Server login based on a `password` with the `CREATE LOGIN` statement, all you need to do is to specify the login `name` immediately after `CREATE LOGIN` and use the `WITH PASSWORD` clause to designate a `password` for the new login.

The `name` for a login must be unique on an SSE instance; you can check for the existence of a login `name` with the `name` column in `sys.syslogins`. After adding a new login, you can verify the existence of the login with either `sys.syslogins` or `sys.server_principals`. These system catalog views provide different kinds of information about logins, and `sys.server_principals` provides information about other kinds of principals besides logins.

■**Note** Despite the fact that you only need to specify a name and a password for a SQL Server login, you can designate additional login options with a `CREATE LOGIN` statement. These include traditional features, such as a default database and a default language, as well as newer options, such as assigning a `CREDENTIAL` object to a login. A `CREDENTIAL` can identify a login for use with data sources outside SQL Server. A traditional way of relating to external data sources is with the `OPENROWSET` function. See the "Specifying Queries from Another Server Instance" section in Chapter 5 for more discussion of the `OPENROWSET` function.

To invoke the `CREATE LOGIN` statement successfully, you must first log in as a principal with permission for the statement. In particular, the login you are using when you invoke `CREATE LOGIN` must have a permission named `ALTER ANY LOGIN`. Any member of the sysadmin group, such as sa or the Windows login for the Windows administrator, has this permission. All the `CREATE LOGIN` samples were tested with the login for the Windows administrator.

The following script shows the use of the `CREATE LOGIN` statement to create a SQL Server login named sqllogin1. You can run the `CREATE LOGIN` statement from any database context because the statement operates at the server level. The essential elements of the script are the two middle batches.

- The first middle batch searches for an existing login named sqllogin1. If the `EXISTS` operator finds the login, the batch invokes the `DROP LOGIN` statement to remove the sqllogin1 login from the server.

- The second middle batch invokes the `CREATE LOGIN` statement to create a new login named sqllogin1 with a `password` of pass_sqllogin1.

- Before and after the two middle batches, two SELECT statements return noninternal principals.

```
SELECT name, principal_id, type_desc
FROM sys.server_principals
WHERE LEFT(name, 4) <> '##MS'
GO

IF EXISTS(SELECT * FROM sys.syslogins
    WHERE name = N'sqllogin1')
    DROP LOGIN sqllogin1
GO

CREATE LOGIN sqllogin1
    WITH PASSWORD = 'pass_sqllogin1'
GO

SELECT name, principal_id, type_desc
FROM sys.server_principals
WHERE LEFT(name, 4) <> '##MS'
GO
```

The result sets from the beginning and ending SELECT statements in the preceding script appear one behind the other below. The sqllogin1 login does not appear in the first result set before the code creates the login, but it does appear in the second result after the invocation of a CREATE LOGIN statement to generate the login. The type_desc column value for the new login is SQL_LOGIN, which denotes a SQL Server login.

Note If you compare either of the following result sets with an earlier result set for the same view appearing in the "Exploring Principals" section, you will notice that the BUILTIN\Users principal, which is a built-in Windows login, has a different principal_id column value (259 in the earlier result set versus 294 here). The new principal_id value follows from the fact that I dropped and restored the BUILTIN\Users principal between the former result set listing and the result set listing that follows. The restored principal entered the view with a new, higher principal_id value.

```
name                            principal_id type_desc
------------------------------- ------------ ------------------------
sa                              1            SQL_LOGIN
public                          2            SERVER_ROLE
sysadmin                        3            SERVER_ROLE
securityadmin                   4            SERVER_ROLE
serveradmin                     5            SERVER_ROLE
setupadmin                      6            SERVER_ROLE
processadmin                    7            SERVER_ROLE
diskadmin                       8            SERVER_ROLE
dbcreator                       9            SERVER_ROLE
bulkadmin                       10           SERVER_ROLE
BUILTIN\Administrators          257          WINDOWS_GROUP
NT AUTHORITY\SYSTEM             258          WINDOWS_LOGIN
BUILTIN\Users                   260          WINDOWS_GROUP
```

```
name                            principal_id type_desc
------------------------------- ------------ ------------------------
sa                              1            SQL_LOGIN
public                          2            SERVER_ROLE
sysadmin                        3            SERVER_ROLE
securityadmin                   4            SERVER_ROLE
serveradmin                     5            SERVER_ROLE
setupadmin                      6            SERVER_ROLE
processadmin                    7            SERVER_ROLE
diskadmin                       8            SERVER_ROLE
dbcreator                       9            SERVER_ROLE
bulkadmin                       10           SERVER_ROLE
BUILTIN\Administrators          257          WINDOWS_GROUP
NT AUTHORITY\SYSTEM             258          WINDOWS_LOGIN
BUILTIN\Users                   260          WINDOWS_GROUP
sqllogin1                       300          SQL_LOGIN
```

The preceding listing is from the execution context of the Windows administrator login for the master database. SQL Server 2005 editions, including SSE, introduce a means of simulating different execution contexts from a single login session. The EXECUTE AS statement permits the running of T-SQL code in a different execution context than the context of the login or user for a session, which is beyond the scope of this chapter, but the following listing (and others in this section) apply the EXECUTE AS statement to demonstrate the affect of running under a different login.

- The syntax for the EXECUTE AS statement in the following script shows how to run two SELECT statements—one for sys.server_principals and the other for sys.syslogins—from the sqllogin1 login without opening a new session with that login or closing and reopening the current session from that login.

- The first SELECT statement is highly similar to the preceding two SELECT statements, but its WHERE clause adds a criterion expression that removes all SERVER_ROLE rows, which are not of interest for this comparison.

- The second SELECT statement returns several column values from sys.syslogins. Notice the column names in the two views are not the same. Although both SELECT statements return information about the logins on a server, sys.server_principals and sys.syslogins provide complementary information about the logins.

- The closing batch with a REVERT statement transfers control from the sqllogin1 execution context to the original Windows administrator login execution context.

```
EXECUTE AS login = 'sqllogin1'
GO

SELECT name, principal_id, type_desc
FROM sys.server_principals
WHERE LEFT(name, 4) <> '##MS' AND
    type_desc <> 'SERVER_ROLE'
GO
```

```
SELECT name, hasaccess, isntname, isntgroup,
    isntuser, sysadmin
FROM sys.syslogins
WHERE LEFT(name, 4) <> '##MS'
GO

REVERT
GO
```

The result sets from the two SELECT statements in the preceding script appear one after the other in the following listing.

- The most important point to note is that each listing shows just two logins. Recall that the listing of principals after adding the sqllogin1 login included six logins. Therefore, changing the execution context from that for a Windows administrator to sqllogin1 reduces the number of logins that are visible.

  - The administrator can see all logins on a server.

  - The sqllogin1 can see only its own login and the sa login.

- The next most important point to take away from the two result sets is that they contain different column values for the two logins.

  - The result set from sys.server_principals includes principal_id, which is not available from sys.syslogins. In addition, the result set for sys.server_principals characterizes both of the logins that it shows as SQL Server logins (SQL_LOGIN).

  - The result set for sys.syslogins has more granular detail than the one from sys.server_principals. For example, the result set from sys.syslogins shows sa is a member of the sysadmin fixed server role. The result set for sys.server_principals enumerates the server principals, including logins and server roles, but it does not indicate if any login principals are assigned to any fixed server roles.

- The result set for the sys.server_principals is filtered to suppress the display of server roles. These would show for sqllogin1 if it were not for criterion expression in the SELECT statement's WHERE clause.

name	principal_id	type_desc
sa	1	SQL_LOGIN
sqllogin1	300	SQL_LOGIN

name	hasaccess	isntname	isntgroup	isntuser	sysadmin
sa	1	0	0	0	1
sqllogin1	1	0	0	0	0

Creating Windows Logins

SQL Server Express integrates tightly with Windows users by default.

- The BUILTIN\Users login, installed by default with SSE, makes it possible for any local Windows user to connect to the SSE instance running on the computer. You don't have to create a Windows login to enable this feature. In fact, you have to drop the BUILTIN\Users login to disable this feature.

- In spite of this feature, there are distinct benefits to creating a Windows login for a Windows user. For example, you can grant distinct permissions to individual Windows users who have a Windows login on a SQL Server instance that corresponds to their individual Windows user account.

- When a user tries to connect to a SQL Server instance with a Windows login, there is no need to specify a password to facilitate the process of authenticating the user. This feature makes it easier to connect to an SSE instance with a Windows login than with a SQL Server login.

The syntax for the CREATE LOGIN statement is slightly different for a Windows login than for a SQL Server login. In addition, the different naming convention for Windows versus SQL Server logins creates other subtle differences for formatting CREATE LOGIN and DROP LOGIN statements as well as searching for existing logins. Despite these differences, there are numerous points of similarity, such as the ability to define a default database for a login. As with earlier SQL Server versions, the default database is the master database for a login, unless you specify otherwise in a CREATE LOGIN statement or an ALTER LOGIN statement.

As with SQL Server logins, the name of all Windows logins must be unique on a server instance. The following script shows the syntax for checking for the existence of a Windows login named winlogin1 on a computer named computername. Replace computername with the name of the computer that you are using to run SSE (my computer is called cab233a). You can specify the name of a Windows login in single quotes within the WHERE clause of a SELECT statement for an EXISTS operator.

> **Note** You can use the Windows Computer Management Administrative tool to graphically create a Windows user named winlogin1 before running the following script. The CREATE LOGIN statement requires a Windows user account before you use the statement to create a login.

When you specify the name for a Windows login in a CREATE LOGIN statement or a DROP LOGIN statement, you must embrace the name in brackets. Follow the name of a Windows login with the FROM WINDOWS clause. There is no need for a WITH PASSWORD clause because a Windows login is authenticated by Windows, not SQL Server. The SSE instance trusts Windows to authenticate a user correctly.

```
SELECT name, hasaccess, isntname, isntgroup, isntuser, sysadmin
FROM sys.syslogins
WHERE LEFT(name, 4) <> '##MS'
GO

IF EXISTS(SELECT * FROM sys.syslogins
    WHERE name = N'computername\winlogin1')
    DROP LOGIN [computername\winlogin1]
GO

CREATE LOGIN [computername\winlogin1] FROM WINDOWS
GO
```

```
SELECT name, hasaccess, isntname, isntgroup, isntuser, sysadmin
FROM sys.syslogins
WHERE LEFT(name, 4) <> '##MS'
GO
```

The code for creating a new Windows login resides between SELECT statements that let you confirm the outcome of the CREATE LOGIN statement for a Windows login. The result sets for these before-and-after SELECT statements follow:

- The main point is that cab233a\winlogin1 appears in the second result set, which is returned after the CREATE LOGIN statement runs. Recall that cab233a is the computer on which I am running SSE.

- The rows for sqllogin1 and cab233a\winlogin1 both have access to SSE (hasaccess), but the cab233a\winlogin1 row is for a login name that is a Windows user (isntuser) and is an explicit Windows name (isntname). Neither of these created logins are members of the sysadmin fixed server role.

- The Windows administrator for the local computer connects to SSE through the BUILTIN\Administrators login. This login has access and is a Windows name, a Windows group, and a member of the sysadmin fixed server role. Because the BUILTIN\Administrators login is for a Windows group, the login enables connections by other Windows accounts on the local computer that belong to the Windows Administrators group even if they do not have an explicit login for the SSE instance.

- Just as the BUILTIN\Administrators login enables connections by all members of the Administrators group on the local computer, the BUILTIN\Users login permits all members of the Users group on the local computer to access the server. Notice that the BUILTIN\Users login does not belong to the sysadmin group, but you can customize its permissions in whatever way you wish.

name	hasaccess	isntname	isntgroup	isntuser	sysadmin
sa	1	0	0	0	1
MS_AgentSigningCertificateLogin	1	0	0	0	0
BUILTIN\Administrators	1	1	1	0	1
NT AUTHORITY\SYSTEM	1	1	0	1	1
BUILTIN\Users	1	1	1	0	0
sqllogin1	1	0	0	0	0

name	hasaccess	isntname	isntgroup	isntuser	sysadmin
sa	1	0	0	0	1
MS_AgentSigningCertificateLogin	1	0	0	0	0
BUILTIN\Administrators	1	1	1	0	1
NT AUTHORITY\SYSTEM	1	1	0	1	1
BUILTIN\Users	1	1	1	0	0
sqllogin1	1	0	0	0	0
cab233a\winlogin1	1	1	0	1	0

The previous two result sets explore the logins on the server from the Windows administrator account. However, you can also explore server logins from the two user-created logins to explore the logins (sqllogin1 and cab233a\winlogin1). In fact, the availability of the BUILTIN\Users login permits you to explore server logins from any member of the Windows Users group on the local computer—even one that does not have an explicit Windows login on the SSE instance. To test this capability and demonstrate how it worked, I created another Windows account named winlogin2 on the cab233a computer.

The following script shows the syntax for exploring server logins from three different execution contexts: cab233a\winlogin1, sqllogin1, and cab233a\winlogin2. The simulation of each execution context begins with EXECUTE AS. After exploring the logins with a SELECT statement for sys.syslogins, the code returns control to the Windows administrator context with a REVERT statement.

```
EXECUTE AS login = 'cab233a\winlogin1'
GO

SELECT name, hasaccess, isntname, isntgroup, isntuser, sysadmin
FROM sys.syslogins
WHERE LEFT(name, 4) <> '##MS'
GO

REVERT
GO


EXECUTE AS login = 'sqllogin1'
GO

SELECT name, hasaccess, isntname, isntgroup, isntuser, sysadmin
FROM sys.syslogins
WHERE LEFT(name, 4) <> '##MS'
GO

REVERT
GO


EXECUTE AS login = 'cab233a\winlogin2'
GO

SELECT name, hasaccess, isntname, isntgroup, isntuser, sysadmin
FROM sys.syslogins
WHERE LEFT(name, 4) <> '##MS'
GO

REVERT
GO
```

The result sets from the three preceding SELECT statements appear one after the other in the following listing. All three execution contexts show the sa login, but the other logins that appear depend on the execution context.

- The cab233a\winlogin1 execution context shows its own login along with the login for BUILTIN\Users to which cab233a\winlogin1 also belongs.

- Besides the sa login, the sqllogin1 execution context shows just its own login.

- The cab233a\winlogin2 execution context also shows just one additional login beyond sa, namely, BUILTIN\Users. The winlogin2 Windows user can connect to the server and explore logins, but it has no login created specifically for its Windows account.

- The general rule is that any normal individual connecting to SSE can explore its own login, any other logins to which it belongs, and the sa login for the system administrator. If you connect as the administrator of an SSE instance, then you can explore all the logins on the server.

name	hasaccess	isntname	isntgroup	isntuser	sysadmin
sa	1	0	0	0	1
BUILTIN\Users	1	1	1	0	0
cab233a\winlogin1	1	1	0	1	0

name	hasaccess	isntname	isntgroup	isntuser	sysadmin
sa	1	0	0	0	1
sqllogin1	1	0	0	0	0

name	hasaccess	isntname	isntgroup	isntuser	sysadmin
sa	1	0	0	0	1
BUILTIN\Users	1	1	1	0	0

As previously mentioned, the ability to connect to an SSE instance by members of the Windows Users group depends on the status of the BUILTIN\Users login. If you drop the BUILTIN\Users login, you will not be able to log in as a member of the Windows Users group unless the Windows Users group member has an explicitly created Windows login in the SSE instance, such as the Windows login for cab233a\winlogin1. You can verify the inability to connect by attempting to access an SSE instance with a client, such as the SSMS-based query tool for SSE or the sqlcmd utility, from the winlogin2 Windows user account after first dropping the BUILTIN\Users login.

Creating Users

Just as logins grant access to an SSE instance, users grant access to a database on a server instance. The user represents a principal just as a login represents a principal. The principal for a login can point at the same individual as a database user, because a single login can be a user in multiple databases. You explore user principals in the sys.database_principals and sys.sysusers catalog views, which operate in an analogous way to sys.server_principals and sys.syslogins for logins.

Users are database objects that are scoped at the level of a database, instead of a server. Schemas are another type of object at the database level, and users can populate schemas with database objects. The names for classic database objects, such as tables, views, and stored procedures, must be unique within a schema inside a database. This means that a single database can have two different tables with the same name—so long as they are in different schemas. However, a database can have only one user per name—just as a database can have only one schema per name.

To create a new user, you need a database context. If you inadvertently fail to specify a desired database context, your new user enters the current database context, such as the default master database. It is good practice to have only the users that you need in a database, because leaving an unnecessary user in a database makes your database, and ultimately your server, vulnerable to attack by a hacker.

You can create a new user by invoking the CREATE USER statement. At the time that you create a new database, such as NewDB from this chapter's "Exploring Principals" section, the database has two built-in schemas for typical users—dbo and guest. By default, these schemas are set up for dbo and guest users, but other users, such as the user for the sqllogin1 login, can reference these schemas as their default schema. Of course, you can create additional schemas in a database with the CREATE SCHEMA statement. See the "Creating and Owning Schemas" section in this chapter for additional details on managing schemas and their relationships to users.

The following script includes a CREATE USER statement that shows the syntax for creating a new user named sqllogin1 in the NewDB database for the sqllogin1 login. The script specifies the NewDB database for the user by the USE statement at the top of the code sample. The sqllogin1 user has the guest schema as its default schema. The "Creating Objects in Owned Schemas" and the "Creating Objects in Any Schema" sections describe and demonstrate the relationships between schemas and user permissions to create objects. You specify the name for a new user immediately after CREATE USER. The CREATE USER statement also requires a FOR LOGIN clause in which you specify the login to which the user maps. The sample code below includes an optional WITH DEFAULT_SCHEMA clause used to designate that the sqllogin1 user has the guest schema as its default schema.

An IF statement with an EXISTS operator checks for the existence of a current user just before the CREATE USER statement. If the user already exists, the IF statement drops the user by invoking the DROP USER statement. The SELECT statement for the EXISTS operator searches the sys.sysusers catalog view for a user with a name column value of sqllogin1. There is no need to search for users within schemas because you cannot have two users in a single database with the same name even if the users have different default schemas.

```
USE NewDB
GO

SELECT name, principal_id, type_desc,
    default_schema_name, is_fixed_role
FROM sys.database_principals

IF EXISTS(SELECT * FROM sys.sysusers WHERE name = 'sqllogin1')
    DROP USER sqllogin1
GO

CREATE USER sqllogin1 FOR LOGIN sqllogin1 WITH DEFAULT_SCHEMA = guest
GO

SELECT name, principal_id, type_desc,
    default_schema_name, is_fixed_role
FROM sys.database_principals
```

The result sets for the two SELECT statements are shown next. Notice that the first result set lists the default database principals. The "Exploring Principals" section has a review of these principals. Although prior code samples added two new logins to the server, these logins have no direct impact on sys.database_principals.

The second result set shows sys.database_principals column values after the CREATE USER statement. Notice the new sqllogin1 principal with a principal_id column value of 0. This user is a SQL_USER because it maps to a SQL Server login. Note also that the default_schema_name column value for the sqllogin1 user is guest.

```
name                 principal_id type_desc     default_schema_name is_fixed_role
-------------------- ------------ ------------- ------------------- -------------
public               0            DATABASE_ROLE NULL                0
dbo                  1            WINDOWS_USER  dbo                 0
guest                2            SQL_USER      guest               0
INFORMATION_SCHEMA   3            SQL_USER      NULL                0
sys                  4            SQL_USER      NULL                0
db_owner             16384        DATABASE_ROLE NULL                1
db_accessadmin       16385        DATABASE_ROLE NULL                1
db_securityadmin     16386        DATABASE_ROLE NULL                1
db_ddladmin          16387        DATABASE_ROLE NULL                1
db_backupoperator    16389        DATABASE_ROLE NULL                1
db_datareader        16390        DATABASE_ROLE NULL                1
db_datawriter        16391        DATABASE_ROLE NULL                1
db_denydatareader    16392        DATABASE_ROLE NULL                1
db_denydatawriter    16393        DATABASE_ROLE NULL                1
```

```
name                 principal_id type_desc     default_schema_name is_fixed_role
-------------------- ------------ ------------- ------------------- -------------
public               0            DATABASE_ROLE NULL                0
dbo                  1            WINDOWS_USER  dbo                 0
guest                2            SQL_USER      guest               0
INFORMATION_SCHEMA   3            SQL_USER      NULL                0
sys                  4            SQL_USER      NULL                0
sqllogin1            5            SQL_USER      guest               0
db_owner             16384        DATABASE_ROLE NULL                1
db_accessadmin       16385        DATABASE_ROLE NULL                1
db_securityadmin     16386        DATABASE_ROLE NULL                1
db_ddladmin          16387        DATABASE_ROLE NULL                1
db_backupoperator    16389        DATABASE_ROLE NULL                1
db_datareader        16390        DATABASE_ROLE NULL                1
db_datawriter        16391        DATABASE_ROLE NULL                1
db_denydatareader    16392        DATABASE_ROLE NULL                1
db_denydatawriter    16393        DATABASE_ROLE NULL                1
```

The next script drops the sqllogin1 user created in the preceding sample and replaces it with a new one. The new CREATE USER statement is identical to the previous one, except that it does not include a WITH DEFAULT_SCHEMA clause. As a result, the new sqllogin1 user belongs to the dbo schema instead of the guest schema. The result set from the SELECT statement after the CREATE USER statement confirms that the sqllogin1 user now belongs to the dbo schema.

```
IF EXISTS(SELECT * FROM sys.sysusers WHERE name = 'sqllogin1')
    DROP USER sqllogin1
GO

CREATE USER sqllogin1 FOR LOGIN sqllogin1
GO

SELECT name, principal_id, type_desc,
    default_schema_name, is_fixed_role
FROM sys.database_principals
WHERE name = 'sqllogin1'
GO
```

name	principal_id	type_desc	default_schema_name	is_fixed_role
sqllogin1	5	SQL_USER	dbo	0

Creating a new user for a Windows login, such as `cab233a\winlogin1`, is basically the same as creating a new user for a SQL Server login. The only distinction in syntax relates to using a two-part name for a Windows login as opposed to a one-part name for a SQL Server login. In terms of the outcome, the `type_desc` column value for a user based on a Windows login is `WINDOWS_USER` instead of `SQL_USER`. The following listing demonstrates the syntax for creating a user based on the `cab233a\winlogin1` login and shows a filtered set of rows that excludes all rows with a `DATABASE_ROLE` column value for `type_desc`. As a consequence, the result set shows only users—based on either SQL Server or Windows logins.

```
IF EXISTS(SELECT * FROM sys.sysusers WHERE name = 'cab233a\winlogin1')
    DROP USER [cab233a\winlogin1]
GO

CREATE USER [cab233a\winlogin1] FOR LOGIN [cab233a\winlogin1]
GO

SELECT name, principal_id, type_desc,
    default_schema_name, is_fixed_role
FROM sys.database_principals
WHERE type_desc <> 'DATABASE_ROLE'
GO
```

name	principal_id	type_desc	default_schema_name	is_fixed_role
dbo	1	WINDOWS_USER	dbo	0
guest	2	SQL_USER	guest	0
INFORMATION_SCHEMA	3	SQL_USER	NULL	0
sys	4	SQL_USER	NULL	0
sqllogin1	5	SQL_USER	dbo	0
cab233a\winlogin1	6	WINDOWS_USER	dbo	0

Assigning Permissions to Principals

SQL Server Express administrators can enable principals to perform tasks by assigning permissions to them. Without permission, a principal can do little more than connect to a server and perform `SELECT` statements for some system catalog views. A permission allows a principal to do something to a securable. For example, you can assign a permission that enables a principal to create a database or table or write to a table or even just read from a table. SQL Server Express offers multiple ways to assign permissions to principals.

Before diving into the details of assigning permissions to principals, this section starts with a brief overview of securables and permissions. The overview aims to help you evaluate the suitability of different approaches to assigning permissions. After the overview, I describe different ways to assign permissions to securables.

Overview of Securables and Permissions

You already know that SSE supports a hierarchy of principals. A login principal operates at the server level, and a user principal operates at the database level. One login can serve as the parent for multiple users—each in a different database. There are also hierarchies for securables and permissions.

Securables

The securable hierarchy has multiple levels. The main levels that SSE users are likely to encounter include the following:

- Server
- Database
- Schema
- Database object, such as table, view, or stored procedure

Securables are the elements of a database solution, such as a table. You can think of a securable as a database object, including the database server itself. Even principals can serve as securables. For example, you need permission to create a login. Therefore, a login is a securable, and the ALTER ANY LOGIN permission enables another principal to create a new login.

Understanding the hierarchical relationships among securables can help you appreciate which way to assign permissions to achieve a desired security outcome. Schemas within a database illustrate the hierarchical relationships among securables. By default, all databases have at least two schemas (dbo and guest), but you can add more schemas to a database. Schemas nest hierarchically within a database. In turn, each schema can contain multiple database objects. Objects of the same type, such as tables, within a schema must have unique names, but there is no requirement for unique database object names across schemas.

Assigning SELECT permission to a user for a table in one schema will not have any effect on the ability of that user to run a SELECT statement on a table with the same name in a different schema.

Assigning a user to a database role, such as db_datareader, can enable the user to run SELECT statements on all tables, views, and user-defined functions returning a table. This is because the db_datareader role resides at the database level, and any user in the db_datareader role inherits the database-level permissions associated with the role.

Permissions

There are three sets of topics that you need to grasp when working with permissions.

- You have to learn about the different kinds of permissions. These can range from granular ones, such as permission to read an individual table, to coarse ones, such as permissions to perform any task on a database server.

- Next, you have to learn how to assign permissions to a principal. There are different approaches depending on the type of principal and granularity of the permission that you want to assign.

- Finally, it is very helpful to be able to explore the permissions that belong to principals. This helps you to assess whether existing permissions meet your current and likely future database security requirements.

There are two popular ways to assign permissions to principals.

- One way is to assign permissions directly to principals. This technique works best for a small group of users that require distinctly different permissions. In addition, the administrative burden of this approach is least when there is relatively little turnover among group members, and the number of permissions you need to manage per principal is relatively small.

- Another approach to managing permissions is to assign a principal to a role. You can use either fixed roles, such as fixed server roles and fixed database roles, or custom roles. In either case, the principal inherits the permissions of the role to which you assign it. This second approach is easier to administer than the first approach as the number of users grows large, turnover among users grows large, and the number and types of permissions you are managing per principal becomes either large or complex.

Just as with principals and securables, there is a permission hierarchy. One especially useful source for exploring the permission hierarchy is the sys.fn_builtin_permissions system catalog view. This view can return a description for any individual permission in the permission hierarchy, which is the set of all permissions that you can assign to a principal with T-SQL. When you run a SELECT statement for the view, you must specify a securable class as an argument. See ShowingPermissions.sql for samples demonstrating the use of sys.fn_builtin_permissions.

When you run a SELECT statement for sys.fn_builtin_permissions with an argument of either DEFAULT or NULL, the statement returns all permissions in the permission hierarchy. The syntax for a SELECT statement with the DEFAULT argument is shown next. The result set comprises more than 180 permissions that you can assign to principals with T-SQL.

```
SELECT * FROM sys.fn_builtin_permissions(DEFAULT)
```

Not only does the preceding query return all the permissions in the permission hierarchy, but it also contains multiple instances of all the securable classes—one instance per permission for each class. Therefore, a slight adaptation of the preceding query can return the names of the 21 securable classes. Some familiar items from the result set include LOGIN and SCHEMA. The OBJECT designator pertains to such database objects as tables, views, and stored procedures. You can use the result set from the following query as a starting point for exploring permissions for the items that you know about and use in your application development.

```
SELECT DISTINCT class_desc
FROM sys.fn_builtin_permissions(DEFAULT)
ORDER BY class_desc
```

The next code sample and result set show the set of permissions for the LOGIN securable. Notice the character string for LOGIN as a parameter for sys.fn_builtin_permissions. Four permissions apply to the login securable. The CONTROL permission confers all permissions for an object.

- A principal with CONTROL permission has the same permission as a login's owner, which is usually the principal who created the login.

- A principal with IMPERSONATE permission can use an EXECUTE AS statement to act as the designated login.

- The VIEW DEFINITION permission grants read access for meta data about securables for which a principal does not explicitly own or have CONTROL permission.

- The ALTER permission enables a principal to modify a login securable.

The following result set references both the permissions and securable hierarchies. The parent_class column designates SERVER as the parent of LOGIN. The covering permissions for a permission are analogous to the parent of a permission. When a principal has a covering permission, such as CONTROL, the principal with the covering permission automatically inherits any covered permissions. Similarly, a principal with a covering permission for a parent securable inherits any covered permission for a child securable. Therefore, the ALTER ANY LOGIN for a server securable grants a principal permission to modify any particular login as if the principal had CONTROL permission for the login.

```
SELECT class_desc 'class',
    permission_name,
    covering_permission_name 'covering_permission',
    parent_class_desc 'parent_class',
    parent_covering_permission_name 'parent_covering_permission'
FROM sys.fn_builtin_permissions(N'LOGIN')
```

class	permission_name	covering_permission	parent_class	parent_covering_permission
LOGIN	IMPERSONATE	CONTROL	SERVER	CONTROL SERVER
LOGIN	VIEW DEFINITION	CONTROL	SERVER	VIEW ANY DEFINITION
LOGIN	ALTER	CONTROL	SERVER	ALTER ANY LOGIN
LOGIN	CONTROL		SERVER	CONTROL SERVER

You can also use sys.fn_builtin_permissions to drill down on any particular permission. For example, the next SELECT statement and its result set drill down on the properties of the ALTER ANY LOGIN permission. Notice the WHERE clause criterion explicitly references the designated permission. In addition, the securable class is now SERVER, which is the securable class with the ALTER ANY LOGIN permission. The covering permission, or parent of the ALTER ANY LOGIN permission, is the CONTROL SERVER permission.

```
SELECT class_desc 'class',
    permission_name,
    covering_permission_name 'covering_permission',
    parent_class_desc 'parent_class',
    parent_covering_permission_name 'parent_covering_permission'
FROM sys.fn_builtin_permissions(N'SERVER')
WHERE permission_name = 'ALTER ANY LOGIN'
```

class	permission_name	covering_permission	parent_class	parent_covering_permission
SERVER	ALTER ANY LOGIN	CONTROL SERVER		

Assigning Permissions via the Fixed Server Roles

Perhaps the easiest way to administer permissions for server-level tasks is to assign logins to fixed server roles. SQL Server Express defines eight fixed server roles. Each of these roles has a set of permissions associated with it. By assigning a login to a fixed server role, you cause the login to inherit the permissions associated with the role.

You can use the `sp_addsrvrolemember` system-stored procedure to add a login to a fixed server role. You can add a single login to multiple fixed server roles in successive executions of `sp_addsrvrolemember`. You can remove a login from a fixed server role with the `sp_dropsrvrolemember` system-stored procedure. As mentioned in the "Exploring Principals" section earlier in this chapter, there are three system-stored procedures to help you explore fixed server roles and the logins within each role (`sp_helpsrvrole`, `sp_srvrolepermission`, and `sp_helpsrvrolemember`).

When you initially create a login, the login can connect to a server instance, but it usually has no permissions associated with it. This section shows you how to empower a login to create another login as well as how to create a database. Instead of granting these precise permissions, you learn how to assign a login to fixed roles that include these permissions along with others because it is often reasonable to assign clusters or related permissions. For example, you may want a login that can create other logins to also be able to drop logins and to be able to add and drop users associated with those logins. The samples for this section reside in AssigningFixedServerRoles.sql.

Enabling a Login to Create Other Logins

This section empowers the `sqllogin1` login to create other logins. You can use the code for creating the `sqllogin1` login presented in the "Creating SQL Server Logins" section to create this login. For your convenience, the code is available at the top of AssigningFixedServerRoles.sql. Even if you previously created the login, it may be best to create the login again so that you are sure you have a fresh version of it.

After verifying the existence of a fresh version of the `sqllogin1` login, you can demonstrate `sqllogin1`'s initial inability to create another login (`sqllogin2`) with the following script. You can test the code by connecting as the Windows administrator, but the script starts by setting the execution context so that the code runs under the `sqllogin1` login.

- The `IF` statement with the `EXISTS` operator tests for a prior instance of the `sqllogin2` login. If `sqllogin2` exists, the script attempts to drop the login. If you are following the samples to this point in the chapter, the `DROP LOGIN` statement is never reached because `sqllogin2` does not exist.

- Next, control passes to a `CREATE LOGIN` statement for `sqllogin2` after the `IF` statement. At this point, SSE generates an error because the `sqllogin1` login does not have permission to create another login, such as `sqllogin2`.

- The `REVERT` statement in the final batch transfers the execution context back to that for the Windows administrator.

```
EXECUTE AS login = 'sqllogin1'
GO

IF EXISTS(SELECT * FROM sys.syslogins
    WHERE name = N'sqllogin2')
    DROP LOGIN sqllogin2
GO

CREATE LOGIN sqllogin2
    WITH PASSWORD = 'pass_sqllogin2'
GO

REVERT
GO
```

You can enable sqllogin1 to create another login by adding sqllogin1 to a fixed server role. However, if you are just starting out with SSE, or you have not made the particular assignment you need recently, you may not know precisely which fixed server role to use. In this kind of situation, it is useful to know how to explore the fixed server roles.

The sp_helpsrvrole system-stored procedure can generate a list of the fixed server role names, which you need for assigning a login to a role, as well as an indication of the kinds of permissions associated with each role. The following listing shows the syntax for sp_helpsrvrole as well as its output.

As you can see, the securityadmin fixed server role is for security administrators. To benefit from this listing, you need to understand that creating a login is a security function. An SSE administrator should develop at least a basic understanding of the kinds of tasks enabled by these roles. One way to learn more about what each role enables is to run the sp_srvrolepermission system-stored procedure, which is described and demonstrated next.

■**Note** Some system administrators have a way of assigning all or many users to the sysadmin fixed server role, which conveys permission to perform any task within a server. This practice ensures that users can perform whatever they need to do, and it relieves system administrators from learning the kinds of tasks that other fixed server roles enable. Despite the convenience of assigning all or many users to the sysadmin fixed server role, this is not a good practice for a couple of reasons. First, you are exposing your SSE instance and all its databases to someone who may cause damage accidentally or on purpose to the server or its databases. Did you know that the majority of computer hacks occur within an organization—not outside of it? Second, by making the sysadmin role widely available, you offer more opportunities for hackers to gain control of your server at a high level.

```
EXEC sp_helpsrvrole
```

```
ServerRole     Description
------------   --------------------------
sysadmin       System Administrators
securityadmin  Security Administrators
serveradmin    Server Administrators
setupadmin     Setup Administrators
processadmin   Process Administrators
diskadmin      Disk Administrators
dbcreator      Database Creators
bulkadmin      Bulk Insert Administrators
```

The output from the sp_ helpsrvrole system-stored procedure qualifies the securityadmin fixed server role for further examination. You can use the sp_srvrolepermission system-stored procedure to learn more about the specific permissions conveyed by a fixed server role; to do so, you have to name the role as its argument. The following example shows the syntax for requesting the permissions associated with the securityadmin fixed server role.

The output from the EXEC statement for sp_srvrolepermission shows the specific permissions associated with the role. Notice that two permissions are for sp_addlogin and sp_droplogin. These names refer to system-stored procedures that are analogous to CREATE LOGIN and DROP LOGIN statements. Therefore, assigning the sqllogin1 login to the securityadmin fixed server role will enable the login to add and drop other logins on an SSE instance.

```
EXEC sp_srvrolepermission 'securityadmin'
```

```
ServerRole     Permission
-------------  --------------------------------
securityadmin  Add member to securityadmin
securityadmin  Grant/deny/revoke CREATE DATABASE
securityadmin  Read the error log
securityadmin  sp_addlinkedsrvlogin
securityadmin  sp_addlogin
securityadmin  sp_defaultdb
securityadmin  sp_defaultlanguage
securityadmin  sp_denylogin
securityadmin  sp_droplinkedsrvlogin
securityadmin  sp_droplogin
securityadmin  sp_dropremotelogin
securityadmin  sp_grantlogin
securityadmin  sp_helplogins
securityadmin  sp_password
securityadmin  sp_remoteoption (update)
securityadmin  sp_revokelogin
```

The sp_addsrvrolemember system-stored procedure adds a login to a fixed server role, such as securityadmin. You can only invoke this stored procedure from a login that belongs to the sysadmin fixed server role, such as the login for the Windows administrator or the sa login. The sp_addsrvrolemember system-stored procedure takes two arguments, which you can designate as characters in single quotes.

- The first argument is the name of the login that you want to assign to a role.

- The second argument specifies the fixed server role to which you want to assign the login.

The syntax for adding sqllogin1 to the securityadmin fixed server role is shown next.

```
EXEC sp_addsrvrolemember 'sqllogin1', 'securityadmin'
```

After you add sqllogin1 to the securityadmin fixed server role, you will be ready to create a fresh copy of the sqllogin2 login from the execution context for sqllogin1. The following script repeats the logic of the preceding attempt to create a login named sqllogin2 from the sqllogin1 execution context, but this script also adds a couple of SELECT statements to confirm the success of the attempt to add the login. Each SELECT statement returns the logins on the server, including

- Their name

- Whether the login is for a Windows group (isntgroup)

- Whether the login is for a Windows user (isntuser)

- Whether the login belongs to the securityadmin fixed server role

- Whether the login belongs to the sysadmin fixed server role

```
EXECUTE AS login = 'sqllogin1'
GO

IF EXISTS(SELECT * FROM sys.syslogins
    WHERE name = N'sqllogin2')
    DROP LOGIN sqllogin2
GO

SELECT name, isntgroup, isntuser, securityadmin, sysadmin
```

```
FROM sys.syslogins
WHERE LEFT(name, 4) <> '##MS'
GO

CREATE LOGIN sqllogin2
    WITH PASSWORD = 'pass_sqllogin2'
GO

SELECT name, isntgroup, isntuser, securityadmin, sysadmin
FROM sys.syslogins
WHERE LEFT(name, 4) <> '##MS'
GO

REVERT
GO
```

The result sets from the two SELECT statements in the preceding script are shown next, one after the other.

- The first result set shows the login on the server before the execution of the CREATE LOGIN statement. Although the SELECT statement generating the result set executes from the sqllogin1 execution context, the result set shows all the existing logins on the server instead of just the sqllogin1 and sa logins. This is because sqllogin1 was previously added to the securityadmin fixed server role.

- The second result set shows a new login, sqllogin2, added to the previous result. This result set confirms the success of the CREATE LOGIN statement from the sqllogin1 execution context.

name	isntgroup	isntuser	securityadmin	sysadmin
sa	0	0	0	1
BUILTIN\Administrators	1	0	0	1
NT AUTHORITY\SYSTEM	0	1	0	1
BUILTIN\Users	1	0	0	0
sqllogin1	0	0	1	0
cab233a\winlogin1	0	1	0	0

name	isntgroup	isntuser	securityadmin	sysadmin
sa	0	0	0	1
BUILTIN\Administrators	1	0	0	1
NT AUTHORITY\SYSTEM	0	1	0	1
BUILTIN\Users	1	0	0	0
sqllogin1	0	0	1	0
cab233a\winlogin1	0	1	0	0
sqllogin2	0	0	0	0

Enabling a Login to Create a Database

Before a login can invoke either the DROP DATABASE or CREATE DATABASE statements, the login needs permission. One way to grant the permission is by adding the login to the dbcreator fixed server role. You can use the sp_helpsrvrole and sp_srvrolepermission system-stored procedures to determine that the dbcreator role is the appropriate one. Next, you can invoke the sp_addsrvrolemember system-stored procedure to add a login, such as sqllogin1, to the role.

The following script starts with an EXEC statement for the sp_addsrvrolemember system-stored procedure that adds sqllogin1 to the dbcreator role. Then, the procedure changes the execution context to that for sqllogin1. After changing the database context to master, the script adds a new database, NewDB1, to the server. Two SELECT statements—one before and the other after the CREATE DATABASE statement—confirm that sqllogin1 can successfully create a new database.

Attempting to create a new database to a server without first enabling the login to perform this task generates an error. The script in AssigningFixedServerRoles.sql includes T-SQL code that demonstrates this feature before adding sqllogin1 to the dbcreator fixed server role.

```
EXEC sp_addsrvrolemember 'sqllogin1', 'dbcreator'
GO

EXECUTE AS login = 'sqllogin1'
GO

USE master
GO

IF EXISTS(SELECT name FROM sys.databases
    WHERE name = N'NewDB1')
    DROP DATABASE NewDB1
GO

SELECT COUNT(*) 'NewDB1 is there = 1'
    FROM sys.databases
    WHERE name = N'NewDB1'
GO

CREATE DATABASE NewDB1
GO

SELECT COUNT(*) 'NewDB1 is there = 1'
    FROM sys.databases
    WHERE name = N'NewDB1'
GO

REVERT
GO
```

Assigning Permissions via the Fixed Database Roles

Just as you can assign server-level permissions to fixed server roles, you can assign database-level permissions by assigning database users to fixed database roles. One important distinction between assigning database-level and server-level permissions is the requirement for a login to map to some user within a database to gain access to a database. It is not possible to assign database-level permissions to an individual unless the individual has a login that maps to a user within a database.

There are at least three ways to map a login to a fixed database role.

- First, you can explicitly create a user account with the CREATE USER statement for a login. This approach maps a newly created user account to a login.

- Second, you can enable the guest user account in a database so that a login with no explicit user account in a database can gain access to a database through the guest user.

- Third, you can add a login to the sysadmin fixed database role by executing the sp_addsrvrolemember system-stored procedure. All members of the sysadmin fixed database role automatically belong to the dbo user in each database.

Note A deprecated means of mapping a login to a user is with the sp_addalias system-stored procedure. Consider using the newer CREATE USER statement instead of sp_addalias in SSE solutions.

This section drills down on techniques for granting database access to logins. You also learn about system-stored procedures that help you explore fixed database roles as well as the permissions associated with them. Finally, you learn how to add users to fixed database roles to assign the permissions for a role to a user. The samples for this section reside in AssigningFixedDataRoles.sql.

Granting Database Access to Logins

Perhaps the easiest way to enable a login without an associated database user to access a database is by enabling the database's guest user. SQL Server Express automatically makes the guest user available in all databases. Earlier versions of SQL Server required you to explicitly create the guest user and allowed you to drop the guest user.

With SSE, the guest user is always available, and you cannot drop it. However, the guest user is disabled in new databases.

- Before using the guest user, you must enable it by executing the sp_adduser system-stored procedure for the guest user.

- You can disable, but not drop, the guest user with the sp_dropuser system-stored procedure for the guest user.

The sqllogin1 login has been both created ("Creating SQL Server Logins" section) and assigned to fixed server roles ("Assigning Permissions via the Fixed Server Roles" section) earlier in this chapter. If you wish to run the samples in the "Assigning Permissions via the Fixed Database Roles" section, please run the earlier samples using the sqllogin1 login. Next, open SSE from the Windows administrator, sa, or another login in the sysadmin fixed server role. Then, run the following script to connect to the AdventureWorks database and confirm the login's ability to perform a SELECT statement for a table (i.e., ProductCategory) in the AdventureWorks database.

```
USE AdventureWorks
GO

SELECT * FROM Production.ProductCategory
GO
```

Because you run the preceding script from a member of the sysadmin fixed server role, you can perform any task, including those specified by the preceding script, on a server instance. Not all logins have the same range of permissions.

- For example, the sqllogin1 login has significant permissions, as shown in earlier use in this chapter, such as the ability to define a new login and the ability to create a new database. In addition, the sqllogin1 login is the owner of the NewDB1 database, and you can therefore perform any task within the NewDB1 database after connecting to the server instance with the sqllogin1 login.

- However, the sqllogin1 login does not have permission to connect to the AdventureWorks database.

- Attempting to run the following script immediately after the preceding one generates an error precisely because the sqllogin1 login does not have permission to access the AdventureWorks database.

```
EXECUTE AS login = 'sqllogin1'
GO
```

One way to allow the sqllogin1 login to connect to the AdventureWorks database is to enable the guest user within the AdventureWorks database. After enabling the guest user, the hasdbaccess column value for the guest user row in the sys.sysusers view changes from 0 to 1. In addition, the sqllogin1 login and any other login without an AdventureWorks user mapped to it can access the database.

The following script performs tasks that demonstrate the impact that the sp_adduser system-stored procedure can have on the guest user and its ability to work with logins that have no user mapped explicitly to them.

- The script starts by wrapping an execution of the sp_adduser system-stored procedure between two SELECT statements. The sp_adduser statement enables the guest user.

  - The first SELECT statement returns a result set showing the status of the users prior to the enabling of the guest user.

  - The second SELECT statement returns a result set showing sys.sysusers after the enabling of the guest user.

- The EXECUTE AS login = 'sqllogin1' statement executes successfully because the sqllogin1 login can now connect to the AdventureWorks database.

- However, the SELECT statement from the ProductCategory table in the Production schema generates an error because the guest user does not have permission to perform any SELECT statements.

- The final batch with a REVERT statement restores the execution context of the initial login from the sysadmin fixed server role that you initially used to connect with the SSE instance.

```
SELECT name, hasdbaccess, isntuser, issqluser
FROM sys.sysusers
WHERE issqlrole = 0

EXEC sp_adduser 'guest'

SELECT name, hasdbaccess, isntuser, issqluser
FROM sys.sysusers
WHERE issqlrole = 0

--You can now connect
```

```
EXECUTE AS login = 'sqllogin1'
GO

--but you cannot select
SELECT * FROM Production.ProductCategory
GO

REVERT
GO
```

The following pair of result sets shows the `sys.sysusers` rows from the two `SELECT` statements before and after the enabling of the `guest` user with the `sp_adduser` system-stored procedure.

- The initial result set shows a `hasdbaccess` column value of 0 for the `guest` user row. This value indicates that the `guest` user account is inactive.

- The second result set has a `hasdbaccess` column value of 1 for the `guest` user row. The change from 0 to 1 indicates the `guest` user is now enabled.

- It is the enabling of the `guest` user that permits the `EXECUTE AS login = 'sqllogin1'` statement in the preceding script to succeed.

name	hasdbaccess	isntuser	issqluser
dbo	1	0	1
guest	0	0	1
INFORMATION_SCHEMA	0	0	1
sys	0	0	1

name	hasdbaccess	isntuser	issqluser
dbo	1	0	1
guest	1	0	1
INFORMATION_SCHEMA	0	0	1
sys	0	0	1

In general, it is not a good practice to enable database access with the `guest` user account. The `guest` user does not allow you to fine-tune the permissions that you assign to individual logins that connect to a database through it. Every database can have just one `guest` user. Furthermore, any login without a user mapping to it connects to a database through the `guest` user. This feature makes it difficult to know who will connect to a database with whatever permissions you assign to the `guest` user. A much better practice is to create a user for a login and add the user to a fixed server role. The next sample illustrates this approach to granting database access. However, you should invoke the `sp_dropuser 'guest'` statement to disable the `guest` user before proceeding.

The next script shows the syntax for creating a user, `sqllogin1`, which points at the `sqllogin1` login. See the "Creating Users" section for an explanation of the `CREATE USER` statement syntax. The `SELECT` statements before and after the syntax for creating a fresh user based on the `sqllogin1` login allow you to see the addition of a new user to the `sys.sysusers` view that has access to the current database—namely, AdventureWorks. See the result sets from the `SELECT` statements following the script for creating the fresh `sqllogin1` user. Notice the second result set adds a row for the `sqllogin1` user that has 1 for its `hasdbaccess` column value.

```
SELECT name, hasdbaccess, isntuser, issqluser
FROM sys.sysusers
WHERE issqlrole = 0

IF EXISTS(SELECT * FROM sys.sysusers
    WHERE name = 'sqllogin1')
    DROP USER sqllogin1
GO

CREATE USER sqllogin1 FOR LOGIN sqllogin1
    WITH DEFAULT_SCHEMA = dbo
GO

SELECT name, hasdbaccess, isntuser, issqluser
FROM sys.sysusers
WHERE issqlrole = 0
```

name	hasdbaccess	isntuser	issqluser
dbo	1	0	1
guest	0	0	1
INFORMATION_SCHEMA	0	0	1
sys	0	0	1

name	hasdbaccess	isntuser	issqluser
dbo	1	0	1
guest	0	0	1
INFORMATION_SCHEMA	0	0	1
sys	0	0	1
sqllogin1	1	0	1

Permitting a User to Run SELECT Statements

The main value in granting a user access to a database is that you can then assign permissions to the user. The sqllogin1 user has access to the AdventureWorks database, but the user does not have permission to do anything in the database. The fixed database roles offer prespecified clusters of permissions that you can assign to users. Just add a user to a fixed database role to empower a user with any of these prespecified permission clusters. If you want a selection of permissions from more than one prespecified cluster, then add a user to multiple fixed database roles.

This section demonstrates how to explore fixed database role permissions as well as how to assign a user to a fixed server role. There are three system-stored procedures to assist with these tasks. The sp_helpdbfixedrole system-stored procedure provides a list of the nine fixed database roles along with a brief description of each role. The role name and description provide an overall summary of each role.

The following listing includes the EXEC statement for invoking the sp_helpdbfixedrole system-stored procedure. You do not need to specify an argument for this system-stored procedure. The db_owner fixed database role is a critical role because it has the permissions for all the other roles as well as the permission to assign users to any fixed database role. The db_owner role at the database level is comparable to the sysadmin fixed server role at the server level.

```
EXEC sp_helpdbfixedrole
```

```
DbFixedRole         Description
----------------    --------------------------
db_owner            DB Owners
db_accessadmin      DB Access Administrators
db_securityadmin    DB Security Administrators
db_ddladmin         DB DDL Administrators
db_backupoperator   DB Backup Operator
db_datareader       DB Data Reader
db_datawriter       DB Data Writer
db_denydatareader   DB Deny Data Reader
db_denydatawriter   DB Deny Data Writer
```

The definition of a fixed database role is a listing of specific permissions conveyed by membership in a role. You can generate such a list by executing the sp_dbfixedrolepermission system-stored procedure. This system-stored procedure takes the name of a fixed database role for which you seek a list of permissions, and you can specify this with the output returned from the sp_helpdbfixedrole system-stored procedure.

The following listing shows the execution of the sp_dbfixedrolepermission system-stored procedure for both db_datareader and the db_datawriter fixed database roles.

- As you can see, the db_datareader role conveys a single permission, but this permission has broad applicability in that it allows SELECT statements against any of several database objects that permit SELECT statements, including tables, views, and table-valued functions.

- The db_datawriter role endows its members with the permission to perform DELETE, INSERT, and UPDATE statements against any object that will allow the use of these statements—again, including tables, views, and inline table-valued functions.

- Both the db_datareader and db_datawriter fixed database roles apply a permission to all the objects within a database. Therefore, if you need to apply SELECT, DELETE, INSERT, and UPDATE permissions for some but not all tables, views, and inline table-valued functions, these fixed database roles are not appropriate. You can apply individual permissions for specific database objects in these kinds of scenarios.

```
EXEC sp_dbfixedrolepermission 'db_datareader'
```

```
DbFixedRole    Permission
-------------  -------------------------------
db_datareader  SELECT permission on any object
```

```
EXEC sp_dbfixedrolepermission 'db_datawriter'
```

```
DbFixedRole    Permission
-------------  -----------------------------
db_datawriter  DELETE permission on any object
db_datawriter  INSERT permission on any object
db_datawriter  UPDATE permission on any object
```

To empower the sqllogin1 user to perform a SELECT statement against any table in the AdventureWorks database, you can assign the sqllogin1 user to the db_datareader fixed database role. Use the sp_addrolemember system-stored procedure to make the assignment. The following script shows you the correct syntax for adding sqllogin1 to the db_datareader role from the AdventureWorks database context, and it completes the following steps.

- After adding sqllogin1 to the role, the script invokes an EXECUTE AS statement to open a connection to the AdventureWorks database from the sqllogin1 login. This statement succeeds because the sqllogin1 login maps to the sqllogin1 user in the AdventureWorks database.

- Then the script executes a SELECT statement for the ProductCategory table in the Production schema of the AdventureWorks database. This statement works properly because the sqllogin1 user is a member of the db_datareader role in the AdventureWorks database.

- The script concludes with a REVERT statement that transfers control back to a login from the sysadmin fixed server role that you used when you first started running the code samples in AssigningFixedDatabaseRoles.sql.

```
EXEC sp_addrolemember 'db_datareader', 'sqllogin1'

--You can connect from sqllogin1 to the AdventureWorks database
EXECUTE AS login = 'sqllogin1'
GO

--You can also select from tables
SELECT * FROM Production.ProductCategory
GO

REVERT
GO
```

Permitting a User to Run Both SELECT and INSERT Statements

Enabling a user with permissions from two fixed database roles is as simple as executing the sp_addrolemember system-stored procedure twice—once for each role to which you want to assign a user. If you want a user to be able to perform SELECT and INSERT statements within a database, then you can assign the user to db_datareader and db_datawriter fixed database roles.

SELECT statements are enabled by assigning the user to the db_datareader, and INSERT statements are permitted by assigning the user to the db_datawriter role. You must execute the following in the database context where you want to assign permissions.

```
EXEC sp_addrolemember 'db_datareader', 'cab233a\winlogin1'
EXEC sp_addrolemember 'db_datawriter', 'cab233a\winlogin1'
```

Granting, Denying, and Revoking Permissions

Fixed server roles and fixed database roles offer powerful shortcuts to assigning permissions to principals. However, the very feature that makes fixed server roles and fixed database roles so powerful is also a source of weakness. These fixed roles are powerful because they offer clusters of permissions that are predefined. Instead of having to learn more than 180 individual SSE permissions, you can learn just eight fixed server roles and another nine fixed database roles. However, assigning principals to fixed roles does not allow the precision security settings that are possible by working with individual permissions.

This section introduces you to the three key statements for handling individual SSE permissions, such as those returned by the sys.fn_builtin_permissions system catalog view. These statements allow you to grant and deny permissions on securable objects to principals. You can also revoke a granted or denied permission.

- GRANT assigns a permission for a securable object to a principal, such as a login, a user, or a role. You can optionally grant a permission to a principal so that the principal is able to assign the permission to other principals.

- DENY enables an application to block a principal from performing an action enabled by a permission. The DENY statement draws on the same set of permissions available to the GRANT statement.

- REVOKE removes a granted or denied permission for a securable object to a principal. Both GRANT and DENY statements make entries in the sysprotects table to record the granting or denial of a permission. A REVOKE statement removes an entry made in the sysprotects table by a GRANT statement or a DENY statement. The sys.sysprotects system catalog view lets you examine the contents of the sysprotects table.

You will often assign permissions to logins and users. However, you can also assign permissions to custom database roles that you create. Custom database roles are exceedingly useful because they permit you to create your own clusters of permissions. Furthermore, you can add and drop users as members of these custom database roles with the same techniques that you use for fixed database roles. Custom database roles allow you to benefit from the advantages associated with fixed database roles, but you are not locked into using a predefined set of permissions that only approximately matches your requirements.

Assigning Individual Permissions vs. Using Permissions in a Role

You can enable a user to perform SELECT statements by granting the SELECT permission for a particular object to a user principal or by adding a user principal to the db_datareader role. Just as with the db_datareader role, the SELECT permission can apply to any object that supports the use of a SELECT statement, such as a table, view, or table-valued user-defined function.

When you use the GRANT statement to assign the SELECT permission, you specify the permission for just one object per statement. If you need SELECT permission for more than one object, then you can invoke multiple GRANT statements—one for each object. Recall that the assignment of a user to the db_datareader role automatically grants permission to perform SELECT statements for all database objects that support a SELECT statement in a database.

Note Each GRANT statement applies to an individual securable object, but you can assign multiple permissions for an object to multiple principals with a single GRANT statement.

The sample for this section uses the sqllogin2 login and user in the AdventureWorks database. The script in PermissionsOrRoles.sql begins by setting the database context to AdventureWorks and re-creating the sqllogin2 login and user to make fresh copies of both principals. The most significant part of this portion of the script is that it sets the database context to the AdventureWorks database with the USE statement. The sample uses this context throughout the file. Recall that a login can have different permissions in different databases depending on the permissions associated with the database users that map to the login from different databases.

```
USE AdventureWorks
GO

IF EXISTS(SELECT * FROM sys.syslogins
    WHERE name = N'sqllogin2')
    DROP LOGIN sqllogin2
GO

CREATE LOGIN sqllogin2
    WITH PASSWORD = 'pass_sqllogin2'
GO

IF EXISTS(SELECT * FROM sys.sysusers
    WHERE name = 'sqllogin2')
    DROP USER sqllogin2
GO

CREATE USER sqllogin2 FOR LOGIN sqllogin2
    WITH DEFAULT_SCHEMA = dbo
GO
```

After setting up the principals, the sample runs two EXECUTE AS statements for the sqllogin2 login. The first EXECUTE AS statement confirms that the slqlogin2 user can connect to the AdventureWorks database, but an attempt to run a SELECT statement for the ProductCategory table in Production schema generates a failure because SELECT permission for the table is not granted yet. In fact, a new user, such as sqllogin2 user, lacks SELECT permission for all tables in a database. After the SELECT statement, the code block for the first EXECUTE AS statement concludes with a REVERT statement that returns control to the original execution context (e.g., one for a member of the sysadmin role).

```
EXECUTE AS login = 'sqllogin2'
SELECT ProductCategoryID, Name FROM Production.ProductCategory
GO

REVERT
GO
```

A GRANT statement can remedy the inability of the sqllogin2 user to perform a SELECT statement against the ProductCategory table in the Production schema. The following line of code shows the syntax for assigning SELECT permission on the ProductCategory table to the sqllogin2 user. The GRANT statement takes three arguments.

- First, you specify one or more permissions. The GRANT statement shown next designates the SELECT permission. If you assign multiple permissions with a single GRANT statement, you need to comma-delimit the permission names. Specify the permission(s) immediately after the GRANT keyword.

- Second, you designate a securable object to which the one or more permissions apply. The following GRANT statement designates the ProductCategory table in the Production schema of the current database context (AdventureWorks) as the securable object.

- Third, you specify a principal in the TO clause of the GRANT statement. The sample GRANT statement designates a single principal, the sqllogin2 user in the current database context. You can designate multiple principals with commas separating the principals.

```
GRANT SELECT ON Production.ProductCategory TO sqllogin2
```

■**Note** Recall that you can generate a full list of the permissions available for any securable class object. See the "Permissions" section for the T-SQL statement that does this.

A second EXECUTE AS code block for the sqllogin2 login demonstrates the impact of the preceding GRANT statement. The following code block allows the sqllogin2 login to connect to the AdventureWorks database and run a SELECT statement for the ProductCategory table. Another attempt to perform a SELECT statement for the ProductSubcategory table generates a failure, because the sqllogin2 user has permission to run a SELECT statement for only one securable object, the ProductCategory table. As you see, a GRANT statement allows you to specify the permission for a user in a very granular way. The concluding REVERT statement returns control to the principal having the execution context prior to the EXECUTE AS statement.

```
EXECUTE AS login = 'sqllogin2'
SELECT ProductCategoryID, Name FROM Production.ProductCategory
GO
SELECT COUNT(*)
FROM Production.ProductSubcategory
GO

REVERT
GO
```

Contrast the outcome of the preceding two SELECT statements run under different execution contexts. The other execution context is for the sqllogin1 user that belongs to the db_datareader role. Recall that this role lets a user perform SELECT statements against any database object that supports such a statement.

The following EXEC statement for the sp_helprolemember system-stored procedure allows you to verify whether the sqllogin1 user belongs to the db_datareader role. If not, you can run the sp_addrolemember system-stored procedure to add the sqllogin1 user to the db_datareader role. The "Permitting a User to Run SELECT Statements" section includes a sample showing how to achieve this task.

```
EXEC sp_helprolemember 'db_datareader'
```

The final EXECUTE AS code block in PermissionsOrRoles.sql is identical to the preceding one, except that the execution context is for the sqllogin1 instead of the sqllogin2 login. Because the sqllogin1 user belongs to the db_datareader role, it can successfully run both SELECT statements. Contrasting the success of both SELECT statements in this code block with the success of just the first SELECT statement in the preceding code block for the sqllogin2 login confirms that the permission granted with membership in the db_datareader role is broader than that provided by a single GRANT statement. If you do not need SELECT permission for all or even most of the tables, views, and table-valued user-defined functions in a database, then using a GRANT statement for one or a small number of SELECT statements is a more precise way of assigning permissions.

```
EXECUTE AS login = 'sqllogin1'
SELECT ProductCategoryID, Name FROM Production.ProductCategory
GO
SELECT COUNT(*)
FROM Production.ProductSubcategory
GO

REVERT
GO
```

Fine-Tuning Role Permissions with GRANT and DENY Statements

Instead of choosing to use either fixed roles or the assignment of individual permissions to principals, you can choose to rely on a combination of the two approaches to managing security. For example, a fixed role may have most of the permissions that you need a principal to have. However, the fixed role may also have permissions that you do not want the principal to have, and the fixed role can concurrently fail to have other permissions that you want the principal to have. In this kind of scenario, you can do the following:

- Assign a principal to a fixed role as a starting point for the principal's security settings.

- Specify DENY statements for permissions that you do not want a principal to have but that are provided by the fixed role.

- Add permission that the fixed role does not provide through one or more GRANT statements.

- Use one or more REVOKE statements to retire obsolete individual security settings that were previously made with GRANT and DENY statements.

This section illustrates techniques for implementing a fine-tuning strategy for designing the security settings for a principal. You can find the code for this section in PermissionsAndRoles.sql.

The sample for the section modifies the settings of a principal that belongs to both the db_datareader and db_datawriter fixed database roles. These two fixed roles convey the right to invoke a SELECT statement as well as to run INSERT, UPDATE, and DELETE statements for any object in a database. The principal is the cab233a\winlogin1 user in the NewDB1 database associated with the cab233a\winlogin1 login. The code for creating the NewDB1 database initially appears in the "Enabling a Login to Create a Database" section. The "Permitting a User to Run Both SELECT and INSERT Statements" section contains code to add a table named TrackPersons to the NewDB1 database and add the cab233a\winlogin1 user to the db_datareader and db_datawriter fixed roles in NewDB1.

The demonstration for this section shows repeated attempts to modify the contents of the TrackPersons table in NewDB1. Each attempt is with a slightly different array of security settings for the cab233a\winlogin1 user. Initially, the cab233a\winlogin1 user modifies the TrackPersons table based solely on security settings derived from membership in the db_datareader and db_datawriter fixed database roles. Two more attempts are made based on the fine-tuning of the permissions in the fixed database roles with GRANT and DENY statements as well as REVOKE statements that roll back earlier GRANT or DENY statements.

Before each attempt to modify the TrackPersons table, the code reinitializes the contents of the table with the RestoreTrackPersons stored procedure, the code for which appears next. The stored procedure begins by deleting all rows from the TrackPersons table. Then, four INSERT statements add four new rows to the table. These new rows are the only rows in the table after the RestoreTrackPersons stored procedure runs.

```
USE NewDB1
GO

CREATE PROC RestoreTrackPersons
AS

DELETE FROM TrackPersons

INSERT TrackPersons VALUES(1, 'Rick Dobosn')
INSERT TrackPersons vALUES(2, 'Virginia Dobson')
INSERT TrackPersons VALUES(3, 'Name to change')
INSERT TrackPersons VALUES(4, 'Name to delete')
GO
```

It is important to initialize the security settings for the cab233a\winlogin1 user so that it belongs to just the db_datareader and db_datawriter fixed database roles in the NewDB1 database. The following three statements verify the role members of the fixed database roles before initializing the contents of the TrackPersons table. If the cab233a\winlogin1 user does not appear in the proper roles, use the sp_addrolemember or sp_droprolemember system-stored procedure to achieve the proper role memberships for the user. A SELECT statement confirms the initial values in the TrackPersons table inserted by the RestoreTrackPersons stored procedure. The four INSERT statements in the RestoreTrackPersons stored procedure define the values returned by the SELECT statement.

```
EXEC sp_helprolemember

EXEC RestoreTrackPersons
SELECT * FROM TrackPersons
```

The first block of code running an EXECUTE AS statement is shown next. This block runs with the cab233a\winlogin1 user belonging to the db_datareader and db_datawriter roles and having no additional fine-tuning of its security settings. The code block performs four tasks.

- It updates the name column value in the TrackPersons table for the row with a tpid column value of 3.

- It deletes the row with a tpid column value of 4.

- It displays the contents of the modified version of the TrackPersons table.

- It restores the execution context of the login that invoked the initial EXECUTE AS statement in the code block.

The same block of code is rerun two additional times by the script within PermissionsAndRoles.sql. Before each rerun, there is some fine-tuning of the security settings for the cab233a\winlogin1 user with GRANT, DENY, or REVOKE statements.

```
EXECUTE AS login = 'cab233a\winlogin1'

UPDATE TrackPersons
SET name = 'Name changed'
WHERE tpid = 3

DELETE FROM TrackPersons WHERE tpid = 4
GO
SELECT * FROM TrackPersons
GO

REVERT
GO
```

The following listing shows the result set from the SELECT statement in the preceding code block. Notice that both the UPDATE and DELETE statements in the code block succeeded. This is because the name column value for the row with a tpid value of 3 changed from Name to change to Name changed. In addition, there is no fourth row because it was deleted by the DELETE statement in the block. This output confirms the success of both data modification statements within the code block whereas the cab233a\winlogin1 user is a member of the db_datareader and db_datawriter fixed database roles with no fine-tuning.

```
tpid        name
----------- ----------------
1           Rick Dobosn
2           Virginia Dobson
3           Name changed
```

The next couple of lines of code in PermissionsAndRoles.sql are shown next. These lines restore the initial values in the TrackPersons table and invoke a DENY statement. A DENY statement operates similarly to a GRANT statement in that it enforces a rule about the operation of a permission for an object by a principal. In the case of the following DENY statement, the rule is that UPDATE statements are not allowed for the TrackPersons table. The DENY statement instructs SSE to enforce this rule for the cab233a\winlogin1 user. The DENY statement overrides the UPDATE permission granted by the membership of the cab233a\winlogin1 user in the db_datawriter role. A denied permission always overrides a granted permission.

```
EXEC RestoreTrackPersons
DENY UPDATE ON TrackPersons TO [cab233a\winlogin1]
```

The output for the preceding EXECUTE AS code block with the UPDATE and DELETE statement is shown next. The result set below is for a fine-tuned set of permissions that enforces a rule against changes to column values in the TrackPersons table by the cab233a\winlogin1 user. Therefore, the UPDATE statement from the code block does not succeed, but the DELETE statement does. As a consequence, the name column value for the row with a tpid column value of 3 is the same as its initial value. However, the fourth row is missing because the DELETE statement was successful.

```
tpid        name
----------- ----------------
1           Rick Dobosn
2           Virginia Dobson
3           Name to change
```

The next three statements show the operations that take place before the second rerunning of the previous EXECUTE AS code block.

- The first statement restores the initial column values for the TrackPersons table.

- The second statement removes the rule denying updates to TrackPersons column values by the cab233a\winlogin1 user. The removal of this rule allows the underlying permission to update TrackPersons column values by the cab233a\winlogin1 user membership in the db_datawriter role to operate.

- The third statement enforces a new rule for the cab233a\winlogin1 user that denies the operation of DELETE statements for the TrackPersons table. Like the rule for the preceding DENY statement, this rule overrides the underlying permission to delete rows in NewDB1 tables based on cab233a\winlogin1 user membership in the db_datawriter role.

```
EXEC RestoreTrackPersons
REVOKE UPDATE ON TrackPersons TO [cab233a\winlogin1]
DENY DELETE ON TrackPersons TO [cab233a\winlogin1]
```

The result set from the last EXECUTE AS code block is shown next. This result includes four rows because the DELETE statement in the code block fails. The preceding DENY statement blocks the successful operation of the DELETE statement in the code block. However, the name column value for the third row changed to reflect the successful operation of the UPDATE statement in the code block. The REVOKE statement in the preceding code block enables the underlying permission from cab233a\winlogin1 user membership in the db_datawriter role.

```
tpid        name
----------- ------------------------------
1           Rick Dobosn
2           Virginia Dobson
3           Name changed
4           Name to delete
```

The script in PermissionsAndRoles.sql concludes by executing the following statement. This final instruction removes the rule blocking DELETE statements on the TrackPersons table by the cab233a\winlogin1 user. In other words, the final instruction restores the underlying permissions for the cab233a\winlogin1 user by virtue of its membership in the db_datawriter role. After executing the following instruction, you can rerun the EXECUTE AS code block so that it runs as it did initially in this section.

```
REVOKE DELETE ON TrackPersons TO [cab233a\winlogin1]
```

Assigning Permissions to Custom Database Roles

Instead of using fixed database roles you can create your own custom roles. A custom role is a database object that serves as a principal. Custom database roles are similar to fixed database roles in that you can add and drop users from membership in either type of role. In fact, you use the same system-stored procedures to add and drop members in fixed database roles as you do for custom database roles.

There are two especially important distinctions between fixed and custom database roles.

- First, fixed database roles cannot be added to or dropped from a database whereas custom database roles can be added and dropped from a database. Use the CREATE ROLE, ALTER ROLE, and DROP ROLE statements to add, modify, and drop a custom database role.

- Second, permissions associated with a custom role are not fixed. You can configure a role to confer to its members any set of permissions that you want. You can configure the permissions for a custom database role with the same GRANT, DENY, and REVOKE statements that you use to manage permissions for a user. Just designate a role name instead of a user name in the TO clause of the statement.

The sample for demonstrating the use of custom roles uses three custom roles, three permissions, and three users. The roles and users are added to the AdventureWorks database. Two permissions include SELECT permission for the ProductCategory and ProductSubcategory tables in the Production schema. The sample adds a new stored procedure, named ProcHello, which uses the PRINT statement to return the string with a value of Hello from ProcHello. The third permission grants EXEC permission for ProcHello.

The script in UsersRolesPermissions.sql starts by setting the database context to the AdventureWorks database and adding ProcHello to the database with a CREATE PROC statement. The code for these steps does not appear in the book to conserve space, but the code is available at the top of UsersRolesPermissions.sql. If you want a reminder about how to use the CREATE PROC statement, see the "Creating and Using Stored Procedures" section in Chapter 7.

After setting up the sample by completing the two preceding steps, the sample creates three custom database roles called ReadCats, ReadCatsSubCats, and SayHello. Each database role has its own CREATE ROLE statement. The CREATE ROLE statement requires one argument, which is the name of the custom role, and allows an optional second argument for its AUTHORIZATION clause. The argument for the AUTHORIZATION clause designates a user or role to serve as the owner of the new custom role. If you do not specify an AUTHORIZATION clause in a CREATE ROLE statement, the principal invoking the statement is the owner of the custom role.

```
CREATE ROLE ReadCats
CREATE ROLE ReadCatsSubCats
CREATE ROLE SayHello
```

Next, three GRANT statements assign permissions to the roles. The first GRANT statement conveys permission to perform a SELECT statement with the ProductCategory table as a data source. The second GRANT statement enables permission to run a SELECT statement against the ProductSubcategory table. The third GRANT statement confers permission to run the ProcHello stored procedure with an EXEC statement.

The permissions designated by the three GRANT statements are assigned to various subsets of the three custom database roles. The first GRANT statement with SELECT permission for the ProductCategory table assigns its permission to all three custom roles. The second GRANT statement with SELECT permission for the ProductSubcategory table assigns its permission to the ReadCatsSubCats and SayHello roles. The third GRANT statement confers EXEC permission for the ProcHello stored procedure to just one role—SayHello.

```
GRANT SELECT ON Production.ProductCategory
    TO ReadCats, ReadCatsSubCats, SayHello
GRANT SELECT ON Production.ProductSubcategory
    TO ReadCatsSubCats, SayHello
GRANT EXEC ON dbo.ProcHello TO SayHello
```

The setup for the demonstration of custom database roles includes two more kinds of steps.

- First, the script creates three logins and matching AdventureWorks users named sqllogin3, sqllogin4, and sqllogin5. Again, to conserve space, the code for creating the logins and users is not included in this book, but it is available in UsersRolesPermissions.sql. See the "Creating Principals" section for a review of the process for creating logins and users if you want to review the topic.

- Second, the script assigns the new database users to the custom database roles. Each new user gets assigned to one of the three custom roles with the sp_addrolemember system-stored procedure.

```
EXEC sp_addrolemember 'ReadCats', 'sqllogin3'
EXEC sp_addrolemember 'ReadCatsSubCats', 'sqllogin4'
EXEC sp_addrolemember 'SayHello', 'sqllogin5'
```

This kind of basic security design is actually quite common in database solutions. It contains three levels of security, represented by three roles. Each role can confer at least one permission to its members. One role, SayHello, is analogous to an administrator because its members have all possible permissions. This kind of role typically has one or just a very few members. Another role, ReadCatsSubCats, conveys a subset of the full set of permissions to its members. The number of members of this role is typically greater than those in the first role. Finally, a third role, ReadCats, is for any user who has access to the database solution. This kind of role typically has substantially more members than either of the other two roles.

Three EXECUTE AS code blocks complete the main part of the demonstration. Each of the three code blocks is the same, except that they are meant for different login principals and their associated user principals. The following listing shows the EXECUTE AS code block for the sqllogin3 login. As you can see, the code block implements three tasks before reverting control to an execution context that invokes the EXECUTE AS statement. The first task is to invoke a SELECT statement for the ProductCategory table. The second task is to run another SELECT statement for the ProductSubcategory table. The third task is to run the ProcHello stored procedure.

- Because the sqllogin3 user belongs to the ReadCats role, the sqllogin3 login execution context can only successfully complete the first task to perform a SELECT statement for the ProductCategory table. Recall that the ReadCats role receives its sole permission from a single GRANT statement.

- If you use the sqllogin4 login instead, it can successfully perform the first two SELECT statements, but not the third statement, to run the ProcHello stored procedure. This is because sqllogin4 belongs to the ReadCatsSubCats role, which receives permissions from two of the three GRANT statements.

- The sqllogin5 login can complete all three statements successfully because sqllogin5 belongs to the SayHello role. This custom database role receives permissions from all three GRANT statements.

```
EXECUTE AS login = 'sqllogin3'
SELECT ProductCategoryID, Name FROM Production.ProductCategory
GO
SELECT COUNT(*) '# of Subcategories'
FROM Production.ProductSubcategory
GO
EXEC ProcHello
GO

REVERT
GO
```

The script in UsersRolesPermissions.sql concludes with some clean-up code, which follows. This code is interesting for a couple of reasons.

- First, it allows you to rerun the script successfully multiple times without any manual intervention, except to start the code in the file. This is because the clean-up code removes objects that the code in the main body of the script creates. Failing to run the clean-up code can cause the failure of an attempt to create an object, such as a custom role that already exists.

- Second, the following code shows the proper order of dropping role members before dropping roles, users, and logins. Other sequences for dropping objects can cause a script failure that may require manual intervention.

```
EXEC sp_droprolemember 'ReadCats', 'sqllogin3'
EXEC sp_droprolemember 'ReadCatsSubCats', 'sqllogin4'
EXEC sp_droprolemember 'SayHello', 'sqllogin5'

DROP ROLE ReadCats
DROP ROLE ReadCatsSubCats
DROP ROLE SayHello

DROP USER sqllogin3
DROP USER sqllogin4
DROP USER sqllogin5

DROP LOGIN sqllogin3
DROP LOGIN sqllogin4
DROP LOGIN sqllogin5

DROP PROCEDURE ProcHello
```

Creating and Using Schemas

The term *schema* can have multiple meanings in databases. This section focuses on schemas as containers for database objects within a single database and as the second part of four-part names for database objects. Schema can also mean a catalog representing the structure of a database or an XML document representing the structure of other XML documents. These two meanings are outside the scope of this section.

The introduction of schemas in SSE and other SQL Server 2005 editions offers a major distinction between ownership and containership. The four-part name for objects in earlier versions was servername.databasename.username.objectname. The new four-part name is servername.databasename.schemaname.objectname. Objects, such as tables and views, belong to their preceding name part—either username or schemaname. *Belonging* can have two distinct meanings.

- First, an object can belong in the sense of being contained so that no two objects in the same container have the same name. The container represents a namespace.

- Second, an object can belong as a possession belongs to its owner.

Earlier versions of SQL Server mixed both meanings in the username qualifier for objects. All SQL Server 2005 editions, including SSE, allow the schemaname qualifier to represent only the first meaning of belonging—namely, containership. In SQL Server 2005, users do not directly own database objects, and schemas contain objects. In turn, a schema can be owned by a principal, such as a user or a database role.

The separation of containership from ownership delivers a very practical database administration benefit. In the past, when users left an organization or were transferred and therefore no longer had responsibility for database objects in their container, it was necessary to change the username qualifier for those objects. However, this name change could break applications, which referred to the object with the old username qualifier. By removing users from the name for objects, you can manage ownership separately from containership. This, in turn, allows you to change ownership for objects without any impact on the names for objects.

Creating and Owning Schemas

When you initially create a database, your new database includes several built-in schemas. You can also add schemas and assign ownership for the new schemas in multiple ways. This section traces the schemas in a database from its initial creation and through various actions for creating a schema and transferring the ownership of the schema among database users and a database role. The sample scripts covered in this section appear in OwningSchemas.sql.

The following script creates a new database (NewDB2), as well as the schemas in the database, which will set up a baseline that will help you track the ownership of schemas in a database. After changing the database context to the new database, a SELECT statement returns the schema_id, schema name, and owning principal_id of each schema in the database from sys.schemas along with the name of the principal owning a schema from sys.database_principals.

```
USE master
GO

IF EXISTS(SELECT * FROM sys.databases
    WHERE name = 'NewDB2')
    DROP DATABASE NewDB2
GO

CREATE DATABASE NewDB2
GO

USE NewDB2
GO

SELECT s.schema_id, s.name 'Schema name', s.principal_id,
    dp.name 'Principal name'
FROM sys.schemas s RIGHT JOIN sys.database_principals dp
ON s.principal_id = dp.principal_id
WHERE dp.is_fixed_role = 0 AND dp.name <> 'public'
```

The following listing shows the result set from the preceding SELECT statement. The four rows in this result set document the four built-in schemas for a new database. The Schema name column shows the names of the built-in schemas, and the Principal name column shows the principal that owns each built-in schema. The principal_id column is an identification number for the principal owner.

The INFORMATION_SCHEMA and sys schemas make available built-in views of system data. The "Processing Meta Data with System Views" section in Chapter 7 introduces you to using these views. Although the dbo and guest users own the schemas named after them, these schemas are available for use by any database user. For example, you can even designate the guest schema as the default schema for a new user (see "Creating Users" for a sample demonstrating this).

schema_id	Schema name	principal_id	Principal name
1	dbo	1	dbo
2	guest	2	guest
3	INFORMATION_SCHEMA	3	INFORMATION_SCHEMA
4	sys	4	sys

The real power of using schemas comes with creating your own schemas and then making database users the owners of your schemas. The following script shows one approach to this task and creates a login, a user, and a schema. The login, user, and schema all have the name sqllogin3. There is no name conflict because these are different types of securables. The script establishes the sqllogin3 user as the owner of the sqllogin3 schema.

The script starts by creating a fresh login named sqllogin3. Instead of proceeding directly to creating a NewDB2 user named sqllogin3 for the login, the script drops the sqllogin3 schema if it exists. If an existing sqllogin3 user owns a schema (or any other SSE securable), you will not be able to drop the user to make a fresh copy. Therefore, dropping the sqllogin3 schema before attempting to create a new sqllogin3 user helps to make the script more capable of running under different conditions, such as whether the user already owns the sqllogin3 schema or not.

The CREATE USER statement for the sqllogin3 user specifies the sqllogin3 schema as the default schema for the user. Notice that the sqllogin3 schema will definitely not exist at this point because a prior statement dropped the schema if it did exist. The successful operation of the CREATE USER statement demonstrates its ability to designate a default schema even if the schema does not exist at runtime for the CREATE USER statement.

> ■**Note** A default schema for a user is the schema that a user references by default. Therefore, if a user creates a new object without a schema qualifier, SSE creates the new object in the default schema for the user.

The CREATE SCHEMA statement makes a new schema named sqllogin3 and includes an optional AUTHORIZATION clause that specifies the sqllogin3 user as the schema's owner. There are two ways to designate a user as the owner of a schema with CREATE USER and CREATE SCHEMA statements.

- First, you can specify a user as the owner with the AUTHORIZATION clause in the CREATE SCHEMA statement.
- Second, you can specify a schema as the default schema for a user in a CREATE USER statement. If the schema does not have another owner, then this clause makes the user the schema's owner.

Schema ownership is important because it allows a user to create new objects in a schema.

```
IF EXISTS(SELECT * FROM sys.syslogins
    WHERE name = N'sqllogin3')
    DROP LOGIN sqllogin3
GO

CREATE LOGIN sqllogin3
    WITH PASSWORD = 'pass_sqllogin3'
GO

IF EXISTS(SELECT * FROM sys.schemas
    WHERE name = 'sqllogin3')
    DROP SCHEMA sqllogin3
GO

IF EXISTS(SELECT * FROM sys.sysusers
    WHERE name = 'sqllogin3')
    DROP USER sqllogin3
GO

CREATE USER sqllogin3 FOR LOGIN sqllogin3
    WITH DEFAULT_SCHEMA = sqllogin3
GO

CREATE SCHEMA sqllogin3 AUTHORIZATION sqllogin3
GO
```

The following result set shows the outcome of the preceding script. The SELECT statement for
the result set is the same as the preceding SELECT statement that shows the four built-in schemas in
a new database. Notice there are now five rows in the result set. The new row is for the sqllogin3
schema, which is owned by the sqllogin3 user, whose principal_id value is 5.

schema_id	Schema name	principal_id	Principal name
1	dbo	1	dbo
2	guest	2	guest
3	INFORMATION_SCHEMA	3	INFORMATION_SCHEMA
4	sys	4	sys
5	sqllogin3	5	sqllogin3

The next script presents another way to designate a user as the owner of a schema. The primary value of this approach is that it allows you to override a previously designated owner for an
existing schema. The script also highlights the ability of a single user to have relationships with
more than one schema.

The following script starts by creating a fresh sqllogin4 login. The CREATE USER statement for the sqllogin4 user designates the dbo schema as its default schema in its WITH DEFAULT_SCHEMA clause. This syntax explicitly designates the dbo schema as the default schema for the sqllogin4 user, but you can achieve the same result implicitly by not specifying a WITH DEFAULT_SCHEMA clause.

Notice that there is no IF statement to drop the sqllogin3 schema before attempting to drop any previous version of the sqllogin4 user. This script actually assumes that the sqllogin3 schema already exists. The concluding ALTER AUTHORIZATION ON SCHEMA statement modifies the owner of the sqllogin3 schema. The statement assigns the sqllogin4 user as the new owner of the sqllogin3 schema. Because a schema can have only one principal as an owner, the ALTER AUTHORIZATION ON SCHEMA statement implicitly drops the sqllogin3 user as the schema's owner.

```
IF EXISTS(SELECT * FROM sys.syslogins
    WHERE name = N'sqllogin4')
    DROP LOGIN sqllogin4
GO

CREATE LOGIN sqllogin4
    WITH PASSWORD = 'pass_sqllogin4'
GO

IF EXISTS(SELECT * FROM sys.sysusers
    WHERE name = 'sqllogin4')
    DROP USER sqllogin4
GO

CREATE USER sqllogin4 FOR LOGIN sqllogin4
    WITH DEFAULT_SCHEMA = dbo
GO

ALTER AUTHORIZATION ON SCHEMA::sqllogin3 TO sqllogin4
GO
```

The following listing shows the schemas and their owners after the preceding script is run. The listing is returned by the same SELECT statement that generated the prior two listings of schemas.

- The most noteworthy item is that there is a new principal named sqllogin4. The listing shows the new principal as the owner of the sqllogin3 schema.

- You can tell from a query of sys.database_principals that the dbo schema remains the default schema for sqllogin4 although sqllogin4 owns the sqllogin3 schema. This outcome indicates that a single principal can have relationships with multiple schemas.

- Because of a RIGHT JOIN in the SELECT statement generating the result set, the sqllogin3 user shows as a principal, which no longer owns a schema. Although the sqllogin3 user no longer owns the sqllogin3 schema, a query of sys.database_principals confirms that the sqllogin3 schema remains the default schema for the sqllogin3 user.

schema_id	Schema name	principal_id	Principal name
1	dbo	1	dbo
2	guest	2	guest
3	INFORMATION_SCHEMA	3	INFORMATION_SCHEMA
4	sys	4	sys
NULL	NULL	NULL	sqllogin3
5	sqllogin3	6	sqllogin4

Although a single principal can have relationships with multiple schemas, and even own multiple schemas, a single schema can have only one owner. Recall that schema ownership is important because it can enable the ability to add new objects to a schema. If you need to have multiple users own the same schema so that they can jointly add objects to the schema, then you can designate a custom database role as the schema's owner and add multiple users to the role. Each member of the custom database role that owns a schema will be able to create objects in the schema.

The following script creates a custom role named sqllogin3SchemaOwner. Next, it adds two users, sqllogin3 and sqllogin4, to the role. The script closes with an ALTER AUTHORIZATION ON SCHEMA statement to designate the sqllogin3SchemaOwner role as the new owner of the sqllogin3 schema. Both members of the sqllogin3SchemaOwner role inherit the ability to add objects to the sqllogin3 schema.

```
CREATE ROLE sqllogin3SchemaOwner
EXEC sp_addrolemember 'sqllogin3SchemaOwner', 'sqllogin3'
EXEC sp_addrolemember 'sqllogin3SchemaOwner', 'sqllogin4'
ALTER AUTHORIZATION ON SCHEMA::sqllogin3 TO sqllogin3SchemaOwner
GO
```

The following listing shows the standard listing of schemas and principals for this section after a modification to the sqllogin3 schema owner.

- The first point to note is that the sqllogin3SchemaOwner role, with a principal_id value of 7, appears as the new owner of the sqllogin3 schema.

- The sqllogin3 user and the sqllogin4 user both appear as principals, but neither owns a schema directly.

schema_id	Schema name	principal_id	Principal name
1	dbo	1	dbo
2	guest	2	guest
3	INFORMATION_SCHEMA	3	INFORMATION_SCHEMA
4	sys	4	sys
NULL	NULL	NULL	sqllogin3
NULL	NULL	NULL	sqllogin4
5	sqllogin3	7	sqllogin3SchemaOwner

Creating Objects in Owned Schemas

Aside from the fact that you can contain objects in a schema, you may be wondering what's special about schemas. Schemas can integrate tightly with CREATE DDL statements for objects, such as tables, to control who can create a new object in a schema. CREATE DDL statements can be enabled for a principal within a schema exclusively based on ownership of a schema and a CREATE permission for objects of a certain type. The syntax for naming new objects can be slightly different if an owned schema is also the default schema for a user. The code samples in this section can be found in CreatingObjectsInOwnedSchemas.sql.

The samples in this section illustrate syntax and permission settings for adding new objects to a schema from sqllogin3 and sqllogin4 users. The first two samples are for sqllogin3, and the next two are for sqllogin4. The first sample in each pair is meant to succeed. By contrast, the second member is meant to fail. The differences between each member in a pair of samples for a user highlight a particular issue to help you understand your options in using schemas to control the addition of new objects to a schema.

> **■Note** The samples are meant to be run in the order of presentation, and they are meant for use immediately after the running of the samples in OwningSchemas.sql. To repeat the samples in CreatingObjectsInOwned-Schemas.sql, first run the script in OwningSchemas.sql.

Recall that the concluding sample in the preceding section makes the sqllogin3SchemaOwner role the owner of the sqllogin3 schema. In addition, this sample makes sqllogin3 and sqllogin4 database users members of the sqllogin3SchemaOwner role. So long as these users have the CREATE TABLE permission, they can add new tables to the sqllogin3 schema. The CREATE TABLE permission operates at the schema level in this sample, so it empowers users to add new tables to any schemas they own, but it does not enable users to create new tables in schemas that they do not own.

The first sample illustrates the process for making a table in the sqllogin3 schema by the sqllogin3 user. The sample starts by setting the database context to NewDB2 before granting CREATE TABLE permission to the sqllogin3 user. These two tasks are meant to be run by a member of the sysadmin group.

Recall that the sqllogin3 user has the sqllogin3 schema as its default schema. This setting affects how the sqllogin3 user can designate the name of a new table for inclusion in the sqllogin3 schema. An EXECUTE AS block simulates a connection by the sqllogin3 login.

- A CREATE TABLE statement within the block designates a new table name as TrackPersons. Although the table name appears without a schema qualifier, the CREATE TABLE statement adds the new table to the sqllogin3 schema instead of the dbo schema. This is because the sqllogin3 schema is the default schema for the sqllogin3 user.

- A SELECT statement after the CREATE TABLE statement queries sys.tables to return the table name and schema_id value of tables in the NewDB2 database.

```
USE NewDB2
GO

GRANT CREATE TABLE TO sqllogin3
GO

EXECUTE AS login = 'sqllogin3'

CREATE TABLE TrackPersons (
    tpid int Primary Key,
    name nvarchar (30)
    )
GO

SELECT name, schema_id FROM sys.tables

REVERT
GO
```

The following listing shows the output from the preceding script. As you can see, the CREATE TABLE adds the table to the database. The table resides in the schema with a schema_id value of 5 for the sqllogin3 schema as opposed to schema_id 1 for the dbo schema.

```
name         schema_id
------------ -----------
TrackPersons 5
```

The next sample tries to clarify what was special about the preceding one that made it work. It essentially reruns the EXECUTE AS block from the first sample, but it performs two tasks before doing so. The two preparatory steps run from a member of the sysadmin fixed server role.

- The first step is to drop the TrackPersons table from the sqllogin3 schema. This action removes the possibility of the second sample failing from a name conflict. After all, the second sample reruns the EXECUTE AS block, which can add a table named TrackPersons to the sqllogin3 schema. However, the first sample already added a table with that name to the sqllogin3 schema.

- The setup code for the second sample also drops the sqllogin3 user from the sqllogin3SchemaOwner role by executing the sp_droprolemember system-stored procedure. Being in this role, along with having CREATE TABLE permission, conveys the authority to create a new table in the sqllogin3 schema.

```
IF EXISTS(SELECT * FROM sys.tables
    WHERE name = 'TrackPersons' AND schema_id = 5)
    DROP TABLE sqllogin3.TrackPersons

EXEC sp_droprolemember 'sqllogin3SchemaOwner', 'sqllogin3'
```

In this case, rerunning the EXECUTE AS block fails. The only significant change is that the sqllogin3 user is not a member of the sqllogin3SchemaOwner role. Because this role is the owner of the sqllogin3 schema, the role conveys that status to its members. Successfully using CREATE TABLE permission to add a new table in a schema requires owner status for a user.

The third sample in this section adds the TrackPersons table to the sqllogin3 schema from the sqllogin4 user. After confirming whether the CREATE TABLE statement succeeds, the script erases the table to help simplify the interpretation of the next sample.

- The script begins by granting CREATE TABLE permission to the sqllogin4 user. This occurs from a sysadmin member (or other login with permission to assign this permission).

- There is no need to remove a copy of the TrackPersons table in the sqllogin3 schema before the CREATE TABLE statement because the second sample failed to add a new table.

- The EXECUTE AS block for the third sample is nearly the same as the one for the first sample.

  - This sample designates the table name as sqllogin3.TrackPersons instead of just TrackPersons as in the first sample. It is necessary to specify a schema qualifier as part of the table's name in the third sample because the sqllogin3 schema is not the default schema for the sqllogin4 user.

  - After a query of the sys.tables view, an IF statement with an EXISTS operator removes the table added by the CREATE TABLE statement. Using an IF statement makes the execution of the DROP TABLE statement conditional in case the CREATE TABLE statement fails for any reason.

```
GRANT CREATE TABLE TO sqllogin4
GO

EXECUTE AS login = 'sqllogin4'

CREATE TABLE sqllogin3.TrackPersons (
    tpid int Primary Key,
    name nvarchar (30)
    )
GO

SELECT name, schema_id FROM sys.tables
```

```
IF EXISTS(SELECT * FROM sys.tables
    WHERE name = 'TrackPersons' AND schema_id = 5)
    DROP TABLE sqllogin3.TrackPersons

REVERT
GO
```

The output from this script is the same as that of the first sample in this section and confirms the addition of one table named TrackPersons to the sqllogin3 schema with a schema_id value of 5. Using the schema name qualifier in the preceding script does not affect the table name in any way, because the qualifier merely designates the schema in which to create a new table.

The last sample in this section attempts to add another table from the sqllogin4 user. This attempt takes advantage of the fact that sqllogin4 has a default schema name of dbo. The CREATE TABLE statement does not designate a schema qualifier. Therefore, the table will enter the dbo schema if the statement succeeds.

Recall that the sqllogin4 user already has permission to create tables. Unfortunately, this permission is not enough to add a new table to the schema. For CREATE TABLE permission to empower a user to create a new table in a schema, the user must be an owner of the schema. Because sqllogin4 is not the owner of the dbo schema, which is implicitly referred to in the following script, the attempt to add a new table to the dbo schema fails.

```
EXECUTE AS login = 'sqllogin4'

CREATE TABLE TrackPersons (
    tpid int Primary Key,
    name nvarchar (30)
    )
GO

SELECT name, schema_id FROM sys.tables

REVERT
GO
```

Creating Objects in Any Schema

As you can see in the preceding section, combining CREATE object permissions with schema ownership for users is a very precise way of specifying in what schemas a user can create objects. The precision of this approach is attractive when you want to tightly constrain the choice of where users can create objects, such as for novice users. However, experienced developers may benefit from another approach that makes it easy for a user to create objects in multiple schemas. This section illustrates one way to make it possible for a single user to enter all kinds of objects in multiple schemas. The sample for this section resides in CreatingObjectsInAnySchema.sql.

The section has a single sample with three major elements.

- In the initial element, code sets up an environment that will allow the other two elements to work. This initial setup element also makes it easy to rerun the sample with different assignments for a local variable (@sname), which designates a schema name.

- The second element conditionally drops a table from a schema. This element reads the @sname local variable and conditionally drops one of two tables—dbo.TrackPersons or sqllogin3.TrackPersons. The second element also detects and warns with a return message if @sname is set to a value other than dbo or sqllogin3.

- The solution's third element adds a table to the schema specified by the @sname local variable. The approach used here allows a single user to add a table to either of two schemas without direct ownership of either schema.

The code for the initial element of the solution follows.

- As you can see, the first element starts by making NewDB2 the database context.

- Next, the code conditionally drops TrackPersons tables from the dbo schema (schema_id = 1) and the sqllogin3 schema (schema_id = 5).

- Critically, the code assigns the sqllogin4 user to the db_ddladmin fixed database role. The permissions for this role, which include CREATE, DROP, and ALTER for all database objects, operate at the database level and are not confined to any individual schema. As a consequence, a user that is a member of the role can apply its permissions in any schema.

- The initial element opens an EXECUTE AS code block that holds the code for the other two solution elements.

  - The initial element concludes by opening an EXECUTE AS block for the sqllogin4 login. You can adapt the sample in multiple ways to accommodate more than one user, such as using a stored procedure with a parameter to designate the user name.

  - A REVERT statement, which does not show in this excerpt, after the second solution's elements, returns the execution context to that for the user invoking the EXECUTE AS statement.

```
USE NewDB2
GO

IF EXISTS(SELECT * FROM sys.tables
    WHERE name = 'TrackPersons' AND schema_id = 1)
    DROP TABLE dbo.TrackPersons
IF EXISTS(SELECT * FROM sys.tables
    WHERE name = 'TrackPersons' AND schema_id = 5)
    DROP TABLE sqllogin3.TrackPersons
GO

EXEC sp_addrolemember 'db_ddladmin', 'sqllogin4'
GO

EXECUTE AS login = 'sqllogin4'
```

The code for the second solution element is shown next. It's a little lengthy, but the code is relatively easy to follow. The first two statements declare the @sname local variable and assign a value to it of sqllogin3. This points the second and third solution elements at the sqllogin3 schema. By changing the SET statement for @sname to a value of dbo, you can use the code with the dbo schema instead of the sqllogin3 schema. An IF...ELSE IF...ELSE IF statement implements the core logic for the second solution element.

- The IF clause drops the dbo.TrackPersons table if the @sname variable points at the dbo schema and the TrackPersons table exists in the dbo schema. A BEGIN...END block groups two statements for execution when the EXISTS operator returns a Boolean value of 1.

- The first ELSE...IF clause performs the same kind of task as the IF clause for the TrackPersons table in the sqllogin3 schema.

- The second ELSE…IF clause returns a message reminding the user to assign a value of either dbo or sqllogin3 for the @sname local variable.

```
DECLARE @sname nvarchar(18)
SET @sname = 'sqllogin3'

IF EXISTS(SELECT *
    FROM sys.tables t
    JOIN sys.schemas s
    ON t.schema_id = s.schema_id
    WHERE t.name = 'TrackPersons' AND s.name = @sname
    AND @sname = 'dbo')
BEGIN
    DROP TABLE dbo.TrackPersons
    print 'Dropped TrackPersons table in dbo schema'
END
ELSE IF EXISTS(SELECT *
    FROM sys.tables t
    JOIN sys.schemas s
    ON t.schema_id = s.schema_id
    WHERE t.name = 'TrackPersons' AND s.name = @sname
    AND @sname = 'sqllogin3')
BEGIN
    DROP TABLE sqllogin3.TrackPersons
    print 'Dropped TrackPersons table in sqllogin3 schema'
END
ELSE IF (@sname <> 'dbo' AND @sname <> 'sqllogin3')
    PRINT 'Specify schema name of dbo or sqllogin3.'
```

The third solution element also uses an IF…ELSE IF…ELSE IF statement.

- The IF clause creates a new TrackPersons table in the dbo schema.

- The first ELSE…IF clause creates a new TrackPersons table in the sqllogin3 schema.

- The second ELSE…IF clause displays a message that no table is created if the @sname local variable is neither dbo nor sqllogin3.

```
IF @sname = 'dbo'
BEGIN
    CREATE TABLE dbo.TrackPersons (
    tpid int Primary Key,
    name nvarchar (30)
    )
    Print 'Created TrackPersons table in dbo schema.'
END
ELSE IF @sname = 'sqllogin3'
BEGIN
    CREATE TABLE sqllogin3.TrackPersons (
    tpid int Primary Key,
    name nvarchar (30)
    )
    Print 'Created TrackPersons table in sqllogin3 schema.'
END
ELSE print 'Did not create table.'
```

The code in CreatingObjectsInAnySchema.sql is designed to be easy to rerun. If you run code as shown in the preceding sample, after first running the code in OwningSchemas.sql once, you'll get a message confirming the creation of the TrackPersons table in the sqllogin3 schema. Changing the value of @sname to equal dbo and rerunning the script will return a message about the creation of the TrackPersons table in the dbo schema. Assigning a value other than sqllogin3 or dbo to @sname and running the script generates a couple of warning messages.

You can also change the user name manually just to evaluate its impact on the code. You have to modify the code in two places to change the user name. Update the EXEC sp_addrolemember and the EXECUTE AS statements toward the end of the first code block. In the context of the users previously created, you can change the user from sqllogin4 to sqllogin3. Although the samples in the preceding section gave different results for one of these users or the other, this sample works equally well with either user.

Using Encryption Keys and Certificates

Encryption keys and certificates complement the techniques described earlier in this chapter for securing SSE. I presented techniques for determining how to validate a user before granting them access to a server. After validation, SSE offers other security techniques to determine if a user has permission to make different types of requests to an SSE instance, such as access data, manipulate data, or make new database objects. If an invalid user (hacker) pierces the security for a server and discovers a way to access data, encryption offers yet another level of security that protects your data.

Encryption is a process of transforming plain text, such as varchar or nvarchar data, to meaningless character sequences, sometimes called ciphertext. You can think of encryption as a padlock that you apply to your data. With an encryption key or a certificate, you can lock and unlock the padlock. Encrypting data is analogous to locking the padlock on your data, and unencrypting data is analogous to unlocking the padlock on your data. The data are locked in ciphertext format and unlocked in plain text format.

Just as there are different types and sizes of locks, there are also different encryption techniques. Some encryption techniques are distinct by their algorithms; these distinctions are analogous to the types of locks. You can also differentiate encryption techniques by the length of the key. These key length differences correspond to the size of a lock: The bigger the lock, the harder it is to break.

A technique related to encryption is known as signing data. You can sign data with certificates that you can also use to encrypt data. Users can view signed data without a certificate, but they need to unencrypt encrypted data before viewing it. A teacher may want to sign student grades so that students can view their grades easily, but the teacher can see if anyone tampered with a posted grade. If anyone alters a grade, the teacher will be able to detect the change. Signing data is like putting data in a glass box: anyone can see the data, but they cannot change them without breaking the glass box. SQL Server Express has functions that let you assess whether data changed since they were last signed.

All encryption and data-signing techniques require some computation. Although SQL Server Express hides the details of the computation, it does not eliminate the time to make the computation. Furthermore, the most thorough encryption techniques, which are analogous to the biggest, most complex locks, are more computationally intensive than other techniques that are easier to unencrypt without a legitimate encryption key or a certificate. The computational costs for encryption raise the need to assess if encryption security benefits justify the performance impact of the added security that they provide in your application contexts.

Encrypting and signing data are very rich topics. This section quickly introduces you to the basics of encrypting and signing data and has two goals. First, it presents samples to get you started using these techniques. Second, it provides a foundation so that you can go on and learn more about the rich ways that SSE enables the encrypting and signing of data. The sample code for this section is in SettingUpEncSignDemo.sql, EncryptingDecryptingData.sql, and SigningData.sql.

Encrypting Data

SQL Server Express lets you encrypt data with a symmetric key, an asymmetric key, or a certificate. You can sign data and verify that the data is unchanged since last signed with either a certificate or an asymmetric key.

- A symmetric key uses the same secret value to both encrypt and decrypt data.

- An asymmetric key uses public and private key pairs. You can encrypt data or sign data with one member of a key pair and decrypt data or verify a signature for data with the other member of a key pair.

- A certificate serves as a wrapper for a public asymmetric key.

Just as there are hierarchies for principals, securables, and permissions, there is also an encryption hierarchy. Higher elements in the encryption hierarchy can secure lower elements.

- The Service Master Key is at the top of the hierarchy. This key is installed when you create an SSE instance on a computer. The Service Master Key is unique to a server instance.

- Each database within a server can have its own Database Master Key. The Service Master Key secures the Database Master Key.

- Certificates and asymmetric keys are at the same level in the encryption hierarchy—right below the Database Master Key. SQL Server Express can use the Database Master Key to secure both asymmetric keys and certificates.

- Both certificates and asymmetric keys can secure symmetric keys. Additionally, one symmetric key can secure another symmetric key.

You can create, drop, and modify certificates, asymmetric keys, and symmetric keys with CREATE, DROP, and ALTER statements. The CREATE DDL statements let you specify such properties as encryption algorithms, the length of your encryption key, and passwords (if you use them). The property settings for symmetric keys, asymmetric keys, and certificates are distinct. Review the Books Online documentation for the details about which property settings are available and the proper syntax for making the settings.

Specialized T-SQL functions facilitate encrypting and decrypting data with symmetric keys, asymmetric keys, and certificates that you generate with CREATE DDL statements. For example, the EncryptByCert and DecryptByCert functions let you encrypt and decrypt character sequences with certificates. Parallel functions are available for symmetric keys and asymmetric keys that you generate with CREATE ASYMMETRIC KEY and CREATE SYMMETRIC KEY statements.

The EncryptByPassPhrase and DecryptByPassPhrase functions substantially simplify the encrypting and decrypting of data with symmetric keys. One special advantage of these functions is that you do not need to previously invoke a CREATE SYMMETRIC KEY statement before you can invoke the functions. In addition, you must explicitly open a symmetric key created with a CREATE SYMMETRIC KEY statement before you can use the key, but the EncryptByPassPhrase and DecryptByPassPhrase functions have no such requirement. SQL Server Express automatically makes a symmetric key available whenever you invoke either function.

Additionally, you can explore certificates and keys with the system catalog views. Three system catalog views for keys and certificates are sys.asymmetric_keys, sys.certificates, and sys.symmetric_keys. These views are useful for determining if a key or certificate already exists

Encryption keys and certificates depend on a secret, such as a password or another key, to validate encryption, decryption, adding signatures for data in tables, and verifying data signatures. You can let SSE manage your key and certificate secrets for you, or you can manage the secrets yourself. When SSE manages the security of your keys, it will base them on the Database Master Key and Service Master Key of the database and server in which the keys are used. If you use passwords to secure encryption keys and certificates, your certificates and keys are not bound to one database or server. The latter approach makes it easier to use keys and certificates in multiple databases and on different servers. However, you are responsible for devising techniques to manage the security of your passwords.

Both the encryption and data-signing samples rely on tables in the NewDB3 database. There are two tables in the NewDB3 database—one for each type of sample. The following excerpt from SettingUpEncSignDemo.sql shows the code for creating the ForEncDemo table.

- Aside from the primary key column, the table contains columns for the names of individuals, along with two more columns to store identity data for the individuals in plain text and encrypted formats. One of the most common applications for encryption is protecting identity data.

- Notice the id_data_orig column can store up to 11 characters, but its encrypted counterpart is much longer.

- The encrypted format must store information about the encryption key along with the actual encrypted values.

- Also notice that the id_data_orig column has a nvarchar data type, but the id_data_enc column has a varbinary format. SQL Server Express stores ciphertext output from encryption functions in varbinary format.

```
CREATE TABLE ForEncDemo (
    rowid int IDENTITY(1,1) PRIMARY KEY,
    name nvarChar(20),
    id_data_orig Nvarchar(11),
    id_data_enc varbinary(70)
)
```

The next code segment from EncryptingDecrypting.sql illustrates the use of the EncryptByPassPhrase function. The code segment depends on the prior execution of the code in SettingUpEncSignDemo.sql. The @name and @in_id_data local variables are for the name and id_data_orig column values.

Note The @pp_value local variable has a very simple value for this demonstration. However, in actual practice, it is better to use a longer, more complex password for encrypting and decrypting data.

The script inserts a single row into the ForEncDemo table. Then, the segment applies the EncryptByPassPhrase function to encrypt the inserted value for the id_data_orig column. The function has four arguments. The first two arguments denote the pass phrase value and the column to encrypt. The third and fourth arguments specify values for authenticating the encryption. The third argument value of 1 indicates the use of authentication, and the fourth argument value points at the primary key for the row. Authentication in this context makes it more difficult for a rogue user to copy over an encrypted value with another invalid value in a way that can avoid detection. In order for the DecryptByPassPhrase function to decrypt a value encrypted by an EncryptByPassPhrase function, both functions must have identical authentication arguments.

```
USE NewDB3
GO

DECLARE @name nvarchar(20), @in_id_data nvarchar(70)

SET @name = 'Rick Dobson'
SET @in_id_data = '111-11-1111'
INSERT ForEncDemo (name, id_data_orig) VALUES(@name, @in_id_data)
GO

DECLARE @pp_value nvarchar(10)

SET @pp_value = 'passphrase'

UPDATE ForEncDemo
SET id_data_enc = EncryptByPassPhrase(@pp_value, id_data_orig,
    1,
    CONVERT( varbinary, rowid))
WHERE rowid = 1
GO
```

The second code segment from EncryptingDecryptingData.sql focuses on the recovery of encrypted data. The code decrypts data from the ForEncDemo table. A SELECT statement with a WHERE clause specifies a row from which to decrypt a column value. The SELECT list has three items: the original column value (id_data_orig), the encrypted column value (id_data_enc), and the decrypted column value. The DecryptByPassPhrase function uses the arguments in the same order as the EncryptByPassPhrase function.

```
DECLARE @pp_value nvarchar(10);
SET @pp_value = 'passphrase';

SELECT id_data_orig, id_data_enc AS "Encrypted data",
    CONVERT(nvarchar, DecryptByPassphrase(@pp_value, id_data_enc,
    1,
    CONVERT(varbinary, rowid))) AS "Decrypted data"
FROM ForEncDemo
WHERE rowid = 1;
GO
```

The following output listing shows the result sets from the preceding SELECT statement. The
result set shows an excerpt from the encrypted value in varbinary format in its second column.
The full encrypted value is much longer than the original value.

```
id_data_orig Encrypted data Decrypted data
------------ -------------- --------------
111-11-1111  0x010000004ADF 111-11-1111
```

Signing Data

When you sign data, each column that you sign requires an extra column for that column's
encrypted signature. If anyone updates a signed column value in a row, its value becomes unsynchronized with the corresponding encrypted signature's value. Someone can sign a row again after
altering a column value, but the row's editor must have access to a valid certificate or asymmetric
key to re-sign the signature for a row.

You can sign a column value in a row with either the SignByAsymKey or SignByCert function,
depending on whether you are using an asymmetric key or a certificate. Matching functions
(VerifySignedByAsymKey and VerifySignedByCert) exist for verifying that a signature has not
changed since it was last signed.

The code in this section works with the SignedData table created in
SettingUpEncSignDemo.sql. Three critical column values will be necessary for any application that
uses signed data.

- The mysignature column has a varbinary type for holding the data signature.

- The mytext column contains the value that you sign.

- The certname column contains the name of the certificate used to generate the signature
  column value. A column for a certificate's name is not strictly necessary. This is obviously the
  case if you have only one certificate or your organization uses a specific certificate for each
  type of data it signs.

Note When working with tables with many rows, you may want to discover the smallest column width that
allows your signing function to succeed without causing your column to overflow. In any event, the signature
column width must be wider than the width of the data in the column for which the signature column validates
no changes.

```
CREATE TABLE SignedData (
    rowid int IDENTITY(1,1) PRIMARY KEY,
    certname nvarChar(128) NOT NULL,
    mytext nvarchar(256),
    mysignature varbinary(1024)
)
```

The following excerpt from SigningData.sql shows the code to create two certificates named HisCert and HerCert. The code for creating both certificates has the same format, but the detailed settings are different. Notice that the code uses standard DDL statement types.

- The code begins by checking for an existing certificate with the name for the new certificate. SQL Server Express does not allow two certificates on a server instance with identical names.

- The following CREATE CERTIFICATE syntax demonstrates how to secure a certificate with a password. Use the ENCRYPTION BY PASSWORD argument to specify the password value for a certificate. Recall that this approach makes the certificate available for use on other server instances.

- It is useful, but not mandatory, to specify an expiration date for a certificate. This practice forces the users of certificates to reauthenticate themselves at some reasonable point in the future.

```
IF EXISTS(SELECT * FROM sys.certificates
    WHERE name = 'HisCert')
    DROP CERTIFICATE HisCert
GO

CREATE CERTIFICATE HisCert
    ENCRYPTION BY PASSWORD = 'his secret'
    WITH SUBJECT = 'Rick Dobson',
    EXPIRY_DATE = '12/31/2007'
GO

IF EXISTS(SELECT * FROM sys.certificates
    WHERE name = 'HerCert')
    DROP CERTIFICATE HerCert
GO

CREATE CERTIFICATE HerCert
    ENCRYPTION BY PASSWORD = 'her secret'
    WITH SUBJECT = 'Virginia Dobson',
    EXPIRY_DATE = '12/31/2007'
GO
```

The demonstration for signing data utilizes a stored procedure named SignandInsert for inserting new rows in the SignedData table. The stored procedure has three input parameters.

- @myinput is the value for the signed column.

- @CertName is the name of the certificate used to generate a value for the mysignature column in the SignedData table.

- @CertSecret is the password for the certificate.

The stored procedure contains an INSERT statement for adding a new row to the SignedData table. The SignByCert function in the INSERT statement assigns a value to the mysignature column for the new row. Notice that the SignByCert function takes arguments for the certificate's name, the column value being signed, and the certificate's password.

```
CREATE PROCEDURE SignandInsert
     @myinput nvarchar(256),
     @CertName nvarchar(128),
     @CertSecret nvarchar(128)
AS
INSERT SignedData VALUES(@CertName,
    @myinput, SignByCert( Cert_Id( @CertName),
    @myinput, @CertSecret))
GO
```

Four successive sets of statements add or modify rows in the SignedData table; the last of these sets is shown only in SigningData.sql. These statements illustrate the syntax and outcome for populating rows in the SignedData table with and without certificates (and even wrong certificates). The output from the last statement (and in one case the next to the last statement) in a set illustrates the impact of the syntax for preceding statements in a set. The precise formulation of the statements generating a result set depends on the certificate used to sign the data in a row.

The DECLARE, SET, and EXEC statements in the first set appear in the next script, followed by a SELECT statement that generates a result set to confirm the impact of the EXEC statement. This first code block adds a new row to the SignedData table with the HisCert certificate that has a password of 'his secret'. The @myinput local variable sets a mytext column value of This is my story. The EXEC statement passes these values to the parameters for the SignandInsert stored procedure.

After the SignandInsert stored procedure has finished, the SELECT statement executes. This statement returns the rowid column value along with the certificate's name (certname) and the value in the mytext column for all rows in the SignedData table with a certname column value of HisCert.

A VerifySignedByCert function assigns a value to the fourth column (IsSignatureValid) in the result set. This function takes three values: the name of the certificate used to originally generate the mysignature column value for a row, the original mytext column value used as input to the signature, and the mysignature column value. When you are initially signing a row with a certificate, the function always returns a value of 1 to indicate a valid signature.

```
DECLARE @myinput nvarchar(256)
SET @myinput =
     N'This is my story'
EXEC SignandInsert
     @myinput, 'HisCert', 'his secret'
GO

SELECT rowid, CONVERT(nvarchar(10), certname) 'certname',
    CONVERT(nvarchar(20), mytext) 'mytext',
    VerifySignedByCert(Cert_Id('HisCert'),
    mytext, mysignature ) as IsSignatureValid
FROM SignedData
WHERE certname = 'HisCert'
GO
```

rowid	certname	mytext	IsSignatureValid
1	HisCert	This is my story	1

The next set of statements inserts a second row in the SignedData table. This second set of statements uses the HerCert certificate to sign the mytext column value. Notice the EXEC statement passes HerCert and her secret to the SignandInsert stored procedure to develop a signature for the mysignature column. Notice the result set includes just one row although there are two rows in the table. This is because the SELECT statement includes a filter for rows with a certname column value of HerCert. When you are verifying the rows in a table for unaltered signatures, you can check for only one certificate at a time, because the VerifySignedByCert function takes the name of a certificate as one of its arguments.

```
DECLARE @myinput nvarchar(256)
SET @myinput =
        N'This is my song'
EXEC SignandInsert
        @myinput, 'HerCert', 'her secret'
GO

SELECT rowid, CONVERT(nvarchar(10), certname) 'certname',
    CONVERT(nvarchar(20), mytext) 'mytext',
    VerifySignedByCert(Cert_Id('HerCert'),
    mytext, mysignature ) as IsSignatureValid
FROM SignedData
WHERE certname = 'HerCert'
GO
```

rowid	certname	mytext	IsSignatureValid
2	HerCert	This is my song	1

The next code segment shows an update to the second row of the SignedData table. Therefore, this segment is different from either of the two preceding ones because it performs an update instead of an insert. Anyone can sign a change that they make to a row. However, the following code segment signs the updated row with a different certificate than the one initially used to sign the row. Therefore, the signature is invalid relative to the original certificate.

The UPDATE statement in the following script changes two column values in the second row (with a rowid column value of 2). The changed values are for the mytext and mysignature columns. Notice that the SignByCert function assigns a new value to the mysignature column value. However, the initial signature was generated with the HerCert certificate (see the certname column value), but this SignByCert function references the HisCert certificate. Therefore, the new signature is invalid relative to the HerCert certificate.

The first SELECT statement in the following code segment checks the signature relative to the HerCert signature. Because the user signed with the HisCert certificate, the VerifySignedByCert function returns a value of 0—meaning not valid. With this kind of output from the function, you know that the row was not signed by someone with access to the proper certificate or the person signing the change used the wrong certificate.

If you have the password for other possible certificates, you can check the signature to see if the change was signed with one of these. The second SELECT statement shows a check of the validity of the signature with the HisCert signature. As you can see from the second result set, this certificate verifies the validity of the signature. If you believe the signer could have accidentally used the wrong certificate, then you can perform additional checks. Otherwise, you can dispose of the row with modified column values.

```
DECLARE @myinput nvarchar(256), @CertSecret nvarchar(128)
SET @CertSecret = 'his secret'
SET @myinput =
      N'All the day long'
UPDATE SignedData
SET mytext = @myinput,
mysignature = SignByCert( Cert_Id( 'HisCert'), @myinput, @CertSecret)
WHERE rowid = 2
GO

SELECT rowid, CONVERT(nvarchar(10), certname) 'certname',
    CONVERT(nvarchar(20), mytext) 'mytext',
    VerifySignedByCert(Cert_Id('HerCert'),
    mytext, mysignature ) as IsSignatureValid
FROM SignedData
WHERE certname = 'HerCert'
GO

SELECT rowid, CONVERT(nvarchar(10), certname) 'certname',
    CONVERT(nvarchar(20), mytext) 'mytext',
    VerifySignedByCert(Cert_Id('HisCert'),
    mytext, mysignature ) as IsSignatureValid
FROM SignedData
WHERE rowid = 2
GO
```

rowid	certname	mytext	IsSignatureValid
2	HerCert	All the day long	0

rowid	certname	mytext	IsSignatureValid
2	HerCert	All the day long	1

The SigningData.sql file has one additional sample that I leave for you to study on your own. This shows the outcome of someone making a change and not signing the row—say, because the person doesn't have a certificate. In this case, the updated row is shown as an unsigned row. Using the VerifySignedByCert function returns a value of 0 to signify an invalid signature.

Summary

This chapter covered five major security topics in two major groups. The first two topics address traditional security issues, but SSE still introduces several innovations, such as much more granular permissions. The second set of topics highlights three major areas of security innovations.

The first two topics are the most widely used ones for security. The first topic showed you how to create and track the principals in a database, where principals represent users in your database applications. The second essential topic covered the assigning of permissions to principals. SQL Server Express checks the permissions for users before executing requests by principals. Only principals with valid permissions have their requests executed.

The next two security topics introduced SSE security innovations. Schemas allow you to assign names for database objects that do not reflect the owner of objects. This, in turn, makes your applications more robust in the event that employees leave a company or change positions within your company. Encryption is a way of securing your data so that even if hackers somehow break into a server, they will not be able to use your data.

PART 2

Working with Visual Basic Express and Visual Web Developer Express

■■■

CHAPTER 9

Introduction to Visual Basic Express and Windows Forms

Just like SQL Server Express, Visual Basic Express (VBE) is an exciting innovation from Microsoft that is of special benefit to database developers serving the needs of departments in large and mid-sized organizations, as well as those working in or offering consulting to small businesses. VBE also especially targets those who program solutions for themselves or a small group of others, such as database administrators and decision support analysts.

This chapter gives you a feel for how to perform typical kinds of tasks with VBE, but it also provides a firm grounding in the basics of programming Visual Basic (yes, VBE is pure Visual Basic). It also describes the creation of a new Windows application with multiple Windows forms. Each form illustrates a set of related Visual Basic programming topics. After examining the elements associated with each Windows form, you will be familiar with several common programming techniques, including

- Computing results with and converting between variables that have different data types
- Catching runtime errors and gracefully handling them as part of a solution
- Tapping the new My namespace to simplify programming solution

Starting, Saving, and Exploring a Solution

A solution is a fundamental organizing unit for files within VBE. After initially opening VBE from the Windows Start button, you can choose File ➤ New ➤ Project from the VBE menu to start a new solution that wraps your new project. A solution can contain one or more projects (choose File ➤ New ➤ Project to add a new project to an existing solution). Typical VBE solutions consist of a single project per solution. Solutions with multiple projects are especially useful when you are working on a solution as part of a team, and each team member has responsibility for one or more projects within the overall solution.

Starting and Saving a New Solution's Project

When you choose File ➤ New ➤ Project, VBE responds by opening the New Project dialog box. You can choose from several templates for different types of projects as well as some starter kits for demonstrating solution techniques. Selecting a starter kit loads a project with a set of comments about what the kit does and how to use it, as well as suggestions for changing it. The templates configure VBE to start a particular kind of solution.

- A Windows Application template configures VBE to create a solution with Windows forms and controls.

- A Class Library template configures VBE to create a .dll file that can be reused by any other solution with a reference to the .dll file.

- A Console Application creates a solution that enables users to manipulate the solution with command-line instructions from a command prompt.

The New Project dialog box allows you to choose templates or starter kits (described in the preceding paragraph) by clicking their icon in the Templates pane. VBE assigns a default project name consistent with the project type, such as WindowsApplication1, for a Windows application. You can override the default name for a project in the Name text box.

Because VBE does not actually create a permanent solution folder for a project when you start it from a template, the project name in the New Project dialog box is a draft one. When you need to stop working with a project on your first use of the project, you can choose to close the project (File ➤ Close Project), and VBE will prompt you to save or discard your changes. In the Close Project dialog box for a new project, you can elect to save your changes or discard them. Figure 9-1 shows the Save Project dialog box.

■**Note** If you prefer not to wait until you complete your initial use of a project in order to name it, you can choose File ➤ Save All to open the Save Project dialog box at any time after you open a project. The key point is that VBE, along with the other Visual Studio 2005 editions, does not create a project folder when you initially open a project. This is different from earlier versions of Visual Studio, which automatically created a project folder when you started a project—whether or not you meant to keep it.

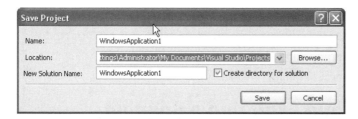

Figure 9-1. *The Save Project dialog box lets you specify project and solution names for a new project along with the location for the top-level project folder.*

Adding Items to a Solution

You develop a solution by adding items to the projects in it. For example, you can add Windows forms to a Windows application, classes to a class library, or modules to a console application. As you add new items to a project, you will populate the project. Inserting new items into a solution adds files for the items to a project's solution folders.

You can add new items to a project from the Project ➤ Add New Item menu command in VBE. This lets you pick from a menu of item types, such as a Windows form, a class, or a text file. These items become the elements of your solution. The Project menu also offers items for directly creating selected items, such as a form or a class. The Project ➤ Add Existing Item menu command lets you import an item from another project. This menu item is very convenient when you want to quickly incorporate a form originally created in another project.

Exploring a Solution

Solution Explorer, a window in the VBE integrated development environment (IDE), gives you a graphical tool for managing the projects in a solution. With Solution Explorer, you can navigate between and explore the items in a project. You can open Solution Explorer by choosing Solution Explorer on the View menu in VBE.

Figure 9-2 shows Solution Explorer for a Windows application before it is saved for the first time:

- A Windows application always initially has a class named `Form1` as its startup form.

- As you add more Windows forms and other items to the solution, these will populate Solution Explorer.

- Figure 9-2 shows the file immediately after a project is started, but before it is saved for the first time (all of the items appearing are created by VBE).

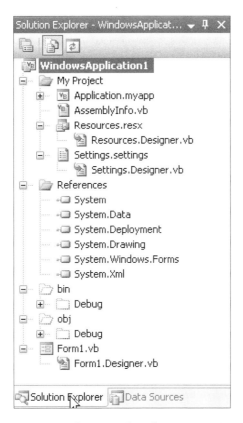

Figure 9-2. *Solution Explorer lets you examine the items within a solution.*

Using Visual Basic Data Types in VBE

A common set of tasks in Visual Basic applications involves declaring variables as data types, and then processing those variables by assigning values to the variables, performing computations with them, and formatting them. Coding these kinds of tasks requires a grasp of the data types that are available to you in VBE and its underlying .NET Framework. This section covers these topics. It is impossible to create solutions with VBE without a grasp of the topics addressed in this section.

VBE IS FOR CLASSIC VB AND VBA DEVELOPERS

VBE is an application development package. However, VBE especially targets the Visual Basic 2005 language within the Visual Studio Express Suite. Although Visual Basic 2005 does not have .NET in its title like Visual Basic .NET from Visual Studio 2002/2003, Visual Basic 2005 is very much a .NET version of the Visual Basic programming language. Therefore, VBE contains the most recent version of Visual Basic for the .NET Framework.

Some other Visual Studio Express Suite packages exclusively support different languages, such as C#, J#, or C++. The Visual Web Developer package (VWDE) within the Visual Studio Express Suite supports multiple languages, including Visual Basic, C#, and J#. VBE is the only edition of Visual Studio 2005 in the Express Suite or otherwise that explicitly targets Visual Basic 2005. In fact, you can think of VBE as a development package exclusively for Visual Basic 2005 much as the classic Visual Basic package was an implementation of the classic VB programming language.

You can use Visual Basic in both VBE and VWDE. VBE is primarily for creating Windows applications, as with prior classic versions of Visual Basic. The main way of interacting with users of a VBE solution is through a Windows form, which is very similar to a form in classic VB. VWDE lets you program in Visual Basic, but it does not require you to program solutions in Visual Basic. In addition, the primary visual interface for interacting with solution users is a web page, which is fundamentally different than a Windows or VB form. As similar as VWDE is to VBE, VWDE still has many features that distinctly identify it as a web development package. This is good, because the main purpose of VWDE is to create web solutions—not solutions that run on a desktop like classic VB.

Visual Basic has grown up over the years from its initial introduction, but a substantial majority of classic VB developers work by themselves or in very small groups. The ease of getting started with classic VB makes it appealing to non-professional programmers who use classic VB to solve simple problems that do not require a professional programmer. The size of the classic VB developer community is matched by another one of roughly comparable size—VBA developers. VBA is an add-in edition of classic Visual Basic. Therefore, VBA developers are classic VB developers, except that VBA developers use the add-in edition.

The defining characteristic of many classic VB and VBA developers is that they work on solutions for themselves or their department. Some classic VB and VBA developers also create solutions as consultants for small businesses and departments in larger organizations. This is also the primary target market for VBE. There are literally millions of developers who use either or both the stand-alone version of classic VB or VBA.

The bottom line is that VBE is the Visual Studio 2005 package of choice for the vast majority of classic VB and VBA developers migrating to .NET.

Data Types Are Objects

If you are migrating to VBE from a classic programming language, such as Visual Basic 6.0, VBA, or even T-SQL, you are used to thinking of data types as specifying storage formats for values. VBE provides this kind of functionality as well, but it also enables data types as objects. Because data types are objects in VBE, they have members that you can use. For example, non-`String` data types have a `ToString` method. This method can convert a number or a `Date` value to a `String` value. Other data type members are useful for learning about data types. The `MinValue` and `MaxValue` fields return the smallest and largest values for a data type.

Note The ToString method is also available for variables with a String data type. This is because all data types inherit members from the Object type, which has a ToString method.

Data types divide into two broad groups: value types and reference types. Both broad groups of value types derive from the Object type.

- Value types, such as in Integer and Double variables, denote variables that are stored in memory along with their values. This type of memory is called stack memory.

- Reference types, such as String variables, are not stored in memory along with their values. Instead, a reference type variable stores a pointer to the location of the variable's value in heap memory.

- Two different reference variables can point at the same reference instance. For example, two String variables can point at the same sequence of characters in memory. In contrast, a value variable points at a memory location with the value for that specific variable.

- An Object type is a reference type that can hold other reference types as well as value types. You can think of an Object type as the base type for all other data types in the .NET Framework.

Note Boxing is the process of converting a value type, such as Integer, to a reference type, such as an Object type. You can cause your application to box a value type by assigning a value type variable to an Object type or any other reference type variable. This kind of assignment forces the .NET Framework to move a value from stack memory to heap memory, which is time consuming. If you need to restore a value from a reference type to a value type (so that you can do computations or numeric comparisons), you can unbox the value by assigning the boxed variable to a value type variable, another time-consuming process. Boxing offers a unified way of representing values, whether they are value types or reference types. This benefit is offset by the computational time required to box and unbox values. One bit of good news is that boxing and unboxing is faster in Visual Basic 2005 than in Visual Basic 2002/2003.

Overview of Data Types

VBE supports 11 data types for storing numbers, and additional data types for storing character data, Boolean values, and dates. Beyond these built-in VBE data types, supplementary .NET Framework types enhance your data-processing capabilities. The best way to understand a data type is to know the range of values that it can represent. Last, you'll want to consider the nominal memory requirements associated with data types. The .NET Framework can dynamically adjust the memory associated with data types depending on the computer hardware (64-bit versus 32-bit systems) or whether the data type represents a stand-alone value or a value that belongs to a user-defined type in a structure or an array.

Note An array can store a table of values in one, two, three, or more dimensions. A structure can define a user-defined type comprising multiple native VBE data types.

Number Data Types

The default value for all number data types is 0. Number values that have no precise representation, such as 1 divided by 3 (.333 . . .), require a data type that allows for the approximate representation of values.

Visual Basic developers often use precise data types that can represent both positive and negative numbers. VBE offers 5 of these data types in lengths of 1, 2, 4, 8, and 16 bytes. The 1-, 2-, 4-, and 8-byte data types are exclusively for integer values without a decimal point. The 16-byte-size data type can represent values with numbers before and after a decimal point.

- Visual Basic 2005 introduces the new SByte data type for values that can be represented by 1 byte. It is for values from –128 through 127.

- The Short data type is a 2-byte data type. This data type corresponds to the Integer type in classic Visual Basic. It is for values from –32,768 through 32,767.

- The Integer data type has a 4-byte data type. This data type corresponds to the Long type in classic Visual Basic. It is for values from –2,147,483,648 through 2,147,483,647.

- The Long data type is an 8-byte data type, which was not available in classic Visual Basic, for values from –9,223,372,036,854,775,808 through 9,223,372,036,854,775,807.

- The Decimal data type is a 16-byte data type, but it holds numbers of 96 bits scaled by a power of 10 from 0 through 28.

  - With a scale of 0, the Decimal data type represents values in the range of +/– 79,228,162,514,264,337,593,543,950,335.

  - With a scale of 28, the Decimal data type represents values in the range of +/– 7.9228162514264337593543950335.

  - This data type is appropriate for currency values. Unlike classic Visual Basic, VBE offers no data type that explicitly targets currency values. Its 96-bit length and precise values make the Decimal data type especially well suited for currency computations that cannot allow rounding errors.

Visual Basic has a set of four additional integer data types. These data types have lengths of 1, 2, 4, and 8 bytes. The maximum values scale based on the length of the data type. Because these data types do not have to reserve a bit for the sign of a value (they are all unsigned), their maximum values are double the maximum values corresponding to integer data types that can represent either positive or negative numbers. The Byte data type was available with classic Visual Basic, but the remaining three data types are new with VBE.

- Byte represents 1-byte values up to 255.

- UShort represents 2-byte values up to 65,535.

- UInteger represents 4-byte values up to 4,294,967,295.

- ULong represents 8-byte values up to 18,446,744,073,709,551,615.

VBE permits the representation of approximate values with its Single and Double data types. These two data types correspond to 4-byte and 8-byte formats for representing values with numbers to the left or right of the decimal point. Because Single and Double data types allow for representing values as powers of a number, they can represent very large numbers.

- The Single data type represents numbers in a 4-byte format with up to 7 digits of accuracy. Values representing more than seven digits of accuracy contribute to rounding error. Values can range between –3.402823E-38 and 3.402823E+38.

  - The Double data type stores values in an 8-byte format with up to 17 decimal digits of accuracy. Values with precision beyond 17 digits of accuracy contribute to a rounding error. Values for this data type can occur between –1.7976931348623157E+308 and 1.7976931348623157E+308.

Boolean Data Types

The Boolean data type represents variables that can take a value representing one of two states, such as on/off, yes/no, or true/false. The two keywords used to denote the states for a variable with a Boolean data type are True and False. The default value for a Boolean variable is False.

Date Data Types and the TimeSpan Structure

A Date data type represents both date and time values. Date values can extend from January 01, 0001 at midnight (00:00:00) through December 31, 9999 at 23:59:59. Date values are instances in time. The smallest increment of a Date value is 1 tick, which is the equivalent of 100 nanoseconds. Any Date instance is equal to the cumulative number of ticks from January 1, 0001 at midnight to that particular instance in time. The datetime structure offers a side variety of members to help you manipulate and extract date and time components from a Date value. For example:

- The AddDays, AddMonths, and AddYears methods let you increment a Date value by days, months, or years.
- The AddMilliseconds, AddSeconds, AddMinutes, and AddHours methods let you modify the time associated with a Date value.
- The Date property returns the date element of a Date value, and the TimeOfDay property returns the time element of a date value.
- The Second, Minute, and Hour properties return the correspondingly named time element from a Date value.
- The Day, Month, and Year properties return the correspondingly named date element from a Date value.

The .NET Framework also offers a TimeSpan structure that VBE developers can use. This structure was not available with classic Visual Basic, but it was available in prior versions of Visual Basic .NET. A TimeSpan instance represents an interval of time. Internally, a TimeSpan value is the number of ticks within an interval. The ToString method for the TimeSpan structure returns a TimeSpan value in days, hours, minutes, seconds, and fractions of a second; the values for days and fractions of a second do not display when they are 0. TimeSpan values can have a positive or negative value, depending on whether the TimeSpan value derives from moving forward or backward in time.

Char and String Data Types and the StringBuilder Class

The Char data type is a value type for representing single Unicode characters. Each variable with a Char data type can hold just one character value at a time. You can change the value stored by a Char variable with an assignment statement that updates the value for the variable. The Char data type is a value type so that the variable's value is stored with the variable.

■**Note** Recall that Unicode characters permit a single character set to represent characters for all typical business languages throughout the world. Unicode characters represent characters in a 2-byte format. To learn more about Unicode characters, navigate your browser to www.unicode.org.

You can represent sequences of characters as either an array of Char variables or as a String data type. The .NET Framework offers a Char structure with a collection of members for manipulating Char values. You can process Char values in variables via Char structure members.

- One set of Char structure members helps you identify the type of character in a Char variable. Selected members in this set include IsDigit, IsLetter, IsLetterOrDigit, IsPunctuation, and IsWhiteSpace. These members are overloaded so that you can apply them to both an individual Char variable as well as a single character within a String variable. The overloaded versions allow you to pass the following arguments to the methods:

  - A single argument for a Char value or an element in an array of Char values.

  - Two arguments for a specific character within a String value.

- Additional Char structure members let you compare two Char values or determine if one Char value equals another.

■**Tip** You can use the IsDigit function to determine if a Char character can be represented as a value from 0 through 9. Char.IsDigit("8"c) returns a value of True. Char.IsDigit("a"c) returns a value of False. Other Char members, such as IsLetter and IsPunctuation, have a similar syntax.

Although a String data type contains a collection of Char values, there are a couple of critical distinctions between Char and String data types.

- The String data type is a reference type, while the Char value is a value type. This means that a variable with a String data type points at another memory location with the String value, while a variable with a Char data type stores its value along with the variable.

- Another major distinction between Char and String data types is that String values are "immutable." In the context of the .NET Framework, immutable means that a String value cannot change after you instantiate it.

  - When you assign a new set of characters to a String variable with an assignment statement, the .NET Framework creates a new String value and points the old String variable at the new String value.

  - When you update a Char value with an assignment statement, the .NET Framework revises the existing Char value instead of creating a new Char value. The assignment statement does not cause the Char variable to point at a different memory location.

When an application requires numerous changes to a large set of character values, you will often be able to achieve performance benefits by using the StringBuilder class rather than the String class. This is primarily because each time you update a String value, the .NET Framework must create a new String value. You can insert String values and Char values into a StringBuilder instance, and you can convert a StringBuilder instance to a String value.

VBE allows you to manipulate `String` values with classic VB `String` functions through the `Microsoft.VisualBasic.Strings` class or the VBE `String` class.

- If you are already familiar with classic VB string-processing techniques, you should be aware that the `Microsoft.VisualBasic.Strings` class permits you to use such familiar functions as `Len`, `Left`, `Right`, `Mid`, `LTrim`, `RTrim`, and `UCase`.
- If you are not already very familiar with these classic functions, or you want to make sure you are using the most current .NET-based techniques, you can spend your time learning the `String` class members to process `String` values.
    - The `TrimStart` and `TrimEnd` methods for the `String` class behave analogously to the `LTrim` and `RTrim` functions in the `Microsoft.VisualBasic.Strings` class.
    - The `ToUpper` method in the `String` class performs similarly to the `UCase` function in the `Microsoft.VisualBasic.Strings` class.
    - The `String` class also offers several richer or unique feature sets not available from the `Microsoft.VisualBasic.Strings` class. For example, there are three functions for copying `String` values in different ways: `Clone`, `Copy`, and `CopyTo`. Additionally, `Concat` and `Join` methods enable the creation of new `String` values based on two or more original `String` values inputs.

Declaring Variables and Assigning Data Type Values

The major reason for learning about data types is so that you can declare variables with one type or another, compute values with the variables based on their type, and then display or otherwise use the results of the computation. This section includes code samples and demonstrations that help you to achieve these goals, and that build on the preceding content about VBE data types.

Dim Statements

Use `Dim` statement to specify a data type for a variable. You can also initialize the value of a variable at the time that you declare it with a `Dim` statement. The `Dim` statement is very flexible. You can also use a single `Dim` statement to declare several variables as belonging to the same data type, or one or more variables as belonging to different data types. The following statement shows a general representation of the syntax for designating the data type for a variable. The data type can be any of those covered in the previous "Overview of Data Types" section.

```
Dim var1 As data type
```

Other examples of `Dim` statements follow. The first `Dim` statement that follows declares two variables—var1 and var2. Each variable has a different data type. The second `Dim` statement also declares two variables—var3 and var4. However, both of these variables have the same data type. The third `Dim` statement illustrates the syntax for assigning a value (5) to a variable at the same time that you declare it.

```
Dim var1 As data type1, var2 As data type2
Dim var3, var4 As data type
Dim var5 As Integer = 5
```

Variable names must follow the rules for declared VB elements. These rules are as follows:

- A name must begin with an alphabetic character or an underscore (_). If the name begins with an underscore, it must contain at least one alphabetic character or digit.
- A name can contain only alphabetic characters, decimal digits, and underscores.
- The maximum number of characters in a name is 1,023.

Option Explicit and Option Strict Settings

The Option Explicit On VBE setting (which is the default) requires the declaration of a variable name before you can use it. While you can relax this default setting, it is better coding practice to leave the restriction in effect to let the VBE environment know the names of your variables. If you do not specify a data type for a declared variable, the default data type is Object. You improve the clarity of your code by always explicitly designating a data type for a variable—even if the data type you wish to specify is Object.

VBE also allows you to restrict how it processes the data type assignments for variables. As you assign one variable to another, VBE attempts to convert between data types if the variables on both sides of the assignment statement are not the same data type. Conversions can be either widening or narrowing. A widening conversion assigns a variable with a smaller data type, such as Byte, to a larger data type, such as Short. A narrowing conversion is one in which your code assigns a variable with a wider data type, such as Integer, to a smaller data type, such as Short. You can encounter runtime errors when a narrowing conversion assigns a value to the smaller data type that it cannot represent, such as 32,769 to a Short variable.

Use the Option Strict On setting to disallow the specification of assignment statements that designate narrowing conversions at compile time. The Option Strict setting is not on by default, but it is another example of good coding practice because it can prevent runtime errors in your applications.

■Note If you want to take advantage of the benefits of the Option Strict On setting, but you occasionally need to assign variables with wider types to variables with narrower types, then convert the wider type to the smaller type before the assignment statement or as part of the assignment statement. This convention will force a runtime error if the wider data type cannot convert to the smaller data type, but the compiler will see the converted value as compliant with the Option Strict On setting. If you prefer, you can catch the runtime error and make appropriate adjustments, such as letting the user know about the problem.

You can manually designate Option Explicit On or Option Strict On settings through the VB Defaults folder in the Projects and Solutions folder of the Options dialog box. Within the VBE IDE, open the Options dialog box by choosing Tools ➤ Options. If the Show All Settings check box in the lower-left corner of the dialog box is not selected, click it. Expand Projects and Solutions to expose the VB Defaults folder so that you can select it. Use the Option Explicit and Option Strict drop-down boxes to make the settings you prefer. Figure 9-3 shows the VB Defaults folder with the default Option Explicit and Option Strict settings.

■Note The Option Compare setting in Figure 9-3 determines how String variable values are compared in a project. The two possible settings are Binary and Text. The Binary setting enforces a case-sensitive sort order (A <> a). The Text setting enforces a case-insensitive sort order (A = a).

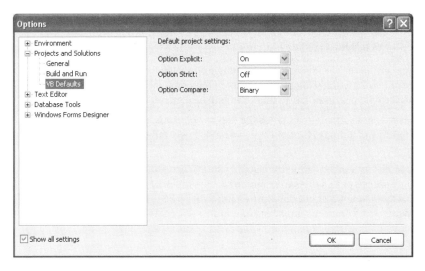

Figure 9-3. *Use the Options dialog box to manually designate Option Explicit and Option Strict settings for a project.*

You can also programmatically set either Option Explicit or Option Strict settings for a module or class within a project with an Option Explicit or Option Strict statement, as appropriate. These statements must appear at the top of the module or class. Conclude either statement with the On keyword to specify the setting. The scope of the statement applies to the module in which the statement appears. An Option Explicit or Option Strict statement within a class or module overrides, for that class or module, the project-level setting in the VB Defaults folder of the Options dialog box.

Assignment Statements

In an assignment statement, you can specify the value of one variable as equal to the value of another variable, literal, or constant. The samples for this section reside in the Button Click event procedures of Form1 within the WindowsApplication1 project started and saved in the "Starting and Saving a New Solution's Project" section.

A String variable can contain a combination of literal Char values, constants defined by a Char literal value, and another String literal. The following code excerpt for the Button1_Click procedure in Form1 introduces the use of the Const statement after the application of a Dim statement to define a variable (varString) as having a String data type. The Const statement assigns the character e as a Char data type to the constant named eAsChar. The literal must appear in quotes, and the trailing letter c designates the literal e as a Char data type. Without this trailing type designator, the .NET Framework interprets the literal as a String data type before transforming it to a Char data type for assignment to the eAsChar constant. The difference between a constant and a variable of any type is that a constant cannot be changed.

■Note A Click event procedure fires when a user clicks an object, such as a Button control named Button1. By default, VBE assigns a name of Button1_Click to the Click event procedure for Button1.

The body of the procedure consists of three assignments to the varString variable. After each assignment, the sample invokes the Show method of the MessageBox class, which presents a message box to show the current value of the varString variable.

- The first assignment to the varString variable changes its value from the default value of Nothing to a String value consisting of a single Char character—namely, H. This assignment uses the character type designator, c, to mark the single character as having a Char data type.

- The second assignment statement appends the eAsChar constant to the H value already in varString. After the assignment, the varString variable has a value based on two Char type values (He).

- The third assignment statement appends a String literal consisting of llo to the preceding characters. The absence of a Char type designator causes the .NET Framework to interpret the literal value as a stream of more than one character with a String data type. A String literal can consist of one or more characters, in contrast to a Char literal, which can consist of just one character. The final Show method displays the value of varString as Hello in a message box.

```
Dim varString As String
Const eAsChar As Char = "e"c

varString = "H"c
MessageBox.Show(varString)

varString &= eAsChar
MessageBox.Show(varString)

varString &= "llo"
MessageBox.Show(varString)
```

You can instantiate instances of the StringBuilder class and use the instances similarly to the way that you use variables with String data types. Recall that using StringBuilder instances will often yield performance benefits as compared to using String variables. The following sample from the Button2_Click procedure contrasts selected syntax and performance differences for specifying variables based on String versus StringBuilder classes.

- The differences between String and StringBuilder types start in the Dim statement. VBE does not require the New keyword when creating an instance of the String class, but you cannot use an instance of the StringBuilder until you first create one with the New keyword. The Dim statement creates two String variables (str1 and str2) as well as two StringBuilder instances (sbd1 and sbd2).

- The manipulation of the String variable values starts by assigning Rick to str1 and then pointing the str2 variable at the String instance (str1) that points at Rick. The Show method for the MessageBox class confirms that both str1 and str2 have values of Rick.

- The Button2_Click event proceeds by invoking the Concat method of the String class to append a y to the end of str1. The .NET Framework implements this appending process by creating a new String value of Ricky, and then pointing the str1 variable at Ricky. However, the str2 variable still points at the initial instance of the String value for str1, which is Rick. The second invocation of the Show method therefore displays the different values of Ricky and Rick for the str1 and str2 variables.

- Next, the Button2_Click event procedure demonstrates the use of the Insert method to add a value of Rick to the beginning of the sbd1 StringBuilder instance. An assignment statement points the sbd2 variable at the sbd1 StringBuilder instance. The third Show method in the procedure confirms that the sbd1 and sbd2 variables both have values of Rick.

- The final processing illustrates the syntax for invoking the Append method of the String-Builder class to add a value of y to the end of the value in sbd1. This process achieves the same kind of result as the use of the Concat method for the String class. However, the .NET Framework does not create a new instance of the value at which the sbd1 variable points—it merely updates the original sbd1 value in memory. Because sbd2 points at the original value of sbd1, which is now changed, the fourth Show method confirms that the values of both sbd1 and sbd2 are Ricky.

```
Dim str1, str2 As String, sbd1, _
    sbd2 As New System.Text.StringBuilder

str1 = "Rick"
str2 = str1

MessageBox.Show("str1: " & str1 & ControlChars.Cr & _
  "str2: " & str2)

str1 = String.Concat(str1, "y")

MessageBox.Show("str1: " & str1 & ControlChars.Cr & _
  "str2: " & str2)

sbd1.Insert(0, "Rick")
sbd2 = sbd1

MessageBox.Show("sbd1: " & sbd1.ToString & ControlChars.Cr & _
  "sbd2: " & sbd2.ToString)

sbd1.Append("y")

MessageBox.Show("sbd1: " & sbd1.ToString & ControlChars.Cr & _
  "sbd2: " & sbd2.ToString)
```

The next excerpt from the Form1 module is from the Button3_Click procedure. This procedure demonstrates assignment statements for the Short and UShort data types, as well as the Boolean data type.

- The initial assignment statement sets varShort, a variable with a Short data type, to the output from the Short structure's MaxValue method. The Show method for the MessageBox class confirms the maximum positive Short data type value. VBE implicitly converts the Short data type to String for display by the Show method.

- The second and third assignment statements are for UShort and Boolean variables named varUShort and varBool.

    - The UShort data type can hold a value approximately twice as large as the Short data type. Therefore, the second assignment statement approximates the maximum value for the UShort data type by multiplying the value of varUShort by 2.

    - The assignment for varBool is the result of an equality (=) statement that indicates whether the value for varUShort is equal to the maximum UShort value. The outcome is False because you need to add one to the value of varUShort to achieve the maximum UShort data type value.

    - The invocation of the Show method immediately after the second and third assignment statements confirms that 2 multiplied by Short.MaxValue is not equal to UShort.MaxValue.

- The last two assignment statements in the Button3_Click procedure increment the value in varUShort by one, and retest the new varUShort value to verify if it equals the maximum UShort value. The final Show method confirms the maximum UShort value for varUShort is achieved by showing a value of True for varBool.

```
Dim varShort As Short, varUShort As UShort, varBool As Boolean

varShort = Short.MaxValue
MessageBox.Show(varShort)

varUShort = varShort * 2
varBool = (varUShort = UShort.MaxValue)
MessageBox.Show(varUShort & ControlChars.Cr & _
  "Is it maximum UShort value: " & varBool)

varUShort += 1
varBool = (varUShort = UShort.MaxValue)
MessageBox.Show(varUShort & ControlChars.Cr & _
   "Is it maximum UShort value: " & varBool)
```

The Button4_Click procedure performs similar kinds of operations for Long and Decimal data types. This procedure is not shown in the book, both to conserve space and because the principles that it demonstrates are similar to those in the Button3_Click procedure.

The Button5_Click event procedure demonstrates the use of the Date data type, and how Date values interact with TimeSpan structure instances.

- The procedure starts by declaring a pair of Date variables, dat1 and dat2, and another variable, ts1, for a TimeSpan instance. Notice that there is no need for the New keyword when you are using a variable based on a structure. The New keyword is required for an instance of a class, such as an instance of the StringBuilder class.

- The Today property, which operates like a function, assigns a Date data type to dat1 with the following:

  - A date value of the computer's system clock

  - A time value of midnight (0 hours, 0 minutes, and 0 seconds)

- The subsequent two statements illustrate two contrasting methods for formatting Date data type values.

  - The first statement using the Show method of the MessageBox class invokes the FormatDateTime function to format dat1 in a LongDate format that displays the day's name, date, and time for dat1. You can replace LongDate with one of four other names to reference other formats for Date values. Look up FormatDateTime in VBE Help for more information on this function and links for other prespecified formats that you can use for different data types, such as FormatCurrency and FormatPercent.

  - The second Show method statement illustrates the use of a custom format for a Date data type value with the ToString method. This syntax returns just the full name—such as Monday or Tuesday—corresponding to dat1's date value. Numerous other options, which are specified in the VBE Help, document alternative values to dddd for designating the format of a Date data type value.

- The next two assignment statements illustrate the use of a couple of Date structure methods.
  - The AddHours method adds a designated number of hours to a Date value. The sample adds 8 hours to the time element of dat1. In the context of this sample, dat2 has a time of 8:00 a.m. on the same day as dat1.
  - The Subtract method computes the difference of dat2 less dat1. This syntax generates a TimeSpan structure instance of 8 hours.
- The final Button5_Click procedure statement illustrates the syntax for displaying the time span between dat2 and dat1. The ToString method reports the span as 8 hours, 0 minutes, and 0 seconds.

```
Dim dat1, dat2 As Date, ts1 As TimeSpan

dat1 = Today

MessageBox.Show("The full long date is " & _
    FormatDateTime(dat1, DateFormat.LongDate))
MessageBox.Show("Just the day name is " & _
    dat1.ToString("dddd"))

dat2 = dat1.AddHours(8)
ts1 = dat2.Subtract(dat1)

MessageBox.Show( _
    "The interval between the start of today, " & _
    ControlChars.Cr & _
    "and eight hours from the start of today is: " & _
    ts1.ToString)
```

Building and Testing a Windows Form Calculator

While the previous section did explain the syntax and operation of the assignment statements, it did not explain how to add a Click event procedure to a form in a Windows Application project. This section systematically examines the process of building Click event procedures for a form in a Windows project.

This section uses the WindowsApplication1 project initially created in the "Starting and Saving a New Solution's Project" section and subsequently used in the "Assignment Statements" section. When you start a Windows Application project, VBE automatically provides Form1, which is the startup form for the project. This section adds a new form, Form2, to the project, and makes the new form the startup form for the project. This means that Form2, instead of Form1, will open whenever you start the project.

The section demonstrates the creation of a four-function calculator by adding controls to Form2 and then adding code as Click event procedures behind the form. You also learn how to test and debug an application after initially building it.

Creating a New Startup Form

You can add a new form to WindowsApplication1 by choosing Project ➤ Add New Item. Select the Windows Form template. If there are no other forms in the project besides Form1, VBE designates a name of Form2 for the new form. You can optionally override this default name in the Name text box on the Add New Item dialog box. Clicking OK adds the new form to the project.

Form2 is not available when you start the WindowsApplication1 project. This is because the project automatically starts Form1, and this form has no code for transferring control to Form2. In many Windows applications, it is common to have a switchboard form that lets you switch between other forms in an application. Another simpler approach when you are prototyping a solution and you want to initially open a form, such as Form2, is to designate the form as the startup form for the project.

You can specify a form as the startup form for a Windows application from the Application tab of the project settings window for a project.

1. Open the project settings window for a project by double-clicking My Project in Solution Explorer.

2. Next, select the Application tab in the WindowsApplication1 window with the project's setting.

3. Then, choose a form, such as Form2, from the Startup Form drop-down box.

Populating a Windows Form with Controls

When you initially start to work with Windows forms, the easiest approach to populating a form with controls and assigning values to control properties may be manually with the Toolbox and the Properties window. The Toolbox contains a selection of built-in controls, such as labels, text boxes, and buttons, which you can add to a Windows form. The Properties window shows the property settings for the currently selected control or even the form containing the controls. You add a control type to a form by dragging the control's icon in the Toolbox to a position on the form. You can also assign control property values in the Properties window.

■Note If the Toolbox and Properties windows are not open, you can open them by selecting their names from the View menu in the VBE IDE.

Form2 implements a four-function calculator. The functions are add, subtract, divide, and multiply. The form includes two text boxes for entering values with which to perform arithmetic. A third text box shows the result of calculation. Four buttons below the third text box allow you to specify a type of calculation to perform on the two text boxes that accept input values.

Figure 9-4 shows Form2 in Design view with the Toolbox on the left and the Properties window below Solution Explorer on the right.

- The selected Button control in Figure 9-4 is the first Button control added to the form. Therefore, its Name property is Button1. The Windows Form Designer also assigns the control name to the Text property for a control.

- Figure 9-4 shows a setting in the Properties window to override the default Text property value of Button1 with a new value that indicates the function of the button—namely, +. The Text property for a control has a String data type.

- The same technique used to assign a nondefault Text property to Button1 is also used for the other three Button and the three Label controls.

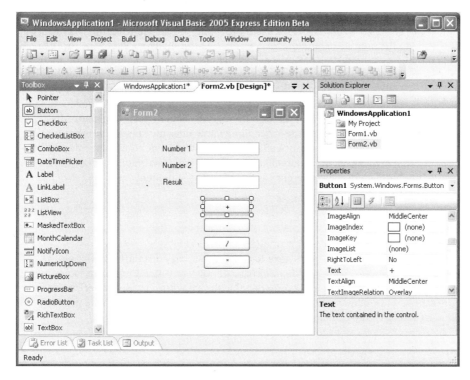

Figure 9-4. *Use the Toolbox to add controls to a form, and the Properties window to set control property values.*

Adding Button Click Event Procedures to a Form

The four-function calculator in Form2 performs addition, subtraction, division, and multiplication with Double data types.

- When you enter values in a TextBox control, such as TextBox1 and TextBox2, the Text property value for the control has a String data type.

  - Therefore, the code behind the form needs to convert the String data type in the TextBox control to some numeric data type, such as Double.

  - The sample code uses the built-in CDbl function to transform a String value returned by the Text property of a TextBox control to a Double value to perform arithmetic.

- An arithmetic operation between two Double values returns a new value of the same type—Double.

  - Although Form2 displays the outcome of the calculation as the Text property of TextBox3, there is no need to explicitly convert the Double value to a String value.

  - VBE performs this transformation automatically as part of the assignment of the arithmetic result to the Text property of TextBox3.

Form2 allows you to enter values into TextBox1 and TextBox2 and then click one of the Button controls on the form. The click launches a Click event procedure associated with the clicked Button control. You can add to the module behind the form by altering the shell for a Button control's Click event procedure. To do so, double-click the Button control in Design view. As VBE adds the shell, it switches to the form's Code view so that you can start adding code to the Click event procedure shell.

The following script shows the automatically generated Click event procedure shell for Button1. The Sub procedure name is Button1_Click. Although the default procedure name does denote the control name and event name, the procedure's name does not specify the event that the control invokes. Instead, the Handles clause after the closing right parenthesis specifies the event for the object that invokes the procedure (Button1.Click). You place your custom code for your event procedure between the Sub statement and the End Sub statement.

```
Private Sub Button1_Click(ByVal sender As System.Object, _
    ByVal e As System.EventArgs) Handles Button1.Click

End Sub
```

The code inside Button1_Click appears next. Recall that Button1 adds the numeric values represented by the Text property values for TextBox1 and TextBox2. The CDbl functions wrapping the Text property values for TextBox1 and TextBox2 enable the + operator to use numeric rules for combining the values. Without the CDbl conversion functions, VBE would combine the two Text property values as String values instead of Double values.

```
Me.TextBox3.Text = CDbl(Me.TextBox1.Text) + CDbl(Me.TextBox2.Text)
```

Note Me is a VBE keyword that can invoke IntelliSense behind a form module. In a form module, Me refers to the form class instance. After you type Me followed by a period (.), IntelliSense shows the members of the form instance. The term Me.TextBox3 refers to TextBox3 on the current form instance, just as Me.TextBox1 refers to TextBox1 on the current form instance.

Figure 9-5 shows the four Click event procedures for Button1 through Button4. The procedures appear in the Code view for the form. All the procedures are very similar and only differ in the operator they use. From Button1 through to Button4 , the operators are +, -, /, and *.

Notice the two drop-down boxes above the code in Figure 9-5. These boxes allow you to create the shell for any event procedure for any control on the form. Select the control name from the left drop-down box (Class name), and select the event type from the right drop-down box (Method name).

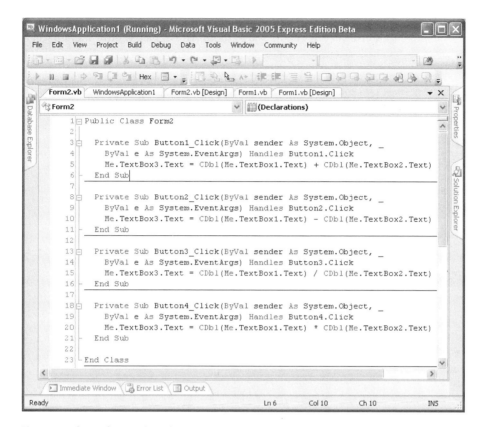

Figure 9-5. *The Code view for a form shows the code behind a form, such as the Click event procedures for Button controls.*

Testing the Code Behind a Form

After you write any code, it is natural to want to test it and then run it. Visual Studio Express offers a rich environment for debugging your code. As part of the debugging process, you can run your code.

- To open Form2 in the WindowsApplication1 project, choose Debug ➤ Start Debugging, or just press F5 as a shortcut to the menu command.
- After the startup form (Form2) opens, you can enter values into TextBox1 and TextBox2.
- Next, you can click one of the four buttons on the form.
- If you enter valid values into TextBox1 and TextBox2, the Click event procedure for the clicked button assigns the result of a calculation to TextBox3, which, in turn, displays the value on the form.

For example, if you enter 2 and 5 in the first and second text boxes for Form2, and click the button with a +, the application displays a value of 7 in the third text box on the form. Because you are running the application in debug mode, special support is available if you make an error.

- If you change the value in the first text box from 2 to 2a and click the + button, the Button1_Click event procedure generates a runtime error. There is nothing inherently wrong with Button1_Click. However, it does not handle invalid user input.

- When the project attempts to convert 2a to a Double value, the .NET Framework raises an InvalidCastException because the .NET Framework cannot recast a String value of 2a to a Double value.

- VBE highlights the line that throws the InvalidCastException object and displays an Exception Assistant dialog box that points to the line generating the runtime error. Figure 9-6 displays the Exception Assistant dialog box.

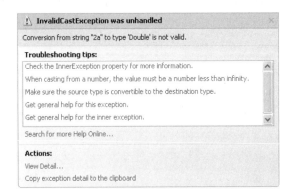

Figure 9-6. *The Exception Assistant dialog box can help you diagnose and resolve the cause of an Exception object thrown by the .NET Framework in response to a runtime error.*

Handling Exceptions

While the Exception Assistant is a nice convenience for a developer debugging an application, it is not available when a user runs the application from its .exe file, such as WindowsApplication1.exe in the Release folder of the WindowsApplication1 project directory. A typical user will run the application from the .exe file after your project is installed. Without any special handling of Exceptions, the error message a user views is not under your control.

You can simulate the typical user experience by running the .exe file for your solution. Before running a project's .exe file, make sure the project's .exe file contains the most recent updates by choosing Build ➤ Build project name from the VBE. Project name is a place marker for the name of your project, such as WindowsApplication1. Then, open the Windows Run window by choosing Start ➤ Run. Next, navigate to the .exe file in the Release folder of your project's directory. Finally, run the .exe file by clicking OK in the Run window.

Note Normally, a user will use the .exe file for your solution after you deploy it. Application deployment is an advanced topic that is beyond the scope of this book. With Visual Studio 2005, including the VBE edition, developers can use the new "ClickOnce" technology that helps to simplify some deployment scenarios. You can start to experiment with this technology by invoking the Publish wizard from the Publish tab of your project's Properties window. To open a project's Properties window, right-click the Project name in Solution Explorer and choose Properties.

Both Try...Catch...Finally and On Error GoTo statements allow your code to exit gracefully from runtime errors or even to dynamically adapt to runtime errors. With either type of statement, you can block a runtime error from causing your application to lose control, such as when the Exception Assistant takes control in response to a runtime error.

Classic Visual Basic as well as VBE supports the On Error GoTo statement for processing runtime errors, but this approach to handling runtime errors leads to spaghetti code that is hard to read and maintain.

New to Visual Basic .Net 1.0, a Try...Catch...Finally statement can have up to three distinct types of clauses.

- The Try block of code represents a set of VBE statements for which you want to trap Exception objects resulting from runtime errors.

- Any Try...Catch...Finally statement instance can have one or more Catch statements. Each Catch clause can test for a specific type of Exception, such as InvalidCastException or OverflowException. The code in a Catch block responds to, or handles, an Exception object. The Catch clause can also have an optional When clause to further filter the runtime errors to which it responds.

    - If you have only one Catch clause, consider catching an Exception object, which responds to any type of runtime error.

    - You can use multiple Catch clauses to catch two or more different types of runtime errors. Use the beginning Catch clauses to trap progressively more specific or common exception types. It is common to use the last Catch clause to trap an Exception object, which catches any runtime error not detected by a previous Catch clause.

- The Finally clause is optional. Only use this clause when there is some code that needs to run whether control passes through the Try clause or any of the Catch clauses in a Try...Catch...Finally statement. In many cases, you are likely to have only Try...Catch statements.

Tip The Finally clause is particularly convenient for managing ADO.NET Connection objects. See the "Getting Help with Constructing a Connection String" section of Chapter 12 for additional commentary and a code sample illustrating the use of the Finally clause to help manage an ADO.NET Connection object.

It is widely known that catching Exception objects can slow an application. One way to mitigate this delay is to anticipate specific types of user errors in your code and respond to them before they throw an Exception. Of course, it is not possible to anticipate all runtime errors. Therefore, you should include some Exception trapping in all your important solutions that are run by other users.

A Form for Running Try...Catch Statements

To illustrate the syntax and use of Try...Catch statements, I'll present an adaptation of the sample implemented with Form2. The new form is Form3 in the WindowsApplication1 project. In order to run the sample form, change the startup form for the WindowsApplication1 project to Form3.

Form3 has the same text boxes and labels as Form2, but the new form has three instead of four buttons. All three buttons add the values represented by the Text property values of TextBox1 and TextBox2 and display the result in TextBox3. If there is something wrong with the input values, the application recovers gracefully and displays feedback about the problem in TextBox3. The Click event procedure for Button3, which is the bottom button on the form, also detects if the calculation generates a runtime error (each of the numbers are valid, but their addition is outside the range of a data type).

■**Note** Try...Catch and Try...Catch...Finally statements keep your solution in control even when a runtime error occurs. You can typically provide more specific guidance to a user about how to recover in your application than the more general help from VBE. You may even be able to recover from a runtime error without user intervention.

Figure 9-7 shows a Design view of Form3. The Button control whose Text property is Integer + converts the values in TextBox1 and TextBox2 to Integer data types. The conversion of the String value in the Text property value for each text box to an Integer value takes place within a Try...Catch statement. The Try...Catch statement traps invalid String values, such as values that are not numbers or values that are outside the range of legitimate Integer values.

The second button in Figure 9-7 has a Text property value of Double +. This button's Click event procedure converts the Text property values for TextBox1 and TextBox2 to Double values. Because Double values can be much larger, they eliminate surpassing the relatively low upper limit for Integer values (2,147,483,647). Recall that the upper limit for Double values is 1.7976931348623157E+308.

The third Button control's Click event procedure computes the sum of the String values in TextBox1 and TextBox2 as either an Integer data type or a Double data type (Int/Dbl +). The user doesn't need to know if Integer arithmetic will work; the procedure automatically uses the smaller data type to get the required result. First, the procedure tries to compute the sum as an Integer data type. Integer arithmetic is preferable because it requires less space (4 versus 8 bytes). Second, if Integer arithmetic fails, either because the procedure cannot convert the value in either TextBox control to an Integer data type, or because the sum of the two Integer data types is outside the range of Integer numbers, the procedure automatically attempts to sum the values with Double data types. If either conversion to a Double data type fails, the application displays an appropriate reminder in TextBox3.

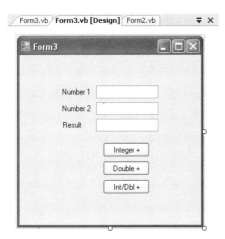

Figure 9-7. *Using Try...Catch statements, you can trap all kinds of Exception objects to make smarter, better-performing forms.*

Using Try...Catch Statements Directly

The Button1_Click procedure applies a Try...Catch statement twice: once for the conversion of the Text property for TextBox1 to an Integer value, and again for the conversion of the Text property value for TextBox2. The addition operation for Button1 in Form3 is superior to the addition operation for Button1 in Form2 because Button1_Click traps conversion errors before they end the application abnormally.

To expose you to more options for converting between data types, the function uses the Parse method for the Integer data type. This method allows you to convert a String data type, such as a Text property value, to an Integer data type. One nice feature of the Parse method is that it works the same for all numeric data types. Therefore, once you learn how to use the method for one data type, it applies equally well to the other numeric data types.

The following listing shows the code inside Button1_Click. As you can see, there are four parts to the procedure.

- The procedure commences with the declaration of int1 and int2 variables as Integer data types.

- Next, a Try...Catch statement tests an assignment statement with the Parse method. The Parse method attempts to convert the Text property of TextBox1 to an Integer value.

  - If the assignment statement operates without throwing an Exception object, control passes to the End Try statement.

  - If the assignment statement throws an Exception object of any type, the Catch clause gains control and assigns the error message "Fix number 1" to the Text property of TextBox3 before exiting the procedure.

- If the first Try...Catch statement does not catch a runtime error, the second Try...Catch statement gains control. This statement performs the same operations as in the first Try...Catch statement, except the focus is on TextBox2 and int2.

- If neither `Try...Catch` statement detects an error, control passes to the last statement, which adds `int1` and `int2` and assigns the result to the `Text` property of `TextBox3`. The .NET Framework automatically recasts the `Integer` sum of `int1` and `int2` to a `String` value.

```
Dim int1, int2 As Integer

Try
  int1 = Integer.Parse(Me.TextBox1.Text)
Catch ex1 As Exception
  Me.TextBox3.Text = "Fix number 1"
  Exit Sub
End Try

Try
  int2 = Integer.Parse(Me.TextBox2.Text)
Catch ex1 As Exception
  Me.TextBox3.Text = "Fix number 2"
  Exit Sub
End Try

Me.TextBox3.Text = int1 + int2
```

Invoking a Try...Catch Statement in a Function Procedure

The `Button2_Click` procedure extends the techniques introduced with the `Button1_Click` procedure in several ways.

- First, `Button2_Click` demonstrates the use of the `Parse` method for the `Double` data type instead of the `Integer` data type. You can confirm for yourself how similar the syntax for the `Parse` method is across different data types—namely, `Integer` and `Double` data types.

- Second, `Button2_Click` invokes the `Try...Catch` statement from within a `Function` procedure, `StrToDbl`, so that there is no need to repeat the `Try...Catch` statement elements twice within the event procedure. All you need to do is pass the correct value to the `Function` procedure, and then process results from the `Function` procedure.

- Third, `Button2_Click` references a variable declared at the module level (`ErrMsg`). Variables declared at the module level can be referenced by multiple procedures, such as a `Click` event procedure and a `Function` procedure invoked by the `Click` event procedure.

The next code listing is the `StrToDbl` `Function` procedure. After declaring the `dbl1` variable as a `Double` data type, the code assigns an empty `String` value to the `ErrMsg` variable, which is declared at the module level. This procedure uses the `Parse` method to extract a `Double` value from a `String` value passed to it. If the `Parse` method fails because of a `FormatException`, the procedure assigns `Invalid double` to `ErrMsg`. The .NET Framework throws a `FormatException` class instance if the `String` value of `str1` does not represent a valid `Double` value. If the method fails for any other reason, the second `Catch` clause can trap the resulting `Exception` object.

```
Function StrToDbl(ByVal str1 As String) As Double
    Dim dbl1 As Double

    ErrMsg = ""

    Try
      dbl1 = Double.Parse(str1)
      Return dbl1
    Catch ex1 As FormatException
      ErrMsg = "Invalid double"
    Catch ex1 As Exception
      ErrMsg = "Not known"
    End Try

End Function
```

The code inside the `Button2_Click` procedure appears next. After declaring a pair of variables (dbl1 and dbl2), the code uses the `StrToDbl` procedure to assign values to each variable. If `ErrMsg` is a value other than an empty `String` value (""), the code sample assigns a `String` literal to the `Text` property of `TextBox3`, reminding the user to fix the input value. If both the `Text` property values for `TextBox1` and `TextBox2` convert to `Double` values successfully, `Button2_Click` concludes by summing the two variables together and assigning the result to the `Text` property of `TextBox3`.

```
Dim dbl1, dbl2 As Double

dbl1 = StrToDbl(Me.TextBox1.Text)
If ErrMsg <> "" Then
  Me.TextBox3.Text = "Fix number 1"
  Exit Sub
End If

dbl2 = StrToDbl(Me.TextBox2.Text)
If ErrMsg <> "" Then
  Me.TextBox3.Text = "Fix number 2"
  Exit Sub
End If

Me.TextBox3.Text = dbl1 + dbl2
```

Dynamically Adapting to Runtime Errors

Sometimes you are able to blend runtime error processing into the fabric of a solution. After all, a runtime error is not really an error in the logic or syntax of some code. Instead, a runtime error can result from unanticipated user input or other environmental issues. More robust solutions anticipate factors that less robust solutions don't.

The `Click` event procedures for `Button1` and `Button2` do not anticipate that both input values can be valid but their sum invalid. This can happen if the sum of two valid numbers exceeds the maximum value of a data type. The `Click` event procedure for `Button3` demonstrates the syntax for handling this type of runtime error when calculating with `Integer` data types.

The following listing shows the code inside `Button3_Click`. The procedure initially tries to compute the sum of the value representations in `TextBox1` and `TextBox2` as if they represent `Integer` values. The first step is the use of the `StrToInt` Function procedure to convert the `Text` property values to `Integer` values. The `StrToInt` Function procedure has a similar design to the `StrToDbl` Function procedure, except the `StrToInt` Function procedure converts to an `Integer` value instead of a `Double` value. Because of the similarity of the `StrToInt` function to the `StrToDbl` function in design and purpose, the listing for the `StrToInt` function does not appear in the book, but it is available in the `Form3` module within the WindowsApplication1 project.

After verifying that the `Text` property values for `TextBox1` and `TextBox2` both convert to `Integer` value types, the procedure computes the sum of the converted `Integer` values in the `Try` clause of a `Try...Catch` statement.

- If the `Integer` sum is valid, the procedure is done (see the first `Exit Sub` statement).

- However, if the .NET Framework throws an `Exception` object with `Overflow` in its name when summing the `Integer` variable values, the procedure exits the `Try...Catch` statement (see the `Exit Try` statement) to convert the `Text` property values to `Double` values and compute the sum as a `Double` data type.

By embedding the statement that assigns the sum of the two `Integer` values in the `Try` clause, the code can exit the `Try...Catch` statement in the event of a runtime error, but continue processing within the procedure.

■**Note** The sum returned to `TextBox3` by the `Button3_Click` procedure has a suffix of either `Int` or `Dbl` to indicate whether `Integer` or `Double` data type values were used to compute the sum.

The `Try` clause in `Button3_Click` contains two lines with comment markers (`'`). One of these commented lines demonstrates the syntax for the `Throw` statement. You can use a `Throw` statement to generate `Exception` objects that test your logic for catching different `Exception` types. If you remove the comment marker from the `Throw` statement and enter valid `Integer` representations in `TextBox1` and `TextBox2`, then the `Click` event procedure for `Button3` will assign `Immediate window` to the `Text` property of `TextBox3`. The Immediate window will document that an `Exception` called Test exception was thrown. This use of the `Throw` statement demonstrates the failure of the procedure for another reason besides an `OverflowException` object.

■**Note** To view the Immediate window, open the windows control on the Debug toolbar within the VBE IDE. Next, select Immediate from the list of windows. After you open the Immediate window, you can change its position, hide it, or close it just like other VBE IDE windows.

```
Dim int1, int2 As Integer, dbl1, dbl2 As Double

    int1 = StrToInt(Me.TextBox1.Text)
    If ErrMsg = "" Then
      int2 = StrToInt(Me.TextBox2.Text)
      If ErrMsg = "" Then
        Try
          'Test Throw statement to simulate an error
          'Throw New Exception("Test exception")
```

```
            Me.TextBox3.Text = int1 + int2 & " Int"
            Exit Sub
        Catch ex1 As Exception
          Debug.WriteLine(ex1.ToString)
          If InStr(ex1.ToString, "Overflow") <> 0 Then
            Exit Try
          Else
            Me.TextBox3.Text = "Immediate window"
            Exit Sub
          End If
        End Try
      End If
  End If

  dbl1 = StrToDbl(Me.TextBox1.Text)
  If ErrMsg <> "" Then
    Me.TextBox3.Text = "Fix number 1"
    Exit Sub
  End If

  dbl2 = StrToDbl(Me.TextBox2.Text)
  If ErrMsg <> "" Then
    Me.TextBox3.Text = "Fix number 2"
    Exit Sub
  End If

  Me.TextBox3.Text = dbl1 + dbl2 & " Dbl"
```

Using the File System

The .NET Framework and Visual Basic .NET 2002/2003 empowered developers like never before to explore any aspect of the file system. However, the .NET Framework provided this superior capability at the cost of simplicity.

This section introduces two new approaches for handling files in the context of two sample applications.

- The first sample is a file explorer for the current project. It lets you examine the folders and subfolders in a project. You can additionally display the text in any selected file. This first solution treats the text in a file as a stream of characters.

- The second sample reads data from fixed-width files, such as SQL Server Express result sets output from Part 1 of this book. The sample application delivers access to individual column values—not just the overall stream of text characters within a file.

Design and Formatted Views of an Application Form

You can see the Design view of the form in Figure 9-8. The following short block of code in the Load procedure formats the form controls to describe their role and make file exploration results easy to read. Figure 9-9 shows the form just after it initially opens.

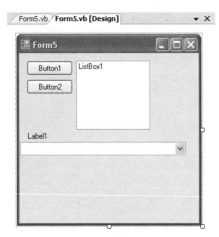

Figure 9-8. *It is often quick and easy to drag controls from the Toolbox and format them programmatically.*

Figure 9-9. *Just a few lines of code can dramatically improve the usefulness of a form and simplify its maintenance in the future.*

The code in the Load procedure appears next. Two types of statements perform different types of formatting. The first three assignment statements merely assign strings to the Text properties for Button1, Button2, and Label1. The second set of assignment statements resizes the form, ListBox1, ComboBox1 within the form. These transformations also reposition ListBox1 and ComboBox1 within the form. By programmatically transforming a form and its controls, you avoid the need for manual formatting.

- The ClientRectangle property is the client area of a control, minus system features including borders, menus, and scroll bars. The following code uses the ClientRectangle property for the form to center ComboBox1 between its borders.

- The Width property refers to the number of pixels between the left and right borders of a control. The Form class inherits its Width property from the Control class.

- The Left property for a control describes the control's left border displacement in pixels from the left border of its parent container.

  - The parent container for a Windows form, such as a Form object, is the Windows desktop.

  - The parent container for a form control, such as ComboBox1, is the Windows form containing the control.

After you become familiar with control properties, you may very well find it faster and more convenient to program form and control layout than to manually implement design changes with the help of the Properties window.

```
Me.Button1.Text = "Fill Combo"
Me.Button2.Text = "Read File"
Me.Label1.Text = "Fill ListBox"

Me.Width = 450
intWidth = Me.ClientRectangle.Width
Me.ComboBox1.Left = intWidth * 0.02
Me.ComboBox1.Width = intWidth * 0.96
Me.ListBox1.Width = Me.ComboBox1.Width - _
   Me.ListBox1.Left + (Me.Width - intWidth)
```

Exploring Folders and Viewing Files

There are four steps to demonstrating the sample application. When you open the solution's form, it appears as in Figure 9-9. Notice that the ComboBox control, which is named ComboBox1, is empty.

- Clicking Button1 (the one with a Text property of Fill Combo) populates ComboBox1 with a succession of path names from the path for the .exe file for the current application to the path just below C:\. You can optionally change the path of the top folder from C:\ to another one. The instructions for doing this are in the "Populating a ComboBox Control with Path Names" section, which follows.

- Selecting a path from ComboBox1 populates the list box (ListBox1) with a list of files in that path. See Figure 9-10 for the selection of the C:\ProSSEApps\Chapter09\WindowsApplication1\WindowsApplication1 folder, which contains project files for forms in the current application. The full path can change depending on where you save the project solution folder for the WindowsApplication1 project.

- The selection of a path from ComboBox1 assigns file names from that path to ListBox1. Figure 9-11 shows the selection of Form2.vb in ListBox1. This file name is available because of the path selection in ComboBox1. A different ComboBox1 selection lists a different set of files in ListBox1.

- Clicking a file name such as Form2.vb populates the Quick Console window with the stream of text characters from the selected file. The Quick Console window shows the output from Console.Writeline and Console.Write unless you explicitly designate otherwise. Figure 9-12 shows an excerpt from Form2.vb in the Quick Console window.

■**Note** Quick Console window is not supported in the initial release of VBE (although it was supported in at least release during the beta program). You can instead direct output from Console.Writeline to the VBE Output window. You can display the Output window by choosing the Output menu item from the Other Windows menu of the View menu. The book retains the screenshot and commentary for the Quick Console window because of my hope Microsoft will restore the Quick Console feature from the beta program in a future update to VBE.

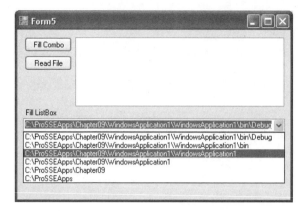

Figure 9-10. *Clicking the Fill Combo button populates ComboBox1 so that you can select a path.*

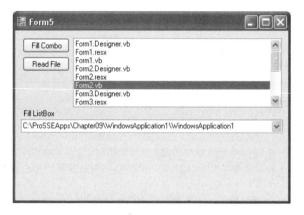

Figure 9-11. *Selecting a path in ComboBox1 populates ListBox1 so that you can select a file name.*

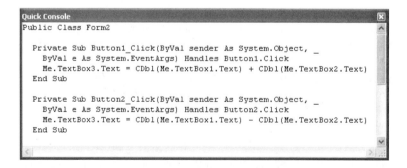

Figure 9-12. *Selecting a file name appends the text for the file to the Quick Console window.*

Populating a ComboBox Control with Path Names

ComboBox1 contains a set of paths from an innermost path to an outermost path. There are three main tasks, and an optional one, to perform when assigning paths to ComboBox1.

1. First, you need to initialize the innermost and outermost paths to variables that help you iterate through intermediate paths.

2. Second, you need to walk along the path from the innermost path to the outermost path and extract the name for each path as you walk the paths.

3. Third, you need to assign the path names to ComboBox1.

4. Unless you want ComboBox1 to appear empty initially after you populate it with paths, you must select a path to show. This is an optional fourth step that the sample solution implements.

The Button1_Click procedure populates ComboBox1. The procedure uses the new Visual Basic 2005 My namespace in a couple of ways to simplify the task. The My namespace exposes many built-in .NET and application elements in an easy-to-access way, in the style of an object property. There are 10 major resource categories accessible through the My namespace. Within these 10 major categories, there are numerous additional types and methods you can easily access in a way that allows you to bypass one or more levels of intermediate objects.

The ability to leave out one or more intermediate objects, along with the benefit of a common interface across such a wide span of resources, makes the My namespace a compelling Visual Basic innovation. This innovation is not available in other .NET languages, nor is it available in versions of Visual Basic .NET prior to Visual Basic 2005. VBE developers will be able to make excellent use of the My namespace feature.

THE MY KEYWORD: TEN MAJOR CATEGORIES

The My namespace exposes properties and methods for 10 major categories of information about a solution, the user running it, and the computer running it. The following list briefly summarizes each major category and shows the top-level syntax for designating the category.

- My.Application exposes information and services available from the current application.

- My.Computer gives a solution access to data, services, and resources—such as file resources—on the computer running a solution.

- My.Forms lets your solution view and change settings for forms in the current solution.

- My.Log grants access to an application's logs.

- My.Request exposes the current application's HttpRequest object in ASP.NET solutions.

- My.Resources enables read-only access to global application resources, such as culture settings.

- My.Response complements My.Request. With My.Request, you receive information about a web-based request, but with My.Response, you can send information to any web-based client, including IE and other browsers.

- My.Settings offers properties and methods for viewing and manipulating an application's settings.

- My.User allows access to the security settings for the current user.

- My.WebServices provides properties for connecting to an existing web service or creating a new one.

The code for populating ComboBox1 takes advantage of two different My categories. The DirectoryPath property of the My.Application.Info object returns the path for the current .exe file running an application. The GetParentPath method of the My.Computer.FileSystem object returns the parent path of a path that you designate as an argument for the method. The My.Computer.FileSystem object is a particularly powerful and friendly resource for working with a file system.

The Button1_Click procedure starts by assigning the directory path for the current project to the strFolderName variable, and the path name of C:\ to the topFolder. If you wish, you can designate a top folder path such as C:\parentfolderforprojectfolder. If you set up your file system with a folder for the book of ProSSEApps and a subfolder for each chapter, you can use a folder name such as C:\ProSSEApps\Chapter09 for the topFolder assignment.

A Do loop passes from the initial innermost folder, which is the directory path that contains the .exe file for the current project, up until the topFolder path. The first statement in the loop adds the current path name in strFolderName to the Items collection for ComboBox1. Then, the GetParentPath method returns the name of the parent folder for the current path (strfolderName). This loop continues until the path returned by the GetParentPath method matches the topFolder path.

The final two lines of code perform the optional step of exposing a path name in the ComboBox control. Without this step, ComboBox1 initially appears unpopulated. Setting the SelectedIndex property of ComboBox1 to 0 selects the top item in the ComboBox1 Items collection. This property assignment raises the SelectedIndexChanged event for ComboBox1. Since this event is used in the application to react to a user selection from ComboBox1, the project's code uses the initComboBox1 Boolean variable to differentiate between the programmatic and user selection of a ComboBox1 item selection. Because initComboBox1 is used in two different procedures, it is declared at the module level.

```
Dim strFolderName As String = My.Application.Info.DirectoryPath, _
   topFolder As String = "C:\"
'Can use a more specific topFolder value, such as the following one,
'if it is known
'topFolder As String = "C:\ProSSEApps\Chapter09"

Do
   Me.ComboBox1.Items.Add(strFolderName)
   strFolderName = _
      My.Computer.FileSystem.GetParentPath(strFolderName)
Loop Until strFolderName = topFolder

initComboBox1 = True
Me.ComboBox1.SelectedIndex = 0
```

Populating a ListBox Control with File Names

Populating ListBox1 with file names is roughly comparable to populating ComboBox1 with path names. However, there are several critical differences. One of these differences is the GetFiles method of the My.Computer.FileSystem object. The GetFiles method returns a read-only Collection object with the full path and file name for each file in a designated directory. Therefore, passing the selected path from ComboBox1 to the GetFiles method returns all the files from the selected path.

The next code listing shows the detailed syntax for populating ListBox1 with file names based on the selection of a path from ComboBox1. The code is from the ComboBox1_SelectedIndexChanged procedure, which fires whenever there is a programmatic or manual change to the index for the currently selected item. All the code within the procedure resides within an If...Then...Else statement. The condition for the If statement evaluates whether this is for an initial programmatic selection (initComboBox1 = True) or a manual programmatic selection (initComboBox1 = False). If the procedure runs because of a manual selection, the following actions take place:

1. The procedure clears the Items collection for ListBox1 to remove files from any prior manual selection.

2. Next, the procedure uses a For Each...Next loop to pass successively through the items of the Collection object returned by the GetFiles method of the My.Computer.FileSystem object.

3. The Add method for the Items collection of ListBox1 populates ListBox1 with file names. In order to show just file names without their full path, the procedure uses the Right method from the Microsoft.VisualBasic library.

```
If initComboBox1 = True Then
  initComboBox1 = False
Else
  Me.ListBox1.Items.Clear()
  For Each foundFile As String In _
    My.Computer.FileSystem.GetFiles(Me.ComboBox1.SelectedItem)
    Me.ListBox1.Items.Add( _
      Microsoft.VisualBasic.Right(foundFile, _
      Len(foundFile) - Len(Me.ComboBox1.SelectedItem) - 1))
  Next
End If
```

Reading a Text File Based on ComboBox and ListBox Selections

The final task in the sample application is to show the text for a file that a user selects. While the user picks a file to show from ListBox1, that control only contains the names for files, not their full paths. Therefore, this part of the solution must use the currently selected items from both ComboBox1 and ListBox1. ComboBox1 contributes the name of the path, and ListBox1 contributes the name of the file.

The process of showing a file is initiated by a user clicking an item in ListBox1 to select a file. Therefore, the code for this part of the solution resides in the ListBox1_SelectedIndexChanged procedure. The code from this procedure appears next. Again, the My.Computer.FileSystem object reduces and simplifies the amount of code needed to perform the task. In addition, the sample takes advantage of the Quick Console window, which is the default window for showing content written to the Console in VBE. Aside from a Dim statement, it takes just three lines of code to read a file based on the selections from the ComboBox and ListBox controls and display the results.

- The first line creates a full path and file name for the selected file with the help of the CombinePath method for the My.Computer.FileSystem object.

- The next line returns a String value with the contents of the selected file represented by the output generated in the first line (strPathFile). The ReadAllText method for the My.Computer.FileSystem object returns the contents of a file as a String variable (fileReader).

- The last line displays the contents of `fileReader` in the Quick Console window within VBE. The `WriteLine` method for the `Console` object directs its output to this window by default in VBE. If the Quick Console window is not open, VBE automatically opens the Quick Console window as it processes the `Console.WriteLine` statement.

```
Dim fileReader As String, strPathFile As String

strPathFile = My.Computer.FileSystem.CombinePath( _
    Me.ComboBox1.SelectedItem, Me.ListBox1.SelectedItem)
fileReader = My.Computer.FileSystem.ReadAllText(strPathFile)
Console.WriteLine(fileReader)
```

Reading Fixed-Width Reports

The preceding sample application demonstrated one way to read a file composed of text characters. Basically, it processed the file as a stream of characters. However, you sometimes have more refined needs than simply reading a stream of characters. For example, the first part of this book included numerous T-SQL samples that generated fixed-width reports from a SQL Server Express database. It is possible to direct the result set output from a T-SQL statement to a file. Using a more advanced set of file-reading resources than in the preceding sample, you can use VBE to read column values from files generated with T-SQL instructions. This section illustrates one approach to the task.

Generating a File with a Result Set

The following listing from the SalesByPersonTerritoryRegion.sql file begins with a `USE` statement to set the database context to the `AdventureWorks` database. Next, a `SELECT` statement lays out a report with seven columns. The columns are of fixed width, with the maximum width of each column set by a `CAST` function, the column's title, or the width that the T-SQL interpreter assigns to a column based on the data type of the values in a column.

```
USE AdventureWorks
GO

SELECT CAST(cr.Name AS nvarchar(14)) 'Region',
    CAST(st.Name AS nvarchar(14)) 'Territory',
    s.SalesPersonID,
    CAST(c.FirstName AS nvarchar(8)) 'FirstName',
    CAST(c.LastName AS nvarchar(17)) 'LastName',
    s.SalesYTD,
    s.SalesLastYear
FROM Sales.SalesPerson s JOIN HumanResources.Employee e
ON e.EmployeeID = s.SalesPersonID JOIN Person.Contact c
ON c.ContactID = e.ContactID LEFT JOIN Sales.SalesTerritory st
ON st.TerritoryID = s.TerritoryID LEFT JOIN Person.CountryRegion cr
ON cr.CountryRegionCode = st.CountryRegionCode
```

The following `sqlcmd` statement invokes the code in SalesByPersonTerritoryRegion.sql and saves the output to a file named SalesByPersonTerritoryRegion.rpt in the C:\ProSSEApps\Chapter09 path. The `-i` switch designates the source file for the instructions to generate a fixed-width report, and the `-o` switch specifies the path and file in which to save results. See the "Using the sqlcmd Utility" section in Chapter 2 for more detail on how to use the sqlcmd utility.

```
sqlcmd -S .\sqlexpress -i c:\ProSSEApps\Chapter09\SalesByPersonTerritoryRegion.sql
-o c:\ProSSEApps\Chapter09\SalesByPersonTerritoryRegion.rpt
```

The preceding `sqlcmd` generates a text-based file with fixed-width columns in SalesByPerson-TerritoryRegion.rpt. You can view the file with the Notepad utility because it is just a text file. An excerpt from the report appears in Figure 9-13.

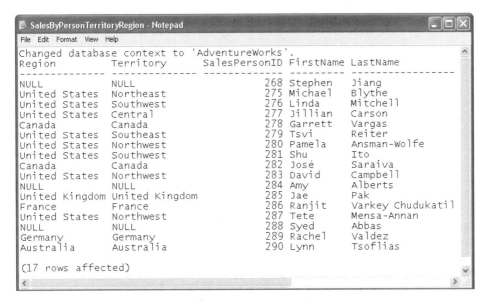

Figure 9-13. *T-SQL can generate report files with fixed-width columns that you can read with VBE.*

Reading the Values from a File with a Result Set

The code for reading the columns of data from the report showing in Figure 9-13 runs from the Click event procedure for `Button2`. VBE refers to these columns as fields. The code does two things. First, it reads the report columns depicted in Figure 9-13 with the `TextFieldParser` class in the `Microsoft.VisualBasic.FileIO` namespace. Second, it writes the column values read from the SQL Server Express report to a new report generated by VBE. In the process, you learn how to extract individual column values from the rows of a fixed-width text file.

■**Note** The `TextFieldParser` class in the `Microsoft.VisualBasic.FileIO` namespace has special properties and methods to help VBE solutions read fixed-width and delimited text files with columns of data.

`Button2_Click` commences with three `Dim` statements that appear in the following code block.

- The first `Dim` statement initializes the `strPathFile` variable to the file with the report that the procedure reads.

- The second `Dim` statement initializes the `SalesWidths` Integer array with a separate element value for each column in the report to be read. The elements in the array appear in the order of the report column to which they refer (for example, the first element references the first column).

  - The first six element values are each one greater than the number of dashes (-) in a column's heading. The extra value of 1 allows the `TextFieldParser` class instance to account for the single blank space at the end of each of the first six columns.

- The seventh element value of –1 specifies a variable width for the seventh and last column of the report. When using the `TextFieldParser` class with fixed-width reports, it is standard to designate the last column as having a variable width.

- The third `Dim` statement initializes the `maxColWidths` Integer array with maximum column widths for the report generated by VBE.

  - This array is used to compute the number of blanks to append so that columns stay in alignment.

  - The `maxColWidths` array element values match those in the `SalesWidths` array, except for the last column.

  - The last `maxColWidths` array element equals the maximum number of characters that you want in the last column of the report from VBE.

    ```
    Dim strPathFile As String = "c:\ProSSEApps\Chapter09\" & _
        "SalesByPersonTerritoryRegion.rpt"
    Dim SalesWidths() As Integer = {15, 15, 14, 10, 18, 22, -1}
    Dim maxColWidths() As Integer = {15, 15, 14, 10, 18, 22, 21}
    ```

All the rest of the code in `Button2_Click` appears within a `Using...End Using` block.

- The `Using` statement in a `Using...End Using` block can acquire a resource for use within the code inside the `Using...End Using` block. In this case, the `Using` statement reserves an instance of the `TextFieldParser` class with the name of `Reader`.

- The `TextFieldType` property of the `TextFieldParser` class designates whether to process fixed-width or delimited data, such as comma-delimited data. The following code segment indicates the use of the `TextFieldParser` for a fixed-width report.

- If you use a `TextFieldParser` instance to process a fixed-width report, as in the current case, then you need to specify column widths for successive report fields. You can specify column widths with the `SetFieldWidths` method for a `TextFieldParser` instance (`Reader`). This sample uses the widths in the `SalesWidths` array.

- The `ReadFields` method of the `TextFieldParser` class returns an array of column values for the current row and advances the text file pointer to the next row. The `Dim` statement for the `currentRow` String array declares an array to hold return values from the `ReadFields` method.

- The `int1` variable, declared in the line following the `Dim` statement for the `currentRow` array, tracks the current column being processed. This variable points at an appropriate element in the `maxColWidths` array for the current output column being generated.

- A `Do...Loop` statement contains the bulk of the processing code within the `Using...End Using` block. There are no conditions on the `Do` or `Loop` elements of the statement because the condition testing for an exit from the loop occurs within the code in the `Do...Loop` statement.

- The `Do...Loop` statement contains a `Try...Catch...Finally` statement with two `Catch` clauses.

  - The `Try` block clause reads a row of column values with the `ReadFields` method from the input report, stores the result in the `currentRow` array, and writes the array elements to the Quick Console window one column at a time. The syntax for the `Try` block shows you how to extract individual column values from a fixed-width report.

  - The `ReadFields` method can generate a single `Exception` type—the `Microsoft.VisualBasic.FileIO.MalformedLineException`. However, it can occur for multiple instances, such as no more data or badly formed data.

- The first Catch clause handles a MalformedLineException resulting from no more data. In this case, Reader.EndOfData is True. A When clause in the Catch clause evaluates this condition. If the condition is True, the procedure exits the Do loop, which in turn passes control to the End Using statement.

- The second Catch clause handles a line with values that cannot be read with the settings for the TextFieldParser instance. This outcome also throws a MalformedLineException object. The Debug.Print statement writes a message to the Immediate window about the line causing the error. This output stream allows a user to know which lines were not processed from the original report.

- The Finally clause inserts a carriage return after each row in the default Output window (see Figure 9-14). The rows of the report are double-spaced. No special coding is required for this benefit.

Note The Using statement is a new Visual Basic statement introduced with Visual Basic 2005. The syntax for this statement is Using resource specification...statements using the resource...End Using. The resource specified is available after the Using clause up until the End Using clause, which disposes of the resource. The Using statement is particularly convenient for automatically disposing of unmanaged resources, such as a file handle or an ADO.NET Connection object (see Chapter 12). This is because the .NET Framework disposes of a resource specified in the Using clause during the execution of the End Using clause.

```
Using Reader As New Microsoft.VisualBasic.FileIO. _
    TextFieldParser(strPathFile)
    Reader.TextFieldType = _
    Microsoft.VisualBasic.FileIO.FieldType.FixedWidth
    Reader.SetFieldWidths(SalesWidths)
    Dim currentRow As String()
    Dim int1 As Integer
    Do
      Try
        currentRow = Reader.ReadFields()
        Dim currentField As String
        For Each currentField In currentRow
          Console.Write(currentField & _
            StrDup((maxColWidths(int1) - currentField.Length), " "))
          int1 += 1
        Next
        int1 = 0
      Catch ex1 As _
      Microsoft.VisualBasic.FileIO.MalformedLineException _
      When Reader.EndOfData = True
        Exit Do
      Catch ex1 As _
      Microsoft.VisualBasic.FileIO.MalformedLineException _
      When Reader.EndOfData = False
        Debug.Print("Line " & ex1.Message & _
        "is not valid and will be skipped.")
      Finally
        Console.WriteLine(ControlChars.Cr)
      End Try
    Loop
End Using
```

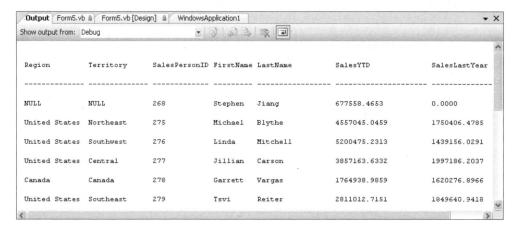

Figure 9-14. *This excerpt from the Output window displays a field-based echo generated by VBE of the text file excerpt in Figure 9-13.*

Summary

This chapter had two main objectives. First, it covered the basics of Visual Basic programming for Windows forms. Second, it presented a series of samples that illustrated several typical kinds of tasks suitable for development with VBE. Among the major topics this chapter addressed were

- VBE data types, including
  - In-depth coverage of how to use them in Dim statements and assignment statements
  - Samples and best practices for converting between data types
  - A couple of calculator samples, including a four-function calculator
- Runtime error processing via the Catch...Try...Finally statement
- File processing techniques, including
  - Coverage of how to simplify file processing with the My namespace
  - A project explorer for learning about the paths and files in a solution
  - A fixed-width column reader for reading SQL Server Express result sets

■ ■ ■

CHAPTER 10

Introduction to Visual Web Developer Express, Web Pages, and Web Forms

Visual Web Developer Express (VWDE) provides an IDE for building Web applications that is comparable to the one Visual Basic Express provides for building Windows applications. To create solutions with VWDE, you code with ASP.NET 2.0, which is a significant improvement over the ASP model that was popular among classic Visual Basic developers for building Web applications.

The first two sections in this chapter give a quick introduction to Web development concepts and show how to create and open a Web application. After the first two introductory sections, the rest of the chapter presents a series of sample applications that demonstrate common solutions and helpful Web development skills for creating any solution. Some sample applications or techniques that you are likely to find especially useful include

- Building and testing a Web application without a Web server
- Using a Calendar control to accept dates on Web Forms
- Letting users pick a message or tip for the day
- Creating hyperlinks between Web pages (.htm) and Web Forms (.aspx)
- Copying Web Forms and pages from a file-based website to a server-based website
- Managing properties for Web Forms and their controls
- Sharing data across multiple round trips for the same page and between different pages
- Validating a Web page's data before sending the page to a Web server
- Querying a fixed-width data report, such as one from SQL Server Express (SSE)

ASP.NET Development Concepts

The term ASP.NET derives from two sources:

- First, ASP stands for Active Server Pages, a technology that allows you to create special kinds of pages that hold content, such as words and tables of numbers, and facilitate navigating to other parts of the same page or different pages on the same or another site in a network—particularly, the Internet. Over time, the ASP technology adapted to accommodate dialogs or conversations between clients and servers via forms on a page.
  - Users can request information to which a server has access, and the server can retrieve and serve the information to a user's browser.

- Users can also input information on a page with their browser, such as Internet Explorer, and the server can store that information.

- An ASP page can also dynamically change its appearance at runtime by showing the time of day, a user's name, or some other content programmed to appear on a page.

- Second, the .NET in ASP.NET refers to an upgrading of ASP technology to take advantage of the .NET Framework in general, as well as specific ASP.NET features that target Web development.

- ASP.NET pages are faster to use because they are compiled rather than interpreted, as the older ASP pages were.

- ASP.NET pages have built-in, smarter caching relative to ASP pages to simplify the display of data in Web Form controls.

- ASP.NET introduces rich Page and Web Form classes to simplify common tasks and to more easily perform advanced tasks. Web Forms offer many of the advantages of Windows forms, and you use them in a similar fashion. However, Web Forms are optimized for use with the Microsoft IIS Web server.

ASP.NET projects always require a folder for storing the pages in a project. The folder for storing the pages for a project is typically called a website. Prior to ASP.NET 2.0, developers required access to a Web server to test an ASP.NET project. ASP.NET 2.0, as implemented through VWDE, can use the built-in ASP.NET Development Server. This Web server can process page files on the local computer from a regular directory folder as if they were in a Web directory.

The fundamental flow of pages in an ASP.NET project is that a server renders a page for a browser to view. The browser can display a page and send back a request with some information in it to a server for additional processing. The server processes instructions from a browser, using a language such as Visual Basic 2005, to render a page that is sent as HTML (Hypertext Markup Language) to the browser. On the client end of an ASP.NET page, the browser reads a page as HTML with any client-side scripts and completes the presentation and processing of a page.

A single Web page can contain HTML or HTML and ASP.NET code. By definition, Web servers render HTML. However, ASP and ASP.NET require a Web server that knows about their syntax for specifying instructions. ASP and ASP.NET are a part of IIS, the Microsoft Web server; IIS is a free Web server for Windows 2000, Windows XP, and Windows 2003.

To run ASP.NET code on a server, you also need to have an appropriate version of the .NET Framework. For example, ASP.NET 2.0 requires the corresponding version of the .NET Framework. Once you have a computer properly configured with IIS and the .NET Framework, it can run ASP.NET code to serve pages to browsers. The computers running the browsers do not require either IIS or the .NET Framework.

Note In case you were wondering, you can code ASP.NET in multiple languages, including Visual Basic 2005, which you learned about in Chapter 9.

ASP.NET both complements and extends HTML features for empowering authors and developers to create Web pages. For example, HTML and ASP.NET enable forms. Although HTML forms provide basic form-processing capabilities, ASP.NET forms provide much richer form-processing features that are easier to use.

There are also HTML controls and ASP.NET controls. VWDE provides separate page templates that are optimized for the use of HTML controls (HTML Page) or ASP.NET controls (Web Form). Pages created with an HTML Page template do not support ASP.NET controls without the addition of special page directives. However, pages created with a Web Form template support both ASP.NET controls and HTML tags without any special page directive. As a general rule, create all your pages with the Web Form template so that you can use either type of control without having to modify a page with a special page directive.

■**Note** ASP.NET extends not only HTML but also ASP. In fact, a single Web solution, that is, one in a folder on a Web server, can have both ASP and ASP.NET pages. The capability of ASP.NET and ASP to run side by side allows you to take advantage of the more advanced features available with ASP.NET in an application that was originally started with ASP.

Starting and Exploring ASP.NET Projects

Before you can get started adding page files to an ASP.NET project, you need to create a website for your project. This section describes how to perform this task by using VWDE IDE (integrated development environment). The good news is that the IDE is similar to the one for Visual Basic Express. Many of the skills you learned in Chapter 8 carry over to VWDE. This section briefly discusses three critical VWDE IDE windows and relates their contents to the items present in a new project. You also learn about the Source and Design views for a page in the VWDE IDE.

Starting an ASP.NET Project

You can start an ASP.NET project by choosing Project ➤ New ➤ Web Site from the VWDE Standard menu. This menu selection opens the New Web Site dialog box. Recall that a website is a repository for the files in an ASP.NET project. You can use the New Web Site dialog box to specify the type of ASP.NET project to start. These templates are

- ASP.NET Web Site

- ASP.NET Web Service

- Personal Web Site Starter Kit

- Empty Web Site

Figure 10-1 shows the New Web Site dialog box with the selections for a new ASP.NET website in the file system. The default language selection for the site is Visual Basic 2005. You can choose C# (or J# as well if you install J# with VWDE). The destination folder for the website is c:\ProSSEApps\Chapter10\WebSite1. Click Browse to navigate to any path for the project folder, and then give the folder any legitimate folder name. All the ASP.NET project files reside in this folder (c:\ProSSEApps\Chapter10\WebSite1). Because of the File System selection in the Location drop-down box, VWDE uses the ASP.NET Development Web Server to run the files in the project. Later, you can copy the folder to a directory on a Web server, or you can designate the current project file folder as a virtual Web directory for additional testing on a Web server.

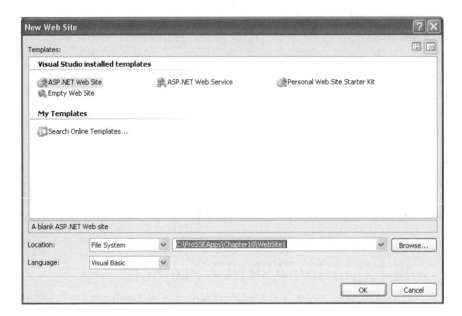

Figure 10-1. *The New Web Site dialog box lets you start a new ASP.NET project with the help of a template or you can open a starter kit project.*

The ASP.NET Web Site template is the template to select when you want to start an ASP.NET project from scratch. This template creates a folder with one file, default.aspx, and an App_Data folder, which is a folder within the website for holding data files. The default.aspx file is the default home page for a website. Web masters typically use this page to describe their site and provide links for resources at their site and elsewhere.

■**Tip** Users cannot directly request files from the App_Data folder. Therefore, it is a secure place to locate database files within a website.

If you select HTTP from the Location drop-down box, VWDE additionally creates an IIS project, which allows others to use the project by connecting to a Web server storing the project's website. ASP.NET distinguishes between two types of IIS website types:

- Website on the local computer
- Website on a remote computer

To create a website on either a local or a remote computer, you need to have administrator privileges on the Web server. You must be able to connect to a remote computer via a LAN connection, and the computer must have FrontPage 2002 Server Extensions installed. For the ASP.NET project to run from a remote computer, the computer must have the appropriate .NET Framework installed, such as .NET 2.0. However, client computers do not require the installation of the .NET Framework to run Web pages.

Other templates besides the ASP.NET Web Site template complete the functionality available from the New Web Site dialog box.

- The ASP.NET Web Service template helps you to start the design of an XML Web Service with VWDE. An XML Web Service is a class library that you can invoke from an Internet connection.

- The Personal Web Site Starter Kit template creates a new ASP.NET project based on a Microsoft-supplied template that includes a home page, resume, and photo album. Substantial resources within the VWDE Help files assist you in learning about and extending the Starter Kit project.

- The Empty Web Site template does what its name implies. It creates an empty website, which does not have a default.aspx file or an App_Data folder. Typically, VWDE developers are not likely to use this option often.

Exploring a New ASP.NET Project

Figure 10-2 shows an ASP.NET project opened to default.aspx. This view becomes available immediately after you click OK in the New Web Site dialog box in Figure 10-1.

The .aspx file extension for default.aspx denotes the Web page file as an ASP.NET page, which gives the page special features. For example, the page contains a `<form>` tag with a `runat` attribute equal to `server`. `Text` and other tags between the starting and ending form tags (`<form>` and `</form>`) are part of the Web Form associated with the default.aspx page.

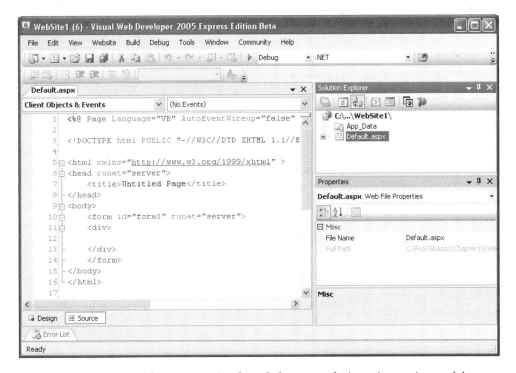

Figure 10-2. *The VWDE IDE lets you examine the code for a page, the items in a project, and the properties of the currently selected item.*

An @Page directive at the very top of Source view for default.aspx specifies attributes for the page. You can see the Language and AutoEventWireUp attribute settings. Two settings cropped from view include CodeFile and Inherits.

- The Language attribute corresponds to the Language setting in the New Web Site dialog box that appears in Figure 10-1.

- The AutoEventWireUp attribute setting designates how VWDE infers which procedures handle object events.

  - The AutoEventWireUp attribute assignment is false in Figure 10-1, which means that a Handles clause designates the event that a procedure processes (see Chapter 9 for more on the Handles clause).

  - A setting of true for the AutoEventWireUp attribute, which is the default value, indicates a procedure responds to an event by its name instead of its Handles clause. Therefore, the procedure handling the Click event for Button1 must have the name Button1_Click instead of any name with a Handles clause argument of Button1.Click.

- The CodeFile attribute designates the file name containing the code behind the page.

  - In this case, the name for the file is default.aspx.vb. You can view the CodeFile attribute by right-clicking in Source view and choosing View Code.

  - The CodeFile setting defines a partial class that inherits from the base class for a page.

- The Inherits clause instructs the .NET runtime which base class to use for page attributes and layout features.

On the right side of Figure 10-2 are Solution Explorer and the Properties window. Within Solution Explorer, you can see that the ASP.NET website contains an App_Data folder in addition to default.aspx. Recall that the App_Data folder's purpose is to hold data files in an ASP.NET project. Clicking the plus (+) next to default.aspx exposes default.aspx.vb in Solution Explorer.

The Properties window shows the two properties for the selected item in Solution Explorer. The Full Path property is cropped from its setting of C:\ProSSEApps\Chapter10\WebSite1\Default.aspx. You can select tags in the Source view of default.aspx to view tag attribute settings that serve as properties for the tags.

If you click the Design control next to the Source control at the bottom of the IDE, you can change the view of default.aspx so that you can type text into the page. VWDE will automatically assign tags as appropriate for the content that you type. Design view provides a view that is similar to one from a browser for a page file. You can also enter text and tags for a page in Source view. Design view and Source view are two different views of the same file and VWDE opens pages by default in Source view. You can control which view VWDE opens initially with the Options dialog box:

- Choose Tools ➤ Options to open the Options dialog box.

- Make sure the Show all settings check box is selected.

- Then, select HTML Designer. Select either Source View or Design View in the Start pages in group.

Creating Pages for an ASP.NET Project

Creating and designing pages for a website is a very deep topic. After all, the main purpose for navigating to a site is what's at the site, and Web pages compose what's at a site. ASP.NET projects offer tools for creating rich interactive experiences that go beyond what is typical for other types of Web projects. In addition, it is particularly easy to engineer this interactivity with VWDE. One main vehicle for making pages interactive is through the use of ASP.NET controls on a special type of Web page known as a Web Form. This section demonstrates how to create Web Form pages and offers samples that highlight different techniques for making pages interactive.

Changing a Page by Clicking a Button

ASP.NET simplifies how a Visual Basic developer can manage a website. You can program pages on the server with special built-in controls and the ASP.NET object model. The sample for this section manages the `Title` property of a Web Form. The `Title` property value is the text that appears in the top-left corner of a Web browser showing a page. This property maps to the `title` element within the `head` block of the HTML for a page; see Figure 10-2 for the tags defining the title element within the head block.

■**Note** HTML tags define the elements and sections or blocks of a Web page. Tags often nest within one another. The opening and closing `html` tags (`<html>` and `</html>`) define the outermost HTML tags for a page. Within the `html` block is the `head` block (`<head>` and `</head>`). An element designates a set of opening and closing tags without another element or block within it. The `title` element (`<title>` and `</title>`) can exist within the `head` block.

By default, ASP.NET initializes the `title` element (or `Title` property) to "Untitled page." The sample application initializes the `Title` property to "Title not assigned" during the `Load` event for a page. The `Click` event procedure for an ASP.NET Button control on the page changes the page's `Title` property value to "Title assigned."

■**Note** You can view the properties of a block or an element that are available for manipulation by clicking the element or block's opening tag. The Properties window shows the properties for the selected block or element.

Starting a Web Form with a Single-file Code Model

You can run Visual Basic 2005 server-side code from a Web Form page. This is a page configured to run ASP.NET controls. You can place server-side code for a page on the same page as your HTML or in a different, but coordinated, file. When you initially create a Web Form, you can choose:

- The default language for the page
- Whether your server-side code appears in the same file as the HTML or in a different, related file
- Whether the page is a master page

■Note Master pages are a formatting aid to help website authors develop a consistent look for the pages at a website. See the "Master Pages" section of the online chapter available at `http://www.apress.com/book/bookDisplay.html?bID=459` for additional coverage of the topic.

To add a new Web Form to a project, right-click the solution name in Solution Explorer and choose Add New Item. You can also open the Add New Item dialog box with the File ➤ New ➤ File menu command. Figure 10-3 shows the Add New Item dialog box with a Web Form item selected. The name for the new file in the WebSite1 project will be AssignPageTitle.aspx. Notice that the check box is unselected for Place code in separate file. This means that the Visual Basic 2005 code for the page will be in the same file as the HTML for the page.

As you can see from Figure 10-3, ASP.NET offers two models for where your server-side code goes.

- The single-file code model includes server-side code and HTML in a single file. Leaving the Place code in separate file check box unselected invokes this model.

- Selecting the check box for Place code in separate file creates separate, but coordinated, page files for the HTML and the server-side code for an ASP.NET page. This approach is the code-behind-page code model.

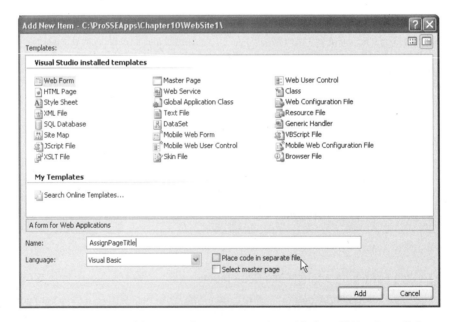

Figure 10-3. *When you add a new Web Form to a project with the Add New Item dialog box, you can specify either a single-file or code-behind-page code model.*

If you have significant experience with either classic Visual Basic or Visual Basic .NET, you are likely to find the code-behind-page code model more familiar. This approach isolates your Visual Basic code from your page layout code. In contrast to Visual Basic developers, many Web developers come from a background in which it is common to mix HTML and other code in a single file. These two different approaches to managing page content appeal to different development styles:

- On the one hand, Visual Basic developers may prefer the single-file code model for simple files with just a few lines of Visual Basic 2005 and HTML code because of the convenience of having all content in a single file.

- On the other hand, as the number of lines of code grows, this convenience will be offset by the drudgery of scrolling back and forth between script blocks with Visual Basic 2005 code and page blocks with page layout code for formatting text and controls.

Another advantage of isolating the HTML and Visual Basic 2005 code pertains to teams made of HTML authors and VB developers. In this scenario, an HTML author can work on one file, and a VB developer can work on another file. However, ASP.NET can integrate the two files when rendering pages to a browser.

Formatting a Page

A typical ASP.NET page has one or more ASP.NET controls and several associated event procedures. The ASP.NET object model has a `Page` object that, in turn, has properties corresponding to the HTML for a page. Although you can assign page property values at design time from the VWDE IDE, you cannot change these properties at runtime from the IDE. Event procedures in the sample for this section illustrate how to dynamically change these attributes at runtime.

The sample application uses an ASP.NET Button control to let a user specify when to change a page property. Before the `Click` event procedure for the Button control fires, the `Load` event procedure for the page initializes the `Title` property to a different default value than the one assigned by the Web Form template in the Add New Item dialog box (see Figure 10-3). The implementation of this sample involves three steps:

- Add an ASP.NET Button control to the page. The default identifier for this control is `Button1`.

- Add shells for the `Page_Load` and `Button1_Click` event procedures.

- Add code to each procedure that assigns a value to the page's `Title` property.

You can drag a Button control to an ASP.NET page from the Standard group in the toolbar. The layout for the sample solution positions the Button control between two built-in tags for the page.

You can re-create the layout for the Button control in the sample solution by dragging a Button from the Standard group in the Toolbox to an empty line that you insert between the `</div>` and `</form>` tags (a `div` block is a generalized container for text and other items, such as controls, that can also accept formatting and pass it on to its contents).

- Make the empty line by pressing Enter with your cursor immediately after `</div>`.

- If the toolbox is not already open, choose View ➤ Toolbox.

- If the Standard group is not already open, click the plus (+) next to Standard.

- Drag a Button control from the Standard group to the empty line.

- Change the `Text` attribute in the Button control tag from Button to Assign title.

Next, you can add `Page_Load` and `Button1_Click` event procedure shells to a script block that appears between the `@Page` directive and the `html` block. You can use the Object drop-down box at the top of the Source view to specify the object and the Event drop-down box to designate the object-event pair for a procedure shell. When you complete your selection from the Event drop-down box, the VWDE IDE automatically adds the corresponding event procedure shell to the script block.

The final formatting step for the page is to add a single line of code to each event procedure shell. Figure 10-4 shows the Source view for the AssignPageTitle.aspx file.

- The `Me` keyword in the two event procedure shells refers to the current ASP.NET page. You can select the `Title` property for `Me` with the help of IntelliSense.

- The `head` block nested in the `html` block shows the default assignment for the `Title` attribute by an ASP.NET page. Without the `Page_Load` event procedure, the page's title would initially be the value designated in the `head` block.

- The Button control tag and its settings illustrate several interesting features.

  - The Button control's tag appears with an `asp` prefix. A colon delimits the prefix from the control name. The tags for other ASP.NET controls also have an `asp` prefix. This `asp` prefix designates a special namespace for processing these tags versus standard HTML tags.

  - The `Text` attribute value for the Button control is `Assign title`.

  - The `OnClick` attribute designates the procedure for processing the Button control's `Click` event. The `OnClick` attribute value points at the `Button1_Click` procedure.

  - There is no closing Button tag (`</asp:Button>`). Using a forward slash (`/`) at the end of an opening tag represents a closing tag.

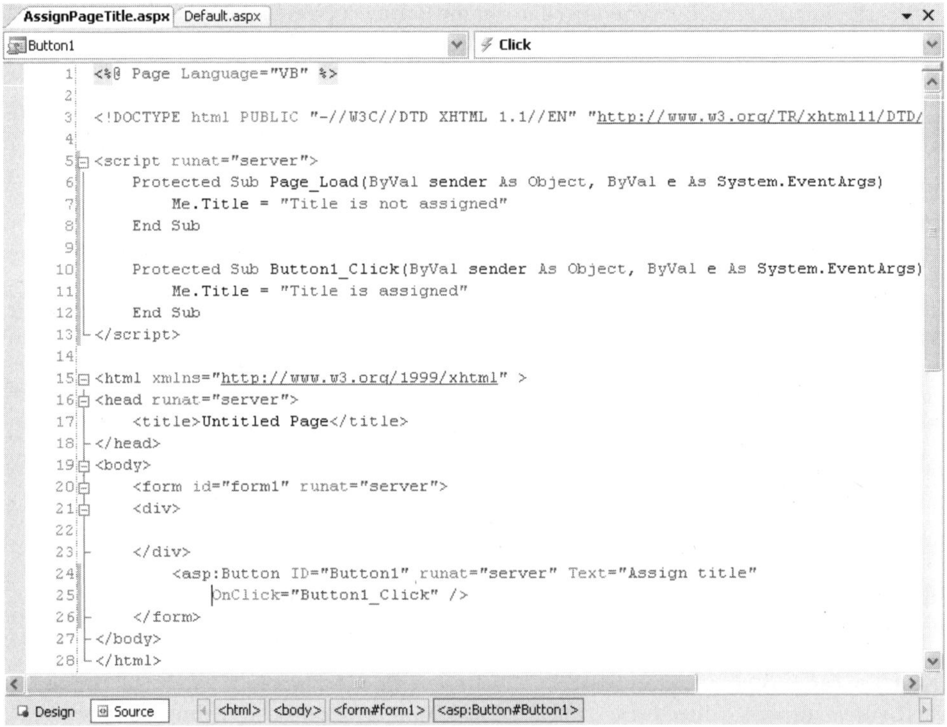

```
AssignPageTitle.aspx  Default.aspx                                          ▼ X
Button1                                    ▼    Click                        ▼
 1  <%@ Page Language="VB" %>
 2
 3  <!DOCTYPE html PUBLIC "-//W3C//DTD XHTML 1.1//EN" "http://www.w3.org/TR/xhtml11/DTD/
 4
 5  <script runat="server">
 6      Protected Sub Page_Load(ByVal sender As Object, ByVal e As System.EventArgs)
 7          Me.Title = "Title is not assigned"
 8      End Sub
 9
10      Protected Sub Button1_Click(ByVal sender As Object, ByVal e As System.EventArgs)
11          Me.Title = "Title is assigned"
12      End Sub
13  </script>
14
15  <html xmlns="http://www.w3.org/1999/xhtml" >
16  <head runat="server">
17      <title>Untitled Page</title>
18  </head>
19  <body>
20      <form id="form1" runat="server">
21      <div>
22
23      </div>
24          <asp:Button ID="Button1" runat="server" Text="Assign title"
25              OnClick="Button1_Click" />
26      </form>
27  </body>
28  </html>
 Design   Source    <html> <body> <form#form1> <asp:Button#Button1>
```

Figure 10-4. *With a single-file code model, your event procedures appear in a script block above the HTML code formatting a page.*

■**Note** ASP.NET control attributes correspond to ASP.NET control properties. The Text property for a Web Form control is similar to the Text property for a Windows form control. Both Text properties serve as control captions. However, the ID property for Web Form controls acts similarly to the Name property for Windows form controls in that both the ID and Name properties provide a programmatic handle for a control.

Running an ASP.NET Page

After you build a solution, it is natural to want to test it. This step helps you to detect and eliminate bugs and faulty program logic, preview the solution with a client to get additional feedback, or fine-tune the solution for your own needs.

When running a file-system website, as is the case for WebSite1, you do not actually have a website to which users from other computers can connect. However, you can easily run the AssignPageTitle.aspx file. This will show whether the page compiles and, if so, the result it generates. When you run the page file in a file-system folder instead of a Web-server folder, VWDE invokes the ASP.NET Development Web Server instead of either a local or a remote Web server. You can run the page by choosing Debug ➤ Start Without Debugging. The shortcut keystroke for this menu command is Ctrl+F5.

Figure 10-5 shows a browser session after a click to the Assign title button. Notice the page's title reads "Title is assigned." This is the outcome of the Button1_Click procedure. Before a click to the button, the title was "Title is not assigned." The change of title is the outcome of the Page_Load procedure. VWDE automatically populates the Address box, which references the AssignPageTitle.aspx file in the WebSite1 website. Notice the button on the page displays the name of the corresponding Button control's Text attribute setting.

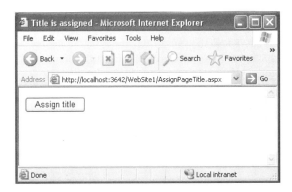

Figure 10-5. *You can test an ASP.NET page with the ASP.NET Development Web Server when you are running from a file-system location.*

Returning a Formatted Date from a Calendar Control

One of the great features of ASP.NET is its rich set of controls. Among the most interesting of the ASP.NET controls is a Calendar control that enables a user to pick a date from a calendar and returns a corresponding Visual Basic 2005 Date value. Recall from the "Date Data Types and the Timespan Structure" section in Chapter 9 that this data type returns both the date and time. When there is no time element for a Date value, as with the return value from a Calendar control, VWDE sets the time element to midnight, the first time instance within a day. The sample in this section shows how to display the return value from a Calendar control before and after formatting to hide the time element.

Starting a Web Form with a Code-Behind-Page File

You can start the building of the sample by adding a new Web Form item to the WebSite1 project. In the Add New Item dialog box, assign the name `CalendarFormattedDate` to the new Web Form page. In addition, select the check box for placing code in a separate file. Recall that this selection causes the creation of a separate, coordinated file for the code behind the Web Form page.

This sample uses three views in two separate files for the `CalendarFormattedDate` page.

- The CalendarFormattedDate.aspx file is the page with the HTML formatting for the page. This page has both Source and Design views.

- The CalendarFormattedDate.aspx.vb file contains the code behind the Web Form in a partial class.

Settings in both the first and second files cause them to reference one another.

■Note The ASP.NET 2.0 code-behind model takes advantage of a new .NET Framework version 2.0 language feature known as partial classes. The code-behind file for a page is not a complete class definition. You can designate the file implementing a partial class with the `CodeFile` attribute setting for a Web Form `@Page` directive. The `Inherits` attribute for a Web Form `@Page` directive denotes the base class for a Web Form page. See the "Exploring a New ASP.NET Project" section for additional coverage of Web Form `@Page` directive attributes.

VWDE specifies a set of `@Page` directive attributes for the `CalendarFormattedDate` page in response to the settings on the Add New Item dialog box during the creation of the Web Form. You can view these settings at the top of Source view for CalendarFormattedDate.aspx.

- The `Language` attribute equals VB, for the persisted Visual Basic setting in the Add New Item dialog box.

- The `AutoEventWireUp` attribute setting is `false`. Recall that this setting designates reliance on the `Handles` clause for determining which procedure replies to an event for an object. The `OnClick` attribute for a control tag cannot reference a procedure in another file, but the `Handles` clause can reference an object in another file. The two files in this sample are

  - CalendarFormattedDate.aspx

  - CalendarFormattedDate.aspx.vb

- The `CodeFile` attribute setting points at CalendarFormattedDate.aspx.vb from CalendarFormattedDate.aspx.

- The `Inherits` attribute setting is `CalendarFormattedDate`, which is the class name for the current page. VWDE creates the `CalendarFormattedDate` class in response to the Add New Item dialog box settings.

The following excerpt from the CalendarFormattedDate.aspx.vb file shows a `Partial Class` declaration at the top of the file. The name following `Partial Class` is `CalendarFormattedDate`. This statement designates the class referenced by the CalendarFormattedDate.aspx.vb file as the same one referenced by the CalendarFormattedDate.aspx file.

```
Partial Class CalendarFormattedDate
    Inherits System.Web.UI.Page
```

Using a Calendar Control

Using the Calendar control involves several steps. First, you need to add the control to a Web Form. Second, you need to add the shell for an event procedure that detects the selection of a date in the control. Third, you need to add some code to the event procedure that responds to the selection of a date. For example, you can display the selected date.

The following excerpt from the Source view shows the HTML code in the body block of the `CalendarFormattedDate` page. In addition to the standard code for a Web Form page generated by VWDE, the excerpt includes three lines of custom code that add and layout controls on the page.

- The important lines add two ASP.NET Label controls (`Label1` and `Label2`) to the form along with a Calendar control (`Calendar1`).
  - You can drag these controls from the Standard group of the Toolbox to the page as described in the preceding sample.
  - You drag all controls to a page in the same way.
- The `<br \>` tag forces a break of the current line so that each of the three controls appears on a separate line within the Web Form. You can add HTML tags to a page with the help of IntelliSense.
  - Open an IntelliSense list box for HTML by typing an open angle bracket (`<`).
  - Then, select the br element from the IntelliSense list box.
  - Complete the tag with a closing angle bracket (`>`).
  - VWDE responds by trailing br with a space and a forward slash (`\`) before the closing angle bracket (`>`). This convention is consistent with XHTML, which is the HTML dialect used within ASP.NET projects.

■**Note** XHTML is a dialect of HTML that reproduces and extends HTML 4. The WC3 (World Wide Web Consortium) maintains the standards for XHTML. You can learn more about XHTML from the WC3 website at `http://www.w3.org/TR/xhtml1/`.

```
<body>
    <form id="form1" runat="server">
    <div>

    </div>
        <asp:Label ID="Label1" runat="server" Text="Label"></asp:Label><br />
        <asp:Label ID="Label2" runat="server" Text="Label"></asp:Label><br />
        <asp:Calendar ID="Calendar1" runat="server"></asp:Calendar>
    </form>
</body>
```

Figure 10-6 shows the Calendar control along with the two Label controls on the page in Design view. If you hover your cursor over many ASP.NET controls, including the Calendar control, you see a smart tag, which appears as a right-facing arrow (until you click it when the arrow direction points left). Clicking a smart tag for a control opens a short list of actions and settings that you can make graphically.

Figure 10-6 shows the Auto Format task available for the Calendar control. Clicking the Auto Format item opens the Auto Format dialog box with a list of format names and a preview screen showing the impact of each selection. I use the Professional 2 format, which highlights all days for the current month relative to days before and after the current month, which are grayed out.

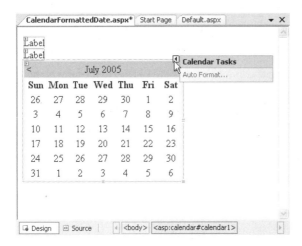

Figure 10-6. *The Calendar control features a smart tag that facilitates formatting the calendar control.*

Double-clicking the Calendar control in Design view of CalendarFormattedDate.aspx opens CalendarFormattedDate.aspx.vb and adds an event procedure shell for the Calendar control's default event. The default event for a Calendar control is the SelectionChanged event. You can see the full list of events for the Calendar control by clicking the Method name drop-down box on the top right-hand side of the Code window in CalendarFormattedDate.aspx.vb with Calendar1 selected in the Class name drop-down box. The Class name drop-down box appears to the left of the Method name drop-down box.

The following listing shows the Calendar1_SelectionChanged event procedure. Notice the Handles clause at the end of the Sub statement. This clause connects the procedure with the SelectionChanged event for the Calendar1 control. Label1 shows the unformatted Date value returned by Calendar control. Label2 displays the Date value returned by the Calendar control formatted to suppress the display of the time element.

■**Note** See the DateTimeFormatInfo Class topic in VWDE Help for a set of examples showing the full range of formatting options available for Date values with the ToString method.

```
Protected Sub Calendar1_SelectionChanged(ByVal sender As Object, _
    ByVal e As System.EventArgs) Handles Calendar1.SelectionChanged
    Me.Label1.Text = "Unformatted date: " & _
        Me.Calendar1.SelectedDate.ToString
    Me.Label2.Text = "Formatted date: " & _
        Me.Calendar1.SelectedDate.ToString("d")
End Sub
```

Running the Calendar Control Sample

There are several ways to start a solution. You learned how to start an application without debugging (e.g., press Ctrl+F5). Yet another option is to view the page in a browser. You can view a page in a browser from multiple starting points, but one way is to right-click the page file name in Solution Explorer, such as CalendarFormattedDate.aspx. After selecting View in Browser, VWDE will prompt you to save any unsaved changes before attempting to display the page in a browser. If the page compiles properly, you will see the page in a browser.

■Note The first time VWDE opens a page or after any edit to a page, there will be a pause associated with the compiling of the code for the page. If there are no further changes to the page, subsequent attempts to run the page proceed much more quickly because VWDE references the compiled copy for the page instead of the uncompiled source code.

Figure 10-7 shows the CalendarFormattedDate.aspx page file after the selection of July 21. The top label, `Label1`, shows the `Date` value for the selection in its unformatted version with both date and time values. However, selections from a Web Form Calendar control do not designate a time of day. Therefore, all unformatted values will have the same time element of midnight. Because the time element presents no useful information about the selected date, it is preferable to suppress its display. Figure 10-7 shows this outcome for the second Label control on the Web Form. The assignment statement for generating this outcome is the one for `Me.Label2.Text` in the `Calendar1_SelectionChanged` procedure.

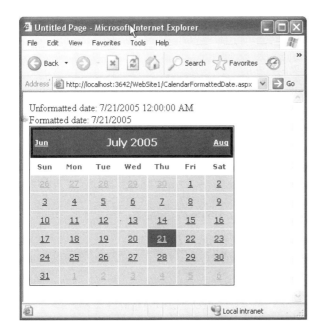

Figure 10-7. *You can use members of the DateTimeFormatInfo class to customize the appearance of the return value from a Calendar control.*

Programming a Message-for-the-Day Application

The Calendar control lends itself nicely to a message-for-the-day application. The need for this type of application is quite common. Because I teach both Sunday school and prayer classes, my messages are a collection of some of my favorite Bible verses. However, you can easily adapt this sample to present any kind of messages that you choose.

The code for the sample is remarkably simple. The most cumbersome part is adding your messages to the sample. There are several reasonable approaches for achieving this kind of task, but this sample implementation uses a `String` array with each message populating an element in the array. In addition to the `SelectionChanged` event for the Calendar control, the sample also demonstrates the use of the `Load` event for the Web Form's `Page` class instance as well as the `Form` instance within the `Page` object. The sample's implementation could have just used the `Load` event for the `Page` object, but using both `Load` event procedures gives you a chance to see the use of `Load` event procedures for two different objects.

Laying Out a Page in Design View

Add a new Web Form to the WebSite1 project whose name is `MessageForTheDay`. Use the same settings as the previous sample so that the default language for the page is Visual Basic, and the sample uses a code-behind-page code model. After the Web Form opens in Source view, switch immediately to Design view. If you do not see the opening and closing `div` tags (`<div>` and `</div>`), choose View ➤ Details. Showing tags often makes the precise positioning of controls on a page easier.

The page will use three Label controls and a Calendar control as well as some formatted text in the `div` block as a title preceding the controls.

- Start by positioning your cursor between the opening and closing `div` tags.
- Type "Message for the Day."
- Select Message for the Day so the text appears highlighted.
- Choose Heading 3 <H3> from the Block Format control on the Format toolbar.

■**Tip** Recall that you can tell the name of a toolbar control by hovering your cursor over it.

Now that you have a title on the page, add the controls to the Web Form. You can subsequently return to format the controls. Figure 10-8 displays the Design view after the addition of text and formatting of text in the `div` block as well as the following steps for the addition of controls to the page.

- Drag a Label control from the Toolbox immediately after the closing `div` tag (`</div>`).
- Press the Enter key twice to create a separation between the first label control and the Calendar control. Each of the Enter keystrokes adds a `br` tag to the page. The `br` tags appear on the page as a carriage return symbol from a keyboard.
- Drag a Calendar control to the page after the marker for the second `br` tag.
- With your cursor immediately below the Calendar control, press the Enter key twice.
- Drag a second Label control to the page.
- Press the Enter key again.
- Drag a third Label control to the page.

Figure 10-8. *You can lay out pages in Design view with the help of the Toolbox and the Format toolbar.*

The next step is to format the controls. The Calendar control is formatted as in the preceding sample (see, in particular, the "Using a Calendar Control" section, for the instructions on how to format a Calendar control). Each of the three Label controls receives an assignment to its Text property, from the Properties window in Design view.

- Assign a value of Pick a day to view a message to the Text property value of Label1.

- Then, designate a value of Your message is: to the Text property of the second Label control.

- Finally, clear the default value in the Text property of Label3 to make the control initially appear empty when the page opens.

Programming the MessageForTheDay Code Module

The ASP.NET Development Web Server serves the MessageForTheDay.aspx file in a Web browser if you invoke the server by pressing the Ctrl+F5 keystroke. However, nothing happens when you click a day on the Calendar control. To enable the application to work, you need to populate the code module in the MessageForTheDay.aspx.vb file. You can navigate to the code module from Design view by right-clicking any blank area in Design view and choosing View Code.

There are four elements to the solution's code:

- A module level declaration of a String array

- A Load event procedure for the Page object

- A Load event procedure for the Form object

- A SelectionChanged event procedure for the Calendar control

A Dim statement at the top of the module declares a String array named Verses (see the following statement). Specifying an upper bound value of 30 in the Dim statement allows 31 array elements with index values of 0 through 30. By declaring the String array at the module level, more than one procedure in the module can reference it.

```
Dim Verses(30) As String
```

Instead of returning to the Design view of the page and double-clicking the page in a blank area to create the Load event procedure shell for the Page object, you can create the shell directly from the code module. Select (Page Events) from the Class Name drop-down box at the top left of the code module. Then, select Load from the Method Name drop-down box at the top right of the code module. Immediately after selecting Load, VWDE populates the code module with the Load event procedure shell for the Page object. The following single line of code assigns a Title property value for the Web Form page.

```
Me.Title = "Message for the day"
```

You can populate the code module with a Load event procedure shell for Form1 with the same general approach used for the page Load event procedure shell. Recall that Form1 is the name that the Web Form template assigns to the Form object in a Web Form page. The page Load event occurs before the page initially loads. Similarly, a form Load event occurs before a form on a page loads. Form Load event procedures are useful for allocating or assigning values used by a form.

In the current application, the Form1_Load procedure assigns values to the Verses array elements. The index values for the array elements commence at 0 and extend through 30 for a total of 31 array elements. The following listing shows the first couple and last couple of array element assignments. The full list of element assignments is in the Form1_Load procedure of the MessageForTheDay.aspx.vb file in WebSite1.

```
'Assign array members
Me.Verses(0) = _
    "Whatsoever things are true, whatsoever things are honest, " & _
    "whatsoever things are just ... think about such things. " & _
    "Philippians 4:8"
Me.Verses(1) = _
    "...whosoever believeth in Him should not perish, " & _
    "but have eternal life. John 3:15"
...
Me.Verses(29) = _
    "For my son was dead, and is alive again; he was lost, " & _
    "and is found.  And they began to be merry. Luke 15:24"
Me.Verses(30) = _
    "For God sent not his Son into the world to condemn the world; " & _
    "but that the world through Him might be saved. John 3:17"
```

The final event procedure is for the Calendar control, which has an ID property value of Calendar1. The event is the SelectionChanged event. You can create the shell for this procedure with the help of the Class Name and Method Name drop-down boxes at the top of the code module.

The sole line of code in the procedure extracts the number of the day selected in a month with the Day member of the SelectedDate object returned from Calendar1. Because the days in a month can extend from 1 through 31, but the index values in the Verses array extend from 0 through 30, the procedure uses the Day property value minus 1 for the Verses array index to assign a String value to the Text property of Label1. This code allows the user to determine which message appears in the third label control on the Web Form page. By successively changing the selected date, a user can view a series of messages.

```
Me.Label3.Text = Verses(Me.Calendar1.SelectedDate.Day - 1)
```

Demonstrating the Message for the Day Application

The demonstration of this application is a fun exercise. In particular, you have 31 messages to review, and I hope that one or two of them will soothe your soul. Even more important, I hope that you derive value from the sample in learning about ASP.NET and in gaining a sample application that you can repopulate with your own messages for each of the days in a month.

Figure 10-9 shows the message for the tenth day in a month. This is the one that helps me a lot as I struggle to meet deadlines and devise meaningful and informative samples for those who read my books and articles as well as attend my seminars. The message for the tenth day of the month corresponds to the ninth element in the Verses array.

Figure 10-9. *A message-for-the-day application is easy to implement and fun for site visitors. In addition, it enables you to communicate with site visitors about topics that interest both of you.*

Creating and Linking HTML Pages

Web Form pages should compose the majority of pages at most sites that you build with VWDE. The IDE for VWDE has special built-in features, such as the Web Form template in the Add New Item dialog box and the Standard group in the Toolbox, that facilitate the use of ASP.NET controls on Web Form pages. Nevertheless, the Internet became popular based, in large part, on its ability to simply transfer control from one Web page with HTML to another page with HTML. You implement this basic kind of functionality with the anchor element (<a>) in HTML. The anchor element works equally well on Web Form pages and other kinds of Web pages.

This section illustrates the use of the anchor element with two HTML pages (OnePage.htm and AnotherPage.htm). Hyperlinks implemented by anchor elements on each page enable the transfer of focus between pages. An HTML page is a different kind of page than a Web Form page, and you use a different template to create an HTML page rather than the template for a Web Form page. One of the most important differences between the two page types is that you cannot have any server-side code behind an HTML page that you create with VWDE. Also, the file extensions are different for Web Form pages (.aspx) and HTML pages (.htm).

You can create OnePage.htm by right-clicking the solution's name in Solution Explorer and choosing Add New Item. Notice that the controls for Language and whether to place the code for the page in a separate file are disabled. You can create the page by clicking OK. Then, you can repeat the process with AnotherPage as the name for a second page file (AnotherPage.htm). VWDE automatically adds an .htm extension when you select HTML Page from the page templates.

The following excerpt from the OnePage.htm file shows the HTML for that page. The HTML Page template does not automatically add div and a (for anchor) blocks to the page. However, you can add these to the page in Source view. You can adapt the instructions for adding a br tag in the "Using a Calendar Control" section to add any HTML code to a page.

After you add HTML tags to a page, you can use the Properties window to assist in formatting them. The sample HTML that appears next includes text within its div block, as well as a style attribute for the opening div tag to format how the text appears on the page. Instructions for customizing the div and a tags for the HTML markup code appear in the following two bullets.

- To format the text within a div block, select the text within the block in Source view. Then, click the ellipsis button (…) next to the Style property in the Properties window. This click opens a Style Builder dialog box with eight tabs for different groups of formatting features.

- After selecting an anchor element in Source view, use the Properties window to assign an href property value to the anchor element. Click the ellipsis button (…) next to the href property to open a dialog box for selecting another page at the same site to which to transfer focus. Alternatively, you can type in a URL in the box next to the href property when you want a hyperlink to transfer control to a page at another site.

Corresponding HTML exists in AnotherPage.htm to transfer control back to OnePage.htm.

```
<html xmlns="http://www.w3.org/1999/xhtml" >
<head>
    <title>One Page</title>
</head>
<body>
<div style="font-size: 24pt;">This is the Title on One Page</div>
To go to another page <a href="AnotherPage.htm">click here.</a>
</body>
</html>
```

Figure 10-10 shows OnePage.htm in a browser, and Figure 10-11 shows AnotherPage.htm in a browser. Click the hyperlink on either page to transfer control to the other page.

Figure 10-10. *OnePage.htm includes a hyperlink for transferring focus to AnotherPage.htm.*

Figure 10-11. *AnotherPage.htm includes a hyperlink for transferring focus to OnePage.htm.*

Interacting with Data

You will often want your Web applications to interact with data. Chapters 11, 12, and 13 drill down on interacting with SSE databases from the perspective of ADO.NET 2.0 as well as Windows and Web Forms. The samples in this chapter examine working with data from the perspective of processing input to Web Form pages and both reading data from and writing data to a file from within a Web application. In the process of learning how to read fixed-width data report files from Web Forms, you also learn about application variables, an efficient way to share values with all the users of a Web application.

Before diving into demonstrations of how to interact with data from Web applications, the section starts out with an introduction of how to create server-based websites. You also learn how to copy files to a server-based website from another Web application, such as a file-based website.

Creating a Server-Based Website and Copying Files to It

Up until this point in the chapter, we used the built-in ASP.NET Development Web Server to test all the ASP.NET pages. This approach is highly convenient for a developer. One main advantage of the approach is that a local copy of the IIS Web server is not required on the developer's computer. Another advantage is that developers do not have to obtain administrative privileges for a website after they release the solution to the System Administrators group.

Offsetting the advantages of using the ASP.NET Development Web Server are some disadvantages. The site is not available for connection by other users –including even testers—besides the registered user of VWDE. In addition, there are a variety of subtle variations between ASP.NET Development Web Server and IIS. Some of these distinctions appear in the Troubleshooting the ASP.NET Web Server topic within VWDE Help. Other distinctions are at multiple Internet sites (I found several reported differences with a search on Google for ASP.NET Development Web Server).

■**Caution** As a consequence of the distinctions between ASP.NET Development Web Server and IIS, you should always test a solution with IIS before deploying it.

There are multiple approaches to migrating all or some of the files in a file-system website to a website running on a Web server. This section demonstrates an approach based on creating a new website with VWDE on the local IIS, and then copying all or some files from the file-system website to the local IIS website. Because the approach deploys all or part of a solution as easily as copying files, it reinforces the idea that an ASP.NET solution is basically just a set of application files, perhaps including a Web.config file that contains settings for a whole website.

Start the process of deploying the file-system WebSite1 website to a server-based website by creating a new website. Open the New Web Site dialog box by choosing File ➤ New ➤ Web Site. Select HTTP from the Location drop-down box. Designate the name of the new site as http://localhost/WebSite1FromChapter10. The term *localhost* refers to the local IIS. Figure 10-12 shows the selections for creating a new server-based website.

■**Note** Recall that IIS is a free Microsoft-supplied Web server for Windows 2000, Windows XP, and Windows 2003. See http://www.microsoft.com/resources/documentation/windows/xp/all/proddocs/en-us/iiiisin2.mspx for installing IIS on a Windows XP computer. See http://www.microsoft.com/windows2000/en/server/iis/default.asp for installing IIS on a Windows 2000 computer. Installing IIS on Windows 2003 is more complex because of the variety of editions of this operating system as well as the fact that IIS initially installs in locked down mode (meaning you have to unlock it to make it operational for selected features, such as IIS). To learn more about IIS for Windows 2003, see http://msdn.microsoft.com/library/en-us/rsinstall/htm/gs_installingrs_v1_8k82.asp.

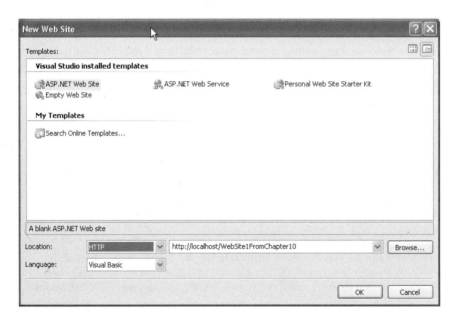

Figure 10-12. *It is nearly as easy to create a new website at the local IIS as in the file system. Of course, you must have IIS installed locally.*

The next step in deploying your solution from a file-system to a server-based website is to copy all or some of the file-system website files to the server-based website folder. The server-based folder will be in the ..\inetpub\wwwroot\ path on the local computer. For example, if IIS is on the C: drive, the folder for the website created with the settings in Figure 10-12 will be c:\inetpub\wwwroot\WebSite1FromChapter10. This folder will have two files, default.aspx and default.aspx.vb, as well as an App_Data folder. Recall that this is the status of a file-system website immediately after its creation.

To complete the deployment of the file-system website to the server-based website all you need to do is copy the .aspx, .aspx.vb, and .htm files, excluding those with a file name of default, from the path for Website1 to the c:\inetpub\wwwroot\WebSite1FromChapter10 path.

- You can start this task by right-clicking the project name in Solution Explorer for the new project in VWDE and choosing Add Existing Items.

- Next, navigate to the WebSite1 path.

- Then, highlight the files for the items that you want to copy.

- Clicking Add launches the copying of the files. For a recently started file like WebSite1, this process should take less than a minute.

Saying Hello Dynamically to a Web Form User

One place to read data in a Web application is from a `TextBox` in a Web Form. The sample for this section demonstrates how to achieve this task. After reading the `Text` property of a `TextBox` control, the form responds dynamically. This is a basic example of the rich functionality that you can achieve with ASP.NET.

The SayHelloDynamically Web Form is dynamic in several respects.

- First, it reads a value and then changes the form's display in response to what it reads. A Label control asks for the entry of a user's name in a `TextBox` control. If the user enters a name, the code behind the page returns the same page with a greeting (Hello) and the name of the user.

- It verifies that there is input to the `TextBox` control. If the user does not enter a name before clicking the Web Form's Button control, the application reminds the user to enter a name. Otherwise, the form goes on to process the value in the `TextBox` control.

- It changes the controls that are visible on the form between the initial view of the form and any subsequent view of the form. The `IsPostback` property for `Page` class instances helps an ASP.NET application determine if a form is appearing for the first time or not, so that it can vary the page's formatting.

Laying out the Form for Saying Hello Dynamically

The following HTML script shows the `body` block from SayHelloDynamically.aspx. Changes were made to no other section of the default Web Form layout. The changes consist of the addition of ASP.NET controls to the Web Form between the closing `div` tag and the closing `form` tag. Two groups of controls are added to the form.

- `Label1`, `TextBox1`, and `Button1` appear when the Web Form page initially opens. These fields facilitate the collection of a user's name. A fourth control, `RequiredFieldValidator1`, is available to assist with a user's name, but this fourth control only shows when there is no user-supplied input to the `TextBox1` control after the user clicks the `Button1` control.

- Label2 and Hyperlink1 appear after the user has successfully entered a name in TextBox1. The Label control greets the user, and the Hyperlink control offers a link for changing the focus to another Web page.

■Note Hyperlink1 is an instance of the ASP.NET Hyperlink control class. This class is analogous to the HTML anchor element. The Hyperlink control class uses its NavigateUrl property similarly to the way the anchor element uses its href attribute.

```
<body>
    <form id="form1" runat="server">
    <div>

    </div>
        <asp:Label ID="Label1" runat="server" Text="Label"></asp:Label>
        <asp:TextBox ID="TextBox1" runat="server"></asp:TextBox>
        <asp:RequiredFieldValidator ID="RequiredFieldValidator1"
            runat="server" ErrorMessage="RequiredFieldValidator">
            </asp:RequiredFieldValidator>
        <asp:Button ID="Button1" runat="server" Text="Button" /><br />
        <asp:Label ID="Label2" runat="server" Text="Label"></asp:Label><br />
        <asp:HyperLink ID="HyperLink1" runat="server"></asp:HyperLink>
    </form>
</body>
```

Figure 10-13 shows the basic layout of the form graphically in Design view. In the preceding page layout code, the form controls appear with their default values. However, the Page_Load event procedure manipulates the control property values. For example, the procedure assigns a meaningful string value to the Text property of Label1 so that the control does not appear in a browser with its default Text property value of Label.

Figure 10-13. *Adding all the controls to a Web Form with their default settings is a fast way of laying out a form. You can later change the default property values manually or programmatically.*

The RequiredFieldValidator control is one example of several different types of validator controls. The RequiredFieldValidator will not send a Web Form to a server until the required field is supplied. Each of the other validator controls verifies a different aspect of input. Besides verifying that a field value is entered with the RequiredFieldValidator control, there are four more controls for validating data.

- The RangeValidator control detects if a value is between a minimum value and a maximum value.

- The RegularExpressionValidator control allows you to use regular expression syntax for detecting if string values conform to a specified format.

- The CompareValidator control can compare two values to determine if they are equal.

- The CustomValidator control allows you to add code to specify your own custom requirements for validating data.

A fifth validator control, the ValidationSummary control, provides a mechanism for summarizing the results for multiple validation controls that can be on the same Web Form page.

Using the IsPostBack Property to Dynamically Manage a Form

The code behind the form depicted in Figure 10-13 exists in SayHelloDynamically.aspx.vb in the WebSite1FromChapter10 website. The code for the page consists of a single event procedure named Page_Load. There is no explicit Click event procedure for the Button1 control. Clicking the Button1 control causes the page to make a round trip to the server and fires the Page_Load event procedure because of the round trip. All ASP.NET controls can generate page round trips when their default events fire even if there's no event procedure for them on the server.

In reviewing the Page_Load event procedure, it is useful to have a basic grasp of the IsPostBack property for a Page class instance. The first time a page loads in a browser, the IsPostBack property value is False. Any other time a page loads in a browser after a sequential round trip, the IsPostBack property value is True. In this case, the server is posting back any changes to the form by a user. In our sample, this means the form posts back the value entered as a name in the TextBox1 control.

An If…Then…Else statement executes one of two code blocks, depending on the IsPostBack property value. If the IsPostBack property is False, then the If…Then…Else statement executes instructions in the Else clause for handling an initial page presentation. If IsPostBack is True, the If…Then…Else statement transfers control to statements in the Then clause.

The code in the Else clause for an initial presentation of the Web Form performs three types of tasks.

- First, this code block overrides Text property values for controls with static, default values, such as Label1, Button1, and Hyperlink1.

- Second, the code assigns False to the Visible property value of two controls that are not to appear during an initial presentation of the Web Form. These two controls are Hyperlink1 and Label2.

- Third, the code initializes essential property settings for the RequiredFieldValidator1 control.

  - This type of control must know to which input control it applies. The ControlToValidate property designates the control to check for valid input, which means in this case that the control must be populated with a value.

  - If you do not designate dynamic display, the validator control takes up a constant space on the form. By assigning ValidatorDisplay.Dynamic to the validator control's Display property, you display the validator control on the form only when it detects an error.

  - The Errormessage property lets you assign a String value as a custom error message to help users recover from an invalid input error.

The If…Then…Else statement executes the code in the Then clause for each time it renders a page beyond the initial page presentation in a browser session. This code block has three main purposes.

- First, it greets a user with a custom salutation based on the name that the user initially input to the form. The code for Label2 handles this task.

- Second, the Then clause makes the HyperLink1 control visible.

- Third, the Then clause suppresses the visibility of three controls used to gather a user's name.

```
If Page.IsPostBack Then
    With Me.Label2
        .Visible = True
        .Text = "Hello " & Me.TextBox1.Text & "!"
    End With
    Me.HyperLink1.Visible = True
    Me.Label1.Visible = False
    Me.TextBox1.Visible = False
    Me.Button1.Visible = False
Else
    Me.Label1.Text = "Enter name:"
    Me.Button1.Text = "Click me"
    With Me.HyperLink1
        .Visible = False
        .Text = _
            "Go to OnePage.htm that links to AnotherPage.htm"
        .NavigateUrl = "OnePage.htm"
    End With
    Me.Label2.Visible = False
    With Me.RequiredFieldValidator1
        .ControlToValidate = "TextBox1"
        .Display = ValidatorDisplay.Dynamic
        .ErrorMessage = "Enter name and click button twice."
    End With
End If
```

Verifying the Operation of the SayHelloDynamically Sample

There are basically two paths that you can take through the sample application:

- First, you can input a name and see the form change in response to the valid input. Figures 10-14 and 10-15 confirm the application in this mode.

- Second, you can click Button1 without entering a name in TextBox1. Figure 10-16 shows the reminder to enter name along with instructions for recovering from the error. Click the button twice after entering a name.

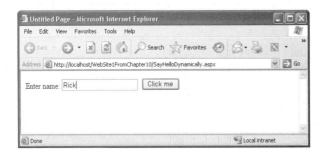

Figure 10-14. *One common use for Web Forms is to collect data from users, such as their name.*

Figure 10-15. *Sometimes an application uses collected data to customize its presentation to a user.*

Figure 10-16. *The RequiredFieldValidator control is a convenient tool for making sure users complete required fields on a form.*

Populating an Application Variable and Reading from It

A common application requirement is to have all users be able to read some data. Although it is common to access data in databases, data sometimes arrive at an organization from an external source as a file with a fixed-width report. Chapter 9 in its "Reading Fixed-Width Reports" section presents a sample that parses a fixed-width report file into distinct field values in the process of echoing the report in the Quick Console window.

This section presents a sample that allows Web users access to the same report from their browser. The report file is available as SalesByPersonTerritoryRegion.rpt. The original report is saved from Notepad with UTF-8 encoding to make it easy to represent extended characters, such as the acute accent in a name like José. On the test computer for this chapter's resource files, SalesByPersonTerritoryRegion.rpt is saved in c:\ProSSEApps\Chapter10.

■**Note** Chapter 9 did not perform the extra save to encode the SalesByPersonTerritoryRegion.rpt file in UTF-8 format (instead, the Chapter 9 version was encoded as ANSI). Therefore, the sample in that chapter does not properly display extended characters. Of course, this extra step is only necessary when your application needs to display properly extended characters, such as an e with acute accent (é) or an o with an umlaut (ö).

The sample in this section stores the report as a String value in an application variable. Application variables are like global variables: Anyone who can use the application can read from an application variable. Application variables have a lifetime that starts when the application first begins and extends until the application closes. You can create and populate application variables from the global.asax file. The global.asax file handles application-level events for ASP.NET applications. This file is an optional ASP.NET file. If it exists, it should reside in the root folder for an ASP.NET project.

Note The Application class has several events, including Application_Start and Application_End. The Application_Start event fires for the very first request to an application in its life cycle. The Application_End event is called just before the application is unloaded. You can use procedures for these events to perform special processing at the start and close of an application. For example, you can create an application variable in an Application_Start event.

There's one last issue to consider before describing the project. The application needs read access permission to the SalesByPersonTerritoryRegion.rpt file. Recall that the application reads the file and saves the file characters in an application variable, which it can't do if it doesn't have read access to the file. One general approach to this issue is to grant all Windows users read access permission for the file. Because the project runs under a Windows user account, this approach grants the project read access permission to the report file. The sample in the next section discusses a more precise method of giving a project access to a file.

Setting up for the Sample to Read an Application Variable

There are three steps to setting up the sample solution.

- First, create a global.asax file if one does not already exist. You can add a global.asax with the following instructions.

  - Right-click the project name in Solution Explorer and choose Add New Item.

  - In the Add New Item dialog box, select the Global Application Class template. VWDE responds by inserting Global.asax in the Name box. Make sure the Language box says Visual Basic. See Figure 10-17 for the proper settings.

- Second, create a Web Form named ReadAppVariable. Complete this task in the same way that added previous Web Form pages to the WebSite1 project.

- Third, update your file permissions so that all members of the Windows Users group have read access to the SalesByPersonTerritoryRegion.rpt file in the c:\ProSSEApps\Chapter10 path or wherever else you have the report file saved. You can do this with the following instructions.

  - Right-click the SalesByPersonTerritoryRegion.rpt file in Windows Explorer and choose Properties.

  - Select the Security tab in the file's Properties dialog box and select Users in the Groups and user names list box. Make sure that the Read permission check box is selected as in Figure 10-18.

  - If you do not see Users in the Groups and user names list box, click Click Add below the list box. Then, type Users in the Enter object names to select box and click OK. After returning to the Security tab, make sure the Read check box is selected for the Users group as in Figure 10-18.

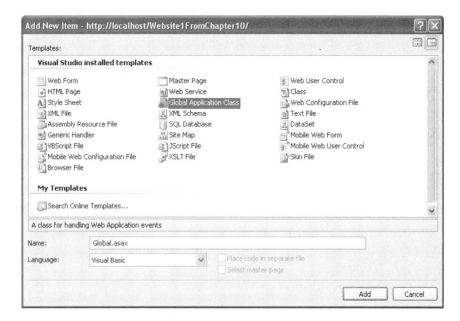

Figure 10-17. *Make these selections to add a global.asax file to an ASP.NET project.*

Figure 10-18. *The application needs permission to read the SalesByPersonTerritoryRegion.rpt file.*

Creating an Application Variable Containing the Report

You can place the code for creating the application variable in the `Application_Start` event procedure within the global.asax file. If you did not already use the `Application_Start` event procedure, then this will be the first code in the `Application_Start` event procedure. Otherwise, you can add the code for creating the application variable to the end of any existing code in the `Application_Start` event procedure.

The code in the `Application_Start` procedure is an adaptation and extension of the code in the sample from Chapter 9 that echoes the SalesByPersonTerritoryRegion.rpt file's contents to the Quick Console window. In this case, the report is not echoed. Instead, it is divided into fields for each row, and saved one field value at a time for all the fields in a row across all the rows in the report.

The `Application_Start` procedure starts with three `Dim` statements.

- The first `Dim` statement specifies a report path and file name.

- The second `Dim` statement designates column width parameters for reading field values from the fixed-width report. The value of –1 for the final column signals the last column and allows the field parser to detect the column's width automatically.

- The third `Dim` statement is for a `String` array with the field names as values. The output from the procedure uses these names for identifying to which field a value belongs.

```
Dim strPathFile As String = "c:\ProSSEApps\Chapter10\" & _
    "SalesByPersonTerritoryRegion.rpt"
Dim SalesWidths() As Integer = {15, 15, 14, 10, 18, 22, -1}
Dim FieldNames() As String = {"Region", "Territory", "SalesPersonID", _
    "FirstName", "LastName", "SalesYTD", "SalesLastYear"}
```

The main code for the procedure takes place inside a `Using…End Using` block, which appears after the following description.

- The `Using` statement declares a `TextFieldParser` object with the variable named `Reader`. The report becomes available to the procedure through this variable. The two statements following the `Using` statement ready the `TextFieldParser` variable for use with the report in SalesByPersonTerritoryRegion.rpt.

- Next, several `Dim` statements declare variables for assisting in extracting field values from the report and in saving the report field values. The `str1` variable ultimately contains a copy of all report field values.

- A `Do` loop after the `Dim` statements declaring variables for extracting and saving the report field values iterates through successive report lines. The code for exiting the loop is inside the loop. The report has 7 field values for each of 17 rows sandwiched between 3 header lines and a couple of trailer lines. Even when a field value is technically missing from a row, the report marks its place with the `NULL` keyword.

  - A variable named `introw` keeps track of the current line being processed.

  - The first header line cannot be parsed, and it generates an `Exception` that a `Try...Catch...Catch...End Try` statement catches in its second `Catch` clause. Therefore, the initial line does not increment the `introw` value from its starting value of 0.

  - The next two header lines, with `introw` values of 0 and 1, are header lines for the field values.

  - Notice the `If` statement inside the `For…Each …Next` statement discards lines with `introw` values of 0 or 1 or more than 19. This statement retains just the first 17 lines after the 2 header lines.

- The code within the If block accumulates successive field values within str1. The &= operator appends a new String value to an existing String value. Three columns of comma-separated values represent each field value. The first column is an arbitrary index value (introw – 2) that starts at 0 and increases by 1 for each new row. The second column is the field name from the FieldNames array. The third column is the current field value. A br tag follows each set of columns for a field value to simplify writing successive field values on a Web page with each field value on a separate line.

- The Do loop continues reading lines past the 17th row of data, but the first Catch clause ultimately detects a malformed line, which signals the end of the data. Control transfers out of the Do loop at this point.

- After exiting the Do loop, an assignment statement copies the value in str1 to the SQLrpt application variable.

```
Using Reader As New Microsoft.VisualBasic.FileIO. _
    TextFieldParser(strPathFile)
        Reader.TextFieldType = _
        Microsoft.VisualBasic.FileIO.FieldType.FixedWidth
        Reader.SetFieldWidths(SalesWidths)
        Dim currentRow As String()
        Dim int1 As Integer
        Dim introw As Integer
        Dim str1 As String = ""
        Do
            Try
                currentRow = Reader.ReadFields()
                Dim currentField As String
                For Each currentField In currentRow
                    If introw > 1 And introw < 19 Then
                        str1 &= introw - 2 & ", " & _
                            FieldNames(int1) & ", " & _
                            currentField & "<br \>"
                    End If
                    int1 += 1
                Next
                int1 = 0
                introw += 1
            Catch ex1 As _
            Microsoft.VisualBasic.FileIO.MalformedLineException _
            When Reader.EndOfData = True
                Exit Do
            Catch ex1 As _
            Microsoft.VisualBasic.FileIO.MalformedLineException _
            When Reader.EndOfData = False
                'Place marker for error processing in
                'non-global.asax file version
            End Try
        Loop

        Application("SQLrpt") = str1

End Using
```

Laying out the Form to Read an Application Variable

The following excerpt from the HTML for ReadAppVariable.aspx describes the user interface for the Web Form.

- The form includes two buttons. The first button is to write out all field values for all rows to a Web page. Each row in the original report is for a sales person, and one of the field values for each row is a SalesPersonID value. A single row in the original report corresponds to seven rows in the deserialized copy of the report stored in the Application("SQLrpt") variable.

- A TextBox control below the second button is available for a user to input a SalesPersonID number. Then, a click to the second button writes to the Web Form just the seven field values for the corresponding sales person.

```
<body>
    <form id="form1" runat="server">
    <div>

    </div>
        <hr /><hr />
        <asp:Button ID="Button1" runat="server" Text="Button" /><br />
        <hr />
        <asp:Button ID="Button2" runat="server" Text="Button" /><br />
        <asp:Label ID="Label1" runat="server" Text="Label"></asp:Label>
        <asp:TextBox ID="TextBox1" runat="server"></asp:TextBox>
    </form>
</body>
```

Reading an Application Variable

Three event procedures automate this sample. The Page_Load event procedure merely assigns String values to controls. This procedure does not show because you can infer its code from the sample output that follows this section. The Button1_Click procedure writes all the field values in the application variable to the Web Form page. The Button2_Click procedure filters the field values in the Application("SQLrpt") variable to write to the Web Form page just those field values for the sales person denoted by the SalesPersonID value represented by the Text property value of the TextBox1 control.

The Button1_Click event procedure contains just two lines of code, which appear next. The first line is a Dim statement that assigns to the str1 String variable the value of the Application("SQLrpt") variable. Recall that this value contains all the field values for all sales persons. Each field value terminates with a br tag. This enables the Write method for the Response class in the second line to insert the three column values for each field value on a separate line in the Web page. These values for successive fields in successive rows appear downward from the top of the page.

```
Dim str1 As String = Application("SQLrpt").ToString
Response.Write(str1)
```

The code for the Button2_Click event procedure is a bit more complicated. However, it contains nothing but standard string-processing techniques, and a For…Next for extracting seven field values for the sales person whose SalesPersonID value appears in the text box on the Web Form page. There are three blocks of code in the procedure.

- The first block assigns the application variable to the str1 String, which is parsed to extract just the field values for one sales person.

- The second block declares four Integer variables and a String variable to help in parsing the values in the final block of code. The strStart variable value is the first column value of the three columns for a field value of the selected sales person. These values start at 0 for the first sales person and extend through 16 for the 17th sales person.

- The third block is a For…Next loop that iterates through the str1 variable seven times to extract the three column values for each of the seven field values for the selected person whose SalesPersonID value appears in the Web Form's text box. The strStart value helps to locate the first column value in a set of three columns for a field value for the designated sales person.

```
Dim str1 As String = Application("SQLrpt").ToString

Dim intStart As Integer = InStr(str1, _
    "SalesPersonID, " & Me.TextBox1.Text) - 3
Dim intEnd As Integer = InStr(InStr(str1, _
    "SalesPersonID, " & Me.TextBox1.Text), str1, "<br \>")
Dim int3 As Integer = InStr(intEnd, str1, ",")
Dim intBeg As Integer = 1
Dim strStart As String = Mid(str1, intEnd + 6, int3 - _
    (intEnd + 6) + 1)

intEnd = 1
For intLoop As Integer = 1 To 7
    intStart = InStr(intEnd, str1, strStart)
    intEnd = InStr(InStr(intStart, _
        str1, strStart), str1, "<br \>")
    Response.Write( _
        Mid(str1, intStart, intEnd - intStart + 6))
Next intLoop
```

Output from the Sample to Read an Application Variable

Figure 10-19 shows selected output from a click to Button1. It shows field values for the first two sales persons with SalesPersonID values of 268 and 275.

Figure 10-19. *The Button1_Click procedure starts writing field values from the top of the Application variable.*

Figure 10-20 shows the result of a click to the second button after inserting 275 in the text box. Recall that 275 is the `SalesPersonID` for the second sales person. You can see that the name of this sales person in Figure 10-20 is Michael Blythe. You can verify this by checking the field values for the second sales person in Figure 10-19. If you changed the text box value to 290 and clicked the second button, the Web Form would show the data for Lynn Tsoflias.

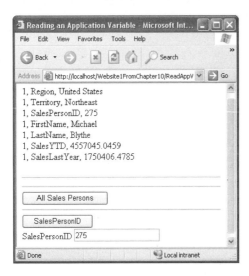

Figure 10-20. *Using the text box and the second button on the Web Form, you can return the field values for just one sales person from the Application variable.*

Summary

The primary focus of this chapter is to give you the skills to feel comfortable building Web solutions on your own with VWDE. Therefore, the chapter reviews the VWDE IDE and drills down on the use of Web Form pages to create Web applications. Because VWDE is optimized for creating ASP.NET solutions, you also gain exposure to ASP.NET development techniques through a series of samples. Some of the core Web development topics covered in this chapter are

- Creating websites and copying files between websites
- Adding different types of pages (.aspx, .htm, .asax) to a website
- Populating Web pages with Web Form controls and HTML tags to simplify common tasks, such as collecting data, showing data, formatting text and data, and linking between pages
- Writing ASP.NET code with Visual Basic 2005 behind pages to make your pages interactive and dynamic
- Using validator controls to verify user input before generating a round trip to a Web server
- Reading from and writing to text files from Web pages
- Managing state between page round trips, from one page to another, and across all the pages in a Web application
- Creating multipage solutions that share information across pages

This concludes our introduction to VWDE, but I have provided an online chapter that drills down into three more advanced VWDE topics. You can view this chapter at `http://www.apress.com/ book/bookDisplay.html?bID=459.`

■■■

CHAPTER 11

Programming ADO.NET

A main motivation for database developers and administrators wanting to learn VBE or VWDE is the need to create database solutions. These solutions typically involve retrieving, inserting, updating, and deleting data. In addition, database administrators, and to a lesser extent developers, have a need to create database objects and perform database server administration. Visual Basic 2005 programmers can put ADO.NET to use implementing data access, data manipulation, database definition, and server administration tasks.

The primary database focus is on SQL Server Express, but the samples apply to other databases as well—particularly other SQL Server 2005 editions, SQL Server 2000, and even Access databases.

Overview of ADO.NET

ADO.NET is a programming model for processing data within .NET languages, such as Visual Basic 2005. While there are subtle differences between VWDE and VBE, you can take advantage of the ADO.NET programming model from Windows applications and web applications. The ADO.NET model is suitable for use with stand-alone data generated from within VBE or VWDE, file-based data, and data in databases such as SQL Server Express, Microsoft Access, and other OLE DB or ODBC-compatible data sources.

This chapter drills down on the use of ADO.NET with SQL Server Express databases, and to a much lesser extent, OLE DB databases as represented by Microsoft Access. Both SQL Server Express and Microsoft Access permit you to work with stand-alone database files, but SQL Server Express also permits you to process data that is continuously managed by a database server.

ADO.NET Providers

ADO.NET offers a provider-based model for interacting with databases. While the different providers offer highly comparable programming interfaces, the whole idea behind provider-specific classes is that you can take advantage of the special features of each type of database with a provider tailored for it.

There are four providers supplied along with VBE and VWDE. Each provider targets a different type of resource. The four provider classes are summarized in the following bullet points.

- .NET Provider for SQL Server works with SQL Server 7.0 + databases, including SQL Server Express. The objects for this provider reside in the `System.Data.SqlClient` namespace.

- .NET Provider for OLE DB works with any data source that you can connect with via OLE DB, such as Microsoft Access, SQL Server versions prior to SQL Server 7.0, and Oracle versions prior to 8.1.7. The objects for this provider reside in the `System.Data.OleDb` namespace.

- .NET Provider for ODBC works with any data source that you can connect with via ODBC (which is just about every database), and selected file types, including .csv, .xls, and even .txt. The objects for this provider reside in the `System.Data.Odbc` namespace.

- .NET Provider for Oracle is optimized to work with Oracle databases running Oracle client software 8.1.7 or later. The objects for this provider reside in the `System.Data.OracleClient` namespace, which resides in the `System.Data.OracleClient.dll` assembly. Solutions using .NET Provider for Oracle must add references to the `System.Data.dll` and `System.Data.OracleClient.dll` assemblies.

The providers deliver a set of ADO.NET objects that Visual Basic 2005 developers can program. The ADO.NET object model can connect VBE and VWDE solutions with databases. On one end, you can program with these objects in VBE and VWDE with Visual Basic 2005 (and other .NET languages). On the other end, the ADO.NET objects communicate with a type of database server.

The topic of ADO.NET database providers has the potential to be very rich for those who require something other than the standard database providers. Two major themes characterize this richness.

- One ADO.NET 2.0 innovation is the introduction of provider-independent data access. At some escalation in the coding difficulty and abstraction level, provider-independent coding allows you to use one model to access different types of data sources. If you regularly work with different types of data sources, and optimized performance for each data source is not an issue, this approach may have some appeal.

- Second, multiple third parties offer highly optimized providers for specific data sources that are not provided with either VBE or VWDE. Some of the specialized providers are for databases, such as MySQL, Informix, Sybase, DB2, and Oracle.

ADO.NET Architecture

There are a couple of significant ways to segment the ADO.NET classes. Some classes are tied to providers, which makes them specialized for one type of data source or another. For example, you cannot connect to a SQL Server data source with an instance of the `OleDbConnection` class. Another type of ADO.NET class is independent of the provider type. `DataSet` and `DataTable` classes are not tied to a specific data source. A single `DataSet` instance can contain multiple `DataTable` objects. Each of the `DataTable` objects can contain data from a different type of data source. Furthermore, it is not even necessary to populate a `DataTable` object from a remote data source because you can populate a `DataTable` with local data. These classes will be discussed further momentarily.

Another way to divide ADO.NET classes is to see whether they permit forward-only access or disconnected access. Forward-only access is very rapid. When you use forward-only access to connect to a data source, you cannot modify the data source values. Disconnected access is not as fast as forward-only access, but it provides a richer set of features. One significant reason that disconnected access is slower is that it stores the data from a data source locally in one or more `DataTable` objects that can reside in a `DataSet` object.

There are four key provider-specific ADO.NET classes. These classes are duplicated in each of the four standard data providers. The four classes complement one another in the type of functionality that they provide. The names that follow refer to the classes by their generic name, such as `Connection` or `DataReader`. However, remember that the names of the classes within a provider are specific to a class. Therefore, the name `OleDbConnection` references a `Connection` object from the `System.Data.OleDb` namespace, but the `SqlConnection` name applies to the name of a `Connection` object in the `System.Data.SqlClient` namespace.

- `Connection` class instances point at a data source from a client application. You will typically use a `Connection` object along with one or more other ADO.NET objects.

- `Command` class instances permit the execution of SQL commands (or statements) within a database from a client application. You can think of a `Command` object as a wrapper for a SQL statement. You must associate a `Connection` object with a `Command` object in order to be able to execute the SQL instruction within a database.

- `DataReader` classes provide forward-only access to a data source, such as a table or a view, within a database. A `DataReader` instance requires both a `Command` object and a `Connection` object. The `Command` object specifies a SQL instruction to retrieve data, and the `Connection` object designates a database from which to retrieve the data.

- `DataAdapter` classes serve as two-way pumps between a database and a client application. You can use a `DataAdapter` object to initialize a `DataTable` in a `DataSet` from data sources in a database. By using multiple `DataAdapter` objects, you can initially populate multiple `DataTable` objects within a `DataSet`. You can also use a `DataAdapter` to pass changes back to a data source from a disconnected `DataTable` object. In addition, you can refresh a local data store, such as a `DataTable` object, with changes made by other users.

A `DataTable` object in a client application is similar to a table database object. Each `DataTable` has a `Rows` collection. You can reference individual rows from a zero-based index. Within each row, there is a `Columns` collection. You can refer to the columns by a zero-based index or by name. Different columns can have individual .NET Framework data types. `DataTable` objects can also have constraints. A `PrimaryKey` property for a `DataTable` can specify one or more columns that serve as a primary key for a `DataTable`.

A single `DataSet` instance can contain multiple `DataTable` objects in its `Tables` collection. Your code can reference the `DataTable` instances within a `DataSet` by name or a zero-based index. In fact, you can use the zero-based index for the `DataTable` objects, and the `TableName` property for a `DataTable`, to discover the names of the `DataTable` objects within a `DataSet` object. You can also designate a `DataRelation` object to specify the relationship between the `DataTable` objects in a `DataSet`. Through these `DataRelation` objects, `DataTable` objects can model hierarchical relationships between objects, such as orders for a customer or order details for an order. Just as a `DataTable` has a `Rows` collection of `DataRow` objects, a `DataSet` can have a `Relations` collection of `DataRelation` objects.

Note The samples in this chapter use what's commonly called untyped `DataSet` objects. Another type of `DataSet` object is a typed `DataSet` that is based on an instance of an XML schema. There are advantages to both kinds of `DataSets`, but one advantage of untyped `DataSet` objects is that they require no use of XML. You'll see some designer-based sample applications of typed `DataSet` objects in Chapter 13.

There are numerous other objects within the ADO.NET architecture. However, the core ones mentioned previously provide the most important functionality. One of the most versatile of these other objects is the `DataView` object. A `DataView` object allows you to represent the values in a `DataTable` in a special way, such as sorted or filtered. You can create multiple `DataView` objects to represent the values in a `DataTable` object in different ways.

Programming Connection Objects

Making a connection to a database is the first step of any client database application. As a minimum, this step involves identifying the type of database to which you want to connect, such as SQL Server or Microsoft Access. You may also need to identify yourself. By specifying your identity, you can receive the permissions associated with a known identity within a database server or a secured file server database application, such as Access.

To make a connection to a database from either VBE or VWDE, you need a reference to the System.Data namespace, which contains the ADO.NET object model. A new project may not automatically have a reference to the System.Data namespace. To add a reference to a VBE project, choose Project ➤ Add Reference. This opens the Add Reference dialog box. From the .NET tab, scroll to the System.Data component, and then click OK. Within a VWDE WebSite project, start the process for adding a reference for the ADO.NET object model by choosing WebSite ➤ Add Reference. After the initial menu selection, the process for adding a reference to VWDE is the same as for VBE.

Even after you add a reference to a project for the ADO.NET object model, it is often convenient to explicitly denote the use of a namespace for a provider at the top of a module with an Imports statement. For example, to use ADO.NET objects for SQL Server databases, you should have an Imports System.Data.SqlClient statement before any class declaration in a module.

Connection objects are provider specific. Therefore, the namespace that you denote must be tailored to the type of database in an application. Use the System.Data.SqlClient namespace for a SqlConnection object pointing at a SQL Server Express database, the System.Data.OleDb namespace for an OleDbConnection object directed at an Access database, and so on.

This section's samples reside in the WinCh11 Windows application project and are associated with Form1. To demonstrate the use of local databases for both SQL Server Express and Access, the sample project folder has the database files for the Northwind SQL Server database and the Northwind Access database. The database files reside in the project folder for Windows form objects.

■**Note** See the "Getting Meta Data About Databases" section in Chapter 3 for commentary and samples using the is_auto_close_on setting.

Opening and Closing a Connection to a SQL Server Database

Form1 in the WinCh11 project has four Click event procedures behind it. Figure 11-1 shows the form in Design view and when it initially opens. The Design view (in the left pane) indicates the names of each of the Button controls for the Click event procedures. The open view of Form1 (in the right pane) shows the captions that users see. These captions explain the role of each Button control.

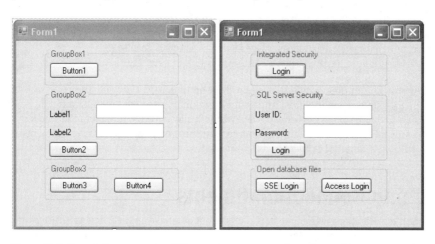

Figure 11-1. *Form1 demonstrates different syntax conventions for making a connection to a SQL Server database.*

The `Click` event procedure for `Button1` demonstrates the logic for managing a `SqlConnection` object connecting to a SQL Server instance with integrated security. When you connect this way, SQL Server identifies the user by their Windows login. Any permissions assigned to the individual, or a Windows group to which an individual belongs, are assigned to the login representing the individual.

The following Visual Basic 2005 code is from `Button1_Click`. The procedure resides in a module that commences with two `Imports` statements for the `System.Data.SqlClient` and `System.Data.OleDb` namespaces. The code in `Button1_Click` relies on the `Imports` statement for the `System.Data.SqlClient` namespace.

The code sample begins by instantiating an instance of the `SqlConnection` class as a variable named `cnn1`. The `New` keyword references the class, and the argument inside the parentheses is a connection string with three arguments.

- The first argument, `Data Source`, specifies the server name. In this case, the connection string points at the default instance of SQL Server on the local computer. You can refer to the local default SQL Server instance with either `(local)` or `localhost`. On the test computer for this chapter, the instance happens to be a SQL Server 2000 instance.

- The second argument designates integrated security. You can set `Integrated Security` to `True` or `SSPI` and achieve the same result.

- The `Initial Catalog` setting refers to the `Northwind` database. This is an attached database (recall that only SQL Server Express supports working with unattached databases).

▓Note If you install SQL Server Express as a named instance on a computer with a default instance of MSDE (or some other SQL Server 2000 edition), `(local)` or `localhost` will refer to the MSDE or SQL Server 2000 default instance. Then you can refer to the SQL Server Express instance as `.\sqlexpress`.

After you create an instance of a `SqlConnection` object, you will often need to explicitly open it before you can use it. Invoke the `Open` method of the `SqlConnection` class instance to make the object available for use with a `SqlCommand` object. If you do explicitly open a `SqlConnection` object, then you should explicitly close the object before exiting the procedure. Two programming practices that can help reduce the load on a database instance are as follows:

1. Open an ADO.NET `Connection` object just before you need it.
2. Close the `Connection` object immediately after completing your need for it.

▓Tip You do not need to open a `SqlConnection` object when you use it with a `SqlDataAdapter` object. This is because the `SqlDataAdapter` manages the status of its associated `SqlConnection` object. Other `SqlClient` objects, such as `SqlCommand` or `SqlDataReader`, do not manage the status of an associated `SqlConnection` object.

```
Dim cnn1 As SqlConnection = _
  New SqlConnection("Data Source=(local);" & _
  "Integrated Security=True;" & _
  "Initial Catalog=northwind")
```

```
'Open connection
cnn1.Open()
MessageBox.Show("Connection succeeded.")

'Place code to use connection here

'Close connection
cnn1.Close()
MessageBox.Show("Connection closed.")
```

Getting Help with Constructing a Connection String

It is very easy to forget the connection string for pointing a SqlConnection object at a SQL Server database. The ease of forgetting is multiplied when you need to use integrated security in some cases and SQL Server security in other cases. Therefore, it is useful to know how to get help with constructing a connection string.

Note Recall that with integrated security, SQL Server trusts the Windows verification of the identity of a user. In the case of SQL Server security, SQL Server manages the identity of a user.

When you connect to a SQL Server instance with SQL Server security, you need a different connection string than with integrated security. In particular, you can replace the assignment for integrated security with assignments for UserID and Password. Recall that Figure 11-1 shows Form1 with two text boxes for the input of UserID and Password values. Whenever you accept input for a SQL Server database server, you expose an application to potential attack by SQL injection. In this kind of attack, a hacker can inject some illegitimate SQL instructions into a connection string in an attempt to gain entry to a SQL Server instance. The extra input overloads a valid connection string specification.

The SqlConnectionStringBuilder class can both help you to remember valid SQL Server connection string conventions and substantially reduce the possibility of a hacker attack by SQL injection. In this way, a SqlConnectionStringBuilder class instance delivers benefits at both design time and runtime. In addition, you can pass a SqlConnectionStringBuilder object a previously saved connection string, and then modify the connection string through the SqlConnectionStringBuilder object.

The SqlConnectionStringBuilder class knows all the valid key/value pairs for a connection string argument. Therefore, a hacker attack that relies on entering invalid key/value pairs will automatically be rejected at runtime as invalid. If a hacker overloads either the user name or password with invalid input, the SqlConnectionStringBuilder object used to construct the full connection string will detect the extra input as invalid. By detecting overloaded values as invalid, a SqlConnectionStringBuilder object can defeat a hacker attack.

The following code from the Button2_Click procedure for Form1 illustrates the use of the SqlConnectionStringBuilder class for constructing the connection string for a SqlConnection object. This connection string uses SQL Server security instead of integrated security syntax and a Try...Catch...Finally clause for managing the SqlConnection object. This approach is superior to the preceding example in that it guards against a runtime error that causes your application to lose control of the computer, and it can automatically close a SqlConnection object after it is no longer needed.

The code segment starts by declaring cbd1 as a SqlConnectionStringBuilder object and cnn1 as a SqlConnection object. Notice the variable for the SqlConnectionStringBuilder object exposes members, such as Data Source, for assigning values to key/value pairs in a connection string. The .\sqlexpress assignment to the Data Source member assigns a named SQL Server

Express instance as the name of the database server. Notice that the code merely assigns the `Text` property values of `TextBox1` and `TextBox2` to the `UserID` and `Password` members of the `cbd1` `SqlConnectionStringBuilder` instance. There is no need for any cleaning of the input values because the `SqlConnectionStringBuilder` object automatically validates the input! After you finish specifying the member values for a `SqlConnectionStringBuilder` object, you can assign the `ConnectionString` property of the `SqlConnectionStringBuilder` object to the `ConnectionString` property of the `cnn1` `SqlConnection` object.

The `Try...Catch...Finally` statement illustrates how to open a `SqlConnection` object so that you can recover from a runtime error. One reason for a runtime error in this case could be that the SQL Server Express instance is temporarily stopped or paused. In either case, the SQL Server Express instance could not respond successfully to an attempt to connect to it. By invoking the `Open` method of the `cnn1` `SqlConnection` object in the `Try` clause, you allow the `Catch` clause to provide feedback about the source of the problem without relinquishing control of the computer by your application.

The `Finally` clause of the `Try...Catch...Finally` statement executes whether the attempt to open the `SqlConnection` succeeds or not. When working with `SqlConnection` objects, it is important to understand that they have client-side and server-side components. If an attempt to open a connection fails, then your code does not generate a server-side component. However, the client-side component still exists because of the `New` keyword in the second `Dim` statement at the top of the sample. By invoking the `Close` method in the `Finally` clause, you can remove both server-side and client-side elements of a `SqlConnection` object, or just the client-side object if there is no server-side element (because a connection attempt failed).

```
Dim cbd1 As New SqlConnectionStringBuilder()
Dim cnn1 As New SqlConnection

'Build connection string
cbd1.DataSource = ".\sqlexpress"
cbd1.InitialCatalog = "northwind"
cbd1.UserID = Me.TextBox1.Text
cbd1.Password = Me.TextBox2.Text

'Assign connection string
cnn1.ConnectionString = (cbd1.ConnectionString)

'Open connection and always close it when done;
'catch exceptions from attempt to connect
Try
 cnn1.Open()
 MessageBox.Show("Connection succeeded.")
 'Insert code to use connection string here
Catch ex As Exception
 MessageBox.Show(ex.Message, "something is wrong")
Finally
 cnn1.Close()
 MessageBox.Show("Connection closed.")
End Try
```

Connecting to SQL Server Express and Access Database Files

Both of the preceding samples demonstrated how to connect to an attached SQL Server database. One of the distinct advantages of SQL Server Express is that it enables you to work with database files that are not always attached to a database server. This capability is the basis of the SQL Server Express XCopy deployment feature. You can copy the .mdf and .ldf files in a project folder and then attach them to a SQL Server Express instance when necessary. You can apply a comparable technique for connecting to a Microsoft Access database file (.mdb). In the case of the Access database file, you will use the System.Data.OleDb namespace. This section discusses two samples that illustrate how to connect to SQL Server Express and Microsoft Access database files in a Windows application folder. *Use to migrate my data!*

Connecting to SQL Server Express Database Files

One of the major advantages of SQL Server Express XCopy deployment is that you can locate the database files for a solution with the application folder instead of in a database server. Deployment of a database solution is a simple matter of copying the application folder, including its database files. It is possible to dynamically compute the path for an application folder so that you can automatically update the path to database files on a new computer. If the new computer has the default name of .\sqlexpress for a SQL Server Express installation, then the deployed solution can run automatically. Otherwise, you will need to update the name of the SQL Server Express instance name in the connection string.

These concepts are not difficult to grasp, but a concrete example may help to clarify how to apply them. The WinCh11 project with Form1 has its initial folder (\WinCh11) in the C:\ProSSEApps\ Chapter11 path on my test computer for this book. Two project-level files and another folder (\WinCh11) with the project's form files reside in the C:\ProSSEApps\Chapter11\WinCh11 path. The project's form files reside in the C:\ProSSEApps\Chapter11\WinCh11\WinCh11 path. You can copy stand-alone database files to any folder for a project, such as the one for the form files. This demonstration relies on copying the SQL Server Express northwnd.mdf and northwnd.ldf files to the folder for form files. You can find additional background on techniques for copying database files in the "Copying Files, the Auto-Close Feature, and sp_detach_db" section of Chapter 3.

One safe way to perform XCopy deployment of a VBE Windows application solution involves copying the top-level \WinCh11 folder and all its child folders to another path on the same or a different computer. When the database files are in the application folder, they automatically go along with the solution—it's just that simple.

To enable a SQL Server Express instance to work with database files that are not permanently attached, you need to attach the database files when you run the solution. You can do this by specifying the AttachDBFileName argument in a connection string. Set the argument equal to the path for a primary data file (the .mdf file for a SQL Server Express database).

The following code from the Click event procedure for Button3 in Form1 illustrates the syntax for using the AttachDBFileName argument in a connection string. The sample begins by computing the character position for the start of the bin folder in the application's directory path. The bin folder is the child folder of the folder with the form files (...\WinCh11\WinCh11\). The strPath variable contains the full path for the project's form files (where the database files are copied). The pdbfph variable contains the path and file name for the primary data file. The expression for the connection string (cst) assigns the pdbfph variable to the AttachDBFileName argument. After computing the appropriate connection string, the procedure uses it to instantiate a SqlConnection object (cnn1). The remainder of the Click event procedure opens and closes the cnn1 SqlConnection object.

```
'Compute top-level project folder and use it as a prefix for
'the primary data file
Dim int1 As Integer = _
 InStr(My.Application.Info.DirectoryPath, "bin\")
Dim strPath As String = _
 Microsoft.VisualBasic.Left( _
 My.Application.Info.DirectoryPath, int1 - 1)
Dim pdbfph As String = strPath & "northwnd.mdf"
```

```
'Then, assign the path to the primary data file as the
'AttachDBFileName argument value in a connection string
Dim cst As String = "Data Source=.\sqlexpress;" & _
  "Integrated Security=SSPI;" & _
  "AttachDBFileName=" & pdbfph
Dim cnn1 As SqlConnection = New SqlConnection(cst)

'Open and close the connection to a SQL Server
'Express  database file
Try
 cnn1.Open()
 MessageBox.Show("Connection succeeded.")
 'Insert code to use connection string here
Catch ex As Exception
 MessageBox.Show(ex.Message, "something is wrong")
Finally
 cnn1.Close()
 MessageBox.Show("Connection closed.")
End Try
```

Connecting to Microsoft Access Database Files

Connecting to an Access database is similar to the process for connecting to stand-alone SQL Server Express database files. In both cases, you point a connection string at a file instead of an attached database on a server. Indeed, Microsoft Access is a file server system, so there are no attached databases in the traditional SQL Server sense. In spite of the similarity of working with a stand-alone file that is not attached by a server, there are also some important differences. First, you deal with the System.Data.OleDb namespace instead of the System.Data.SqlClient namespace. Second, there is a special OLE DB database driver that you must reference in your connection string. The Button4_Click procedure demonstrates the use of both of these points and the syntax for connecting to the Northwind.mdb file.

```
Dim cnn1 As New OleDbConnection

'Compute the path to an Access database inside the project
Dim int1 As Integer = _
  InStr(My.Application.Info.DirectoryPath, "bin\")
Dim DSPath As String = _
  Microsoft.VisualBasic.Left( _
  My.Application.Info.DirectoryPath, int1 - 1)
DSPath += "Northwind.mdb"

'Compose connection string and open connection
'using the OleDb data provider
cnn1.ConnectionString = "Provider = Microsoft.Jet.OLEDB.4.0;" & _
  "Data Source = " & DSPath
Try
 cnn1.Open()
 MessageBox.Show("Connection succeeded.")
Catch ex As Exception
 MessageBox.Show(ex.Message, "something is wrong")
Finally
 cnn1.Close()
 MessageBox.Show("Connection closed.")
End Try
```

Programming Command Objects

A Command object wraps a SQL statement and allows you to execute it from ADO.NET in VBE or VWDE. When creating a Command object, you must specify a Connection object before you can actually invoke the Command object. The Command object specifies what to do, and the Connection object specifies where to do it.

A SqlCommand class instance is the SqlClient entity that corresponds to a SqlConnection object in the System.Data.SqlClient namespace. There are four constructors for SqlCommand objects and a set of related properties that help you specify a property. As you may have noticed with the samples from the "Programming Connection Objects" section, you can construct a SqlConnection object with or without a connection string. Whether or not you construct a SqlConnection object with a connection string, you can't use the SqlConnection object without an assignment for its ConnectionString property. Similarly, for a SqlCommand object, you can construct a SqlCommand object with or without assignments for its CommandText and Connection properties. However, you cannot execute a SqlCommand object until you have assignments for both of these properties.

- The CommandText property can take different forms depending on the value of the CommandType property.

- The CommandType property in the System.Data.SqlClient namespace can assume one of two values: Text and StoredProcedure.

    - With a value of Text for CommandType, CommandText can be any SQL expression. The Text setting is the default.

    - With a value of StoredProcedure for the CommandType property, the CommandText property can be the name of any stored procedure in the database at which the Command object's Connection property points. You can represent parameter values for a stored procedure through the Parameters collection for a Command object. See Chapter 7 for coverage directed explicitly at stored procedures in SQL Server Express databases. See the following link for a slide deck examining how to program parameters for stored procedures and user-defined functions with VB .NET and ADO.NET: www.programmingmsaccess.com/Presentations/ProgramParameters.htm.

■**Tip** Other provider namespaces besides System.Data.SqlClient support a TableDirect CommandType setting. With the TableDirect CommandType setting, the CommandText property can be the name of any table in the database at which the Command object's Connection property points.

You can execute the SQL instructions for a SqlCommand object synchronously or asynchronously. When using the synchronous approach, you return either an individual value or a collection of rows. Another option when invoking a SqlCommand synchronously is to execute a T-SQL instruction that performs a task that does not return a result. Examples of such instructions are INSERT, UPDATE, DELETE, or CREATE TABLE and DROP TABLE. Methods for executing a SqlCommand synchronously include: ExecuteScalar, ExecuteReader, ExecuteNonQuery, and ExecuteXmlReader.

The asynchronous approach for invoking SqlCommand objects is for long-running commands. By invoking these commands asynchronously, you free your solution for other tasks. There is no event to signal the completion of SQL instructions within a SqlCommand object running asynchronously. Therefore, your code must poll the SqlCommand object to determine when execution completes. You also must explicitly end the execution of any SqlCommand objects that you begin to execute asynchronously. Methods for invoking a SqlCommand object asynchronously include: BeginExecuteReader, BeginExecuteNonQuery, and BeginExecuteXmlReader.

This section's samples highlight programming techniques for invoking the ExecuteScalar, ExecuteReader, and ExecuteNonQuery methods. You'll see samples operating in both Windows and web applications. You'll also see coverage of the System.Data.SqlClient and System.Data.OleDb namespaces, with the greatest emphasis on the System.Data.SqlClient namespace. Samples for this section reside on Form2, Form3, Form4, Default.aspx, and Default2.aspx of the WebCh11 WebSite solution.

Returning a Single Value with a Command Object

One of the easiest tasks that you can perform with a Command object is returning a single value. The most typical need for this is when you want to return a single aggregate value, such as the sum or count of the values in a column. Another typical scenario for returning a single value is when you want just a single column value from a row in a table or view.

The ExecuteScalar method for ADO.NET Command objects can return a single value. If the query statement for a Command object returns just a single value, then you get just that value. However, you can also invoke the ExecuteScalar method for a query statement that returns multiple column values and even multiple rows. In either of these cases, the ExecuteScalar method returns just the top-left column value from the result set.

This section drills down on the use of the ExecuteScalar method with the SqlCommand object for SQL Server Express databases. Particular emphasis goes to the use of the method in Windows applications, but coverage also goes to the use of the ExecuteScalar method with the OleDbCommand objects. In addition, this sections highlights the comparability of the ADO.NET model in both Windows and web applications.

Returning a Value in a Windows Application

Form2 in the WinCh11 project includes three Button controls. Figure 11-2 contrasts the Design view of Form2 (left pane) with its appearance immediately after it opens (right pane). See the Form2_Load procedure for code that transforms the Design view into the form's appearance after opening. Notice, for example, that Form2_Load increases the height of the form to show the bottom of the GroupBox3 control. The Click event procedures for the Button controls include increasingly sophisticated solutions for retrieving a value with the ExecuteScalar method of a SqlCommand object.

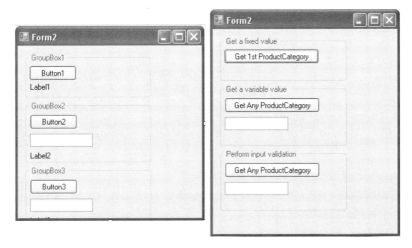

Figure 11-2. *Form2 demonstrates different approaches to instantiating a SqlCommand object and using the object with its ExecuteScalar method.*

All the Click event procedures in Form2 process data from the AdventureWorks database. The Form2 module instantiates the cnn1 SqlConnection object at the module level so that it can be used in the Click event procedures for all three Button controls on the form. The cnn1 SqlConnection object points at the AdventureWorks database in a SQL Server Express instance. The Dim statement for cnn1 appears next.

```
Dim cnn1 As SqlConnection = _
    New System.Data.SqlClient.SqlConnection( _
    "Data Source=.\sqlexpress;" & _
    "Integrated Security=True;" & _
    "Initial Catalog=AdventureWorks")
```

A click to Button1 returns the name column value from the row with a ProductCategoryID value of 1 in the ProductCategory table of the Production schema. The data source for the query is the ProductCategory table in the Production schema of the AdventureWorks database. The contents of the Click event procedure for Button1 appear next. As you can see, the code is very basic.

- First, the procedure constructs a SqlCommand object (cmd1) by specifying a SQL text string and referencing a SqlConnection object (cnn1).

- Second, the procedure opens the cnn1 Connection object. This is necessary because you cannot execute the SQL code in a SqlCommand object, such as cmd1, until the Command object has an open Connection object.

- Third, the code invokes the ExecuteScalar method for cmd1 to return the name of the category with a ProductCategoryID value of 1. The sample invokes the ExecuteScalar method, which returns a value of type System.Object. The ToString method casts the output as a String value and then assigns that value to the Text property of Label1.

- After populating the Text property of Label1, the code sample concludes by closing the cnn1 Connection object for the cmd1 Command object.

```
Dim cmd1 As New SqlCommand( _
    "SELECT Name FROM Production.ProductCategory Where ProductCategoryID = 1", _
    cnn1)

cnn1.Open()

Dim str1 As String = cmd1.ExecuteScalar.ToString
Me.Label1.Text = str1

cnn1.Close()
```

The Click event procedure for Button2 collects the value in a TextBox control, and then returns the product category name for the corresponding ProductCategoryID value from the ProductCategory table. Although this procedure is substantially more flexible than the preceding one, the code is nearly the same as in the preceding sample. The two changes are the declaration of a String variable named str1 and the use of the str1 variable in the SQL expression for the construction of the SqlCommand object.

- The initial Dim statement assigns the Text property value of TextBox1 to str1.

- The SQL expression uses the str1 value to specify for which ProductCategoryID value to return a Name column value.

```
Dim str1 As String = Me.TextBox1.Text

Dim cmd1 As New SqlCommand( _
    "SELECT Name FROM Production.ProductCategory Where ProductCategoryID = " & _
    str1, cnn1)
```

```
cnn1.Open()
str1 = cmd1.ExecuteScalar.ToString
Me.Label2.Text = str1

cnn1.Close()
```

The `Button2_Click` procedure provides superior flexibility over the `Button1_Click` procedure. However, its advantage comes at a cost. The `Button2_Click` procedure can fail easily. If a user does not enter a valid `ProductCategoryID` value in the `TextBox1` control, or does not enter any value in `TextBox1` before clicking `Button2`, the `Click` event procedure returns a runtime error and the application loses control to the operating system. This outcome is potentially confusing and discouraging to users. (Why doesn't this app accept my input and why do I have to restart the app to continue my work?)

The `Button3_Click` procedure remedies some of the problems with the `Button2_Click` procedure while still maintaining the same flexibility. The new approach in `Button3_Click` offers improvements in two areas. First, it carefully checks the contents of `TextBox1` to make sure that it is valid in two ways and sends helpful feedback about how to fix invalid input. Second, if an error occurs even after screening the input, a `Try...Catch...Finally` statement traps the error and provides feedback about the error. In addition, the `Finally` clause guarantees that the `SqlConnection` object associated with the `SqlCommand` object is closed.

Note A good general rule is that you should always close ADO.NET `Connection` objects after you declare and instantiate them—even if the attempt to open an ADO.NET `Connection` object fails.

It is often not possible to anticipate all the variations in input that can generate an error. Therefore, in addition to trapping for specific invalid input, you will also want to trap for unanticipated runtime errors. Use `Try...Catch` blocks in your code to trap for these errors, and then display the associated error message for the trapped errors. Some developers may prefer to just use `Try...Catch` blocks since they may need to use them anyway. No matter how you implement it, always consider following this design guideline: provide feedback for invalid input to users as your application recovers gracefully from any associated errors.

The code within the `Button3_Click` procedure appears next. Despite the fact that the `Button3_Click` procedure performs the same task as the `Button2_Click` procedure if the user enters valid input, the code in `Button3_Click` is substantially longer than the code in `Button2_Click`. All the extra code is to enable `Button3_Click` to recover gracefully instead of relinquishing control to the operating system when invalid input generates a runtime error. In addition, the `Button3_Click` procedure also provides context-sensitive help about how to fix invalid input. These refinements are the hallmarks of well-designed applications.

The `Button3_Click` procedure starts by assigning the `Text` property of the `TextBox2` control to the `str1` `String` variable. Next, a `Try...Catch` block attempts to convert the `str1` value to an `Integer` value with the `CInt` function. If the conversion attempt fails, a message box reminds the user to input an integer before the procedure ends with an `Exit Sub` statement.

After the `str1` value passes the preceding test to verify if it can convert to an `Integer` value, the `str1` value is passed as an argument to the `InColRange` function. This function checks if the `Integer` value represented by the `str1` value is between the minimum and maximum `ProductCategoryID` column values in the `ProductCategory` table of the `Production` schema in the `AdventureWorks` database. The `InColRange` function is a very flexible procedure that can check any `String` value for any column in any table in any database. The three arguments after `str1` specify the column name, table name, and `Connection` object for checking the `Integer` value represented by `str1`.

The `InColRange` function returns a `String` value that the `Button3_Click` procedure stores in the `strReturn` `String` variable. The two `String` values that the function can return are `Value in range` and `Value out of range`. If the `InColRange` function generates an error of any kind, the return value from the function is the error message. If the database server that the `InColRange` function references is stopped or paused, this can cause the return of an error message.

A `Select Case...End Select` statement processes each of the three types of return values from the InColRange function.

- For a `strReturn` value of `Value in range`, the code runs the `SELECT` statement to retrieve the Name column value corresponding to the `ProductCategoryID` column value in TextBox2. There is no need to open the cnn1 `SqlConnection` object because the `InColRange` function procedure opens the object. If the connection is successful, then the `InColRange` function leaves the cnn1 `SqlConnection` open for use by its calling procedure. By running the query in a `Try...Catch...Finally` statement, the code can recover from any unanticipated errors and close the cnn1 `SqlConnection` object even if there is an error.

- For a `strReturn` value of `Value out of range`, the code issues a message box instructing the user to enter another `ProductCategoryID` value.

- If the `InColRange` function generates a runtime error, control passes to the `Case Else` clause of the `Select Case...End Select` statement. This clause displays in a message box the error message for the runtime error generated by the `InColRange` function.

■**Note** The `Try...Catch...Finally` block detects an invalid input of `2.2` in TextBox2. The explicit input validity checks do not detect this kind of value as invalid (it converts to an `Integer` value, and it is between the upper and lower bounds of `ProductCategoryID` values in the `ProductCategory` table). The invocation of the `ExecuteScalar` method for the cmd1 object generates an `Exception`, and the `Catch` clause displays a message box with the system-provided feedback.

```
Dim str1 As String = Me.TextBox2.Text
Dim int1 As Integer

'Verify that an Integer value is input
Try
 int1 = CInt(str1)
Catch ex As Exception
 MessageBox.Show("Please input an integer as a ProductCategoryID value.")
 Exit Sub
End Try

Dim strReturn As String = _
  InColRange(str1, "ProductCategoryID", _
  "Production.ProductCategory", cnn1)

Select Case strReturn
 Case "Value in range"
  'Define cmd1 and execute it
  Dim cmd1 As New SqlCommand( _
    "SELECT Name FROM Production.ProductCategory Where ProductCategoryID = " & _
    str1, cnn1)
  Try
   str1 = cmd1.ExecuteScalar.ToString
   Me.Label3.Text = str1
  Catch ex As Exception
   MessageBox.Show(ex.Message)
```

```
    Finally
      cnn1.Close()
    End Try
  Case "Value out of range"
    MessageBox.Show("Enter another ProductCategory value.")
  Case Else
    MessageBox.Show(strReturn)
End Select
```

The final block of code to be reviewed for Form2 is the InColRange function procedure. This function's declaration includes the Friend keyword. This keyword makes the function procedure available for use as a Form2 member elsewhere in the WinCh11 project. You can reference the InColRange function elsewhere within the module by writing Form2.InColRange.

Nearly all the code within the InColRange function occurs within a Try...Catch block. This is significant for all three of the possible return value types from the function procedure.

- First, if the .NET Framework throws an exception because of a runtime error, the Catch clause causes the function procedure to return the message associated with the Exception object as a return value.

- Second, if the function procedure runs without an exception, an If...End If statement in the Try...Catch block determines the return value.

  - If the If...End If statement detects an integer equivalent of the strValue argument less than the smallest ProductCategoryID value or greater than the largest ProductCategoryID value, the procedure returns a value of Value out of range.

  - Otherwise, the Try...Catch block ends without assigning a return value. In this case, a Return statement after the Try...Catch block designates a return value of Value in Range.

The InColRange function procedure defines two SqlCommand objects: cmdMin and cmdMax. The cmdMin SqlCommand object returns the smallest value in the ColName column of the TabName table. ColName and TabName are arguments set to ProductCategoryID and Production.ProductCategory in the Button3_Click procedure. The cmdMax SqlCommand object returns the largest value in the ProductCategoryID column of the ProductCategory table of the Production schema in the AdventureWorks database.

Before either SqlCommand object (cmdMin or cmdMax) in the InColRange function can return a value, the SqlConnection object, cnn1, needs to be open. Therefore, the procedure invokes the Open method for cnn1 immediately after declaring and instantiating cmdMin and cmdMax. By invoking the ExecuteScalar method for each SqlCommand object, the procedure computes the upper and lower bounds for values in the ProductCategoryID column of the ProductCategory table.

The next segment of the function procedure compares the Integer value transformation of the strValue argument with the computed minimum and maximum values for the ProductCategoryID column. The logic described previously assigns a return value for the function.

```
Friend Function InColRange(ByVal strValue As String, _
  ByVal ColName As String, _
  ByVal TabName As String, _
  ByVal cnn1 As SqlConnection) As String

  Try
    Dim strMin As String = "SELECT MIN(" & ColName & ") " & _
      "FROM " & TabName
    Dim cmdMin As New SqlCommand(strMin, cnn1)
    Dim strMax As String = "SELECT MAX(" & ColName & ") " & _
      "FROM " & TabName
    Dim cmdMax As New SqlCommand(strMax, cnn1)
```

```
   cnn1.Open()
   Dim intMin As Integer = CInt(cmdMin.ExecuteScalar)
   Dim intMax As Integer = CInt(cmdMax.ExecuteScalar)
   If (CInt(strValue) < intMin Or CInt(strValue) > intMax) Then
    cnn1.Close()
    Return ("Value out of range")
   End If
  Catch ex As Exception
   cnn1.Close()
   Return (ex.Message)
  End Try
  Return ("Value in range")

End Function
```

Returning a Value in a Web Application

ADO.NET syntax follows the same conventions for web applications as for Windows applications. This section describes a web application with a single web page (Default.aspx) in a WebSite project that illustrates the basic principles for connecting to a data source and running a command against the data source. The two samples for this section illustrate how to connect to database files in the APP_Data folder of the WebCh11 website. I copied the Microsoft Access Northwind sample database file to the folder as well as the .mdf and .ldf files for the Northwind SQL Server sample database. Because the two code samples work with Access and SQL Server databases, the module behind the page begins with Imports statements for the System.Data.SqlClient and System.Data.OleDb name-spaces.

Figure 11-3 shows the Default.aspx web page from the Design tab of VWDE. Notice there are two Button controls—one for making a connection to and using an Access database, and another for performing the same tasks for a comparable SQL Server Express database. The OleDbCommand object behind the Query Access button counts the number of rows in the Shippers table, and related code displays the result in a Label control. The text announcing that the connection is closed results from a My.Response.Write statement.

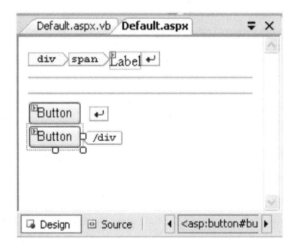

Figure 11-3. *Connecting to and using a database from a WebSite project uses the same ADO.NET syntax as from a Windows application project.*

The following listing shows the code in the Button1_Click procedure for Default.aspx. The code starts by declaring and instantiating an OleDbConnection object (cnn1) and an OleDbCommand object (cmd1). Next, the sample computes the path to the Northwind.mdb file in the project's APP_Data folder, and uses the path to help compute a connection string for the ConnectionString property of cnn1.

The remaining code in the sample puts the cnn1 object to use with the cmd1 object.

- First, the code opens a connection to the Northwind.mdb file.

- Next, it specifies an OleDbCommand object (cmd1) that can count the rows in the Shippers table.

- Then, the code invokes the ExecuteScalar method for cmd1 to compute a count of the shippers and assigns the result to the Text property of the Label control.

- If the procedure ends normally, the code closes the cnn1 Connection object.

- Otherwise, the code writes a message about the reason the code does not end normally.

```
Dim cnn1 As New OleDbConnection
Dim cmd1 As New OleDbCommand

'Compute path to and create connection for Access database file
Dim DSPath As String = _
    My.Computer.FileSystem.CombinePath( _
    Server.MapPath("/WebCh11/App_Data"), "Northwind.mdb")
cnn1.ConnectionString = "Provider = Microsoft.Jet.OLEDB.4.0;" & _
    "Data Source = " & DSPath

'Open connection, use it, close it
Try
 cnn1.Open()
 cmd1.CommandText = "SELECT Count(*) FROM Shippers"
 cmd1.Connection = cnn1
 Me.Label1.Text = "Number of Shippers: " & _
   cmd1.ExecuteScalar().ToString
Catch ex As Exception
 My.Response.Write(ex.Message)
Finally
 cnn1.Close()
 My.Response.Write("Connection closed.")
End Try
```

The code for Button2_Click connects to the SQL Server Northwind database instead of the Access Northwind database. However, it computes the count of Shippers and displays its results in an identical fashion. If it were not for the Button2 Text property, you could not tell whether you were using SQL Server Express database files or an Access database file.

The following excerpt from Button2_Click shows the part of this click procedure that is different from the one in Button1_Click.

- The excerpt starts by declaring and instantiating SqlConnection and SqlCommand objects instead of OleDbConnection and OleDbCommand objects.

- Next, the code computes the path to the Northwnd.mdf file instead of the Northwind.mdb file.

- Then, the code computes a connection string that ties the SQL Server Northwind database files to the .\sqlexpress SQL Server Express instance with integrated security.

- Finally, the code assigns the connection string to the cnn1 SqlConnection object.

```
Dim cnn1 As New SqlConnection
Dim cmd1 As New SqlCommand

'Compute top-level project folder and use it as a prefix for
'the primary data file in the connection string for cnn1
Dim pdbfph As String = _
    My.Computer.FileSystem.CombinePath( _
    Server.MapPath("/WebCh11/App_Data"), "Northwnd.mdf")
Dim cst As String = "Data Source=.\sqlexpress;" & _
    "Integrated Security=SSPI;" & _
    "AttachDBFileName=" & pdbfph
cnn1.ConnectionString = cst
```

Returning Forward-Only, Read-Only Rowsets

Instead of returning a single value from a SQL string wrapped in an ADO.NET command object, it is more common to want to retrieve one or more rows of data. If there is no need to update the retrieved data, the fastest way to accomplish the job in ADO.NET is with a DataReader object. Because DataReader objects are provider specific like the Connection and Command ADO.NET objects, you must use a different DataReader object type for each ADO.NET provider. For example, you can use the SqlDataReader object for SQL Server databases and the OleDbDataReader object for databases connected via the .NET OLE DB provider.

DataReader objects do not have a constructor that you invoke with the New keyword. Instead, you invoke the ExecuteReader method for an ADO.NET Command object to instantiate a new DataReader. Before you can invoke the ExecuteReader method for an ADO.NET Command object, the Command object must have an open connection. You cannot typically use a Connection object for any other purpose while a DataReader is using it.

■Tip A new, advanced Connection object feature in ADO.NET 2.0 allows for the use of multiple active result sets (MARS) with a single Connection object. By using MARS, you can have more than one DataReader object use the same Connection in an interleaved fashion. If you require true parallel processing of multiple DataReader objects, Microsoft recommends using a separate Connection object for each DataReader. By using a separate Connection object for each DataReader, you can achieve faster performance.

The ExecuteReader method is the same across all providers, but the Command and DataReader types are unique for each provider. While the general process for creating a DataReader object is the same for all databases, you must use the proper ADO.NET provider for the database that you are using. The following two cases describe the use of the ExecuteReader method for SQL Server Express and Access databases:

- For a SQL Server Express database, create a SqlDataReader object by invoking the ExecuteReader method for a SqlCommand object.

- For an Access database, create an OleDbDataReader object by invoking the ExecuteReader method for an OleDbCommand object.

After you create a DataReader object, you can pass through successive rows in a forward-only manner by repeatedly invoking the Read method for a DataReader object. If the Command object for a DataReader wraps a single SELECT statement, your DataReader object returns a single result set. In this case, the DataReader points at the first row of its result set after you initially invoke the Read method. For all rows until the last one, each successive invocation of the Read method returns a value of True and moves to the next row in the result set. Invoking the Read method from the last row of a result set returns a value of False. When you are finished reading data with a DataReader object, invoke the Close method. You can also invoke the Close method for the Connection object associated with a DataReader to release the connection resources associated with the DataReader object.

You can retrieve column values for the current row of a DataReader object with a variety of GetXXX methods, such as GetInt32 or GetSqlInt32. Using the GetInt32 method returns a column value as a 32-bit signed .NET Framework Integer data type. Using the GetSqlInt32 method returns a column value as a 32-bit signed Integer value from within SQL Server 2005. Other methods for returning column values in popular SQL Server database formats include GetSqlMoney, GetSqlDouble, and GetSqlDateTime. For columns with a varchar or nvarchar data type, you can retrieve values with the GetSqlString method. SQL Server data types do not necessarily correspond to .NET Framework data types without conversion. For example, to process a value retrieved with the GetSqlString method, you must convert the value to a .NET Framework String value with the ToString method.

You can denote columns by a zero-based ordinal index value for the GetXXX methods, such as GetSqlInt32. If rdr1 represents a DataReader object, then rdr1.GetSqlString(0).ToString can retrieve an nvarchar column value into ADO.NET as a SqlString value from the first column of the current row, and convert the value to a .NET Framework String value. Invoke the GetDataTypeName method with an ordinal column index value to retrieve the database data type name for values from a column. Invoke the GetOrdinal method to return the ordinal index value of a column that corresponds to the name you supply.

Tip Use the GetOrdinal method to return the ordinal index value nested within a GetXXX method that returns a column value so that your code can represent a column value by its column name instead of its column index value. For example, use rdr1.GetSqlString(rdr1.GetOrdinal("column_name")).ToString to return the .NET Framework converted String value for a column named column_name from the current row of the rdr1 DataReader object.

You can use a single DataReader object to successively return multiple result sets. Use two nested loops; in the inner loop, read the rows of the current result set, and in the outer loop, navigate from one result set to the next. Here's the process:

- Start by specifying a SQL string with multiple query statements for the CommandText property of a Command object; delimit each successive query statement after the first one by a semi-colon.

- Next, invoke the ExecuteReader method to create a DataReader object for the Command object. This locates the DataReader just before the first result set.

- Then, use the Read method to iteratively pass through successive rows of the result set until there are no more rows in the current result set.

- After reading the last row in the current result set, invoke the NextResult method. This advances the DataReader to the next result set (if there is one).

  - Return to reading the rows of the current result set in the inner loop.

  - When there are no remaining result sets, exit the outer loop instead of returning to the inner loop.

Several `DataReader` members deserve special mention.

- The `HasRows` property returns a value of `True` when the current result set has one or more rows, and a value of `False` when it doesn't.
- The `FieldCount` property returns the number of columns in the current row.
- The `IsDBNull` method returns a value of `True` for a column value that is missing. The method has the same syntax as the `GetXXX` methods for retrieving column values from the current row.

Reading Column Values Returned by a Single SELECT Statement

The Design view of `Form3` appears in Figure 11-4. The form contains three `Button` controls—one to launch each of the three samples. The `ListBox` control is for use for the third sample, which writes the values from one column in a `SqlDataReader` as elements in the `Items` collection of the `ListBox` control. A `DataReader` permits forward-only access to its column values. However, you can save the column values on the current row to a class instance, such as a Windows Form control for use after passing from the current row.

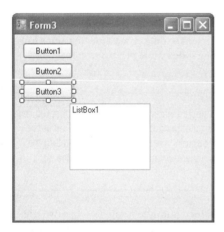

Figure 11-4. *A DataReader object lets a VBE or VWDE solution read data from a database and display it locally, such as in a ListBox control.*

The organization of the code behind `Form3` is straightforward. The `Click` event procedure for each button corresponds to the code for a sample. Because a `SqlDataReader` object depends on a `SqlConnection` object and a `SqlCommand` object, you need a reference to the `System.Data.dll` assembly. In addition, it is convenient to have an `Imports` statement pointing at the `System.Data.SqlClient` namespace. Because all three samples use the same SQL Server Express AdventureWorks database, the code behind `Form3` declares and instantiates a `SqlConnection` object at the module level. The `Dim` statement for the `SqlConnection` object has the same syntax as for `Form2`.

Tip I found it useful to add a reference to the `System.Xml.dll` assembly to the WinCh11 project for working with the code behind `Form3`. Without the reference to this assembly, using a `GetSqlXXX` method, such as `GetSqlString`, returned a compiler error. However, the code still executed properly. The compiler error did not occur for `GetXXX` methods (such as `GetString`) that worked with .NET Framework data types.

The `Button1_Click` procedure reads the `ProductCategoryID` and `Name` column values from the ProductCategory table in the `Production` schema and displays the values in a message box. The code within the procedure divides the task into three parts.

- The first part creates a `SqlDataReader` object for the required data.

- The second part reads the data from the `SqlDataReader` object and computes a `String` value based on the read values.

- The third part displays the `String` value computed in the second part with the `Show` method of the `MessageBox` class.

The code for the first part of the `Button1_Click` procedure appears next. The code segment starts with the declaration of a query `String` variable (strQuery). This `String` variable designates the data source for the `SqlDataReader`. In order to achieve this outcome, you must designate strQuery as the `CommandText` property for the `SqlCommand` object (cmd1) serving as the source for the `SqlDataReader` (rdr1).

The code uses a `SqlCommand` constructor to specify strQuery as the `CommandText` property of the cmd1 SqlCommand object. While the excerpt uses a `Dim` statement to declare rdr1 as a `SqlDataReader` type, notice that the `Dim` statement for rdr1 does not contain the `New` keyword. The only way to instantiate a new `SqlDataReader` object is with the `ExecuteReader` method.

```
Dim strQuery As String = "SELECT ProductCategoryID, Name " & _
  "FROM Production.ProductCategory " & _
  "ORDER BY ProductCategoryID"
Dim cmd1 As New SqlCommand(strQuery, cnn1)
cnn1.Open()
Dim rdr1 As SqlDataReader
rdr1 = cmd1.ExecuteReader()
```

The code for the second part of the `Button1_Click` procedure computes a `String` value (str1) that contains values from the `SqlDataReader` object formatted for display in a message box. This code block starts by assigning an empty string to str1 to avoid an initial null value for the `String` variable. The reading of the values from the `SqlDataReader` occurs within a `Try...Catch...Finally` statement. Within the `Finally` clause, the code closes the `SqlDataReader` (rdr1) and its SqlConnection object (cnn1). This step releases the resources associated with the cnn1 SqlConnection object.

The `Read` method applies to the rdr1 SqlDataReader as the condition for a `While` loop within the Try clause. As long as the `Read` method returns a value of `True`, the `While` loop continues reading the next row in the reader. A return value of `False` passes control to the first statement after the `End While` statement at the bottom of the `While` loop.

An expression within the `While` loop concatenates column values from the current row to the str1 variable. Two different `GetXXX` methods extract values from the current row, and each `GetXXX` method demonstrates a different syntax for retrieving values from the current row. Because the code assigns the column values to a `String` variable (str1), the `ToString` method is applied to the output from each `GetXXX` method for retrieving a value.

- The `GetSqlInt32` method extracts the first column value from the current `SqlDataReader` row. The index value of 0 designates the first column. The value for this column corresponds to the `ProductCategoryID` column in the `ProductCategory` table within the `AdventureWorks` database. This column has an int SQL Server data type, which is a signed 32-bit `Integer` data type.

- The `GetSqlString` method uses the `GetOrdinal` method to specify a column index value. The advantage of the `GetOrdinal` method is that you can use a column name in your code even while you pass a column index value to the `GetXXX` method for retrieving a value.

- At the end of each row, the expression for concatenating to str1 appends carriage return and linefeed characters. These are special control characters that you can designate with the ControlChars constants. If you are more familiar with or prefer classic VB conventions, you can also use vbCrLf as well.

```
Dim str1 As String = ""
Try
  While rdr1.Read()
    str1 += rdr1.GetSqlInt32(0).ToString _
    & ", " & _
    rdr1.GetSqlString(rdr1.GetOrdinal("Name")).ToString & _
    ControlChars.CrLf
  End While
Catch ex As Exception
  MessageBox.Show(ex.Message)
Finally
  rdr1.Close()
  cnn1.Close()
End Try
```

The third part of the Button1_Click procedure consists of a single statement. This statement invokes the shared Show method of the MessageBox class. The expression for the Show method discards the carriage return and linefeed characters from the end of the str1 variable. These special characters are not necessary because no other row appears after them.

The output consists of four comma-delimited rows—one for each row in the ProductCategory table. The first value in each row is the ProductCategoryID column value, and the second row value is the Name column value.

```
MessageBox.Show( _
Microsoft.VisualBasic.Left(str1, str1.Length - 2), _
"Product Categories")
```

Reading Column Values Returned by Multiple SELECT Statements

Downloading multiple result sets from a single database connection one after another is more efficient that reconnecting multiple times to download multiple result sets. Happily, the process for returning multiple result sets with a single SqlDataReader is strikingly similar to the process for returning a single result set. Therefore, you can enhance the productivity of your solutions with very little work for coding the more productive technique.

The Button2_Click procedure demonstrates one approach to returning multiple result sets from a single connection with a SqlDataReader. Just as with the Button1_Click procedure for returning a single result set, there are three parts to the task.

- The first part creates a SqlDataReader object for the required data. The only distinction for returning multiple result sets is to specify multiple SELECT statements. Assign these SELECT statements to the CommandText property for the SqlCommand object.

- The second part reads the data from the SqlDataReader object and computes a String value based on the read values. This part uses the Read method to read the rows within a result set, and the NextResult method to move from one result set to the next.

- The third part displays the String value computed in the second part with the Show method of the MessageBox class. This part can be almost identical to the comparable part in Button1_Click.

The code for the first part of `Button2_Click` is nearly identical to that for the first part of `Button1_Click`. In fact, the only difference is in the assignment of a `String` value to `strQuery`. In the `Button1_Click` procedure, the `String` value assigned to `strQuery` consists of a single `SELECT` statement for two column vaues from the `ProductCategory` table.

In the case of `Button2_Click`, the assignment for `strQuery` starts with the same SQL statement, but it follows the initial SQL statement with a semicolon delimiter before specifying a second SQL statement. The second `SELECT` statement also has two column names in its `SELECT` list; these are the `ProductSubcategoryID` and `Name` columns from the `ProductSubcategory` table in the `Production` schema. You can include as many SQL strings as you wish so long as they are delimited from one another by semicolons.

```
Dim strQuery As String = "SELECT ProductCategoryID, Name " & _
    "FROM Production.ProductCategory " & _
    "ORDER BY ProductCategoryID;" & _
    "SELECT ProductSubcategoryID, Name " & _
    "FROM Production.ProductSubcategory " & _
    "ORDER BY ProductCategoryID, ProductSubcategoryID"
Dim cmd1 As New SqlCommand(strQuery, cnn1)
cnn1.Open()
Dim rdr1 As SqlDataReader
rdr1 = cmd1.ExecuteReader()
```

The second part of `Button2_Click` differs in structure from the second part of `Button1_Click`. The two procedures are also distinct in how they format output for display. The most important distinction is the structural one to accommodate multiple result sets. Notice that an inner `Do` loop resides within an outer `Do` loop.

- The inner `Do` loop reads the column values from successive rows of the current result set. This loop corresponds to the `While...End While` loop in the `Button1_Click` procedure.

- The outer `Do` loop contains a `While` clause as part of its `Loop` instruction. The argument for the `While` clause is true as long as there are unread result sets.

  - So long as there are unread result sets, control passes to the top of the outer loop and eventually to the inner loop for reading the unread result set.

  - If there are no additional result sets, control passes to the `Finally` clause of the `Try...Catch...Finally` statement.

In this particular sample, the statement for parsing column values from the `rdr1` `SqlDataReader` is the same for both result sets. This is so because both result sets have two columns with the same data types. It will be more common to require different code for parsing the values for each result set. When this need arises, you can use a variable to track the result set and select an appropriate parsing expression for a result set based on the tracking variable's value. This sample illustrates a similar approach in its use of the `bolSecondRSStarted` Boolean variable to control the addition of content to the `str1` variable after all rows for the first result set are read.

The differences in how results are formatted between `Button2_Click` and `Button1_Click` pertain mostly to the addition of labels to identify each result set in `str1`.

- Instead of initializing `str1` to an empty string, `Button2_Click` initially sets `str1` to the string `Product Categories` followed by a carriage return and a linefeed.

- As mentioned previously, the declaration of the `bolSecondRSStarted` variable tracks the result set being processed. This Boolean variable is initially `False`.

- The inner `Do` loop in `Button2_Click` for parsing values has similar—but not identical—parsing code to the parsing code in `Button1_Click`.

- There is no use of the GetOrdinal method to permit the use of a column name instead of a column index value. You can use either approach depending on your personal preference.

- The Button2_Click procedure parses the Name column value with the GetString method instead of the GetSqlString method used in Button1_Click. Because the GetString method automatically returns a .NET Framework String data type, there is no need to invoke the ToString method as there is with the return value from the GetSqlString method.

- After the second part of Button2_Click finishes reading the first result set, the code tests the value of bolSecondRSStarted as the condition of an If...End If statement.

  - If the value is False, the code writes another String constant to str1 to label the values from the second result set, and resets the value of bolSecondRSStarted to True.

  - Therefore, the next time the code reaches the If...End If statement with bolSecondRSStarted as a condition, the flow bypasses the code within the If...End If statement.

■**Caution** Don't forget the preceding tip about the need for a reference to System.Xml.dll when using a GetSqlXXX method. If your project does not have that reference, the GetSqlInt32 method for the rdr1 SqlDataReader will generate an error in the following listing. If you prefer not to add the reference to the System.Xml.dll, then you can replace the GetSqlInt32 method with the GetValue method.

```
Dim str1 As String = "Product Categories" & ControlChars.CrLf
Dim bolSecondRSStarted As Boolean
Try
 Do
  Do While rdr1.Read()
   str1 += rdr1.GetSqlInt32(0).ToString & _
    ", " & _
    rdr1.GetString(1) & _
    ControlChars.CrLf
  Loop
  If bolSecondRSStarted = False Then
   str1 += ControlChars.CrLf & "Product Subcategories" & ControlChars.CrLf
   bolSecondRSStarted = True
  End If
 Loop While rdr1.NextResult
Catch ex As Exception
 MessageBox.Show(ex.Message)
Finally
 rdr1.Close()
 cnn1.Close()
End Try
```

The code from the third part of Button2_Click is essentially the same as the third part of Button1_Click procedure. The only difference is the addition of a label for the message box in Button2_Click.

```
MessageBox.Show( _
 Microsoft.VisualBasic.Left(str1, str1.Length - 2), _
 "Product Categories followed by Product Subcategories")
```

Despite the similarity in the design of the third parts of `Button1_Click` and `Button2_Click`, the output from the `Show` method is strikingly different. The main distinction is that the output from `Button2_Click` has two result sets instead of just one. An excerpt from the message box displayed by `Button2_Click` appears in Figure 11-5. You can see all four rows from the first result set and the first six rows from the second result set.

Figure 11-5. *You can use a single ADO.NET DataReader object to return values from multiple result sets.*

Populating the Items Collection of a ListBox with a SqlDataReader

Chances are that your main reason for using a `SqlDataReader` object won't be to display database values in a message box. Therefore, you may be thinking that the preceding two examples are somewhat artificial—or at least not relevant to common development tasks. That would be a mistake.

The main objective of the preceding two samples and their discussions is to give you a good foundation in understanding `SqlDataReader` objects and, more generally, any type of ADO.NET `DataReader` objects. Given that understanding, you can readily adapt `SqlDataReaders` for other purposes besides displaying results in a message box.

The last sample in this section reinforces this notion by adapting the code sample to display the `ProductCategoryID` and `Name` column values from the `ProductCategory` table in a message box so that you can show the `Name` column values in a `ListBox` control. It is actually pretty common to want to display database results in Windows Form controls. Furthermore, this is a task that you are likely to want to perform quickly because your main objective for having a `ListBox` control is to make a selection from it, not to populate it. One of the best features about ADO.NET `DataReader` objects is that they offer the fastest way for ADO.NET developers to retrieve data from a database.

Because the object of the last `SqlDataReader` sample is to read values from the `ProductCategory` table, it makes sense to adapt the first `SqlDataReader` solution, which also reads values from the same database table. However, please understand that this sample readily generalizes to any situation in which you need to display a column of values from a database table in a `ListBox` control. All you need to do is make two changes, as follows:

1. Revise the `Connection` object for the `SqlCommand` object from which you derive the `SqlDataReader`. Make the `SqlConnection` object point at the database you want to use.

2. Then, specify a new `CommandText` property value with a SQL string that extracts the column of values that you want to display in the `ListBox` control.

The sample for populating a `ListBox` control with product category names needs just the first two parts of the `Button1_Click` procedure. The third part, which displays a message box, is no longer necessary. Furthermore, the first part, which creates a `SqlDataReader`, is useful for this sample without any changes. To adapt the `Button1_Click` procedure, all you need to do is modify the second part of the sample. The `Button3_Click` procedure shows the completed adapted sample.

The modified code for the second part of the sample appears next. A critical part of the solution is the `While...End While` statement. This loop successively passes through column values for all the rows for the `ProductCategory` table. The second column value, with a column index value of 1, contains the `Name` column values. Therefore, on each pass through the `While` loop, the code adds the value from the second column to the `Items` collection for `ListBox1`. After passing through all the rows (there are only four of them), the `ListBox` control displays the `Name` column values from the `ProductCategory` table.

There are a couple of other design features that are worthy of mention.

- First, the code clears the `Items` collection of `ListBox1` just before populating the `Items` collection of `ListBox1`. If this task weren't performed, each time a user clicked `Button3`, it would add to the existing items in the `ListBox` control instead of replacing the items in the control.

- Second, the sample sets the height of `ListBox1` to 65 pixels just after populating the control. By resizing the `ListBox` control, you can avoid displaying empty white space below the items. The default height of a `ListBox` control in VBE is 95 pixels.

```
Try
  Me.ListBox1.Items.Clear()
  While rdr1.Read()
    Me.ListBox1.Items.Add(rdr1.GetString(1))
  End While
  Me.ListBox1.Height = 65
Catch ex As Exception
  MessageBox.Show(ex.Message)
Finally
  rdr1.Close()
  cnn1.Close()
End Try
```

Figure 11-6 shows `Form3` after the `Click` event for `Button3` completes. Notice that the `ListBox` control displays the names of the four product categories from the `ProductCategory` table. Also, notice that the `ListBox` is sized so that it fits just those four items. If you added additional rows to the `ProductCategory` table, VBE would automatically add a vertical scroll bar to the `ListBox` control, or you could assign a new, larger value to the `Height` property for the `ListBox` control. On the test computer used for these samples, I need to add between 16 and 17 pixels per new item added to the `Items` collection for the `ListBox` control. The pixel size on your computer may dictate different sizing for the `ListBox` control and the amount to add for each new item.

Figure 11-6. *It is easy to adapt the samples for showing SqlDataReader contents in message boxes for other purposes, such as populating a ListBox control.*

Performing Data Definition and Database Maintenance

In its most general sense, an ADO.NET Command object is a wrapper for one or more SQL statements. Anything that you can do with SQL, you can do with ADO.NET Command objects. Up until this point in the chapter, the focus has been on data retrieval—namely, recovering single values and rowsets from a database with a Command object. However, you can do much more.

This section introduces you to using the ExecuteNonQuery method for a Command object. This method is appropriate for any ADO.NET Command object that does not return any data from a query statement. Therefore, the ExecuteNonQuery method especially targets Command objects wrapping SQL statements that perform data maintenance (inserts, updates, and deletes), as well as data-definition tasks, such as creating a table. Both of these topics were covered extensively with T-SQL in Chapter 4 and Chapter 7. The objective of this section is to present a set of simple samples that show you how to get started performing data maintenance and database definition with the SqlCommand object.

The samples for this section reside in Form4 of the WinCh11 project. In this section, you'll learn how to add and drop a table from a database. In addition, you'll learn how to insert rows in your newly created table. You'll also learn how to search for a row in your table and then either update the row or delete it.

Opening the Sample with Conditionally Enabled Controls

Figure 11-7 shows Form4 both in Design view and after the form initially opens. In addition to helping you to map Button, Label, and GroupBox control names to Form4, this screenshot also illustrates how some controls are initially disabled. On any form with more than a few controls, it is typical for some controls to be relevant only some of the time. With Form4, the Update and Delete buttons (Button4 and Button5, respectively) are only relevant after a user finds a row to change or delete. Therefore, the Update and Delete buttons along with their associated TextBox and Label controls are disabled when Form4 initially opens.

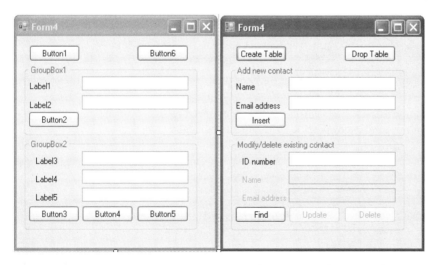

Figure 11-7. *You can specify whether a control on a form operates by manipulating its Enabled property. A disabled control appears dimmed.*

■**Note** The Enabled property for a control can be either True or False. Controls, such as Button and TextBox controls, are enabled by default. This allows users to operate controls normally. For example, users can enter and edit values in a TextBox control. Your code can set the Enabled value for a control to False. In this case, the control appears dimmed, and users cannot operate the control. For example, users cannot enter and edit values in a TextBox control. If a Label control describes a TextBox control on a form, you may care to set its Enabled property to the same value as the TextBox control's Enabled property. In this way, a Label for a TextBox control will become dimmed when the TextBox it describes is disabled.

The Connection object for this sample points at the local copy of the SQL Server Northwind database files that are opened with a SQL Server Express instance. The following code excerpt from the module behind Form4 illustrates how to make the Connection object available to all procedures within the application, and how to disable selected controls on the form when it initially opens. The code excerpt is a little lengthier than normal, but it is very easy to understand.

- The excerpt includes a module-level variable declaration for a SqlConnection object (cnn1), but the Form4_Load event procedure actually instantiates the object.

  - The code within the Load event procedure for instantiating the object dynamically computes the path to the Northwnd.mdf file.

  - Next, the Load event procedure uses the path to create a connection string for and instantiate the cnn1 SqlConnection object.

- The bulk of the code in the Load event procedure merely assigns Text property values to controls. Recall that form controls are enabled by default. The final line of code in the procedure calls the DisableEnableUpdateDeleteControls procedure with an argument of Disable.

- The DisableEnableUpdateDeleteControls procedure in the following listing either disables or enables selected controls on a form.

  - Disabled controls are dimmed and do not operate. The Button4, Button5, Label4, Label5, TextBox4, and TextBox5 controls in right pane of Figure 11-7 are disabled.

  - Passing a value of Disable disables the controls listed in the preceding sub-bullet and clears TextBox3, TextBox4, and TextBox5 in GroupBox2.

  - Passing any other String value to the function procedure, such as Enable, enables all the controls disabled by passing an argument of Disable.

```
Dim cnn1 As SqlConnection

 Private Sub Form4_Load(ByVal sender As Object, _
 ByVal e As System.EventArgs) Handles Me.Load

 'Compute top-level project folder and use it as a prefix for
 'the primary data file
 Dim int1 As Integer = _
  InStr(My.Application.Info.DirectoryPath, "bin\")
 Dim strPath As String = Microsoft.VisualBasic.Left( _
  My.Application.Info.DirectoryPath, int1 - 1)
 Dim pdbfph As String = strPath & "northwnd.mdf"
 Dim cst As String = "Data Source=.\sqlexpress;" & _
   "Integrated Security=SSPI;" & _
   "AttachDBFileName=" & pdbfph
```

```
        cnn1 = New SqlConnection(cst)

        Me.Button1.Text = "Create Table"
        Me.Button2.Text = "Insert"
        Me.Button3.Text = "Find"
        Me.Button4.Text = "Update"
        Me.Button5.Text = "Delete"
        Me.Button6.Text = "Drop Table"

        Me.GroupBox1.Text = "Add new contact"
        Me.GroupBox2.Text = "Modify/delete existing contact"

        Me.Label1.Text = "Name"
        Me.Label2.Text = "Email address"

        Me.Label3.Text = "ID number"
        Me.Label4.Text = "Name"
        Me.Label5.Text = "Email address"

        DisableEnableUpdateDeleteControls("Disable")

    End Sub

    Sub DisableEnableUpdateDeleteControls(ByVal str1 As String)

        If UCase(str1) = "DISABLE" Then
         Me.Label4.Enabled = False
         Me.Label5.Enabled = False
         Me.TextBox4.Enabled = False
         Me.TextBox5.Enabled = False
         Me.Button4.Enabled = False
         Me.Button5.Enabled = False
         Me.TextBox3.Clear()
         Me.TextBox4.Clear()
         Me.TextBox5.Clear()
        Else
         Me.Label4.Enabled = True
         Me.Label5.Enabled = True
         Me.TextBox4.Enabled = True
         Me.TextBox5.Enabled = True
         Me.Button4.Enabled = True
         Me.Button5.Enabled = True
        End If

    End Sub
```

Adding and Dropping a Table

One of the most common data-definition tasks is to create a table. Creating a table provides a repository for your application to store and retrieve data. You may also need to retire tables from use by dropping them. It is always a good idea to remove objects from an application that you no longer need because it leaves fewer objects for a hacker to attack.

A click to `Button1` creates a table named `DotNetTable` in the database pointed at by the `cnn1` `SqlConnection` object. The code inside the `Button1_Click` procedure appears next. There are two parts to the procedure, which are as follows:

- First, the code instantiates a `SqlCommand` object (`cmd1`). The `cmd1` `CommandText` property includes the code for creating the `DotNetTable`. The `Connection` property equals `cnn1` so that the table is added to the version of the `Northwind` database files within the current project. The table has three columns.

  - The `ContactID` column with an `IDENTITY` property serves as the source for the table's primary key.

  - The `ContactName` column holds up to 25 Unicode characters for a contact's name.

  - The `ContactEAddr` column holds up to 60 Unicode characters for a contact's email address.

- After defining the `cmd1` `SqlCommand` object, the code executes the command with the `ExecuteNonQuery` method. Before invoking the method, you must open the `SqlConnection` object for the `SqlCommand` object. The code to execute the `cmd1` `SqlCommand` object occurs within the `Try` clause of a `Try...Catch...Finally` statement.

  - Whether the attempt to execute succeeds or fails, the `Finally` clause will always close the `cnn1` `SqlConnection` object.

  - If the T-SQL for the `CommandText` property cannot execute, the `Catch` clause provides some feedback. For example, if the `DotNetTable` database table already exists, you'll receive a message alerting you about this. No special code is required for this feedback. It is a normal error message that SQL Server Express returns to the client application through ADO.NET.

```
Dim cmd1 As New SqlCommand
cmd1.CommandText = "CREATE TABLE DotNetTable (" & _
  "ContactID int IDENTITY PRIMARY KEY, " & _
  "ContactName nvarchar(25) NOT NULL, " & _
  "ContactEAddr nvarchar(60) NOT NULL)"
cmd1.Connection = cnn1

'Invoke the command
Try
 cnn1.Open()
 cmd1.ExecuteNonQuery()
 MessageBox.Show("Command succeeded.", "Outcome", _
   MessageBoxButtons.OK, MessageBoxIcon.Information)
Catch ex As Exception
 MessageBox.Show(ex.Message)
Finally
 cnn1.Close()
End Try
```

Figure 11-8 shows `Form4` after two successive clicks to `Button1`. If there is not already a table named `DotNetTable` in the database pointed at by `cnn1` before the first click, then the attempt to execute the SQL in the `CommandText` property for `cmd1` succeeds. The procedure presents a message box like the top one on the right side of Figure 11-8. Notice that the icon and caption for the message box follow from the settings for the `Show` method in the `Try` clause of the preceding code segment. A second successive click to Button1 will fail because the DotNetTable will already exist from the prior click to the button. A native error message appears in the bottom-right pane to report this outcome. You can add any custom code you prefer to replace the message box generated in the Catch clause of the preceding code segment to display a more tailored message or even perform some remedial action.

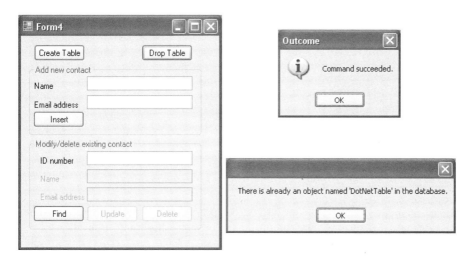

Figure 11-8. *It is good programming practice to provide feedback to users after they perform an action.*

The Click event procedure for Button6 is nearly identical to that for Button1. Recall that the Button6_Click procedure drops the DotNetTable. The only item that needs to change from Button1_ Click to Button6_Click is the SQL string assignment to the cmd1 SqlCommand object. The following excerpt from the Button6_Click procedure shows the new SQL statement for the CommandText property along with the statements just before and after it. The rest of Button6_Click is identical to the rest of Button1_Click.

```
Dim cmd1 As New SqlCommand
cmd1.CommandText = "DROP TABLE DotNetTable"
cmd1.Connection = cnn1
```

Inserting New Rows in a Table

After adding a table, such as DotNetTable, to a database, you normally want to add rows to it. GroupBox1 in Form4 contains two TextBox controls and a Button control to help accomplish this task. Users can specify the ContactName and ContactEAddr column values for a new row in the TextBox1 and TextBox2 controls within the GroupBox1 control. Clicking Button2 adds the designated column values to DotNetTable. SQL Server Express automatically populates the ContactID column value because of its IDENTITY property setting.

Figure 11-9 shows Form4 just before the addition of a new row to the DotNetTable with Rick Dobson and rickd@cabinc.net as the ContactName and ContactEAddr column values. If this is the first attempt to add a row to the table, the ContactID column value will be 1. Users can successively add new rows to the DotNetTable after clicking Insert. Clicking the Insert button clears the TextBox controls to ready them for the insertion of a new row.

Figure 11-9. *It's easy to collect values for a database with TextBox controls, but remember to verify your input values before submitting them to your database server.*

When you accept input from TextBox controls, it's good programming practice to include some code to validate the input. Failing to verify incoming data values can expose your application to hacker attacks. In addition, verifying incoming data can sometimes allow you to detect faulty input.

The Button2_Click procedure has code to verify both ContactName and ContactEAddr column values.

The following excerpt from the Button2_Click procedure shows the code for verifying ContactName and ContactEAddr column values. Several Dim statements precede an If...ElseIf... Else...End If statement. The Dim statements define a SqlCommand object, as well as several quantities used to verify email addresses. The expressions for verifying the ContactName and ContactEAddr column values are conditions for the If and ElseIf clauses of the If...ElseIf...Else...End If statement.

- The If condition has four criteria for verifying ContactName column values.

  - A ContactName cannot contain a semicolon (;). This is a common character used in hacker attacks for input to databases. In addition, most names do not have a semicolon within them.

  - A ContactName with an equal sign (=) is rejected for the same reasons that semicolons are rejected.

  - A third criterion for a ContactName value is that its number of characters is greater than zero. If the ContactName field length equals 0, then a user did not input a value into TextBox1. The DotNetTable definition requires an entry for ContactName.

  - The last ContactName criterion rejects a ContactName column value with greater than twenty-five characters. The nvarchar(25) setting for ContactName in the table's CREATE TABLE statement limits ContactName column values to no more than twenty-five characters.

- The ElseIf condition has three criteria for verifying email addresses as ContactEAddr column values.

  - All email addresses must have an @ sign. The int_at quantity will be 0 for ContactEAddr values that do not contain an @ sign.

- Every email address must have at least one period (.) after its @ sign, such as @cabinc.net. The int_period quantity is 0 if this condition is not satisfied.

- Finally, the length of an email address must be at least eight characters (c@ccc.cc). Email addresses with less than eight characters are therefore not valid.

Tip It is popular among advanced developers to use regular expressions for verifying email addresses (and other String values). However, regular expressions are still not widely used by most developers, and using them makes your code difficult to maintain. In addition, much more familiar Visual Basic String expressions can sometimes allow more precise validation criteria.

The Else clause in the If...ElseIf...Else...End If statement assigns CommandText and Connection property values to the cmd1 SqlCommand object declared and instantiated at the top of the excerpt. The CommandText property value is a SQL string that uses the Text property values of TextBox1 and TextBox2 to construct an INSERT statement for the DotNetTable. The Else clause assigns the cnn1 SqlConnection object instantiated at the top of the Form4_Load procedure to the Connection property for the cmd1 SqlCommand object.

```
Dim cmd1 As New SqlCommand

Dim int_at As Integer = InStr(Me.TextBox2.Text, "@")
Dim int_period As Integer = InStr(int_at, Me.TextBox2.Text, ".")
Dim int_len As Integer = Len(Me.TextBox2.Text)

If InStr(Me.TextBox1.Text, ";") > 0 Or _
 InStr(Me.TextBox1.Text, "=") > 0 Or _
 (Len(Me.TextBox1.Text) = 0) Or _
 (Len(Me.TextBox1.Text) > 25) Then
 MessageBox.Show("Invalid Name.  Please fix name.")
 Exit Sub
ElseIf Not (int_at > 0 And int_period > 0 And int_len >= 8) Then
 MessageBox.Show("Invalid email address.", "Please fix it")
 Exit Sub
Else
 cmd1.CommandText = "INSERT DotNetTable " & _
   "(ContactName, ContactEAddr) VALUES " & _
   "('" & Me.TextBox1.Text & "', '" & Me.TextBox2.Text & "')"
 cmd1.Connection = cnn1
End If
```

After exiting the If...ElseIf...Else...End If statement with valid ContactName and ContactEAddr column values, the procedure is ready to execute the cmd1 SqlCommand that inserts a row into DotNetTable. The final code segment from Button2_Click, which appears next, accomplishes this task.

- Before invoking the ExecuteNonQuery method for the SqlCommand object, it is necessary to open the cnn1 SqlConnection that the SqlCommand object uses to interact with the SQL Server Express database.

- If the ExecuteNonQuery method completes successfully, the code clears TextBox1 and TextBox2. Clearing the TextBox controls gives visual confirmation that something happened. In this case, the something is the insertion of the new row. Reasons that the ExecuteNonQuery might fail could include a paused or stopped SQL Server Express instance, or a moved—or even deleted—database file.

- Whether or not the ExecuteNonQuery method completes successfully, the Try...Catch...Finally statement always closes the cnn1 SqlConnection object in its Finally clause.

```
Try
 cnn1.Open()
 cmd1.ExecuteNonQuery()
 Me.TextBox1.Clear()
 Me.TextBox2.Clear()
Catch ex As Exception
 MessageBox.Show(ex.Message)
Finally
 cnn1.Close()
End Try
```

Updating Column Values and Deleting Rows

The GroupBox2 control at the bottom of Form4 enables three functions through its Button controls. From left to right, these functions work to do the following:

- Find a row in the DotNetTable database table based on the row's ContactID value

- Update either or both the ContactName and ContactEAddr column values for the currently found row

- Delete the currently found row

Before you can update the ContactName and ContactEAddr column values for the currently found row or delete the currently found row, you must first find a row that matches the ContactID column value designated in TextBox3, the first TextBox control in the GroupBox2 control. You can find a row by entering a value in the TextBox3 control and clicking the Find button. If a row exists in the DotNetTable database table with a ContactID value matching the value in TextBox3, then clicking the Find button populates the other two TextBox controls in GroupBox2 with the ContactName and the ContactEAddr column values for the matched row.

Until you successfully find a row, the Update and Delete buttons along with their associated Label and TextBox controls remain disabled. After a user successfully finds a row, the Update and Delete buttons along with TextBox4 and TextBox5 become enabled.

Figure 11-10 shows Form4 after the row with a ContactID column value of 1 is found. Notice the Update and Delete buttons are now enabled (they are no longer dimmed as in the right pane of Figure 11-7). In addition, the two TextBox controls below the TextBox control with the matching ContactID column value have the corresponding ContactName and ContactEAddr column values for the matched row.

The Button3_Click procedure does a lookup in the DotNetTable database table based on the value in TextBox3. A SqlDataReader object based on a SqlCommand object with SELECT list items of ContactName and ContactEAddr and a WHERE clause with a criterion based on the value in TextBox3 returns the ContactName and ContactEAddr column values corresponding to the value in TextBox3.

Before performing a lookup in the DotNetTable based on the value in TextBox3, the Button3_Click procedure does a couple of verification checks on the value in TextBox3.

- First, the code confirms that the value in the TextBox control represents an integer.

- Second, the code makes sure the represented Integer value is within the range of Integer values for the ContactID column in DotNetTable.

Figure 11-10. *By using ADO.NET capabilities to assign values to form control properties, you can create richly interactive forms.*

The following excerpt is from the top of the `Button3_Click` procedure. This excerpt assigns the value of the `Text` property for `TextBox3` to the `str1` `String` variable before passing the value of `str1` to the `IsInteger` function procedure as the argument of an `If` clause in an `If...End If` statement. If the `IsInteger` function procedure returns a value of `False`, the `Button3_Click` procedure displays a message box about inputting an `Integer` value for the `ContactID` column value before exiting the procedure.

```
Dim str1 As String = Me.TextBox3.Text

'Verify that an Integer value is input and is in
'proper range of values
If IsInteger(str1) = False Then
 MessageBox.Show("Please input an integer as an ID value.", _
   "Warning notice", MessageBoxButtons.OK, MessageBoxIcon.Warning)
 Exit Sub
End If
```

The test in this section for identifying a `String` value as representing an `Integer` value is more rigorous than similar code in the "Returning a Value in a Windows Application" section. The next listing is the code for the `IsInteger` function procedure. Instead of just verifying whether the `str1` `String` value can convert to an `Integer` data type, this function procedure also verifies that the `CDbl` transform of `str1` equals the `CInt` transform of `str1`. Unlike just using the `CInt` function by itself, this test about the equality of the `CDbl` and `CInt` function values correctly detects that 2.2 is not an `Integer` data type value. Using `CInt` by itself cannot rule out 2.2 as an `Integer` data type value.

```
Function IsInteger(ByVal str1 As String) As Boolean
 Dim int1 As Integer

 Try
  int1 = CInt(str1)
  If CDbl(str1) = CInt(str1) Then
   Return True
  End If
 Catch ex As Exception
  Return False
 End Try

End Function
```

The second check for the value in TextBox3 ties together tightly with the code to return the ContactName and ContactID column values, as well as the code to enable the control for editing column values and deleting rows.

- After the check for str1 being an Integer data type value, the Button3_Click procedure invokes the InColRange function from Form2. This function was originally discussed in the "Returning a Value in a Windows Application" section.

- Then, a Select Case...End Select statement processes the return value from InColRange (strReturn).

  - In the event of a Value in range return value from InColRange, the procedure uses a SqlDataReader to extract the ContactName and ContactEAddr values corresponding to the ContactID column value in TextBox3. The procedure assigns the retrieved values to the Text property values for TextBox4 and TextBox5. The procedure also invokes the Sub procedure named DisableEnableUpdateDeleteControls with an argument of Enable. This Sub procedure call enables the controls for editing column values and deleting a row.

  - Any InColRange return value other than Value in range generates helpful feedback via a message box about how to get the return value to Value in range.

```
Dim strReturn As String = _
Form2.InColRange(str1, "ContactID", _
"DotNetTable", cnn1)

Dim rdr1 As SqlDataReader
Select Case strReturn
 Case "Value in range"
  'Define cmd1 and execute it
  Dim cmd1 As New SqlCommand( _
           "SELECT ContactName, ContactEAddr " & _
           "FROM DotNetTable Where ContactID = " & str1, _
           cnn1)
  rdr1 = cmd1.ExecuteReader()
  Try
   If rdr1.HasRows Then
    rdr1.Read()
    Me.TextBox4.Text = rdr1.GetString(0)
    Me.TextBox5.Text = rdr1.GetString(1)
    DisableEnableUpdateDeleteControls("Enable")
   Else
    MessageBox.Show("No contact corresponds to ID value.", _
    "Warning notice", MessageBoxButtons.OK, _
    MessageBoxIcon.Warning)
   End If
  Catch ex As Exception
   MessageBox.Show(ex.Message, "Error message", _
     MessageBoxButtons.OK, MessageBoxIcon.Error)
  Finally
   rdr1.Close()
   cnn1.Close()
  End Try
 Case "Value out of range"
  MessageBox.Show("Please enter another ID value.", _
    "Warning notice", MessageBoxButtons.OK, _
    MessageBoxIcon.Warning)
 Case Else
  MessageBox.Show(strReturn)
End Select
```

The `Button4_Click` procedure updates the `ContactName` and `ContactEAddr` column values for the row with a `ContactID` column value equal to the value represented by the contents of `TextBox3`. While the details of this implementation are unique to this task, the overall process should be very familiar.

- First, you check the input values to make sure they are valid. In this case, that means the values in `TextBox4` and `TextBox5`. Recall that `Button4` is not even enabled until it is known that the value in `TextBox3` is valid.

- Second, you perform an `ExecuteNonQuery` method for a SQL statement that modifies the `DotNetTable` database table. In this case, the modification is to update the `ContactName` and `ContactEAddr` column values with the entries in `TextBox4` and `TextBox5` for the row whose `ContactID` column value matches the entry in `TextBox3`.

The code for the `Button4_Click` procedure is very similar to the code for the `Button2_Click` procedure. However, there are also some critical differences.

- Both procedures use identical code to verify the `TextBox` entries representing `ContactName` and `ContactEAddr` column values. In a production solution, it would be best to invoke this code from a common source, such as a function procedure. In this context, the code is duplicated to simplify the process of understanding each procedure separately.

- The `Button4_Click` procedure is different than the `Button2_Click` procedure in a couple of ways.
  - First, the `Button4_Click` procedure assigns an `UPDATE` statement instead of an `INSERT` statement to the `CommandText` property of a `SqlCommand` object.
  - Second, the `Button4_Click` procedure manages the enabled status for the controls that permit the updating of column values and the deleting of rows.

The following listing shows the first part of the code in `Button4_Click`. As you can see, it checks the values in `TextBox4` and `TextBox5` with condition expressions in an `If...ElseIf...Else...End If` statement. If the `Text` property values for `TextBox4` and `TextBox5` are valid, the `Else` clause assigns a SQL string expression to the `CommandText` property of the `cmd1` `SqlCommand` object declared and instantiated at the top of the listing. The SQL string expression is for an `UPDATE` statement that relies on `Text` property values for `TextBox3`, `TextBox4`, and `TextBox5`.

■**Caution** To keep the focus on the update process and for the sake of simplicity, the following script copies user input directly into a SQL statement. This exposes you to a potential SQL injection attack in which a user inserts SQL statements along with or instead of a requested value. There are multiple defenses against SQL injection attacks, including cleaning and verifying the input before using it in a SQL statement. See the code for the `Button2_Click` procedure in `Form4` for an example of how to filter name and email address input values.

```
Dim cmd1 As New SqlCommand
Dim int_at As Integer = InStr(Me.TextBox5.Text, "@")
Dim int_period As Integer = InStr(int_at, Me.TextBox5.Text, ".")
Dim int_len As Integer = Len(Me.TextBox5.Text)

'Verify name and email and display reminder to fix if not valid;
'otherwise, update existing row
If InStr(Me.TextBox4.Text, ";") > 0 Or _
 InStr(Me.TextBox4.Text, "=") > 0 Or _
 (Len(Me.TextBox4.Text) = 0) Or _
 (Len(Me.TextBox4.Text) > 25) Then
```

```
  MessageBox.Show("Invalid Name.   Please fix name.")
  Exit Sub
ElseIf Not (int_at > 0 And int_period > 0 And int_len >= 8) Then
  MessageBox.Show("Invalid email address.", "Please fix it")
  Exit Sub
Else
  cmd1.CommandText = "UPDATE DotNetTable " & _
    "SET ContactName = '" & Me.TextBox4.Text & "', " & _
    "ContactEAddr = '" & Me.TextBox5.Text & "' " & _
    "WHERE ContactID = " & Me.TextBox3.Text
  cmd1.Connection = cnn1
End If
```

The remainder of the Button4_Click procedure executes the SQL statement in the cmd1 SqlCommand object and manages the Enabled property for the controls, permitting the updating of column values and the deleting of a row. A Try...Catch...Finally statement contains the code for these tasks. The code in the Try clause invokes the ExecuteNonQuery method for the SQL string in the cmd1 SqlCommand object. After this code completes successfully, the Finally clause closes the cnn1 Connection and disables the controls for changing the DotNetTable database table. If a runtime error occurs for any reason, the Catch clause provides feedback about the source of the problem before executing the code in the Finally clause.

```
Try
  cnn1.Open()
  cmd1.ExecuteNonQuery()
Catch ex As Exception
  MessageBox.Show(ex.Message)
Finally
  cnn1.Close()
  DisableEnableUpdateDeleteControls("Disable")
End Try
```

The Button5_Click procedure allows users to delete a row from the DotNetTable. It divides this task into three steps.

1. First, the procedure verifies that the user specifies a row in DotNetTable. The procedure accomplishes this by checking that the entry in TextBox3 is an integer and is in the range of values for the ContactID column of DotNetTable.

2. Then, the procedure constructs a SQL string to delete a row based on the verified ContactID value.

3. Third, the procedure executes a SqlCommand object to complete the task and manage the Enabled property value of selected controls on Form4.

This chapter previously discussed the pieces of code cobbled together in the Button5_Click procedure. For example, code to verify that the user specifies a row in the DotNetTable database table was described initially in the discussion of the Button2_Click procedure. Button2_Click, Button3_Click, and Button4_Click demonstrated how to construct a SQL statement for use with a SqlCommand object. The code for invoking a SqlCommand object and managing controls in Button5_Click is exactly the same as in Button4_Click. Because of these similarities, the code for Button5_Click appears without further comment (except for the comments in the code sample).

```
'Verify that an Integer value is input and is in
'proper range of values
Dim str1 As String = Me.TextBox3.Text
If IsInteger(str1) = False Then
 MessageBox.Show("Please input an integer as an ID value.", _
    "Warning notice", MessageBoxButtons.OK, MessageBoxIcon.Warning)
 Exit Sub
End If

Dim strReturn As String = _
Form2.InColRange(str1, "ContactID", _
"DotNetTable", cnn1)


'Create a command to delete a row
Dim cmd1 As New SqlCommand
cmd1.CommandText = "DELETE FROM DotNetTable " & _
  " WHERE ContactID = " & Me.TextBox3.Text
cmd1.Connection = cnn1

'Invoke the command
Try
 'cnn1.Open()
 cmd1.ExecuteNonQuery()
Catch ex As Exception
 MessageBox.Show(ex.Message)
Finally
 cnn1.Close()
 DisableEnableUpdateDeleteControls("Disable")
End Try
```

Summary

This chapter introduced you to the basics of programming ADO.NET, which is your database programming interface from VBE and VWDE. In addition to teaching you about ADO.NET classes, the chapter demonstrated how to use ADO.NET classes to perform many traditional kinds of database chores. You learned how to use ADO.NET to retrieve data from a database and manipulate data in a database. You also focused on using ADO.NET in coordination with Windows and Web Forms—especially Windows Forms.

The next chapter will add to this discussion by describing DataAdapter and DataSet objects. These objects allow you to work with the data from a database on the client side and give you a rich set of functions to do so.

CHAPTER 12

Programming DataAdapter and DataSet Objects

As we saw in the previous chapter, Command objects offer the ability to run any SQL statement within a database server, such as SQL Server Express (SSE), and DataReader objects provide a fast way of retrieving data from a database. However, neither Command nor DataReader classes offer a rich client-side representation of database data, nor do they simplify client-side editing of the data in a database. The combination of the DataAdapter and DataSet classes provides these and other benefits to database developers.

You can think of a DataAdapter object as a two-way pump for exchanging data between a database and a client application. Each DataAdapter object can handle the exchange of data between one data source in a database and one DataTable object, which may optionally reside in a DataSet object. Think of the data source as the list items in a SELECT statement for a Command object. In fact, the Fill method for a DataAdapter object can create a DataTable object when it initializes the DataTable object.

Any one DataSet object can hold multiple DataTable objects. You can populate each DataTable object with an associated DataAdapter object. Each DataAdapter object has a SelectCommand property, which gets or sets a Command object wrapping a SQL statement or a stored procedure name used to select data from a database.

- Use a CommandType property value of CommandType.Text for a SqlCommand object wrapping a SQL statement.

- For a SqlCommand object wrapping a stored procedure name, use CommandType.StoredProcedure for the CommandType setting of the SqlCommand for the SelectCommand property.

The data pumped to a client-side data repository, such as a DataTable object in a DataSet object, are disconnected from the server-side database. That is, the DataAdapter object opens a Connection object to a database before attempting to retrieve data from a database. Then, the DataAdapter object closes the Connection object after the attempt completes. The retrieved data are available for manipulation while they are disconnected from the database server. You can add new rows to a DataTable object, change column values for one or more rows in a DataTable, or delete one or more rows in a DataTable.

Tip Your code does not need to open and close a Connection object that a DataAdapter object uses, because a DataAdapter object manages its own Connection object.

After an application makes one or more changes to a disconnected data source, it is common to want to pass the changes back to the database. You can use the Update method for a DataAdapter object to return data from a disconnected data source to a database table or view. Again, the DataAdapter object manages the status of a Connection object for the task by opening the object before the attempt to pass changes back to a database.

The Update method can process one updated row or multiple updated rows at a time. Processing multiple rows yields performance benefits but can complicate matters when passing the local changes to the data source.

■Tip Because batch processing updates can complicate the transfer of any changes, avoid batch processing updates until you become very familiar with the basics of data manipulation for DataAdapters and DataSets.

Just as data retrieval with a DataAdapter relies on the SelectCommand property of a DataAdapter, transferring local inserts, updates, and deletes to a database from a DataSet object depends on the InsertCommand, UpdateCommand, and DeleteCommand properties of a DataAdapter object. These DataAdapter properties correspond to Command objects that wrap SQL INSERT, UPDATE, and DELETE statements.

ADO.NET requires the use of parameters for SQL statements implementing data manipulation through a DataAdapter object. Some parameters, such as those denoting primary key values for a row, typically need to point at original values copied from a database source. Other parameter values need to represent new or changed values so that they can update the database.

When designating parameters, you must give their name, data type, value, and version (original or changed). The settings are not the same for parameters referring to the InsertCommand, UpdateCommand, and DeleteCommand properties. For example, parameters for an UpdateCommand must have at least one parameter referencing a new or updated value and one or more parameters referencing an original value. The original value enables your application to find the row in the database source to which to apply the new or updated value. By contrast, the parameters for an InsertCommand property can all reference new values, because there are no old values to match.

This chapter introduces you to the basics of creating DataSet objects, such as creating one and using more than one DataTable object in a DataSet object. You'll also learn how to sort and filter the values in a DataTable object with a DataView object. Next, this chapter illustrates how to make changes to a table in a database from a DataTable in a client application. The next-to-last sample in the chapter shows how to enable a user to browse through data one row at a time with a form. The chapter closes with a sample that demonstrates how to use the new SqlBulkCopy class to populate a database table from an Excel workbook. This sample relies on a DataTable object to facilitate the data transfer.

Creating, Populating, and Using DataSet Objects

The samples to this point in the chapter used Imports statements for the System.Data.SqlClient or System.Data.OleDb namespaces. Connection and Command objects reside in these namespaces for SQL Server and OLE DB data sources. The SqlDataAdapter class also resides in the System.Data.SqlClient namespace. However, the DataSet class resides in the System.Data namespace. All the samples are for SqlDataAdapters and DataSet objects, so our module starts with two Imports statements for the System.Data and System.Data.SqlClient namespaces.

Creating, Populating, and Iterating Through DataSets

The first SqlDataAdapter sample works from the Click event procedure for Button1 in a new form. It starts by specifying two String values. Each String value specifies a SQL statement for the AdventureWorks database. We declare a variable (cnn1) for connecting to the AdventureWorks database at the module level. The first SQL statement (strQuery1) returns two columns from the ProductCategory table in the Production schema. The second SQL statement (strQuery2) also returns two columns from the ProductSubcategory table in the Production schema.

The SQL statements along with the cnn1 variable are necessary for instantiating two SqlDataAdapters. Each SqlDataAdapter creates a DataTable object in the das1 DataSet object, which is also declared at the module level. The process of creating the DataTable objects with a SqlDataAdapter takes place in the TwoDTsInADS function procedure. This procedure takes two String arguments for the SQL statements and returns a DataSet object containing two DataTable objects corresponding to the SQL statement.

```
'Specify query statements to populate DataTables in DataSet
Dim strQuery1 As String = _
 "SELECT ProductCategoryID, Name " & _
 "FROM Production.ProductCategory"
Dim strQuery2 As String = _
 "SELECT ProductCategoryID, " & _
 "ProductSubcategoryID, Name " & _
 "FROM Production.ProductSubcategory"

das1 = TwoDTsInADS(strQuery1, strQuery2)
```

The code inside TwoDTsInADS is shown next. By the way, this procedure has a Friend access modifier to facilitate its use elsewhere. The TwoDTsInADS procedure uses one of the constructors for SqlDataAdapter objects. The constructor specifies the SQL statement for the SelectCommand property of each SqlDataAdapter object with one of the String arguments passed to the function procedure. The dapCategories SqlDataAdapter corresponds to strQuery1 in the Button1_Click procedure, and the dapSubcategories SqlDataAdapter uses strQuery2 from the Button1_Click procedure.

Before using the SqlDataAdapter objects to pump data from the AdventureWorks database to the client application, the code needs a receptacle to store the data. The declaration for das1 at the top of the module declares the variable, but the module-level statement does not instantiate the DataSet object (the New keyword is not used as part of the declaration). Therefore, TwoDTsInADS performs this task after instantiating the two SqlDataAdapter objects.

By invoking the Fill method for each SqlDataAdapter, TwoDTsInADS copies data from the database to a DataTable in the das1 DataSet. The Fill method can take two arguments: the name of the DataSet in which to transfer data and the name of the DataTable. If the DataTable object does not already exist, the Fill method can create and populate the DataTable in a single step. The dapCategories SqlDataAdapter creates a DataTable named ProductCategories, and the dapSubcategories SqlDataAdapter creates a second DataTable named ProductSubcategories. The concluding Return statement passes the populated das1 DataSet back to the calling procedure (Button1_Click).

```
'Declare and instantiate first DataAdapter object
Dim dapCategories As SqlDataAdapter = _
New SqlDataAdapter(strQuery1, cnn1)

'Declare and instantiate second DataAdapter object
Dim dapSubcategories As SqlDataAdapter = _
New SqlDataAdapter(strQuery2, cnn1)

'Declare and instantiate the das1 DataSet
Dim das1 As New DataSet

'Fill the das1 DataSet with two different DataAdapter objects
dapCategories.Fill(das1, "ProductCategories")
dapSubcategories.Fill(das1, "ProductSubcategories")

Return das1
```

After `Button1_Click` receives the das1 DataSet, the procedure examines the DataSet object from three different perspectives. The following excerpt illustrates the syntax for two ways of examining the das1 DataSet. A call to the `DisplayDTsInADS` implements a third way to examine the DataSet.

- The first way of examining the contents of the das1 DataSet iterates through the Tables collection in the DataSet.

  - On each pass through the Tables collection, the code saves the TableName property value for the current DataTable in a String variable that is formatted with carriage returns and linefeeds for display in a message box.

  - The invocation of the Show method for the MessageBox class displays the String variable containing the DataTable names.

  - These names, ProductCategories and ProductSubcategories, are assigned during the two invocations of the Fill method in the TwoDTsInADS procedure.

- The second way of examining the contents of the das1 DataSet is to display the first column value in the first row of the first DataTable (4) and the last column in the last row of the last DataTable (Tires and Tubes) within the DataSet.

  - The expression for the first value is das1.Tables(0).Rows(0)(0). You can refer to the DataTables within a DataSet by a zero-based index number, meaning zero points at the first table. Each DataTable has a Rows collection with a zero-based index. The last zero in the expression points at the first column in the Columns collection within the first row.

  - The expression for the last column value in the last row of the last DataTable is das1.Tables(das1.Tables.Count - 1).Rows(36)(2). The das1.Tables.Count - 1 part of the expression points at the last DataTable in the das1 DataSet. Similar syntax is available in the following note for designating the last row and the last column, but I elected to simplify the expression and use constant values to designate the last row and column index values.

Tip The following expression shows the syntax for computing the index value of the last row in the DataTable with an index value of int1 within the das1 DataSet: das1.Tables(int1).Rows.Count - 1. The next expression shows the syntax for computing the index value of the last column in the DataTable with an index value of int1 within the das1 DataSet: das1.Tables(int1).Columns.Count - 1.

```
Dim str1 As String = ""
For Each dtb1 As DataTable In das1.Tables
 str1 += dtb1.TableName & ControlChars.Cr
Next
MessageBox.Show( _
 "The das1 dataset has " & das1.Tables.Count.ToString & _
 " table(s).  The table name(s) are:" & ControlChars.CrLf & str1)

MsgBox("First cell in first row of first table:" & _
 ControlChars.CrLf & das1.Tables(0).Rows(0)(0).ToString & _
 ControlChars.CrLf & _
 "Last cell in last row of last table:" & _
 ControlChars.CrLf & _
 das1.Tables(das1.Tables.Count - 1).Rows(36)(2).ToString)

DisplayDTsInADS(das1)
```

As you can see from the preceding statement, a call to the `DisplayDTsInADS` procedure implements the third way of examining the contents of the `das1` `DataSet`. Instead of just displaying two values, the `DisplayDTsInADS` procedure displays all the column values for each row within all the `DataTables` within a `DataSet` object. While the current sample `DataSet` has two `DataTables` with 4 rows in the first `DataTable` and 37 rows in the second `DataTable`, the following code from the `DisplayDTsInADS` procedure will work with any number of `DataTables` having any number of rows and columns. The code contains three nested loops.

- The outer loop iterates through the `Tables` collection of a `DataSet` object.

- The middle loop iterates through the `Rows` collection of each successive `DataTable`.

- The inner loop iterates through the `Columns` collection of each successive `DataTable` for each row within a `DataTable`.

```
Dim str1 As String
'Demo the syntax for iterating through all cell values in all
'DataTable objects within the das1 DataSet object
str1 = ""
For Each dtb1 As DataTable In das1.Tables
 str1 += "Rows for " & dtb1.TableName & _
  Microsoft.VisualBasic.StrDup(2, ControlChars.CrLf)
 For Each drw1 As DataRow In das1.Tables(dtb1.TableName).Rows
  For Each dcl1 As DataColumn In _
   das1.Tables(dtb1.TableName).Columns
   str1 += drw1(dcl1.ColumnName).ToString & ", "
  Next
  str1 = Microsoft.VisualBasic.Left(str1, Len(str1) - 2)
  str1 += ControlChars.CrLf
 Next
 str1 += ControlChars.CrLf
Next dtb1
MessageBox.Show(str1)
```

The output from the `ProductCategories` `DataTable` is shown in alphabetical order by `Name` column values. The output from the `ProductSubcategories` `DataTable` is shown in the order of `ProductSubcategoryID` column values from 1 through 37. The most significant point is that the rows appear in a different sort order depending on which database table is used as the source for a `DataTable`.

Returning Sorted Values to a DataTable

One way of obtaining consistently sorted column values across `DataTables` is to work with sorted values. When working with ADO.NET `DataSet` objects, there are at least a couple of ways of generating rows in a `DataTable` sorted by one or more column values.

- First, you can sort the values on a database server. This approach returns a sorted list of values from a database server to a `DataTable` in a client application. The sample in this section demonstrates this approach.

- Second, you can sort the values locally in a client application. This approach can save time from recovering values from a database server by re-sorting the values in a `DataTable` without having to repopulate the `DataTable` from a database server. The "Setting Up to Use DataViews" section demonstrates how to sort `DataTable` values with a `DataView` object.

The GroupBox control below Button1 contains two radio buttons and a Button control (Button2). RadioButton1 has a Text property value of Alphabetical, and RadioButton2 has a Text property value of ProductCategoryID. The form's Load procedure initially selects RadioButton1 when the form loads. However, the user can change the default selection so that rows from both sets appear sorted by ProductCategoryID column values instead of Name column values. Clicking Button1 generates a DataTable of sorted column values based on either ProductCategoryID or Name column values.

Figure 12-1 shows the output from clicking Button2 on two successive occasions. The output displays the rows for the ProductCategories and ProductSubcategories DataTable objects in alphabetical order on the left and ProductCategoryID column values on the right. Because several different factors can control the sort order of rows in a DataTable, it is always wise to specify a sort order when you need the results sorted one way or another.

Figure 12-1. *You can change the order of values in a DataTable by using a different ORDER BY clause to populate a DataTable.*

The next listing shows the code inside the `Button2_Click` procedure. The most novel feature of the procedure is an `If…Else…End If` statement. The condition for the `If` clause of the statement evaluates whether `RadioButton1` has been selected. If `RadioButton1` is checked, the code will assign SQL statements to the `strQuery1` and `strQuery2` variables that sort the rows of a result set by `Name`. Otherwise, the `Else` clause will use SQL statements that sort the rows for the `ProductCategories` and `ProductSubcategories` DataTables by `ProductCategoryID` column values.

After assigning statements to the `strQuery1` and `strQuery2` variables, the code uses the statements with two procedure calls. First, a call to the `TwoDTsInADS` procedure generates the `ProductCategories` and `ProductSubcategories` DataTables. Second, a call to the `DisplayDTsInADS` procedure displays the values of both DataTables in a single message box. Figure 12-1 shows the output sorted by `Name` column values or `ProductCategoryID` column values.

```
Dim strQuery1 As String = ""
Dim strQuery2 As String = ""

'Order DataTable rows by Name or ProductCategoryID
'column values
If Me.RadioButton1.Checked Then
  strQuery1 = _
    "SELECT ProductCategoryID, Name " & _
    "FROM Production.ProductCategory " & _
    "ORDER BY Name"
  strQuery2 = _
    "SELECT ProductCategoryID, " & _
    "ProductSubcategoryID, Name " & _
    "FROM Production.ProductSubcategory " & _
    "ORDER BY Name"
Else
  strQuery1 = _
    "SELECT ProductCategoryID, Name " & _
    "FROM Production.ProductCategory " & _
    "ORDER BY ProductCategoryID"
  strQuery2 = _
    "SELECT ProductCategoryID, " & _
    "ProductSubcategoryID, Name " & _
    "FROM Production.ProductSubcategory " & _
    "ORDER BY ProductCategoryID"
End If

'Dim das1 As DataSet
das1 = TwoDTsInADS(strQuery1, strQuery2)

DisplayDTsInADS(das1)
```

Assigning DataTable Values to ListBox Controls

One of the most popular reasons for downloading data from a database server is to display it in a control on a form. This section describes two approaches to populating a `ListBox` control on a Windows Form. The first is how to assign a column of values from a `DataTable` to display in a `ListBox`. One especially nice feature of this approach is that you do not have to iterate through the rows in the `DataTable`. The second is demonstrated by a sample that conditionally populates a second `ListBox` control based on the currently selected item in the first `ListBox` control. The contents of the second `ListBox` control are updated whenever a user picks a new item from the first `ListBox` control.

Figure 12-2 shows the two ListBox controls in operation. Clicking the Button control (Button3) above the first ListBox on the left (ListBox1) populates ListBox1 with the Name column values from the ProductCategories DataTable. Initially, ListBox1 opens with the Accessories item selected. This item is from the first row in the ProductCategories DataTable. After populating ListBox1, the second ListBox control (ListBox2) shows the Name column values for matching items by ProductCategoryID from the ProductSubcategories DataTable. When a user selects another ListBox1 item, such as Bikes, the items showing in ListBox2 update to show Name column values for the most recently selected item from the ProductSubcategories DataTable.

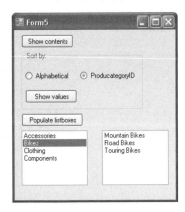

Figure 12-2. *You can conditionally populate a second ListBox control based on a selection from an initial ListBox control.*

The code to achieve the functionality depicted in Figure 12-2 is remarkably easy. The code in the Button3_Click procedure, which is shown next, initially populates ListBox1. This procedure has two parts.

- The procedure begins by populating the ProductCategories and ProductSubcategories DataTable objects. The code does this by calling the TwoDTsInADS procedure after specifying two String variables with SQL statements.

- The last two statements in the Button3_Click procedure assign the Name column values from the ProductCategories DataTable to ListBox1. No iterating is required with this approach.

  - The ProductCategories DataTable is the first DataTable in the das1 DataSet, so it has a table index value of 0. The following code uses the das1.Tables(0) expression to assign the whole DataTable to the DataSource property of ListBox1.

  - To show a particular column, you must specify the column name as the DisplayMember property for ListBox1.

```
Dim strQuery1 As String = _
  "SELECT ProductCategoryID, Name " & _
  "FROM Production.ProductCategory"
Dim strQuery2 As String = _
  "SELECT ProductCategoryID, " & _
  "ProductSubcategoryID, Name " & _
  "FROM Production.ProductSubcategory"
das1 = TwoDTsInADS(strQuery1, strQuery2)

Me.ListBox1.DataSource = das1.Tables(0)
Me.ListBox1.DisplayMember = "Name"
```

The `ListBox1_SelectedIndexChanged` procedure controls the items that show in `ListBox2`. The procedure runs whenever there is a change to the selected item in `ListBox1`. This happens when the `Button1_Click` procedure initially populates `ListBox1`. It also happens when a user selects a new item from `ListBox1`.

The code for the `ListBox1_SelectedIndexChanged` procedure is shown next. It starts by clearing the `Items` collection for `ListBox2` to remove any prior items showing in `ListBox2`. Next, a loop iterates through the rows of the second `DataTable` in the `das1` `DataSet` (`das1.Tables(1)`). This is the `ProductSubcategories` `DataTable`. An `If...End If` statement within the loop copies the `Name` column value for any row in the `ProductSubcategories` `DataTable` with a matching `ProductCategoryID` column value to the currently selected item in `ListBox1`.

```
Me.ListBox2.Items.Clear()
For Each drw1 As DataRow In das1.Tables(1).Rows
 If CInt(drw1("ProductCategoryID")) = _
 CInt(das1.Tables(0).Rows( _
 Me.ListBox1.SelectedIndex)("ProductCategoryID")) Then
 Me.ListBox2.Items.Add(drw1("Name"))
 End If
Next
```

Sorting and Filtering DataTables with DataViews

Sorting and filtering are two core tasks of any database application. Therefore, it is not unsurprising that ADO.NET gives you more than one way to perform these tasks. This section highlights how to implement sorting and filtering for values in `DataTable` objects. Unlike the preceding sorting and filtering samples, the approaches described in this section do not sort data in a database and then transfer the sorted or filtered values to a `DataTable` object. Instead, they operate on `DataTables` that can be populated from any source, including a database.

This section depicts `DataView` objects as a way of sorting and filtering values in a `DataTable`. A `DataView` object returns the values in a `DataTable` object. There are two main approaches to implementing sorting and filtering with `DataView`.

- You can dynamically assign sorting and filtering criteria to a single `DataView` object so that it can show the same values sorted or filtered in different ways.

- You can instantiate multiple `DataView` objects for the same `DataTable`. Then, you can assign different sorting or filtering criteria to each `DataView`. This approach allows you to recover a specialized view of a `DataTable` object without performing any new sorting or filtering each time you use the `DataView` object.

You may be wondering why you need more than one way to implement sorting and filtering. Why isn't it good enough to always retrieve data from a database whenever you need data sorted or filtered?

- If your data do not come from a database, then the ability to sort and filter data in a database before transferring them to a `DataTable` is totally useless.

- Another consideration is that there is a performance cost of retrieving data from a database. If you can reuse data that you already retrieved, you can save the cost of retrieving the same data again with a different sort order or slightly different filtering.

Tip You can drag a `DataGridView` control to a form from the Data section of the Toolbox.

Setting Up to Use DataViews

A DataView is an ADO.NET object. As such, you must declare, instantiate, and specify it before you can use it. Furthermore, it is quite common to instantiate a view in one procedure, such as a Load event procedure for a form, and then use the DataView object in another procedure, such as the Click event procedure for a Button. As a result, it's common to declare DataView objects at the module level or with a Public access modifier so that you can refer to them throughout a module or project or even from other projects.

The module-level declarations and the beginning of the Load event procedure for our DataView example are shown next. The end of the Load event procedure merely formats the controls on the form. You declare a variable as having a DataView type with a Dim statement. Three module-level declarations for vewOName, vewOProductCategoryID, and vewFiltered illustrate this syntax. Notice these declarations do not include the New keyword so that they do not populate the variables with DataView objects.

The code to assign DataView objects to the module-level variables declared at the module level is shown within the Load procedure after the creation of the das1 DataSet based on two SQL statements used in the last several examples. You can instantiate a DataView object with the New keyword and by basing it on a DataTable. For example, the assignment statement vewOName = New DataView(das1.Tables(0)) creates a new DataView based on the first DataTable in the das1 DataSet.

The next statement specifies an ascending sort order based on Name column values for the rows in the vewOName DataView. The specification of the vewOProductCategoryID DataView is the same as the vewOName DataView, except that the sort order is ascending based on ProductCategoryID column values.

The vewFiltered Dataview is based on the second DataTable (das1.Tables(1)) in the das1 DataSet. A New keyword instantiates the DataView object. However, there is no specification of how the view is supposed to work, because the Button4_Click procedure dynamically assigns a filter to the DataView object at runtime. In this way, the rows in the DataView can change based on the currently selected item from a ListBox.

```
Dim cnn1 As SqlConnection = _
    New System.Data.SqlClient.SqlConnection( _
    "Data Source=.\sqlexpress;" & _
    "Integrated Security=True;" & _
    "Initial Catalog=AdventureWorks")

Dim das1 As DataSet
Dim vewOName As DataView
Dim vewOProductCategoryID As DataView
Dim vewFiltered As DataView

Private Sub Form6_Load(ByVal sender As Object, _
ByVal e As System.EventArgs) Handles Me.Load

 Dim strQuery1 As String = _
  "SELECT ProductCategoryID, Name " & _
  "FROM Production.ProductCategory"
 Dim strQuery2 As String = _
  "SELECT ProductCategoryID, " & _
  "ProductSubcategoryID, Name " & _
  "FROM Production.ProductSubcategory"

 das1 = Form5.TwoDTsInADS(strQuery1, strQuery2)
```

```
vewOName = New DataView(das1.Tables(0))
vewOName.Sort = "Name"

vewOProductCategoryID = New DataView(das1.Tables(0))
vewOProductCategoryID.Sort = "ProductCategoryID"

vewFiltered = New DataView(das1.Tables(1))
```

Showing the Values in a DataView

A DataView object offers a view of the values in a DataTable. Therefore, a DataView has the same number and order of columns as the DataTable used to define the DataView. This is an important consideration because a DataTable has a richer structure than a DataView. You can use the structure of a DataTable used to define a DataView and to navigate through the elements of a DataView.

The Button1_Click and the PrintView procedures jointly demonstrate how to view the values in the vewOName and vewOProductCategoryID DataView objects.

- The Button1_Click procedure has two calls for the PrintView procedure.
  - The first call invokes the PrintView procedure for the vewOName DataView.
  - The second PrintView call is for the vewOProductCategoryID DataView.
- The PrintView procedure takes three arguments: the name of a DataView for which to display values, the index value for a DataTable in the das1 DataSet, and a String value that specifies a heading for the report of the DataView values.
  - The declaration of the das1 variable as a DataSet is at the module level. The variable is assigned a value in the Load procedure.
  - The PrintView procedure is quite general and will work for any DataView based on a DataTable in the das1 DataSet.

The following listing shows the code inside the Button1_Click procedure. Each procedure call for PrintView specifies three argument values.

```
PrintView(vewOName, 0, _
 "ProductCategory by Name")

PrintView(vewOProductCategoryID, 0, _
  "ProductCategory by ProductCategoryID")
```

The PrintView procedure uses two nested For loops to iterate through successive columns of each row within the name of the DataView passed to it. The outer For loop passes through the rows of the view. The Count property returns the number of rows in a DataView. A DataView object does not have a Columns collection, but you can use the Columns collection for a DataView's underlying DataTable to pass through the columns of a DataView.

The inner loop for the code in the PrintView procedure demonstrates the syntax for accomplishing this goal. The PrintView procedure constructs a String variable (str1) with the column values for successive rows in a DataView. The procedure concludes by passing str1 to the Show method of the MessageBox class to present a message box with the values.

```
Sub PrintView(ByVal vew As DataView, _
ByVal tabindx As Integer, _
ByVal RepTitle As String)
```

```
Dim str1 As String = RepTitle & StrDup(2, ControlChars.CrLf)

For int1 As Integer = 0 To vew.Count - 1
 For int2 As Integer = 0 To das1.Tables(tabindx).Columns.Count - 1
  str1 += vew(int1)(int2).ToString & ", "
 Next
 str1 = Microsoft.VisualBasic.Left(str1, Len(str1) - 2)
 str1 += ControlChars.CrLf
Next

MsgBox(str1)

End Sub
```

Changing the Sort Order in a DataGridView Control

The DataGridView control is a new control introduced with Visual Basic Express (the control is also available in other Visual Studio 2005 editions). The DataGridView is Microsoft's latest generation of a grid control for displaying data in a tabular format. A comparable ASP.NET control, the GridView control, exists with the same name for Web Forms that you can use with Visual Web Developer Express.

As mentioned previously, you can instantiate multiple views of a DataTable to present values in any of several different sorted orders. Although you can display DataView values with a message box, it is more common to see them in grids. There is a natural congruence between a DataGridView control and a DataView object. A DataView object holds multiple column values for multiple rows, and a DataGridView control can display multiple columns of data for multiple rows. This congruence makes it especially easy to assign a DataView for display in a DataGridView control.

If you have more than one DataView object based on a DataTable object, it is especially easy to dynamically change the view showing in a DataGridView control based on user actions or environmental variables. For example, you can show one view of data for one user or for users in one role, and you can show a different view of data for another user or users in another role. Another scenario is one where you display sales data by sales person, region, or customer. You can provide other controls, such as a Button control or a ListBox control, to let a user determine which view of some data will be shown in a DataGridView control.

Button2 and Button3 populate the DataGridView1 control with ProductCategories DataTable values sorted by Name column values or ProductCategoryID column values. Recall that two DataView objects created in the Load event procedure create two views that show values these two different ways. The vew0Name DataView makes rows of data available sorted by Name column values. The vew0ProductCategoryID DataView makes rows of data available sorted by ProductCategoryID column values.

By assigning either the vew0Name DataView or vew0ProductCategoryID DataView to the DataSource property of a DataGrid control, you can dynamically change how data display in a DataGridView control. Figure 12-3 shows DataGridView1 control with two different views of values from the same DataTable. Clicking the Sort by name button assigns the vew0Name DataView to the DataSource property of DataGridView1, and the rows instantly appear sorted as they are in the left pane. Clicking the Sort by ID button assigns the vew0ProductCategoryID DataView to the DataSource property of DataGridView1. The new assignment to the DataSource property instantly arranges the rows in the order shown in the right pane of Figure 12-3.

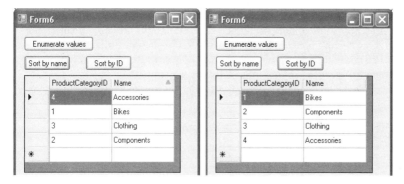

Figure 12-3. *DataView objects can facilitate controlling the order of rows in a DataGridView control.*

The Sort by name and Sort by ID buttons correspond, respectively, to the `Button2` and `Button3` controls. The `Click` event procedure for these `Button` controls requires just one line of code to change the order of the rows in the `DataGridView1` control. For example, the statement in the `Button2_Click` procedure is

```
Me.DataGridView1.DataSource = vewOName
```

By contrast, the instruction in the `Button3_Click` procedure is

```
Me.DataGridView1.DataSource = vewOProductCategoryID
```

Dynamically Filtering ListBox Items

The bottom portion of our form works identically to the bottom portion of the form from the "Creating, Populating, and Iterating Through DataSets" section. However, the code behind the operation of the form is radically different. The code for making the items showing in the second `ListBox` control conditional on the currently selected item in the first `ListBox` control is shorter. This is because we're using `DataView` objects to populate the `ListBox` controls.

Figure 12-4 shows the Button control and two `ListBox` controls. Clicking the Populate listboxes button (`Button4`) populates `ListBox1`, the `ListBox` control on the left, with the contents of `Name` column values from the `vewOName` `DataView` object. The population of the `ListBox1` control by the `vewOName` view fires the `SelectedIndexChanged` event procedure for `ListBox1`. This procedure also fires whenever a user changes the selected item in `ListBox1`. For example, Figure 12-4 shows `ListBox2` showing component items because of the selection of the Components item from `ListBox1`.

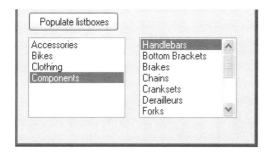

Figure 12-4. *A DataView object can simplify conditionally populating a second ListBox control based on a selection from an initial ListBox control.*

The `Button4_Click` procedure has just two lines of code (see the following listing). To ensure that product category names appear in alphabetical order, the code assigns the `vewOName` DataView object to the `DataSource` property for `ListBox1`. In addition, the `DisplayMember` property is set equal to `Name` for the column with the same name in the DataView. This syntax is similar to using a `DataTable` object to define the items in a `ListBox` control. However, using a `DataView` object as the data source for a `ListBox` control allows you to specify a sort order without relying on an `ORDER BY` clause in the `SELECT` statement used to define `DataTable` object.

```
Me.ListBox1.DataSource = vewOName
Me.ListBox1.DisplayMember = "Name"
```

The `ListBox1_SelectedIndexChanged` procedure assigns a `String` variable to the `RowFilter` property of the `vewFiltered` DataView. The syntax for the contents of the `String` variable is similar to that for the `WHERE` clause of a `SELECT` statement—that is, a column name is set equal to some criterion value. In the case of the event procedure, the criterion value is the `ProductCategoryID` column value from `vewOName` that matches the currently selected item from `ListBox1`.

By setting the `vewFiltered` DataView object as the `DataSource` property for `ListBox2` and the `DisplayMember` property of `ListBox2` to the value of "Name," `ListBox2` shows product subcategory items conditional on the product category selected in `ListBox1`.

```
vewFiltered.RowFilter = _
  "ProductCategoryID = " & _
  vewOName(CInt(Me.ListBox1.SelectedIndex)) _
  ("ProductCategoryID").ToString

Me.ListBox2.DataSource = vewFiltered
Me.ListBox2.DisplayMember = "Name"
```

Inserting, Updating, and Deleting Rows

`DataAdapter`, `DataSet`, and `DataTable` objects team up together to facilitate inserting, updating, and deleting rows in a data source in a database. Modifying a database via a `DataAdapter` is a three-step process.

- First, specify one or more `DataTables` based on data sources in a database.

- Next, insert, change, or delete rows for the `DataTables` in the client application.

- Finally, send the changes made to the `DataTables` to the corresponding database data sources.

One nice feature of using a `DataAdapter` to make changes to databases is that you do not have to be familiar with SQL. All you need to do is modify a `DataTable` using ADO.NET features. Sending changes to a database can be as simple as executing one method (`Update`) for a `DataAdapter`.

Another benefit of using `DataAdapters` to update a database is that this technique scales well as you add more users. Because Express suite packages, such as Visual Basic Express and even SSE, are primarily for small groups of users, this is less of a consideration than for Visual Studio 2005 developers using one of the commercial versions of SQL Server 2005. With Web applications, be particularly careful about using `DataAdapters` as a vehicle for making changes to a database, because the values in one or more `DataTable` objects may have to make a round trip as a page goes from the server to the browser and back again to the server. As the amount of data in `DataTable` objects becomes large, performance may slow down.

A DataAdapter that enables data modification needs specifications for its InsertCommand, UpdateCommand, and DeleteCommand properties. Just as the SelectCommand property supports transferring data from a database to a DataTable in a client application, the InsertCommand, UpdateCommand, and DeleteCommand properties support transferring changes from a DataTable object to a database table. The Command objects for the properties enabling data modification wrap INSERT, UPDATE, and DELETE statements for a database.

Note If you have permission to create stored procedures, or if someone else created them for you, the InsertCommand, UpdateCommand, and DeleteCommand properties can refer to stored procedures instead of INSERT, UPDATE, or DELETE statements. See the beginning of the "Programming Command Objects" section in Chapter 11 for a reference to a slide presentation covering this topic. You can also review the "Performing Data Manipulation" section in Chapter 7 for T-SQL of stored procedures that perform data manipulation.

The SQL statements for the InsertCommand, UpdateCommand, and DeleteCommand properties involve the use of parameters for the Command objects. Some parameters need to refer to values originally copied from a database. Other parameters need to refer to new values for adding to, modifying, or deleting values within a database; the mix of different types of parameters changes for InsertCommand, UpdateCommand, or DeleteCommand properties. In addition, if you are modifying more than one table, you will need a whole new set of these tricky parameter specifications for each DataAdapter that you use.

One way to avoid specifying parameters for the InsertCommand, UpdateCommand, and DeleteCommand properties of a DataAdapter object is to use a CommandBuilder object. A CommandBuilder object automatically constructs these properties based on the SelectCommand property for a DataAdapter object.

CommandBuilder objects are provider specific, so there is no generic CommandBuilder type for use with all kinds of databases, which means you should use a SqlCommandBuilder object when working with an SSE database and an OleDbCommandBuilder object when using an Access database. A CommandBuilder object works against a single database table, so you cannot use a CommandBuilder object with a SelectCommand property based on a database view that references two or more tables.

Tip The DataAdapter Configuration Wizard can automatically create a DataAdapter object, including its InsertCommand, UpdateCommand, and DeleteCommand properties. Chapter 13 drills down on the use of graphical development tools, including the DataAdapter Configuration Wizard.

Another way of avoiding the writing of SQL statements for InsertCommand, UpdateCommand, and DeleteCommand properties is to perform data modification with Command objects that wrap SQL INSERT, UPDATE, and DELETE statements. The syntax for these wrapped SQL statements is often less complicated than is necessary for the InsertCommand, UpdateCommand, and DeleteCommand properties of a DataAdapter. Review the "Inserting New Rows in a Table" and "Updating Column Values and Deleting Rows" sections in Chapter 11 to refresh yourself on the techniques for performing data modification with Command objects. The concluding sample for this section builds on the content in these earlier sections.

When using Command objects for data modification, you do not strictly need local data caches. Nevertheless, these caches in DataTables can be quite convenient for simplifying application development or even speeding up application performance—particularly via DataView objects. However, it is possible to have the best of both worlds so that you perform data modification with Command objects and still have DataTable objects available for local use with DataView objects.

Setting up for Data Modification Samples

There are three parts to the initial setup for the data modification samples in the "Inserting, Updating, and Deleting Rows" section. The first part is a series of Dim statements at the module level. The Dim statements in the next code segment are for variables used in multiple procedures or to persist values beyond the scope of a single procedure.

- The dap1 and dap2 variables denote two SqlDataAdapter objects.

- The SqlDataAdapter objects rely on a cnn1 variable for a SqlConnection object pointing to the AdventureWorks database. However, you can point the cnn1 variable to any database because the sample code creates its own database tables exclusively for use with the sample.

- A das1 variable represents a DataSet object that stores DataTables created by the dap1 and dap2 SqlDataAdapters.

- The int1 and int2 variables represent Integer values that retain their values between successive runs of a procedure in the final data modification sample.

```
Dim cnn1 As SqlConnection = _
    New System.Data.SqlClient.SqlConnection( _
    "Data Source=.\sqlexpress;" & _
    "Integrated Security=True;" & _
    "Initial Catalog=AdventureWorks")

Dim dap1 As SqlClient.SqlDataAdapter
Dim dap2 As SqlClient.SqlDataAdapter
Dim das1 As DataSet
Dim int1, int2 As Integer
```

The beginning part of the Load procedure, which is shown next, creates a database table named DotNetTable in the database to which the cnn1 SqlConnection object points (AdventureWorks). To help ensure the success of the attempt to create a new table named DotNetTable, the procedure starts by trying to drop a previous version of the table. A single SqlCommand object with different CommandText property settings implements both attempts. The invocation of an ExcecuteNonQuery executes the SQL code assigned to the CommandText property. Wrapping the ExecuteNonQuery statement for each attempt in a separate Try…Catch…Finally statement provides feedback about failed attempts and facilitates the management of the cnn1 SqlConnection object.

The DotNetTable database table has three columns.

- The first column, ContactID, serves as the basis for the table's primary key. This column has an IDENTITY column property.

- The second and third columns are both nvarchar variables for storing the names and e-mail addresses of contacts.

```
Dim cmd1 As New SqlCommand
cmd1.CommandText = "DROP TABLE DotNetTable"
cmd1.Connection = cnn1

Try
 cnn1.Open()
 cmd1.ExecuteNonQuery()
Catch ex As Exception
 MessageBox.Show(ex.Message)
Finally
 cnn1.Close()
End Try
```

```
cmd1.CommandText = "CREATE TABLE DotNetTable (" & _
    "ContactID int IDENTITY PRIMARY KEY, " & _
    "ContactName nvarchar(25) NOT NULL, " & _
    "ContactEAddr nvarchar(60) NOT NULL)"
cmd1.Connection = cnn1

Try
  cnn1.Open()
  cmd1.ExecuteNonQuery()
Catch ex As Exception
  MessageBox.Show(ex.Message)
Finally
  cnn1.Close()
End Try
```

The final setup segment places the DotNetTable database table in the context of the client application.

- First, a DataSet object is instantiated to populate the das1 variable.

- Next, a SELECT statement helps to populate the dap1 SqlDataAdapter variable.

- Then, the code invokes the Fill method to make a DataTable in the das1 DataSet based on the DotNetTable database table. Because no name is assigned to the DataTable, this table has a default of Table.

- The Load procedure concludes by creating a new instance of a SqlCommandBuilder object based on the SelectCommand property of the dap1 SqlDataAdapter.

Tip Only one DataTable object in a DataSet object can have the default name of Table, because all the DataTable objects in a DataSet must have unique names.

```
das1 = New DataSet
dap1 = New SqlDataAdapter("SELECT * FROM DotNetTable", cnn1)
dap1.Fill(das1)
Dim bld1 As SqlCommandBuilder = New SqlCommandBuilder(dap1)
```

Adding a Row to a Database Table Through a DataTable

After the Load procedure concludes, the database table named DotNetTable will be empty. In addition, the corresponding DataTable named Table in the client application has no rows, but the DataTable columns do map to the database table columns. Therefore, you can

- Create a new DataRow based on the DataTable.

- Populate the DataRow columns with values.

- Add the DataRow to the Rows collection for the DataTable.

- Send the change to the DataTable to the database table.

The following code from the Button1_Click procedure performs these steps along with an extra one—namely, calling another procedure to display the final result. The first statement creates a new DataRow object based on the Table DataTable, which is the first and only DataTable in the das1 DataSet. The next couple of statements populate the ContactName and ContactEAddr column values.

You should not attempt to populate the ContactID column value in the client application because that column in the database table has an IDENTITY property value, which means the server populates the column.

The invocation of the Add method for the Rows collection of the first DataTable in the das1 DataSet inserts the drw1 DataRow into the Rows collection of the DataTable. Finally, the invocation of the Update method transfers the change in the Table DataTable to the DotNetTable database table.

After the Update method concludes, the new row for Rick Dobson is in the database table. However, the Table DataTable is slightly out of synchronization with the database table. This is because the ContactID column value is added at the server—not the client. The client DataTable does not know what value the server specified for the ContactID column. One solution to this lack of synchronization is to clear the Table DataTable and refill it from the database. The two statements after the one invoking the Update method illustrate this process:

```
Dim drw1 As DataRow = das1.Tables(0).NewRow
drw1("ContactName") = "Rick Dobson"
drw1("ContactEAddr") = "rickd@cabinc.net"

das1.Tables(0).Rows.Add(drw1)

dap1.Update(das1, das1.Tables(0).TableName)

das1.Tables(0).Clear()
dap1.Fill(das1)

DisplayTableValues()
```

The last statement in the preceding code listing calls the DisplayTableValues procedure. This procedure loops through all the rows in all the DataTables in the das1 DataSet. Although this procedure serves a purpose similar to the preceding DisplayDTsInADS procedure, the structure of the code here is different enough to not allow the reuse of the DisplayDTsInADS procedure. In particular, the DisplayDTsInADS procedure instantiates the das1 DataSet object, but here we use a das1 DataSet object instantiated elsewhere—namely, in the Load procedure. In addition, the DisplayTableValues procedure uses a das1 variable declared at the module level, instead of a das1 variable passed to it, as is the case for the DisplayDTsInADS procedure.

Both versions of the code are declared with a Friend access modifier. This makes it simple for you to use either version of the code in your projects by copying the procedure to a module in your project. For completeness, the listing for DisplayTableValues procedure is shown next.

```
Friend Sub DisplayTableValues()

  Dim str1 As String = ""
  For Each dtb1 As DataTable In das1.Tables
   str1 += "Rows for " & dtb1.TableName & _
    Microsoft.VisualBasic.StrDup(2, ControlChars.CrLf)
   For Each drw1 As DataRow In das1.Tables(dtb1.TableName).Rows
    For Each dcl1 As DataColumn In das1.Tables(dtb1.TableName).Columns
     str1 += drw1(dcl1.ColumnName).ToString & ", "
    Next
    str1 = Microsoft.VisualBasic.Left(str1, Len(str1) - 2)
    str1 += ControlChars.CrLf
   Next
   str1 += ControlChars.CrLf
  Next dtb1
  MessageBox.Show(str1)

End Sub
```

Updating a Column Value in a Row Through a DataTable

At the completion of the `Button1_Click` procedure in the preceding sample, you have a database table and a `DataTable` in your client application with the same information. This information includes one row for a contact with a `ContactName` column value of Rick Dobson. It is often necessary with database applications to revise values in a database. When working with an application that has a disconnected copy of a database table, it is highly desirable to synchronize a disconnected data store, such as a `DataTable`, before attempting to update a local value and then send the updated value to the database table.

Whether or not you synchronize first, you can attempt to pass one or more changed local values from a `DataTable` to a database table with the `Update` method for the `DataAdapter` object. As with nearly all .NET methods, the `Update` method is overloaded. One common pair of arguments to pass the `Update` method is a `DataSet` object and the name of a `DataTable` object within the `DataSet`. The syntax for this approach is `dap1.Update(dasname, "TableName")`.

■ **Caution** The `Update` method for a `DataAdapter` object does not just pass along updates from a `DataTable` object to a database table. It also attempts to pass along other changes, such as inserts and deletes, to the `DataTable` since the last time the `DataTable` was synchronized with its corresponding database table. Make sure your local `DataTable` object only has changes that you wish to make to the database source before invoking the `Update` method.

The following code from the `Button2_Click` procedure illustrates the syntax for making a change to the last and only row to the `Table DataTable` that changes Rick Dobson to Rickie Dobson. Then it passes the local change to the corresponding database table, `DotNetTable`. There are six lines of code in this very simple sample:

- The first two lines of code refresh the `Table DataTable` in the `das1 DataSet` with the `DotNetTable` database table. This is not required, but it is a recommended best practice.

- The next pair of lines assigns Rickie Dobson to the `ContactName` column value of the last and only row in the `Table DataTable`. This statement assumes that you clicked the `Button1` control just prior to clicking the `Button2` control.

- The next statement invokes the `Update` method for the name of the first table in the `das1 DataSet`. The `das1.Tables(0)` expression points at the first `DataTable` in the `das1 DataSet`. The `TableName` property returns a `String` value with the name of the `DataTable`.

- The last statement calls the `DisplayTableValues`. Notice there is no need to resynchronize the local `DataTable` with the database, because the database server does not perform any additional changes, such as adding an `IDENTITY` column value.

```
das1.Tables(0).Clear()
dap1.Fill(das1, das1.Tables(0).TableName)

Dim intLast As Integer = das1.Tables(0).Rows.Count - 1
das1.Tables(0).Rows(intLast)("ContactName") = "Rickie Dobson"

dap1.Update(das1, das1.Tables(0).TableName)

DisplayTableValues()
```

The two message boxes in Figure 12-5 are from two clicks. The first click is to the Button1 control immediately after the form loads. Recall that the Button1_Click procedure adds a row for Rick Dobson. The second click is to the Button2 control immediately after the click to the Button1 control. Notice the second comma-delimited value in the second message box is Rickie Dobson instead of Rick Dobson. This revision is the result of the change to the column value in the DataTable followed by the invocation of an Update method for the das1 DataSet object.

 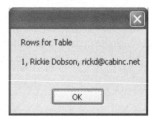

Figure 12-5. *A DataAdapter object facilitates changes to a database table based on modifications to a DataTable object in a client application.*

Concurrently Transferring Multiple Types of Changes

Each of the preceding two samples demonstrate how to move a single change made to a DataTable in a client application to a database. The type of change is different in each sample (an insert versus an update), but each sample conveys just one change at a time. However, sometimes users want to make multiple changes before submitting them to the database from the client application. The Button3_Click procedure illustrates the concurrent submission of an insert and a delete change at one time from a DataTable to a database table.

The core code segment for this sample is shown next. The first change for this sample involves the insertion of a new row. The syntax for this process is similar to the syntax for inserting the first row in that you add a new row to the Table DataTable, but it is different in that you do not immediately send the change from the DataTable object to the database table. Instead, the code invokes the Delete method for the first row in the first DataTable of the das1 DataSet.

Up until this point in the code, the changes exist solely on the client side. Invoking the Update method for the dap1 SqlDataAdapter attempts to transfer the two changes from the DataTable object to the DotNetTable database table. Refreshing the local DataTable from the database recovers the ContactID IDENTITY value inserted by the database server.

```
Dim drw1 As DataRow = das1.Tables(0).NewRow
drw1("ContactName") = "Virginia Dobson"
drw1("ContactEAddr") = "virginiad@cabinc.net"

das1.Tables(0).Rows.Add(drw1)

das1.Tables(0).Rows(0).Delete()

dap1.Update(das1, das1.Tables(0).TableName)

das1.Tables(0).Clear()
dap1.Fill(das1)
```

A call to the `DisplayTableValues` procedure is clipped from the preceding code excerpt from the `Button3_Click` procedure. Figure 12-6 shows the message box that appears after you initially open the form and then successively click `Button1`, `Button2`, and `Button3` while, of course, clearing the intervening message boxes. Notice that the new row with Virginia Dobson as a contact appears in the message box. The previously inserted row for Rick or Rickie Dobson is deleted. This is consistent with the code for the `Button3_Click` procedure.

Rows for Table

2, Virginia Dobson, virginiad@cabinc.net

OK

Figure 12-6. *A single invocation of the Update method can transfer one change or multiple changes from a DataTable in a client application to a table in a database.*

■**Caution** When working with a disconnected data source, such as a `DataTable`, your disconnected data source and the database can become unsynchronized. One common reason for the lack of synchronization is a change by another user. If your application tries to make any changes from an unsynchronized data source, one or more of the attempted changes can fail. The failure of an attempted change generates an `Exception` object. You can trap the `Exception` object with a `Try…Catch` statement and then resubmit the changes. From a programming perspective, one easy way to do this is to alert the user that an error occurred, along with a request to resubmit the changes after your application refreshes the local data source from the database.

Processing Changes to Two Tables

The last data modification sample tackles several issues. The core part of the sample highlights one approach to changing two database tables from a client application. Although there is no explicit foreign key relationship between the tables, they are implicitly related. The input for the child table requires the recovery of an `IDENTITY` value from the parent table. This concluding sample also shows how to jointly use data modifications through a `Command` object with disconnected data sources. By using this technique, applications can benefit from the advantages of making changes directly to a database while concurrently offering the benefits of a disconnected data source. Finally, the changes implemented through a `Command` object demonstrate the basic syntax for using parameters with a `Command` object.

Two procedures implement the sample:

- The first procedure, `Button4_Click`, sets up the sample.
  - This involves creating a second table, `DotNetTable2`, which can act as a child table to the `DotNetTable` database table.
  - In addition, the first part creates a disconnected data source that maps to the `DotNetTable2` database table in the same way that the `Table DataTable` maps to the `DotNetTable` database table.

- The second procedure, `InsertWithSQL`, performs the database modification tasks via a `Command` object with SQL statements and synchronizes the two database tables with the two local, disconnected data sources that map to them.

The `Button4_Click` procedure starts by creating the `DotNetTable2` database table. The procedure implementing this object is shown next. Initially, the code drops any prior table in the database pointed at by the `cnn1` `SqlConnection` object. If the table doesn't already exist, the `Try…Catch…Finally` statement displays an error message about that fact. Next, the code excerpt runs the SQL statement for creating the `DotNetTable2` database table.

The `CREATE TABLE` statement for the `DotNetTable2` database table designates three columns and a primary key constraint. The `SalesID` and `ContactID` columns jointly define the primary key that makes each row in the table unique. The `Amount` column stores information about the amount of a transaction defined by the combination of `SalesID` and `ContactID` column values. The `ContactID` column from the `DotNetTable2` database table contains values that should link back to a row in the `DotNetTable` database table. The primary key constraint specifies that rows must be unique by the combination of their `SalesID` and `ContactID` column values.

```
Dim cmd1 As New SqlCommand
cmd1.CommandText = "DROP TABLE DotNetTable2"
cmd1.Connection = cnn1

Try
 cnn1.Open()
 cmd1.ExecuteNonQuery()
Catch ex As Exception
 MessageBox.Show(ex.Message)
Finally
 cnn1.Close()
End Try

cmd1.CommandText = "CREATE TABLE DotNetTable2 (" & _
  "SalesID int NOT NULL, " & _
  "ContactID int NOT NULL, " & _
  "Amount dec(7,2) NOT NULL," & _
  "CONSTRAINT PK_TwoIDs PRIMARY KEY(SalesID, ContactID))"
cmd1.Connection = cnn1

Try
 cnn1.Open()
 cmd1.ExecuteNonQuery()
Catch ex As Exception
 MessageBox.Show(ex.Message)
Finally
 cnn1.Close()
End Try
```

After creating the `DotNetTable2` database table, the `Button4_Click` procedure creates a `DataTable` in the client application based on the database table. The name of the local `DataTable` mapping to the `DotNetTable2` database table is `Table2`. The `Table2` `DataTable` is a local data cache for the `DotNetTable2` database table in the same sense that the `Table` `DataTable` is a local cache for the `DotNetTable`.

```
dap2 = New SqlDataAdapter("SELECT * FROM DotNetTable2", cnn1)
dap2.Fill(das1, "Table2")
```

The final line in the Button4_Click procedure calls the InsertWithSQL procedure. It is this second procedure that performs inserts for the DotNetTable and DotNetTable2 database tables. The InsertWithSQL procedure also synchronizes the Table and Table2 DataTable objects with their corresponding database tables.

The following excerpt from the InsertWithSQL procedure shows the syntax for populating the DotNetTable database table with values and synchronizing the updated database table with the first DataTable in the das1 DataSet. The code segment demonstrates the use of parameters in an INSERT statement:

- You must reference the parameters in the INSERT statement for the SqlCommand object.
- You must add the named parameters to the Parameters collection for the SqlCommand object.
  - Use the Add method for the Parameters collection of a SqlCommand object to add a new parameter to the collection.
  - As with arguments for the Add method, you can specify the parameter name, the SQL Server data type, and the maximum length in characters if you are dealing with a parameter that has an nvarchar data type.
- You must assign a value to each parameter. The following syntax combines this step with the addition of a parameter to the Parameters collection, but you can also assign a value to a parameter in a separate statement. The parameters are for the ContactName and ContactEAddr columns in the DotNetTable database table.
- After parameters are added to a SqlCommand object, you must assign values to them before invoking the ExecuteNonQuery method for the SqlCommand object.
  - The addition of a second row by the procedure illustrates the syntax for using this approach.
  - You can contrast the syntax with the syntax for the first row added by the procedure. Notice that with the reuse of the previously created parameters all you have to do is reference a parameter name and assign a value to the Value property of a parameter.
- After adding both rows to the DotNetTable database table, the procedure invokes the Fill method for the dap1 SqlDataAdapter. This step synchronizes the Table DataTable values with the current values in the DotNetTable database table.

```
Dim cmd1 As SqlCommand = New SqlCommand
cmd1.CommandText = "INSERT DotNetTable VALUES(@Name, @EAddr)"
cmd1.Connection = cnn1

cmd1.Parameters.Add("@Name", SqlDbType.NVarChar, 25).Value = _
  "Rick Dobson"
cmd1.Parameters.Add("@EAddr", SqlDbType.NVarChar, 60).Value = _
  "rickd@cabinc.net"
cnn1.Open()

cmd1.ExecuteNonQuery()

cmd1.Parameters("@Name").Value = "Virginia Dobson"
cmd1.Parameters("@EAddr").Value = "virginiad@cabinc.net"
cmd1.ExecuteNonQuery()

cnn1.Close()

das1.Tables(0).Clear()
dap1.Fill(das1, das1.Tables(0).TableName)
```

The next excerpt from the InsertWithSQL procedure shows comparable code for adding two rows to the DotNetTable2 database table. This excerpt also synchronizes the Table2 DataTable with the DotNetTable2 database table after adding the two new rows. The SQL syntax for adding a new row to the DotNetTable2 database is different from that for the DotNetTable database table for three reasons:

- First, there is no column in the DotNetTable2 database table with an IDENTITY property. Therefore, an INSERT statement must specify values for every column in the database table.

- Second, the ContactID column value in the DotNetTable2 database table must match at least one corresponding value in the ContactID column value of the DotNetTable database.

- Third, the rows of the DotNetTable2 database table must be unique by the combination of SalesID and ContactID, because the code for creating DotNetTable2 database table has a primary key based on both its SalesID and ContactID columns. The sample values inserted with the following code has unique SalesID column values, but it is permissible for the SalesID column values to duplicate within the column so long as they are unique for any given ContactID column value.

```
Dim cmd2 As SqlCommand = New SqlCommand
cmd2.CommandText = _
 "INSERT DotNetTable2 VALUES(@SalesID, @ContactID, @Amount)"
cmd2.Connection = cnn1

If das1.Tables(1).Rows.Count = 0 Then
 int1 = 1
 cmd2.Parameters.Add("@SalesID", SqlDbType.Int).Value = int1
Else
 int1 += 10
 cmd2.Parameters.Add("@SalesID", SqlDbType.Int).Value = int1
End If
cmd2.Parameters.Add("@ContactID", SqlDbType.Int).Value = _
 das1.Tables(0).Rows(das1.Tables(0).Rows.Count - 2)("ContactID")
cmd2.Parameters.Add("@Amount", SqlDbType.Decimal).Value = 75
cnn1.Open()

cmd2.ExecuteNonQuery()

If das1.Tables(1).Rows.Count = 0 Then
 cmd2.Parameters("@SalesID").Value = 2
 int2 = 2
Else
 int2 += 10
 cmd2.Parameters("@SalesID").Value = int2
End If
cmd2.Parameters("@ContactID").Value = _
 das1.Tables(0).Rows(das1.Tables(0).Rows.Count - 1)("ContactID")
cmd2.Parameters("@Amount").Value = 26

cmd2.ExecuteNonQuery()

cnn1.Close()

dap2.Fill(das1, das1.Tables(1).TableName)
```

The last line of code in the `InsertWithSQL` procedure calls the `DisplayTableValues` procedure. The results shown by the `DisplayTableValues` procedure depend on the synchronization of SQL Server tables with client-side `DataTable` objects.

- The repeated invocation of the `ExecuteNonQuery` method for the `cmd1` and `cmd2` `SqlCommand` objects implements all the updates to the `DotNetTable` and `DotNetTable2` database tables based on values supplied from the client application.

- Immediately after closing the `cnn1` `SqlConnection` object for `cmd1` or `cmd2` `SqlCommand` objects, the invocation of the `Fill` method for either the `dap1` or `dap2` `SqlDataAdapter` objects copies a SQL Server table to the `Table` or `Table2` `DataTable` object in the `das1` `DataSet` object.

- The invocation of these two `Fill` methods makes data available for the `DisplayTableValues` procedure.

Figure 12-7 shows the output from the `DisplayTableValues` procedure following three successive clicks to `Button4` immediately after the form opens. The top part of the message box shows six rows in the Table `DataTable`. The rows are unique by `ContactID` column values, which are assigned by the database server.

The bottom part of the message box in Figure 12-7 displays values for the `Table2` `DataTable`. Notice that the second column value on each row matches a corresponding `ContactID` column value in the `Table` `DataTable`. These matching values implicitly relate the `Table` and `Table2` `DataTable` objects. Also, notice that there are no two rows in the `Table2` `DataTable` object with the same `SalesID` and `ContactID` column values. This outcome results from the primary key constraint for the `DotNetTable2` database table. The `Table2` `DataTable` is merely a copy of the `DotNetTable2` database table.

Rows for Table

1, Rick Dobson, rickd@cabinc.net
2, Virginia Dobson, virginiad@cabinc.net
3, Rick Dobson, rickd@cabinc.net
4, Virginia Dobson, virginiad@cabinc.net
5, Rick Dobson, rickd@cabinc.net
6, Virginia Dobson, virginiad@cabinc.net

Rows for Table2

1, 1, 75.00
2, 2, 26.00
11, 3, 75.00
12, 4, 26.00
21, 5, 75.00
22, 6, 26.00

Figure 12-7. *You can use ADO.NET to manage input to multiple database tables and to synchronize multiple database tables with client-side DataTable objects.*

Bulk Loading Data from Excel

When you are initially building a new database solution, it is not uncommon for the data to come from another source. It is likely that at least some SSE solutions will be migrations from Excel. Excel has a limit on the number of rows for a worksheet (65,536). In addition, VBA in Excel does not offer the rich, safe development environment available with .NET development tools. By creating solutions with SSE and Visual Basic Express or Visual Web Developer Express, you can migrate Excel solutions while keeping the cost low and level of resources required low compared with other editions of SQL Server 2005 or Visual Studio 2005.

One important step in migrating data from Excel to SSE is the data transfer. The ADO.NET SqlBulkCopy class can help to transfer data from Excel to SSE. This class is attractive for more than migrating data from Excel. Any type of data that you can read and copy to a DataTable makes a good candidate for processing with the SqlBulkCopy class. In addition, SqlBulkCopy class instances can also transfer data to SSE using a DataReader as their data source.

The SqlBulkCoply class is new with ADO.NET 2.0 and is an ADO.NET front end to the bcp command-line utility. It can be tricky to get the syntax correct for the bcp utility, so if you are proficient at reading data from files and copying it to a DataTable, the SqlBulkCopy class may significantly simplify copying of data to SSE or any other SQL Server 2005 edition. In addition, the SqlBulkCopy class delivers the performance benefits associated with the bcp command-line utility when transferring data.

When using the SqlBulkCopy class to copy Excel data to SSE, you are likely to find it most convenient to output the data as a .csv file from Excel. This is a text file with commas separating its column values. Each row of data from a worksheet is on a separate line in the text file. The new TextFileParser object in Visual Basic 2005 makes reading and parsing .csv files particularly easy.

The SqlBulkCopy class can be very easy to use as well.

- You can instantiate a new instance of the class by designating a SqlConnection object as an argument with the New keyword in a constructor. This specifies which database the class instance will copy data to.

- You can specify the DestinationTableName property for the class instance to indicate the table within a database to receive new rows through the class instance. You can qualify a table name with schema name. You can also use a database name qualifier if you wish to copy data to a table in another database besides the one at which the SqlConnection points. If your destination table name includes any special characters in its name, then put the table name and its qualifiers in brackets ([DatabaseName.SchemaName.TableName]).

- After specifying a DestinationTableName property, you can invoke the WriteToServer method to transfer values to a destination. You can copy data from a DataTable object, a DataReader object, or an array of DataRow objects.

■**Caution** You will throw an Exception object if you invoke the WriteToServer method before specifying the DestinationTableName property for a SqlBulkCopy class instance.

This section's sample for the SqlBulkCopy class reads a short .csv file named Book1.csv. The file resides in the project folder (the one with the form files) for the WinCh12 project. Our form for this example, Form9, has three Click event procedures for Button1 through Button3 and a Load event procedure for the form. The sample relies on a copy of the Northwind SQL Server database whose database files reside in the project folder.

- The Load event procedure points the cnn1 SqlConnection object at the Northwind database files in the project folder. See the "Connecting to SQL Server Express Database Files" section in Chapter 11 for commentary on how to accomplish this. The cnn1 variable is declared at the module level for its use with multiple procedures.

- The Button1_Click procedure creates a database table named FromExcel that has columns matching the columns of the Book1.csv file.

- The Button2_Click procedure drops the FromExcel database table.

- The `Button3_Click` procedure is the workhorse component of the sample. It performs four tasks, including one that uses a `SqlBulkCopy` instance to copy data from a client application to an SSE database.

Creating a Database Table for an Excel Worksheet

Figure 12-8 shows the `Book1.csv` file open in Excel. The file has a single worksheet named `Book1`. The worksheet has three columns for first name, last name, and an identification number. The worksheet has five rows. The `SqlBulkCopy` class is ideal for cases in which there are many rows, but it is easy enough to use that you may want to consider it for small worksheet files, such as the one in this demonstration. In any event, the syntax for using a `SqlBulkCopy` instance is the same whether you are dealing with 5 rows or 50,000 rows.

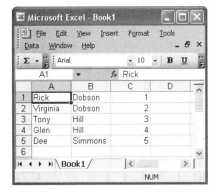

Figure 12-8. *You can export a .csv file from Excel for populating a database table via a SqlCopyBulk instance.*

Although the Book1.csv file can be opened with Excel in a spreadsheet, it is actually a text file with the column values on each row separated by commas. Figure 12-9 shows the same Book1.csv file open as a text file within Visual Basic Express.

Figure 12-9. *Although a .csv file can open as a worksheet from within Excel, its underlying format is that of a simple text file with commas separating the values on a row.*

The following excerpt from the `Button1_Click` procedure includes a `CREATE TABLE` statement for the `FromExcel` database table. The procedure creates the table in the `Northwind` database files inside the WinCh12 project, because the `cnn1 SqlConnection` object points at these files.

The procedure generates a message confirming success or a reminder that the attempt to create the table did not succeed. One reason an attempt to generate the table might fail is because it already exists. In this case, you can click `Button2` to drop the existing version of the `FromExcel` database table.

```
Dim cmd1 As New SqlCommand
cmd1.CommandText = "CREATE TABLE FromExcel (" & _
  "FirstName nvarchar(15), " & _
  "LastName nvarchar(20), " & _
  "PersonID int Not Null)"
cmd1.Connection = cnn1

Try
 cnn1.Open()
 cmd1.ExecuteNonQuery()
 MessageBox.Show("Command succeeded.", "Outcome", _
   MessageBoxButtons.OK, MessageBoxIcon.Information)
Catch ex As Exception
 MessageBox.Show(ex.Message)
Finally
 cnn1.Close()
End Try
```

Using a SqlBulkCopy Instance

The `Button3_Click` procedure does nearly all the work for the sample application. It is the only procedure within the sample to actually use a `SqlBulkCopy` instance. There are four parts to this procedure. This section reviews the code for each part separately.

- It creates a `DataTable` for storing the data from the Book1.csv file.

- It reads and parses the Book.csv file as it copies a worksheet's column values to the `DataTable` created in the first step.

- It sends the `DataTable` contents to the database table by invoking the `WriteToServer` method for a `SqlBulkCopy` instance.

- Finally, it reads the values from the `FromExcel` database table and displays the result in a message box to confirm the success of the bulk copy operation.

The code from the top of the procedure declares a `DataTable` named `FromExcel`. This `DataTable` will accept data from the Book1.csv file before its contents are sent to a database table with the same name by the `SqlBulkCopy` instance. Three successive `Add` methods for the `Columns` collection of the `FromExcel DataTable` adds three columns that correspond to the `FromExcel` database table. The `SqlString` data type is a variable length stream of characters. The `RowForExcel DataRow` variable helps to populate the `FromExcel DataTable` from the Book1.csv file in the procedure's second part.

```
Dim FromExcel As New DataTable
Dim RowForExcel As DataRow

FromExcel.Columns.Add("FirstName", GetType(SqlTypes.SqlString))
FromExcel.Columns.Add("LastName", GetType(SqlTypes.SqlString))
FromExcel.Columns.Add("PersonID", GetType(SqlTypes.SqlInt32))
```

The code for the second part creates a TextFieldParser object that points at the Book1.csv file in the project folder. A TextFieldParser object is a new type of file reader introduced with Visual Basic Express and other Visual Studio 2005 editions. It radically simplifies the reading of fixed-width and variable-width text files with delimiters, such as commas, separating the values on a row. The settings for the TextFieldType and Delimiters properties of the crd1 TextFieldParser instance enable the object to read comma-delimited data.

After declaring and specifying the crd1 TextFieldParser, the code excerpt loops through the file one row at a time. Within each row, the code loops through the field values within a row and assigns the values to the columns of the RowForExcel DataRow. The structure of this DataRow is based on the FromExcel DataTable. When the code concludes reading the column values on a row into the DataRow object, the code appends the DataRow object to the Rows collection of the FromExcel DataTable until there is no further data in the Book1.csv file (Do Until crd1.EndOfData).

```
Dim crd1 As Microsoft.VisualBasic.FileIO.TextFieldParser
Dim strPath As String = _
 Microsoft.VisualBasic.Left( _
 My.Application.Info.DirectoryPath, _
 InStr(My.Application.Info.DirectoryPath, "bin\") - 1)
crd1 = My.Computer.FileSystem.OpenTextFieldParser _
(My.Computer.FileSystem.CombinePath(strPath, "Book1.csv"))
crd1.TextFieldType = Microsoft.VisualBasic.FileIO.FieldType.Delimited
crd1.Delimiters = New String() {","}

Dim currentRow As String()
Do Until crd1.EndOfData
 Try
  currentRow = crd1.ReadFields()
  Dim currentField As String
  Dim int1 As Integer = 1
  RowForExcel = FromExcel.NewRow
  For Each currentField In currentRow
   Select Case int1
    Case 1
     RowForExcel("FirstName") = currentField
    Case 2
     RowForExcel("LastName") = currentField
    Case 3
     RowForExcel("PersonID") = CInt(currentField)
   End Select
   int1 += 1
  Next
  int1 = 1
  FromExcel.Rows.Add(RowForExcel)
  RowForExcel = FromExcel.NewRow
 Catch ex As Microsoft.VisualBasic.FileIO.MalformedLineException
  MsgBox("Line " & ex.Message & _
  "is not valid and will be skipped.")
 End Try
Loop
```

After populating a DataTable, such as the FromExcel DataTable, it is very simple to populate a database table with a SqlBulkCopy instance. The following excerpt from the Button3_Click procedure illustrates how simple it can be to copy the FromExcel DataTable values to the FromExcel database table. In fact, if you were willing to run without a Try…Catch…Finally statement, you could further simplify this short code excerpt (all you really need is the code in the Try clause). However, it is a good practice to use Try…Catch statements to trap errors, and the Try…Catch…Finally statement helps to remind you to close a SqlConnection object.

```
Try
 cnn1.Open()
 Using sqc1 As SqlBulkCopy = New SqlBulkCopy(cnn1)
  sqc1.DestinationTableName = "dbo.FromExcel"
  sqc1.WriteToServer(FromExcel)
 End Using
Catch ex As Exception
 MessageBox.Show(ex.Message)
Finally
 cnn1.Close()
End Try
```

The final segment of the Button3_Click procedure merely uses a SqlDataReader to populate a String variable (str1) to demonstrate the success of the attempt to copy the values to the FromExcel database table. This final step is not necessary in a production application. It is provided here just so that you can confirm the operation of the sample when you run it.

```
Dim strQuery As String = "SELECT * " & _
    "FROM dbo.FromExcel "
Dim str1 As String = ""

Dim cmd1 As New SqlCommand(strQuery, cnn1)
cnn1.Open()
Dim rdr1 As SqlDataReader
rdr1 = cmd1.ExecuteReader()
Try
 While rdr1.Read()
  str1 += rdr1.GetString(0) & ", " & _
    rdr1.GetString(1) & ", " & _
    rdr1.GetSqlInt32(2).ToString & ControlChars.CrLf
 End While
Finally
 rdr1.Close()
 cnn1.Close()
End Try
MessageBox.Show(str1, "FromExcel")
```

Summary

This chapter continued with our discussion of ADO.NET and introduced the DataAdapter and DataSet objects. It closed with a sample reviewing how to use the SqlBulkCopy class to transfer data from an external data source, such as Excel, to a database, such as SSE.

CHAPTER 13

■■■

Using Visual Database and Form Design Tools

Whether you are a beginning database user or an experienced database professional, there is always a place for visual database development tools and graphical form development techniques. *Quicker* and *easier* are the two hallmarks of visual database tools and graphical form development techniques. Visual database tools can help you to quickly examine and modify both the structure of and the values in a database. Graphical form development tools offer rapid application development techniques for building prototype solutions. In fact, you may find that prototypes created with graphical form development techniques work well enough to become final solutions.

This chapter has three major sections for examining and demonstrating visual database tools and graphical form development techniques.

- The first section presents Database Explorer for use with VBE. The rich Query Designer is like a jewel among the visual database tools because of the ease with which it permits the construction and testing of SQL statements.

- The second section drills down on the use of data sources with VBE. You learn how to tap data sources for expediting database development with graphical form development techniques.

- The third section introduces the use of Database Explorer and graphical form development techniques with VWDE. In fact, this section starts by demonstrating the tight integration between Database Explorer and ways of presenting data-bound controls on a Web Form page.

Visual Database Tools in VBE

Visual database tools are available in VBE from Database Explorer. The Database Explorer window is one of the major, defining windows of the VBE integrated development environment (IDE). You can open Database Explorer from the View menu (View ➤ Database Explorer).

Database Explorer offers VBE users a subset of SQL Server Management Studio (SSMS) capabilities. You do not need an open VBE project to work with a database file, but VBE must, of course, be open. The graphical capabilities supported by Database Explorer enable such tasks as

- Connecting to database files

- Showing and editing the values within database files

- Permitting some data-definition capabilities, including the ability to create tables, views, stored procedures, user-defined functions, and even triggers

Database Explorer is not a DBA tool in that its graphical capabilities do not target server administration topics. For example, Database Explorer focuses more directly on database files than on a server instance. You can graphically explore the tables in a database file and view as well as edit the values in tables, but you cannot graphically explore the databases on a server or show the logins for a server.

■Tip The Create New SQL Server Database item on the right-click menu for Data Connections in Database Explorer permits you to create a SQL Server Express database in the current VBE project or VWDE website. If you have difficulty connecting to SQL Server Express from Database Explorer, try setting the user instance in the connection string to False. See Chapters 2 and 3 for alternative, richer techniques for creating and managing SQL Server databases.

Dialog Boxes for Creating Connections

The Database Explorer toolbar contains three tools, with tooltips of Refresh, Stop Refresh, and Connect to Database. You can start the process of connecting to a database by clicking the Connect to Database tool. This opens the Add Connection dialog box. You can also open the Add Connection dialog box by right-clicking Data Connections in Database Explorer and choosing Add Connection.

The Add Connection dialog box makes available the normal settings for creating a database connection. You can specify a type of data source, the path to a database file, and a type of authentication. If you select SQL Server Authentication, you need to designate a user name and password. After you browse to a database file, you can click OK to add the connection to the database to Database Explorer. Click Test Connection to evaluate whether your settings can successfully create a connection.

Click the Advanced button on the Add Connection dialog box to refine your connection settings more granularly than is possible with the Add Connection dialog box. In addition to the main Add Connection dialog box settings, the Advanced Properties sheet enables you to determine whether

- To allow multiple active result sets on a connection

- A server maintains a connection pool for your connection string as well as the minimum and maximum number of items in the pool

- To persist the security settings for a connection after its use

- To connect with a user instance or via a connection to a server instance (the initial default mode is user instance)

■Tip User instance is a special connection string setting available for database files used with a SQL Server Express instance. When user instance equals True, the database file runs under a special instance of SQL Server Express just for the user. This setting completely isolates users from each other because each user has their own separate instance of SQL Server Express for working with database files. Each user can have just one user instance, and the user instance goes out of scope when there are no connections to it.

The Add Connection dialog box enables one of two built-in choices for connecting to a database. These are for SQL Server and Access databases. Click Change in the Add Connection dialog box to open the Change Data Source dialog box that appears in Figure 13-1.

- If you choose a SQL Server data source, VBE uses the .NET Framework Data Provider for SQL Server to connect to a SQL Server database, including a SQL Server Express database.

- If you choose a Microsoft Access database, VBE uses the .NET Framework Data Provider for OLE DB to connect to an Access .mdb file.

- By selecting a data source provider and also selecting the "Always use this selection" check box before clicking OK, you establish the selected data source provider as the default for future uses of the Add Connection dialog box.

- You can override the default data provider by clicking Change on the Add Connection dialog box.

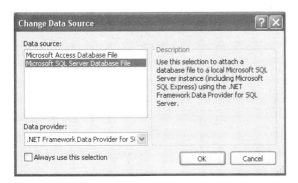

Figure 13-1. *The Change Data Source dialog box permits you to change the data source provider for connecting to a database and set one of two providers as the default.*

Exploring a SQL Server Express Database

After navigating to the .mdf file for the AdventureWorks database in the local SQL Server Express instance, you can have a node something like AdventureWorks_Data.mdf. This file resides in the Data folder for the local SQL Server Express instance. You can expand the AdventureWorks_Data.mdf node in Database Explorer to reveal additional folders for exploring categories of items, such as tables and stored procedures, within the database. You can, in turn, expand any of these folders to display the items in a folder.

To the right of Database Explorer is the data for the ProductCategory table in the Production schema. You can show the data for any table by expanding the Tables folder. Then, right-click the table and choose Show Table Data. You can edit the data for the ProductCategory table by revising column values, adding new rows, and dropping existing rows. The representation of the table data acts like a bound form.

Other right-click menu items of special interest for Tables folder items are Open Table Definition and Add New Trigger. The Open Table Definition menu item opens a Design view of a table, which allows you to examine the overall table and column settings. The menu item also makes it possible for you to modify a table's design, such as the data type for a column or the maximum number of characters for a column with an nvarchar data type. The Add New Trigger menu item opens a trigger with a template for an AFTER trigger for the selected table. You specify the trigger with T-SQL. See the "Creating and Using Triggers" section in Chapter 7 for sample SQL Server triggers.

In addition to exploring tables, you can also examine other types of objects, such as views, stored procedures, and user-defined functions. The right-click menu items vary depending on the type of database object. Figure 13-2 shows the expansion of View items within the `AdventureWorks` database. By expanding the `vEmployeeDepartmentHistory` view, you can see the columns returned by the view. The parentheses after the view's name denote the schema containing the view (`HumanResources`). The items in the Tables folder return the same information about them.

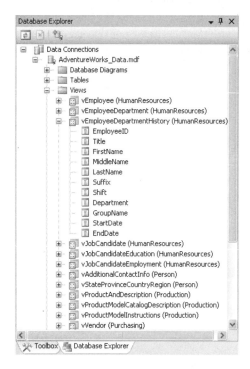

Figure 13-2. *Database Explorer enables you to explore the objects within a database connection.*

Selected items in the right-click menu for a view include Open View Definition, Show Results, and Add New Trigger. The Add New Trigger item specifies an `INSTEAD OF` trigger for a view, but the menu item with the same name for a table presents a template to create an `AFTER` trigger. The Show Results menu item presents a whole window to the right of Database Explorer with the result set returned by a view. The OpenView Definition menu item can open a display with as many as four panes (Diagram, Criteria, SQL, and Results). You can toggle the visibility of individual panes through toolbar controls.

Figure 13-3 shows the Diagram, Criteria, and SQL panes for the `vEmployeeDepartmentHistory` view. The Diagram pane on top shows the data sources that the view relies on to return results. The names for the sources are actually aliases. The SQL pane at the bottom shows the SQL statement for the view along with the assignment of alias names to data sources. For example, e refers to the `Employee` table in the `HumanResources` schema, and c refers to the `Contact` table in the `Person` schema. The Criteria pane between the Diagram and SQL panes shows an excerpt of the selected items from the data sources in the view. The names going down the column with a `Column` heading in the Criteria pane are items in the list for the `SELECT` statement defining the view.

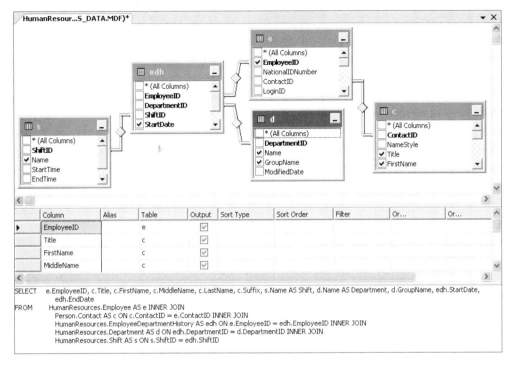

Figure 13-3. *The Database Explorer Open View Definition menu item provides a variety of different perspectives to help you understand a view.*

Adding Objects to a SQL Server Express Database

Just as you can explore existing objects in a SQL Server Express database, you can also add new objects to a SQL Server Express database. The visual database tools in Database Explorer are particularly convenient for developers who want to add tables and views without a detailed knowledge of T-SQL. Even when Database Explorer does not provide a rich graphical interface for the creation of database objects, it provides a template to reduce the amount of T-SQL code that you must enter to complete the definition of a new object, such as for a trigger or a stored procedure. In the case of triggers, Database Explorer presents different trigger types depending on whether you are adding a trigger for a table or a view.

With Database Explorer, you create objects at design time. In some circumstances, this has advantages over creating database objects at runtime. First, it is typically easier to create objects at design time. This, in turn, can reduce your development effort and leave more time to think about the project objectives and the best way to meet them. Creating objects at runtime is typically more code intensive than creating them at design time. If you are only creating an object once, or just a few times, design-time creation of objects with a tool such as Database Explorer offers a definite advantage.

Here we'll create a table called `DotNetTable`. This table has just three columns and a primary key based on a column with an `IDENTITY` property setting. If necessary, drop a prior version of the table by right-clicking the table and choosing Delete.

The `DotNetTable` example in this section creates the new table in the `AdventureWorks` database. The files for this database reside in the Data folder of the SQL Server Express instance on the test computer for this book.

- Start the process by right-clicking the Tables folder in Database Explorer and choosing Add New Table. This selection opens a window for specifying the new table to the right of Database Explorer.

  - The top of the window contains the first row of a table for specifying the table's first column. The column headings for the rows in the table are Column Name, Data Type, and Allow Nulls.

  - The bottom of the window initially contains an empty properties sheet with a tab labeled Column Properties.

- Figure 13-4 shows the Design view settings for the first row in the DotNetTable database table. The top of the Design view shows the process of adding a primary key specification for the first row. The bottom of the Design view shows the Identity Specification property for the first column in the table.

- Figure 13-5 displays the Design view after finishing the specification of the third and final column (ContactEAddr) for the new table. The bottom part of the Design view shows the selection of Length immediately after the specification of a maximum length of 60 characters for this nvarchar column.

- None of the columns allow nulls, so all three Allow Nulls check boxes in the top of the Design view are clear or unselected. These check boxes are checked by default.

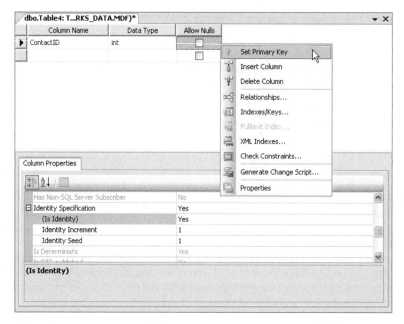

Figure 13-4. *Database Explorer facilitates specifying an IDENTITY property for a column and allows you to design a column as the basis for a primary key in a table.*

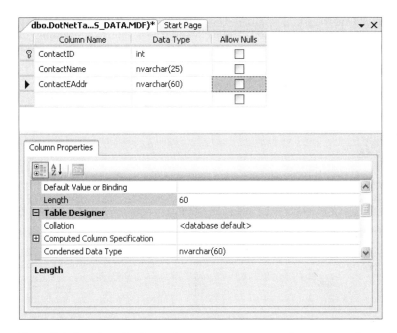

Figure 13-5. *Database Explorer allows you to set many column properties, such as the maximum number of characters in a column with an nvarchar data type.*

After completing the specification of a new table, you can close the window. Database Explorer asks if you want to save your changes to the item. Click Yes. Then, assign a name, such as DotNetTable, to your new table.

You can open a new empty table, such as DotNetTable, with the Show Table Data menu item. Later you can manually add data to the table by opening the table with the Show Table Data menu item. Then, just type values into the columns for each new row. Remember to omit entering values for columns with an IDENTITY property setting because SQL Server adds values to columns with an IDENTITY property setting.

You can add a new view for showing the values populating the DotNetTable database table.

1. Start the process by right-clicking the Database Explorer Views folder and choosing Add New View.

2. From the Tables tab of the Add table dialog box, choose DotNetTable as the source for the new view.

3. In the Diagram tab, select the check boxes for all three columns in the DotNetTable. These selections add the column names to the Criteria pane and populate the SQL pane with a SELECT statement defining the new view.

4. Then, click the Execute SQL control on the View Designer toolbar. This populates the Result pane in the designer.

Figure 13-6 shows the Query Designer after a click of the Execute Sql control. The SQL pane shows the T-SQL for this very simple view. You can specify sort orders, filters for including column values in the view, calculated column values, grouping, and column aggregates. The Results pane shows the values added to the `DotNetTable` for the `ContactName` and `ContactEAddr` columns as well as the `ContactID` column values added by the SQL Server Express instance. You can save a new view in the same way that you save a table. Assign a name, such as `vDotNetTable`, to the new view.

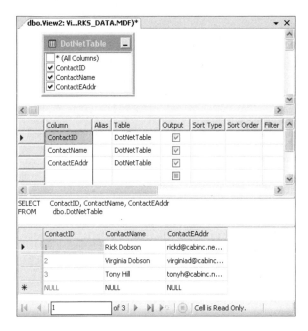

Figure 13-6. *Database Explorer makes it easy to specify a new view for a database without any T-SQL code.*

While the Query Designer will automate the creation of a T-SQL statement for you, you can also type T-SQL into the SQL pane and have your code automatically populate the Diagram and Criteria panes. See Chapters 5 and 6 for numerous T-SQL query samples.

Migrating and Revising an MSDE Database

One scenario for some SQL Server Express applications involves migrating an MSDE database, which has a SQL Server 2000 binary file format, to a SQL Server Express instance, which uses a SQL Server 2005 binary file format. MSDE is the predecessor to SQL Server Express in many respects. Because SQL Server Express can run side by side on the same computer with MSDE, you will not need to migrate an MSDE database unless you want to upgrade your solution—perhaps to take advantage of new SQL Server Express features. Another reason for migrating is to benefit from innovations associated with VBE and VWDE, which both integrate tightly with SQL Server Express—but not with MSDE.

Before migrating from MSDE to SQL Server Express, you should understand that the migration is not reversible. The MSDE and SQL Server Express binary file formats are incompatible. The incompatibility is such that SQL Server Express can read database files in a SQL Server 2000 binary file format, but MSDE cannot reliably read database files in SQL Server 2005 format. Connecting to MSDE database files with SQL Server Express, such as with Database Explorer, can make those files unusable by MSDE. On the other hand, being able to use database files in the way Database Explorer permits is, in itself, a powerful incentive for migrating from MSDE to SQL Server Express.

You can follow a four-step process for migrating and revising MSDE databases to SQL Server Express.

1. Detach the files for a database from MSDE. You can use the sp_detach_db system-stored procedure to detach a database.

2. Make a copy of the original MSDE files while they are detached. I recommend you copy them to your VBE project folder with the forms for the project.

3. Reattach the original database files to MSDE. The sp_attach_db system-stored procedure can facilitate this task.

4. Connect to the copied MSDE files with Database Explorer. You may get a time-out on your initial attempt. If you do, just try to make the connection again.

■**Tip** See the "Attaching and Detaching Databases" section in Chapter 3 for guidance on how to detach and reattach database files. Also look in Books Online (the SQL Server documentation files) for help with the sp_detach_db and sp_attach_db system-stored procedures.

Figure 13-7 shows the pubs database in Database Explorer after the selection of the Modify Connection right-click menu item. This opens a dialog box with the name of the menu command. As you can see, the pubs.mdf file is in a folder of the WinCh13 project, which is a Windows application used later in this chapter. You can place your copied MSDE database files anywhere that is convenient. Placing the database files in a project folder is convenient if you want the database files to move whenever you copy or move the folders for a project. For example, to work with the copied pubs database files, all you need to do is copy the WinCh13 folders to your computer.

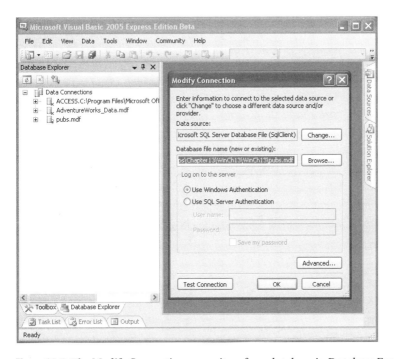

Figure 13-7. *The Modify Connection menu item for a database in Database Explorer can remind you where the database files reside.*

The "Adding Objects to a SQL Server Express Database" section described the steps for adding a new table named `DotNetTable` to the `AdventureWorks` database. You can follow these steps for the `pubs` database to add the `DotNetTable` to the `pubs` database and populate the table with data values. Recall that one main advantage of using Database Explorer to create a table is that no T-SQL is required to create or populate the table. Similarly, you can add a view as described previously.

Figure 13-8 shows the completed design for the view in the visual Query Designer that you can open from Database Explorer. You can override the default name with a name of your choosing, such as `vTitleSales`.

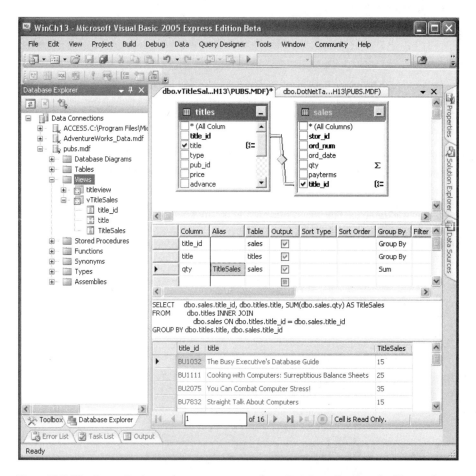

Figure 13-8. *The Query Designer that you can open from Database Explorer facilitates the specification of a new view for a database.*

Adding a Stored Procedure

Database Explorer allows you to add a stored procedure to a database from VBE. In the initial release of VBE, Database Explorer does not offer a graphical designer for stored procedures— T-SQL coding is required. Choosing Add New Stored Procedure from the Stored Procedures folder can open the upcoming template in a window to the right of Database Explorer.

■**Tip** You can learn more about the use of T-SQL with stored procedures in the "Creating and Using Stored Procedures" section of Chapter 7. In addition, Chapters 4 through 7 include many T-SQL samples that you may care to adapt for your own custom stored procedures.

The following listing shows the template that the Add New Stored Procedure command generates for you. You can edit this template to create your custom stored procedure. The template begins with a CREATE PROCEDURE statement. After the statement, the template specifies a stored procedure name of StoredProcedure1 in the dbo schema. You can override the suggested stored procedure and schema names. When you initially save and subsequently open your stored procedure, the built-in stored procedure designer revises the CREATE PROCEDURE statement to an ALTER PROCEDURE statement. Therefore, any changes you make change the previously saved stored procedure instead of creating a new stored procedure (that may have a name conflict with an existing stored procedure).

Between two multiline comment markers (/* and */), the template specifies the syntax for adding an input-output parameter (@parameter1) with a default value of 5 and an output parameter (@parameter2). You can write over either of the parameter specifications to create parameters for your custom stored procedure. If your stored procedure does use parameters, remember to remove the comment markers.

The AS keyword denotes a transition between the declaration and the code for a stored procedure. You can write over the content in the template after the AS keyword to specify what your stored procedure does. Use T-SQL statements, such as a SELECT statement, to specify what the stored procedure does. For those who are just starting to learn T-SQL, you can use the Query Designer to help compose SELECT statements. Then, you can edit these statements, if necessary, for use in your stored procedure.

```
CREATE PROCEDURE dbo.StoredProcedure1
        /*
        (
        @parameter1 int = 5,
        @parameter2 datatype OUTPUT
        )
        */
AS
        /* SET NOCOUNT ON */
        RETURN
```

Figure 13-9 shows a stored procedure named SalesForATitleID in the dbo schema for the copied pubs database. The stored procedure has a single parameter named @titleid used in a SELECT statement after the AS keyword.

When you are writing a stored procedure that is very similar to the one for an existing view, you can copy the SELECT statement from the view to the stored procedure and then edit the SELECT statement. In this case, there are two changes—one for the SELECT list and the other for the addition of a WHERE clause. The SELECT list for the stored procedure omits the title_id item. The WHERE clause appears just before the GROUP BY clause. The syntax for the WHERE clause specifies the return of a row that matches the value of the @titleid parameter value.

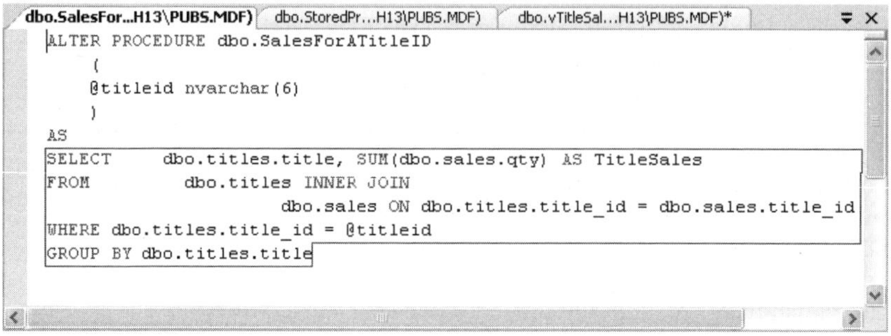

```
dbo.SalesFor...H13\PUBS.MDF)    dbo.StoredPr...H13\PUBS.MDF)      dbo.vTitleSal...H13\PUBS.MDF)*              ▼ ×
ALTER PROCEDURE dbo.SalesForATitleID
    (
    @titleid nvarchar(6)
    )
AS
SELECT      dbo.titles.title, SUM(dbo.sales.qty) AS TitleSales
FROM        dbo.titles INNER JOIN
                    dbo.sales ON dbo.titles.title_id = dbo.sales.title_id
WHERE dbo.titles.title_id = @titleid
GROUP BY dbo.titles.title
```

Figure 13-9. *The stored procedure designer that you can open from Database Explorer facilitates the specification of a new stored procedure for a database.*

Unlike with a view, Database Explorer does not permit you to show the values returned by a SELECT statement within a stored procedure. The "Using a Stored Procedure to Perform a Lookup" section that appears later in this chapter will use both the vTitleSales view and the SalesForATitleID stored procedure on a Windows Form. Through this demonstration, you'll see how to use in a Windows application the database objects that you can create with Database Explorer and its associated designers.

Working with Data Sources and Windows Forms

The Data Sources window in Visual Studio 2005 is an innovation that is also available in VBE. If you ever used the graphical tools for enabling the display and updating of data in Visual Studio 2002 or Visual Studio 2003, you may notice that those tools are no longer available. Microsoft replaced them with a new, richer set of graphical tools that do much more than the former graphical tools. The new Data Sources window is at the heart of the new graphical tools.

Interestingly (and happily), Microsoft did preserve database programming techniques that relied on the ADO.NET model. While the new graphical techniques benefit from an understanding of ADO.NET, you can largely bypass programming ADO.NET for many simple tasks. A working knowledge of the fundamentals of ADO.NET, such as Chapter 11 provides, can help you extend the built-in functionality of the new graphical tools for working with forms. Also, understanding some of the data display innovations with VBE, such as TableAdapters, build on a working knowledge of ADO.NET.

A TableAdapter component, which a Data Source wizard can automatically create, acts like a "super" DataAdapter object. While a DataAdapter can relate one database table, view, or stored procedure to a DataTable in an untyped (or typed) DataSet object, a TableAdapter can relate multiple database tables, views, and stored procedures to a typed DataSet. A typed DataSet is based on the DataSet class as well as an XML schema file (.xsd) that stores specific information about the content with the DataTables within a DataSet as well as the relationships between DataTables. The DataSet Designer in VBE provides a graphical representation of the contents within a typed DataSet object.

The new Data Sources window allows you to specify data sources that you can drag and drop on a Windows Form or assign to the Windows Form controls. When you drag and drop data from the Data Sources window, it can actually create a form control that automatically displays data. Through the combination of the data sources and the Windows Form controls, you can

- Display data unconditionally from a data source.

- Make the display of data conditional and interactive, such as with a form that filters data.

- Allow the two-way communication between your database application and the data source to pass updates in both directions.

When you add a new data source to the Data Sources window, the data source can depend on any one of multiple types of sources, including a database, a business object, or a Web Service. This chapter focuses exclusively on using a database source for a data source. When basing a data source on a database, you can work with connections previously created with the Database Explorer, or you can create new connections directly from the Data Source wizard. In the process of creating a data source, you automatically build a typed `DataSet` object.

When you have data sources populating a Data Sources window, it gives you data sources to which you can graphically bind controls. If there are no data sources in the Data Sources window of your project, you can use new smart tag actions on selected controls, such as a `ListBox` control, to create a new data source that you can, in turn, bind to the control. The new `DataGridView` control is an exceedingly rich control for displaying data in a tabular format and updating data on a Windows Form through a `TableAdapter`.

Creating a Data Source for the Data Sources Window

The default location for the Data Sources window is along the right-hand border of the IDE. If the Data Sources window does not show (even for being hid), you can choose Show Data Sources or Add New Data Source from the Data menu. You can launch the Data Sources Configuration wizard with the Add New Data Source menu item or by clicking the Add New Data Source link in the Data Sources window.

- The initial wizard screen enables you to select a type of source. This book focuses on the use of the database source. Other source types include web service and object.

- The next screen lets you select from a drop-down control any existing connection previously specified in Database Explorer or add a new connection. If you choose to add a new connection, you have access to the same Add Connection dialog box and Change Data Source dialog box previously described in the presentation of Database Explorer.

  - This second wizard screen creates a connection string for you based on your selections.

  - If you choose an existing connection for a database file not in the current project, you may be prompted whether you want to add a copy of the database file to the project folders, and the connection string will be updated to point at the local copy.

- The third screen offers the option of saving the connection string in the project's application configuration file. This screen also allows you to change the default name for the connection string, which is initially based on the primary database file (.mdf) name.

- The fourth screen lets you specify database objects to which your data source provides access. You can also use this screen to specify the name of the typed `DataSet` with which your data source interacts. Figure 13-10 shows the selection of `ProductCategory` and `ProductSubcategory` database tables from the `AdventureWorks` database. Besides tables, you can also populate a data source with views, stored procedures, and user-defined functions. Clicking Finish on this screen commits your data source to the project.

▥**Caution** In order for VBE to populate the Data Sources window with your Data Sources Configuration wizard selections, you'll need to save or build a project at least once.

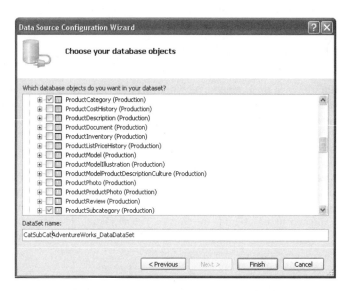

Figure 13-10. *The last Data Source Configuration wizard screen lets you specify the items to which your data source provides access.*

Completing the preceding steps adds a data source to the Data Sources window named CatSubCatAdventureWorks_DataDataSet (see Figure 13-11). Notice this is the DataSet name for the fourth wizard screen in Figure 13-10. This clarifies that the data source is based on the DataSet object. Figure 13-11 shows the Data Sources window with all its nodes expanded.

- Directly below the topmost node (CatSubCatAdventureWorks_DataDataSet) for the DataSet is a pair of nodes named ProductCategory and ProductSubcategory.
    - These names correspond to DataTable names within the DataSet for the data source.
    - The DataTable names are, in turn, based on database table names.
- Within the ProductCategory and ProductSubcategory nodes are end points listing the column names within each DataTable. These DataTable column names correspond to the database column names.
- An additional ProductSubcategory node exists within the ProductCategory node. This nested node represents the relationship of the ProductSubcategory DataTable to the ProductCategory DataTable.

After adding the CatSubCatAdventureWorks_DataDataSet data source to the project, Solution Explorer also changes in a couple of obvious ways. An app.config file appears in Solution Explorer. This file has an XML format with one element having the name ConnectionStrings. Within this element, the Data Sources Configuration wizard adds a new connection string for each new data source that you use. The first connection string points at the AdventureWorks_Data.mdf file in the Data folder for the first SQL Server instance named SQLEXPRESS.

The second new item in Solution Explorer is an entry for the XML schema file for the data source's DataSet. The file's name is CatSubCatAdventureWorks_DataDataSet.xsd. If you show all the files in Solution Explorer, you'll see several files related to it, but the most important file is the one for the XML schema. Double-clicking the file opens a graphical representation of the `DataSet`.

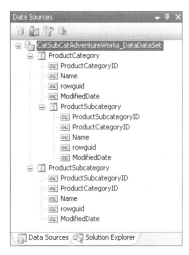

Figure 13-11. *A data source in the Data Sources window maps to a DataSet that you specify in the Data Source Configuration wizard.*

In this screen, you will see the relation between the `DataTables` and a `TableAdapter` object associated with each `DataTable`. The `TableAdapters` are named after the `DataTables` with which they are associated. In spite of this initial correspondence between a `DataTable` and a `TableAdapter`, one `TableAdapter` has the potential to populate multiple `DataTable` objects. A `GetData` method for a `TableAdapter` defines a new `DataTable` instance and populates the new instance with data, and a `Fill` method populates an existing `DataTable` instance.

■**Note** If you prefer, you can open the .xsd file for a `DataSet` in XML format by right-clicking the file in Solution Explorer and choosing Open With. Then, select XML editor from the Open With dialog box for the .xsd file.

Dragging Data Source Items to a Windows Form

One of the most exciting features of the Data Sources window is the ability to drag items from the window to a form and to immediately enable the viewing of data. There is no need for any code. While you can make settings to enrich the functionality to enhance user interactivity with the data, you can obtain a form for displaying, browsing, and editing data just by dragging items from the Data Sources window.

You can drag the `ProductCategory` node to `Form1` from the `CatSubCatAdventureWorks_DataDataSet` node in the Data Sources window of the WinCh13 project. This adds a `DataGridView` control to `Form1` that automatically has a horizontal scrollbar for viewing all the columns in the `ProductCategory` `DataTable`. Furthermore, a `BindingNavigator` control just below the top border of `Form1` enables a user to edit column values in rows as well as add and delete rows with the help of the automatically supplied `BindingNavigator` control. If there were more rows that appeared in the display area on `Form1`, then the `BindingNavigator` control would allow a user to navigate between rows, such as from the first row to the last row.

Figure 13-12 shows `Form1` with an edit in progress. An X is appended to the end of the `Name` column value in the first row. Moving off the row shows the value as committed (the pencil marker on the left border goes away). However, closing and opening `Form1` shows the `Name` column value without the appended X. In order to commit a change to the underlying database table from a form and not just change the intermediate DataTable in the local DataSet, users must press the Save button on the far right of the BindingNavigator control after editing a column value. Then, closing and opening Form1 shows the change is saved in the database. The same rule applies to the addition and the deleting of rows. No change is final until a user clicks the Save control on the BindingNavigator control after making the change.

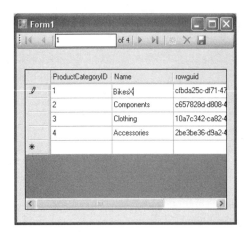

Figure 13-12. *You can browse and edit data in the new DataGridView control just by dragging the node for a DataTable to a Windows Form.*

If you look at Form1 in Design view, you'll notice that several controls exist in a tray below the form. If you developed database solutions with Visual Studio 2002 or Visual Studio 2003, this may remind you of these earlier Visual Studio versions. However, in this case, the controls are automatically added to the tray below the form. Furthermore, the control names are different from what they were in the earlier Visual Studio versions. This is not your grandfather's version of Visual Studio! For this basic databinding example, developing a solution is faster than ever before.

In addition to representing the values in a DataTable by a DataGridView control, you can also specify a Details control. A drop-down list after nodes for DataTable names in the Data Sources window enables you to select either the DataGridView or Details view for displaying the values in a DataTable on a form. By selecting Details just before dragging the ProductCategory node to Form2 in the WinCh13 project, you get a layout like the one in Figure 13-13. The Details control has a separate TextBox for each column in the DataTable along with a corresponding label.

A Details control represents DataTable values one row at a time. This makes it easier to tell which row is currently active and removes potentially distracting information from other rows. The Details control has the same BindingNavigator control to help with navigating through rows and editing the values in a database table underlying the DataTable values showing in the form.

You cannot selectively remove individual columns from the Details control representation of the values in a DataTable object. However, you can also drag individual columns to a form. The default representation for column values in a DataTable is a TextBox control. Whether you use Details or DataGridView controls to show all the columns in a DataTable or you drag individual columns to a form to show data in TextBox controls, the form still enables the browsing and editing of data values with the BindingNavigator control.

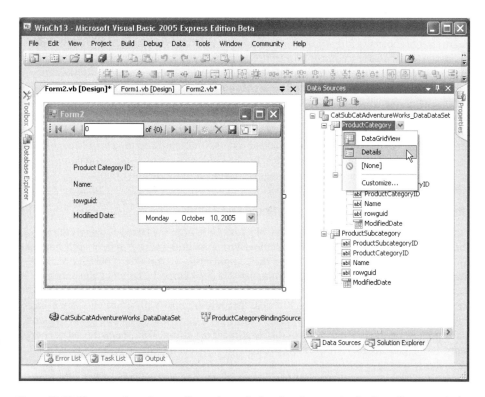

Figure 13-13. *You can drop down a list at the end of an item's name in the Data Sources window to select the form control used to display the values in a DataTable.*

Figure 13-14 shows Form3 in the WinCh13 project with a couple of bound TextBox controls. You can add these TextBox controls to the form by dragging the ProductCategoryID and Name items within the ProductCategory node of the Data Sources windows. The form shows an edit to the Name column value for the first row in the ProductCategory DataTable. Clicking the Save button will commit the change to the database table in the AdventureWorks database underlying the ProductCategory DataTable in the CatSubCatAdventureWorks_DataDataSet data source.

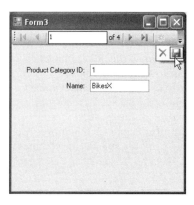

Figure 13-14. *By dragging individual column names to a form, you can select a subset of the columns in a DataTable for display on a form.*

Modifying Control Behavior with Smart Tags

Smart tags are a set of shortcuts for performing common tasks or actions with a control. You can view the smart tag shortcuts for a control by selecting the control and clicking its smart-tag glyph, which appears as a right-facing arrow towards the top-right border. The smart tag shortcuts can vary according to the control that you select. The list of shortcuts can even vary depending on which prior shortcuts you select.

Microsoft did a good job of making the smart tag shortcut names self-documenting. Therefore, just opening the smart tags for a control makes it apparent what you can do. The best way to learn about these shortcuts is to use them. This section illustrates several shortcuts for a couple of controls in database applications to give you a firsthand feel for the kinds of tasks that you can accomplish with smart tags. Previous examples using smart tags with Web Forms appear in Chapter 10.

Limiting the Columns That Appear in a DataGridView Control

As Figure 13-12 demonstrated, dragging the name for a DataTable from the Data Sources window to a form can populate a DataGridView control with all the columns in the DataTable. It frequently happens that an application only needs to show a subset of the columns from a DataTable. A DataGridView binds to a set of columns—not an individual column like a TextBox control. Therefore, the only source from the Data Sources window suitable for populating the control is a node for a DataTable.

You can restrict the columns that appear in a DataGridView control with smart tags. After dragging a DataTable name, such as ProductCategory, to a form, open the smart tags display by clicking the right-facing arrow on the top-right side of the DataGridView control. This opens the list of shortcuts that appear in Figure 13-15. Here's a short summary for each of the smart tag actions in the DataGridView shortcut list.

- Choose Data Source lets you choose from any existing data source in the Data Sources window or add a new data source if you want to use one not currently available.

- Edit Columns lets you modify the columns that appear and their properties.

- Add Column opens a dialog box to help you add a new column.

- Enable Adding, Enable Editing, and Enable Deleting control the ability to modify the local DataTable source for a control.

- Enable Column Reordering permits a user to rearrange the order of columns.

- Dock in parent container docks the control so that it fills the available space within its parent.

- Add Query lets you add a query so that you can make the rows displayed in a control conditional on runtime input from a user.

- Preview Data opens a dialog box for previewing data returned by queries in a data source.

By clicking the Edit Columns shortcut for DataGridView tasks, you open the Edit Columns dialog box. You can use the Selected Columns list box in this dialog box to remove columns.

After removing the rowguid and ModifiedDate columns, Form4 in the WinCh13 project opens looking like Figure 13-16. This new version of the DataGridView control for the ProductCategory DataTable contrasts with the initial version of the DataGridView control for the ProductCategory DataTable in Figure 13-12. In particular, the new version of the control in Figure 13-16 removes two columns that most users are not likely to want to see. However, the DataTable still has the columns available for other forms that may need to display those columns.

Figure 13-15. *The smart tag tasks for a DataGridView control cover several different topics, including the ability to edit the columns appearing within the control.*

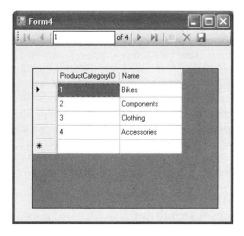

Figure 13-16. *After removing the rowguid and ModifiedData columns, a DataGridView control for the ProductCategory DataTable shows just two remaining columns.*

Restricting Updating with the DataGridView Control

There are multiple approaches to restricting the ability to update data from a control. The next example shows how to accomplish this task by removing features with smart tags from a DataGridView control and its corresponding BindingNavigator control. This example removes the ability to edit existing values as well as add new rows and remove existing rows from the DataTable for a DataGridView control. While these actions are sufficient for restricting the ability to make data modifications from the DataGridView control, they do not restrict the ability to make any kind of data modification from the form.

In order to fully lock out the ability to make changes from the form, you need to alter the BindingNavigator control as well. This control is bound to the same DataTable as the DataGridView control. Even if changes through the DataGridView control are disabled, users can still select a row, delete the row, and then save the changes to the database table corresponding to the DataTable in the client application. The BindingNavigator control enables these features through its own controls without the assistance of the DataGridView control. In order to remove the ability to delete rows and propagate those changes to the database, you need to remove the controls enabling the deletion of the currently selected row and the ability to save changes in the local DataTable to the corresponding database table.

Two sample forms demonstrate how to fully restrict the ability to make local changes to a DataTable and propagate those changes to a corresponding database table.

- The first form, Form5, just clears the Enable Adding, Enable Editing, and Enable Deleting check boxes in Form5. This restricts the ability to make changes through the DataGridView control.

- The second form, Form6, removes the bindingNavigatorAddNewItem, bindingNavigatorDeleteItem, and bindingNavigatorSaveItem controls from the BindingNavigator control.

Both forms use a new data source based on the pubs database, which was initially discussed in the "Migrating and Revising an MSDE Database" section. If you do not have an MSDE version of the pubs database, you can follow the instructions in the "Installing Sample Databases" section of Chapter 1 to download a version of the pubs database that you can use with SQL Server Express. Then, make the design changes to the database described in the "Migrating and Revising an MSDE Database" section. You need these changes for some subsequent examples but not the examples in this section, because this section uses a standard version of the titles table in the pubs database. However, recall that the final revised version of the pubs database files are in the WinCh13 project folder. Therefore, you can make a data source based on the database files in that folder if you prefer.

Adapt the instructions in the "Creating a Data Source for the Data Sources Window" section for populating a new data source. The data source should have the titles and sales tables, the vTitleSales view, and the SalesForATitleID stored procedure. The last two items are added to the pubs database with the instructions in the "Migrating and Revising an MSDE Database" section.

From the Data Sources window in WinCh13, drag the titles node to a new form named Form5. This will populate the form with a BindingNavigator control over a DataGridView control. Use the Edit Columns smart tag action for the DataGridView control to specify that only the title_id, title, type, and pubdate columns show in the DataGridView control. These columns are required for the entry of a new row. Also clear the Enable Adding, Enable Editing, and Enable Deleting check boxes in the smart tag window. Clearing these boxes disables the ability to edit the titles DataTable from the DataGridView control on the form.

In another new form, Form6, repeat the process for creating Form5. After completing these steps, open the smart tag for the BindingNavigator control. Click the Edit Items link at the bottom on the BindingNavigator Tasks window (see Figure 13-17). This click opens the Items Collection Editor dialog box. From the Members list box on the dialog box, select the bindingNavigatorAddNewItem and click the X control to remove the bindingNavigatorAddNewItem. Repeat the process for the bindingNavigatorDeleteItem and bindingNavigatorSaveItem before clicking OK to commit your changes to the BindingNavigator control.

It is helpful to have a new row for the titles table in order to contrast the behavior of Form5 and Form6. Since neither form can add a new row to the titles table (the Adding Items check box is cleared for both forms), you can use Database Explorer to add a row. From Database Explorer, choose Show Table Data from the right-click menu of the titles table in the pubs database. In the row of null values at the bottom of the result set, you can enter new values for the four columns showing the DataGridView controls on Form5 and Form6. The sample for contrasting the two forms uses the following column values for the new row.

- title_id: AA1234
- title: Book by Rick Dobson
- type: popular_comp
- pubdate: 12/15/2005

Figure 13-17. *Click the Edit Items link in the BindingNavigator Tasks window to modify the items that show on a BindingNavigator control.*

Figure 13-18 shows Form5 and Form6 side by side. Form5 is on the left. Both forms have the newly added row with a title_id column value of AA1234. However, Form5 on the left has its Delete control selected. By clicking this control, and then the Save Data control, a user of Form5 can delete the selected row successively from the local titles DataTable and then from the titles table in the pubs database. Notice that the BindingNavigator control in Form6 has no controls for modifying data. Therefore, Form6 demonstrates one appropriate way for allowing form navigation without form editing. This approach also reinforces your understanding of smart tags, and it exposes you to techniques for modifying the BindingNavigator control.

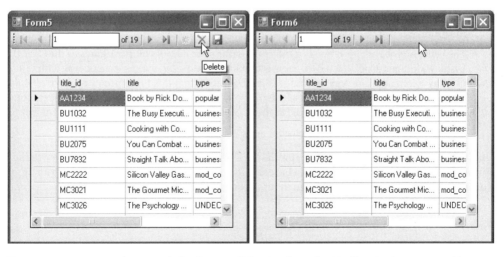

Figure 13-18. *Removing the controls for data modification from the BindingNavigator control is necessary to remove the ability to modify data in a database table.*

Configuring and Using ListBox Controls

Recall that DataTable elements within a data source have multiple form controls that can represent them when you drag them to a form. Similarly, Column elements within a DataTable node have multiple form controls that can represent them when you drag them to a form. While the default form control type for a Column element is a TextBox control, another selectable control type is a ListBox control. When you drag a Column name from the Data Sources window after first designating that you want a ListBox on the form, the Windows Form Designer adds a BindingNavigation control and a Label for the ListBox control with the name of the column. However, the ListBox control is initially unbound. If you open the form without first configuring the ListBox, it appears empty!

To make a ListBox control based on a column from a data source show values, you first have to configure the ListBox control. Surprisingly, the ListBox is not automatically bound to the column that you drag from the Data Sources window to instantiate the ListBox control on the form. The smart tag window for a ListBox offers one of two ways to configure the control.

- You can override the default unbound status of a ListBox control by manually adding items to its Items collection. Select the Edit Items link in the smart tag window to open a dialog box that assists with this task.

- Select the Use data bound items check box to populate the ListBox control with Items based on a data source from the Data Sources window or a new data source that you can add to the project for the control.

If you select the Use data bound items check box, the smart tag window for the ListBox expands to show a Data Binding Mode section.

- Use the Data Source drop-down box to select a DataTable name within a DataSet corresponding to one of the data sources in the Data Sources window. After you select the DataTable, the Windows Form Designer populates the Data Source drop-down box with the name of a BindingSource object, such as ProductCategoryBindingSource1.

- Your selection for the Data Source drop-down box will populate the Display Member drop-down box with column names from the DataTable selected for the Data Source drop-down box. Display Member column values appear as items in the ListBox control when users open the form.

- The Value Member drop-down box offers the same selection of column names as the Display Member drop-down box. Value Members correspond in a one-to-one way with Display Member column values. The currently selected item in a ListBox control normally has contrasting colors to other unselected items. The Value Member column value corresponding to the selected item is available as the SelectedValue property for the ListBox control.

- The SelectedValue entry is normally left at its default value of none.

Figure 13-19 shows the smart tag window for the NameListBox control. The settings will cause the control to display Name column values and have a SelectedValue property corresponding to a row value from the ProductCategoryID column in the ProductCategory DataTable.

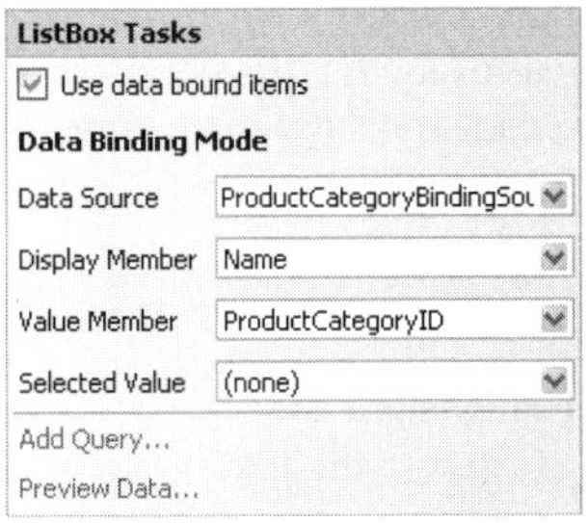

Figure 13-19. *Select the Use data bound items check box in the smart tag window for a ListBox to select display and value members from a binding source.*

Form7 uses a pair of TextBox controls to track the SelectedValue and SelectedIndex property values for the NameListBox control. These two values update when the Form7 loads initially and whenever a user clicks a new item in the ListBox control. The BindingNavigator control does not contribute to this solution. Therefore, Form7's Load event procedure assigns False to the Visible property of the BindingNavigator control. This hides the control.

Figure 13-20 shows Form7 after a click to the Clothing item. Notice the value of 3 for the SelectedValue property. The number corresponds to the ProductCategoryID column value for the row with a Name column value of Clothing. The SelectedIndex value is a zero-based series that is for the ListBox items. The value 0 corresponds to Bikes. Therefore, the value 2 is the index value for Clothing.

Figure 13-20. *A ListBox control updates its SelectedValue and SelectedIndex property values whenever a new item is selected.*

The Windows Form Designer initializes the code in the Load event procedure for Form7. The code for this procedure appears as the following code segment. Despite the fact that the Windows Form Designer initializes the procedure, you can add your own custom code to facilitate the functionality and features illustrated by Figure 13-20.

- The procedure starts by filling the ProductCategory DataTable in the CatSubCatAdventureWorks_ DataDataSet DataSet. This is the code written by the Windows Form Designer.

- Next, the code calls the UpdateTextBoxes procedure. This procedure assigns the SelectedValue property and the SelectedIndex property of the ListBox to the Text property settings for TextBox1 and TextBox2.

- The Load event procedure concludes by formatting some controls on the form.

```
Me.ProductCategoryTableAdapter.Fill( _
 Me.CatSubCatAdventureWorks_DataDataSet.ProductCategory)

UpdateTextBoxes()

Me.Label1.Text = "SelectedValue:"
Me.Label2.Text = "SelectedIndex:"
Me.ProductCategoryBindingNavigator.Visible = False
```

The SelectedIndexChanged event procedure also calls the UpdateTextBoxes procedure. This event procedure fires whenever a user clicks a new item in the ListBox control. The concluding code segment for this sample is the UpdateTextBoxes procedure. Its two most important lines are the two assignment statements in the Try clause for updating the Text property values of TextBox1 and TextBox2. These statements demonstrate the syntax for referencing the SelectedValue and SelectedIndex property values for a ListBox.

Note The .NET Framework raises the SelectedIndexChanged event for a ListBox control whenever a user selects a new item from its Items collection. You can do this by clicking an item with your mouse or by moving the currently highlighted item with arrow keys on the keyboard.

The bolClosed variable is a Boolean variable declared at the module level. This variable initializes by default to False. The FormClosed event procedure for Form7 changes the variable's value to True. The Catch clause allows a graceful exit from a faulty behavior by the Windows Form Designer after the FormClosed event.

```
Sub UpdateTextBoxes()
  Try
   Me.TextBox1.Text = Me.NameListBox.SelectedValue.ToString
   Me.TextBox2.Text = Me.NameListBox.SelectedIndex.ToString
  Catch ex As Exception
   If bolClosed = False Then
    MessageBox.Show(ex.Message)
   Else
    'Test diagnostic output; do not run normally
    'MessageBox.Show(ex.Message)
   End If
  End Try
End Sub
```

Creating and Using Interactive Data Displays

Interactive data displays allow the data on a form to change in response to user input. For example, a user might want to look up information about an item in a database, such as a product or a person. Nearly all the samples to this point in the chapter focus on returning a fixed result set, such as a set of column values from the ProductCategory database table in the AdventureWorks database. This section will demonstrate the application of built-in and customized techniques for allowing users to change the results that they display on a form.

It is one thing to see results change based on user input, but it is also important to be able to change the results in a database based on user input. The default way of committing changes to a database with graphical approaches, such as those covered in this chapter, is through *optimistic concurrency*. This approach is preferred because it increases the number of users that a database can serve in comparison to another popular approach called *pessimistic locking*. However, one disadvantage of optimistic concurrency is that someone else can change data before you commit your change to a database. In this case, your change must be rejected because the database cannot find the base record that you want to modify (after all, someone else modified it already). This chapter demonstrates an easy technique for handling errors resulting from database concurrency, which happen when two different users try to change the same row in a database table or view.

Adding a Parameter Query to Look Up Information

The classic way to make results dynamic at runtime is with a parameter query. A *parameter query* is a regular SELECT statement with a WHERE clause that has one or more key-value pairs. The key is a column name in the data source specified by the FROM clause for the SELECT statement. The value is a parameter or a criterion. The WHERE clause contains an operator, such as an equal sign (=), between each key-value pair that returns a value of True or False. If your parameter query has more than one key-value pair, then you must have operators between pairs so that the overall parameter query returns a value of True or False. The parameter query returns a subset of rows from the original query for parameter expression values equal to True. In a sense, a parameter query looks up information for rows that match its search criteria.

Parameter queries are so popular that Microsoft has traditionally made them very easy to use in its database applications, and the tradition continues with TableAdapters for a DataGridView control. Recall that a DataGridView control relies on a TableAdapter. The Windows Form Designer automatically adds the TableAdapter for the DataGridView control to a Components tray below the form containing the DataGridView control. You can add a new query to the TableAdapter from the smart tag window for the TableAdapter. This query should contain a WHERE clause for a parameter query. After completing the query, the Windows Form Designer adds a control to the form that allows users to specify parameter values and run the parameter query to specify a subset of values from the original query to populate the DataGridView control.

You can start to create your first parameter query graphically by dragging the ProductSubCategory node from the CatSubCatAdventureWorks_DataDataSet data source in the Data Sources window for the WinCh13 project. This adds a DataGridView control and a corresponding BindingNavigator control to a new form, such as Form8. Edit the columns for the DataGridView control to drop the rowguid and ModifiedDate columns. The Load event procedure for Form8 includes the following assignment statement for dynamically resizing the ProductSubcategoryID column in the DataGridView control so that the column is initially wide enough to display its heading without cropping.

```
Me.ProductSubcategoryDataGridView. _
  Columns("ProductSubcategoryID").MinimumWidth = 115
```

In the Components tray, open the smart tag for the ProductSubcategoryTableAdapter and click the Add Query link. After the click, the Search Criteria Builder dialog box opens. You must specify the syntax for a new query, and you must assign the new query a name (or you can use a previously specified query). The query name specifies a FillBy method that you can invoke with code for more customized solutions. However, the basic approach described here requires no code. In the current example, assign the name FillByCatID as the name of the query. The syntax for the query within the Search Criteria Builder dialog box appears in Figure 13-21.

Figure 13-22 shows Form8 after it initially opens and after a value of 1 is entered as an @CatID parameter. The top view of Form8 shows the form when it opens. Notice that the BindingNavigator permits navigation to any one of 37 rows in the DataGridView control. This view of the data returned by the ProductSubcategoryTableAdapter includes no parameters. However, you can see the control for entering a parameter value above the BindingNavigator control. A TextBox is available for specifying an @CatID parameter value, and the text to the right of the TextBox can be clicked to invoke a parameter query that populates the DataGridView control with the results of the query.

After entering a value of 1 for the parameter and clicking FillByCatID1, the DataGridView control displays just three rows. Each of these rows has a ProductCategoryID column value of 1. You can change the contents of the DataGridView control to display any other subset of rows based on ProductCategoryID column values by inputting a new value for @CatID and clicking FillByCatID1.

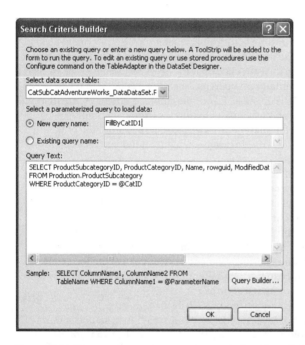

Figure 13-21. *You can create a parameter query for a DataGridView control as simply as naming the query and adding a WHERE clause in a dialog box.*

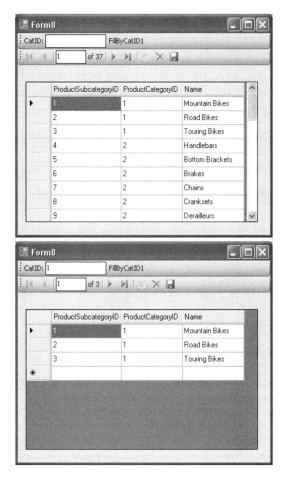

Figure 13-22. *Creating basic parameter queries for a DataGridView control is easy and powerful with the TableAdapter object.*

Performing a Lookup with Two ListBox Controls

You can readily extend the preceding example for parameter queries to all kinds of conditional, interactive displays. This section shows a simple extension that removes the need for a user to type in a number indicating the ProductCategoryID value for the list of product categories to show. Instead of typing in a number, a user can select from a list of product category names. After the selection of the name in one ListBox control, the application populates a second ListBox control with the product subcategory names from the currently selected category in the first ListBox control. In addition, the Click event procedure for a Button control changes the Items collection for the second ListBox to include all product subcategory names. Form9 in the WinCh13 project implements this solution.

Figure 13-23 shows side by side the Design view and Form view of Form9 in the WinCh13 project. The Load event procedure for Form9 formats the controls by assigning Text property values to the Label and Button controls as well as changing the position and size of the Button control. The Load event procedure also populates the first ListBox control on the left (ListBox1), which, in turn, populates the remaining ListBox control (ListBox2). Clicking items in ListBox1 repopulates ListBox2 with items from the most recently selected product category. Clicking the Button control (Button1) above ListBox2 repopulates ListBox2 to show all product subcategory names.

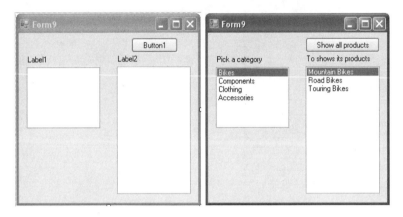

Figure 13-23. *While it is OK to allow a user to enter a value to specify a parameter query, it is generally easier for users to select an item from a ListBox control.*

It is preferable to drag the ListBox controls to a form from the Toolbox. This avoids having the Windows Form Designer generate a BindingNavigator control for each ListBox control (the BindingNavigator controls do not participate in the solution anyway). You can still use the smart tag window to set the bound data for each ListBox control.

Figure 13-24 shows the smart tag settings for ListBox1. This control binds to ProductCategory DataTable through the ProductCategoryBindingSource. The settings in the smart tag ListBox Tasks window cause ListBox1 to display Name column values from the ProductCategory DataTable and return the ProductCategoryID value as its SelectedValue property. The particular ProductCategoryID column value corresponds to the most recently selected item from the ListBox1 control.

The smart tag ListBox Tasks settings for ListBox2 appear in Figure 13-25. ListBox2 binds to the ProductSubcategory DataTable through the ProductSubcategoryBindingSource. You only need to set the Display Member for ListBox2 because its sole purpose is to show column values corresponding to the selected item in ListBox1.

Note A BindingSource class interfaces a Windows Form control with a source of data. The BindingSource can work with all types of databases (SQL Server, OLE DB, and ODBC) and other types of sources as well (web services and business objects). As with the TableAdapter class, particular instances of the class take the name of the source with which they interface. For example, the ProductCategoryBindingSource is a BindingSource class instance that interfaces with the ProductCategory DataTable.

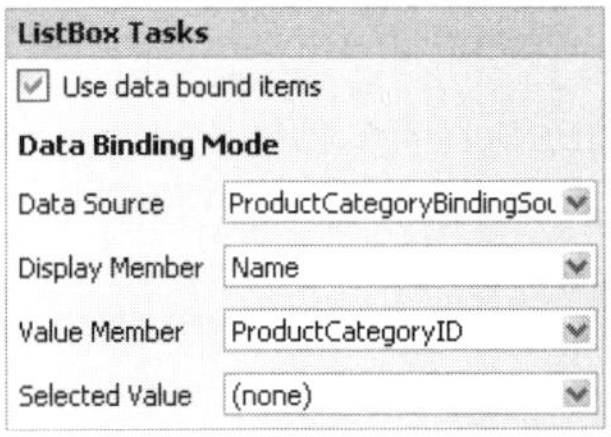

Figure 13-24. *When specifying a parameter through a ListBox selection, it is common to designate the parameter value with the Value Member setting.*

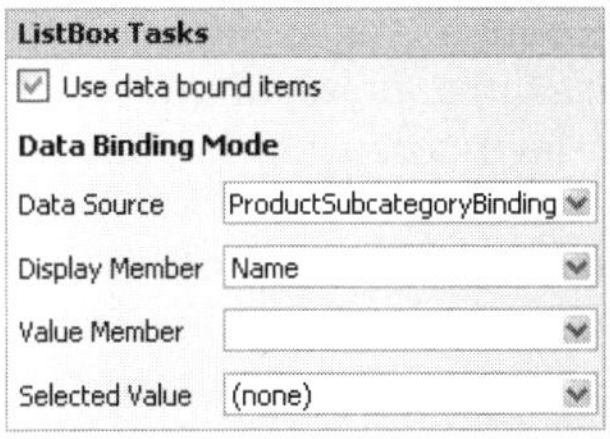

Figure 13-25. *There is no need to specify a Value Member setting when a ListBox control is just meant to show a collection of values.*

The graphical tools for displaying data are so rich that they drastically reduce the amount of code that is necessary. These tools include the Windows Form Designer that writes a substantial amount of code in a partial class that is out of view most of the time (except when Exception objects are thrown to halt normal execution). In addition, the Windows Form designer even inserts some code in the Load event procedure. You can modify or comment out this code as your needs dictate.

The code inside the Load event procedure for Form9 appears as the next code segment.

- The first two statements are generated by the Windows Form Designer.
  - The statement to populate the ProductSubcategory DataTable is commented out because the procedure uses another approach for populating this DataTable. The alternative approach is necessary because the values in the DataTable need to have the option to be conditional.
  - The statement to populate the ProductCategory DataTable is also supplied by the Windows Form Designer. This code is acceptable as supplied for use in the demonstration.
- The call to the UpdateListBox2 procedure populates the ProductSubcategory DataTable based on the currently selected item in ListBox1. When the form loads, the currently selected item in ListBox1 is the first Name column value for the first row in the ProductCategory DataTable.
- The remaining lines of code in the Load event procedure format the controls in Form9.

```
'TODO: This line of code loads data into the
'CatSubCatAdventureWorks_DataDataSet.ProductSubcategory' table.
'You can move, or remove it, as needed.
'Me.ProductSubcategoryTableAdapter.Fill( _
'Me.CatSubCatAdventureWorks_DataDataSet.ProductSubcategory)
'TODO: This line of code loads data into the
'CatSubCatAdventureWorks_DataDataSet.ProductCategory' table.
'You can move, or remove it, as needed.
Me.ProductCategoryTableAdapter.Fill( _
Me.CatSubCatAdventureWorks_DataDataSet.ProductCategory)
```

```
UpdateListBox2()

Me.Label1.Text = "Pick a category"
Me.Label2.Text = "To show its products"
Me.Button1.Text = "Show all products"
Me.Button1.Width = Me.ListBox2.Width
Me.Button1.Left = Me.ListBox2.Left
Me.Button1.BackColor = Color.Transparent
```

The code in the UpdateListBox2 procedure, which consists of a single line, populates the ProductSubcategory DataTable based on the currently selected value in ListBox1. Two types of event procedures invoke the UpdateListBox2 procedure: when Form9 loads (Form9_Load) and every time a user selects an item from ListBox1 (ListBox1_SelectedIndexChanged). The following listing from the UpdateListBox2 procedure shows two different syntax styles for specifying the instruction—one illustrating the use of a traditional Visual Basic function and another presenting a comparable technique using a comparable .NET Framework class. The approach using the .NET Framework class is commented out.

The statement uses the FillByCatID1 method for the ProductSubcategoryTableAdapter. This method was silently created by the steps to add a query to the ProductSubcategoryTableAdapter in Form8. If you did not create that Form8, the Components tray for Form9 also has a ProductSubcategory-TableAdapter components icon. You can use the instructions describing how to add a query from the preceding example for this example. If you did create the method, you can just refer to it with the following syntax. The FillByCatID1 method represents a parameter query that requires a parameter value. The parameter value should match one of the values in the ProductCategoryID column of the ProductSubcategory DataTable.

- The SelectedValue method always returns an Object value, but a CInt function transforms the String value to an Integer value for the parameter value required by the FillByCatID1 method.

- Instead of using the CInt function to transform a String value to an Integer value, you can invoke the ToInt32 member of the Convert class in the System namespace. You can use this approach for making transformations between nearly all kinds of data types by using other members of the System.Convert class. For example, only String values can convert to DateTime values. An attempt to convert any other data type to a DateTime data type throws an InvalidCastException.

```
Me.ProductSubcategoryTableAdapter.FillByCatID1( _
Me.CatSubCatAdventureWorks_DataDataSet.ProductSubcategory, _
CInt(Me.ListBox1.SelectedValue))

'Shows System.Convert.ToInt32 syntax to replace CInt syntax
'Me.ProductSubcategoryTableAdapter.FillByCatID1( _
'Me.CatSubCatAdventureWorks_DataDataSet.ProductSubcategory,
'System.Convert.ToInt32(Me.ListBox1.SelectedValue))
```

The final procedure in the Form9 module is the Click event procedure for Button1. This procedure uses the standard Fill method for the ProductSubcategoryTableAdapter. The query for this method has the same syntax as the one for the FillByCatID1 method, except the Fill method query has no WHERE clause in its SELECT statement. Therefore, the query for the Fill method returns all the rows from the ProductSubcategory DataTable.

```
Me.ProductSubcategoryTableAdapter.Fill( _
Me.CatSubCatAdventureWorks_DataDataSet.ProductSubcategory)
```

Using a Stored Procedure to Perform a Lookup

Instead of looking up values with a SQL statement, it is often preferable to use a stored procedure. A stored procedure can sometimes perform a search faster than using a query string. In addition, it is generally more secure to have a database server accept one or more parameters for a stored procedure than a query statement. This section illustrates the use of a stored procedure to perform a lookup.

The sample for this section uses a stored procedure and a view from the pubs database. These two database objects were added to the pubs database in the "Migrating and Revising an MSDE Database" section. The objects are available with the revised pubs database files that are in the WinCh13 project folder. This sample also assumes you previously added a data source for the pubs database to the Data Sources window. You can run the demonstration for this section by adding the titles and sales tables as well as the vTitleSales view and SalesForATitleID stored procedure to the data source as described in the "Restricting Updating with the DataGridView Control" section.

The sample form for this section is Form10 in the WinCh13 project. Figure 13-26 shows a Design view of Form10 on its left and a Form view on its right. The two main design elements for the form are a ListBox control above a pair of TextBox controls with Label controls to their left. Users can select a title from the ListBox control to make the form display information about the selected title in the TextBox controls. Because the SalesForATitleID stored procedure returns a book's title along with its sales, the TextBox controls display the sales and title for a book. For the purposes of the demonstration, it doesn't matter what column values for a selected row are returned. When you design a variation of this solution for your custom applications, you can write your stored procedure to return any values that your application requires.

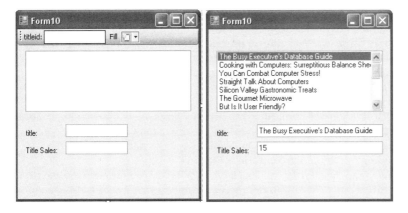

Figure 13-26. *In this sample form, a user can select an item in a ListBox control to show other values, such as sales, for the selected item.*

The vTitleSales view serves as the data source for the ListBox control in Form10. This view uses an inner join to merge the sales and titles tables in the pubs database. Therefore, the view's result set rows are exclusively for books that appear in both the titles and the sales tables. If a book fails to appear in the sales table because it is not in print yet, then the book will not appear as a row in the result set for the vTitleSales view. It is often convenient to do this kind of filtering (excluding rows that do not match a criterion) for a data source that you pass to a form. This practice can simplify the application logic that you need behind a form.

The vTitleSales view and SalesForATitleID stored procedure work together to meet the display requirements for Form10.

- The vTitleSales view has three columns in its result set, including title_id, title, and sales. Therefore, the vTitleSales view can enable the ListBox to
  - Show book titles.
  - Return the title_id column value for the selected title as its SelectedValue property.
- The SalesForATitleID stored procedure accepts a title_id value as an input parameter and returns a result set having a single row with title and sales column values for the book with a title_id specified as an input parameter.
  - The sales column value is from the sales table. The stored procedure sums the sales from multiple stores for a title.
  - The title column value is from the titles table.

■Tip Notice that the SalesForATitleID stored procedure returns two scalar values in its result set. Therefore, you could revise the stored procedure to return the scalar values as output parameters instead of a result set. Because of the ease of returning a result set from a stored procedure, it is common practice to pass back scalar values as column values in a single row of a result set. With this approach, a developer has to learn one technique for retrieving values from a stored procedure instead of two separate approaches for result sets and output parameters.

The two TextBox controls and their matching Label controls were added to Form10 by dragging the SalesForATitleID node from the pubs data source in the Data Sources window. Before dragging the node to the form, you should select Details as the type of control for the data source node. This action binds the TextBox controls to the columns in the result set from the SalesForATitleID DataTable. To change the values appearing in the TextBox controls when the user for the application selects a new title, all you need to do is rerun the stored procedure, which, in turn, repopulates the SalesForATitleID DataTable in the DataSet mapping to the pubs database.

Dragging the SalesForATitleID node from the Data Sources window to Form10 automatically adds a control at the top of the form to accept user input for the SalesForATitleID parameter. Because a selection in the ListBox based on the vTitleSales view supplies an input parameter for the SalesForATitleID stored procedure, there is no need for users to manually input a title_id value as an input parameter. Therefore, the sample application assigns a value of False to the Visible property of the automatically added control at the top of the form.

The code to automate the application depicted in Figure 13-26 relies on three main procedures. The first of these is a Load event procedure for Form10 whose code appears in the next code segment.

- A Windows designer automatically adds code to the form's Load event procedure.
  - In this case, the automatically added code populates the vTitleSales DataTable in the DataSet mapping to the pubs database.
  - Since ListBox1 binds to the vTitleSales DataTable, the ListBox control shows the values in the DataTable.
  - The first item in the ListBox is automatically selected.
- A call to the RunStoredProc procedure runs the stored procedure.
- The last few lines in the Load event procedure perform control formatting, such as making invisible the ToolStrip control for accepting an input parameter.

```
Me.VTitleSalesTableAdapter.Fill(Me.PubsDataSet.vTitleSales)

RunStoredProc()
```

```
Me.FillToolStrip.Visible = False
Dim intLBDisp As Integer = (Me.ListBox1.Left + Me.ListBox1.Width)
Me.TitleTextBox.Width += intLBDisp - _
 (Me.TitleTextBox.Left + Me.TitleTextBox.Width)
Me.TitleSalesTextBox.Width += intLBDisp - _
(Me.TitleSalesTextBox.Left + Me.TitleSalesTextBox.Width)
```

The second procedure is for the SelectedIndexChanged event for ListBox1. This procedure runs whenever a user selects a new item in the ListBox control.

- The most important task the procedure does is to call the RunStoredProc procedure. The call to this procedure appears in the Try clause of a Try...Catch...End Try statement. The procedure call allows the form to update its values for the two TextBox controls to match the most recently selected item from the ListBox.

- Built-in Windows designers can generate some aberrant behavior either before Form10 initially appears or after the form is closed. The Catch clause traps Exception objects resulting from this aberrant behavior and ignores the irrelevant Exception objects. A couple of module-level variable declarations (bolShown and bolClosed) and some code for controlling the value of the variables assist the Try...Catch...End Try statement in managing the aberrant behavior.

```
Try
 RunStoredProc()
Catch ex As Exception
 If bolShown = True And bolClosed = False Then
  MessageBox.Show(ex.ToString)
 End If
End Try
```

The RunStoredProc procedure runs the SalesForATitleID stored procedure. In turn, this populates the SalesForATitleID DataTable in the DataSet for the pubs database. The good news is that it takes just one line of code to run the server-side stored procedure and populate the client-side DataTable. When you dragged the SalesForATitleID node from the Data Sources window, it automatically created the SalesForATitleIDTableAdapter and the Fill method to accomplish this. The Fill method takes two arguments:

- One for the DataTable to populate

- A second for the input parameter for the stored procedure.

```
Me.SalesForATitleIDTableAdapter.Fill(Me.PubsDataSet.SalesForATitleID,
 Me.ListBox1.SelectedValue.ToString)
```

Handling a DBConcurrencyException

The introduction to the "Creating and Using Interactive Data Displays" section identified a potential problem with optimistic concurrency. This optimistic concurrency approach is the default way of updating values in a data source using graphical form development tools, such as those covered in this chapter. The problem occurs when two or more users attempt to change the same row in a database table. If at least two users open a row before either commits a change to the row, the attempt of the second user to commit a change will have their change rejected. The rejection is because the row the second user is attempting to edit is no longer there. The first user just changed it!

This explanation of the problem suggests one solution—refresh the copy of the data that the second user has from the database and resubmit the change. Actually, the complete solution is a little more complicated than that. First, you have to detect the error returned from the database.

Then, your application can refresh the data and ask the user to resubmit the change. The .NET Framework throws a DBConcurrencyException class instance for each attempted change to a database that does not succeed. This applies to inserts, updates, and deletes of the database from the client. Therefore, your client application can catch any DBConcurrencyException instances resulting from the invocation of the Update method for a TableAdapter.

This section demonstrates a way to manually generate a DBConcurrencyException instance. In addition, the demonstration for this section shows how to catch the DBConcurrencyException and refresh the local copy of data from the database. Finally, you'll see how to prompt users to resubmit their change after the local copy of the refreshed data is available. In order to expand the coverage of the chapter, this last sample of a Windows Form uses a connection to the Microsoft Access Northwind database. Once you have one or more database objects specified as a data source, it doesn't matter what kind of database you use. Therefore, the same approach demonstrated in this section applies a data source based on a SQL Server Express database.

Start the process of creating a data source for the Customers table in the Access Northwind database by opening the Data Source Configuration wizard in the WinCh13 project. Choose Data ➤ Add New Data Source to open the wizard.

- Click New Connection on the first wizard screen.
  - This click opens the Add Connection dialog box.
  - Then, navigate to the Northwind.mdb file.

After specifying a connection, you can accept the default name (Northwind) that the Data Source Configuration wizard assigns to the connection string. This name forms part of the name for the DataSet that is the basis of the data source. On the third wizard screen, select just the Customers table to become a member of the data source's DataSet.

Figure 13-27 shows the NorthwindDataSet diagram in the WinCh13 project on the left. This image is from the VBE DataSet Designer.

- The left side of Figure 13-27 shows the Customers table name and the column names within the Customers table. If you had selected a subset of database columns in the Data Sources Configuration wizard, then just the selected columns would show. Notice that the process of creating a DataSet for the data source created a CustomersTableAdapter. This object is critical for data manipulations, such as those that are the focus of this section.

- The right side of Figure 13-27 shows the same data source in the Data Sources window. Notice that the name of the data source is the same as the file name for the DataSet (NorthwindDataSet.xsd). In addition, the Data Sources window shows the same DataTable name (Customers) and the same column names as in the DataSet Designer window.

- These parallel representations of the data source and its DataSet underscore the relationship between a data source and its DataSet. As you can see, the data source name refers to the DataSet name.

CHAPTER 13 ■ USING VISUAL DATABASE AND FORM DESIGN TOOLS **549**

Add `Form11` to the WinCh13 project and drag the Customers node in the `NorthwindDataSet` data source to the form. This populates the form with a `DataGridView` control and a `BindingNavigator` control. Edit the columns for the `DataGridView` control with the Edit Columns dialog box that you open from the `DataGridView` control's smart tag Window. Show just the `CustomerID`, `CompanyName`, and `ContactName` columns.

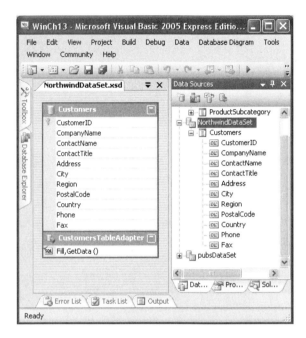

Figure 13-27. *A data source and its DataSet are like two different sides of the same coin.*

Drag two `Button` controls to `Form11` so that the form appears as in Figure 13-28. This example adds code to three event procedures behind `Form11`. The event procedure shell for the `Load` event is already created and populated by the Windows Form Designer. The example needs `Click` event procedure shells for the `Button1` and `Button2` controls, which will enable users to update the database from `Form11` and refresh the data showing in the form from the database. These `Button` controls allow you to customize the form in a way that no longer requires the `BindingNavigator` control added by the Windows Form Designer.

1. Create the `Button1_Click` procedure shell by double-clicking the `Button1` control in Design view.

2. After VBE changes the focus to the `Form11` module in the `Button1_Click` procedure shell, return to Design view.

3. Create the `Button2_Click` procedure shell by double-clicking the `Button2` control in Design view.

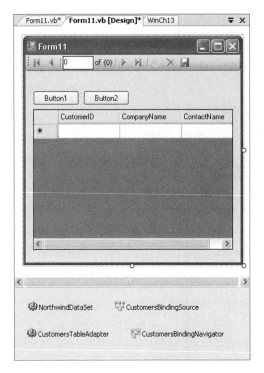

Figure 13-28. *To permit updates to a database, you will need at least two buttons—one to pass updates to the database (Button1) and another to refresh the form from the database (Button2).*

The code inside Form11's Load event procedure, which appears in the next code segment, performs two functions.

- First, the procedure begins with a line of code written by the Windows Form Designer. The statement fills the DataGridView control with values from the Customers table in the Northwind database.

    - The initial statement in the procedure performs this task by invoking the Fill method for the CustomersTableAdapter so that values from the Customers database table populate the Customers DataTable in the NorthwindDataSet DataSet.

    - The DataGridView control, in turn, displays the values from Customers DataTable.

- Second, the procedure formats controls on the form.

    - Initially, the formatting instructions hide BindingNavigator control automatically added by the Windows Form Designer (by setting the Visible property of the CustomersBindingNavigator to False).

    - The next two lines describe the purpose of each button by assigning String values to the Text property of the Button1 and Button2 controls.

- The last formatting instruction assigns a width for the `CustomerID` column for the `DataGridView` control that is smaller than the default value (65 versus 100 pixels) to make more room available for showing values from the other two columns.

```
Me.CustomersTableAdapter.Fill(Me.NorthwindDataSet.Customers)

    Me.CustomersBindingNavigator.Visible = False
    Me.Button1.Text = "Update"
    Me.Button2.Text = "Refresh"
    Me.CustomersDataGridView.Columns("CustomerID").Width = 65
```

The `Button1_Click` procedure fires when the user clicks the `Button` control with a `Text` property of Update. The procedure's code consists of a `Try...Catch...End Try` statement. This `Try...Catch...End Try` statement is critical to recovering from the throwing of a `DBConcurrencyException` instance resulting from the attempt to change a row that no longer exists in the database.

- The `Try` clause of the statement invokes the `Update` method of the `CustomersTableAdapter` object. This method passes any changes to the `Customers DataTable` made with the `DataGridView` control. If this statement succeeds, control transfers to the first line after the `End Try` clause.

- If the .NET Framework throws a `DBConcurrencyException` object because the row to change no longer exists, the code in the `Catch` clause runs.

  - This code invokes the `Fill` method for the `CustomersTableAdapter` to populate the `Customers DataTable` in the `NorthwindDataSet`. The `Fill` method clears a `DataTable` by default before populating the `DataTable` (unless you override the default setting).

  - The `Show` method for the `MessageBox` class displays a message box telling the user how to recover from an error—namely, enter the changed data again and click Update.

```
Try
 Me.CustomersTableAdapter.Update(Me.NorthwindDataSet.Customers)
Catch ex As System.Data.DBConcurrencyException
 Me.CustomersTableAdapter.Fill(Me.NorthwindDataSet.Customers)
 MessageBox.Show("Please enter your changes again and click Update again.")
End Try
```

The purpose of the `Button2_Click` procedure is to populate the `DataGridView` control in the same way as in the `Load` event procedure for the form. In order to do this, the `Button2_Click` procedure must clear any existing values in the `Customers DataTable` before filling the `DataTable` from the Northwind database. A single line of code is all that is necessary, and you do not even have to write the instruction. Just copy the line of code generated by the Windows Form Designer for the `Form11`'s Load event procedure to the `Button2_Click` procedure. This line of code also appears as the first line of code in the `Catch` clause of the `Button1_Click` procedure.

After you add the controls to `Form11` and the code for its event procedures, you are ready to demonstrate the application. This demonstration will be unique from the preceding ones in this chapter from a couple of perspectives.

- First, the demonstration requires two active sessions for `Form11`—not just one.

  - Each session simulates a separate user.

  - You can launch each session from the Run dialog box (Windows Start ➤ Run).

- Second, each session runs a compiled version of the .exe file for the solution in the project's Release folder (..\ProjectName\ProjectName\bin\Release\ProjectName.exe).

  - The Release folder contains the most recently built solution .exe file for a project. This is the distribution .exe for your solution.

  - VBE does not automatically rebuild this .exe file every time that you rerun the application.

  - Therefore, to ensure a current .exe file reflects the most recent changes to a project, invoke the Build ➤ Build ProjectName menu item from the VBE Standard toolbar.

To start the two sessions for the WinCh13 project, you'll invoke the WinCh13.exe file twice from the Release folder. If Form11 is the Startup form, the project will open to Form11. Figure 13-29 shows the two Form11 sessions. The CompanyName column for the first row is selected in each instance, but there are no edits to the original data. To track the steps to each form separately, the description of the process for throwing and handling a DBConcurrencyException object refers to the form sessions as leftForm11 and rightForm11.

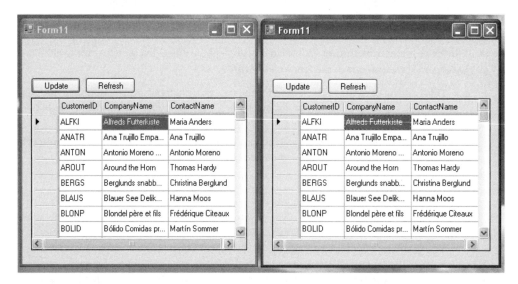

Figure 13-29. *Two Form11 sessions for demonstrating how to generate and handle DBConcurrencyException instances*

Here's a series of steps to run the demonstration.

1. Append an L to the CompanyName column value in leftForm11. There are no changes so far—even the change to leftForm11 is not committed.

2. Click Update on leftForm11.

   - This commits the change to leftForm11 and copies the change from the DataGridView control to the Customers DataTable for the instance of WinCh13 running for leftForm11.

   - This step also updates the Northwind database file with the change in the Customers DataTable.

   - At this point, rightForm11 has no knowledge of either the change to the database table or the change to the Customer DataTable in leftForm11's instance of the WinCh13 project.

3. Click Refresh on `rightForm11`.

- This copies the updated values from the `Customers` database table to the instance of the WinCh13 project running for `rightForm11`.

- The `DataGridView` control in `rightForm11` shows the change made in `leftForm11`.

4. Next, make edits to `leftForm11` and `rightForm11` without clicking Update on either form.

    1. Append a 1 to the `CompanyName` column value in `leftForm11` so that the new suffix to the original `CompanyName` column value is L1.

    2. Replace the L suffix in the `rightForm11` instance with R. The cursor shows after the R suffix in `rightForm11`.

5. Click Update on `rightForm11`.

- This commits the change on `rightForm11`.

- In addition, the local instance of the `Customers DataTable` changes to reflect the edit to the form.

- Finally, the `Customers` database table changes to reflect the edit on `rightForm11`.

- After the `Customers` database table changes, the `Customers DataTable` associated with `leftForm11` is unsynchronized with the `Customers` database table.

6. Click Update on `leftForm11`.

- This generates a `DBConcurrencyException` object because the original value of `CompanyName` for the first row in `leftForm11` is no longer the current value of `CompanyName` in the first row of the `Customers` database table.

- The `Catch` clause in the `Button1_Click` procedure refreshes the `leftForm11` project instance to obtain a new copy of the `Customers` database table in its `Customers DataTable` and presents the prompt that appears in Figure 13-30.

- At this point, the user of `leftForm11` can re-enter the change and click Update to successfully commit the change to the database.

Figure 13-30. *A custom error message to recover from a DBConcurrencyException instance*

Visual Web Developer Visual Database Tools

Visual database tools for VWDE are similar, but not identical, to VBE visual database tools. Despite different ways of configuring database solutions in VBE and VWDE, VWDE still enables you to

- Make connections graphically to databases.

- Explore databases and add objects, such as tables, to databases.

- Drag and drop items representing database objects on to a form to show and manipulate data.

- Manipulate data by editing values as well as deleting and inserting rows.

Because the tools for implementing these actions are visual, you can perform all these actions without code. Because you can get the basics performed visually, adding a little code can leverage the benefits of the visual database tools to generate truly compelling solutions.

Making Database Connections

VWDE features a Database Explorer window that simplifies making connections to a database. In addition, every ASP.NET website has an App_Data folder. The App_Data folder, which VWDE automatically creates for each new Website project, can work together with Database Explorer to add connections automatically to a project. In addition, the Add Connection dialog box for Database Explorer in VWDE does not work identically to VBE. The good news about this difference is that you have even more flexibility with VWDE than VBE for the types of databases to which you can connect. This section illustrates several approaches for making connections to different types of databases, and highlights the enhanced functionality available from VWDE relative to VBE.

VWDE developers can open Database Explorer as in VBE. You choose View ➤ Database Explorer from the Standard VWDE toolbar. Just as with VBE, VWDE does not require that you have a project open in order to use Database Explorer. Therefore, you can use nearly all the functionality of Database Explorer without even having a project open.

When you do create a new or open an existing Website project, Database Explorer plays a special role in VWDE that partially overlaps with the Data Sources window in VBE.

With VWDE:

- There is no Data Sources window for a project.

- You can drag and drop items directly from Database Explorer to a Web Form.

- When you drag and drop a database object to a Web Form from Database Explorer, VWDE populates the form with a data source and a `GridView` control, which resembles the `DataGridView` control in VBE.

- The scope of a data source is restricted to the page on which it resides, but you can copy a data source from one page to another.

You may see database connections from a prior session when you open Database Explorer in a new Website project or with a previously created Website project that you are opening again. You can remove these database connections or leave them in Database Explorer at your preference. Deleting a database connection from Database Explorer does not affect the database. It just removes the connection from Database Explorer for the current session. Any Website project can still have and use the database connection that you removed from Database Explorer in another Website project. In addition, you can subsequently add any database connections that you drop.

All the VWDE samples for this section were designed from the WebCh13 Website project. To add a new connection to Database Explorer, you can right-click Data Connections in Database Explorer and choose Add Connection to Open the Add Connection dialog box. Add a connection to the AdventureWorks database in the Data folder for the first named instance of SQL Server on a computer. Click OK to add the connection to Database Explorer in the WebCh13 Website project.

The default SQL Server instance on the test computer for this book is an MSDE instance. It is instructive to contrast the graphical process for using an MSDE database with VBE versus VWDE.

- VBE requires a fairly elaborate process for working with legacy SQL Server database files, such as MSDE databases. You need to

  - Detach the files for a database.

  - Copy them to a new location for use by VBE with SQL Server Express.

  - Then, attach the detached files to restore them for use with the original MSDE instance.

- VWDE in contrast allows you to connect directly to an MSDE database server without the need to make a copy of the original MSDE database files.

  - You must first change your data source setting so that it points at a database server instead of a database file. Figure 13-31 shows the Change Data Source dialog box for designating a SQL Server instance instead of the primary SQL Server database file (.mdf).

  - Notice also that VWDE offers you additional database connection settings not available in VBE. Compare Figure 13-1 for VBE to Figure 13-31 for VWDE to see the full scope of the differences.

  - Figure 13-32 shows the completed Add Connection dialog box after selecting a data source for a Microsoft SQL Server instance.

  - The designation of (local) as the server name is a traditional way of referring to the default instance of SQL Server on a computer.

  - After selecting the server name and identifying how to log on to the computer, you can use a drop-down box to select a database name. In this case, it is the pubs database.

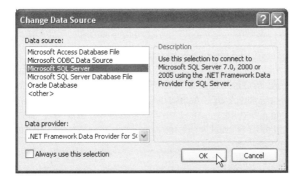

Figure 13-31. *The Change Data Source dialog box in VWDE offers more data source types than the same dialog box in VBE.*

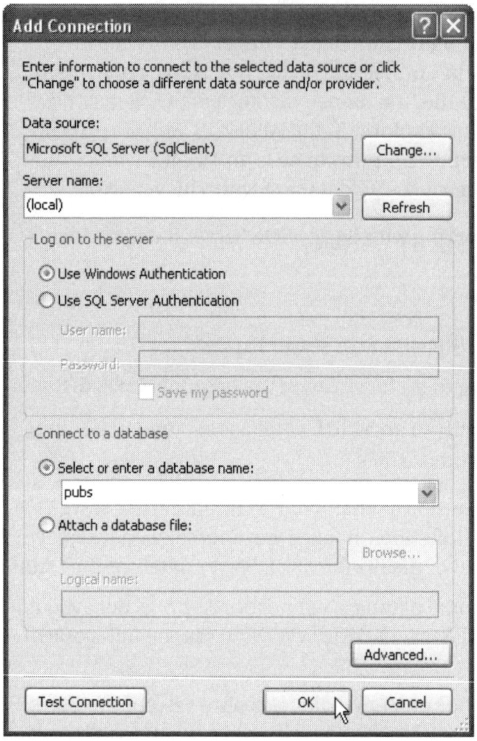

Figure 13-32. *The Add Connection dialog box for Database Explorer in the VWDE Website project can reconfigure depending on the type of data source that you select.*

If you are working with database files that can remain local to a solution, such as SQL Server Express or Microsoft Access database files, you can copy them into the App_Data folder for a VWDE Website project. One easy way to copy database files to a VWDE project is with Windows Explorer.

■**Tip** A database connection in Database Explorer to an Access database in the App_Data folder of the current VWDE project does not persist beyond the current session. However, a database connection to another folder outside the current project can persist across multiple sessions. As a result of this behavior, you have two options for working with Database Explorer database connections to Access database files. First, you can just re-create the database connection whenever you need it. Second, you can save the database file to another location, such as one outside the current VWDE project, in order to avoid having to re-create the database connection in Database Explorer whenever you need it between sessions.

Figure 13-33 shows the WebCh13 Website project in VWDE with the App_Data folder expanded and selected.

- You can see the two primary database files. The northwnd_log.ldf file is related to the north-wnd.mdf file. You can show the .ldf file by clicking the Expansion node (+) next to northwnd.mdf.

- The four database connections created for the WebCh13 Website project show in Database Explorer.

- The AdventureWorks_Data.mdf node points at the Adventure works database in the Data folder for a SQL Server Express instance.

- The cab233a.pub.dbo node points at the pubs database attached to an MSDE database server named cab233a. This node is expanded to remind you of the Database Explorer capability for exploring databases. Although this database name (pubs) is identical to the one used in the "Migrating and Revising an MSDE Database" section, the two databases are based on different database files and have some nonoverlapping content.

- The Northwind.mdb node points at the sample Access Northwind database file copied to the App_Data folder of the WebCh13 project. You can see this file in Solution Explorer.

- The northwnd.mdf node points at the sample SQL Server Northwind database file copied to the App_Data folder of the WebCh13 project. Like the Northwind.mdb file node, you can also see the file for this node in Solution Explorer.

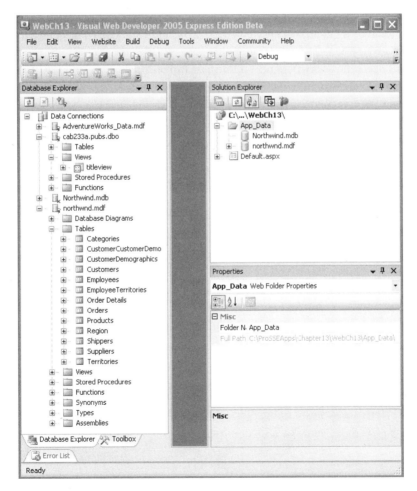

Figure 13-33. *Database Explorer for a VWDE project can display connections to local database files, files attached through a connection string, and databases attached to a database server.*

Viewing Data and Modifying Databases

Two major reasons for connecting to databases in Database Explorer are so that you can view data values and modify databases (both data values and objects). You can view data in a variety of ways, including showing the data in a table. When you want to examine the data values from multiple tables, you can design a custom query to join two or more tables or views. If you want to use the query repeatedly, perhaps as the source for a form's data source, you can save the query as a view. Database Explorer permits you to perform these kinds of tasks and more. One additional capability that is particularly convenient is the ability to modify database values as well as new rows and delete existing rows. This section will highlight these features. One view created in this section will be used as the source for a Web Form in a subsequent section.

After you add a database connection to Database Explorer, you can use the connection in the same way whether you are working from VBE or VWDE. The Northwind sample database includes values in the Orders table and Order Subtotals view that are useful when merged together in a single query.

1. Because this demonstration will save the query as a view for reuse with a Web Form, you can start by right-clicking the Views node in the northwnd.mdf connection and choosing Add New View.

2. This opens the Query Designer for Database Explorer in the background with the Add New Table dialog box in the foreground.

3. Select the Orders table from the Tables tab and click Add.

4. Then, select the Order Subtotals view from the Views tab and click Add.

5. Close the Add New Table dialog box by clicking Close.

Figure 13-34 shows the Add Table dialog box in front of the Query Designer after the addition of the Orders table and the Order Subtotals view. You can see the icons for the two database objects in the Diagram pane and the beginning of a SQL statement with an inner join between the table and the view.

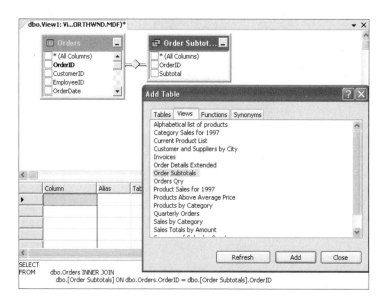

Figure 13-34. *You can use the Database Explorer Query Designer to join a table and a view that forms a new view.*

The query that we seek to create includes a computed column that is the sum of the Freight column value from the Orders table to the Subtotal column value from the Order Subtotals view. Figure 13-35 shows the design of the query, which includes OrderID, CustomerID, OrderDate, and Freight columns from the Orders table along with the Subtotal column from the Order Subtotals view. Notice the full SQL query statement in the SQL pane. Even if you do not wish to save the query as a view, the query designer is often useful for quickly designing SQL statements that you can cut from the SQL pane and use elsewhere in a database application.

Complete the process of saving a new view by closing the query. Database Explorer prompts for a view name before it initially closes the query. Designate the name vOSubtotals for the new view.

Figure 13-35 also shows in its Results pane the outcome of running the query statement in the SQL pane. Notice from the footer in the Results pane that the Freight column value in the first row is read-only. The Query Designer does not allow data modification for cells in queries with joined database objects even if they can normally be modified. There are at least a couple of solutions for allowing the modification of Freight column values.

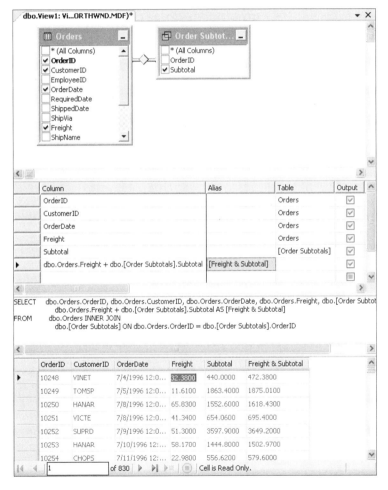

Figure 13-35. *The Database Explorer Query Designer offers multiple views of a query statement in different panes along with a preview of the result set from a query statement.*

- First, you open a new window from Database Explorer by choosing the Show Table Data right-click menu item for the Orders table. Then, you can modify any Freight column value (or any other column value, except for the OrderID column with an IDENTITY property value).

- Second, you can open another new window by choosing the Show Results right-click menu item from vOSubtotals view. This window will allow you to make a change, but you will be prompted to rerun the Show Results command.

You are most likely to be successful making changes to column values in a window from the Show Table Data menu command. The approach of making changes to columns in individual tables is a very robust solution for making changes to a database. However, even in this very limited scenario, issues such as IDENTITY property settings, referential integrity, and other database design issues can inhibit your ability to change column values. Your best defense against some of these issues is to learn database design techniques and how databases work. Chapter 3 through Chapter 8 in this book cover many issues that you will find useful as you ramp up the database design learning curve.

Displaying Data on a Web Form Page with a GridView Control

Three major distinctions characterize the way that VWDE works graphically with data-bound controls from the way that VBE deals with them.

- VWDE does not support a Data Sources window, such as the one enabled by VBE. One reason for this is that a data source in VWDE does not have a scope at the project level. A data source is scoped to a web page. You can't use the data source on one Web Form on another Web Form.

- VWDE does let you drag and drop items on to a Web Form in a way that corresponds generally to the way that VBE lets you drag and drop a data source to a Windows Form. However, you drag and drop from Database Explorer in VWDE—not a Data Sources window as in VBE.

- Yet another major distinction between the ways VWDE implements data-bound controls as different from VBE is that VWDE lets you drag items to a Web Form to appear in a single control type—namely a GridView control. Recall that VBE allowed you to select from multiple control types as you drag a data source element to a Windows Form.

  - The GridView control corresponds generally to a DataGridView control in VBE. The GridView control is optimized for use with web applications.

  - Although the data source for a GridView control initially populates a Web Form along with the GridView control, you can delete the GridView control and reuse the data source with other controls, such as a ListBox.

It can be exceptionally easy to populate a Web Form with a GridView control. Start by creating a page with a Web Form in the WebCh13 project (see the "Creating Pages for an ASP.NET Project" section in Chapter 10 if you need instructions on how to do this). The initial sample assigns a name of ShortGridView.aspx to the Web Form page. The easiest way to populate a Web Form with a GridView control is particularly appropriate for a short table having just a few columns with about a dozen or fewer rows. The GridView control looks like a table on a Web Form—especially if you do not perform any special formatting.

The Shippers table in the Northwind database has just three rows and three columns. Therefore, it displays nicely in a short table, and there is no need for extensive vertical scrolling to view rows at the end of the table. Since there are just three columns in the Shippers table, you can show all the columns without any concern for whether users will have to scroll horizontally to view all the data on a single row.

Figure 13-36 shows the VWDE IDE after dragging the Shippers table from the northwnd.mdf database connection in Database Explorer to between the opening and closing div tags on a Web Form page in Design view. The dragging adds two controls to the Web Form.

- The GridView control correctly represents column names, but the control does not represent either the number of rows or the values on a row correctly in Design view.

- A control named SqlDataSource1 exists right below the GridView control in Design view. The SqlDataSource1 control appears as a gray rectangle in Design view, but the data source control is invisible when the page renders in a browser. Its sole purpose is to provide data for the GridView control.

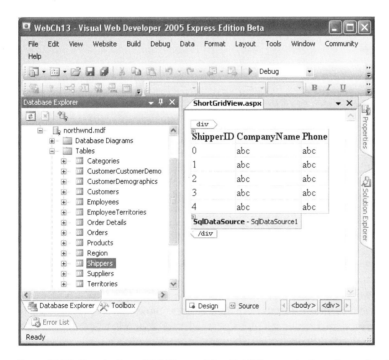

Figure 13-36. *Populating a Web Form with a GridView control can be as simple as dragging a table name from a database connection in Database Explorer.*

Figure 13-37 shows the ShortGridView.aspx page in a browser. You can open the page in a browser by right-clicking the Design view of the page in a blank area and choosing the View in Browser menu item. If prompted to save your changes, reply Yes. In addition to having the correct column headers, the GridView control in Figure 13-37 has the correct number of rows—three. You can verify that the GridView control binds directly to a database table by editing one or more table values, saving your changes, and then refreshing the page. You can make the change in Database Explorer.

Figure 13-37. *VWDE can bind a GridView control directly to a database table that has a SqlDataSource control.*

It is common that the data source for display on a Web Form page has more than a few columns and more than 20 or so rows. In this case, it may be effective to edit the columns that appear in a GridView control to minimize or eliminate the need to scroll horizontally to view all the column values on a single row. Similarly, if you have more than 20 rows or so, users are likely to need to scroll to view rows of data at the bottom on a data source. The more rows in your data source for a Web Form page, the more browsing users will have to do to view row values at the bottom of the data source. Giving users the ability to sort rows based on column values is one way to enable them to minimize the amount of vertical scrolling necessary to view rows that they seek.

The PagedSortedEdited.aspx file in the WebCh13 project demonstrates three simple techniques to ease the viewing of medium-sized tables. The GridView control in this sample page displays an excerpt from the Customers table in the Northwind sample database. The GridView control displays a subset consisting of the first three columns from the Customers table. The GridView control for this page implements paging so that a user can pick a set of 10 rows to view in a browser. The GridView control makes it especially easy to determine whether a browser renders a GridView control to a web page with paging. Sorting is another exceptionally easy feature to add to a GridView control.

After dragging the Customers table from the northwnd.mdf connection in Database Explorer, the PagedSortedEdited.aspx page can appear in Design view as in Figure 13-38. The smart tag window is open, and there are buttons for enabling paging and sorting. Click each of these buttons.

To select just the first three columns for display in the GridView control, click the Edit Columns link in the smart tag window. This click opens the Fields dialog box. You can use the ListBox control with a Label control showing Selected fields within the dialog box to select any row that you want to make invisible on the Web Form. Start by selecting an entry in the ListBox control, such as Fax, and clicking the Button control with a Text property of X to the right of the ListBox control. Repeat this process for each entry that you want to remove from display in the GridView control. The sample GridView control in the PagedSortedEdited.aspx page removes all columns, except for the first three named CustomerID, CompanyName, and ContactName.

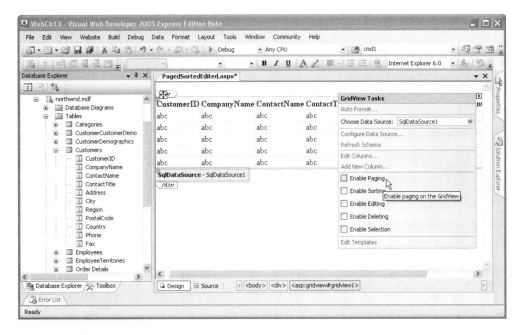

Figure 13-38. *Use the smart tag window for a GridView control to enable paging and sorting of the rows from a browser.*

By default, the GridView control groups rows into pages of up to 10 rows each for display in a browser. The last page may have fewer than 10 rows. You are not restricted to a page size of 10. Use the Properties window for the GridView control to designate a different number of rows per display. Figure 13-39 shows the second page of rows sorted in their default order by CustomerID. You can select a page by clicking the numbers at the bottom of the GridView control.

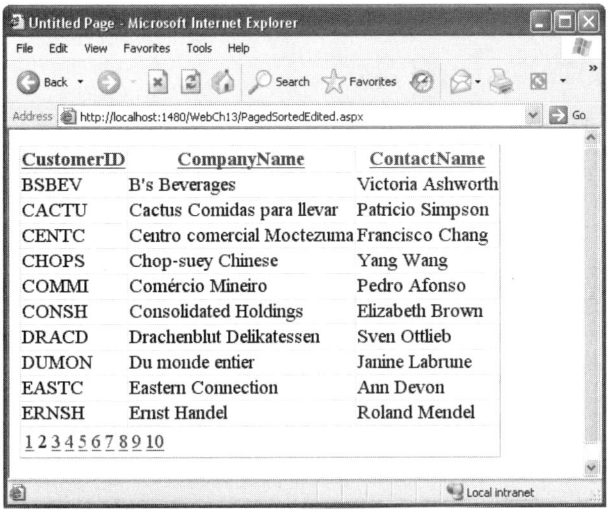

Figure 13-39. *The paging control numbers at the bottom of a GridView control let users select a page of rows to display.*

The `CustomerID` and `CompanyName` sort orders for the rows in the `Customers` table are nearly the same. However, the `ContactName` order is substantially different than the `CustomerID` sort order. If you click the `ContactName` column header, the rows rearrange in ascending order based on `ContactName`. Clicking the column header a second time changes the sort order of rows to descending order by `ContactName`. Successive clicks to the `ContactName` column header toggles the sort order between ascending and descending order based on company name. Figure 13-40 shows the PagedSortedEdited.aspx page after the user clicks the `ContactName` column header to sort the rows in ascending order by their `ContactName` column values. After the click, the `GridView` shows the first page of rows in the new sort order.

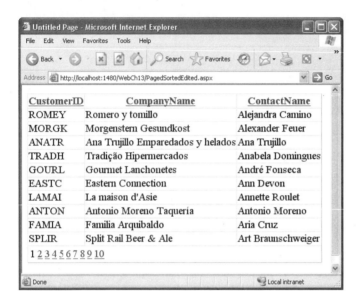

Figure 13-40. *When sorting is enabled for a GridView control, users can click the column headers to toggle the sort order from ascending to descending for the values in a column.*

Performing Lookups on a Web Form Page

Aside from showing a fixed set of rows from a data source, another common database solution is to enable users to look up some values. This section shows a couple of approaches to letting a user look up the order history for a customer. Given some information from a user specifying a customer, the order history samples return a result set showing the dates and amounts of prior orders from the customer.

Looking Up Order History in an Access Database

The Access order history sample joins a table and a view in a query statement. As is common of relational databases, the solution requires information from both database objects to compose the result that a user wants to generate. In addition, the Access solution uses a parameter query to let a user specify a `CustomerID` value that determines for which customer to return an order history. The VWDE graphical form design features for working with data make it possible to create the solution without the developer writing a single line of code.

Start to create the solution by adding a new Web Form page to a Website project whose name is LookupAccessData.aspx.

1. Switch to the Design view of the page.

2. From the Toolbox, drag a `TextBox` control and then a `Label` control to the page before the opening `div` tag.

3. Use the Properties window to assign a `Text` property value of `Enter CustomerID:` to the `Label` control.

   - You could make this assignment programmatically behind the form.

   - However, one major objective of this sample is to emphasize that you can build a useful solution without manually specifying a single line of code.

4. Populate the form with the `Orders` table from the Access `Northwind` database.

   1. Drag the `Orders` table node in the Access database connection to the `Northwind` database from Database Explorer.

   2. Drop the `Orders` table on the page between the opening and closing `div` tags.

Figure 13-41 shows the LookupAccessData.aspx page in Design view at the end of the preceding steps. The label control prompts the user to input a `CustomerID` value into the `TextBox` control (`TextBox1`). The `TextBox` control has its default `AutoPostBack` setting of `False`, but a reference to `TextBox1` causes any committed value to the control to update the values in the `GridView` control below it. Normally, a `False` setting for the `AutoPostPack` property of a server-based control, such as `TextBox1`, does not let the control operate automatically after you commit a value to it. However, a special setting on a Define Parameters wizard screen causes `TextBox1` to return its value to the server immediately after a user presses the Enter key on the keyboard. The Define Parameters wizard screen is one of a series that you can pass through when you reconfigure a data source with a wizard.

The `AccessDataSource1` control sits right below the `GridView` control in Figure 13-41. This control connects the `GridView` control to the columns of the `Orders` table in the `Northwind` Access database file within the WebCh13 project. By reconfiguring `AccessDataSource1`, we can make the `GridView` control suitable for the order history lookup task.

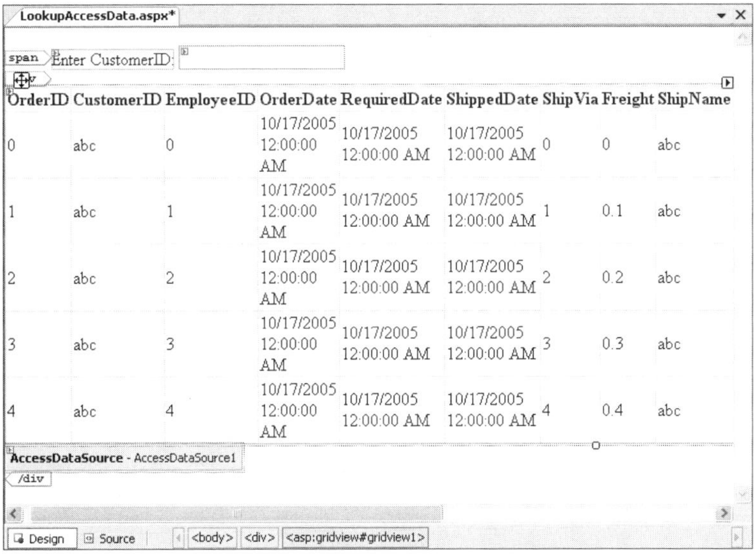

Figure 13-41. *A draft initial version of a Web Form page that will be revised by using a wizard to reconfigure the GridView control's data source.*

You can start to reconfigure a data source control by clicking the Configure Data Source link from the data source control's smart tag window. This opens a wizard for reconfiguring the data source. In the context of this solution, the reconfiguration should

- Remove columns from the data source that are not necessary for the order history report.
- Add the Subtotal column from the Order Subtotals view that joins with columns from Orders table having at least one order with a Subtotal value.
- Specify a calculated column for the data source based on the sum of the Freight column from the Orders table and the Subtotal column from the Order Subtotals view.
- Designate a parameter for the CustomerID column so that a user can input a CustomerID value and return orders just for that customer.

■**Tip** SQL Server and SQL Server Express databases allow you to designate parameters in SQL statements differently than other types of databases. Therefore, be sure to follow the rules for an Access database when denoting parameters for it, but do not apply these same rules for a SQL Server database.

You can start to accomplish the preceding tasks by reconfiguring AccessDataSource1.

1. Clicking the Configure Data Source link for the control opens a wizard that indicates the database connection for AccessDataSource1. Click Next to move on to the next wizard screen.

2. On the Configure the Select Statement screen, select the radio button that lets you create a custom SQL statement and click Next.

3. On the screen to define a custom statement, click Query Builder. This opens a Query Designer that is highly similar to the one you can open from Database Explorer. Perform the following steps to make the Query Builder dialog box appear like Figure 13-42.

   1. Right-click in a blank area within the Diagram pane and choose Add Table. Then, from the Views tab add the Order Subtotals view.

   2. Next, make column selections from the check boxes next to the field names in the Diagram pane so that just the following columns are selected from the Orders table: OrderID, CustomerID, OrderDate, and Freight. Make an additional selection of Subtotal from the Order Subtotals view.

   3. Create a calculated column by typing its expression for the last row of the Criteria pane. The expression is Freight + Subtotal. The wizard automatically modifies this basic expression so that column names appear with database object qualifiers as in Figure 13-28.

   4. Insert a question mark (?) in the Filter column for the CustomerID row in the Criteria pane. This adds a WHERE clause to the SQL pane that converts the SELECT statement to a parameter query. The question mark denotes the parameter.

   5. Click OK to commit your query design and return to the regular flow of wizard screens. Then, click Next to open the Define Parameters screen.

4. The Define Parameters screen lets you control how the parameter in the parameter query acquires its value. Figure 13-43 shows the completed version of the dialog box for the order history solution.

   • You need to designate that the parameter will come from a control named `TextBox1`.

   • The default value for the parameter is `ALFKI`. Any valid `CustomerID` value setting allows the query to run before the user actually assigns a value to the parameter, and it avoids having an empty `GridView` control when the LookupAccessData.aspx initially opens.

5. When a user clicks Next on the Define Parameters screen, you move to a screen that lets you check how your query runs before leaving the wizard.

   • If the query runs as desired, you can exit the wizard by clicking Finish.

   • Otherwise, you can click one or more Previous buttons and redefine your query and its parameters.

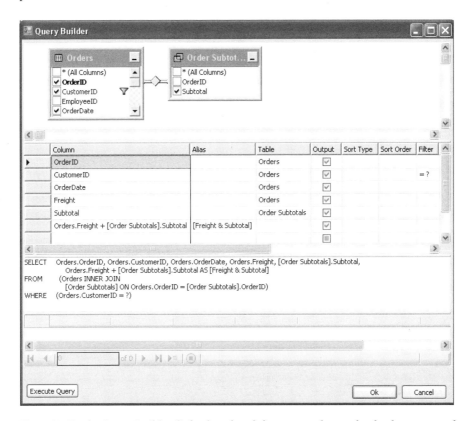

Figure 13-42. *The Query Builder dialog box that defines new columns for the data source of the GridView control in the LookupAccessData.aspx page*

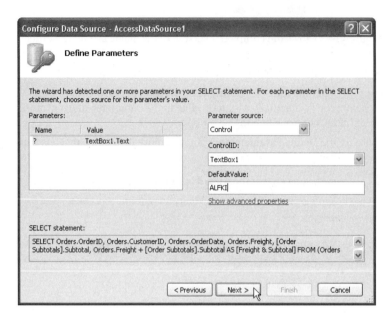

Figure 13-43. *With the Define Parameters wizard screen you can link controls on a Web Form page to the query statement in a data source control.*

When you return to the LookupAccessData.aspx page in the VWDE IDE, you will be prompted whether to regenerate the column fields for the GridView control. Click Yes to commit your settings from the wizard to the Web Form page. Figure 13-44 shows the redesigned page. You can contrast this page with the one in Figure 13-42 to see the affect of your wizard selections. If the form's design has the fields you want, right-click the page in a blank area and choose View in Browser. If prompted to save changes, click Yes.

LookupAccessData.aspx*						▾ ×

span ▸ Enter CustomerID: [2]
div ▸

OrderID	CustomerID	OrderDate	Freight	Subtotal	Freight & Subtotal
0	abc	10/17/2005 12:00:00 AM	0	0	0
1	abc	10/17/2005 12:00:00 AM	0.1	0.1	0.1
2	abc	10/17/2005 12:00:00 AM	0.2	0.2	0.2
3	abc	10/17/2005 12:00:00 AM	0.3	0.3	0.3
4	abc	10/17/2005 12:00:00 AM	0.4	0.4	0.4

AccessDataSource - AccessDataSource1
/div

▣ Design	▣ Source	◂	<body>			▸

Figure 13-44. *The revised version of the LookupAccessData.aspx page based on an updated query statement with a WHERE clause to designate a parameter*

When the LookupAccessData.aspx page initially opens, it shows the order history for the customer with a CustomerID value of ALFKI. The TextBox control above the GridView control is blank. Figure 13-45 shows the Web Form page after the entry of a CustomerID value of ANATR followed by a press of the Enter key. The press of the Enter key sends the ANATR value to the parameter query specified in Figure 13-42.

Built-in VWDE behavior and the settings on the Define Parameters wizard screen repopulate the GridView control based on the parameter value in the TextBox control.

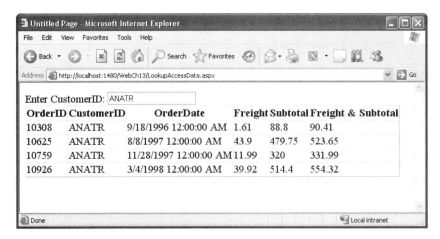

Figure 13-45. *You can build a parameter query for a Web Form page with VWDE without manually entering a single line of code.*

Looking Up Order History in a SQL Server Express Database

The northwnd.mdf file in the App_Data folder of the WebCh13 project has very nearly the same structure and contents as the Northwind.mdb file. As a result, you can build the same order history solution for either database. However, this section presents an enhanced solution from a couple of different perspectives. Switching from Access to SQL Server Express is an improvement all by itself. One significant reason for the superiority of SQL Server Express is because it supports multithreading. Access does not have built-in support for multithreading with IIS (http://support.microsoft.com/default.aspx?scid=kb;en-us;299973). This distinction makes SQL Server Express better able to handle multiple requests at the same time.

Beyond the native capabilities of SQL Server Express versus Access, three other areas improve the SQL Server Express solution.

- The SQL Server Express Northwind database file in the WebCh13 project was enhanced with a special view, vOSubtotals, which facilitates the development of customer order histories. The "Viewing Data and Modifying Databases" section describes the process for creating the vOSubtotals view.

- The SQL Server Express solution uses a ListBox control to show the CompanyName column value from the Customers table, but returns the CustomerID column value for the selected item. This relieves users from needing to know the CustomerID before they can query for the order history of a company.

- Special formatting is applied to the GridView columns so that the results are easier to read in the SQL Server Express solution.

  - All column values are right justified.

  - The OrderDate column has a format to strip the time component of datetime values.

  - The Freight, Subtotal, and Freight & Subtotal columns have a format setting for displaying currency values in the local regional setting for the local Windows operating system.

You can start the solution by creating a Web Form page named LookupSSEData.aspx. The presentation of the solution for this page emphasizes graphical development techniques. As a consequence, you'll see just how easy it can be to create web-based database solutions with VWDE. In spite of the enhanced functionality from the SQL Server Express solution relative to the Access database solution, you still do not need to write a single line of code.

As mentioned, the SQL Server Express solution includes a ListBox control to let a user select a customer.

1. Start the solution by dragging a ListBox control to the LookupSSEData.aspx page before the opening div tag.

2. Then, use the Properties window to make three property settings for the ListBox control.

   - Set the width to 250 pixels.

   - Set the height to 150 pixels.

   - Assign True to the AutoPostBack property.

3. Next, you can open the smart tag window for the ListBox control and click the Choose data source link. This click opens a wizard that allows you to create a bound data source for the ListBox. On a series of successive screens, make these selections.

   1. Select New Data Source from a drop-down box.

   2. Select a Database as the type of source.

   3. From the Choose Your Data Connection screen select northwnd.mdf. This database connection was created in the "Making Database Connections" section. It points at the northwnd.mdf file in the App_Data folder for the WebCh13 project.

   4. You can choose to have the wizard save the connection string for the northwnd.mdf database connection. This selection can make access to your databases more secure by not including the connection string in the Web Form page.

   5. Next, you need to specify the database resource, such as a table or view, which will provide data for display in the ListBox and for the return of a selected value. In this case, select the CompanyName and CustomerID column values from the Customers table.

   6. You can optionally test your query before viewing one last screen that lets you specify CompanyName column values for display in the ListBox and CustomerID column values for return as the SelectedValue property. Click OK after making these selections to return to the VWDE IDE.

After you finish specifying the ListBox control so that it can show CompanyName column values and return CustomerID column values for the selected item, you can switch your attention to the GridView control that actually displays the order history data. The data source for the GridView control will rely on the vOSubtotals view. Recall that this view returns the order history for all customers. However, the sample application returns the order history for the customer with a CustomerID value specified by the selected item from the ListBox control above the GridView control. Therefore, the data source for the GridView control must wrap the vOSubtotals view in a parameter query of the filter statement that returns just the rows from vOSubtotals for the selected customer.

1. Start working with the GridView control by dragging it from the Toolbox to between the opening and closing div tags on the LookupSSEData.aspx page.

2. Select New Data Source from the Choose Data Source drop-down box in the smart tag window for the GridView control.

3. Select Database as the data source type. Specify a SQL Server Data Source as opposed to an Access database file or several other types of nondatabase data sources.

4. As with the data source for the `ListBox` control, select the northwnd.mdf database connection.

5. Also, specify whether to save your connection string so that it does not appear on the web page along with the data source.

6. Next, select all the columns from the `vOSubtotals` view as the data source for the `GridView` control by clicking *. However, because you will not be showing all the rows from the view in the `GridView` control, click the WHERE button.

7. In the Add WHERE Clause dialog box, designate `CustomerID` as a filter column for returning rows, and the `SelectedValue` property for `ListBox1` as the filter value for which rows to return. After making these selections, click the Add button to commit your settings. Figure 13-46 shows the settings for the Add WHERE Clause dialog box immediately prior to a click to the Add button.

8. After testing your query with the default parameter and any other parameters you want to try, click Finish to exit the wizard for designating and configuring a data source.

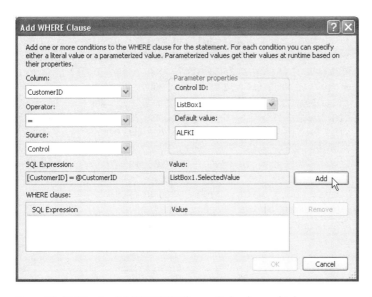

Figure 13-46. *Use the Add WHERE Clause dialog box, which you can open from the Configure the Select Statement screen, to specify a WHERE clause that filters rows for a data source.*

Once you complete the preceding steps, LookupSSEData.aspx is ready to operate and present the order history for a selected customer. Of course, there is still no column formatting. Results appear with the lack of any special formatting to improve their appearance. In order to fully convey the impact of the formatting, Figure 13-47 shows the initial page prior to the application of column formatting settings.

The screen shot in Figure 13-47 is for the `ListBox` and `GridView` after the selection of a customer named Around the Horn.

- Notice that all columns are left justified.

- The `OrderDate` column values all show the same time: 12:00 AM.

- The last three columns, which each represent currency values, do not include a currency sign to indicate they represent money.

The application of very straightforward format settings can remedy each of these weaknesses with the appearance of results in the GridView control.

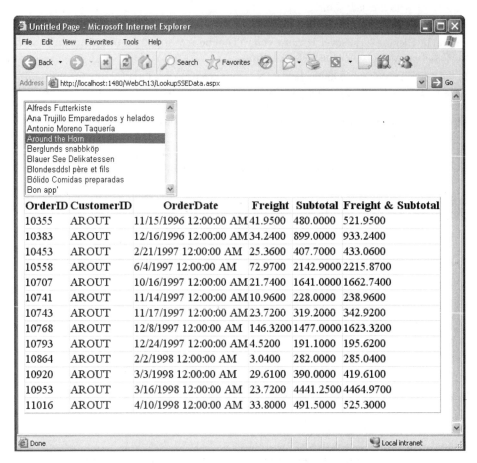

Figure 13-47. *The LookupSSEData.aspx page can return order history data for any selected customer from a ListBox control.*

Close the browser session showing in Figure 13-47, and open the smart tag window for the GridView control. From the smart tag window, click Edit column to open the Fields dialog box. This box allows you to apply formatting to individual columns within the GridView control.

1. Select a column to which to apply formatting, such as OrderID, from the Selected fields ListBox control. From the BoundField properties ListBox control

    1. Scroll to the HorizontalAlign property in the ItemStyle group of properties.

    2. Open the drop-down selector next to the property and choose Right.

2. Repeat the preceding property selection for each of the remaining columns in the Selected fields ListBox to assign right justification to each of the columns in the GridView control.

3. Then, select the OrderDate column in the Selected fields ListBox.

    1. Scroll to the DataFormatString property.

    2. Enter {0:d} as a property setting to set the format to a date representation in the style of the local Windows regional setting without showing any time values, such as 12:00 AM.

4. Next, select the Freight column in the Selected fields ListBox.

    1. Scroll to the DataFormatString property.

    2. Enter {0:c} to format column values as currency values in the local Windows regional setting.

5. Repeat the DataFormatString property setting for the Freight column for the Subtotal and Freight & Subtotal columns.

Figure 13-48 shows the LookupSSEData.aspx page after the application of the formatting. By contrasting the appearance of output in Figure 13-48 with the same output in Figure 13-47, you can verify the impact of the formatting settings. In addition, you can use this approach as a guideline for evaluating the affect of other formatting settings for the GridView control columns.

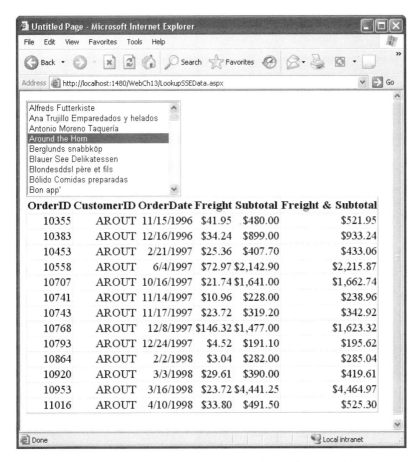

OrderID	CustomerID	OrderDate	Freight	Subtotal	Freight & Subtotal
10355	AROUT	11/15/1996	$41.95	$480.00	$521.95
10383	AROUT	12/16/1996	$34.24	$899.00	$933.24
10453	AROUT	2/21/1997	$25.36	$407.70	$433.06
10558	AROUT	6/4/1997	$72.97	$2,142.90	$2,215.87
10707	AROUT	10/16/1997	$21.74	$1,641.00	$1,662.74
10741	AROUT	11/14/1997	$10.96	$228.00	$238.96
10743	AROUT	11/17/1997	$23.72	$319.20	$342.92
10768	AROUT	12/8/1997	$146.32	$1,477.00	$1,623.32
10793	AROUT	12/24/1997	$4.52	$191.10	$195.62
10864	AROUT	2/2/1998	$3.04	$282.00	$285.04
10920	AROUT	3/3/1998	$29.61	$390.00	$419.61
10953	AROUT	3/16/1998	$23.72	$4,441.25	$4,464.97
11016	AROUT	4/10/1998	$33.80	$491.50	$525.30

Figure 13-48. *The LookupSSEData.aspx page after the application of three formatting settings to a mix of columns in the GridView control*

Summary

This chapter introduced you to rapid application database development techniques for use with VBE and VWDE. The introduction to Database Explorer showed you how to use this powerful visual database tool to add database connections to a project, examine and modify the data in a project, and revise or add database objects in a project. Step-by-step instructions and numerous screen shots demonstrated how to use visual database tools and graphical form development techniques. Rich graphical techniques were demonstrated for presenting data, looking up data, and modifying data. You saw the use of graphical development tools with both VBE and VWDE.

Index

forums.apress.com

JOIN THE APRESS FORUMS AND BE PART OF OUR COMMUNITY. You'll find discussions that cover topics of interest to IT professionals, programmers, and enthusiasts just like you. If you post a query to one of our forums, you can expect that some of the best minds in the business—especially Apress authors, who all write with *The Expert's Voice™*—will chime in to help you. Why not aim to become one of our most valuable participants (MVPs) and win cool stuff? Here's a sampling of what you'll find:

DATABASES
Data drives everything.

Share information, exchange ideas, and discuss any database programming or administration issues.

PROGRAMMING/BUSINESS
Unfortunately, it is.

Talk about the Apress line of books that cover software methodology, best practices, and how programmers interact with the "suits."

INTERNET TECHNOLOGIES AND NETWORKING
Try living without plumbing (and eventually IPv6).

Talk about networking topics including protocols, design, administration, wireless, wired, storage, backup, certifications, trends, and new technologies.

WEB DEVELOPMENT/DESIGN
Ugly doesn't cut it anymore, and CGI is absurd.

Help is in sight for your site. Find design solutions for your projects and get ideas for building an interactive Web site.

JAVA
We've come a long way from the old Oak tree.

Hang out and discuss Java in whatever flavor you choose: J2SE, J2EE, J2ME, Jakarta, and so on.

SECURITY
Lots of bad guys out there—the good guys need help.

Discuss computer and network security issues here. Just don't let anyone else know the answers!

MAC OS X
All about the Zen of OS X.

OS X is both the present and the future for Mac apps. Make suggestions, offer up ideas, or boast about your new hardware.

TECHNOLOGY IN ACTION
Cool things. Fun things.

It's after hours. It's time to play. Whether you're into LEGO® MINDSTORMS™ or turning an old PC into a DVR, this is where technology turns into fun.

OPEN SOURCE
Source code is good; understanding (open) source is better.

Discuss open source technologies and related topics such as PHP, MySQL, Linux, Perl, Apache, Python, and more.

WINDOWS
No defenestration here.

Ask questions about all aspects of Windows programming, get help on Microsoft technologies covered in Apress books, or provide feedback on any Apress Windows book.

HOW TO PARTICIPATE:
Go to the Apress Forums site at **http://forums.apress.com/**.
Click the New User link.